DRAWING DOWN THE MOON

DRAWING DOWN THE MOON

MAGIC IN THE ANCIENT GRECO-ROMAN WORLD

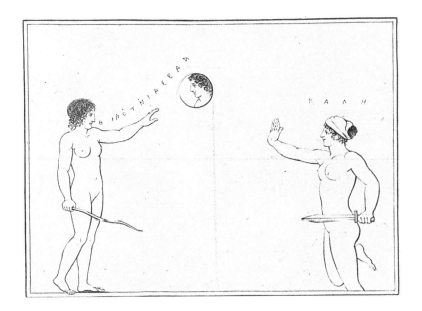

Radcliffe G. Edmonds III

PRINCETON UNIVERSITY PRESS
PRINCETON & OXFORD

Copyright © 2019 by Princeton University Press
Published by Princeton University Press
41 William Street, Princeton, New Jersey 08540
6 Oxford Street, Woodstock, Oxfordshire OX20 1TR
press.princeton.edu
All Rights Reserved
LCCN 2018964391
First paperback printing, 2021
Paper ISBN 9780691230214
Cloth ISBN 9780691156934
British Library Cataloging-in-Publication Data is available
Editorial: Rob Tempio and Matt Rohal
Production Editorial: Debbie Tegarden
Text Design: C. Alvarez-Gaffin
Jacket/Cover art: This is the only image from antiquity identified as drawing
down the moon. It is a line drawing (#44 from Hamilton and
Tischbein 1791, courtesy of the Bryn Mawr Library)., but the original Greek vase itself was
lost when the ship carrying it and other spoils back to England in the eighteenth century
sunk off the coast of Italy.
Jacket/Cover Credit: C. Alvarez-Gaffin
Production: Erin Suydam
Publicity: Jodi Price
Copyeditor: Hank Southgate
This book has been composed in Charis SIL

Contents

4

BEWITCHED, BOTHERED, BEWILDERED
LOVE CHARMS AND EROTIC CURSES 91

5

HEALING AND PROTECTIVE MAGIC
DEFENSE AGAINST THE DARK ARTS 116

6

RELATIONSHIPS WITH THE DIVINE
PRAYER AND MAGIC 149

7

THROUGH A GLASS DARKLY
DIVINATION AND MAGIC 188

8

MYSTERIES OF THE HEAVENLY SPHERES
ASTROLOGY AND MAGIC   236

9

TRANSMUTATIONS OF QUALITY
ALCHEMY AND MAGIC   269

10

THE ILLUMINATIONS OF THEURGY
PHILOSOPHY AND MAGIC   314

11

THE LABEL OF 'MAGIC' IN THE ANCIENT GRECO-ROMAN WORLD   378

Figures

Acknowledgments

Iowe thanks to many people for the help and encouragement they have provided over the years I have been working on this project, but my most profound gratitude goes to those whose contributions came before I ever began. First of all, I must thank my teachers who helped lead me into the study of magic in the ancient Greco-Roman world, especially Hans Dieter Betz, Chris Faraone, Bruce Lincoln, and J. Z. Smith. I learned so much from each one of them, starting from my first seminar in graduate school, which was on the Greek Magical Papyri with Professor Betz. But I have also learned immensely from my students, particularly those students in my course on Magic in the Greco-Roman World at Bryn Mawr College. I have taught that course many times now, both at the undergraduate and graduate level, and each time my understanding has been enriched and illumined by the questions, confusions, digressions, and insights of my students. The book has grown from the class, and I hope that it will be usable by others who wish to teach such courses on magic in the ancient Greco-Roman world as well as by those who wish to learn about this fascinating subject outside the classroom.

This book owes its existence to that class, but in particular to the vision of my editor at Princeton University Press, Rob Tempio, who more than a decade ago saw the syllabus I had for the course online and asked me if I had ever thought of turning it into a book. "No," I replied, "but what a great idea!" I am grateful for his patience as I finished the other two book projects I was engaged in before beginning this one, for his patience and support as the writing took longer than planned, and for his support as the project ended up rather larger in scale than had been envisioned. His energy and encouragement have been fundamental to this project, and his patience and trust that I would accomplish it have been empowering.

I am also grateful to the large number of colleagues who have lent their aid, advice, or just an ear along the way. I want to thank the members of the Tri-College Mellon Working Group on Magic, who allowed me to try out a number of my chapters in progress on them, and especially Shiamin Kwa, Sibelan Forrester, and Tracey Hucks, who provided me with insights from their different disciplines. I am also grateful to all those who read chapters and responded with their expertise, especially Werner Riess, Chris Faraone, Matteo Martelli, Raquel Martin, Roger Beck, Michael Flower,

Marilynn Lawrence, and Sarah Iles Johnston. Sarah has been a mentor and an inspiration for me ever since I was still a graduate student, and I am particularly thankful to her for the care and attention she put into reviewing the whole manuscript, her extensive comments, and well-deserved critiques. I am also grateful to the anonymous reviewer from the Press, whose comments I found both thorough and insightful.

I would also like to thank those who gave me the opportunity to present my work in progress, especially Peter Struck at the University of Pennsylvania, Pat and Steve Ahearne-Kroll at the University of Minnesota, and Luc Brisson, who arranged for me to speak at the École Normale Supérieure in Paris during the spring of 2017. An earlier version of chapter 4 appeared in the *Blackwell Companion to Greek and Roman Sexualities*, and I am grateful to the editor, Thomas Hubbard, for prompting me to write that piece, which served as the basis for the book chapter. I am also grateful to the graduate students in my Ancient Magic seminar in the fall of 2016 who read through each chapter of the manuscript (on top of all their other assigned reading) and provided me with feedback from the student's perspective. I am particularly grateful to R. J. Barnes and Dan Crosby for their comments—and to Dan and Kate Dolson for the work they have done on the indices. I appreciate the generosity of Attilio Mastrocinque, Genevra Kornbluth, Chris Faraone, and Marina Piranomonte, in giving me permission to use the images that they have created, and I thank all those who have granted me permission to make use of images from their museum collections. I am thankful for the supportive environment of Bryn Mawr College, especially for the semester of leave during the spring of 2017 that enabled me to bring the draft of the manuscript to completion. Finally, such a project could never have been completed without the love and support of my family—there is no greater magic. . . .

Works Cited

Titles and Abbreviations

Note: Most of the titles and abbreviations in the citations follow the conventions of the *Oxford Classical Dictionary*, but not all titles appear in that reference work. I have also made use of the conventions in the Packard Humanities Institute (PHI) Epigraphic database and the Thesaurus Linguae Graecae (TLG) database. As a default, I have made use of the texts and translations in the Loeb Classical Library series when possible, on the grounds that such works are the most easily accessible to the broadest audience. However, I have at times made alterations to the translations or provided my own translations whenever I felt that I needed to bring out some nuance of the text not captured in the Loeb translation. For other works, I have made use of other published translations, but any deviation from the default should be marked in the note. For the Greek Magical Papyri, I have used the translations in Betz 1992 (GMPT) unless otherwise noted. I have generally made use of the editions found in the PHI Epigraphic database (https://inscriptions.packhum.org/) and the TLG database (stephanus.tlg.uci.edu) for other texts.

AP = *Peri Asēmou Poiēseōs* in Martelli, Matteo. 2013. *The Four Books of Pseudo-Democritus*. Leeds: Maney Publishing.

CAAG = Berthelot, M., and C. E. Ruelle. 1888. *Collection des anciens alchimistes grecs*. 4 vols. Paris: Steinheil.

CMA = Berthelot, M. 1893. *Histoire des sciences: La chimie au moyen âge*. 3 vols. Paris: Imprimerie nationale.

DT = Audollent, Auguste, ed. 1904. *Defixionum Tabellae Quotquot Innotuerunt Tam in Graecis Orientis Quam in Totius in Corpore Inscriptionum Atticarum Editas*. Luteciae Parisiorum: Albert Fontemoing.

DTA = Wünsch, Richard, ed. 1897. *Inscriptiones Atticae Aetatis Romanae, Defixionum Tabellae. Inscriptiones Graecae, iii. 3*. Appendix. Berlin: Reimer.

FGrH = Jacoby, Felix. 1923–1958. *Die fragmente der griechischen Historiker*. Berlin: Weidmann.

Gager = Gager, John G., ed. 1992. *Curse Tablets and Binding Spells from the Ancient World*. New York and Oxford: Oxford University Press.

GMA = Kotansky, Roy. 1994. *Greek Magical Amulets: The Inscribed Gold, Silver, Copper, and Bronze Lamellae: Text and Commentary.* Abhandlungen der Rheinisch-Westfälischen Akademie der Wissenschaften. Sonderreihe Papyrologica Coloniensia 22. Opladen: Westdeutscher Verlag.

GMPT = Betz, Hans Dieter, ed. 1986. *The Greek Magical Papyri in Translation: Including the Demotic Spells.* Chicago and London: University of Chicago Press.

I. Kourion = Mitford, Terence B. 1971. *The Inscriptions of Kourion.* Memoirs of the American Philosophical Society 83. Philadelphia: American Philosophical Society.

IG I² = *Inscriptiones Graecae I: Inscriptiones Atticae Euclidis anno (403/2) anteriores.* 1924. 2nd ed. Ed. Friedrich Hiller von Gaertringen. Berlin: Prussian Academy of Sciences.

IG I³ = *Inscriptiones Graecae I: Inscriptiones Atticae Euclidis anno anteriores.* 1981, 1994. 3rd ed. Berlin: Prussian Academy of Sciences. Fasc. 1, ed. David Lewis, *Decreta et tabulae magistratuum (nos. 1–500).* Fasc. 2, ed. David Lewis and Lilian Jeffery, *Dedicationes. Catalogi. Termini. Tituli sepulcrales. Varia. Tituli Attici extra Atticam reperti. Addenda (nos. 501–1517).*

IG II = *Inscriptiones Atticae aetatis quae est inter Euclidis annum et Augusti tempora.* 1877–1895. Ed. Ulrich Koehler. Parts I–V. Berlin: Prussian Academy of Sciences.

ILS = Dessau, Hermann. 1892–1916. *Inscriptiones latinae selectae.* 3 vols. in 5 parts. Berlin: Prussian Academy of Sciences.

LSAM = Sokolowski, F. 1955. *Lois sacrées de l' Asie Mineure.* Ecole française d' Athènes, 9. Paris: E. de Boccard.

MA = Mertens, Michèle. 1995. *Les Alchimistes Grecs. Tome IV, 1ère Partie. Zosime de Panopolis. Mémoires Authentiques.* Paris: Les Belles Lettres.

Meiggs and Lewis 1969 = Meiggs, Russell, and David Lewis. 1969. *Selection of Greek Historical Inscriptions to the End of the Fifth Century B.C.* Oxford and New York: Clarendon Press.

PG = Migne, J.-P., ed. 1856–1866. *Patrologiae cursus completus. Series graeca.* Paris: Imprimerie Catholique.

PGM = Preisendanz, Karl, and Albert Henrichs, eds. 1973. *Papyri Graecae Magicae: Die Griechischen Zauberpapyri.* 2nd ed. Stuttgart: Teubner.

PM = *Physika kai mystika* in Martelli, Matteo. 2013. *The Four Books of Pseudo-Democritus.* Leeds: Maney Publishing.

SEG = *Supplementum Epigraphicum Graecum.* Vols. 1–11, ed. Jacob E. Hondius. Leiden, 1923–1954. Vols. 12–25, ed. Arthur G. Woodhead. Leiden, 1955–1971. Vols. 26–41, eds. Henry W.

Pleket and Ronald S. Stroud. Amsterdam, 1979–1994. Vols. 42–
44, eds. Henry W. Pleket, Ronald S. Stroud, and Johan H. M.
Strubbe. Amsterdam, 1995–1997. Vols. 45–49, eds. Henry W.
Pleket, Ronald S. Stroud, Angelos Chaniotis, and Johan H. M.
Strubbe. Amsterdam, 1998–2002. Vols. 50–, eds. Angelos
Chaniotis, Ronald S. Stroud, and Johan H. M. Strubbe.
Amsterdam 2003–.

SIG = *Sylloge inscriptionum graecarum*. 1915–1924. Ed. Wilhelm
Dittenberger. 3rd ed. Eds. Friedrich Hiller von Gaertringen,
Johannes Kirchner, Hans Rudolf Pomtow, and Erich Ziebarth.
4 vols. Leipzig: S. Hirzel.

SM = Daniel, Robert, and Franco Maltomini, eds. 1992. *Supplementum Magicum*. 2 vols. Papyrologica Coloniensis, XVI. Cologne:
Westdeutscher Verlag.

TAM V.1 = *Tituli Asiae Minoris, V. Tituli Lydiae linguis Graeca et Latina
conscripti*. 1981 and 1989. Ed. Peter Herrmann. 2 vols. Vienna:
Österreichische Akademie der Wissenschaften. Vol. 1, nos. 1–
825, *Regio septentrionalis, ad orientem vergens*.

DRAWING DOWN THE MOON

1

Drawing Down the Moon: Defining Magic in the Ancient Greco-Roman World

She strives with the reluctant moon, to bring it down from its course in the skies, and makes hide away in shadows the steeds of the sun; she reins the waters in, and stays the down-winding stream; she charms life into trees and rocks, and moves them from their place. Among sepulchres she stalks, ungirded, with hair flowing loose, and gathers from the yet warm funeral pyre the appointed bones. She vows to their doom the absent, fashions the waxen image, and into its wretched heart drives the slender needle—and other deeds 'twere better not to know.

(Ovid, *Heroides* 6.84–93)[1]

INTRODUCTION

Magic—the word evokes the mysterious and the marvelous, the forbidden and the hidden, the ancient and the arcane—deeds that it is better not to know. Drawing down the moon and reversing the rivers' flow, like sticking pins into wax images and stealing bones from funeral pyres, are typical examples of magic, and Ovid's Hypsipyle accuses Medea, her rival for her lover, Jason, of doing such terrible things. Drawing down the moon from

---

[1] *illa reluctantem cursu deducere lunam nititur et tenebris abdere solis equos; illa refrenat aquas obliquaque flumina sistit; illa loco silvas vivaque saxa movet. per tumulos errat passis discincta capillis certaque de tepidis colligit ossa rogis. devovet absentis simulacraque cerea figit, et miserum tenuis in iecur urget acus—et quae nescierim melius* (Loeb).

the sky is a familiar trope in discussions of the weird and extra-ordinary activity that is often labeled 'magic,' and it appears, either as part of a list of magical acts or as a single act representative of the whole scope of magical possibilities, in sources throughout the ancient Greco-Roman world, by which I mean the peoples of the Mediterranean region who expressed themselves in Greek or Latin between the eighth century BCE and the fifth century CE.

So what did 'magic' mean to the people who first coined the term, the people of ancient Greece and Rome? In this study, which takes its title of *Drawing Down the Moon* from the most famous of the magical tricks known from the ancient world, I survey the varieties of phenomena labeled 'magic' in the ancient Greco-Roman world, seeking ways to form a definition of magic to understand the uses of the label. I discuss ancient tablets and spell books as well as literary descriptions of magic in the light of theories relating to the religious, political, and social contexts in which magic was used. I also examine the magicians of the ancient world and the techniques and devices they used to serve their clientele. Bindings and curses, love charms and healing potions, amulets and talismans—from the simple spells designed to meet the needs of the poor and desperate to the complex theurgies of the philosophers, the people of the Greco-Roman world did not only imagine what magic could do, they also made use of magic to try to influence the world around them.

The study of magic in the Greco-Roman world is not merely an exploration into the weird and wonderful, an antiquarian search for the colorful corners of the ancient world. Understanding why certain practices, images, and ideas were labeled as 'magic' and set apart from the normal kinds of practices provides insight into the shifting ideas of normal religion in the Greco-Roman world. Normative religion is that which both follows the model of socially accepted religious activity and expresses that model for the community, and, from our own contemporary cultural context, we tend by default to think of normative religion in terms of institutionally sanctioned correct ways of believing (orthodoxy) and of practicing religion (orthopraxy). However, in societies with no notion of orthodoxy and even limited modes of orthopraxy, normative religion could only be defined by this kind of practice of labeling, and 'magic' was one of the more important labels that was used, in different ways by different people at different times. The study of ancient magic therefore provides a crucial perspective on normative practices of religion in the ancient Greco-Roman world—on ritual practices such as sacrifice, purification, and prayer, on theological elaborations of the hierarchies of divinities, and on the underlying cosmologies that structured human interactions with both the material world and the divine.

The evidence for magic comes not only from the familiar literary traditions of the classical world, the spectacular and memorable images of witches, ghosts, and demons and the fantastic powers of metamorphosis, erotic attraction, or reversals of nature such as the famous trick of drawing down the moon. The archaeological record provides evidence that attests to the ideas of people in the ancient world who never had a chance to contribute to the literary tradition, the non-elites or marginal figures whose expressions were never preserved and recopied throughout the millennia of reception of classical materials. In the curses scrawled on sheets of lead, seeking to restrain rivals in business, law courts, athletics, or erotic affairs, we can see the hopes and fears of a group of people whose voices have been lost in the intervening centuries. In the elaborate formulations of the spell books or alchemical recipes, we can see the complex workings of intellectuals who remained at the margins of society, engaging in complex speculations about the nature of the world and the gods. In the jumbled lists of powers invoked, we can see the dynamics of cultural fusion that occurred in the rich multicultural environment of the ancient Mediterranean world, where an ancient Mesopotamian goddess Ereškigal might be invoked alongside the Greek Persephone and the Egyptian Isis, right next to a prayer to the supreme deity Iaō, the Greek rendering of the Hebrew Jehovah.

Understanding the category of magic in its ancient Greco-Roman context is important for understanding not only the ancient world itself, but also the ways in which the ideas and controversies have influenced later periods. The ways in which things and ideas are labeled 'magic' in the ancient world are replicated in religious controversies throughout the later Western tradition. Most famous of these is perhaps the critique of Catholic ritualism that plays a central role in the Protestant Reformation, but even in the witch hunts that are used to reinforce (or invent) orthodoxy, we can see the reuse of ancient categories for normative and non-normative religion in the accusations of magic. On the more positive side, the esoteric traditions of ancient wisdom that manifested in the astrological, pharmacological, and alchemical practices of ancient magic play an important part in the history of science from antiquity through the Enlightenment and beyond. A deeper understanding of the category of magic in its ancient contexts provides a richer understanding of its reception.

Drawing down the moon provides an illustrative example of the issues involved with understanding magic in the ancient Greco-Roman world and its later receptions. This act, which appears in the contemporary world as an important ritual in certain Wiccan and Neopagan traditions, appears first in the evidence from the ancient world as a joke. In Aristophanes's *Clouds*, the scoundrel Strepsiades explains his cunning plan for getting out of his debts. He'll hire a Thessalian witch to draw down the moon and keep it in a box so that the new moon day, on which debt payments are due, will never come.[2]

STREPSIADES: I have an idea for cheating them of the interest.
SOCRATES: Explain it.
STREPSIADES: Tell me now, then. . . .
SOCRATES: What?
STREPSIADES: If I should hire a Thessalian witch woman and draw down the moon at night, and then I lock it up in a round case, like a mirror, and then I keep it guarded . . .
SOCRATES: And what would you gain from that?
STREPSIADES: Why, if the moon should never rise anywhere, then I would not pay interest.
SOCRATES: And why is that?
STREPSIADES: Because the money is lent month by month.

This joke reveals several things about the idea of drawing down the moon in Aristophanes's Athens. First, the procedure was familiar enough to his audience that it could be mentioned without explanation: everyone knows that Thessalian witches draw down the moon. Secondly, Strepsiades proposes this idea as an extra-ordinary solution to his debt problem; drawing down the moon is a dramatic reversal of the natural order that will get him out of an otherwise insoluble crisis. Thirdly, however, Strepsiades is a comic idiot, which means that his plan won't work, even within the fiction of the comedy; the extra-ordinary feat of drawing down the moon is actually a worthless sham, good only for a laugh at Strepsiades's expense.

This same constellation of familiarity within the tradition coupled with either extra-ordinary power or worthless superstition appears repeatedly in evidence for magic throughout the ancient Greco-Roman world. It is worth probing, however, how exactly this extra-ordinary nature of magic appears throughout the evidence—what is magic? To answer this question, we must start with a definition of magic that can help us make sense of the evidence. I therefore propose that:

---

[2] Aristophanes, *Nub.* 746–757. Στρεψιάδης: ἔχω τόκου γνώμην ἀποστερητικήν. ‖ Σωκράτης: ἐπίδειξον αὐτήν. ‖ Στρεψιάδης: εἰπὲ δή νύν μοι — ‖ Σωκράτης: τὸ τί; ‖ Στρεψιάδης: γυναῖκα φαρμακίδ᾽ εἰ πριάμενος Θετταλὴν‖ καθέλοιμι νύκτωρ τὴν σελήνην, εἶτα δή‖ αὐτὴν καθείρξαιμ᾽ ἐς λοφεῖον στρογγύλον,‖ ὥσπερ κάτοπτρον, κᾆτα τηροίην ἔχων — ‖ Σωκράτης: τί δῆτα τοῦτ᾽ ἂν ὠφελήσειέν σ᾽; ‖ Στρεψιάδης: ὅ τι; εἰ μηκέτ᾽ ἀνατέλλοι σελήνη μηδαμοῦ,‖ οὐκ ἂν ἀποδοίην τοὺς τόκους. ‖ Σωκράτης: ὁτιὴ τί δή; ‖ Στρεψιάδης: ὁτιὴ κατὰ μῆνα τἀγύριον δανείζεται. For a study of drawing down the moon in modern Neopaganism, see Adler 1981.

> Magic is a discourse pertaining to non-normative ritualized activity, in which the deviation from the norm is most often marked in terms of the perceived efficacy of the act, the familiarity of the performance within the cultural tradition, the ends for which the act is performed, or the social location of the performer.

Each piece of this definition needs unpacking, and its usefulness can be demonstrated through a closer examination of some of the evidence for drawing down the moon.

DEFINING MAGIC IN THE ANCIENT GRECO-ROMAN WORLD

Magic and the Art of Bicycle Maintenance

In her review of several scholarly works on magic in the ancient world, Sarah Iles Johnston refers to Marvin Meyers's comparison of the scholarship on magic to riding a rather rickety bicycle; we continue to make progress in understanding ancient magic as we pedal forward working with the evidence, but every once in a while, we need to stop and do some maintenance on the bicycle itself, our definition of the category of magic. The definition will always be a bit rickety, but if we spend all our time and energy in trying to fix it up, we will never make any progress.[3] Nearly fifteen years after her reflection, however, it may be time for some more work on the definition of magic.

Defining magic is notoriously problematic, and the comparison is often made to Supreme Court Justice Stewart's famous comment on pornography: he couldn't quite define it, but he knew it when he saw it.[4] When people see an example of drawing down the moon, most would know it as magic, even if they can't articulate why. This sort of intuitive definition is the starting point for any kind of classification, but if it remains the end point as well, the definition will be full of tacit and unexamined presuppositions that do more or less violence to the subject under investigation. We can move, however, from an intuitive to an analytic definition by making explicit and examining the presuppositions we bring to it—why does it feel like magic, smell like magic, look like magic? What distinguishes

---

[3] Meyers was calling for more pedaling forward while setting aside the question of definition, or even the use of the term 'magic' itself, while Johnston calls for some renewed attention to the definitions. "So although I remain an enthusiastic cyclist ten years after Meyer's remark, I now ride with a closer eye on my chain and sprocket" (Johnston 2003: 54).

[4] Cp. C. Phillips 1991, who refers n. 34 to Stewart's legal opinion in Jacobellis v. Ohio, 378 U.S. 184 (1964), at 197.

the things that we know as magic when we see them from the things that we don't classify as magic?

If we are looking at magic in the ancient Greco-Roman world, we face the further problem that our categories and classifications do not necessarily align with the classifications made in those cultures during those times. What did those people define as magic, and by what criteria did they make their distinctions? Anthropologists distinguish between emic and etic perspectives on a culture, between the cultural insider's perspective and the outside, scholarly perspective.[5] An account from a member of the community, using the terms and categories of the culture, provides an emic perspective, while someone examining the culture from the outside, using the terms and categories of his or her own culture, takes an etic perspective. Ideally, to understand another culture, we must understand the way that the people in that culture think, but, as anthropologists have shown, an outsider can never fully adopt an insider perspective. In the case of the ancient Greco-Roman world, we are separated too far in time (and, for many of us, in space as well) to merge seamlessly into the world of those we study; the gaps in the evidence are too enormous, and the cultural shifts over the centuries are too great and too complex.

Thus, we must start with etic definitions, since those are the presuppositions we bring to any inquiry from our own culture and upbringing. Ultimately, we must end up with etic definitions as well, since we cannot analyze another culture as though we were part of it. So, for the modern scholar, 'magic' will always be an etic category, formulated for the purposes of analyzing and understanding the ancient Greco-Roman world.[6] If we want to make sense of the evidence for ourselves, we cannot do without definitions altogether; any attempt to do so just ends up bringing back in implicit—and therefore unexamined—etic definitions.[7] However, we can

---

[5] The terminology of emic and etic are borrowed from linguistics, which differentiates the phon*emic* and phon*etic* qualities of a word, the meaning comprehensible to one who knows the language and the sounds audible even to outsiders who don't know the language. See Pike 1967, especially 37–41.

[6] J. Z. Smith makes the same point of of religion in general: "Religion is solely the creation of the scholar's study. It is created for the scholar's analytic purposes by his imaginative acts of comparison and generalization" (J. Smith 1982: xi). One might also compare the concepts of *parole* and *langue* from structural linguistics; the particular examples of *parole* are real individual speech acts, but the *langue* is an idea of a system deduced by the one who examines the *paroles*.

[7] Cp. Johnston 2003: 54: "Taking a crack at defining 'magic'—that most provocative of chimeras—is simply irresistible; we should at least learn to do it better. The second reason is that we need definitions of magic, at least for heuristic purposes. Truly emic research is impossible; we are condemned to look at other cultures from the outside, and are better off confronting that fact and turning each attempt to define magic into an exercise in examining our conceptions about the practices and beliefs we categorize under that term."

come up with better etic definitions if we look to the way the ancient Greeks and Romans made their own emic definitions and drew their own categories.[8] If we refine our intuitive modern etic definitions with reference to the evidence for the ancient emic classifications, the bicycle may still end up a bit wobbly, but we will be able to make better progress.

Magic as a Discourse

One of the most useful adjustments in the recent scholarship on magic has been the turn to considering magic as a dynamic social construct, instead of some particular reality.[9] Magic is not a thing, but a way of talking about things. It is thus a 'discourse,' like sexuality, or religion, or science, or literature—or, indeed, pornography. Such a discourse, as Foucault points out, always has a history, since such a way of talking about things shifts over time as different people do the talking.[10] When we speak of 'magic,' therefore, we should always explain: 'magic for *whom*?' Any specific piece of evidence from the ancient Greco-Roman world provides an example of magic for that particular person, from one particular persepctive. To speak of 'magic in the ancient Greco-Roman world' is thus to refer (loosely) to the whole range of things that various people in those cultures during those times could label as 'magic.'

Scholarship over the past few decades has pointed to the ways the discourse of magic has been used to denigrate the Other. Magic has been a colonialist tool to denigrate the colonized (we have real religion; they just have magic), but even before that, magic was a Reformation tool to denigrate traditional Catholic religion (barren ritualism) or an Enlightenment tool to denigrate religion in general (primitive superstition).[11] All of these

[8] As Bremmer 1999: 9, points out, "In order to be workable, the etic definition of a concept should always be as close as possible to the actors' point of view: if not, it will soon cease to be a useful definition."

[9] "Magic is best understood as a discursive formation—a socially constructed body of knowledge that is enmeshed in and supports systems of power. What gets labelled magic is arbitrary and depends on the society in question. Once the label is affixed, however, it enables certain practices to *become* magic by virtue of being regarded as such by memember of the society" (Stratton 2013: 246–247). Gordon 1999a provides the best starting point for this approach, but see also Stratton 2007; Gordon and Marco Simón 2010; Otto 2013; and Kahlos 2016, among others.

[10] Styers 2004 provides perhaps the best overview of the history of the discourse of magic in the modern period, although he has little interest in the ancient world.

[11] Stratton 2007: 4–18 provides a good brief introduction; cp. Collins 2008a: 1–26. Thomas 1997 provides the classic study of the categories of magic and religion in the early modern period following the Protestant Reformation. As Styers 2004: 8 points out, "More than a century of thwarted attempts to reify and define magic—to contain and circumscribe this phenomenon—by many of the West's most prominent cultural theorists would seem to provide a rather clear indication that this enterprise might be suspect."

negative uses remain latent in the discourse whenever we as contemporary scholars make use of it, but it is worth noting that the history of the discourse also includes positive senses of magic. In the Renaissance, for example, 'magic' was used as a term to designate the rediscovered wisdom of the ancients, while in the twentieth century the term 'magic' was at times reappropriated from colonialist discourse to indicate the romanticized Other as positive in contrast to soulless modernity. These conflicting uses of the discourse do not mean that we should (or can) discard 'magic' as a useful way of talking about Greco-Roman antiquity. The shifts between positive and negative evaluations are not merely the pendulum swings of history but inherent in the nature of the discourse of magic itself.

Beyond the Grand Dichotomies: Magic as Non-normative

Throughout the scholarship dealing with magic, not just in the ancient Greco-Roman world, but for cultures in various times and places, magic is often set up in opposition to religion, but the opposition of magic to science often also appears.[12] Intuitively, it seems, we tend to define magic as that which is not (real) science or that which is not (real) religion. Such a negative definition, I would argue, contains an important insight, but applied uncritically to the ancient evidence, as it often has been, this etic definition is not very useful, largely because the discourses of religion and science are likewise modern etic constructions, so distinguishing between them creates divisions that are often alien to the ancient emic distinctions. We must probe further.

The modern distinction between science and religion depends upon a modern distinction between the natural and supernatural, but that distinction does not map onto the categories of the ancient Greco-Roman world without some serious distortions. The ancient Greeks and Romans, like all the peoples of the ancient Mediterranean world (and beyond), certainly distinguished between the mortal and the divine, as well as between the material and the immaterial. The divine and the immaterial, however, were generally considered as an integral part of the cosmos, the natural order of the world.[13] Whereas moderns tend to treat anything that involves

[12] Braarvig 1999 discusses the 'Grand Dichotomy' of magic and religion with reference to many other such dichotomies: primitive/civilized, oral/literate, closed/open, them/us, etc., noting that science often appears in the 'us' side. Cp. also Styers 2004: 6.

[13] "In our own culture, we tend to equate the occult and uncanny with the supernatural: something is uncanny only if it has no obvious explanation within the scientific framework of 'nature,' and so is necessarily 'supernatural' as well. In the Roman world, by contrast, it would have been perfectly possible for people to regard something as occult or uncanny and yet not supernatural" (Rives 2003: 320). Cp. Collins 2003: 21–29.

the divine as religion and anything that involves the perceptible, material world as science, such a distinction does not appear in the ancient evidence. Some philosophers might frame a contrast between the things perceptible by the senses (especially sight and touch) and those perceptible only by the mind and reasoning, but both kinds of things are part of the same cosmic order. Material objects may have divine powers that operate in ways that are not directly perceptible, and divine entities may act in ways that produce direct, material, and perceptible results.

J. Z. Smith points out that if magic is defined in opposition to religion as well as in opposition to science, then, logically, religion and science should share some characteristic that stands in opposition to magic.[14] I would suggest that this shared characteristic is *normativity*, since both science and religion function as normative discourses in our contemporary society; that is, they are held up as models of the normal ways to relate to the divine and to the material world. Someone who stitches up a cut or who goes into a temple to make a prayer is seen as acting in a normal and expected way, making use of normal scientific or religious patterns of action. By contrast, someone who cuts the throat of a puppy and burns it on a tombstone in the middle of the night is engaging in non-normative religious behavior, just as someone who smears the wound with a paste made from the wrappings of an Egyptian mummy, powdered rhino horn, and the intestines of a frog is engaging in non-normative scientific activity. Both such actions might well be labeled 'magic' by an observer, but, whereas a modern observer would draw the distinction between science and religion, an ancient one would simply characterize both actions as abnormal.

What counts as 'normal,' however, differs from culture to culture and era to era, and even within a given culture at a particular time, what is considered normal may depend on a complex of circumstantial factors. Abnormality, moreover, is not absolute; there is a whole spectrum of differences from the norm.[15] The concept of a 'hierarchy of means' is useful here.[16] To achieve any end, there is a whole range of means that might be employed, but some means are more highly valued than others, because of their difficulty, cost, or efficacy. Normal means are in the middle of the hierarchy; the ordinary way to solve a problem is the one most often adopted. Something that is high on the hierarchy of means is only rarely

[14] J. Smith 1995: 13.

[15] Gordon 1999a: 192 makes the important point that "the value of conceptualizing a continuum of possible values between fully normative and wholly illicit is that, while allowing the negative pole to be wholly imaginary, it leaves plenty of room for religious activity which for one reason or another is viewed askance."

[16] Gordon usefully applies this concept from Evans-Pritchard 1937 in a number of his studies of Greek magic; see especially Gordon 1997 and Gordon 1999a.

employed; it may be perceived as having higher efficacy, but it is much more troublesome or expensive or difficult. If you are trying to kill a fly, a grenade launcher will probably take care of it, but there are simpler solutions, like a rolled up magazine. On the other hand, a well-designed fly swatter is more likely to succeed than the magazine, but it may not be immediately at hand, so the choice of means always involves weighing the costs and advantages, especially when opting for something out of the normal.

It is also crucial to remember that abnormality is double-edged; it may be either inferior to the normal or superior. Something that differs from the norm may be considered deviant in a bad way, failing to meet the expectations for ordinary action, but at times the normal way of doing things is insufficient to the situation and an abnormal solution needs to be sought, something better and stronger than the ordinary. Non-normative behavior is thus extra-ordinary, out of the ordinary and normal way of doing things, but it may be extra-ordinary either in a negative or a positive sense. The evidence labeled 'magic' in the ancient Greco-Roman world shows both these positive and negative labels of 'abnormality'; although much of the labeling applies to things considered negatively deviant, in some cases the deviation from the norm is marked as a marvelously positive thing.[17]

Magic as Ritualized Activity

As J. Z. Smith points out, magic is always only one of the ways in which a society can mark deviation; not every social deviation is labeled 'magic' or even could be.[18] The first distinction that must be drawn is to limit the scope of magic as a discourse of non-normative activity to ritualized activity, where 'ritual' is defined very broadly as symbolic action, which may include speech, gesture, movement, or other kinds of symbolic actions.[19] Purely instrumental actions tend not to be characterized as magical; they

---

[17] Cp. Gordon 1999a: 178: "The basic difficulty in making clear to oneself what one takes magic to be is that it is janus-faced, there being little point in choosing to stress exclusively (as has been the recent tendency) one side or the other. One face is that of religious power used illegitimately, the other the dream of power to effect marvellous changes in the real world."

[18] J. Smith 1995: 19: "I wish I could share the confidence of some scholars that, although substantive definition of 'magic' is rendered impossible by a sociological approach, the sorts of social fissures and conflicts revealed by the accusations are generalizable. A review of the ethnographic, historical and analytic literature makes clear that they are not. Any form of *ressentiment*, for real or imagined reasons (see Aberle on 'relative deprivation'), *may* trigger a language of alienating displacement of which the accusation of magic is *just one possibility* in any given culture's rich vocabulary of alterity."

[19] See further discussion of the nature of ritual in ch. 2, pp. 45–52.

are normal ways of dealing with normal situations. Likewise, normal speech acts, while involving the basic symbolic system of language, tend not to involve the more complex layers of symbolism that characterize magical speech. Rituals need not involve contact with divine entities, although most contacts with the divine are indeed ritualized. Any particular act, be it killing an animal, eating a meal, or walking along a path, can be ritualized, given added significance beyond its instrumental effect. Observing the positions of the stars is not in itself a ritual, but interpreting them as signs of divine communication ritualizes the process by adding the extra symbolic level. Likewise, to melt and combine two metals is simply metallurgy, but to perform the procedure as a symbolic re-enactment of the demiurgic process by which the cosmos is ordered turns the mechanical process into a kind of ritual.

As symbolic processes, rituals depend upon a cultural tradition to provide the symbolic material with which to work. One way of understanding magic as a discourse of ritualized activity is on the analogy of language, analyzing rituals like speech acts that draw upon a religious and cultural tradition in the way that linguistic speech acts draw upon the tradition of the language. Saussurean linguistics refers to the speech act as the *parole*, while the language system is called the *langue*.[20] Every *parole* is structured by the system of the *langue* but at the same time contributes to the dynamic change of the system. So, too, every ritual act, be it a prayer or a sacrifice or an elaborate consecration, is a particular articulation of ideas within the system of the religious tradition and, at the same time, serves to shape the continuing tradition. As scholars, we must remember that we only have individual *paroles* for our evidence and that any reconstruction of the *langue* is the result of our analytic activity. The ritual tradition, then, of any particular community may be seen analogously to the language of that community, as a *langue* that structures (and is structured by) every individual ritualized act. Every society has countless rituals in its cultural tradition, most performances of which are normative, acceptable, and expected, while only a few violate the boundaries of normality. To understand what is normative in the ancient Greco-Roman world requires a shift from our preliminary etic categories to something more closely approaching emic ones.

Labeling Magic: Valid Cues

The non-normative is also always a relational category rather than a substantive one. That is, rather than a discourse like magic being a thing

---

[20] Cp., e.g., the general introduction to the concepts in de Saussure 1986: 8–15, or an application to the study of myth in Lévi–Strauss 1963: 209.

that can be defined by a single necessary and sufficient criterion, it is a label applied by one person to another person, act, or thing, who defines it as non-normative for one of a variety of reasons. What is considered non-normative therefore depends on who is labeling whom in what circumstances.

To take account of all of these variables requires a definition that is not monothetic, but polythetic, involving multiple criteria of varying cue validity. Polythetic definitions are best explained by Wittgenstein's famous analogy of family resemblances: all the members of a family share a set of characteristics—hair color, bone structure, nose shapes, eye color, and so forth. Every member of the family has some of these features, but no one member of the family has all the characteristics, nor is there any feature that every family member has. Contemporary cognitive psychologists have shown that humans intuitively make such definitions of complex classes and that some features of the family are given more weight than others in any classification; that is, to use the jargon, some cues have more validity than others.[21] To identify furniture, for example, one might use the cues of having four legs, a flat surface, and a wood or metal frame. Not all things with such cues will necessarily be classified as furniture (e.g., a small water tower), nor will all things identified as furniture have all these features (e.g., a lamp), but things that exhibit such cues are more likely to be identified. Of course, the validity of some cues may shift over time. For the automobile, the internal combustion engine has become less valid a cue with the recent development of electric cars, whereas for the earliest automobiles, it was the most crucial feature. To define magic in the Greco-Roman world, therefore, we must determine what kinds of non-normative activity have the highest cue validity to be classified as magic. The specific cues may vary over time and circumstance, as may their relative validity, but we can nonetheless survey the evidence to assemble a collection of such cues. The valid cues in the ancient world differ notably from those most significant in modern or early modern Europe or in contemporary scholarship, since the ideas of normative behavior have shifted notably.

It is difficult, however, to find good evidence for emic definitions, since few ancient sources are interested in providing systematic definitions, and such sources are invariably polemical texts that are using systematicity as a rhetorical device to validate their arguments. Such polemics tend to focus on specific criteria to distinguish magic from some other practice, but such criteria are often rarefied cosmological or theological points incomprehen-

---

[21] Cp. Rosch and Mervis 1975: 575–576: "The principle of family resemblance relationships can be restated in terms of cue validity since the attributes most distributed among members of a category and least distributed among members of contrasting categories are, by definition, the most valid cues to membership in the category in question."

sible to a general audience, and we should be wary of trying to extrapolate a generally applicable definition of magic from these particular polemics. Such polemics nevertheless provide insights into the contexts in which the discourse of magic appears, as well as some of the ways in which one person labels another as non-normative.

One favorite tactic in the attempt to recreate the emic categories, especially among Classical philologists, is to look to specific words used in contexts that seem to involve magic. Although there is a certain amount of circularity in the process of choosing such contexts, it helps that the modern word for magic (in English and other European languages) is directly related to the ancient Greek term, *magos* or *mageia* or *magikē*, as are the Latin terms *magus, magia, magica*. The *magos/magus* is someone who performs *mageia/magia* or *magikē/magica*. These cognates provide at least a starting point for a lexical study, but, as many scholars have discovered, problems arise almost immediately.[22] *Magos* and related terms appear in only a few of the contexts in which the same kinds of practices are being described; other terms are frequently found instead. Moreover, the term *magos* at times seems to retain its original meaning of a particular kind of priest from Persia, so although it is a cue with fairly high validity, the word is neither a necessary nor a sufficient marker of a magical context.[23]

Philological studies have turned up a collection of other words that often appear in contexts that look like magic to scholars who know it when they see it. Although none of these words provide a necessary or sufficient indicator of magic, a few do seem to correlate best with magical contexts, providing relatively high cue validity. The words *goēs* and *goētia* are often strongly marked with non-normative activity; they might be rendered 'sorcerer' and 'sorcery' in English. The Late Antique encyclopedia, the *Suda*, connects these words with the *goos*, the funeral lament, and with necro-

---

[22] As J. Smith 1995: 20, points out, "Giving primacy to native terminology yields, at best, *lexical* definitions which, historically and statistically, tell how a word is used. But, lexical definitions are almost always useless for scholarly work. To remain content with how 'they' understand 'magic' may yield a proper description, but little explanatory power. How 'they' use a word cannot substitute for the *stipulative* procedures by which the academy contests and controls second-order, specialized usage."

[23] Bremmer 1999 makes a study of the 'birth of the term magic,' while Otto 2013 surveys the same material to create a historical overview. A short summary overview may be found in the introductory sections of the standard treatments of ancient magic, such as Graf 1997: 20–29; Dickie 2001: 12–17; Collins 2008a: 49–63; and Stratton 2007: 26–34 (with an excursus on Hebrew terminology, 34–37); as well as Luck 1999: 97–107. While these studies focus mostly on Greek usage, Rives 2011 usefully surveys the deployment of the Latin terms. Otto has examined in detail the sources from the ancient Greek to the modern period in his dissertation, published as Otto 2011. This study provides a better overview than, e.g., Daxelmüller 1993, but the vast scope of both works nevertheless means that little evidence from the ancient Greco-Roman world can be considered.

mantic activity, but, although some ancient uses of the term fit a necro-mantic context, most just seem to indicate extra-ordinary rituals and those who perform them.[24] Two other groups of words seem particularly relevant, the words for a magical substance (*pharmakon* in Greek or *venenum* in Latin), and the words for incantation (*epaoidē* in Greek or *carmen* in Latin). A *pharmakon* is something that produces an effect without a visible cause; it may be a material substance—a poison, a drug, a medicine, or a potion—but it may also refer to an immaterial incantation or curse. A reference to *epaoidai* or *carmina*, by contrast, always refers to speech acts marked by some special poetic or musical feature, but Homeric epics or Latin lyric poems might be so labeled, as well as the enchantments of sorcerers. These words (and others referring to various rituals and practitioners) all have some cue validity, but their usage must always be examined to determine who is applying them to whom in what circumstances and for what reasons.

In addition to formal, systematic definitions or definitions grounded in the presence of specific terms, the ancient sources provide evidence for more informal definitions in less polemical contexts. Collocation is an important element in these informal emic definitions, since ancient sources often group together a variety of things whose deviation from the norm marks them as liable to receive a label of 'magic.' This kind of definition by association helps expand the range of activities that can be labeled 'magic,' since something explicitly marked as *mageia* in one text may be listed with a number of other things that, even if not explicitly marked, may well be classified as magic. A survey of the things associated with the terminology of magic, with particular systematic definitions of magic in contrast to other practices, and the things collocated with them in the ancient evidence provides the best way to refine the basic definition of magic as a non-normative practice with the cues that are most valid in the Greco-Roman world. Drawing down the moon provides a good test case, since it is often listed among a whole variety of practices that contravene the natural order, and those who perform the drawing down of

---

[24] *Suda* s.v. Γοητεία: μαγεία. γοητεία καὶ μαγεία καὶ φαρμακεία διαφέρουσιν: ἅπερ ἐφεῦρον Μῆδοι καὶ Πέρσαι. μαγεία μὲν οὖν ἐστιν ἐπίκλησις δαιμόνων ἀγαθοποιῶν δῆθεν πρὸς ἀγαθοῦ τινος σύστασιν, ὥσπερ τὰ τοῦ Ἀπολλωνίου τοῦ Τυανέως θεσπίσματα. γοητεία δὲ ἐπὶ τῷ ἀνάγειν νεκρὸν δι' ἐπικλήσεως, ὅθεν εἴρηται ἀπὸ τῶν γόων καὶ τῶν θρήνων τῶν περὶ τοὺς τάφους γινομένων. φαρμακεία δὲ, ὅταν διά τινος σκευασίας θανατηφόρου πρὸς φίλτρον δοθῇ τινι διὰ στόματος. "Goēteia: magic. Sorcery [γοητεία] and magic [μαγεία] and witchcraft [φαρμακεία] differ; Medes and Persians discovered them. So magic is of course invocation of beneficent spirits for the production of something good, like the oracles of Apollonius of Tyana. But sorcery refers to raising a dead person by invocation, whence the word is derived from the wailing [γόοι] and lamentations that are made at burials. But the word witchcraft is used when some death-dealing concoction is given as a potion by mouth to someone."

the moon are often depicted as performing all sorts of other non-normative practices.

The Etic Perspective: Frazer versus Weber and Beyond

However, the inadequacy of the ancient terminology for defining the category, in addition to the basic problem of ever obtaining a sufficiently emic perspective, has led scholars to rely on primarily etic criteria, and such cues have often been used by scholars, explicitly or implicitly, in determining whether something is magical or not. As Versnel and others have shown, the most common criteria are those deriving from Frazer's influential treatment of magic in his *Golden Bough* (these criteria go back further, of course, but Frazer's framing has been particularly formative for later thinkers).[25] Versnel distinguishes four criteria, *attitude, action, intention*, and *social evaluation*, that are most often used to distinguish magic from normative religion, and it is worth briefly summarizing them here. A manipulative or coercive *attitude* in relations with the divine marks magic, in contrast with the submissive or supplicative *attitude* in religion. Magic operates through impersonal *action*, rather than the personal interactions characteristic of religion. The *intention* behind magical practices aims at concrete and individual goals, rather than the intangible long-term goals of religion (such as, for example, blessedness or salvation). Finally, magic is imagined to be antisocial or at least not working for the common good of the society, whereas religion has a cohesive function, so that the *social evaluation* of religion is positive, in contrast to the negative evaluation of magic. In the scholarship, a coercive attitude is most often used as single criterion, but others often appear in supporting roles, especially impersonal or automatic action. As scholars have pointed out, these two criteria have played an important role in the debates over ritual in the Christian theological tradition over the centuries, particularly in Protestant critiques of Catholic ritualism in which the ritual is imagined to be immediately efficacious simply by being performed by the appropriate priest (*ex opere operato*).[26]

The problem is that the contrast between a coercive and a submissive attitude in addressing the divine powers is actually one of the least significant contrasts in the ancient evidence; that is, it matches least well with the emic discourse of magic. An examination of Greek prayers, both in 'magical' and nonmagical contexts shows a mixture of imperatives and

---

[25] Versnel 1991b provides the best treatment. Despite questioning the etic categories, both Braarvig 1999 and Thomassen 1997 end up reverting to some version of Versnel's set.

[26] Versnel 1991b: 179–180. Cp., e.g., Thomas 1997: 52, etc. Styers 2004: 73, 104–119 further points to the way that the contrast between materialistic and other worldly intentions has been deployed within modern capitalist social orders.

supplications scattered throughout both.[27] Intention and social evaluation suffer similar problems as useful criteria for distinguishing magic from normative religious activity, since petitions for very concrete things from the gods appear alongside less tangible benefits, such as divine favor or blessedness. Likewise, performing rituals for the benefit of oneself and one's close friends and family, often at the explicit expense of others, appears both in magical and perfectly normative religious activity.

More importantly, the ancient sources themselves seem to focus on other issues when drawing the lines between magic and other kinds of activity; these Frazerian criteria, so intuitively familiar to modern scholars, do not demonstrate particularly high cue validity. The key, then, to coming up with a definition of magic as a discourse of non-normative activity that reflects the ancient emic perspective is to identify the factors in the ancient sources that seem to make that activity deemed non-normative. Again, a survey of different sorts of things that are labeled 'magic' emically, as well as things that are collocated with them, is needed, and all the evidence must be analyzed to take account of *what* it is, *who* is involved, *where* and *when* it takes place, *why* it is done, and *how* it is imagined to work. These standard analytic questions, applied to the body of evidence from the ancient sources, produce a set of cues that characterize the things that could be labeled as 'magic.'

The criteria that appear in the sources correspond fairly well with the Weberian criteria for legitimate religious activity discussed by Gordon, a set of criteria that are vague and broad enough to apply to the ancient materials without too much distortion.[28] Gordon refers to *objectivity, ends, performance,* and *social or political location* as the arenas in which the validity of any religious activity may be judged, and these criteria are also useful, from an etic scholarly perspective, for gauging the validity of scientific activity, thus providing a way to classify magic in relation to both elements of the grand dichotomies so prevalent in etic definitions of magic. By *objectivity*, Gordon refers to the success rate or efficacy of the activity, judged by an objective observer, but I prefer the term '*efficacy*' as somewhat more transparent. Things labeled 'magic' are characterized by an abnormal success rate or efficacy, whether that abnormality is extraordinarily low efficacy or extraordinarily high. The *ends* are the socially unac-

[27] As Graf 1991 has shown. See further ch. 6, n. 5, p. 152.

[28] Gordon has demonstrated the viability of these criteria in his magisterial essay on imagining Greek and Roman magic. Cp. Gordon 1999a: 191–192: "Legitimate religious knowledge in antiquity can roughly be defined in terms of performance, political-social location, objectivity, and ends. In relation to each, we can posit a normatively ideal form from which actual forms diverge in greater or lesser degree: the ideal form constructs the positive pole of a notional contiuum of legitimacy whose opposite pole is constitiued by fully illegitimate religious knowledge."

ceptable or deviant aims of the magic, in contrast to other more normal and socially acceptable actions. The validity of the *performance* depends on its execution by the actor and reception by its audience, while the *sociopolitical location* of the performer with respect to that audience is the final criterion for its legitimacy.

The criterion of objectivity or *efficacy* addresses the question perennially raised by newcomers to the study of ancient magic: did it work? Such a question, however, properly understood, is not the same as: can we, from our modern perspective, find a way of explaining how it could work? Rather, we must ask whether, from the evidence available to us, those involved with the magic thought it worked or not. At times, the text provides explicit indication of the perceived extra-ordinary efficacy of the magic, but other times we must deduce the evaluation from other evidence. To take an example, people in the ancient Greco-Roman world continued to make curse tablets from our earliest examples in the fifth century BCE to Late Antiquity a millennium later, so we have to conclude that they assumed that the practice was sufficiently effective to continue.[29] Of course, the deviation from the ordinary standard of efficacy may be negative as well as positive; something that does not, in fact, work in the ways that it is expected to (especially by others), is often labeled as 'magic.'[30] Herbal remedies or good luck charms may be derided as 'magic' or 'superstition' because, from the standpoint of scientific causality, they don't actually work in the ways that their users expect them to.

This criterion is also crucial for addressing the etic distinction between magic and science, since modern thinkers often assume that some version of Arthur C. Clarke's famous Third Law must apply: "Any sufficiently advanced technology is indistinguishable from magic."[31] That is, if you can't understand how it works, it counts as magic, so the primitives who cannot understand modern scientific processes regard the operation of those processes as magic. Other critics quibble, pointing out correctly that most of us have no ability to explain the operation of our microwave ovens, automobiles, or cellphones, nor would we have the capacity to replicate their functions. We do not, however, regularly regard such

[29] As Tomlin 1988a: 101 comments of the curse tablets at Roman Bath, "The practice of inscribing them continued for two centuries, from the second to the fourth, which implies that they did work. Or rather, that they were believed to work; and, perhaps, that this belief was justified."

[30] As Gordon 1999a: 210 points out, abnormal religious activity is often assumed to be less effective than the normative. "It is precisely this connection, unquestioned for civic cult, between ritual and efficacy that fails to hold true for illicit religion. There is a vacancy at the centre of illicit cult, a vacancy that is the structural consequence of negating the norm."

[31] The 'law' appears in a footnote at the end of Clarke's essay on "The Hazards of Prophecy: The Failure of the Imagination," in Clarke 1973: 21.

technologies as magic, because they are such familiar and normal parts of our ordinary world. The point here is that anything that works better than our normal expectation appears as magic; it is the deviation from the ordinary that provokes the label, rather than our inability to provide a causal explanation.

It is the deviance from the norms of acceptable behavior that also marks the criterion of *ends*, rather than the dubious concept that true religious action always tends toward the cohesion of the society.[32] In a given social circumstance, it may be completely normal and acceptable to act in one's own interest instead of the imagined greater good of the community, whereas in others to sacrifice one's own interests or life for the greater good of the community might be seen as bizarre and extra-ordinary. It is also crucial to bear in mind that, just because something is agreed upon as non-normative or socially unacceptable does not mean that people won't do it. Adultery, for example, is a non-normative behavior that violates the norms of marriage, but Greco-Roman literature (and indeed history) is full of stories of people choosing to commit adultery.

Likewise, people may deliberately choose deviant modes of *performance* of their actions upon the social stage, or their performance may be adjudged as non-normative by their audience. Someone who mutters a prayer in a foreign language rather than speaking aloud in standard Greek may be suspected of non-normative behavior, but someone who performs an incantation full of incomprehensible words and animal noises must surely be performing magic. Magical words, *voces magicae* or *voces mysticae* as they are often called in the scholarship, are a deliberately deviant verbal performance, since they do not communicate meaning normally, and the more abnormal and exotic they appear, the more magical they seem.[33]

Some scholars have critiqued the 'deviance theory' of defining magic as non-normative because of the existence of evidence in which individuals define their own actions as deviant.[34] Such self-definitions of deviance, however, are far from uncommon in all realms of cultural performance; there are many ways of 'queering' oneself, be it with regard to gender or sexuality or any other facet of one's social identity. Gordon makes use of

---

[32] Such a concept derives from the Durkheimian understanding of religion as an expression of the collective identity and will. If religion is merely a transferred honoring of the collective to imagined gods, then any action against the interests of the collective would logically be an antireligious action. The classic study in Mauss 1972 works out these ideas most fully and influentially.

[33] Malinowski 1935: 218–223 refers to this deviation from normality as the "coefficient of weirdness"; the higher the coefficient, the more likely it is to be magic.

[34] "The deviance theory falls short in at least one respect, in that it fails to account for the fact that some people also apply the concept of 'magic' to themselves and their own practices and beliefs" (Otto and Stausberg 2013: 7). Cp. also Otto's critique of the deviance theory in Otto 2013.

Bourdieu's terminology of 'intentional profanation' to refer to those who intentionally mark themselves as non-normative in the performance of religious ritual as they seek to transcend or subvert the established norms of society.[35]

Bourdieu's concept of profanation is also useful in discussing the criterion of *sociopolitical location,* since someone may be marked as a non-normative member of society, especially by someone who considers himself normative, simply on the basis of that person's place in society. If the mature male citizen is taken as the normative member of society in the Greco-Roman world, then anyone who is not a citizen, not a mature adult, or not a male may be marked as non-normative, objectively profane in Bourdieu's terms. The levels of alterity may be cumulative, so an old, foreign, slave woman has the greatest number of valid cues for her non-normative status and thus most likely to be suspected of using magic.

DRAWING DOWN THE MOON

Criteria for Non-Normative Action

The act of drawing down the moon with which we began furnishes a good example of the usefulness of these criteria adapted from Gordon for understanding the discourse of magic in the ancient Greco-Roman world, the ways the ancient Greeks and Romans defined magic. This act is explictly labeled 'magic' by some of the earliest sources, and many different examples of this Thessalian trick appear throughout the entire range of the evidence. The ability to draw down the moon frequently appears in lists of magical powers, so these collocations provide a wider set of other practices that may be labeled 'magic' from an emic perspective. The various examples stress different aspects of the non-normativity of the act: some the social location of the performers, some the non-normative ends for which it is performed, some for the weirdness of the perfomance, and others for the extra-ordinary power and efficacy of the rite.

In some of the evidence for drawing down the moon, its nature as magic is marked by the sociopolitical location of the ones performing the ritual. *Who* does it indicates the kind of practice it is, and its alterity is marked by various aspects of alterity of the performers, especially their alien status, their gender, and their age. Our earliest witness, Aristophanes, attributes the trick of drawing down the moon to a Thessalian witch (*pharmakis*), and the association persists throughout the evidence. The Thessalian

---

[35] Gordon 1999a refers to the categories of intentional and objective profanation developed in Bourdieu 1971, although the context of Greco-Roman religion differs with respect to forms of institutional control from the examples Bourdieu discusses.

trick is the sort of thing that people in far-off Thessaly do, so that Thessalian women become proverbial as magicians.³⁶ As Pliny notes, magic has long been associated with the Thessalian women, to the extent that Menander called his play about women drawing down the moon *The Thessalian Woman*.³⁷ Lucan digresses on the magical powers of Thessalians in his introduction of the greatest witch of all, his horrible Erictho, while a later scholarly commentator, a scholiast on Apollonius, quotes a passage from the lost *Meleager* of the fourth-century BCE tragedian, Sosiphanes, to the effect that every Thessalian girl with her magic incantations can bring down the moon from the heavens.³⁸ This alien Thessalian origin can serve as a transferred epithet; Horace's witches draw down the moon with Thessalian incantations, and the whirligig, the spinning wheel device that makes a buzzing noise that draws down the moon, is often simply referred to as the Thessalian wheel.³⁹ This whirligig is actually a very common toy found in cultures all over the world, from the Neolithic period through the present day, but, in the evidence from the Greco-Roman world, it is associated with erotic magic and drawing down the moon.⁴⁰

³⁶ Aristophanes, *Nub.* 746–757, ch. 1, p. 4, n. 2. The practice may, like so many of the rites attested in the Greco-Roman tradition, have a precedent in Mesopotamia. A Neo-Assyrian letter to King Esarhaddon in the seventh century BCE refers to women who bring down the moon from the sky; see Reiner 1995: 98.

³⁷ Pliny, *HN* 30.7. *nec postea quisquam dixit quonam modo venisset Telmesum religiosissimam urbem, quando transisset ad Thessalas matres, quarum cognomen diu optinuit in nostro orbe, aliena genti Troianis utique temporibus Chironis medicinis contentae et solo Marte fulminante. miror equidem Achillis populis famam eius in tantum adhaesisse, ut Menander quoque litterarum subtilitati sine aemulo genitus Thessalam cognominaret fabulam complexam ambages feminarum detrahentium lunam.* "And in later times nobody has explained how ever it reached Telmesus, a city given up to superstition, or when it passed over to the Thessalian matrons, whose surname was long proverbial in our part of the world, although magic was a craft repugnant to the Thessalian people, who were content, at any rate in the Trojan period, with the medicines of Chiron, and with the War God as the only wielder of the thunderbolt. I am indeed surprised that the people over whom Achilles once ruled had a reputation for magic so lasting that actually Menander, a man with an unrivalled gift for sound literary taste, gave the name 'Thessala' to his comedy, which deals fully with the tricks of the women for calling down the moon" (Loeb).

³⁸ Cp. Lucan, *Pharsalia* 6.434–506; Scholiast on Apollonius Rhodius 3.533 (234.22–235.6) Σωσιφάνης ἐν Μελεάγρῳ (fr. 1 N.2) 'μάγοις ἐπῳδαῖς πᾶσα Θεσσαλὶς κόρη ψευδὴς σελήνης αἰθέρος καταιβάτις.'

³⁹ Horace, *Ep.* 5.45–46. *quae sidera excantata voce Thessala lunamque caelo deripit.* "She charms the moon and stars with Thessalian incantations and pulls them down from the sky." Cp. Martial 9.29.9–12, 12.57.15–17, with reference to drawing down the moon with a Thessalian or Colchian whirligig (*Thessalo rhombo, Colco rhombo*).

⁴⁰ The Greek terms are *iunx, strophalos,* or *rhombos,* whereas the Latin usually uses *rhombus*. This whirligig, sometimes called a spinner, buzzer, buzz saw or sawmill in English, is sometimes confused with the bullroarer, another simple device that makes sound when it is spun. The bullroarer, however, is a piece of wood or other material swung around at the end of a single string, whereas the whirligig is rotated by pulling the two strings that go through

These sources stress another form of alterity, gender, for it is specifically Thessalian women who are famous for drawing down the moon. Moreover, although Sosiphanes refers to girls, many of the depictions of Thessalian women add another layer of alterity, old age. Such old Thessalian women appear in Apuleius and other Roman sources, culminating in Lucan's horrible hag Erictho, who is old and female and Thessalian. The alterity of age and gender can appear without Thessalian origin; Horace's witches Canidia, Sagana, and Folia are filthy old women, but they are Italian, like Ovid's drunken old bawd-witch, Dipsas. Propertius's gloating description of the death of the bawd-witch Acanthis, who has thwarted his erotic intentions with her magic, dwells in gruesome detail on the ravages of age on the hag's body.[41] In other cases, merely the alterity of alien origin takes the place of gender and age. Lucian describes a (male) Hyperborean magician drawing down the moon, while Nonnos attributes this feat to the Brahmans of India.[42] In all these cases, drawing down the moon is an act characteristic of someone *who* is not in a normative place in the social and political order, not a mature, male citizen but old, female, or alien.

Other indicators of the non-normative status of the act may be *where* and *when* it is performed; it is a perfectly respectable thing for a woman to go to a cemetery to visit the tombs of family members, but for anyone to visit a graveyard in the dead of the night is always suspicious. The scarecrow Priapus statue in Horace's *Satire* complains that, in his spot in the Esquiline gardens by the old pauper's cemetery, he not only is beset with robbers and wild beasts, but, worst of all, the witches come prowling in the light of the moon. Lucian's Hyperborean magician may perform his ritual in the courtyard of his client's house, but he still waits for midnight under a waxing moon to perform his uncanny ritual.[43]

Of course, the motives for performing the drawing down of the moon may be as shady as the time and place in which they are done. The Hyperborean magician summons up the dead, invokes Hekate, and draws down

---

its middle. Both devices generate sound from the speed of their rotation, but the whirligig goes much faster, actually reaching speeds of up to 125,000 rpm (faster than a Ferrari engine) because of the hypercoiling effect of the strings. Scientists have recently devised a way to use such simple whirligigs as centrifuges for processing blood samples in areas without access to regular electricity, since the speed of rotation and the force generated (up to 30,000 g) exceed the capacity of centrifuges costing thousands of times more. See Bhamla et al. 2017.

[41] Cp. Apuleius, *Met.* 1.12 on Meroe and Panthia as *mulieres duas altioris aetatis*, two women of rather advanced age. Horace, *Ep.* 5.98; Ovid, *Amores* 1.8.1–2; Propertius 4.567–572.

[42] Lucian, *Philops.* 14; Nonnos, *Dionysiaca* 36.344–349. θεοκλήτοις δ᾽ ἐπαοιδαῖς πολλάκις ἠερόφοιτον, ὁμοίιον ἄζυγι ταύρῳ, οὐρανόθεν κατάγοντες ἐφαρμάξαντο Σελήνην. "Their inspired incantations have often enchanted Selene as she passes through the air like an untamed bull, and brought her down from heaven."

[43] Horace, *Sat.* 1.8.17–26; Lucian, *Philops.* 14.

the moon to obtain the power to send the pretty young wife of his client's neighbor over to his client's bed, maddened with lust. This kind of illicit inflaming of passion is often *why* magicians draw down the moon. Vergil depicts a woman drawing down the moon to force her errant lover Daphnis to return to her.

> Songs can even draw the moon down from heaven;
> by songs Circe transformed the comrades of Ulysses;
> with song the cold snake in the meadows is burst asunder.
> Bring Daphnis home from town, bring him, my songs![44]

Vergil is adapting the motif from the earlier poem of Theocritus, where Simaetha spins her magic whirligig (called a *iunx* or a *rhombus*) to draw down the moon and bring her errant lover Delphis back to her.

> O *iunx*, drag this man to my house.
> As this wax doll I, with the divinity's power, do melt,
> So may he melt with *eros*, the Myndian Delphis, at once
> And, as whirls round this bronze *rhombos* from Aphrodite,
> So too may he whirl round to my doors.
> O *iunx*, drag this man to my house.[45]

For these girls, forsaken by their lovers, some extra-ordinary means is needed to win back their affections, so they turn to magic and the power gained by drawing down the moon to take control of their lovers' minds and bodies, subjugating these men to female control, something that is always viewed as abnormal in the patriarchal societies of the ancient Greco-Roman world.

The illicit aims of drawing down the moon may have nothing to do with *eros*, however. Strepsiades's plan, in Aristophanes, is to get the Thessalian witch to draw down the moon so that he can hide it in a box, thus enabling him to get out of paying his debts, which are due on the new moon day, when the new moon first appears in a month. No moon in the sky means no payment due date, which, Strepsiades reasons, means no debts.[46]

In other accounts, the aim of drawing down the moon is to collect the lunar power that accumulates from the proximity of the moon to the earth, whether in the form of plants with extra potency from the moon's rays or

[44] Vergil, *Ecl.* 8.69–72. *Carmina vel caelo possunt deducere Lunam;* | *carminibus Circe socios mutavit Ulixi;* | *frigidus in pratia cantando rumpitur anguis.* | *Ducite ab urbe domum, mea carmina, ducite Daphnim.*

[45] Theocritus, *Idyll* 2.27–32. ἶυγξ, ἕλκε τὺ τῆνον ἐμὸν ποτὶ δῶμα τὸν ἄνδρα.| ὡς τοῦτον τὸν κηρὸν ἐγὼ σὺν δαίμονι τάκω,| ὣς τάκοιθ᾽ ὑπ᾽ ἔρωτος ὁ Μύνδιος αὐτίκα Δέλφις.| χὢς δινεῖθ᾽ ὅδε ῥόμβος ὁ χάλκεος ἐξ Ἀφροδίτας,| ὣς τῆνος δινοῖτο ποθ᾽ ἁμετέραισι θύραισιν.| ἶυγξ, ἕλκε τὺ τῆνον ἐμὸν ποτὶ δῶμα τὸν ἄνδρα.

[46] Aristophanes, *Nub.* 746–757.

in a concentrated form as 'moonfoam,' *aphroselenon*. As the early third-century CE Sextus Julius Africanus tells us in his collection of interesting facts entitled *Kestoi*, this moonfoam is gathered from the dew of plants and the rays of moonbeams, and Lucan and other sources refer to the foam of the moon that appears when the moon is drawn down by magic.

> And the clear moon, beset by dread incantations, grew dim and burned with a dark and earthy light, just as if the earth cut her off from her brother's reflection and thrust its shadow athwart the fires of heaven. Lowered by magic, she suffers all that pain, until from close quarters she drops foam upon the plants below.[47]

The third-century CE alchemist Zosimus likewise connects *aphroselenon* with the rays of the moon, since at the waning (or drawing down?) of the moon there is an outflow of light that bears the particular lunar nature.[48] This magical substance might be used for various magical ends, but Lucan depicts his horrid witch Erictho using the moonfoam in her gruesome re-animation of a corpse for necromancy.

> Then she began by piercing the breast of the corpse with fresh wounds, which she filled with hot blood; she washed the inward parts clean of clotted gore; she poured in lavishly the poison that the moon supplies. With this was blended all that Nature inauspiciously conceives and brings forth. The froth of dogs that dread water was not wanting, nor the inwards of a lynx, nor the hump of a foul hyena, nor the marrow of a stag that had fed on snakes; the echenais was there, which keeps a ship motionless in mid-ocean, though the wind is stretching her cordage; eyes of dragons were there, and stones that rattle when warmed under a breeding eagle; the flying serpent of Arabia, and the viper that is born by the Red Sea and guards the precious pearl-shell; the skin which the horned snake of Libya casts off in its lifetime, and ashes of the Phoenix which lays its body on the Eastern altar. These ordinary banes that bear names she added to her

[47] Lucan, *Pharsalia* 6.500–506. *Phoebeque serena Non aliter diris verborum obsessa venenis Palluit et nigris terrenisque ignibus arsit, Quam si fraterna prohiberet imagine tellus Insereretque suas flammis caelestibus umbras, Et patitur tantos cantu depressa labores Donec suppositas propior despumet in herbas.* Cp. the reference to making the moon drop its dew by magic (*magico . . . lunam despumari*) in Apuleius, *Met.* 1.3 and Medea's knowledge of how to make the moon produce foam by magic substances (*Atracio lunam spumare veneno sciret*) in Valerius Flaccus, *Argonautica* 6.447–448. Sextus Julius Africanus, *Kestoi* 9.1.35 apud Psellos, *Opusc.* 32.48. ὁ δὲ ἀφροσέληνον συλλέγει ἐκ τῆς δρόσου τῶν φυτῶν καὶ τῶν σεληναίων αὐγῶν.

[48] On Zosimus, *On Excellence and Interpretation*, CAAG II.123.17–19. ἐπείπερ ἐν σελήνῃ ἐνρωηκὰ ἀπορ < ρο > ία ἐστὶν τοῦ φωτός, καὶ αὕτη ἡ ῥεῦσίς ἐστιν τῆς οἰκείας φύσεως ἐνδικαίως τῶν ἄλλων πάντων τῶν ἄστρων. Cp. ἀφροσέληνον . . . ἀπὸ σεληνιακῆς ἀπορροίας in *Fragmenta Alchemica, On the Dyeing of Stones*, CAAG II,357 Berthelot.

brew; and next she put in leaves steeped with magic unutterable, and herbs which her own dread mouth had spat upon at their birth, and all the poison that she herself gave to the world; and lastly her voice, more powerful than any drug to bewitch the powers of Lethe, first uttered indistinct sounds, sounds untunable and far different from human speech.[49]

Erictho's aims in violating the bounds of life and death are characteristically repulsive, but alchemists like Zosimus used moonfoam for other extra-ordinary aims, such as transmuting silver into gold.

> Unify *aphroselenos* with *komaris*, pounding it fine and softening it and making it solid and washing it, smelt silver, and make a projection from the compound, and you will see the silver transmuted into gold, and you will be amazed. Nature rejoices in nature, and nature conquers nature.[50]

Alchemists can use the magical substance of moonfoam in their processes of the transmutation of qualities, with just a tiny trace amount changing a large quantity of the white shiny metal of silver into the yellow shiny metal of gold.

"You will be amazed," proclaims the alchemical recipe; this procedure is not at all a normal one, but something extra-ordinary and marvelous. The extra-ordinary efficacy of the process is the most significant marker of its magical status, what Weber would term its abnormal *objectivity*.

---

[49] Lucan, *Pharsalia* 6.667–687. *Pectora tunc primum ferventi sanguine supplet Volneribus laxata novis taboque medullas Abluit et virus large lunare ministrat. Huc quidquid fetu genuit natura sinistro Miscetur. Non spuma canum quibus unda timori est, Viscera non lyncis, non dirae nodus byaenae Defuit et cervi pastae serpente medullae, Non puppim retinens Euro tendente rudentes In mediis echenais aquis oculique draconum Quaeque sonant feta tepefacta sub alite saxa; Non Arabum volucer serpens innataque rubris Aequoribus custos pretiosae vipera conchae Aut viventis adhuc Libyci membrana cerastae Aut cinis Eoa positi phoenicis in ara. Quo postquam viles et habentes nomina pestes Contulit, infando saturatas carmine frondes Et, quibus os dirum nascentibus inspuit, herbas Addidit et quidquid mundo dedit ipsa veneni. Tum vox Lethaeos cunctis pollentior herbis Excantare deos confundit murmura primum Dissona et humanae multum discordia linguae.* Cp. the witch's invocation of the moon for necromancy in Heliodorus 6.14. Gordon 1999a: 223 suggests that this substance is the same as the lunar ointment (τῷ σεληνιακῷ χρίσματι) used in PGM VII.874 to anoint a statue of the moon goddess in a spell for attracting women and sending dreams.

[50] *Fragmenta Alchemica, On the Dyeing of Stones*, CAAG II.358.28–359.3. Ἀφροσέληνον ἔνωσον μετὰ κομάρεως, λειῶν καὶ μαλάττων καὶ πηγνύων καὶ βάπτων αὐτὸν, χώνευσον ἄργυρον, καὶ ἐπίβαλε ἀπὸ τοῦ συνθήματος, καὶ ἴδῃς τὴν ἄργυρον εἰς χρυσὸν μεταποιηθεῖσαν, καὶ θαυμάσεις. Ἡ φύσις τῇ φύσει τέρπεται, καὶ ἡ φύσις τὴν φύσιν νικᾷ. This recipe is attributed to Demokritos, the fifth-century BCE thinker to whom many later alchemical works were spuriously atttributed (see ch. 9, p. 272, nn. 4–6). To make a projection (ἐπίβαλε) is to put a tiny portion of the special substance (here, the ἀφροσέληνος) into a larger quantity of another substance (here, silver) that is to be transformed.

While changing silver into gold using the power from the drawn-down moon is indeed an amazing feat, drawing down the moon is associated with even more astounding actions.

They profess to know how to bring down the moon, to eclipse the sun, to make storm and sunshine, rain and drought, the sea impassable and the earth barren, and all other such sorts of things, either by rites or by some knowledge or practice that those accustomed to do such things say they are able to happen.[51]

This Hippocratic critique of rival practitioners is the earliest witness to this kind of catalog of acts that are contrary to the normal order of things in which drawing down the moon has pride of place, but such lists of powerfully abnormal acts becomes a familiar trope, especially in Roman literature. Ovid's Medea proclaims,

When I have willed it, the streams have run back to their fountainheads, while the banks wondered; I lay the swollen, and stir up the calm seas by my spell; I drive the clouds and bring on the clouds; the winds I dispel and summon; I break the jaws of serpents with my incantations; living rocks and oaks I root up from their own soil; I move the forests, I bid the mountains shake, the earth to rumble and the ghosts to come forth from their tombs. Thee also, Luna, do I draw from the sky, though the clanging bronze of Temesa strive to aid thy throes; even the chariot of the Sun, my grandsire, pales at my song; Aurora pales at my poisons.[52]

Medea boasts total control over the cosmos, the ability to reverse every normal condition, whether it be reversing the regular movements of rivers and winds, disrupting the immobility of trees and rocks and mountains, or even making the dead come back to the world of the living. Her power, like that of other witches in Roman literature, is beyond that of any normal mortal, exerting control even over the gods.[53]

---

[51] Hippocratic, *de morb. sacr.* IV.1–8. σελήνην καθαιρεῖν καὶ ἥλιον ἀφανίζειν καὶ χειμῶνά τε καὶ εὐδίην ποιεῖν καὶ ὄμβρους καὶ αὐχμοὺς καὶ θάλασσαν ἄπορον καὶ γῆν ἄφορον καὶ τἆλλα τὰ τοιουτότροπα πάντα ὑποδέχονται ἐπίστασθαι, εἴτε καὶ ἐκ τελετέων εἴτε καὶ ἐξ ἄλλης τινὸς γνώμης καὶ μελέτης φασὶ ταῦτα οἷόν τ᾽ εἶναι γενέσθαι οἱ ταῦτ᾽ ἐπιτηδεύοντες (Loeb trans. adapted).

[52] Ovid, *Met.* 7.199–209. *cum volui, ripis mirantibus amnes in fontes rediere suos, concussaque sisto, stantia concutio cantu freta, nubila pello nubilaque induco, ventos abigoque vocoque, vipereas rumpo verbis et carmine fauces, vivaque saxa sua convulsaque robora terra et silvas moveo iubeoque tremescere montis et mugire solum manesque exire sepulcris! te quoque, Luna, traho, quamvis Temesaea labores aera tuos minuant; currus quoque carmine nostro pallet avi, pallet nostris Aurora venenis.* Cp. Ovid, *Rem. am.* 249–266; Ovid, *Amores* 1.8.5–18; Valerius Flaccus, *Argonautica* 6.439–445; Tibullus 1.2.41–52. Vergil, *Aeneid* 4.483–491 has a similar catalog, but does not explicitly mention drawing down the moon.

[53] Lucan, as usual, provides the most extensive and extravagant catalog of the powers

So disturbing is this level of power that certain sources postulate that some compensation must right the balance. In discussing whether gaining political power in the city is worth the moral cost, Plato refers to a proverb that Thessalian women who draw down the moon do so only at the expense of losing one of their eyes—or one of their children.[54] The Hippocratic author of *On the Sacred Disease*, however, argues that anyone who claims such abnormal powers must either be an impious disrespecter of the gods or, more likely, simply a fraud.

> In any case I am sure that they are impious, and cannot believe that the gods exist or have any strength, and that they would not refrain from the most extreme actions. . . . But perhaps what they profess is not true, the fact being that men, in need of a livelihood, contrive and devise many fictions of all sorts.[55]

The extra-ordinary power of drawing down the moon is too extra-ordinary to be believed, and thus it must simply be a trick of some kind that enables charlatans to make a living by duping the credulous fools who trust in them.

A similar idea appears in other sources that explain away the drawing down of the moon as a trick by which someone pretends, during an eclipse of the moon, to be drawing it down to make it vanish. Plutarch claims that the Thessalian woman Aglaonike used her scientific knowledge of astronomy to predict lunar eclipses and then pretended to other women that she had the power to draw down the moon.[56] Others, like the early Christian apologist Hippolytus, explain the Thessalian trick as an elaborately staged hoax, with smoke and mirrors, designed to dupe the gullible into believing that these practitioners actually have access to divine power.

> They exhibit the moon and the stars on the ceiling in the following fashion. They fix a mirror to the central part of the ceiling and place a bowl of water directly beneath it in the middle of the floor. Then

---

of the Thessalian witches (*Pharsalia* 6.434–506), culminating in Erictho, who goes even beyond. "These criminal rites and malpractices of an accursed race fierce Erictho had scouted as not wicked enough." *Hos scelerum ritus, haec dirae crimina gentis Effera damnarat nimiae pietatis Erictho* (*Pharsalia* 6.507–508).

[54] Plato, *Gorgias* 513a. The proverb itself first appears in Zenobius's collection of proverbs, *Epitome* 4.1.

[55] Hippocratic, *de morb. sacr.* IV. 8–10, 17–19. δυσσεβεῖν ἔμοιγε δοκέουσι καὶ θεοὺς οὔτε εἶναι νομίζειν οὔτε ἰσχύειν οὐδὲν οὔτε εἴργεσθαι ἂν οὐδενὸς τῶν ἐσχάτων. . . . ἴσως δὲ οὐχ οὕτως ἔχει ταῦτα, ἀλλ' ἄνθρωποι βίου δεόμενοι πολλὰ καὶ παντοῖα τεχνῶνται καὶ ποικίλλουσιν ἔς τε τἄλλα πάντα (Loeb).

[56] Plutarch, *Conj. praec.* 145c–d; *de def. orac.* 416f–417a. Hill 1973 argues cogently that the evidence from the ancient Greeks and Romans shows that they did not think that drawing down the moon was an eclipse, but rather that they could interpret an eclipse as a drawing down of the moon.

they put a dimly shining lamp in the middle of the room, suspended above the bowl. In this way the mage makes a moon appear in the mirror from the reflection of the bowl. Also, the mage often suspends a drum from a height and cloaks it with a cover. This is kept covered by an accomplice, so that it should not be seen before the right time. The mage places a lamp behind it. When he gives the agreed signal to his accomplice, the accomplice removes part of the cover, just enough to mimic the phase of the moon at that point. The mage paints the translucent parts of the drum with cinnabar and gum. With a greater degree of preparation, the mage removes the neck and base from a round bottle, puts a lamp inside and covers it with some equipment in such a way that the shape of the moon shines through. . . . One of the accomplices secretly takes up position on high, behind a screen. After receiving the agreed signal, he lowers the apparatus from its suspended position, so that the moon appears to be descending from heaven. A similar trick with a pot is done in wooded places. Tricks can be done with a pot indoors too. An altar is set up and the pot is positioned behind it with a dimly shining lamp. When several lamps are shining, this remains undetectable. Now when the enchanter calls on the moon, he gives the order to extinguish the lamps, but to leave one dim one. Then the light from the pot reflects onto the ceiling and shows an image of the moon to the audience. The pot is kept covered until the time comes for displaying its moon-shaped image on the roof.[57]

These charlatans perform a rite they claim has extra-ordinary efficacy, but, in reality, claims Hippolytus, this procedure has no efficacy at all; it is

[57] Hippolytus, *Haer.* 4.37. Σελήνην δὲ ἐν ὀρόφῳ φαίνεσθαι δεικνύουσι καὶ ἀστέρας τοῦτον τὸν τρόπον· ἐν μέσῳ τῆς ὀροφῆς μέρει προσαρμόσας κάτοπτρον, τιθεὶς λεκάνην ὕδατος μεστὴν ἐν τῷ μέσῳ <κατὰ> τῆς γῆς κατ' ἴσον, λύχνον δὲ μέσον φαίνον<τα> ἀμαυρὸν μετεωρότερον τῆς λεκάνης θείς, οὕτως ἐκ τῆς ἀντανακλάσεως ἀποτελεῖ σελήνην φαίνεσθαι διὰ τοῦ κατόπτρου. ἀλλὰ καὶ τύμπανον πολλάκις ἀφ' ὑψηλοῦ αἰωρηθὲν ὄρθιον περιβαλὼν ἐσθῆτί τινι, σκεπόμενον ὑπὸ τοῦ συμπαίκτου, ἵνα μὴ πρὸ καιροῦ φανῇ, <καὶ> κατόπιν θεὶς λύχνον, ἐπὰν τὸ σύνθημα παράσχῃ τῷ συμπαίκτῃ, <οὗτος> τοσοῦτον ἀφαιρεῖ τοῦ σκεπάσματος, ὅσον ἂν συνεργήσαι πρὸς τὸ μιμήσα<σθαι> κατὰ τὸν καιρὸν τῆς σελήνης τὸ σχῆμα. χρίει δὲ τὰ διαφαίνοντα τοῦ τυμπάνου μέρη κινναβάρ<ει> καὶ κόμμι. καί τις ἑτοιμό<τερος> δὲ ὀλίγης λαγήνου περικόψας τὸν τράχηλον καὶ τὸν πυθμένα, ἐνθεὶς λύχνον καὶ περιθεὶς τι τῶν ἐπιτηδείων πρὸς τὸ διαυγεῖ <τὸ> σχῆμα <*> στὰς <δὲ> ἐφ' ὑψηλοῦ κρύβδην ὑπό τινα σκέπην τις τῶν συμπαικτῶν, μετὰ τὸ λαβεῖν τὸ σύνθημα ἐκ μετεώρου κατάγει τὰ μηχανήματα, ὥ<στ>ε δοκεῖν ἐξ οὐρανοῦ κατιέν(αι) τὴν σελήνην. τὸ δὲ ὅμοιον καὶ διὰ χύτρας γίνεται ἐν ὑλώδεσι τόποις· διὰ δὲ τῆς χύτρας καὶ τὰ κατ' οἶκον παίζεται. βωμοῦ γὰρ κειμένου κατόπιν κεῖται ἡ χύτρα ἔχουσα λύχνον φαίνοντα <ἀμαυρόν>· ὄντων δὲ πλειόνων λύχνων οὐδὲν τοιοῦτον δείκνυται. ἐπὰν οὖν ἐπικαλέσηται ὁ ἐπαοιδὸς τὴν σελήνην, πάντας κελεύει τοὺς λύχνους σβέννυσθαι, ἕνα δὲ ἀμαυρὸν καταλιπεῖν. καὶ τότε ἀντανακλᾷ τὸ φῶς τὸ ἐκ τῆς χύτρας εἰς τὸν ὄροφον καὶ παρέχει φαντασίαν σελήνης [καὶ] τοῖς παροῦσιν, ἐπισκεπασθέντος τοῦ στόματος τῆς χύτρας πρὸς ὃ ἀπαιτεῖν ὁ καιρὸς δοκεῖ, ὡς μηνοειδῆ δείκνυσθαι ἐν τῷ ὀρόφῳ τὴν φαντασίαν (trans. Ogden 2009).

below normal rather than above normal. The enchanter (*epaoidos*) is a magician in the negative sense of the term, one who performs acts that are worthless and useless, mere deceptions that prey on the superstitious, just as Aglaonike is a Thessalian witch who takes advantage of the ignorance of uneducated women by pretending to power she does not (and could not) have.

Polemical Perspectives

In each case, how the act of drawing down the moon is considered magic depends on who is labeling whom and by what criteria, and even in what kind of text the performance is described. Literary descriptions of the rite differ from the kind of references found in polemical arguments that either accuse people of drawing down the moon by magic or try to defend them from such a charge. The polemics are meant to be representing real life, even if the details are exaggerated or just simply fabricated, but the literary imaginings are limited only by the imagination and artistic purposes of the poet. Then again, these labelings of some other as using magic differ from self-labeling of oneself or one's activities as 'magical.'

Depictions of someone else using magic in literary texts provide an implicit definition of magic in various ways, often through the depiction of aspects of the person's sociopolitical location, such as the old, Thessalian woman who sneaks into graveyards in the dead of night. Literary accounts also illuminate the motivations of the characters involved, and so the ends for which the person is acting can also serve to define the action as magic. The description of the extra-ordinary efficacy of the procedure in literary accounts remains unbounded by anything but the author's imagination, so that the most hyperbolic accounts of magical power come from sources such as the Roman poets and novelists, who use the figure of the super-witch (like Canidia, Meroe, or Erictho) for their various literary purposes in their works. A favorite motif is to pile up the astounding and incredible powers of the witch and then to point out that these nearly omnipotent beings are still helpless in the face of love.

> If anyone thinks that the baneful herbs of Haemonia and arts of magic can avail, let him take his own risk. That is the old way of witchcraft; my patron Apollo gives harmless aid in sacred song. Under my guidance no spirit will be bidden issue from the tomb, no witch will cleave the ground with hideous spell; no crops will pass from field to field, nor Phoebus' orb grow suddenly pale. As of wont will Tiber flow to the sea's waters; as of wont will the Moon ride in her snow-white car. No hearts will lay aside their passion by enchantment, nor love flee vanquished by strong sulphur. What availed thee the grasses

of thy Phasian land, O Colchian maid, when thou wert fain to stay in thy native home? What did Persean herbs profit thee, O Circe, when a breeze that favoured them bore the Neritian barks away? Thou didst all, that the cunning stranger should not leave thee: yet he spread full canvas in unhindered flight.[58]

The power of Medea and Circe, which could pull down the moon, reverse the courses of the rivers, and bring dead spirits to the living, cannot empower these women to hold the affections of their lovers, and the more hyperbolic the description of their magical powers, the more the author can enhance the irony of the situation.

The polemical accounts tend to focus on the extra-ordinary efficacy as the most important feature. They either deny any normal efficacy at all, claiming that the performance of drawing down the moon is charlatanry (fakery or eclipse), or they attribute its marvelous efficacy to impious action, a transgression of the natural normal order. Some, like the Hippocratic author, have it both ways, claiming that either the ritual healers who draw down the moon either simply lie about their power to command the divine forces or they impiously treat the gods as inferiors and ask them to do evil things unworthy of a god. In either case, the level of efficacy is out of the ordinary, drastically below in the case of fraud or dramatically above in the case of the real transgressions of the cosmic order. This kind of non-normativity is reinforced by the deviant social location or socially unacceptable ends of the performers. At best they are marginal itinerants who simply want to make a dishonest living; at worst they are pernicious atheists who disrespect the gods and appropriate their power.

By contrast, Marinus does not use the discourse of magic to label Proclus when he describes his activity in drawing down the moon as part of his hagiographic biography of the fifth-century CE head of the Platonic Academy in Athens. Like Simaetha and the Thessalian witches, Proclus was skilled in the use of the *iunx*, the whirligig or spinner that was used in rites of attraction, including the drawing down of the moon. Marinus reports that Proclus described in one of his writings (now lost) the appearance of a luminous form of Hekate, a goddess frequently identified as an aspect of the Moon in this time period. Marinus also recounts some of the miracles

---

[58] Ovid, *Rem. am.* 249–266. *Viderit, Haemoniae siquis mala pabula terrae Et magicas artes posse iuvare putat. Ista veneficii vetus est via; noster Apollo Innocuam sacro carmine monstrat opem. Me duce non tumulo prodire iubebitur umbra, Non anus infami carmine rumpet humum; Non seges ex aliis alios transibit in agros, Nec subito Phoebi pallidus orbis erit. Ut solet, aequoreas ibit Tiberinus in undas: Ut solet, in niveis Luna vehetur equis. Nulla recantatas deponent pectora curas, Nec fugiet vivo sulpure victus amor. Quid te Phasiacae iuverunt gramina terrae, Cum cuperes patria, Colchi, manere domo? Quid tibi profuerunt, Circe, Perseïdes herbae, Cum sua Neritias abstulit aura rates? Omnia fecisti, ne callidus hospes abiret: Ille dedit certae lintea plena fugae.* Cp. Prince 2003 on this theme.

Proclus performed with his rituals for the benefit of Athens, producing rain to end a drought and foretelling earthquakes, as well as the miraculous healing of a young girl.[59] *Who* Proclus is as the respected head of the Platonic Academy and *why* he does his rituals—for the benefit of the community—mark his actions as not transgressing the norms of the community. His extra-ordinary efficacy, his miraculous work, is abnormal, but the fact that his social location is normative and his aims are approved by the community makes his using a whirligig to bring down a lunar power a miracle of philosophical theurgy, not magic—at least, that is, for his faithful disciple and biographer, Marinus. A more hostile source, such as a Christian theologian following the arguments of Augustine, might well classify Proclus as a magician, someone who has dealings with the evil mistress of demons in order to perform his extra-ordinary feats.[60] Marinus indeed relates that Proclus spent a year in exile in Lydia because of the suspicions of certain 'vultures' around him in Athens.[61] Such defenses, relying on normative sociopolitical location and normative ends to counterbalance accusations of non-normative efficacy of practices, show that others must indeed have focused on this kind of Weberian objectivity in their labeling as 'magic' the one being defended. Apuleius's *Apologia*, his speech in his own defense against a charge of using magic, shows a similar defensive strategy, albeit with characteristically Apuleian twists, in his focus on his sociopolitical location (in the broader intellectual world of the Roman Empire) and acceptable ends (of philosophical inquiry).[62]

[59] Marinus, *Vit. Procl.* 28.677–679. ταῖς γὰρ τῶν Χαλδαίων συστάσεσι καὶ ἐντυχίαις καὶ τοῖς θείοις καὶ ἀφθέγκτοις στροφάλοις ἐκέχρητο. 684–686. ὁ φιλόσοφος τοῖς Χαλδαϊκοῖς καθαρμοῖς καθαιρόμενος, φάσμασι μὲν Ἑκατικοῖς φωτοειδέσιν αὐτοπτουμένοις ὡμίλησεν, ὡς καὶ αὐτός που μέμνηται ἐν ἰδίῳ συγγράμματι. ὄμβρους τε ἐκίνησεν, ἰυγγά τινα προσφόρως κινήσας, καὶ αὐχμῶν ἐξαισίων τὴν Ἀττικὴν ἠλευθέρωσεν. "He had made use of the communions of the Chaldaeans and the encounters with the gods and the ineffable spinners.... The philosopher, having been purified by Chaldaean purifications, consorted with the self-manifesting luminous images of Hekate. He moved the rain clouds, spinning a certain whirligig [*iunx*] in the appropriate way, and miraculously freed Attica from droughts" (my trans.). Cp. ch. 29 702–734 for the healing miracle.

[60] Graf 2002a discusses Augustine's arguments, particularly in his *de doctrina Christiana, de divinatione daemonum*, and his sermon of January 1, 403, in Carthage. See also Graf 2002b, as well as more recent studies in Dufault 2006 and Dufault 2008.

[61] Marinus, *Vit. Procl.* 15 370–373. καί ποτε ἐν περιστάσει τινῶν γυπογιγάντων ἐξετασθεὶς ἀπῆρεν, ὡς εἶχε, τῶν Ἀθηνῶν, τῇ τοῦ παντὸς περιφορᾷ πειθόμενος, καὶ τὴν ἐπὶ τὴν Ἀσίαν ἐποιεῖτο πορείαν. "And once having been tested in circumstances with certain opponents like vultures, he left Athens, as he was, and made a journey into Asia."

[62] See further below, in ch. 11, pp. 391–396, with references to the extensive scholarship. Modern philosophy scholars often have trouble with the idea of a respectable philosopher like Proclus engaging in magic rituals with the *iunx*. "It is hard to picture a Neoplatonist like Iamblichus or Proclus uttering inarticulate sounds or imitating an animal or laughing insanely as he rotated his bull-roarer. Perhaps they let someone else do this for them and simply watched and listened" (Luck 2000: 130).

Self-Labeling of Magic

Apuleius's defense of himself points to another type of evidence for the discourse of magic, self-labeling. Such self-labeling of oneself or one's activities as magic is far rarer than the label of 'magic' being applied to another, but the deliberate application of the discourse of magic to oneself is particularly illuminating for an understanding of the category in emic terms.

One spell from the Greek Magical Papyri gives us the evidence of someone who is trying to draw down the moon with a procedure that the text itself labels as 'magic' (*mageia*). The Greek Magical Papyri are a collection of spell books from Greco-Roman Egypt, and this spell appears in the PGM IV, a codex of seventy-two pages of ritual instructions compiled in the fourth century CE from earlier collections of spells in Greek. In one spell, the magician invokes the moon, drawing her down and compelling her to stay until she has fulfilled his demand.

> I whirl the wheel for you; the cymbals I don't touch. . . . The Moirai throw away your endless thread, unless you check my magic's winged shaft, swiftest to reach the mark. For to escape the fate of my words is impossible: happen it must. Don't force yourself to hear the symbols forward and then in reverse again. You'll, willy-nilly, do what's needed. Ere useless light becomes your fate, do what I say, O Maid, ruler of Tartaros. I've bound your pole with Kronos' chains, and with awesome compulsion I hold fast your thumb. Tomorrow does not come unless my will is done. To Hermes, leader of the gods, you promised to contribute to this rite.[63]

The magician stresses the inescapable efficacy of his magic. Just as in Proclus's invocations, the summons is performed with the wheel (a *rhombos* is a spinning whirligig device like a *iunx* or *strophalos*), but the magician also notes that the Moon's descent is guaranteed by her previous agreement with the leader of the gods, a pact marked by the special symbols the magician uses. The magician directs the power of the goddess against his chosen victim, designated in the papyrus—it is a fill-in-the-blank recipe, like many in the Greek Magical Papyri. Other spells in the same section of the spellbook direct the Moon's anger against a female victim for the

---

[63] PGM IV.2291, 2313–2326. ῥόμβον στρέφω σοι, κυμβάλων οὐχ ἅπτομαι, . . . Μοῖραί σου τὸν ἀνέκλειπτον ῥίπτουσι μίτον,| ἂν μὴ μαγείης τῆς ἐμῆς ἀναγκάσῃς| βέλος πετηνὸν ταχύτατον τέλος δραμεῖν. οὐ γὰρ φυγεῖν ἔξεστι μοῖράν μου λόγων.| ὃ δεῖ γενέσθαι· μὴ σα<υ>τὴν ἀναγκάσῃς| ἄνωθεν εἰς ἄνω τ' ἀκούειν συμβόλων.| τὸ δεῖ, ποιήσεις, κἂν θέλῃς κἂν μὴ θέλῃς·| ἀχρείου φωτὸς πρίν σε μοῖρα καταλάβῃ, ποίησον, ὃ λέγω, ταρταροῦχε παρθένε.| ἔδησα δεσμοῖς τοῖς Κρόνου τὸν σὸν πόλον| καὶ ὀπιδνῇ ἀνάγκῃ ἀντίχειρά σου κρατῶ. οὐ γίνεται αὔριον, εἰ μὴ γένηται, ὃ βούλομαι. ἔνευσας Ἑρμῇ, τῷ θεῶν ἀρχηγέτῃ, εἰς τήνδε τὴν πρᾶξιν συμβαλεῖν·

particular purpose of getting the goddess to drive the target insane with a lust that can only be satisfied by sexual subjection to the magician.

While the extra-ordinary efficacy of the spell is the primary marker of its magical nature, this example thus also qualifies on the basis of its socially unacceptable ends. The magician knows full well that he is doing something that his society would consider deviant behavior, if not actually illegal, but he nonetheless proclaims his magical power within the performance of the spell.

CONCLUSIONS: AN OVERVIEW

In all these examples of drawing down the moon, then, the non-normative, extra-ordinary nature of the procedure is marked with regard to its efficacy, its aims, the social location of the performer, or the style of the performance itself. These features provide a good set of criteria by which to evaluate other kinds of ritualized action that appear in the evidence from the ancient Greco-Roman world to determine whether they might have a place within the discourse of magic, that is, whether they might, from an ancient, emic perspective, have been labeled 'magic.'[64] The fragmentary and incomplete nature of the evidence means that modern scholars will never have enough information to determine the entire range of things labeled 'magic' in antiquity or to distinguish all the particular reasons that someone might have labeled a specific thing as 'magic,' but these criteria nonetheless provide a starting point from which we can improve our understanding of the way the people of the ancient Greco-Roman world considered these phenomena.

In each chapter of the book, I explore a type of evidence that may be considered magic to determine the most significant factors in the classifications. While extra-ordinary efficacy often furnishes the most valid cue for the label of 'magic,' in certain kinds of materials the social location of the performer is determinative, while in others particular features of the performance mark its non-normativity. I turn first to cursing, the attempt to inflict harm on a target through ritual, since this activity seems to fit with most intuitive concepts of magic. The evidence, however, shows that only certain forms of cursing appear as magical in antiquity, whereas others

---

[64] While some might criticize the re-establishment of a dichotomy of magic and nonmagic, this dichotomy nevertheless is deployed for a specific analytic purpose, to better understand the categories of thought in the ancient Greco-Roman world. As Braarvig 1999a: 23 notes, "Dichotomies should be coined to represent a certain context: they should be formulated in the process of working with a certain material where they explain certain aspects of the phenomena we have chosen to study."

appear as normative forms of ritual action undertaken by an individual or community. The social and political location of the performer and especially certain aspects of the performance are the most valid cues for marking curses as magical. Curses performed at non-normative times and places as part of a procedure that shows a high coefficient of weirdness, involving strange language or unfamiliar actions, are most likely to be classified as magical, especially if performed by someone of non-normative social status. Such non-normative curses appear as forms of cheating within the competitive contexts of the ancient world, illicit means to socially acceptable ends of success, victory, prosperity, and so forth.

In the following chapter, I consider erotic magic, which bears many resemblances to the tradition of cursing, especially the highly competitive context. Here again the social location or style of the performance may mark a procedure as magical, but more emphasis appears on the extraordinary efficacy of the procedures that differentiate erotic magic from the normal strategies for success in the lists of love. Protective and healing ritual provides the focus for the next chapter, procedures whose aims are generally considered beneficent and socially acceptable. Outstanding claims to efficacy may distinguish the magical from the nonmagical, but, nonetheless, certain kinds of protective or healing rites may be considered magical if performed at non-normative places and times or with non-normative elements in the performance.

These same criteria of performance appear as the distinguishing features of prayers to the gods in magical rituals. Although modern scholarship has most often relied on a coercive rather than supplicative attitude as the defining feature of magical relations with the divine, in contrast to normative religion, an examination of the evidence shows that other aspects of the performance are more significant cues for the label of 'magic.' A more careful and detailed analysis of the rhetoric of ritual contacts with the gods in prayers and sacrifice reveals complexities that go beyond the coercive/supplicative dichotomy and shed light not only upon the nature of magic as a discourse in the ancient Greco-Roman world, but also the discourse of normative religion.

I then turn to divination, a collection of ritual practices for receiving messages from the divine, many of which are considered completely normative within the religions of the ancient Greco-Roman world. Divination becomes marked as magical, however, when the procedure claims extraordinary efficacy, especially if the social location of the performer is marginal, dubious, or otherwise non-normative. The chapter on astrology considers this particular form of divination, where the non-normative status is often enhanced by a rhetoric of extra-ordinary systematicity in the performance. The sources that outline the extremely complex interactions of a vast number of variables within the astrological system bolster the claims to extra-ordinary efficacy with a demonstration of the performer's mastery of their complexity.

The same kind of rhetoric of extra-ordinary systematicity characterizes much of the evidence for alchemy, the process of manipulating matter to transform its qualities. Alchemy appears as magic when the demonstration of mastery of the complex processes of cosmological system produces extra-ordinary results. Non-normative efficacy (whether miraculous transmutations or cheap charlatan's tricks) distinguishes alchemy as a magical process, in contrast to normal ways of working with metals and other materials. Theurgy, the ritual connection of the material world to the divine world, likewise relies on performance that shows the mastery of the complex system of interrelations between the divine and material worlds to produce extra-ordinary results. Non-normative elements of the performance, such as incomprehensible utterances or strange actions like spinning a whirligig, may be used by hostile sources to label the practice as 'magic' in a negative sense, but the defenders of theurgy stress its extra-ordinary efficacy in making contact with the divine.

In the conclusion, I return to issues of definition, exploring the ways in which the evaluation of magic as non-normative is expressed within different contexts in the Greco-Roman world. One of the most important contexts is the legal one, and magic is defined in different ways in different places by laws and prosecutions throughout the time periods of the ancient world. The legal definition is a societal marking of an individual as Other, but we also investigate some of the self-definitions of magic in the ancient Greco-Roman world, the positive claims to non-normative status.

This study can provide only a beginning in its rather superficial survey of the vast and complex evidence for magic in the ancient Greco-Roman world. Further work is needed in each and every one of the areas I examine here, but I hope that our understanding of the discourse of magic in the ancient Greco-Roman world can progress a little further and that my tinkering with the definitions will enable other scholars to pedal the bicycle more effectively in the future.

2

The World of Ancient Greco-Roman Magic

If we are to explore magic in the ancient Greco-Roman world, we must not only define what we mean by 'magic,' but also what we mean by 'the ancient Greco-Roman world.' For the purposes of this study I, more or less arbitrarily, define 'the ancient Greco-Roman world' as a reconstruction of what people thought and did, including both material evidence and the history of ideas, within three parameters of time, space, and language. By 'ancient,' I here mean primarily the period between the fifth century BCE and the fourth century CE, with occasional glimpses back into the Archaic period (eighth to sixth century BCE) and forward into Late Antiquity (fifth to ninth century CE). By 'world,' I mean the territory around the Mediterranean Basin, from Iberia (Spain) in the west to the Levant (Syria to Egypt) in the east, the northern coast of Africa in the south and the Roman provinces of Europe to the north, in effect the Roman Empire at its greatest extent. Within this vast stretch of space and time, I am limiting my investigations to Greco-Roman evidence, by which I mean the cultures of Greece and Rome, whose languages were primarily Greek and Latin.

The limitation to evidence in Greek and Latin, while to some degree an arbitrary choice based on my own linguistic competence (since I am not trained in Egyptian, Phoenician, Hebrew, or any other of the languages used in the ancient Mediterranean during these periods), nevertheless has a certain amount of justification. Greek was the *koinē*, the common tongue of the ancient Mediterranean, from the Hellenistic period onward, while Latin was the language of the dominant imperialist power of the Roman Empire, so even people whose native languages were neither Greek nor Latin were more likely to use these languages than a native Greek speaker to use Hebrew or a Roman Demotic Egyptian. Greek in particular was the language most often used by peoples of all different backgrounds for certain kinds of cultural productions, including many of the things labeled 'magic.' Dieleman has pointed to the linguistic phenomenon known as 'code-switching' to account for the use of the Greek language for certain kinds of spells and rituals by the bilingual scribes of the Greek Magical Papyri; the Greek linguistic and cultural tradition is the background for such expressions, and so they are most naturally and easily expressed in Greek, even by those for whom Greek is not their first language.[1] The Egyptian, Hebrew, Phoenician, and (going further back in time) Babylonian traditions all have non-normative ritual practices that could be labeled 'magic,' and these traditions are rich and fascinating, and worthy of studies in their own right, but beyond the scope of my project here. All of these traditions (and others) influenced the Greco-Roman traditions in a variety of significant ways, but, while I try to point to such influences where the comparisons are illuminating, since these other traditions share in many ways a common set of ideas and practices, I focus on the way such elements are employed within the Greco-Roman tradition, on their reception, adaptation, and reuse, rather than their origin. This reception of other cultural elements is not limited to words or ritual patterns but even includes deities and cosmological structures that are adapted into the polytheistic worldview of the Greco-Roman world. Iaō, the Greek rendering of the Hebrew Jehovah, is the deity most often mentioned within the Greek Magical Papyri, while the Egyptian goddess Isis was given a Greek pedigree in some sources and a Roman temple in some cities throughout the empire. The goddess Isis in the Greek sources or Roman temples is not precisely the same figure that appears in the earlier Egyptian evidence, just as Iaō in the Greek Magical Papyri differs from the figure that appears in the Hebrew scriptures, but, although I acknowledge these other forms of evidence, my focus remains on the figures as they appear in the Greek texts.

Just as I do not focus on the origins and transmission of elements from one culture to another within the ancient Mediterranean world, so too I am not focusing upon the origins and shifts of elements over time, but rather on their particular deployment in specific texts and other kinds of evidence. The particular place and time in which any given piece of evidence was produced is significant, but only in relation to the author, audience, genre, execution and performance, and many other such factors. Despite changes over time, the patterns that appear throughout the entire time span under consideration are significant enough to bring together evidence from very different times, especially since the evidence from any given time and place is hardly ever sufficient in quantity to be compared

---

[1] Cp. Dieleman 2005: 285–294. Brashear 1995: 3425 notes the striking paucity of magical papyri written in Latin, even during the Roman imperial domination of Egypt.

substantively with evidence from another time and place. Our study of curses, for example, addresses the common patterns from the earliest evidence to the latest, noting the shifts in the amount of written material and complexity of the texts as the technology of writing becomes more prevalent but without trying to chart its development.

Therefore, throughout this study, I will discuss examples drawn from the entire range of both space and time within this ancient Greco-Roman world. The definition of magic or the terms employed to label it did not remain constant or even consistent, but such juxtapositions of evidence are useful, despite being so greatly separated in space and time, because the most significant variations occur from text to text, not period to period or place to place. The overall discourse of 'magic' as a label for non-normative ritualized activity remains fairly stable, even as the terminology shifts from age to age and the ways in which the Otherness is imagined vary. The most important factor in each instance of magic as a non-normative ritualized activity is what the one using the label of 'magic' considers to be normative. While ideas of what is normative certainly change over time and differ by region, they also vary from individual to individual and circumstance to circumstance, and examination of the particular criteria or cues that are used to mark the deviations from the norm provides the most insight in each case.

Periodization, Technology, and Space

Scholars have made various attempts at periodization in discussing religious phenomena in the ancient Greco-Roman world, from Murray's five stages of Greek religion to Stratton's more recent division into Greek, Roman, Jewish, and Christian ways of portraying the witch figure.[2] The canonical periods of history provide as useful a set of arbitrary divisions as any, and so I make reference throughout to the Archaic Period (eighth to sixth century BCE), the Classical Period (fifth to fourth century BCE), the Hellenistic Period (third century BCE to first century CE), the Roman Imperial Period (first to fourth century CE), and Late Antiquity (fifth to ninth century CE). Some rough generalizations may be made about the

[2] Cp. Murray 1925, whose five stages trace the rise and fall of Greek religion from the idyllic *Saturnia regna* of the Archaic period to the glorious Olympian Conquest of the Classical to the rationalization in the Great Schools of philosophy to the Failure of Nerve in the Hellenistic and Roman period and the rise of Christianity, with a Last Protest against Christianity in the time of Julian the Apostate. The schema of Stratton 2007 is broader and less teleological in its outlook. Otto calls for historicizing the concept of magic, but his study (both in Otto 2011 and summarily in Otto 2013) goes through the uses of the terminology in certain authors in a roughly chronological order, rather than generalizing about characteristics of the discourse in different periods.

way the label of 'magic' is used in each period, but it would be imprudent to put too much weight on them.

The Classical period is the time in which the term 'magic' first appears, as the Persian term for a Persian priest is adapted into Greek as *magos* and used to indicate a ritual practitioner who makes claim to extra-ordinary religious authority or efficacy.[3] Although the birth of the *term* 'magic' may come in the fifth century in the wake of the Persian War, the category of magic, as I define it here, exists long before the term, *mageia*, comes into use. Descriptions of incantations, magical potions, and even necromancy appear in the earliest Greek textual sources, the Homeric epics, and they are marked in these texts as extra-ordinary elements, not as normative practices. The Classical period also sees the first expansion of the technology of writing, which appears in Greece in the Archaic period, although elements of the oral culture remain significant, particularly in the Greek ritual tradition that shunned the written recording of important matters.

In the Hellenistic period, as contacts with the cultures of the ancient Near East expand with the conquests of Alexander the Great, the expansion of writing brings a great process of systematization of traditional knowledge, both from Greek traditions and from even older traditions, such as those of Babylonian astronomy. This process, as Gordon has pointed out, transforms ancient lore that was marked as magical in the negative sense of the superstitions of the marginal within society into a kind of arcane knowledge that is magical in the positive sense of extra-ordinary collections of wisdom accessible only to the highest levels of society.[4] The evidence from the Hellenistic period, however, is far sparser than the evidence from the Classical period. Like the texts from the Archaic times, many of the Hellenistic texts have been lost and survive only in references or quotations, whereas the Classical texts that had become canonical were preserved and recopied throughout the manuscript tradition.

In the Roman period, the hegemony of the Roman Empire throughout the Mediterranean provides a new presence of Latin materials, along with a resurgence of Greek writings as Greek becomes the common language of culture. The expansion of the uses of writing that began in the Hellenistic period spreads even more during this time, and the shifting political structures also have repercussions for the cosmological ideas of the period. The rise of Christianity coincides with and creates more changes in the theological and cosmological landscape of the Greco-Roman world and

---

[3] See, e.g., the treatment in Bremmer 1999, although the topic is also treated in standard works such as Graf 1997; Dickie 2001; and Collins 2008a.

[4] Gordon 1999a provides the best account of this general process, although his specific studies of astrology (Gordon 1997) and natural lore (Gordon 1987a) also offer valuable insights.

brings a shift in some of the ways the magic is understood, even if many of the new ideas derive originally from within the non-Christian philosophical schools.

In Late Antiquity, the dominance of Christianity shapes the religious ideas of Christians and non-Christians throughout the Mediterranean, but this period provides evidence for ideas of magic in earlier periods because of the number of thinkers looking back, either in nostalgia or critique, to the previous religious traditions. The traditions of the ancient Greco-Roman world, of course, remain a subject of fascination in the Byzantine era and are greeted with renewed interest in the Renaissance, but, except for making use of little tidbits of evidence preserved in these later sources, the complex receptions of earlier ideas of magic in the ancient Greco-Roman world remain beyond the scope of this study.

While the expansion of the technology of writing is one of the shifts that makes the clearest difference over time, other technological advances also have an impact traceable within the sources. The increased precision of mathematical and scientific measurements and the development of a number of mechnical technologies create a marked difference between the evidence from different periods. Practices such as astrology or alchemy can only become incorporated into the discourse of magic after the systematization of lore in the Hellenistic period and the development of the empirical processes and mathematical calculations in astronomy and metallurgy, and technological progress leaves its mark in other varieties of magic as well.

Shifts in technology naturally alter what is considered normal with regard to the material world, but shifts in political and social organization also impact the ideas of normative behavior. In the Greco-Roman world, smaller political units such as city-states predominated during the Archaic and even through the Classical period, although larger kingdoms and leagues began to make an appearance as well. The Hellenistic era saw the geographic spread of Greek political communities, with the conquests of Alexander the Great and the fragmentation of his empire after his death, while in Italy and the western Mediterranean, the Roman power spread. The shift from Republic to Empire marked a shift in political order to a vision of a hierarchical system dominated by a single figure at the top, a model that remained dominant into Late Antiquity despite the religious shift to Christianity.

Theological shifts tend to accompany historical political shifts, since the gods are often imagined to be organized in the cosmos much as mortals are—in heaven as it is on earth. The Homeric poems, originating in the Archaic period (or before), present a loosely organized collection of gods, each with their own conflicting interests and ambitions, under the power of Zeus as the chief god. While this theological model remains influential in every period, other models of the gods and the world develop alongside it, and the idea of an ordered hierarchy of divine powers organized under a single supreme leader develops in philosophy and theology long before its political equivalent becomes a reality in the Greco-Roman world. These shifting ideas of the nature of the gods affects what is considered normative behavior towards these gods in different times and different places, but it is important to remember that older models persist, sustained in part by the literary and mythic tradition that is one of the most significant expressions of theological ideas in every period.[5] By contrast, the speculations of philosophers often present models of the gods that stand far apart from the ideas that many of their contemporaries would have held, and the tendency of writers like Plato to present their own radical theological innovations as the commonly accepted norms that they later came to be can be misleading.

J. Z. Smith provides a useful distinction in cosmological models, between locative and utopian, that appear in the various sources.[6] In the locative model, there is a place for every entity in the cosmos, mortal or divine, and every entity is normatively in its place. Disruptions occur when someone is out of place, be it a peasant on a royal throne, a dead person in the world of the living, or a mortal trying to climb to Olympus. By contrast, a utopian perspective views the proper place of humans as outside this world entirely; their place is no-place (*ou-topia*). Rather than, as in a locative order, the aim of life being to perform optimally in one's proper place, the aim in a utopian model is to escape from this world entirely. The dead are going home to their proper spiritual abode, while religious experts seek to transcend the material world and make contact with the divine perfection above. Traces of such a utopian model appear in Plato (and even before), but there is wider circulation of such ideas in the Roman Imperial Period and Late Antiquity than in earlier periods.

Another useful analytic framework Smith provides is the classification of different types of religious activity by space. Borrowing from the illustrious Dr. Seuss, Smith distinguishes between religion of *here*, religion of *there*, and religion of *anywhere*.[7] The religion of *here* involves the private religious practices individuals perform in their own personal spaces—mostly domestic, but certain forms of family tomb cult would also be included. By contrast, the religion of *there* involves the practices performed in public, in the spaces designated by the community as special, be it a temple in the middle of the city or a pilgrimage site appropriately far away from the center. The religion of *anywhere* involves the practices that de-

---

[5] See the thoughtful comments in Parker 1997.

[6] Smith articulates this model in several different articles; see particularly J. Smith 1978b.

[7] Smith 2003, drawing upon *Green Eggs and Ham*, "I will not eat them here or there, I will not eat them anywhere."

pend neither upon the particular, personal domestic space of *here* nor the public places *there*, but rather can be performed anywhere on any occasion, because their religious efficacy depends not on the place and time but rather on the special authority of the performer. Although some scholars, coming from a Durkheimian perspective, have made public versus private a key difference between religion and magic, Smith's category of religion of *here* provides a space for private religious acts that are nonetheless normative. The religion of *here*, although always present in society, leaves few traces in contrast with the religion of *there*, because it is performed in private, but such private performances do not make the religion of *here* non-normative; many rituals performed beyond the gaze of any outside observer, such as sacrifices to household gods or household purifications are perfectly normal and expected, what good citizens should be doing in the way that they should be doing it. The religion of *anywhere*, by contrast, because it does not rely on places and times sanctified by the normative religious tradition, often provides material for the discourse of magic, be it in the miracles of wandering holy men or in the occult practices of witches. All three modes coexist at any given time and place, but again Smith sees an increased focus on the religion of *anywhere* in the Roman Imperial period and Late Antiquity, especially as the changing political landscape affects the importance of sacred spaces previously hallowed by tradition.

Gordon approaches the same phenomenon from a different perspective, seeing the increased evidence for performers who either mark themselves or are marked by their audience as non-normative in their religious activity as a shift from a pattern of "objective profanation" to more "intentional profanation."[8] That is, whereas in earlier periods magic is associated with those who are in some way marginal within the social and political order (objectively profane or non-normative), later periods witness an increase in evidence for those whose behavior is what marks them as magical (intentionally profane or deliberately non-normative). In the terms of my own definition of magic in this study, I would describe this process as a variation in the validity of the cues of *social location* and *performance*, but I would also note that both sets of cues are significant throughout the whole period of our evidence, even if their relative validity varies over time. Rather than trying to trace an arc of development over time, I think it is important to remain attentive to the multiple cues that are operative in the sources throughout the whole Greco-Roman world, taking into account the particular perspective of each source, which is often more determinative of how the label of 'magic' is used than the period from which the evidence comes.

---

[8] Gordon 1999a: 265–266.

The Varieties of Evidence

In this study, I examine a variety of kinds of evidence, each of which provides its own challenges for interpretation. Literary texts provide the richest and most detailed depictions of magic, but their portrayals are shaped not only by the author's time and place, but also by constraints of genre (epic, comedy, tragedy, lyric, novel, etc.). Since these literary creations are not meant to be realistic portrayals of the ordinary world, their depictions of magic follow the logic of the story, rather than what the author and audience might have understood as real life. Historical accounts and other depictions of real life provide much more limited evidence, both in quantity and in the scope of the magical practices described, which tend to be less sensational than those found in literary fictions.[9] However, sensational and sordid details often appear in polemical treatises designed to denigrate the practices of certain individuals in real life, even if their presence in polemical contexts means that their accuracy must always remain suspect. Another source of evidence comes not from the texts, literary or historical, that were passed down over the centuries in the manuscript traditions, but in the epigraphic and papyrological evidence recovered in archaeological excavations. These texts, along with other kinds of material evidence, provide direct witness to the work of the people of the ancient Greco-Roman world, unmediated by centuries of reception.

The literary evidence provides the richest depictions of magic in the ancient Greco-Roman world, although it can never be taken as accurate reflections of actual practices or people. The literary evidence provides a picture of magic as it appears in the ancient Greco-Roman imaginary, that is, all the familiar ideas and tropes of the discourse as people thought about and imagined it, rather than what they actually did. Richard Gordon indeed has argued that the true home of magic in the ancient Greco-Roman world is in the imaginary:

> In my view, it is much too easy to be distracted by the archaeological survival of curse—and vindicative—tablets, and the remains of Graeco-Egyptian magical receptaries (grimoires), from the essential point, which is that the true home of magic is a body of narrative, what Cicero calls "old women's tales," which construct the social knowledge to which any event, real or supposed, fearful or peculiar, may be referred and in terms of which, if need be, explained.[10]

---

[9] I would include in this category legal speeches, which occasionally mention practices of magic, although the extensive defense speech of Apuleius (discussed in ch. 11, pp. 391–396) provides an exceptional wealth of information.

[10] Gordon 1999a: 167.

The literary evidence constructs a world within the text, and everything can be explained and accounted for within that fictional world, even personal motives, processes of cause and effect, and divine actions that are not transparent or perceptible in the real world. Literary evidence can thus supply explanations of why someone did something and how it worked that are simply not available in descriptive accounts or material records.

At the same time, the imaginary world that the literary text creates is shaped by the constraints of the genre in which it is written as well as by the author's own agenda. Magic in the world of comedy, for example, is almost always a sham, a con by devious charlatans, whereas when magic appears in Greek tragedy or epic, its extra-ordinary efficacy is valid but its deviant elements are often toned down (while in Roman tragedy and epic they are often extravagantly hyped up). Ancient novels provide some of the most detailed and nuanced evidence, and the *Metamorphoses* of the second-century CE Latin author Apuleius (better known as *The Golden Ass*) offers a detailed description of a world simply teeming with magic of all sorts. The hero, Lucius, sets off for Thessaly to find magic, and, after getting turned into a donkey through a magical mishap, he suffers through a series of extra-ordinary adventures before regaining his human form. Apuleius plays with the discourse of magic throughout the novel, presenting magic at times as truly miraculous and other times as absurdly fraudulent, both sides of non-normativity. The novel provides perhaps the best and most comprehensive overview of magic in the Greco-Roman imaginary, but the author's ironic and playful attitude should caution us against uncritically accepting his narrative as a precise and accurate depiction of actual practices.

Apuleius is also a Platonic philosopher who wrote on the nature of the gods and the world, including an important treatise on the nature of demons, *De Deo Socratis*, that became influential in later ages. Such philosophical or cosmological works also provide evidence for ideas and practices of magic in the ancient Greco-Roman world, but they provide a different kind of perspective, with different strengths and limitations than the literary evidence. One of the earliest references to magic and drawing down the moon comes from a treatise in the corpus of works by the doctors of the Hippocratic school, and, in this treatise *On the Sacred Disease*, magicians who draw down the moon are attacked as impious charlatans whose methods in healing patients are fraudulent and ineffective in comparison to the systematic theories of the Hippocratic doctors. Such a text is characteristic of this kind of evidence, a polemic against rival claimants to extra-ordinary power or authority that is grounded in very specific cosmological and theological ideas, even though the particular points at issue differ from text to text. However exaggerated the polemics may be, though, the accounts are nevertheless grounded in the world of practice, rather than the literary world of the imaginary whose excesses are constrained only by the fluid bounds of the tradition. Other texts, such as the compilations of the marvelous properties of plants, herbs, or stars, may appear less polemical, but they nevertheless arise out of the agonistic contexts of the competitions for the authority of superior knowledge, and the attack on rivals is always implict, even if the targets are not specified.

In addition to the texts passed down through the centuries in the manuscript tradition, archaeological excavations have uncovered a variety of evidence that provides vital insights into the way magic as a discourse was imagined in the ancient Greco-Roman world. The corpus of the curses inscribed on lead tablets, for example, provides a fascinating glimpse into the hopes and fears, lusts and anxieties, of individuals in the ancient world, especially those from strata of society that rarely are represented in the canonical texts passed down through the manuscript tradition. Some of the papyri preserved in the arid sands of Egypt provide similar windows into the lives of ordinary folk, but one set of papyri provides a particularly significant body of evidence, coming not from the masses but rather from the educated elite, the trained scribes of Egypt. This collection of papyri, known as the Greek Magical Papyri, provides an unparalleled trove of evidence for ancient magic, a collection of spell books with a variety of recipes for magical rituals. The publication in 1986 of an English translation of this augmented collection of the Greek Magical Papyri by a team of scholars working under the leadership of Hans Dieter Betz at the University of Chicago marked a turning point in the study of magic in the ancient Greco-Roman world by making these texts accessible to a wider audience of scholars.[11]

This peculiar collection of texts, coming from Greco-Roman Egypt in the third through fifth centuries CE, provides, as J. Z. Smith has noted, the largest body of ritual instructions in Greek from the ancient world.[12] Greek religion (and to a lesser extent Roman religion) tended not to commit important ritual procedures to writing; generations of ritual performers learned to perform sacrifice, prayers, and other kinds of rituals through participating in them and through oral instruction. The Greek Magical Papyri, by contrast, make use of a scribal tradition with a long history in Egyptian culture to inscribe ritual instructions in Greek for rituals that seem to have been composed by people working in the Greek ritual tradi-

---

[11] The collection in Betz 1992 provides a translation of the Greek texts collected in Preisendanz and Henrichs 1973, along with many others, both in Greek and Demotic. Some of the texts translated in Betz 1992 are published in the *Supplementum Magicum* (Daniel and Maltomini 1990 and Daniel and Maltomini 1992), but these volumes include other texts as well, and more continue to be published.

[12] J. Smith 1995: 21.

tion.[13] This kind of instruction manual differs from much of the other evidence for similar ritual practices in the same way that a cookbook differs from a cake: that is, instead of a curse tablet, which is the finished product of a ritual process, the Greek Magical Papyri provide instructions for making curse tablets. As a result, the instructions describe elements of the rituals, such as spoken prayers or preliminary purifications for the performer, which leave no trace of evidence in the completed product of the rite. Athough literary texts do provide such elements in their descriptions of characters performing magic, the ritual cookbooks of the Greek Magical Papyri provide evidence that such elements were not merely the product of the literary imagination, but actual parts of the rites performed by people who labeled their own acts as 'magical.'

THE NATURE OF RITUAL

Such collections of ritual instructions make clear the ritual nature of the procedures prescribed within them, but other evidence provides less obvious indications of the ritualized nature of the actions involved. Literary representations of ritual depict the ritual in process, but epigraphic evidence such as curse tablets provides only the end result of a ritual process, and the ritual itself must be deduced from its traces. Other evidence, such as treatises on the properties of stones or on the astrological significance of the positions of the planets, provides only oblique indications of the ritualized processes involved.

The anthropologist S. J. Tambiah defines ritual as a symbolic communication, where those symbols may be not only words but actions and where not merely the presence of these signs but their ordering bears significance.

> Ritual is a culturally constructed system of symbolic communication. It is constituted of patterned and ordered sequences of words and acts, often expressed in multiple media, whose content and arrangement are characterized in varying degree by formality (conventionality), stereotypy (rigidity), condensation (fusion), and redundancy (repetition). Ritual action in its constitutive features is performative

---

[13] The situation of the composition of the PGM is much disputed, but Egyptian lector-priests (*hry hb*) trained in the scribal traditions of the Egyptian temples are the most likely population to have had the necessary linguistic skills to produce these papyri, which have not only Greek but Old Coptic and Demotic. See Frankfurter 1997 and Frankfurter 1998: 248–264. As Dieleman 2005: 285–294 points out, these bilingual (or multilingual) scribes choose to write some kinds of rituals in Greek and others in Demotic, reflecting a distinction between the kinds of procedures appropriate to the different language.

in these three senses: in the Austinian sense of performative wherein saying something is also doing something as a conventional act; in the quite different sense of a staged performance that uses multiple media by which the participants experience the event intensively; and in the third sense of indexical values—I derive this concept from Peirce—being attached to and inferred by actors during the performance.[14]

Any ritualized action, therefore, may be analyzed to discover the ideas signified through the symbols deployed in the communication.

An action is ritualized insofar as a symbolic meaning is communicated through the action. To ask what ritual communicates is like asking what speech communicates; anything and everything may be conveyed in ritual. Kissing the picture of one's beloved signifies, to whomever witnesses the act, the love the performer feels for the beloved. It is not an instrumental action; no one who kisses a picture ever believes that the beloved will feel the kiss. Some ritualized actions still retain some instrumental aspects, even if the symbolic aspect predominates.[15] The youth who goes out with a gang of friends to buy a drink (or several) on reaching the legal drinking age is acting instrumentally to obtain alcohol, but the action is ritualized insofar as it is a symbolic communication (to the individual, the friends, and the world at large) of that person's change in social status. The individual could make the same instrumental action a week later, but it would lack the same symbolic force and thus the ritual aspect.

Analyzing Ritual

The efficacy of ritual thus lies in the success of its symbolic communication, rather than in the effectiveness of its instrumental action.[16] We can gain insights into these ritual symbolic communications through the same kind of poetic and rhetorical analyses used to understand other kinds of symbolic communications, from high literature to advertising. Attention to devices such as metaphor and metonymy, repetition, and vivid imagery shows the ways that the ritual communicates meaning to its audience, not in terms of explicit propositions but rather in symbolic associations of ideas. A car ad, for example, makes no explicit claim that, if you buy

---

[14] Tambiah 1979b: 119.

[15] Thomassen 1997: 58 refers to Habermas for the distinction between instrumental and symbolic action as a way of understanding the problem with Frazer's approach, pointing out that ritual acts may seem instrumental because they involve action.

[16] Cp. Tambiah 1979a: 353: "magical acts are ritual acts, and ritual acts are in turn performative acts whose positive and creative meaning is missed and whose persuasive validity is misjudged if they are subjected to that kind of empirical verification associated with scientific activity."

the car, you will soon be driving through exotic locales and enjoying a lavish lifestyle with attractive partners, but the imagery in the ad associates the sexy partners, the lavish lifestyle, and the exotic locale with the car. Just so, making a lead figurine with its hands and feet bound and placing it in a little lead coffin does not claim to tie up the target of the curse and put him into a coffin, but it expresses quite clearly the intended association of the target with the ideas of binding and incapacity. Rather than viewing these as failed instrumental actions, the car ad, the lead figurine, and kissing the picture of the beloved may all be seen as effective communications.

Previous theories of magical action, however, drawing on the ideas of Frazer, have seen ritual acts (and magical acts in particular) as instrumental acts that fail because of some fundamental misunderstanding of the nature of causality. Frazer articulates two 'laws' of magic, the law of contagion and the law of similarity.[17] He explains the "law of contagion" as the primitive belief that something once part of or connected to another thing will remain somehow in contact—a fingernail or tress of hair, a footprint, or even a shadow. The "law of similarity" or "homeopathy" is the idea that causes and effects resemble one another qualititatively: pouring water on the ground causes rain to fall in a similar manner, while tying up a figurine causes the person whom it resembles to be tied. Frazer, and many of those influenced by him, regard these 'laws' as mistaken understandings of natural causality, but they are better understood as expressive devices such as metonymy (part for a whole) and metaphor (association through qualitative resemblance). Devices such as repetition likewise make more sense when understood as expressive and emphatic, rather than attributed to a primitive anxiety about the inability to control nature or some sort of societal form of obsessive-compulsive disorder.[18] The use of vivid imagery can also be understood in terms of its communicative power for the audience.

Ritual, as a symbolic communication, depends upon the familiarity of the audience with the symbolic system, the *langue*, in Saussurean terms, of which any given act is a *parole*. A speech act is normatively valid insofar as it can be understood by its audience, which means that unfamiliar or extra-ordinary features mark it as non-normative. Again, such features are always to some extent situational; a sentence in French is perfectly valid from one French speaker to another but meaningless gibberish to a barbarian who doesn't know the language. Some features are, however, common markers of extra-ordinary speech, such as poetic meter and song. To sing

---

[17] Cp. Frazer 1979, drawn from vol. 1 of his famous *Golden Bough* (Frazer 1952).

[18] Styers 2004: 176–178 surveys some Freudian theories of ritual repetition as a form of infantile attempts to control the world.

in a conversation with another person is marked as peculiar, even if the sentences uttered are completely meaningful and comprehensible. The inclusion of metaphor or metonymy, repetition or vivid imagery likewise marks a speech as unusual, while the use of incomprehensible words or phrases brings to the speech act what the anthropologist Malinowski would call an even higher "coefficient of weirdness."[19] A speech with a high coefficient of weirdness, for whatever factor, is less likely to be considered normative, although, depending on the circumstances, its efficacy may be considered either higher or lower than normal. A poem or incantation is a far more memorable and affecting speech act than ordinary prose speech, but it is also more likely to be dismissed as a meaningless noise. All ritual, because of its extra symbolic layers, differs from ordinary speech, but rituals labeled 'magic' tend to have a high coefficient of weirdness to their performance, and this deviation from the normative modes of expression helps mark their extra-ordinary status.

Such extra-ordinary performance can also be marked rhetorically by the complexity of the language and the systems set out. By presenting the performer as someone who has learned and mastered a complicated, abstruse, or arcane system unfamiliar to the audience, the performance marks the performer as extra-ordinary, either as a learned master of lore beyond the ken of ordinary mortals or, more negatively, as a hopeless pedant unable to communicate with normal people in an ordinary way. Whether the non-normativity is construed positively or negatively, however, the rhetoric of complex systematicity marks the performance as non-normative, extra-ordinary.

Ritual Performance: Reconstructing Performer and Audience

Any speech act is also a performance, and as such it involves not only a communication but a performer and an audience. A speech act is effective insofar as the intended meaning is communicated through the symbolic elements of the speech act to the audience. If the speaker garbles the pronunciation of the words or fails to structure the sentence properly, the audience might fail to comprehend the message, but the audience might also fail to comprehend a perfectly formed and articulated sentence, if the audience cannot hear it or if the language is unknown to the audience. Deconstructionists have pointed out that no communication ever succeeds in fully transmitting its meaning, but human beings endlessly continue to try to communicate nonetheless, passing along more or less partial messages. It is worth noting that a speech act may have multiple aspects of its

---

[19] Malinowski 1935: 218–223.

symbolic communication, not simply words but gestures, inflections, and even sequences of actions. A sailor, seeing a disheveled man standing on the beach of a tiny island in the midst of the sea, may not be able to hear or understand his words, but if he sees the man leaping up and down and waving his arms, the words are not needed to convey the message adequately.[20] Just so, even if some of the verbal expressions in magical ritual are incomprehensible, we can understand the sort of thing they indicate from their place in the ritual sequence of actions.[21]

A ritual can thus be analyzed to reveal the assumptions about the audience that structure it; just as a text creates its own ideal reader, any speech act, by the way it is put together, indicates the audience for whom it is performed. A sentence in French, for example, indicates that the audience is expected to understand that language, while a complicated explanation that involves the names of several individuals and particular places indicates that the audience is expected to know those individuals and places. Aristophanes's joke about Thessalian witches drawing down the moon shows that he expected his audience to understand the reference, to know stories about Thessaly, about the strange women there, and about their strange powers, as well as to have an understanding of the basic procedure of drawing down the moon on which the joke hinges.

Just as a text sets up its own reader and a ritual creates its own audience, so too a text or a ritual communicates the nature of its own author or performer through the structure and elements of the speech act. A sentence in French must be constructed by a speaker who knows (at least some) French, while a joke about Thessalian witches indicates someone who knows the tropes involved. A ritual thus provides information about the performer's identity and relation to the audience, situating the performer, the audience, and the communication in that relational context. The performer may be indicating through a ritual that she is a young maiden becoming an adult wife or that he is a desperately ill man who stands in dire need of divine healing or even that she is a learned expert who, by imitating the processes by which the divine creator formed the world, is becoming more godlike and pure. Even if these indications of performer and audience are not explicit in the communication itself, they

---

[20] As Pike 1967: 26 comments, "Language is behavior, i.e., a phase of human activity which must not be treated in essence as structurally divorced from the structure of nonverbal human activity."

[21] As Graf 1991 has argued for the *voces magicae* in magical prayers. Elements of meaning may be conveyed by their place in the structure, as may be seen by comparing the start of Lewis Caroll's classic "Jabberwocky": " 'Twas brillig and the slithy toves did gyre and gimble in the wabe," with a scrambled sentence such as "girl the to rose a gave boy." The latter sentence is meaningless, although all the words are familiar, whereas the former conveys a certain sense of the action, even though all the significant words are nonsense.

remain implicit in the way that the act of symbolic communication is structured and performed.

While not all ritualized actions are, in modern terms, religious acts, many rituals are religious acts whose performances are primarily directed at the divine, that is, they are performances for which the divine is the intended audience. Insofar as they are performed by mortals in the world of mortals, however, there is always another audience in this mortal world, an audience that includes the performers themselves as well as others who may be witnessing the ritual. Graf refers to these two audiences for religious acts as the vertical and horizontal axes of communication, since any religious speech act has one form that corresponds to the way it is understood by a divine audience and another that corresponds to the way it is perceived by any audience in the mortal world.[22] The mortal audience can be as large as an entire community or as small as the individual performer, and the divine audience can likewise range from a single specific divinity to an unspecified and undifferentiated mass of divinity, all the divine elements of the entire cosmos.[23]

The question of who is performing the ritual and for whom is thus always crucial in understanding the dynamics of the ritual. Many of the anthropological studies of ritual have focused on the horizontal axis from a functionalist point of view—what function does the ritual have in maintaining (or subverting) the structure of the community? What effect does this performance have on the community of performers and audience? The horizontal axis can thus be analyzed from an etic, scholarly point of view, taking into account various political, social, economic, and other factors, insofar as the scholar has sufficient data to reconstruct them, which is always a problem for the ancient Greco-Roman world. The vertical axis, by contrast, is essentially inaccessible, since it is articulated in the minds of the ancient performers. We might attempt to reconstruct this axis from an etic perspective by using some universalizing theory of how the human mind works, be it Freudian psychology, Levi-Straussian structuralism, or contemporary cognitive science. Such theories provide explanations of why the ancient performers thought (and therefore acted) in the ways that

---

[22] Graf 1997: 214.

[23] While it may seem odd to think of addressing a statement to oneself, the Bath curse tablets that have scratchings on the tablet that resemble letters show that the performer was trying to write the curse in the proper way and that, for the audience of his own illiterate self, the marks that resembled letters sufficed to successfully communicate the idea of writing out the petition. Tomlin 1988b: 253 mentions a set of texts that "all seem to have been intended to look like inscribed tablets: they contain repeated or implausible letter-forms which are best interpreted as an illiterate person's attempt at a *defixio*. The author will have seen others inscribing tablets and throwing them into the sacred spring; for him the mysterious act of writing would have been part of the magic."

they did, allowing us to try to understand them, rather than dismissing them as incomprehensible irrationalities. Some theories of this kind are more helpful than others: Preuss's concept of *Urdummheit* (primitive stupidity) or Frazer's idea of an evolution of mankind from childlike ignorance to adult scientific reasoning seem to provide less insight than structuralist identifications of patterns of opposition or the discoveries of how certain things remain better in human memory because of their cognitive salience. Nevertheless, all these theories translate the thoughts and actions of the ancients into terms that fit into our contemporary understanding of the world and human nature, and, as in any process of translation, we must remain aware of the imperfect fit between our perspective and theirs.

Another option is to attempt to analyze the expressions in the ancient evidence of the ways that the ancient performers conceived of the vertical axis of communication, that is to say, the ways that they imagined the relation of mortals and the divine (be it celestial or infernal, immanent or transcendent).[24] Such an analysis requires us to set aside any question of what they were *really* doing (in our own terms) when they called upon the gods or performed a ritual, in favor of examining what they *thought* they were doing. One problem of trying to reconstruct such an emic perspective is, as always, that most of our evidence does not explicitly address such issues, leaving us to try to reason out the underlying logic, a task that we can only approach using our own ideas. Moreover, we must be careful, even when we do get an explicit explanation of what an ancient performer thought he or she was doing, not to take that particular text as representative of what all performers (male and female, across the span of the centuries in the Mediterranean world) thought they were doing. Nevertheless, close attention to such emic explanations, categorizations, and collocations provides us with the best insight into the structures these ancient thinkers imagined for the nature of the world and the gods.

Any analysis that looks only to the horizontal or vertical component of the communication flattens out the entire contour of the speech act, missing important indicators about the act of communication. Any ritual provides information about the way the performers present themselves both within the mortal world of the horizontal axis and in relation to the divine powers of the vertical axis. The presentation of the performer on the horizontal axis illustrates the sociopolitical location of the performer within

---

[24] Attention to theology in recent scholarship on Greek religion, in, e.g., Henrichs 2010; Eidinow, Kindt, and Osborne 2016 (a collection of essays on theology in ancient Greek religion); or Naiden 2013, etc., turns the focus to the vertical axis, the way that the Greeks imagined the interactions of gods and mortals. Struck 2016 also critiques the functionalist focus in the analysis of divination, calling for attention to what the ancient Greeks and Romans thought they were doing, although he makes use of contemporary cognitive science, rather than attempting an analysis of theological assumptions from an emic perspective.

the mortal world, whereas the level of access to divine favor or power along the vertical axis correlates to the efficacy of the ritual, so both axes provide important insights into the normativity of the rite from an emic perspective.

CONCLUSIONS

When approaching the evidence from the ancient Greco-Roman world for ritualized action, therefore, we must analyze not only *what* kind of evidence we are examining but also what sort of action is depicted in the evidence. We must also analyze *who* is performing it and for whom, *where* and *when* it is performed, *why* it is being performed, and *how* the performance works. In this study, the chapters are organized primarily by what sort of practice is involved, but the analysis probes each of the other factors as well to determine when a ritualized action may be labeled 'magic.' The survey of different varieties within the discourse of magic in the ancient Greco-Roman world provides us with a better sense of the categories and criteria by which the Greeks and Romans evaluated normative and non-normative ritual activity in the ancient world.

3

Curses for All Occasions:
Malefic and Binding Magic

A second-century CE lead table from Roman Beirut (see figure 1, page 54) seeks to curse the charioteer and the horses of the popular Blue team in order to prevent them from winning the high-stakes chariot race. More than 1,700 curse tablets from the ancient Greco-Roman world have been published, and many more remain unpublished, awaiting the analysis of scholars. These tablets of metal inscribed with malevolent wishes present a good body of evidence for scholars of ancient magic, since most of these curses seem to fall within everyone's intuitive definition of magic. They clearly intend harm to the target, they are mostly made and deposited in secret, and they use strange words to compel suprahuman powers to take concrete action against another for the personal benefit of the curser. This large data set provides the opportunity to analyze the features of the curses to help determine the boundaries of the category to which they belong, to clarify what might be labeled 'magic' and which cases fall upon the fuzzy borders. One of the first types of magical evidence to be systematically collected and cataloged, the curse tablets have been the object of scholarly study for over a hundred years, and a number of recent studies have analyzed particular features of the curse tablet, elucidating the rules of the genre and illuminating the characteristic poetics of the magical curse.[1]

---

[1] The earlier collections of Wünsch 1897 (DTA) and Audollent 1904 (DT) have been augmented by, e.g., Jordan 1985 and Cunliffe and Tomlin 1988, but, despite the publication of new curse tablets, many tablets remain unpublished, and there has been no recent com-

ΚΑΤΟΧΟС ΙΠΠΩΝ ΚΕΗΝΙΧΩΝ
ΦΡΙΞ
ΦΩΞ
ΒΕΙΑΒΟΥ
(ΤωΚΤΑΝΕωΤΕ
ΙΤΕΠΟΧΘΩΝ
ΥΠΟΧΘΩΝ
ΛΑΜΝΩ
ΔΑΜΝΑ
ΛΥΚΩΔΑΗΝΑ
Η ΕΝΙΠΠΑ
ΠΥΡΙΠΙΠΑΝΥΞ
ΟΡΕΟΒΑΡΖΑΓΡΑΚΡΑΜΜΑΧΑΔΑΡΙ
ΦΝΟΥΚΕΝΤΑΒΑωΘωΡΑΡΑΒΑΥ
ΑΓΙΟΙΑΝΓΕΛΟΙΕΝΝΟΙΤΣΑΤΕΚΑΙΚΑΤΑΣΧΕΤΕ
ΛΥΛΑΤΑΥΑΥΔωΝΙΣΑΤΑΑΥΤΟΥΣ ΤΟ
ΟΙΑΤΙΤΝΟΥΝΑΜΙΝΤΟΥ ΝΗ Α С ΚΕΛΛΙΗΑСΚΕ
ΦΝΟΥΚΕΝΤΑΜΛ ωΘΟΡ ΕΟΒΑΡΖΑΛΛω
ΚΕΤΑΙΝСΥΝΕΡ Θ ΑΤΕΑ ΗСΑΤΕ ΚΑΙ ΡΑΜΤΕ
ΤΕΤΑСΤΡ ΕΥΑΤΕΛΕΠΤΟΚΟΠΗСΑΤΕΙΦΑΛ Ε
ΙΠΠΟΥСΚΕΗΝΙΟΧΟΥСΧΡΟΑС ΚΑΛΑΕΙΝωΝ
ΝΥΦΙΚΟСΘΑΛΟΦΟΡΟС ΑΗΤΗΤΟСΜΟΥΚΟΤΡΟΦΟС
ΚΑΛΙΜΟΡΦСΦΛΟ ΠΑΡΘΩΝΟС ΠΑΝΤΟΜΕΔΩΝ
ΥΠΑΤΟС ΦΙΛΑΡΗΑΤΟС ΜΑΚΑΡΙ СΟΦΑΛΙΟС ΗΓΕ
ΗωΝ ωΚΕΙΑΝΟС ΤΥΡΑΝΟС ΧωΡΙΚΙСΚΑΛΙΜΟΡΦ
ΑΥΡΙΟС ΑΚΤΙΝΟΒΟΛΟС ΕΓΔΙΚΟС ΖΑΒΑΔΗСΧωΡ
ΙΚΙС ΝΟΜΟΘΕΤΗС ΒΑΡΒΑΡΟС ΕΙΕΡ · ΝΙΚΗСΞΑ
ΕССΑΚΑΡΙСΔω ΝΑΤΟС ΑΝΘΕΡΕΤΟСΨωΦΟΡΥ
ΟΛΥΚΟΤΡΑΗΟС ΓΕΡΜΑΝΟС ΟΗΕΛΙСΚΟСΑСΠΡΟ
ΦΟСΑΝΑΤΥΛΙΚΟСΑΝΤΙΟΧΟСΧΡΑΒΔΗСΟΝΙС
ΧΡΑΒΑ ΗΛΥСΗС
ΧΕΡΑС ΠΟΔΑС ΝΕΥΡΑ ΟΑС·ΚΑΛΛΕ
ΙΠΠΩΝ ΚΕΗΝΙΟΧΩΝ Χ·ΟΛΑΜΑΥΑ ΕΝωΝ

For Restraining Horses and Charioteers.

PHRIX PHÔX BEIABOU STÔKTA NEÔTER
whether above the earth or below DAMNÔ DAMNA
LUKODAMNA MENIPPA PURIPIGANUX

EULAMÔ	EULAMÔ
EULAM	ULAMÔ
EULA	LAMÔ
[EUL]	AMÔ
[EU]	MÔ
[E]	Ô

OREOBARZAGRA AKRAMMACHARI PHNOUKENTABAÔTH
ÔBARABAU, you holy angels, ambush and restrain
LULATAU AUDÔNISTA them. The spell—
OIATITNOUNAMINTOU MASKELLI MASKELLÔ
PHNOUKENTABAÔTH OREOBARZA, now attack, bind
overturn, cut up, chop into pieces the horses and the
charioteers of the Blue colors—Numphikos, Thalophoros,
Aêtôs, Mousotrophos, Kalimorphos, Philoparthenos,
Pantomedon, Hupatos, Philarmatos, Makaris, Omphalios,
Hêgemôn, Ôkeianos, Turanos, Chôrikis, Kalimorphos,
Aurios, Aktinobolos, Egdikos, Zabadês, Chôrikis,
Nomothetês, Barbaros, Eieronikês, Xaes, Makaris, Dênatos,
Antheretos, Phôsphoros, Lukotramos, Germanos, Obeliskos,
Astrophors, Anatolikos, Antiochos—CHRAB, bind and
CHRAB, damage the hands, the feet, sinews of the horses
and charioteers of the Blue colors.

Figure 1. Curse tablet for restraining Horses and Charioteers. Image
by permission from Maricq, "Tablette de defixion de Beyrouth,"
Byzantion 1952, facing p. 368. (Gager #5).

To move from the intuitive sense that anything that involves using
mysterious words to cause chariot horses to stumble and crash must somehow be magical to an analytic understanding of the genre of curses in the
ancient Greco-Roman world, we may analyze the evidence using both
substantive and functionalist criteria, not only asking *what* these things
are and *where* and *when* they appear, but also *who* used them in what
contexts and *how* they were imagined to operate. These basic analytic ques-

---

prehensive listing (although the database in Kropp 2008 helps redress some of this gap for
tablets in Latin). The online database Thesaurus Defixionum Magdeburgensis (http://www.
thedema.ovgu.de/thedema.php?) now provides texts for over 1,700 published curse tablets,
many with translations and additional information, and the database is searchable, which
provides an enormous resource for scholars. Although Gellar-Goad, Papakonstantinou, and
Riess 2018 announce a forthcoming English translation of all the Attic *defixiones*, the translations in Gager 1992 remain the most accessible for a wider range of tablets, and the studies
in Faraone 1991b and Versnel 1991b remain fundamental to understanding the corpus. For
an introductory overview, see Ogden 1999.

tions will help us determine the place of curse tablets within the ancient Greco-Roman world and give us a better understanding of this phenomenon, so peculiar to our modern sensibilities and yet so ubiquitous to the ancients.

WHAT ARE CURSE TABLETS?

The curse tablet, the thin sheet of metal (lamella) with mysterious writings on it, appears as part of the standard equipment of the malevolent magician. When Apuleius describes the workshop of the Thessalian witch Pamphile, these lamellae appear alongside the weird collection of body parts as the stock in trade of the witch.

> First she arranged her deadly laboratory with its customary apparatus, setting out spices of all sorts, *unintelligibly lettered metal plaques,* the surviving remains of ill-omened birds, and numerous pieces of mourned and even buried corpses: here noses and fingers, there flesh-covered spikes from crucified bodies, elsewhere the preserved gore of murder victims and mutilated skulls wrenched from the teeth of wild beasts.[2]

While Apuleius is creating an elaborately imagined literary scene, Plato too refers to binding curses as part of the standard repertoire of the magicians who go to the doors of the rich soliciting clients. "And if he wants to harm some enemy, he will harm just and unjust alike with spells [*epagōgai*] and binding curses [*katadesmoi*] for only a small expense, having persuaded, as they claim, the gods to obey them."[3] These experts claim special powers from the gods to harm and bind any enemy, regardless of whether such harm is justifiable or not (a problem that is central to Plato's purposes here), and their appearance at the doors of the rich is presented within the dialogue as a familiar sight in Socrates's fifth-century BCE Athens. Centuries later, the Roman author Pliny acknowledges that there is no one who does not fear being bound by evil spells, even if Cicero is scornful in condemning as a flimsy excuse his rival Curio's claim that he forgot his whole legal speech because of a magic spell.[4] Such curses were part of the popular imagination in the Greco-Roman world, always to be suspected when dealing with a rival or enemy.

---

[2] Apuleius, *Met.* 3.17. *Priusque apparatu solito instruit feralem officinam, omne genus aromatis et ignorabiliter lamminis litteratis et infelicium avium durantibus damnis <repletam>, defletorum, sepultorum etiam, cadaverum expositis multis admodum membris; hic nares et digiti, illic carnosi clavi pendentium, alibi trucidatorum servatus cruor et extorta dentibus ferarum trunca calvaria.*

[3] Plato, *Republic* 364b–c.

[4] Pliny, *HN* 28.19; cp. Cicero, *Brutus* 217.

These curses, however, were not merely products of the imagination; Greeks and Romans really did employ curse tablets and binding spells in their efforts to defeat their rivals and harm their enemies. When Germanicus, the popular young Roman nobleman and potential heir to the emperor Tiberius, died mysteriously, his friends and family suspected that he had fallen victim to a curse from one of the many other nobles jealous of his power and position. And indeed, they dug up the floor of his house and discovered a number of lead tablets engraved with Germanicus's name, along with the remains of the ritual procedures that set the curses in action, bits of human bodies, "charred and blood-smeared ashes, and other implements of witchcraft, by which it is believed that the living can be devoted to the powers of the underworld."[5] Modern observers may debate whether Germanicus perished from a poison slipped into his food, but, for the Romans, the efficacy of the curse rituals was clear both to his friends and to the enemies who had performed them.

These testimonies, both from literary imaginings and historical sources, provide a sense of the ubiquity of curses, but the material record provides even more evidence for this kind of magic. Not only are there large numbers of curse tablets surviving from all parts of the Greco-Roman world, starting from around the fifth century BCE and going for at least a thousand years thereafter, but the Greek Magical Papyri preserve some of the recipes for creating these tablets. These recipes in the formularies provide witness to parts of the ritual of cursing that left less durable traces than the engraved lead tablets, the sacrifices that provided the bloody ashes beneath Germanicus's floor, as well as the oral incantations that leave no material trace at all. While the recipe books of the Greek Magical Papyri come from the peculiar environment of second- to fourth-century CE Egypt, some of the earlier curse tablets from various places in the Mediterranean provide indications that they too were prepared from formularies. Some lead tablets, such as the chariot race curse from Beirut (p. 54), begin with "For Restraining," the title taken from the recipe book. Others were clearly prepared by professionals making multiple copies from an exemplar, since they have identical texts in the same scribal hand with only different names filled in on different tablets. A few tablets even appear where the magician forgot to write in the name of the target, so there is only a blank space or the generic 'so-and-so' that appears in the recipes of the Greek Magical Papyri.[6] In analyzing our evidence for curses, then, we

---

[5] Tacitus, *Annals* 2.69; cp. Cassius Dio 57.18.

[6] Beirut chariot curse (Gager 5); for such titles in the recipe books, cp. PGM VII.417–422 and VII.429–458, both of which begin with "For restraining." Jordan 1994: 135 notes that many of the two hundred or so unpublished tablets from Amathous seem to have the same formulas executed by the same hand. Most spells from the formularies in the PGM collection have ὁ δεῖνα or ἡ δεῖνα, 'so and so' (either masculine or feminine), rendered as NN in Betz's translation. A first-century CE lead tablet from Carthage (DTA 230) was found with blank

may distinguish between literary depictions like Apuleius, references to actual use like Plato or Cicero, recipes for producing the tablets in the Greek Magical Papyri, and the actual tablets themselves. All four types of evidence provide different perspectives on the nature of curses in the ancient Greco-Roman world.

Although lead is the most popular material for curse tablets, both in the recipes and in the actual examples, curses could be put on other materials as well. Some recipes call for using lead or tin or some other metal, and tablets have been found composed of various metals and alloys, usually corresponding to what was most readily available in the vicinity.[7] The huge collection of curse tablets in Bath, England, for example, seem to be made of a sort of local pewter, formed from a combination of lead, tin, and copper, while a grave shaft in Cyprus held not only over two hundred tablets of lead, but more than sixty inscribed on sheets of the soft mineral selenite. Lead scraps seem to have been fairly easily available from plumbing systems (some recipes even call for taking the lead from a cold-water pipe), and they were used as a handy writing surface for other types of writing as well. Pottery sherds (ostraka) were another readily available substance, used for everything from official public ostracism votes in Classical Athens to jotting down shopping lists in Imperial Egypt. Papyrus could be substituted for a lead tablet in some recipes, but, while both pottery sherds and lead tablets last well through the centuries in various places throughout the Mediterranean world, papyrus survives almost exclusively in the sands of Egypt. Wax writing tablets, another common writing surface, are mentioned in Ovid as inscribed with magical curses, but no examples of such have survived the ages.[8]

The primary ritual involved with the creation of a curse tablet is of course the inscription of the tablet, and some of the tablets simply use the verb for writing down (*katagrapho*) to describe the action of magically binding the target. While the literary testimonies and allusions tend to be vague about what is written, the executed examples and the recipe books

---

spaces left for the name of the target that were never filled in. Jordan 1985: 162 mentions an unpublished tablet from Athens (#38) where the name of the target was clearly written in later, in smaller letters to fit into the space left when the formulaic curse was written out in advance (cp. the formula in examples 24–35, Jordan 1985: 161–162).

[7] For the tablets from Bath, see Cunliffe and Tomlin 1988, while Jordan 1994 explains that the tablets from Amathous earlier thought to be talc or mica are actually selenite. The recipes in PGM VlI.396–404 and 429–458 both call for using lead from a water pipe. On the symbolic significance of using lead (or lack thereof), see ch. 3, p. 83, n. 65 below. For the use of ostraka, see PGM XLVI.4–8; PGM CXIXa.4–6; PGM CXXIV.1–43; and the discussion in Martín Hernández and Torallas Tovar 2014. Some scholars have suggested a connection between the practice of ostracism in Athens and cursing; see Collins 2008a: 65–66.

[8] Ovid, *Amores* 3.7.29; cp. DTA 55a, a lead tablet that refers to binding in both lead and wax—presumably the wax version perished while the lead remained. PGM V.305 allows the substitution of papyrus for lead.

Figure 2. DTAP 475561, Museo Nazionale Romano at the
Baths of Diocletian, room of the fountain of Anna Perenna,
fig. 10 from Piranomonte 2012: 165. (See plate 2.)

Figure 2. P. Oslo 1 (PGM XXXVI.1–34), Courtesy of the University of Oslo Library Papyrus Collection. (See plate 1.)

naturally preserve the text, the words of the curse. The simplest form of inscription is just the name of the target, perhaps with a verb of binding, but some of the later examples contain lengthy and complex texts. The curse's action upon the target is described in a variety of ways: as binding or binding down the target (καταδεσμεύειν, καταδεῖν, *defigere, ligāre*), as registering or writing down the name of the target (καταγράφειν, ἐνγράφειν, ἐπιγράφειν), or as dedicating or devoting the target to some deity (ἀνατιθέναι, ἀνιεροῖν, *dedicāre, demandāre, devotāre*). Sometimes a drawing is added to the text, the image complementing the words in creating the effect.[9]

---

[9] PGM XXXVI provides instructions for illustrations in several spell recipes, including curses in 1–34, 35–68, and 231–255. Cp. PGM VII.940–968; PGM V.304–369. Some of the tablets from the shrine of Anna Perenna (e.g., DTAP 475567) contain elaborate drawings, as do the 'Sethian' tablets from Rome (e.g., Gager 5).

The recipe books confirm that the act of writing is only one part of the spell; incantations must be spoken or sung while the tablet is being prepared or deposited. In the earliest examples, there is little written text—just the name of the target, the oral component probably filled in the rest of the wish, the action of binding, and perhaps the powers invoked to carry it out. In the much later Greek Magical Papyri, the magician is sometimes instructed to speak the text at as well as inscribe it on the tablet: "And take a lead tablet and write the same spell and recite it."[10] While some of the texts on the tablets are clearly designed to be written, rather than pronounced, others show traces of poetic formulae, which point to an oral tradition of magical incantations now largely lost. As Faraone has argued, however, the famous song of the Erinyes in Aeschylus's *Eumenides* echoes this oral tradition, with its repeated refrain of "This is our song over the sacrificial victim—frenzied, maddened, destroying the mind, the Furies' hymn, a spell to bind the soul, not tuned to the lyre, withering the life of mortals." The Erinyes here are cursing Orestes as he prepares to defend himself for the slaying of his mother Clytemnestra, a lawcourt context that seems to underlie many curse tablets. Such reflections, in the high art form of the Greek tragic chorus, are the only remains of this oral incantation tradition that was gradually superseded as the technology of writing grew in importance.[11] As the 'epigraphic habit,' the cultural practice of writing things down, expands across the ancient Mediterranean world, the texts that are written on the tablets grow increasingly longer and more complex, although regional (and perhaps even personal) variations complicate any straightforward progression over time.[12]

Other aspects of the cursing ritual produce more or less visible remains in the evidence. Many tablets are rolled up or carefully folded, which may simply serve to keep the text secret but which may also be a part of the ritual preparation of the tablet. Some tablets are pierced with a nail, which symbolically nails down and binds the target. The nail may have special significance if taken from a gibbet or a shipwreck, like the supply in Pam-

---

[10] E.g., PGM IV.330. Some executed examples have only lists of names, e.g., SEG 54.398 = Gager 57, DT 60 = Gager 42, DTA 38 = Gager 37.

[11] See Faraone 1985 for a more complete discussion of the Furies' curse and the oral tradition. It is worth noting that the Furies in fact succeed in preventing Orestes from defending himself in the play; Apollo must take up the defense.

[12] The earliest Greek curse tablets appear in Sicily around the end of the sixth century BCE, and more start to appear in Attica and other parts of the Greek world in the mid-fifth century. Cp. Faraone 2011c: 50 on the epigraphic habit and the distortions in scholarly interpretations caused by this explosion of textual material. Faraone argues that many of these magical practices existed in oral form long before evidence appears in written form on durable materials. Contacts with cultures, such as Egypt and Mesopotamia, which had writing much earlier, create new ways in which writing is used in these magical rituals. Cp. also Faraone 2012b, and Graf 2015.

Figure 3. Room of the fountain of Anna Perenna, DTAP 500189.
(See plate 3b.)

phile's workshop, and a recipe in the Greek Magical Papyri calls specifically for a nail from a shipwreck. Other tablets are further bound with
string, and one recipe calls for tying 365 knots in the string to ensure that
the spell stays unbroken every day of the year: "Taking a black thread,
make 365 knots and bind the thread around the outside of the tablet, saying the same formula again and 'keep him who is held.' "[13] Any string
wrapped around a lead tablet two thousand years ago has of course perished long since, but traces remain in the archaeological record that suggest that such binding with string was employed in the actual examples as
well as the recipes.

In addition to rolling, nailing, or binding the tablet itself, some of the
curse rituals involved manipulations of other figures. Plato mentions little
wax figurines deposited at the crossroads, and lead versions of such 'voodoo dolls' have survived. Some of these have their hands tied behind their
backs or are even placed in little coffins, but they differ from the modern
popular conception of 'voodoo dolls' in that these manipulations, even

[13] For nails, cp. PGM VII.465–466; Apuleius, *Met.* 3.17 (above). For the knotted string,
cp. PGM VII.453–454.

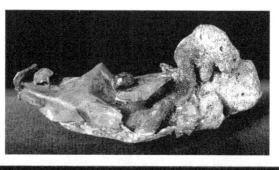

Figure 4. Room of the fountain of Anna Perenna,
DTAP 475550, 475549, 475552, and 475567 M. (See plate 4.)

sticking needles into the figurines, do not seem to have been imagined to produce a direct similar effect on the target. Oftentimes these figurines are very crude, nearly shapeless lumps of metal that vaguely resemble a human form.[14] A few are more well developed, and the cache from the fountain of Anna Perenna in Rome has yielded a few examples of figurines with elaborate treatments. Since the curse tablets and figurines in this fountain were sealed within triple layers of leaden canisters, the figurines of wax or paste have survived. One figurine is blanketed by the tablet, while a serpent twines around the body beneath, its head rearing up out of the tablet to strike the figurine in the face. Serpents are inscribed on some of the tablets as well, and the magician who created these seems to have had a taste for serpent imagery.[15]

While the archaeological record preserves few traces, sometimes actual animals were used for these symbolic manipulations instead of (or in

[14] Plato, *Laws* 933b. For an overview of the figurines, see Faraone 1991b. It is worth noting that, in general, the *less* direct and detailed the image, the more powerful the link to the original; there is an emphasis on symbolism rather than mimesis. Portrait statues are not used for *defixiones*, nor is there even any attempt to make such figurines individualized, for too many complicated details distract from the simple symbolic act of binding.

[15] The initial notice by Piranomonte 2002 has been expanded by the publications of Blänsdorf 2010 and Piranomonte 2010 and Piranomonte 2012, with the most recent discussions of the figurines in Rapinesi and Polakova 2012.

addition to) the manipulations of the tablet or a figurine. When the orator Libanius was prostrated by headaches that prevented him from reading or lecturing, he had a dream that somehow magical spells were involved, and a search of his classroom turned up the mutilated remains of a chameleon. "Its head had been placed between its hind feet. Of its forefeet, one was nowhere to be seen, and the other was closing its mouth to keep it silent." A curse tablet from Carthage describes a rooster bound by its feet, hands, and head, while two curse tablets from Aquitania refer to manipulations with a puppy, turned onto its back and made helpless like the target. The recipe books of the Greek Magic Papyri call for various animals to be subjected to symbolic tortures, such as a frog cut open and stitched back up again after the tablet is deposited within or a bat caught alive and released with its eyes torn out. Another, less violent, recipe calls for the bat simply to have magical drawings and names painted on its wings before it is released.[16] The animals here serve as further symbolic components of the ritual, but such symbols, like the oral incantations, leave little trace after two millennia, in contrast to the unrusting, undecaying lead tablets that form the literal bulk of our evidence.[17]

WHERE AND WHEN WERE CURSE TABLETS DEPOSITED?

Many of the curse tablets found have been uncovered in graves or in well-shafts, and, although Plato mentions crossroads, the recipe books confirm these two types of locations as the favored places for depositing a curse, even if they provide little information as to why such places are preferred. While the principal factor seems to be that both are secret places where a deposited tablet is least likely to be found, scholars have speculated that both provide some connection with the underworld—the graves with the dead body there interred, the wells with the nymphs and other water spirits who dwell beneath the ground. While some texts specify placement in a grave to make use of the dead person therein, others treat the choice of deposit place as optional—"whether you cause the plate to be buried or sunk in river or land or sea or stream or coffin or in a well."[18] Some practitioners clearly had their favorite deposit spots, as the hundreds of tablets, all written in the same hand, in the well at Amathous in Cyprus indicate, or the collection of canisters with tablets and figurines deposited in the

---

[16] Libanius 1.249; Carthage: DT 241 = Gager 12; Aquitania DT 111–112 = Gager 53; PGM XXXVI.231–255; PGM IV.2943; PGM XII.376–396.

[17] Wilburn 2012 provides a set of useful case studies to show how careful material analysis of the archaeological evidence can provide insights into the rituals.

[18] PGM VII.429–458.

spring of Anna Perenna and the nymphs at Rome. While graves account for over half of the extant tablets with known findspots, the other popular place for such deposits seems to have been in the sanctuaries of deities associated with the earth or underworld, such as the sanctuaries of Demeter at Corinth and at Selinous.[19] These curses still seem to have been buried secretly rather than publicly displayed, although there is another group of curses that do seem to have been hung up in public view, a fact that has caused some scholars to argue that these public curses do not fall within the category of magic at all.

The favored time of deposit, according to the recipes, is the middle of the night, even though this detail obviously cannot be corroborated by the archaeological record.[20] Again, the primary impetus seems to be to avoid detection, rather than to make some sort of contact with the powers of the night. Disturbing a grave is likely to garner the anger of the relatives responsible for the tendance and upkeep of the tomb, but any witness of a graveyard deposit might be upset from the fear of the anger of the dead whose rest has been disturbed. The secrecy connected with such deposits stands in contrast to public curses, such as those at Teos, which not only are performed in the sight of the community, but must be performed at certain prespecified times and occasions: "If anyone in office does not perform this curse at the statue of Dynamis when the games are convened at the Anthesteria or the festival of Heracles or that of Zeus, he is to be the object of the curse."[21] The public place where the ritual is performed, along with the specified times when it must be done, seem to differentiate these curses from the magical curse tablets deposited secretly in graves in the dark of night.

WHY DID PEOPLE MAKE CURSE TABLETS?

When we turn from the substantive questions (what, where, and when) to the more functionalist ones (why and how), matters become more complex. The performance of curses is embedded in the social context of the ancient Greco-Roman world, and the motivations that inspire people to turn to such curses must be understood within that cultural context. In

---

[19] Jordan 1985: 207 recounts that around 325 of roughly 625 come from graves. For the *defixiones* at Selinous, see Bettarini 2005; for Corinth, see Stroud 2013. The excavations from the shrine of Anna Perenna and the nymphs have been published in Blänsdorf 2010 and Piranomonte 2010, with further discussion in Piranomonte 2012; Jordan 1994 discusses some of the finds from Amathous, but many remain unpublished. Cp. also the cache of tablets found at the sanctuary of Isis and Magna Mater at Mainz, published in Blänsdorf 2010.

[20] E.g., PGM VII.429–58; VII.862–918; LXX.4–25.

[21] *Dirae Teorum* in Meiggs and Lewis 1969 #30 = SIG III.37–38.

each case, we should ask what motivates this use of cursing and what the curser hopes to achieve.

In general, it is useful to distinguish between curses directed at the present situation and conditional curses meant for future problems. Curses aimed at future contingencies tend to be more public and more dire than those directed at present problems, since part of the strategy involved in performing the curse is to deter anyone from triggering it by creating the future situation that is deemed undesirable. Curses written on tombs warn the passerby not to disturb the grave, calling down death and disaster on anyone who dares to do so. If no one violates the tomb, the curse is more successful than if someone does risk the curse and perishes horribly. Important crises within a community may be resolved with oaths taken by the community members to abide by the resolution, and those oaths are reinforced with vivid curses against any who violate their promises. The Athenian orator Aeschines recalls the actions of the Amphictyonic League when faced with the crisis of the Sacred War, which involved certain parties tilling the sacred land around Delphi that belonged to Apollo.

> Collecting a great force of the Amphictyons, they enslaved the men, destroyed their harbor and city, and dedicated their land, as the oracle had commanded. Moreover they swore a mighty oath, that they would not themselves till the sacred land nor let another till it, but that they would go to the aid of the god and the sacred land with hand and foot and voice, and all their might. They were not content with taking this oath, but they added an imprecation and a mighty curse concerning this; for it stands thus written in the curse: "If any one should violate this," it says, "whether city or private man, or tribe, let them be under the curse," it says, "of Apollo and Artemis and Leto and Athena Pronaea." The curse goes on: That their land bear no fruit; that their wives bear children not like those who begat them, but monsters; that their flocks yield not their natural increase; that defeat await them in camp and court and market-place, and that they perish utterly, themselves, their houses, their whole race. "And never," it says, "may they offer pure sacrifice unto Apollo, nor to Artemis, nor to Leto, nor to Athena Pronaea, and may the gods refuse to accept their offerings."[22]

Once again, this curse will be most successful if it never has to be imposed, if no one ever breaks the oath to preserve the sacred lands. The curse promises a complete breakdown of the normal order—flocks and lands fail to yield their produce, families disintegrate, and even the relations of the

---

[22] Aeschines, *Against Ctesiphon* 3.109–111.

community with the gods become corrupted and ineffective—until ultimate destruction comes.

Such conditional self-cursing is not confined to communities; it could also be an effective way for an individual to add force to an oath sworn in public. In the sanctuary of Demeter at Knidos, a number of metal plaques have been discovered that bear witness to oaths sworn by individuals, many of which include a self-curse if the swearer should be lying. A woman named Antigone calls down a curse upon herself if she is guilty on casting a malicious curse upon a certain Asclepiadas or hiring someone else to do so.[23] Also at Knidos is a stele, on which is recorded the story of another woman, Tatia, who called down curses upon herself in her oath that she had not bewitched her son-in-law Iucundus. When both she and her son perished shortly thereafter, however, her relatives and community took it as a sign that the gods had fulfilled the curses she called upon herself for falsely swearing to her innocence, and they set up the stele relating the story and attesting to the power of the gods that fulfilled the curses.[24]

As with private curse tablets, such public curses may be reinforced with other symbolic gestures. The people of Thera made wax figurines and melted them as they swore the oath to colonize Cyrene.

On these conditions a sworn agreement was made by those who stayed there and by those who sailed to found the colony, and they invoked curses against those transgressors who would not abide by it—whether those settling in Libya or those who remained. They made waxen images and burnt them, calling down the following curse, everyone assembled together, men, women, boys, girls: "The person who does not abide by this sworn agreement but transgresses it shall melt away and dissolve like these images—himself, his descendants and his property; but those who abide by the sworn agreement—those sailing to Libya and those staying in Thera—shall have an abundance of good things, both themselves and their descendants."[25]

Faraone speaks of "a sliding scale of sensory effects, ranging from the auditory alone, to the theatrical or visual, and ending with the tactile or participatory,"[26] to describe the different kinds of symbolic activities that

[23] DT 1 = Gager 89. The practice of erecting such public oaths with curses seems to be a local custom, appearing in the areas of Lydia near Knidos. Gordon 2004 provides the best discussion of the social context.

[24] Confession Stele from Knidos 156/157 CE. TAM V.1 318. See the comments in Gordon 2004: 76.

[25] This text appears on a fourth-century BCE marble stele from Cyrene, purporting to record the initial oath of the citizens of Thera in the seventh century. Meiggs and Lewis 1969 #5.

[26] Faraone 2012a: 127.

may be associated with such curses. The public oath itself is a powerful verbal performance, but its effect is enhanced even more by the spectacle of the wax figurines melting away in the fire in front of the whole populace. Once again, the curses directed at future contingencies are more dramatic and more dire, threatening utter destruction for the transgressor and all his descendants.

By contrast, the curses for immediate and present problems tend to be more restrained, limited to practical solutions for the particular situation rather than hyperbolic threats to prevent a problematic situation from occurring. The most important factor for understanding the use of curses is placing them within the competitive or agonistic context of the cultures of the ancient Mediterranean world, where every aspect of life involves different levels of competition with rivals for resources, power, or status. As scholars have noted, these competitions tend to be seen as zero-sum games, in which one person's success entails the failure of another.[27] While the Roman chariot races, with the fanatical factions who often rioted after a particularly tense win or loss, provide a dramatic illustration of this kind of agonistic context, in which the rivalries of the athletic arena extended into other spheres of life, one of the earliest Greek poets, Hesiod, places this kind of competitive spirit at the basis of all Greek culture. Strife (Eris), he says, is one of the primal powers of the cosmos, the elder daughter of dark Night.

> It rouses even the helpless man to work. For a man who is not working but who looks at some other man, a rich one who is hastening to plow and plant and set his house in order, he envies him, one neighbor envying his neighbor who is hastening towards wealth: and this Strife is good for mortals. And potter is angry with potter, and builder with builder, and beggar begrudges beggar, and poet poet.[28]

The spirit of rivalry is thus imagined as a basic fact of life; success will bring the envy and enmity of those who failed, and they will be continuously seeking to turn the tables and see the prosperous fail while they succeed. The sidelong glance of envy is associated with the 'evil eye,' a basic form of cursing that is simply wishing failure to the successful. Catullus famously exhorts his beloved Lesbia to give him so many kisses that the onlookers, envious of their shared happiness, will not be able to count the kisses and thus bewitch them.[29] Not only does all of life involve these competitions, but Catullus knows that there will always be envious observ-

[27] Faraone 1991b; cp. Versnel 1991a: 62, who cites the amoral familist's principle "maximize the material, short-term advantage of the nuclear family; assume that all others will do the same."

[28] Hesiod, *Works and Days* 11–24.

[29] Catullus 7.11–12; 5.10–13.

ers, gossiping about the success and failure of others. Scholars have noted the importance of such networks of gossip and slander in the competitions for status that pervade every aspect of life.[30]

Competition for status and resources is thus a form of public sport in which everyone engages, and beating out one's rivals in these contests is a good and just goal. Indeed, one of the common definitions of justice (which Plato critiques in the *Republic*) is to help your friends and harm your enemies; defeating your opponents is a moral duty as much as helping those who are dear to you. In this agonistic context, then, winning is indeed everything. However, it is worth noting that, while one may boast of the strength, speed, skill, or even, like Odysseus, the cunning intelligence one has used to defeat one's rivals, no one ever boasts of using curses or magical means to hamper those rivals. A defeated rival may whine that his loss was due to magical interference, like Cicero's rival orator, but the implication is that to use such means is essentially cheating. As with other forms of cheating, many may engage in it secretly (because, after all, winning is winning), but no one would admit it publicly (because to admit that one needed such means is an admission that one's rival was otherwise better). Such curses, then, appear as a desperate move in the competitive contexts of the ancient Greco-Roman world, a form of cheating that rigs the odds of the competition in one's own favor by using some means with extra-ordinary efficacy.

The evidence of the curse tablets provides a look into the many agonistic contexts in which people of the ancient world found it necessary to try to rig the odds in their own favor.[31] Indeed, these texts give voice to the hopes and fears, the desperate anxieties, of those who would not otherwise leave a trace in the historical record. Individuals who would never have anything publicly inscribed in stone, much less write a text that would be transcribed and passed down through the millennia, have their thoughts preserved in the medium of the durable lead curse tablet. Many of the extant curse tablets come from economic contexts, since the competition for business—potter against potter—could mean the success or failure of one's livelihood. A fourth-century BCE curse tablet from the Kerameikos district in Athens binds "the body, the business of Demetrios

---

[30] Eidinow 2007: 231 places the curse tablets within the networks of gossip and slander in Athenian society, pointing out the ways in which reputations are on the line in every context; Eidinow 2016 develops this study to examine accusations of magic in ancient Athens. Cp. also Versnel 1999 on the role of schadenfreude, rejoicing in the failures of one's enemies, esp. 136–140 on the place of envy and slander in the gossip networks. Riess 2012: 164–234 provides a good examination of the ways in which violence factors into such conflicts.

[31] Eidinow has discussed the use of such curses as risk-management strategies in Eidinow 2007 and Eidinow 2012.

the ceramic worker, the hands, the feet, the soul," along with a number of his associates in the business. Other Athenian tablets bind silver workers or bronzesmiths, as well as tavern-keepers and a variety of other shopkeepers, and the evidence shows that, wherever there was a business rivalry, someone might employ a curse tablet to try to hold back his rivals so that he could get ahead.[32]

While economic contexts provide implicit competitions between businesses, public performances were always explicitly competitive contexts, where rivals vied openly against one another for the prizes. Most theatrical performances were part of competitions at festivals, where prizes were awarded, so these competitions have public status at stake, not primarily economic factors as in modern theater. Naturally enough, the archaeological record provides plenty of evidence that many competitors (or their supporters) tried to stack the odds in their favor before the competition. While choruses and their directors may be bound or rival wrestlers, the chariot race perhaps draws the most cursing activity, in keeping with the enormous social prestige involved in the chariot race, not just in the Roman Empire, but all the way back to the funeral games of Patrocles in Homer's *Iliad*. The chariot race was a dangerous and uncertain activity, since chariot crashes could cause spectacular calamities and deaths even for the most highly skilled, so it is little wonder that so many felt impelled to try to influence the outcome.

Sometimes this attempt may just have been seen as a way to level the playing field in an inherently unfair situation, as the myth of Pelops and his winning of Hippodameia suggests. The father of Hippodameia challenged any suitor for his daughter's hand to a chariot race, which he always won because of the marvelous horses given to him by the god Ares. Pelops cannot win by his own merits, but different versions of the myth provide different means for him to succeed. The most familiar account is that Hippodameia cheated by substituting wax linchpins for bronze in the axles of her father's chariot, causing him to crash in the midst of the race. Pindar, however, recounts that Pelops prayed for aid from his former lover, the god Poseidon, to hold back the chariot of Hippodameia's father (and the spear with which he killed the suitors in the race as he caught up with them), while Pausanias preserves an account that Pelops in fact used curse tablets to achieve his unlikely victory. Binding curses become a way to explain a victory against the odds in a traditional story, just as they were actually used by various competitors to try for such a victory against their rivals.[33]

---

[32] Gager 70 = W. Peek 1941 #9. Gager 1992: 151–174 (ch. 4) provides a collection of such 'business' curses.

[33] Pindar, *Olympian* 1; cp. Pausanias 6.20. See the discussion of Howie 1991: esp. 78–80.

Serious rivalries in the ancient Greco-Roman world often ended up in the courts, which, even more than in our litigious modern society, were the social institution for handling personal disputes. Lawsuits might be undertaken to gain vengeance for a wrong done, but the accusation of wrongdoing might itself be a tactic for harming one's rivals. Especially in the ancient Athenian courts, the context from which we have the most evidence preserved, the setup of the legal system meant that a trial was arranged as a contest between two parties. Even in criminal cases such as murder trials, the defendant was prosecuted by an individual who was harmed by the death, rather than by the state. Given the limited possibilities for the use of material evidence, trials hinged on persuading the juries (often large crowds of citizens) through legal speeches. Hence we find that the focus on many judicial curses is on the speaking ability of the target. A curse tablet from Athens names a number of other targets with the same formula before concluding:

> Seuthes, I bind the tongue and soul and speech that he is practicing, and his feet and hands and eyes and mouth. Lamprias, I bind the tongue and soul and speech that he is practicing, and his feet and hands and eyes and mouth. All these I bind, I hide, I bury, I nail down. If they lay any counterclaim before the arbitrator or the court, let them seem to be of no account, either in word or in deed.[34]

From the jokes in Aristophanes and Cicero, we know that speakers did at times become tongue-tied in court, unable to remember their practiced speeches, and that they did blame their lapses in performance upon the malign influence of curse spells.[35] Many of the curse tablets seem designed to create this effect and must have been deposited before the trials in hopes of influencing the outcome.

Other curses in the judicial realm seem, however, to be aimed, not preemptively at an upcoming trial, but rather retrospectively at some injustice done that is beyond the power of the courts to redress. These pleas for justice (or judicial prayers, as Versnel has termed them) resemble other curse tablets in many respects, but some scholars have argued that they belong rather to the sphere of religion than of magic. They often employ the language of 'registering' or 'handing over' the target to some deity, rather than 'binding,' and in some cases it is clear that the target is being devoted to the deity because the one making the tablet has despaired of human justice.[36]

[34] DT 49.12–22 = Gager 44.

[35] Aristophanes, *Vesp.* 946–948 and scholiast; Cicero, *Brutus* 217 (60); and Libanius, *Orat.* 1.245–249.

[36] The standard treatment remains Versnel 1991b, but the category has been challenged in various ways by scholars.

The largest collection of such pleas for justice has been uncovered in the temple of Sulis Minerva in Roman Bath, England, where several hundred such tablets have been found, mostly cursing whoever purloined some personal item. The tablets are formulaic and follow a basic pattern of handing over the stolen item to the goddess, thus making the punishment of the thief a personal matter for the goddess. Sometimes the names of the suspected thieves are mentioned, and in some cases the name of the agent is also listed, as the one who is dedicating the item to the goddess and asking for her help.[37] By contrast, the name of the agent is almost never found in the competitive curses, just as the agent takes care not to be observed depositing the tablet in a hidden place at a secret time, rather than commissioning (and perhaps publicly displaying) the tablet in a public sanctuary. Again, the audience for whom the curse is performed provides the biggest difference between these prayers for justice and the competitive curses; while both kinds of curse address divinities on the vertical axis of the audience to carry out their wishes, the prayers for justice may well have been proclaimed aloud in a sanctuary before deposition to maximize their impact on the horizontal axis of the audience (the people of the community), while the competitive curses sought to avoid any audience on the horizontal axis.[38]

Some tablets include lists of body parts to be affected, much like the curses that bind the tongue or the feet of the rival. A first-century (BCE or CE) tablet from Delos makes a comprehensive list:

> I register with the gods whoever took and stole the necklace. I register those who had any knowledge of it and those who took part in it. I register him, his head, his soul, the sinews of the one who stole the necklace . . . I register the genitals and private parts of the one who stole it, the hands, from head to feet and toenails, of those who took the necklace.[39]

In a tablet from first-century CE Athens, the agent complains of a theft by unknown persons and asks the goddess Hekate, in her triple aspects, to punish the thieves, whoever they may be.

---

[37] Cp. Gager 94 = Tomlin 8, which has a list of suspects; Tomlin's collection from Bath contains many with similar formulae. See also Gager 99 = DT 106, which accuses a man named Senicianius of taking a gold ring. A gold ring inscribed with the name of Senicianus, dating from perhaps around the same period, the late fourth century CE), was discovered in Silchester, only 50 km away from the tablet's location at the temple of Nodens in Lydney. See further Tomlin 2010.

[38] See Chaniotis 2009 for a discussion of the public aspect of some prayers for justice. Gordon 2004 provides the best treatment of the social dynamics involved.

[39] Gager 88 from Versnel 1991a: 66–67.

I hand over to the goddesses and gods of the underworld, and to Hermes the helper; I transfer the thieves who stole from the little house in the street called Acheloou, who stole a necklace, three bedspreads (a new white wool one), gum arabic, tools, white pigments, linseed oil, and three white things: mastic, pepper, and bitter almonds. I hand over those who know about the theft and deny it. I hand over all of them who have received what is contained in this deposition. Lady Hekate of the heavens, Hekate of the underworld, Hekate of the crossroads, Hekate of the triple-face, Hekate of the single-face, cut out the hearts of the thieves or the thief who took the items contained in this deposition. And let the earth be not walkable, the sea not sailable; let there be no enjoyment of life, no increase of children, but may utter destruction visit them or him.[40]

It is interesting to note that the scope of the punishment in this tablet is more like the dramatic extremes of the contingent curses than the targeted effects of the competitive curses; the curser is not merely seeking an edge in competition that could be achieved by a slight binding or holding back of his opponent. So too, he is not asking for an observable result in a face-to-face competition, but rather letting his imagination dwell on what he would like to have happen to those who have wronged him.

In the competitive curses, the death of the target is almost never sought; rather the curse binds down some crucial part of him—the legs of a runner or chariot horse, the tongue of an orator, even the energy and activity of a craftsman—to prevent him from competing successfully with the agent of the curse. The effect is carefully tailored to the context. A chariot race curse includes the plea, "Let him not make the turn properly," while one from a theater context includes the peculiar wish, "May he not be able to play the role of a married woman in a fit of drunkenness upon a young horse."[41] In the pleas for justice, by contrast, the effects are more general and more extreme, up to and including the death of the target and the annihilation of his family for generations to come.

One peculiar type of curse, known as the *diabolē* or slander spell, makes use of some of the features characteristic of the pleas for justice while resembling the agonistic curses in other regards. Such spells are performed in secret and the performer does not include his name, but the harm called

---

[40] SEG 30.326 = Gager 84. I have made a few minor changes in the translation from Gager's, the most significant of which is by reading χρώματα for χώματα on the tablet.

[41] Gager 15 = Wünsch 1898: 50–52, #49. The corrupt text of Gager 16 appears in DT 110, but see Versnel 1985: 247–248 for an improved text (read as Latin rather than Gallic).

down upon the target is dramatic and extreme. Just as the prayers for justice assign stolen property to the deity to make the culprit's offense against the deity instead of the mortal agent, so too in these spells the performer justifies his request by claiming that the target has committed offenses against the deity (usually the moon goddess).[42]

In all these cases, the violence that is described is not merely an outlet for the sadistic malevolence of the agent; the fact that these tablets were ritually inscribed and carefully prepared indicates that it is a carefully considered symbolic gesture rather than an uncontrolled emotional venting. Often, too, it is clear that the tablet was actually created by someone other than the person who wanted it done; the presence of the formulaic patterns of cursing indicates the activity of professional experts, even without such corroboration as at Amathous in Cyprus, where hundreds of tablets with nearly identical phrasing were composed by the same hand. At Bath, too, the recurring patterns of the texts suggest that professionals were working from handbooks or at least written models to provide this service for their clientele. Given that agonistic situations abounded in the ancient Greco-Roman world, the laws of supply and demand suggest that experts would be on hand to satisfy the market for extra-ordinary solutions to the present problems of competition.

Although curse tablets serve to hold back a competitor and prevent his success, other charms are found that promote success and victory for the agent. One recipe in a Greek magical papyrus formulary promises success in a dice game, while another is labeled simply a 'victory charm' for general success. Such charms for victory may seem like the positive side of the negative and malevolent curses, but it is important to remember that in a zero-sum competition, any help to one person is a detriment to the other—victory and success inevitably entail loss and failure for someone else. Eustathius relates the tale of an Ephesian wrestler who consistently defeated his Milesian opponent in the Olympics, until his magic charm was detected and removed from his wrist, at which point he lost the next thirty matches in a row. Such extra-ordinary tampering with the competition appears just as problematic as the curses that bind the opponent, giving an unfair advantage to one competitor.[43]

[42] Cp. the discussion of Versnel 2010: 303–304, who cites as examples the spells recipes in PGM III.5, 113; IV.2475, 2574–2671, 2642–2674; VII.604–612; and the executed *defixiones* in DTA 188.7–12, 140.15–18, and 295.8–10.

[43] PGM VII.423–428 for victory in a dice game; VII.528–539 labeled victory charm for general success. Cp. (Kotansky 1994) GMA #60 = SM 64, a silver lamella that asks for favor, friendship, success, and loveliness for the bearer. For the wrestler's charm, see Eustathius 2.201 on *Odyssey* 19.247. (See the discussion of the Ephesia Grammata in ch. 5, pp. 143–144, n. 66.)

How Did Curse Tablets Work?

The most complicated question of all regarding the curse tablets is how they might be imagined to work. What was the underlying logic that shaped their creation? What did the users expect from them? If they were imagined to provide extra-ordinary power, what was that power and how did it operate? It is essential, when considering these questions, to distinguish between the (etic) perspective of the modern scholar and the (emic) perspective of the ancient users, since the differences of worldview mean that different answers will be valid or meaningful depending on the perspective.

From our modern, etic, and scholarly perspective, the best and simplest answer is the observable fact that ancient Greeks and Romans kept on using these curses in the belief that they worked. Various psychological explanations, from the placebo effect to the counterphobic attitude, have been adduced, but such explanations assume a much better insight into the thoughts of the ancients than our available evidence warrants. Ultimately, these curse rituals were valid and meaningful actions for the ancient Greeks and Romans because they thought they were. Once we turn to the question of *how* they might think they were valid, we must try to gain an understanding of the emic point of view, and the only way to do that is to analyze the underlying logic of the texts they produced and to examine critically the explanations they themselves give.

Fundamentally, a curse is an efficacious wish for someone else's harm, an expression of malevolence, ill-wishing, that produces the desired effect. Now, since it is not within the power of normal human beings to instantaneously bring their wishes to fruition, some extra-ordinary power is required. That power may not be explained or even named within an ancient text itself, but we can at least analyze the different ways in which it appears to work.

The so-called evil eye is the simplest form of cursing, consisting merely of the envious glance at the target without even a verbalized wish. Plutarch and his companions debate the nature and causes of the evil eye in one of Plutarch's *Table Talk* dialogues, coming up with a variety of explanations for the phenomenon, but they are all grounded in the idea that it is caused by envy, that feeling that someone else is doing better than oneself and the subsequent wish to reverse that situation. The rationalizing philosopher Plutarch comes up with an explanation that involves beams coming from the eyes that are generated by internal feelings of envy producing evil within the soul. These rays of malevolence may further be explained by Democritean theories of images (*eidola*) that pass from one eye to another and create harm in the receiver, but it is the feeling of envy that creates the power. The effects of the evil eye (*baskania*) may be diverted by bizarre evil eye protections (*probaskania*) that literally distract the gaze, especially phallic amulets or images of the ejaculating phallus or even phallic gestures or ejaculatory spitting.[44] The Roman figure of Fascinus, the divine personification of the phallus, represents this power to attract and divert the harmful gaze, the power of fascination that charms and protects.[45]

Such explicit explanations as Plutarch's are rare within our sources; more often we get no explanation and must deduce the way a curse operates from the text of the tablet itself. Sometimes this is fairly obvious: if normal human power is insufficient to transform a wish for harm into reality, then some suprahuman power must be called upon, some god or daimon or spirit. Many tablets do invoke the names of such powers, especially underworld divinities such as Hermes Katachthonios (Underworld Hermes) or Hekate. A fourth-century BCE tablet from Attica addresses both Hermes and Hekate with the wish, "Let Pherenikos be bound before Hermes Katachthonios and Hekate Katachthonia. I bind Pherenikos's girl Galene to Hermes Katachthonios and to Hekate Katachthonia I bind her." The tablet has the names of Hermes and Hekate inscribed on the other side, indicating that this prayer is addressed to them. Other deities appear in other tablets; a curse from Rome pleads, "I appeal to you, Phrygian goddess and to you nymph goddess Eidōnea, that you may restrain Artemios, also called Hospēs, son of Sapēda, and make him headless, footless, and powerless with the horses of the Blue colors and overturn his reputation and victory." Another from Carthage invokes a collection of divinities by their secret and powerful names to bind a charioteer from the Blue team there, along with all his horses.

> Semesilam, Damatameneus, Iēsnnallelam, Laikam, Ermoubelē, Iakoub, Ia, Iōbēth, Iōpakerbēth, Ēomalthabēth Allasan. A curse. I invoke you [pl.] by the great names, so that you will bind every limb and every sinew of Victoricus, the charioteer of the Blue team.[46]

The precise identity of the deities invoked by these secret names is uncertain, but they recur in a number of other texts, where they seem to be linked to the Greco-Egyptian Seth-Typhon.[47]

---

[44] Plutarch, *Table Talk* 7 680c–683b. Plato, *Laws* 932e–933b seems to express reservations about whether such curses secure divine aid for harming others, but notes that they nevertheless convince both those who use them and those who are targeted that they have special power.

[45] Cp. Pliny, *HN* 28.39.

[46] DT 241 = Gager 12; Attic tablet: DTA 107 = Gager 40; Roman tablet: Gager 14 from Wünsch 1898: 40–41 #29.

[47] Wünsch thought that a whole collection of curse tablets from Rome was linked to Seth-Typhon because of these names and the images of a donkey (or horse) on several of them (Wünsch 1898, cp. DT 140–187), but his arguments are no longer plausible. Some of these names, however, do appear in association with Typhon, as the hostile aspect of the sun, in

At times the lesser powers of the underworld, such as the Erinyes or other spirits of punishment and vengeance, are invoked to enact the binding of the target, often in company with a whole list of infernal entities, for example, "to Pluto and to the Fates and to Persephone and to the Furies and to every harmful being." Other tablets invoke the holy angels, the *daimones*, or even the *charaktēres*, the personified spirits of the peculiar letter-like shapes that appear on some tablets and in the spell books.[48] A number of tablets invoke the spirits of the dead to carry out the curse, making use of the spirit of the one buried in the grave in which the tablet is deposited. "I invoke you, spirit of one untimely dead, whoever you are," begins one tablet from Carthage, indicating that the magician did not know the identity of the grave into which the tablet was deposited. The spirits of those "untimely dead" (*aōroi*) often appear as the addressees in these tablets, for those who ended their lives prematurely, especially through violence (*biaiothanatoi*) or before marriage (*atelestoi*), were thought to be more restless in their graves than those who lived their full span of years before death. The other class of restless dead are the unburied (*ataphioi*), but for obvious reasons their restless energies could not be harnessed by putting a curse tablet in their graves.[49] The curses in the large cache at Amathous in Cyprus follow a formula that invokes, not an individual dead spirit, but an indeterminate mass of them.

> *Daimones* under the earth and *daimones* whoever you may be; fathers of fathers and mothers who are a match for men, whether male or female, *daimones* whoever you may be and who lie here, having left grievous life, whether violently slain or foreign or local or unburied, whether you are borne away from the boundaries of cities or wander somewhere in the air.[50]

The spirits of the dead are here (and elsewhere) referred to as *daimones*, a word that can refer to anything from Homeric gods to malicious demons but has the basic sense of some unspecified suprahuman entity. The curse tablets at Amathous call on the power of the dead to enact the curse, usually to silence an opponent in court.

---

the magical papyri; cp. PGM IV.277–279 and XII.367–370, which explicitly invoke Typhon (cp. IV.2223); n.b., Gager's citations, n. 76 for #40, are erroneous or missing.

[48] SEG 30.326 = Gager 84. Angels appear in, e.g., SEG 7.213 (15.847) = Gager 5, DT 155 = Gager 13 = DT 187 = Gager 15; *charaktēres* appear in, e.g., SEG 34.1437 = Gager 6, DT 155 = Gager 13. For a discussion of *charaktēres*, see Gordon 2011b.

[49] DT 237 = Gager 9; Johnston 1999 provides the best discussion of the context in which the spirits of the restless dead might be employed to carry out magical spells.

[50] DT 25.1–6 = Gager 46. A handful of the lead tablets from Amathous have been published as DT 22–37 = I. Kourion 127–142.

But how is the power of the dead—or the gods—enlisted to aid the one making the curse? Given the importance, in the history of the scholarship on magic, of the distinction between religious supplicative prayer and magical coercion, it may be surprising that the line is often blurred in ancient curse tablets. Sometimes, the curse is phrased as a command: "give a muzzle to Theodoros the governor of Cyprus and to Timon, so that they will be unable to do anything against me." At other times, however, the curse comes out more as a wish in the subjunctive: "let my opponents be speechless and voiceless, Theodoros the governor and Timon." That these two forms can coexist on the same tablet suggests that the distinction between praying and commanding was less significant to the ones making the tablets than it is to modern scholars who have inherited the distinction through centuries of Christian theological disputes.[51] The precise relationship between the one making the tablet and the powerful entity he calls upon is rarely specified in the curse tablets; the texts take for granted that some relation exists that would incline this power to grant the wish expressed by the curser.

Occasionally, more details of the relationship are spelled out. In some tablets, the curser promises some offering in return for the divinity's aid in effecting the curse. An Attic tablet of unknown date calls upon underworld powers to restrain the target, promising *euangelia*, thank offerings, in return for glad tidings, if the target's work is affected.

> I bind and restrain Manes. You, dear Praxidikai [spirits of vengeance], hold him down, and Hermes Restrainer, restrain Manes and the work which he does and make everything backward and opposite for Manes: I will sacrifice thank-offerings to you, Praxidikai and Hermes Restrainer, if Manes fares badly.[52]

The dread spirits of vengeance known as the Praxidikai (literally, workers of justice) are rarely addressed with so intimate an epithet as 'dear' (*philae*), but this tablet's emphasis on the relationship between curser and divine powers also appears in the explicit mention of a thank offering. Note, however, that this relationship does not preclude the use of imperatives to command these divinities to restrain the target.

Such offerings are not confined to gods such as Hermes or divinities like the Praxidikai. In a tablet from the Black Sea colony of Olbia Pontica, the curser promises to honor and make offerings to the unknown spirit of the dead man in whose grave the tablet is deposited. "If you hold them down and seize them for me, I will honor you and prepare a most excellent gift for you." The curser proposes a bargain with the spirit, offering honor and

---

[51] DT 25.13–14, 16–18 = Gager 46.
[52] DTA/IG3 app. 109 = Gager 61.

gifts in return for the binding force of the curse. Such explicit bargains are the exceptions rather than the rule, but the reciprocal nature of Greek and Roman religion suggests that such offerings are always a possible strategy.[53]

Other curses, however, especially the later tablets and the papyrus spell books from Greco-Roman Egypt, make use of a different rhetorical strategy; the power that effects the curse is constrained to do so by the authority of an even greater power. The magician calls upon the dead spirit or the minor divinity in the name of a great deity of the underworld or even a supreme god of the whole cosmos. A fifth-century CE tablet from Egypt commands the *daimones* of the dead to act in the name of the great god Iaō, the supreme lord of the universe: "I invoke you *daimones* who lie here, who are continually nourished here and who reside here and also you young ones who have died prematurely. I invoke you by the unconquerable god, Iaō." The magical papyri can create even more complex relationships among the divine powers invoked. One spell involves making a food offering of bread from one's meal to "heroes, gladiators, and those who have died a violent death." The magician complements this positive offering with a plea to an underworld goddess (identified with Hekate, Persephone, and even the ancient Babylonian queen of the underworld, Ereškigal), she "who rouses up with fire the souls of the dead, unlucky heroes and luckless heroines, who in this place, who on this day, who in this hour, who in coffins of myrtlewood, give heed to me." The spirits of the dead do the actual work in this spell, but they are roused to do so by Hekate, the mistress of the underworld.[54]

Such a strategy is different from that of the curse tablets that construct themselves as letters to the powers of the underworld, placed in the hand of the buried corpse (or inserted in the wound of an unburied one) to be conveyed by the dead spirit to Hekate or Persephone. A fourth-century BCE lead tablet from Athens lists a number of well-known naval leaders whom the curser wants punished by the powers of the underworld. "I am sending this letter to Hermes and Persephone, since I am presenting wicked people to them, for it is fitting for them to obtain the final penalty."[55] Here

---

[53] Gager 48 = SEG 37.673. Other late curses promise to release the spirit if it performs the deed requested, e.g., SEG 8.574 = SM 46.40–41. Ἐὰν τοῦτό μοι ποιήσῃς, ἀπολύσω σε. "If you do this for me, I will set you free." See ch. 6, especially pp. 153–166, for a discussion of reciprocity.

[54] PGM IV.1390–1495; cp., e.g., SEG 26.1717 = Gager 28; I. Kourion 127 = Gager 45; I. Kourion 134–140; SM 2.54.

[55] DTA/IG3 app. 103 = Gager 38. Another pair of tablets (Gager 43 = SEG 37.351, 352) have a peculiar self-negating form of address. "Whenever you, O Pasianax, read this letter, but neither will you ever read this letter, nor will Neophanes ever direct a lawsuit against Aristandros. But just as you, O Pasianax, lie here idle, so let Neophanes be idle and nothing."

the underworld gods are doing the work, while the spirit is just a messenger. Another tablet from fourth-century Athens addresses the letter to both the spirits of the dead and to Persephone and asks both to restrain the list of targets. "I am sending a letter to the *daimones* and to Persephone. . . . May Persephone restrain all of her. Hermes and Hades, may you restrain all of these. Daimon, may you restrain Galene, daughter of Polykleia." Again, Persephone and Hermes are asked to do the binding themselves, even if in this case the *daimones* (presumably spirits of the dead) also take a hand in restraining the target. Thus, not all letters borne by the dead to the underworld work in the same way.[56] Appeals to complex underworld hierarchies come more often in the complex and hierarchical world of the later Roman Empire, while the earlier tablets have simpler appeals to the powers of the underworld, either individually or collectively, calling for direct action.

Many curse tablets in fact have no mention of divine powers or the dead at all, but simply list the target or targets and the desired effect. Particularly in the earliest of the tablets, ones found in Attica and Sicily in the fifth century BCE, the mere act of writing down the target's name is the primary act of ritual power. There may of course have been verbal components, addressing the gods or spirits and offering justifications or promising recompense, but such things leave no trace. In some, descriptions such as "all the choral directors and assistant choral directors with Theagenes" or "Philippides, Euthykritos, Kleagoras, Menetimos, and all the other others, however many are advocates for them" provide the context, while in others the target is not the person but the relevant part of the person, "the tongue of Eukles and that of Aristophanis and that of Angeilis and that of Alkiphron."[57] The inscription of the target onto the lead tablet serves as the act of magical ritual, even if other ritual actions—prayers, sacrifices, libations, etc.—are likely to have accompanied the inscribing.

While some tablets have just names, others employ verbs of binding, registering, or dedicating that mark the desired action. These verbs are typically in the first-person singular, "I bind" or "I register," and are the perfect example of performative speech acts, since the act of writing the words "I bind" is the act of binding the target. A collection of tablets in the same hand from fourth century Athens bind a series of targets.

Scholars have debated whether Pasianax is the corpse or, as Wünsch suggested, a euphemism for Hades.

[56] Some texts (e.g., Gager 22 = DT 68) use the dead person as a persuasive analogy for the effect on the target, while others direct the request to the deceased as an underworld entity (e.g., Gager 104 = DTA/IG3 app. 102).

[57] SEG 26.1113 = Gager 49; cp. Gager 1 = DTA 34 and Gager 37 = DTA 38 for the theatrical and lawcourt contexts.

Menyllos of Halai I bind, his tongue and his soul.
I bind Philonautes who is with Menyllos.
I bind Kēphisoklēs, the in-law of Menyllos.
I bind, I bind Astyphilos of Halai and Phanias, the tongue.[58]

The curse names the target of the binding and often specifies the part of the body or of the person's identity that is to be bound. Law court curses frequently bind tongues, while race course curses more often bind feet, but at times the target is the mind or soul, or even the business ventures of the person targeted. Some curses elaborate the specification of the target by listing aspects of the person, in and out, from head to toe.

Malcius the son of Nicona: his eyes, hands, fingers, arms, nails, hair, head, feet, thigh, belly, buttock, navel, chest, nipples, neck, mouth, cheeks, teeth, lips, chin, eyes, forehead, eyebrows, shoulderblades, shoulders, sinews, bones, merilas, belly, penis, shin; in these tablets I bind his business profits and health.[59]

This Roman tablet so emphatically lists everything that some parts are listed twice. The aim is clearly to inhibit a rival business competitor, but every element of his person that could be bound is listed, the better to ensure his inability to compete with the curser.[60]

A distinction may be drawn between verbs of binding (*katadesmō* or *katadō*—I bind, or *katexō*—I hold down) and verbs of dedicating (*anatithemi* and *anaiero*—I dedicate, or *engrapho, epigrapho, katagrapho*—I register or write down), since the latter hand the target over to some divinity or spirit to do the binding rather than doing it directly, but both are performative speech acts.[61] One of the oldest curse tablets, a large lead tablet from Selinous in Sicily that may date back to the end of the sixth century BCE, registers a long list of targets with 'the holy goddess,' presumably Demeter Malophoros, in whose sanctuary this was found along with a number of other tablets of the same date. "I record [*katagrapho*] Apelos son of Lukinos with the holy goddess, along with his life and power; and also Lukinos, the son of Halos, and his brother." The curser expects Demeter to deal with these targets who have been assigned to her, but the details of what she is to do are left implicit. In another curse from the same sanctuary, a peculiar round tablet dating perhaps a few decades later, the

[58] Gager 59: 4, 1, 2, 3 = DT 50, 47, 48, 49.

[59] Gager 80 = DT 135. It is unclear what *merilas* is meant to refer to, although Gordon 1999b: 272 plausibly suggests that *medullas* (marrows) is meant.

[60] Cp. Gordon 1999b on the rhetorical force of such lists in curses and their background in the Greek poetic and oratorical tradition.

[61] See Kropp 2010 on the distinction between manipulating and committing formulae. These Greek verbs have Latin equivalents (*defigo* and *ligare* or *dedicare* and *demandare*), which are found in the Latin tablets.

curser is more explicit. "I inscribe [*engrapho*] Timasoi and the tongue of Timasoi, twisted to the point of uselessness." In curses that refer to hierarchies of divine powers, we often find verbs of adjuring (*horkizo* or *adiurare*) by which the less powerful entities are constrained with reference to the greater powers. All these performative utterances make manifest the malevolent wish of the curser, and the act of inscribing them on a lead tablet makes that wish permanent, being uttered continuously for ever and ever.[62]

Not only is the act of writing a performative utterance, but, as a ritual act, it can be embellished and elaborated to reinforce or enhance the symbolic meaning. In a curse aiming to disrupt, confuse, or disable the target named in the spell, the written name becomes the symbol of the target who is bound or confounded. Even the very letters of the name can thus be manipulated with symbolic resonance, and numerous curses appear in which the letters of the target's name have been scrambled or written backwards. Tambiah discusses such an effect as "persuasive analogy," a rhetorical device that, through the vivid imagery of the analogy, whether spoken or symbolically enacted in ritual, enhances the impact of the curse upon the audience, on both the vertical and horizontal axes.[63] By "persuasive analogy," reversing or scrambling the letters of the target's name could enhance the illustrative force of the act of cursing. A Latin tablet from Cologne makes the idea explicit: "Vaeraca, in this way may you undertake your affairs backwards, just as this text is written backwards."[64] Although, when writing first developed in the Greek world, words could be written in any direction, as the technology became more familiar, the direction of left to right became standard. Right to left (retrograde) or even back and forth (boustrophedon—literally, cow tracks, because it was like a plowed field) thus became marked as nonstandard or extra-ordinary, and that extra-ordinary nature could be deployed for symbolic purposes in ritual acts.

Other manipulations of the letters, words, or other elements of the inscribed text could likewise be infused with symbolic resonance. Scholars have speculated that the tablets that identify the target by his mother's name (matronymic) instead of the father's name (patronymic) customarily used in Greek and Roman societies, are not simply borrowing an Egyptian custom but doing so because of its unusual reversal of normal modes of address. So too, some curses exploit even the material of the tablet for symbolic effect. Several tablets from Attica employ the persuasive analogy,

[62] Gager 50 = SEG 16.573; Gager 51 = SEG 4.37–38. Cp. Depew 1997: 243–244.
[63] Cp. Tambiah 1973b: 209–212 and throughout.
[64] Faraone and Kropp 2010: 383. *Vaeraea (or: Uxeraca), sic res tua<s> perverse agas, comodo hoc perverse scriptu<m> est.*

"Just as this lead is cold and worthless, so let him and his things be cold and worthless," in order to transfer the attributes of the lead to the target.[65] Such symbolic resonance cannot be presumed for all tablets made of lead, but the analogy is always there to be exploited by a curser who wishes to add extra force to the curse.

Other manipulations of the tablet, such as rolling or folding the tablet, may have been imbued with significance beyond simply concealing the text, and the practice of pounding a nail through the tablet may often have had a symbolic resonance beyond fixing the tablet in its hiding place (like the tablets nailed down beneath the starting gates in the Carthage hippodrome to affect the chariot races). The act of driving in the nail may have been another way to symbolically express the act of binding or fixing down the target. While the many lamellae discovered with nails through them give us little indication of the idea behind the piercing, a recipe in one of the Greek Magical Papyri provides insight into the process with the instructions of what to say when piercing the tablet (or papyrus sheet) being prepared in the recipe with a metal stylus.

> Piercing it through the character with the pen and tying it, say: "I bind NN with regard to the NN [thing]. Let him not speak, not be contrary not oppose; let him not be able to look me in the face nor speak against me; let him be subject to me."[66]

Here the piercing is combined with tying, another form of persuasive analogy that acts out a symbolic version of the binding of the target. The 365 knots tied around a tablet in one of the recipes of the Greek Magical Papyri represent an elaborate form of such symbolic tying, while another recipe calls for the tablet itself to be trodden underfoot. "The spell to say when the metal leaf with the frog's tongue is put into your right sandal: 'Just as these sacred names are being trampled, so also let him, NN (add the usual) the trouble-maker, be trampled.' "[67]

The various manipulations with animals or figurines work in a similar way, providing persuasive analogies of the effects desired for the target by the curser. A pair of second-century CE tablets from Gaul spell out some of these analogies most extensively.

> I denounce the persons written below, Lentinus and Tasgillus, in order that they may depart from here for Pluto and Persephone. Just as this puppy harmed no one, so [may they harm no one] and may they not be able to win this suit; just as the mother of this puppy

---

[65] καὶ ὡς οὗτος ὁ βόλυβδος ἄτιμος καὶ ψυχρός, οὕτω ἐκε<ῖ>νος καὶ τὰ ἐκε<ῖ>νω ἄτιμα [κ]αὶ ψυρχὰ ἔστω. DTA 107 = Gager 40, cp. DTA 105, 106.

[66] PGM V.319–325.

[67] PGM VII.453–455; PGM X.40–42.

cannot defend it, so may their lawyers be unable to defend them, and so may those opponents be turned back from this suit; just as this puppy is on its back and unable to rise, so neither may they; they are pierced through, just as this is.[68]

The characteristics of the puppy, its helplessness and incapacity to do harm, are projected upon Lentinus and Tasgillus, whom the curser wishes to be as defenseless and vulnerable as a puppy flipped onto its back and pierced through with nails.

These manipulations of material are best understood, not in Frazerian terms as primitive misunderstandings of the laws of causality, but rather in rhetorical terms, as persuasive analogies that express the desired effects in vivid and powerful ways.[69] Rather than analyzing these ritual acts in terms of Frazerian laws of sympathy and contagion, invoking the principle of *similia similibus* or like to like, we can gain a better understanding by analyzing them in terms of literary devices such as simile, metaphor, and synecdoche. Following the basic distinction drawn by Jakobson, metaphoric devices make use of observable similarities while metonymic ones employ associative symbolic links that do not rely on perceptible qualities.[70] For example, melting a wax figurine is a metaphoric action based on the resemblance of the figurine to a person, whereas burning strands of the target's hair involves a metonymic relation of the hair to the person, a synecdoche or part to whole relation, rather than a visual resemblance. The instructions in various recipes to include *ousia*, that is some substance of the target like hair or nail clippings, as well as the few well-preserved examples in which a bit of hair or other substance is actually found, indicate that many curses may have incorporated such metonymic actions in their ritual acts, and the literary record is full of fictional witches always seeking body parts to use in their spells.[71] Just as the various modes of addressing divine powers may be analyzed in terms of rhetorical strategies designed to gain their cooperation, so too we may parse the underlying logic of the curse tablets by understanding the use of devices of metaphors and similes, as well as other devices such as listing and visualization, rep-

---

[68] Gager 53 = DT 111–112.

[69] Faraone 1991a: 8, with the useful phrase in Faraone 2012a: 122n2: " 'persuasive analogy' (magic = good rhetoric) as opposed to 'sympathy' (magic = bad science)." For the Frazerian 'laws,' see the discussion in ch. 2, p. 47, n. 17.

[70] Jakobson [1956] 2002: 46–47 includes Freud's displacement and identification, as well as Frazer's contagion and similiarity, under the general semiotic rubrics of metonymy and metaphor.

[71] The 'superwitches' in Roman literature are often seeking body parts, e.g., Apuleius, *Met.* 2.28–30 and Lucan *Pharsalia* 6.438–830. While most of these examples come from imaginative literature, Ammianus Marcellinus (19.12.14) tells us that people were executed in the fourth century CE for digging up graves for corpse parts.

etition and pleonasm, rhythm and meter, and even the manipulation of word sounds and shapes.[72]

The manipulation of word sounds and shapes underlies one of the most striking features of the curse tablets, and indeed other forms of magic as well. The so-called *voces magicae*, the magical words, although they are absent from the earlier curse tablets, appear in increasing profusion in the later examples. Both sounds and shapes of collections of letters are manipulated in the curse tablets for a variety of rhetorical effects that are both auditory and visual. There are two basic types of *voces magicae*, which may be called the *hocus-pocus* words and the *abracadabra* words (to make use of two magical words that are very familiar to modern audiences but make relatively little appearance in the ancient Greco-Roman world). *Abracadabras* have no referential meaning but derive their effect merely from the sound patterns and visual arrangements of the letters; repetition of syllables, rhyming endings, or chiming sounds provide a striking auditory effect, while patterns of letters such as palindromes provide an effect for the eye. *Hocus-pocus*, on the other hand, comes from a term that originally had a specific meaning and a specific contextual significance. The words from the Christian Latin Mass, *hoc est corpus*, 'this is the body,' were originally a meaningful phrase spoken at a key moment in an important ritual; the words signal the transubstantiation of the Eucharistic bread into the body of Christ. Taken out of context, however, and altered to a rhyming jingle, the words no longer have a specific meaning, but they still carry the weight of the authoritative context from which they derive, a traditional association with power. The outside eyes of modern scholars may have a hard time distinguishing between the types, however, since we are not part of the tradition from which a *hocus-pocus* has been derived. This fact has not stopped scholars from speculating at length on the possible origins of every set of *voces magicae* that appear in the evidence, and the fact that scholars often do not even agree which language family the words come from has not deterred scholars from multiplying their guesses.[73]

Palindromes such as ABLANATHANALBA or scrambled variations of syllables such as PSINŌTHER NŌPSITHER THERNŌPSI are perhaps most likely to be *abracadabras*, while OSORONNOPHRIS appears to be a *hocus-pocus* kind of corruption of the Egyptian *Wsir Wn-nfr*, Osiris the Beautiful Being. Some may in fact be mixtures of the two types; the frequent formula MASKELLI MASKELLŌ PHNOUKENTABAŌ OREOBAZAGRA RĒXICHTHŌN HIPPOCHTHŌN PURIPĒGANUX seems to contain elements, such as

[72] Gordon 1995 draws on the work of Todorov 1978 to analyze the magic charm as a form of allocution; cp. Versnel 2002 on the "Poetics of the magic charm."
[73] Brashear's glossary (in Brashear 1995) provides the most extensive collection of such scholarly guesses.

RĒXICHTHŌN and HIPPOCHTHŌN that could derive from epithets for some deity (the one bursting from the earth, the earth-horse), but others, like MASKELLI MASKELLŌ that seem simply to be sound variations. The depth of our modern ignorance is brought home by the occasional revelation of a coherent origin for apparently incoherent sounds. One of the most famous sets of *voces magicae*, the so-called *ephesia grammata*—ASKI KATASKI LIX TETRAX DAMNAMENEUS AISION—can be traced back to a coherent set of hexameter verses that are found on a fifth-century BCE tablet from Selinous. The tablet also has the *hocus-pocus* version of garbled words on another part of the tablet, so we can see the process of transformation at work.[74] Even in antiquity this meaning was lost, and the term *ephesia grammata* became a general label for incomprehensible words of power, while the words themselves received learned interpretations (ASKI is light, KATASKI is dark, LIX is earth, etc.).[75] The formula, however, retained the protective associations of its original form and continued to be used in contexts where such warding magic was needed.[76]

The significance, if not the actual meaning, of some of these *voces magicae* can be determined by the way they are used in the context of the spell. Many are deployed as special names or epithets for divine powers invoked in the spells, extra-ordinary terms of address that are designed to persuade the entity to assist. A string of incomprehensible words are used as names of divine powers to adjure a restless dead spirit: "I invoke you, spirit of one untimely dead, whoever you are, by the mighty names Salbathbal Authgerōtabal Basuthateō Aleō Samabēthōr." The third-century CE Iamblichus, in his treatise defending the magical practices of theurgy, argues that the incomprehensible words uttered in invocations are in fact ways of communicating with the gods in the languages they prefer.[77] Not all *voces magicae* seem to be used as magical names, but the placement of most within the spells indicates this significance.

The arrangements of letters into shapes, however, are less easily explained in this way, even when the *voces magicae* manipulated may appear elsewhere as part of an invocation. In addition to the address to the divine power within the spell, sets of letters are arranged into a block (*plinthion*) or a triangle (*cardia*, literally heart-shaped, or cluster of grapes, *staphyle*,

---

[74] For the text of the earliest witness and a number of essays commenting on the tradition, see the Faraone and Obbink 2013. More discussion of the *Ephesia Grammata* in ch. 5, pp. 143–144, n. 66.

[75] Cp. Clement of Alexandria, *Stromata* 5.8.43.

[76] See Edmonds 2013 in Faraone and Obbink 2013.

[77] Gager 9 = DT 237; Iamblichus, *de myst.* 7.5, cp. 3.14. The *charaktēres* often seem to function as signs that transcend pronounceable speech. Gordon 2011: 35–36 discusses the importance of the *charaktēres* and ineffable words in terms of semiotic theory, where the extra-ordinary signifier must point to a correspondingly extra-ordinary signified.

or wing-shapes, *pteryges*).[78] The letters often form unpronounceable palindromes, so the effect is clearly intended to be visual. One particular form consists of all seven Greek vowels arranged in ascending and descending pyramids.

A	Ω Ω Ω Ω Ω Ω Ω
E E	Υ Υ Υ Υ Υ Υ
H H H	O O O O O
Ι Ι Ι Ι	Ι Ι Ι Ι
O O O O O	H H H
Υ Υ Υ Υ Υ Υ	E E
Ω Ω Ω Ω Ω Ω Ω	A

One recipe calls for these letters to be written on a scrap of papyrus, but then intoned at the beginning of an invocation, so the effect is both visual and auditory. The seven vowels are associated, in other sources, with the seven musical tones, and scholars have speculated that the sequences of vowels that show up in various invocations (particularly in the Greek Magical Papyri) may in fact represent musical lines to be chanted.[79]

We may not be able to reconstruct with much certainty the meanings of the *voces magicae* and their manipulations from an emic point of view, that is, what precisely they meant to those who employed them in the spells. We can, however, get a sense from our modern, etic point of view of their rhetorical effect. The incomprehensible utterances and outlandish names, the strange arrangements of letters and peculiar palindromes, these all serve to mark the performance as extra-ordinary, unusual, abnormal— in a word, magical. The anthropologist Malinowski's concept of a "coefficient of weirdness" may be useful in this regard; the *voces magicae* raise the coefficient of weirdness in a spell, setting it further beyond the bounds of ordinary speech. The weirdness of the spell has the rhetorical effect of convincing the audience (be it just the magician himself, a client, or even a larger audience) of the extra-ordinary power of the speech act: this is not just a normal wish, but an efficacious one; this is not just an ordinary address to a deity, but a particularly effective one.[80]

[78] References to heart shape: PGM III.70; LXII.82; IV.407; II.68; grapes: PGM LXII.82; III. 69–70; wings: PGM II.2, 6; VII.716; XIII.902. The best overall discussion of these shapes remains Gordon 2002b: 85–95, although Faraone 2012b explores some important complexities of the uses of the wing form.

[79] PGM I.15–20. Cp. Nicomachus of Gerasa, *Excerpta* 6.276.12–18 on the relation of vowels to tones (and the planets).

[80] Malinowski 1935: 218–223. Pliny, *HN* 28.20 provides an ancient expression of this perspective: "It is not easy to say whether our faith is more violently shaken by the foreign, unpronounceable words, or by the unexpected Latin ones, which our mind forces us to consider

In what Versnel has called the "poetics of the magical charm," this coefficient of weirdness must be balanced with familiarity, since the expression must also seem to be a part of the cultural tradition in which it is performed.[81] The structure of the curse, the address to the gods, the implicit context, all must be familiar enough for the audience to recognize, just as a poetic expression must have enough familiar features for the audience to be able to recognize its genre, its allusions to traditional material, and so forth. At the same time, any poetic expression must innovate within the tradition, making use of traditional literary devices to convey its imagery and ideas in striking ways. The 'magic charm,' then, can be evaluated like any other rhetorical performance—what makes the reading of a poem successful or the performance of a political speech? The texts of the curse tablets repay this kind of poetic and rhetorical analysis, which reveals the logical structure of their speech acts and the devices used to enhance their effects. The addresses to divine powers, the acts of performative speech (binding or dedicating), and the expressions of the curser's wish all work together to articulate the curse, while the various symbolic manipulations (be they of the words and images, the tablet, or even of supplemental materials such as figurines or animals) serve to add vividness and persuasive force to the expression. These manipulations can be multiplied, adding visual effects to the basic auditory ones of pronouncing the spell, and even including tactile or participatory effects in the act of tying, piercing, melting, mutilating, or otherwise working with the materials.[82] From this etic point of view, analyzing the poetics of the magical charm helps to explain the recurrent features of the curse tablets as well as the variations between tablets, even allowing us to chart the differences in style between various regions and across the span of time in which our evidence appears.

CONCLUSIONS

This survey of curses in the ancient Greco-Roman world reveals certain common features of the genre, what might be called a poetics of cursing that shapes the individual curses found inscribed on metal and other materials over the course of nearly a thousand years. The techniques by which the curse is elaborated, while they differ in some ways from case to case, seem to come from a common tradition of rituals and images. Many of these techniques may well have been adapted from Near Eastern traditions,

---

absurd, being always on the look-out for something big, something adequate to move a god, or rather to impose its will on his divinity."

[81] Cp. Versnel 2002.

[82] Cp. Faraone 2012a: 127: "a sliding scale of sensory effects, ranging from the auditory alone, to the theatrical or visual, and ending with the tactile or participatory."

such as those found in the Mesopotamian Maqlû, or from the Egyptian cursing traditions that go back for millennia before the earliest Greek evidence. It is worth noting, however, that most of the recipes in the Maqlû are countercharms against cursing, operating in an environment where hostile witchcraft by unidentified magicians is a common cultural assumption.[83] There is surprisingly little evidence in Mesopotamia of the tradition of active cursing that appears in the Greek and Roman contexts. Perhaps the early Greek contacts with the ritual experts of the Near Eastern traditions provoked Greek innovators to, as it were, reverse-engineer the counterspells to create rituals for active cursing, adapting the defensive rituals for offensive use in the agonistic contexts of the Greek and Roman worlds. Such a speculative hypothesis is of course unprovable given the absence of so much evidence from all of the cultures involved, but the abundance of curse tablets found in the Greco-Roman world at least shows that active cursing was not merely in the realm of the imaginary.

While the complexity of the texts inscribed on the tablets increases over time, from the earliest tablets from fifth-century BCE Attica and Sicily bearing only the target's name to the elaborate inscriptions on the tablets from late Roman Egypt, crammed with intricate word formations and abounding with invocations that employ bizarre *voces magicae*, the basic structure of the curses remain the same. A wish for harm is expressed, the target is named, and the curse is effected with reference to some suprahuman power, be it only the force of the words employed. The elements of the curses, from the lead tablets to the inscriptions to the complementary rituals, remain fairly constant throughout the times and places examined. While the what, who, why, and how of curses seems to be the same across the range of evidence, the most significant differences appear in the places where the curses are made and deposited. While most of these curse tablets are made and deposited secretly, without any mention of the curser's name, a significant subset appears to have been created and displayed in public. These curses, whether appeals to the gods for justice against wrongdoers beyond human punishment or contingent curses self-imposed in oaths or other community activities, do announce the name of the one performing the curse. Whereas the personal curses thus appear to have been regarded as a form of cheating in the agonistic contexts of the ancient world, these public curses seem to be regarded as legitimate and normative actions, some of which are even required by the rules of the community, like the Curses of the Teans. Although the mechanics of these curses differ

---

[83] As Thomsen 2001: 23 notes of the Mesopotamian tradition, "References to actually executed witchcraft are very few, instructions for performing evil magic do not exist and only one case of a recorded court trial concerning witchcraft has so far been found. This is in striking contrast to the comprehensive material concerning incantations, rituals and medical recipes against witchcraft which document a profound fear of being bewitched."

little from the personal curses, the public and contingent curses tend to call for more dramatic and powerful results than the more pragmatic personal curses, whose effects are usually limited to the specific situation in which they are produced. The exaggerated rhetoric may perhaps be suited to the larger public audiences to whom it is addressed, in contrast to the personal curse whose text may be seen only by the one inscribing it secretly onto a tablet. The persuasive analogies may need to be more vivid, the verbal effects may need to be enhanced by visual or tactile ones, and the effects can be limited only by the wildest imaginings of the one performing the curse.

If the performance of the curse is regarded, by the performer or any other audience on the horizontal axis, as a way of cheating, of deploying extra-ordinarily efficacious means to gain unfair advantage in the contestive situation, then it is more likely to be labeled as 'magic,' especially if the rhetoric of the curse is not the clear and vivid imagery of a public performance but is marked with a high coefficient of weirdness and performed in a secretive way to limit the audience. This distinction in the performance and context of the curses makes better sense of the evidence than any distinction between magic and religion grounded in the mode of operation, since many of the curses employ both appeals to divine powers and performative speech acts. The generic rules of cursing apply to both the public and private contexts, even if one action is socially acceptable and the other is not. Like marriage and adultery, the basic mechanics may be the same, but the societal evaluation is different, even if the non-normative activity is ubiquitously practiced and even highly valued in some circumstances. Curse tablets were a familiar part of the ancient Greco-Roman world, and the analysis of this body of evidence illuminates aspects of the social dynamic that otherwise remain obscure and unrecorded.

4

Bewitched, Bothered, Bewildered:
Love Charms and Erotic Curses

O *iunx*, drag this man to my house.
As this wax doll I, with the divinity's power, do melt,
So may he melt with *eros*, the Myndian Delphis, at once
And, as whirls round this bronze *rhombos* from Aphrodite,
So too may he whirl round to my doors.
O *iunx*, drag this man to my house.
(Theocritus, *Idyll* 2.27–32)[1]

INTRODUCTION

The betrayed Simaetha, in Theocritus's famous poem, turns to an elaborate
magical spell, complete with spinning whirligig (*iunx* or *rhombos*), to try
to get her lover Delphis back. Her spell is a literary pastiche of many of
the familiar elements of erotic magic that appear in the Greco-Roman
tradition, but Theocritus's poem sheds light upon the situations and the
ways in which erotic magic, real or imaginary, was conceived in the ancient Greco-Roman world.

Magic, as a general rule, is an extra-ordinary practice, a measure one
turns to when ordinary solutions are insufficient for handling the problems
of life. An ancient Greek or Roman would resort to magic either to supplement his or her more mundane efforts, as a kind of hedging of bets, or after
the normal solutions had already failed. Since the field of erotic interactions is so unpredictable, so competitive, and so vital to the whole range
of people in the society, a great deal of evidence attests to the fact that the

---

[1] ἰυγξ, ἕλκε τὺ τῆνον ἐμὸν ποτὶ δῶμα τὸν ἄνδρα.| ὡς τοῦτον τὸν κηρὸν ἐγὼ σὺν δαίμονι τάκω,| ὡς
τάκοιθ᾽ ὑπ᾽ ἔρωτος ὁ Μύνδιος αὐτίκα Δέλφις.| χὠς δινεῖθ᾽ ὅδε ῥόμβος ὁ χάλκεος ἐξ Ἀφροδίτας,| ὡς
τῆνος δινοῖτο ποθ᾽ ἀμετέραισι θύραισιν.| ἰυγξ, ἕλκε τὺ τῆνον ἐμὸν ποτὶ δῶμα τὸν ἄνδρα.

ancient Greeks and Romans not only imagined magical solutions to their erotic problems, but actually engaged in magical practices in the attempt to resolve them. The erotic problems might be simply physical or they might derive from the devastatingly complicated social interactions that attend erotic relationships in every society, so the evidence for these solutions likewise ranges over the whole spectrum.

WHAT IS THE EVIDENCE FOR EROTIC MAGIC?

Literary depictions such as Simaetha's pathetic attempt to win back her faithless lover naturally provide some of the most rich and complex pieces of evidence for understanding the nature of erotic magic in the ancient Greco-Roman world, but literary evidence must be treated carefully, since the depictions contained therein are affected by literary considerations such as genre and narrative. Simaetha's ritual, as various scholars have pointed out, does not match the evidence for such rituals in the nonliterary evidence. Instead of each step following upon the next in the logic of a ritual process, the ritual described in the poem follows rather the narrative logic of Simaetha's story of love betrayed.[2] While Theocritus doubtless makes use of ideas of how erotic magic works that were familiar to his audience, he is first and foremost a poet telling his story. When Vergil, in his Eighth *Eclogue*, tells a similar story, his details are shaped by the dynamics of literary influence of Theocritus's poem (as indeed Theocritus's work seems to be shaped by its reception of earlier poems on the same theme).[3]

Literary depictions of erotic magic, therefore, are shaped by generic concerns, but they also enjoy the freedom of a literary fiction to depict anything within the realm of imagination, unbounded by the constraints of practicality or observable results. However, although Richard Gordon has argued that the true home of magic in the ancient world is in the imaginary rather than in the practices of Greeks and Romans, the evidence for erotic magic that survives for modern scholars is not limited to literary flights of fancy that promise characters a nearly unlimited power to fulfill their desires; nor were accusations of bewitchment by envious rivals or seductive lovers grounded purely in the imagination.[4] Real people turned to practices that they themselves considered magical in the attempt to achieve their goals in the erotic realm.

[2] Cp., e.g., Graf 1997: 175–185.

[3] Sophron's mime "Women saying that they expel the goddess" seems, from the surviving fragments (frr. 3–9 Kock), to have treated a similar story, and certain elements seem to parallel those in Theocritus and Vergil.

[4] Cp. Gordon 1999a: 167.

The evidence for such practices comes from both epigraphic and literary sources, since art and life are always inextricably intertwined. Lead curse tablets in which the wishes of the desperate are scrawled, intricately engraved gems and amulets whose materials and inscriptions symbolize the desired results, and elaborate formularies in which the recipes for performing magical rituals are collected by professional experts—all these are among the materials that provide direct evidence of magical practices, for erotic and other purposes. We also have literary attestations to some of these materials, representations of daily life aiming at verisimilitude, not fantastic fictions of superpowered creatures of the imagination. Of course, just as the magic of literature might be drawn from the practices of life, so too the magic of the imagination might inspire the practices, as practitioners sought to imitate the greatest magicians of legend.

The epigraphic sources, in particular, provide insights into the lives of men and women in parts of society that rarely make it into the pages of the literary sources, giving voice to their hopes and fears and anxieties. Erotic curses make up a large number of the lead tablets discovered with curses from the ancient world. They follow many of the same patterns as the curses concerned with other realms of life, but the agonistic arena in which they are deployed is the complex one of erotic relations, and their effects are tailored to their aims. Those aims are often recounted in graphic detail, enriching our knowledge of the sexual vocabulary of the ancient world and providing a glimpse into a world of private and intimate relations that appears only seldom elsewhere. In addition to the curse tablets, other devices survive in the archaeological record that play a role in erotic magic, from the desire-inducing *iunx* that Simaetha employs to items of adornment that enhance the erotic appeal of the wearer (figure 5). Such items are only rarely inscribed with texts to identify them, so understanding their use depends upon their correlation with other textual sources.

WHY PRACTICE EROTIC MAGIC?

Ancient Greek and Romans turned to erotic magic to grapple with extraordinary crises in the realm of erotic relationships, and the types of erotic magic practiced may be divided according to the problems to which they are addressed. A number of magical practices are attested as solutions to what might be termed the technical difficulties associated with erotic interactions—issues of impotence, fertility, contraception, and even abortion. Beyond these physical problems, many of the magical practices are aimed at the social dynamics of the erotic relations. To handle competition with rivals, restraining curses could be employed; these would bind and hamper the activities of the competitor in the erotic arena in much the

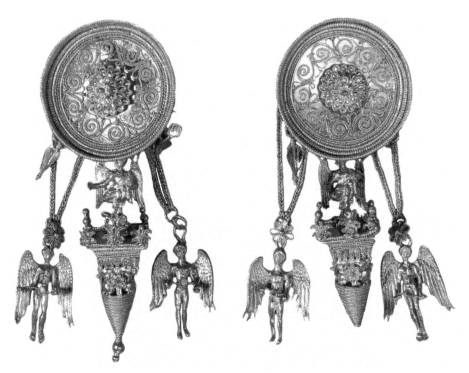

Figure 5. Iunx earring BM 1877,0910.17, by permission
of the British Museum. (See plate 5.)

same way as binding curses would in other venues. Many spells are focused
on retaining the affections of the target, preventing him or her from straying from an established relationship. Of course, one of the most crucial
problems in love is always gaining the affections of the beloved, and a
variety of types of obtaining spells could be used to inflict *eros* on the
beloved and to bring him or her to the lover, past all the obstacles, physical
and social, that might be in the way. Since human relationships are always
complex, the actual spells for which evidence survives do not fall neatly
into these categories, but even the spells that aim, for example, at retaining
the beloved and restraining rivals can be understood as combinations of
the types of spells analyzed here.

Technical Difficulties

The magical solutions for the technical difficulties associated with sex and
reproduction are perhaps the simplest category of erotic magic for which
evidence survives from the ancient world, although even these straightfor-

ward remedies are gendered, providing different kinds of solutions for the problems faced by men and women. For men, there are a variety of recipes to address what would today be termed 'erectile dysfunction'; these remedies of extra-ordinary efficacy range from a preparation of honey and pepper smeared on one's 'business' to Theophrastus's amazing Indian herb, which guarantees as many erections as a man might want, up to twelve (one scientifically minded researcher, Theophrastus tells us, found that he could get as many as seventy before starting to ejaculate blood).[5] Of course, the dysfunction itself might have been caused by magic, either an antaphrodisiac *pharmakon* or a spell. Ovid worries that some magic may have caused his episode of "languid loins," while Encolpius, similarly afflicted, regains his potency from the incantations of an old witch.[6]

For women, magical charms can promise effective contraception, or even abortion, if the woman does not wish for a pregnancy.[7] But magic for enhancing fertility and for promoting conception and healthy delivery appears far more often, since reproduction was so important to the status and position of women within their families and communities, while at the same time pregnancy and childbirth represented some of the greatest hazards to women's health and life. While many of these remedies no doubt remained unwritten traditions for women, some appear in the collections of the learned. Theophrastus lists plants that aid in the conception of a male or a female child. In his list of the useful parts of the hyena, Pliny recommends the eye, in food with anise, as a cure for barrenness that would work in three days, while the sinews of the kidney, taken in wine with incense, would restore fertility damaged by witchcraft. Fat from the loins or the bones from the spine help a woman in labor, as does the right foot—although not the left foot, which could be fatal.[8]

In addition to plant and animal remedies, stones were used, especially hematite (bloodstone), for controlling the flows of blood from the womb, promoting conception, and protecting pregnancy. Some of the most commonly found amulets depict a stylized womb (as an overturned jar) and a large key, either opening the womb to permit conception or sealing it to prevent miscarriage. Spells for the womb appear in the Greek Magical Papyri as well, including a spell to prevent the womb from wandering and a *phusikleidon* (genital key) spell intended to open the womb of the target for the agent only.[9]

[5] PGM VII.191–192; Theophrastus, *HP* 9.18.9. Cf. Ovid's aphrodisiac salad at *Ars am.* 2.415–425. Another recipe is simply "to copulate a lot" (PGM VII.183–185).

[6] Ovid, *Amores* 3.7.27–38; Petronius, *Satyricon* 131.

[7] See PGM LVIII.24–25 for a contraceptive amulet; PGM XXIIa.11–14 prescribes a Homeric line, namely *Iliad* 3.40.

[8] Theophrastus, *HP* 9.18.5; Pliny, *HN* 28.27.92, 102, 103.

[9] PGM VII.260–271 on the wandering womb; *phusikleidon* PGM XXXVI.283–294. For the

Restraining Spells

While the remedies for technical difficulties are concerned mainly with physical performance, magic was also used to address more complicated social problems. Erotic relationships involve complicated social dynamics, and many different kinds of crises can arise that seem beyond the power of ordinary tactics to resolve. Although spells to obtain a desired person are perhaps the most dramatic, spells to retain the affections of a loved one and to restrain rivals make their appearance both in literature and in the epigraphic record.

The restraining spells may target either the rival, preventing him or her from engaging in erotic relations with the beloved, or the beloved, keeping him or her from a particular rival or any potential rivals. These spells, often found engraved on lead tablets buried in graves or deposited in wells, show marked similarities to other kinds of curse tablets, which are designed to hamper the performance of a rival in some other arena of competition. In the context of erotic relationships, it is easy to see the appeal of a magical solution that could eliminate what might seem to the lover to be the primary obstacle to winning the beloved's affections: a rival with superior charms.

One basic form of ill wishing that could be used on an erotic rival was βασκανία or *fascinatio*, what moderns refer to as the 'evil eye.' Simply glancing in envy at another could be sufficient to bring the wished-for harm, to bind back the one who was excelling and thus outdoing the agent. Although various Greeks and Romans came up with rationalizations for how this act could work, they all explain the same basic phenomenon of the sidelong glance of envy—the indirect confrontation with a potential rival. Perhaps the most famous testimony is Catullus's request to Lesbia to give him so many kisses that the envious onlookers would not be able to count them and bewitch their love (*fascinare* or *malus invidere*).[10]

While the envious glance associated with the evil eye is common enough (and even more easily imagined as a cause of one's own misfortune), it leaves little in the way of tangible evidence. Lead curse tablets, on the other hand, provide a durable witness to the rivalries that drove people in the ancient Greco-Roman world to engage in magical practices. A tablet dating from the fourth century BCE, probably deposited in a grave, invokes

---

amulets, Bonner 1950: 79–94 remains the fundamental study, but see Michel 2004: 334–339 for a more recent catalog of examples. Cp. also Dasen 2014a; Faraone 2011a: 135–144 and Faraone 2011c: 56–57, as well as Dasen 2008 on images of Herakles and Omphale that play with ideas of gender and sexuality in protecting female fertility. Dasen 2014b: 210–214 discusses stones thought to be 'pregnant' and thus analogically helpful to women in pregnancy.

[10] Catullus 7.11–12; 5.10–13. See ch. 3, p. 68, n. 29.

the powers of the underworld to bind a certain Theodora and to prevent her from consummating a relationship with Charias.

> I bind Theodora to remain unmarried to Charias, and I bind Charias to forget Theodora, and I bind Charias to forget . . . Theodora and sex with Theodora. And just as this corpse lies useless, so may all the words and deeds of Theodora be useless with regard to Charias and to the other people. I bind Theodora before Hermes of the underworld and before the unmarried and before Tethys. I bind everything, both her words and deeds toward Charias and toward other people, and her sex with Charias.[11]

The unknown agent performing the spell, presumably a woman who wants Charias for herself, wishes that Theodora be as incapable of having sexual relations with Charias as the corpse into whose grave the tablet has been deposited. Theodora's words and deeds are to be bound by the powers of the underworld, which should thus prevent her from competing with the agent.

Other spells, rather than binding all the target's words and deeds, enumerate instead all the specific body parts to be bound and made useless for erotic activity. A lead curse tablet from a fourth-century BCE deposit at Nemea repels one man, Euboles, from every bit of his beloved Aineas.

> I turn away Euboles from Aineas, from his face, from his eyes, from his mouth, from his breasts, from his soul, from his belly, from his penis, from his anus, from his entire body. I turn away Euboles from Aineas.[12]

Enumerations of body parts are common in other curses, but, whereas curses for the law courts target the tongue or the mind of the opponent, erotic curses provide a whole map of the body that may be involved in erotic relations.[13]

Retaining Spells

Although both men and women use spells to win the affections of a beloved by restraining rivals, women seem more often to be the agents in spells designed to preserve an existing erotic relationship and to protect it from outside influences. One example, particularly fascinating on account of its

---

[11] DT 68; trans. Gager 1992: 90.

[12] SEG 30.353; trans. Gager 1992: 92.

[13] Cp. Versnel 1998 for a detailed study of such anatomical lists, esp. 247–264 for the erotic variety.

apparent amateur authorship and lack of formulaic patterns, is a lead tablet from a fourth-century BCE grave near Pella in Macedonia.

> Of Thetima and Dionysophon the ritual wedding and the marriage I bind by a written spell, as well as the marriage of all other women to him, both widows and maidens, but above all of Thetima; and I entrust this spell to Makron and to the *daimones*. And were I ever to unfold and read these words again after digging the tablet up, only then should Dionysophon marry, not before; may he indeed not take another beside myself, but let me alone grow old by the side of Dionysophon and no one else. I implore you: have pity for Phila, dear *daimones*, for I am indeed bereft of all my dear ones and abandoned. But please keep this piece of writing for my sake so that these events do not happen and wretched Thetima perishes miserably; but let me become happy and blessed.[14]

The writer, Phila, pleads with the powers of the dead to prevent Dionysophon from marrying anyone but her, using a binding spell upon him in order to keep him from all her rivals, especially the hated Thetima. Some scholars have speculated that Phila is a *pallakē* (concubine), kept in an informal relationship with Dionysophon and now threatened by the prospect of his marriage to Thetima, and, while other explanations are possible, this scenario highlights a social situation in which restraining spells and their counterparts, retaining spells, might be used.

In the ancient Greco-Roman world, marriage provided for a woman a relatively stable position in society, in which recognition of her claims to that status and support from the family into which she had married were bolstered by the authority of her native family. Without this socially recognized status, her position, even her means of life, might be much more precarious and dependent on the whims of the male with whom she was associated. The category of precariously positioned women included not only prostitutes, who depended on income from their erotic relationships for their livelihood, but also many other women, often referred to as concubines, who formed erotic relationships with men that were not supported by the marriage contract. In such situations, where the legal options were few and the stakes extremely high, we might reasonably expect such women to turn to magical solutions, to use extra-ordinary means to solve their problems, when the normal means available were few and ineffective.

One such magical recourse was the *philtron*, the love potion or spell, whose name suggests not the burning desire of *eros* but the more durable bond of affection termed *philia*. *Philia* can certainly be used of sexual (and,

---

[14] DTA 78; trans. Voutiras 1998, who provides the best study of this tablet.

in that sense, erotic) relationships, but it also can refer to the relationship with family members and friends. Faraone points out the interesting way in which such *philtra* were imagined to work, increasing the benevolence of the target toward the agent by relaxing him and taming his aggressive impulses. Like the effects of wine, which in moderate quantities seems to enhance erotic feelings but in larger quantities can bring about incapacitation, such *philtra* at first made the target relaxed and happy, but further application or overdose could bring about sedation of the target or even, in certain cases, death.[15] A prostitute in Alciphron seeks a potion that will not only keep her client from straying, but also tame his drunken bad temper and make him a more docile lover. In a speech from fourth-century Athens, a concubine anxious about being dismissed puts *pharmaka* in the wine; but, instead of making the man more affectionate, the *philtron* killed him.[16] Later references to cases in which a man was poisoned by an attempt to secure his affections with a love charm show that the woman could either have been acquitted on the grounds that she did not mean to kill him or condemned on the grounds that she did in fact cause his death.[17] Plutarch warns the young bride not to meddle with such *philtra*, since she is likely to end up with a husband whose sedated virility would leave the relationship crippled.[18]

Faraone compares the effects of these *philtra* with a type of spell known as the *thumokatoxon*, the spell for restraining anger, for binding down the *thumos*, the seat of strong emotion.[19] He suggests that the *thumos* can be understood almost as *machismo*, the impulse toward displays of masculine forcefulness, whether sexual or not. Just as modern people might loosely refer to an excess of testosterone as the cause of either violently aggressive or oversexed masculine behavior, so the ancient Greeks might have been concerned about an excess of *thumos* and sought to restrain it, either to prevent violence or to halt indulgence in sexual activity. The *thumokatoxon* spells combine the effect of restraining the anger of a powerful male with

[15] Faraone 1999: 126–129 lists a number of other *pharmaka*, substances used for poison or healing, that have a similar pattern of effect. Theophrastus (*HP* 9.9.1; 9.19.3; 9.19.1; 9.11.6) discusses mandrake, cyclamen, oleander, and another plant, which is probably belladonna: all have a narcotic effect in larger doses but promote good feeling in smaller quantities.

[16] Antiphon 1; Alciphron, *Epist.* 4.10.3. Cf. the mythic parallel of Deianeira, who, anxious about being supplanted in the home by Herakles's war-prize Iole, uses a *pharmakon* to try to recapture his love. In the tragedy, of course, what she thinks is a love charm (*pharmakon*) is really a deadly poison (*pharmakon*), but Deianeira's motivation fits the pattern.

[17] Acquitted—Ps. Aristotle, *Magna Moralia* 16, 1138b29–38; condemned—Basil of Caesarea, *Letter* 188.8.

[18] Plutarch, *Conj praec.* 139a compares using philtra to fishing with poison; it may catch more fish, but it leaves them useless.

[19] See Faraone 1999: 122–131.

an enhancement of the personal charms of the agent. One recipe boasts, "A charm to restrain anger and to secure favor and an excellent charm for gaining victory in the courts—it works even against kings; no charm is greater," while another promises, "The world has nothing greater than this. For when you have it with you you will always get whatever you ask from anybody. Besides it calms the angers of masters and kings."[20] Such magic moves out of the realm of the erotic, but it is worth noting that subordinate males are imagined as employing the same kind of magic to retain the favor of their social superiors in a legal or political context as women are employing to retain the favor of their men in an erotic one.

The combination of restraining anger and securing affection also occurs in the magical *kestos himas*, the adornment of Aphrodite that Hera borrows in the *Iliad*, supposedly to calm the anger and restore the affection of her quarrelling parents, but actually to seduce her husband, Zeus, and to lull him into forgetting the Trojan battlefield.[21] A Hellenistic epigram describes a girl wearing an intricate floral girdle with the inscription, "Love me forever and don't get angry if another man holds me," once again combining the wish to retain love with the restraint of anger. This item blurs the lines between a magic charm and an adornment that merely enhances Hermione's natural charms; ancient moralizers place all such adornments, ranging from ordinary cosmetics and jewelry to magical *philtra* and *thumokatoxoi*, in the spectrum of devices by which women manipulate men's affections.[22]

Obtaining Spells

If women anxious about preserving their relationships use retaining spells to tame their men, and if jealous lovers of both sexes use restraining spells to prevent their rivals from being successful, how would the unsuccessful lover try to obtain the beloved? If normal means of seduction or courtship have failed, magical means can provide solutions for the lover. One spell from the late Greco-Egyptian collection of magical recipes known as the Great Paris Magical Papyrus involves staring into the beloved's eyes while murmuring the name of Aphrodite for seven consecutive days.[23] The erotic gaze that so fascinates modern theorists, penetrating through barriers to ravish the soul of its object, does not seem, however, to have similarly captured the imagination of the ancients. *Eros* may come into the lover

[20] PGM XXXVI.35; PGM XII.277–278.

[21] Homer, *Iliad* 14.197–210. Scholars disagree as to whether this adornment should be imagined as an amulet, a girdle, or even a cross-your-heart breast band. See Faraone 1999: 97–99 for discussion

[22] *Anth. Pal.* 5.158.

[23] PGM IV.1265–1274.

through the eyes, but that is not the route through which most erotic magic attempts to capture the beloved. In most cases, the magic used to obtain the affections of a beloved focuses rather on inflicting the symptoms of *eros* on the target, stirring up her desire and leading her to the agent performing the spell. The gendered pronouns are deliberate here, since the vast majority of "obtaining" spells that have been discovered have a male agent and a female target, and the exceptions—spells that have female agents and male targets, or spells with agents and targets of the same gender—seem to borrow the formulae from the male agent / female target pattern.

While gazing into the beloved's eyes may be one way of signaling the lover's desires, another charm that appears both in the literary sources and in the spell books is the apple charm—a type of spell in which the lover throws an apple (or a quince, a pomegranate, or some other seed-filled sweet fruit) at the target, transferring his love to the one who picks up this token charged with erotic resonances. Ovid recounts the tale of a clever youth, Acontius, who won his bride by tossing an apple inscribed with the words "I vow to marry Acontius" over the garden wall where his beloved would pick it up and read it aloud; the vow was magically effective, to the extent of incurring divine punishment when the girl's parents tried to prevent the marriage. A spell preserved on a first-century (BCE or CE) papyrus makes use of the same idea:

> To whichever woman I give or whichever woman I throw the apple at or hit with it, setting everything aside, may she be mad for my love—whether she takes it in her hand and eats it or sets it in her bosom—and may she not stop loving me. O Lady Kyprogeneia, bring to perfection this perfect incantation.[24]

Again, as with the eye contact spell, we can see the blurring of lines between magical action and simple flirtation—the tossing of the apple to the girl, catching her attention; the girl picking it up and putting it to her lips, or perhaps tucking it away into her bosom. Indeed, in Lucian, one courtesan complains of her boyfriend flirting with another woman by tossing her a bit of apple, which she kissed and put between her breasts. Tossing the apple is the active step in the relationship, signaling one's interest, so a prostitute may toss an apple at a potential client, to catch his attention and express her readiness for sex.[25]

The apple serves as a symbol of sexual desire, perhaps of fertility, certainly of erotic interest, which is why, Plutarch tells us, a quince or an apple was presented to a new bride on her wedding night, symbolizing the awakening of her sexuality, legitimized and sanctioned by the ritual of

---

[24] Ovid, *Heroides* 20 and 21; SM 72 col. i.10–14 = PGM CXXII.
[25] Lucian, *Dial. meret.* 12.1.30–36; cp. Aristophanes, *Nub.* 996–997.

Figure 6. Attic pyxis (London E 774), Eretria Painter 440–415
BCE, by permission of the British Museum.

marriage.[26] Another item associated with the awakened sexuality of marriage is the *iunx*, a little whirligig toy made of a disk that gives off a hum
when spun on a double cord. Depictions of elaborately stylized *iunges* appear on many wedding vases, and on one Attic pyxis depicting the preparation of a bride, the *numpheutria* (maid of honor) spins a little *iunx* as the
bride does her hair (figures 6 & 7).

The whirligig *iunx*, however, also appears as a magical device designed
to attract lovers through its whirling and humming. When the beautiful

[26] Plutarch, *Vit. Sol.* 89c; *Conj. praec.* 138d; *Quaest. Rom.* 279f.

Figure 7. Apulian Red Figure Loutrophoros (Malibu 86.AE.680), Louvre MNB 1148 Painter, 350–340 BCE. Digital image courtesy of the Getty's Open Content Program.

courtesan Theodote asks Socrates how he manages to attract so many handsome young men, he jokes that he is expert in the use of the *iunx* and that perhaps he will show her his tricks some day so that she can be as successful as he is. Theocritus's Simaetha uses it, and Pindar recounts that Aphrodite herself first taught Jason the use of the *iunx* to win Medea. The imagery here is startlingly different from that of idyllic wedding vases or of the flirtatious banter of Socrates and Theodote. Aphrodite takes the *iunx*-bird (the wryneck) and nails it, like Ixion, to a rotating wheel, and the effect is to transfer the maddening torture of the bird to Medea, lashing her with the torments of *eros* and making her forget the respect she owes to her parents in her overwhelming love for Jason. The *iunx* does not merely cause disorientation with its spinning; the target is lashed like a spinning top spun by a whip, while the hum of the wheel becomes a siren song that lures the target in.[27]

This pattern of inflicting violent torture and madness in order to bring the beloved to the lover appears in one of the most common forms of erotic magic: the type of obtaining spell that is often labeled the *agōgē*, the leading spell. With imagery that is often horrifyingly graphic and violent, these obtaining spells wish for the madness and torments of *eros* to be inflicted upon the target.

> Fetch Euphemia, whom Dorothea bore, for Theon, whom his mother Proechia bore, to love me with love and longing and affection and intercourse, with mad love. Burn her members, her liver, her female parts, until she comes to me, longing for me. . . . [D]o not let her eat, or drink, or find sleep, or have fun, or laugh, but make her run away from every place and from every house and leave father, mother, brother, sisters, until she comes to me.[28]

As horrible as these agonies may seem, the torments inflicted on the victim are, by and large, the same torments that *eros* was thought to inflict on a lover—sleeplessness, twisting and turning, a burning feeling, inability to eat or drink, inability to concentrate, to think of anyone else or be with anyone else, and, ultimately, madness. Such symptoms have a long history in the literary tradition; in one of the most famous and moving descriptions, Sappho complains:

> For when I look at you for a moment, then it is no longer possible for me to speak; my tongue has snapped, at once a subtle fire has stolen beneath my flesh, I see nothing with my eyes, my ears hum, sweat pours from me, a trembling seizes me all over, I am greener than grass, and it seems to me that I am little short of dying.[29]

Eros is a passion, something suffered, and a devastating loss of self-control, not the gentle and delightful giddy feeling so often associated in modern thought with "falling in love." Stories abound of the terrible effects of love, and even of love hurled as a curse—such as the story of the poet Homer cursing a priestess who rejected him, dooming her to fall hopelessly in love with ugly old men. So painful and disturbing are the effects of *eros* that some spells, the so-called *diabolē* or slander spells, even ask that *eros* be

[27] Pindar, *Pythian* 4.213–219. Socrates and Theodote in Xenophon, *Mem.* 3.11.16–17. See the discussions in Faraone 1993 and Faraone 1999: 5–15, 55–69.

[28] SM 45.29–32, 45–48 = PGM CI; cp. SM 40.12–21 = PGM LXXI.

[29] Sappho, fr. 31. Such symptoms have a long history in the literary tradition. See, e.g., Anacreon, fr. 413.

Figure 8. Perugia Inv. 1526; collezione Guardabassi.
Image courtesy of Attilio Mastrocinqu. (See plate 61.)

inflicted on the target as a punishment for some imaginary crime of which
the agent accuses the target. Usually invoking a dreadful and dangerous
moon goddess, the agent generally claims that the target has defamed the
goddess or performed obscene sacrifices to her.[30] *Eros* is the first stage of
punishment in this spell, which can also be used to cause illness—or even
death, if the ritual is prolonged.

It is in this context too that we should understand images of the god
Eros, armed not with a little baby-Cupid bow and arrow, but with torches
and a whip, so as to burn and wound the soul (*psuchē*) of the target on
whom *eros* is being inflicted. The tale of Cupid and Psyche, known best
from Apuleius's fable of the trials of the beautiful Psyche seeking to regain
her lost husband, appears in a different form in the spell known as the
Sword of Dardanos. (figure 8) The spell, which "immediately bends and

---

[30] E.g., PGM IV.2474–2492. The curse of *eros* in [Herodotus] *Life of Homer* 30. Although
the idea of inflicting *eros* as a divine punishment appears in the Greco-Roman mythic tradition from Euripides's *Hippolytus* to Apuleius's tale of Cupid and Psyche, this pattern of transferring the slander to the target of the spell does not appear in earlier Greek magical texts;
it has, however, a long history within the Egyptian magical tradition, so it seems to be a
perfect example of the way ritual experts were able to innovate by working within both traditions. Betz 1992: 83n314.

attracts the soul of whomever you wish," instructs the agent to make a gem engraved on one side with images of Psyche dominated by Aphrodite and tormented by the burning torches of Eros, while the other side depicts Psyche and Eros clasped in an embrace. Precisely such a gem has been found, inscribed with a version of the formula directed in the Greco-Egyptian formulary; and other gems depicting a butterfly-winged Psyche bound and tormented by Eros show that the theme was not uncommon.[31] The obtaining spells, then, attempt to dominate the soul of the target and inflict upon it the feeling of burning so characteristic of *eros*.

Many spells, however, target not just the soul, but specifically the body. A clay figurine, now in the Louvre, of a woman bound hand and foot and pierced with nails was discovered in Egypt with a lead tablet, and both the figurine and the tablet correspond remarkably closely to a spell from the Great Paris Magical Papyrus (figures 9 and 10). This recipe book provides the following instructions:

> And take thirteen copper needles and stick 1 in the brain while say-ing, "I am piercing your brain, NN"; and stick 2 in the ears and 2 in the eyes and 1 in the mouth and 2 in the midriff and 1 in the hands and 2 in the pudenda and 2 in the soles, saying each time, "I am piercing such and such a member of her, NN, so that she may remem-ber no one but me, NN, alone."[32]

This recipe, although complex and involving not just the figurine but an inscribed tablet and an elaborate deposition ritual, appears to have been fairly popular, since no less than five examples of the executed spell have been discovered, although only one such figurine has survived.[33]

While the figurine may seem like a voodoo doll of the modern popular imagination, the nails are not sadistically intended to cause piercing pains in the corresponding regions of the target. Rather, they are explicitly de-signed to bind the target magically to the agent and turn her thoughts and memory to him. Like Theon's spell for Euphemia above, the spell here makes the target remember only the agent, forgetting all her other social ties and obligations. The great force, even violence, expressed in the ritual of binding and piercing the figurine represents the impetus that is needed to break the target's internal will and self-control, as well as the external social obliga-tions that prevent her from succumbing to the agent's desires.

---

[31] PGM IV.1716–1870. Cf. Inv. 1526 of the Guardabassi collection (see Mouterde 1930). See also the two gems Inv. No. Ж 316 and Ж 20 in the Hermitage collection.

[32] PGM IV.296–466, lines 321–328. On the correspondences between the executed ex-amples and the formulary, see Martinez 1991 (with detailed commentary).

[33] The versions of the spell are collected in SM 46–50, with further analysis in Martinez 1991. The figurine, now in the Louvre, was found in a clay pot with SM 47.

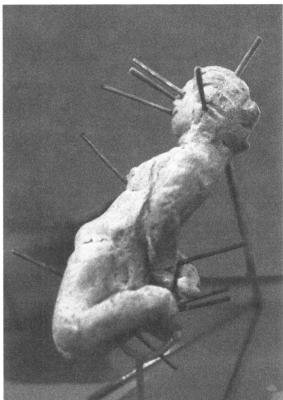

Figure 9 (left). Clay figurine. Louvre E27145b. © Marie-Lan Nguyen /
Wikimedia Commons / CC-BY 2.5.
Figure 10 (right). Clay figurine. Louvre E27145b. © Genevra
Kornbluth, by permission. (See plates 6b and 6c.)

HOW DOES EROTIC MAGIC WORK?

The fact that many of these obtaining spells aim to project upon the target
the feelings of *eros* has led some scholars to imagine a kind of psychological transfer, in which the tormented lover projects his own feelings upon
his beloved in the hopes that she will reciprocate his love. As Winkler
puts it,

> Between the agent and the victim, as depicted in these scenarios,
> there is a curious transference. The rite assigns a role of calm and

masterful control to the performer and imagines the victim's scene as one of passionate inner torment. But if we think about the reality of the situation, the intended victim is in all likelihood sleeping peacefully, blissfully ignorant of what some love-stricken lunatic is doing on his roof; while the man himself, if he is fixated on this particular woman, is really suffering in that unfortunate and desperate state known as *eros*. . . . The typical client for such a rite was not a Don Juan who wanted to increase the sheer number of his conquests but rather some young male who needed it rather desperately.[34]

While not impossible, this scenario imagines far more insight into the psychology of the agent than our evidence can possibly provide. Especially since the symptoms of *eros* described are so traditional and the spells themselves so formulaic, there is no reason to suppose we can uncover anyone's authentic feelings from the texts. However, the same formulaic character prevents us from drawing too many conclusions about the nature of the targets; the graphic list of sex acts prohibited and the injunctions to prevent any other man from sexual contact with the target do not necessarily indicate that the target must be a prostitute.[35] The generic tendency of curses of all types to enumerate or list items and to aim at completeness by covering contingencies provides sufficient explanation of the phenomenon's occurrence in the erotic spells, even if some spells certainly were in fact directed at sex workers, whether by clients or by rival prostitutes. While we may not know much about the individuals who used this kind of magic, we can nevertheless learn much about ancient ideas of how *eros* worked and the kinds of social dynamics involved.

From the etic, modern, scholarly perspective, the pattern of male domination over female sexuality appears strongly in these sources. Although this kind of *agōgē* spell could be adapted for female use upon a male target, the preponderance of the male agent–female target pattern, both in the formularies and in the executed examples, illustrates the cultural protocol, throughout the range of times and places that produced these spells, that assumed male dominance and active role in the erotic relationship.[36] Even if, as Winkler rightly cautions, the gap between social protocol and actual behavior may have at times been very wide, the spells show the force and

---

[34] Winkler 1991: 225–226.

[35] *Pace* Dickie 2000: 571.

[36] Winkler 1991: 216 suggests "that the victimage models enacted in *agogai* paradoxically incorporate rather than suppress women's desire but that they do so only within the models of family competition and male fantasy in which any desire is a dangerous irruption into one's autonomy and in which women's desire in particular must be thought of—that is, by men—as submitting to the pretensions of masculine control."

violence that were imagined to be needed to disrupt the personal and social barriers that inhibit the female target's expression of desire.[37]

While the practical obstacles to men's erotic access to women obviously differed not only from individual to individual, but also between social contexts and time periods, it is notable that the problem of access and of dissolving the social obligations appears far more frequently in spells in which a male is targeting a female, while spells with a female agent and a male target or same-sex spells are concerned less with access, with bringing the target out of the house and dissolving the social obligations, than with restraining rivals or retaining the current partner. It is worth noting that the *agōgē* spells do not envisage physical barriers like locked doors that must be surmounted, nor male guardians or parents who must be circumvented.[38] Any seclusion of the women targeted is therefore likewise a protocol, an imagined inaccessibility. Indeed, since the relative seclusion of women correlates to their desirability, the most desirable maiden would obviously be the most unattainable, the noble, pure, and chaste maiden carefully guarded by her parents rather than the woman who was available to anybody. Inaccessibility thus could be a carefully cultivated posture, whether by upper-class women in Athens in the fourth century BCE or by a *hetaira* in Ptolemaic Alexandria whose careful selectivity with regard to her clientele reinforced, according to the law of supply and demand, her high prices.

In any case, any target for whom the agent must go to the extra-ordinary lengths of commissioning or performing a magical ritual is by that very fact inaccessible enough, at least in the agent's estimation, to require such exercise of power and force. The point is made ironically in Lucian's description of a young man who hires an exotic (and expensive!) sorcerer to perform an elaborate obtaining spell so as to compel the beautiful wife of his neighbor to come banging on his door in the middle of the night for sex, only to have another character comment drily that he knows the woman in question and that she could be had by anyone for a mere twenty drachmas. Nevertheless, for the youth, the obstacles seemed such that he would be willing to pay one hundred times that price to have a Hyperborean sorcerer draw the moon down from the heavens, invoke Hekate, animate an Eros statue, and even call up his father from the dead to ask for permission.[39]

---

[37] Faraone 1999: 78–95 compares abduction marriage as a similar strategy designed to maintain the protocols of paternal control over the daughter's sexuality. The control of the father (or of another *kurios*) is broken only through a violent invasion, which may in fact have been not so violent; it may even have involved the cooperation of the bride.

[38] Faraone 1999: 167–168 discusses the issue of how much or whether women were actually secluded in contrast with the protocols of their separation from masculine spheres.

[39] Lucian, *Philopseudes* 13–15.

Lucian's ludicrous piling up of magical procedures raises the question of the emic perspective on how such erotic magics worked. Like the curse tablets in other arenas, the erotic spells make use of invocations to various deities, particularly chthonic underworld figures like Hekate, to inflict the curse of *eros* upon the target, and both the soul of the target and her body (in its various parts) were imagined as involved in the process. This divine power might be contacted through a dead spirit with whom the curse tablet is deposited, or the divine power might employ spirits of the dead to carry out the task of restraining the target or, alternatively, afflicting her with the symptoms of *eros*. For the latter, however, the spirit involved is often specifically the personification of Eros, rather than some other entity, and Lucian's parody rite has a parallel in the Greek Magical Papyri, where a special statue of Eros is created to serve the magician's ends.[40]

Many of the same *voces magicae* and special arrangements of words and letters are employed in the erotic spells as in the other curses, and symbolic performative ritual manipulations of figurines and other materials are likewise found. The predominance of burning metaphors is significant in the rhetoric of these spells, and scholars have noted the similarities between such metaphors (both in words and in actions) and the descriptions of the symptoms of *eros* in the medical literature.[41]

The emic understanding of retaining magic, as noted above, operates somewhat differently. Rather than a female target whose body and soul must be inflamed with *eros*, such spells more often target a male whose masculine *thumos* must be tamed. While invocations to divine powers may be involved, these procedures often involve particular substances whose sedative power calms the masculine sex drive and thus prevents it from impelling the target to seek other erotic relations. Restraining spells may employ divine aid to target either gender to bind back their sexual activity and restrict it to the agent alone, but retaining spells aim to tame the male erotic drive, while obtaining spells are imagined to be enflaming the erotic passions of a female target.

WHO PERFORMED EROTIC MAGIC?

While the evidence of spell books and material examples seems to show that men were more often using magic to obtain the love of women, the literary evidence presents a very different picture. There are numerous and elaborate depictions of women using erotic magic, in contrast to a definite paucity of men. Even the few men who are depicted as using erotic magic

[40] Cp. PGM XII.14–95.
[41] Cp. LiDonnici 1998.

are generally shown as clients of some powerful female magician. Scholars have explained this gap between the literary imagination and the evidence reflective of real life in a variety of ways; these range from ignoring the epigraphic evidence and assuming that women were indeed the primary users of erotic magic to reading the literary evidence as a systematic projection of men's activities onto women through male anxieties about female sexual power. The predominance of women in the imaginative depictions of erotic magic seems, however, to stem primarily from their place in the Greco-Roman imaginary as Other; it is a way of depicting difference from the male norm.

The essential feature of all the phenomena labeled 'magic' in the ancient Greco-Roman world is their abnormality, their difference from the everyday and ordinary, whether what is at stake is the practices or the people who engage in them. For those who engage in practices they consider magic, these rituals promise solutions beyond the ordinary to problems they have not been able to solve by ordinary means. Others blame magic to explain events inexplicable by ordinary explanations. And when people imagine the power to do things not ordinarily within their ability to perform, that too is magic. As Gordon points out, the imagined power of magic is bounded only by the limits of the imagination, so literature tends to depict magic in more extreme ways, as being more out of the ordinary, more inexplicable, more powerful.[42]

The extra-ordinary nature of magic manifests itself in both the users and the things they do. The characters depicted as using erotic magic are not exclusively female, but gender is one of the markers of alterity, along with age, alien origin, and marginal social status, that indicate the extraordinary status of the one using magic.. Some figures display only a limited alterity, like the male *magoi* from foreign lands, such as Lucian's Hyperborean, while others, like Apuleius's Meroe, pile up the levels of alterity, being not only female but also old, foreign (an inhabitant of Thessaly, notorious for its witches), and a tavern-keeper. Stratton's study of the figure of the witch in Greek and Roman literature provides a good set of types: young and sexy sorceresses; oversexed, superpowered old hags; and male foreigners. The male sorcerers bring the alterity of the foreign, wisdom from the beyond (Egypt or Chaldea, or even Hyperborean lands), as well as a social position outside the normal social hierarchies. They are often depicted as itinerant experts; they come into the community to offer their services to love-struck youths or foolish women, but they do not use their powers for their own sexual satisfaction. In imaginative literature, that is the role of women.[43]

---

[42] Cp. Gordon 1999a: 168 on magic and the marvelous.

[43] Stratton 2007. *Pace* Dickie 2000: 577–582. The only males on his list of experts in erotic

The sexy sorceress has magical powers that are in some way an extension of her sexual attractiveness: nature aided by art. She may be semidivine, like Homer's Circe, or a somewhat marginal figure, like Theocritus's Simaetha, who appears to run her own household; but in either case she is not under a male guardian who controls her sexual relationships. Simaetha casts an elaborate obtaining spell, invoking Hekate and using the *iunx* to drag her faithless lover to her house. Other literary figures, like Deianeira or Medea, still do not use obtaining spells, but rather retaining spells (like Deianeira's accidentally poisoned robe) or magic designed to restrain their rivals (like Medea's intentionally poisoned robe). In literature, the effects of the spells can be more grandiose, as the level of alterity is increased; in particular, Medea, the foreign witch, seems to have nearly limitless powers in some versions of her story.

The older witch types, the oversexed widows and predatory hags, who appear with increasing frequency and increasing power in Roman literature, often share this near-omnipotence. Stratton links this type to fears in late republican and early imperial Rome of the increasing power of elite women, who had more independent control of property and wealth.[44] Apuleius's Pamphile certainly seems to typify such a powerful and wealthy woman; she uses her magic to attract young lovers, even casting an obtaining spell to make a handsome youth come banging on her door in the middle of the night. However, many of these older women are more marginal than elite, Thessalian hags or drunken old bawds who have built up a repertoire of magical powers, and this marginal status may actually serve to emphasize their extra-ordinary power. Horace's Canidia, like the *saga* whom Tibullus's lover employs or the dreadful Meroe in Apuleius, has supreme power over the whole of nature, she can make streams run backward, pull the moon down from the sky, and disrupt the entire order of the cosmos in any way she pleases.[45] Again, none of these women's sexuality is under male control; even the matron Pamphile conducts her affairs entirely unbeknownst to her clueless cuckold of a husband. They use their magical powers to satisfy their sexual desires, unfettered by any social

magic who use it for their own relationships are Jason in Pindar, who actually receives the *iunx* from Aphrodite, and Lucian's Alexander, who does not actually use erotic magic to attract sexual partners, but simply flatters an old woman for money.

[44] Stratton 2007: 96: "the preoccupation with sexually predatory old women and women with money reflects a particularly Roman concern that women who were economically independent and socially emancipated threatened male control over the *domus* and the very structures of society."

[45] Pamphile in Apuleius, *Met.* 3.15–16; Canidia in Horace, *Ep.* 5.17, *Sat.* 1.8; *saga* in Tibullus 1.2; Meroe in Apuleius, *Met.* 2.5. It is worth noting that Apuleius's own defense speech against charges of using erotic magic in his own life (discussed in ch. 11, pp. 391–396) resembles the documentary evidence more than it does his own literary depictions.

constraints or limitations imposed by the cosmic order upon everyday life. Whether this is a fantasy or a nightmare depends on the particular literary depiction—and on the reactions of its audience.

CONCLUSIONS

Of course, the extra-ordinary efficacy of magic in the Greco-Roman imaginary cuts both ways: magic may be powerful beyond all ordinary limitations or it may be a worthless waste of time, incapable of producing any results. Lucian's Hyperborean magician turns out to be a fraud who takes twenty minas from a youth to bring a woman who could be bought for twenty drachmas. Medea's beauty and nearly unbounded magical power do not suffice to keep Jason in a happy erotic relationship with her, an irony that Ovid exploits to its fullest potential.[46] Pliny sneers at those who believe that the various parts of the hyena have any special effects.

Even Pliny, however, admits that everyone fears the power of curses, and even the wise philosopher Sosipatra took steps to guard herself against the love spell cast by Philometor.[47] While there is no way to judge, from a modern perspective, whether any of this erotic magic 'worked,' from the standpoint of cultural history we can nevertheless conclude that erotic magic was a real part of the Greco-Roman world, both in the imagination of its possibilities and in the practices of those seeking extra-ordinary solutions to the endless problems that can arise in erotic relationships. The evidence, in literature and in epigraphic sources, provides insights into those problems as well as into the ways people thought those problems might be solved. This material is a rich source for the understanding of ancient Greco-Roman sexualities, providing glimpses of the underlying patterns of erotic behavior, both in the fantasies of the ancient Greeks and Romans and in the realities of their relationships.

The erotic practices labeled 'magic' show, through their categorization as non-normative, what the boundaries of normative erotics were and how fuzzy they might be. The scene from one of Lucian's *Dialogues of the Courtesans* shows how the line between erotic magic and erotic flirtation might be blurred. One courtesan complains to her lover that he has been making advances to other women.

> I didn't worry particularly at your kissing Cymbalium five times. To kiss a woman like that was an insult to yourself! But oh! the way you kept on making signs to Pyrallis, and would lift up your cup to her,

---

[46] Ovid, *Ars am.* 2.99–107; *Rem. am.* 259–264; *Heroides* 12.163–172; see Prince 2003.
[47] Pliny, *HN* 28.4.19; Eunapius, *Vitae sophistarum* 413.

when you drank, and whisper in the slave's ear, when you returned the cup, telling him not to give anyone a drink unless Pyrallis asked for one! In the end you bit off a piece of your apple, when you saw Diphilus was busy talking to Thraso, and, bending forward, shot it with skilful aim into her bosom, without any attempt to hide it from me. She kissed it, and, dropping it between her breasts, tucked it under her girdle.[48]

Here the gesture of throwing the apple is just simple flirting, but it is the same kind of gesture made in the apple spell preserved on one of the Greek Magical Papyri. The differences between extra-ordinary magic and ordinary love play again lie primarily in the perceived efficacy of the act; Pyrallis may choose to respond to the apple with another flirtatious gesture, but the spell drives the target mad with lust and makes the *eros* a permanent condition. In the papyrus, the efficacy is guaranteed by the story of the spell's origin, since it is entitled, "An excerpt of enchantments from the holy book called Hermes, found in Heliopolis in the innermost shrine of the temple, written in Egyptian letters and translated into Greek."[49] This charm is no mere spur of the moment flirtation; it comes from ancient Egyptian wisdom, preserved within the holy book of divine Hermes in the most secret recess of the temple until it was translated into Greek for the benefit of the user. The performance of the magic is marked with a higher coefficient of weirdness as well, with the formulaic tag of "bring to perfection this perfect incantation," a magical charm in ritualized speech, not flirtatious banter.[50] Other examples of erotic magic pile up the bizarre elements of the performance, adding *voces magicae*, strange ingredients, or vivid persuasive analogies like the nail-pierced figurine, and all of these non-normative elements of the performance bolster the claims to non-normative efficacy.

The social location of the performer is particularly interesting in erotic magic, since the literary evidence would suggest that erotic magic is generally associated with the objectively profane: the female, the old, the foreign. The evidence of the lead tablets and the papyri, however, indicates that many of the performers are intentionally, rather than objectively, profane; that is, they are normative members of society (adult, nonforeign males) who are choosing to act in a way that is non-normative. No male in the ancient Greco-Roman world would boast of winning his lover by means of spells like a woman or foreigner, rather than by his own manly attractions, but the evidence shows that many such males did attempt to

---

[48] Lucian, *Dial. meret.* 12.1.30–36.

[49] PGM CXXII.1–4.

[50] As Faraone 1992a notes, this formula has a long history in the Greek ritual tradition, particularly in association with erotic magic.

win their lovers through magic. The non-normative nature of erotic magic is expressed in the literary sources through the cue of social location; the old Thessalian hags or the exotic sexy sorceresses of a Medean mold are the ones most often depicted performing erotic magic. In reality, however, both males and females made use of erotic magic for its extra-ordinary efficacy in addressing one of the problems in life most difficult to control, the complex relationships of *eros*.

5

Healing and Protective Magic:
Defense against the Dark Arts

If you engrave a flamingo onto the stone hephaestites, also called
pyrites, and at the feet of it a scorpion, and you put a little rootlet
of the plant [*eryngion* or *gorgonion*] under the stone, you will have
a good protective amulet against all venomous creatures. It wards
off night-time hallucinations, and it is also effective for those who
suffer from the stone. It wards off every evil eye.
(Kyranides I.7.17–21)[1]

INTRODUCTION

In the agonistic contexts of the ancient Mediterranean world, the threat of
the evil eye or even more deliberate and elaborate hostile magic from some
rival could seem a constant threat. Some form of defense against these dark
arts would be needed, not to mention the threats from other kinds of dangers, be they venomous beasts or infectious diseases. The flamingo amulet
described in the Roman-era treatise *Kyranides* is a more complicated version of amulets against the evil eye and other hostile influences that appear
in the evidence from the earliest through the latest periods. While the
earliest and simplest magical protective devices might be merely an apotropaic image of the gorgon's head or a phallic gesture, the evidence provides witness to an increasingly elaborate tradition of protective and healing magic in the Greco-Roman world, tightly interwoven with the traditions

---

[1] Εἰς δὲ τὸν ἡφαιστίτην λίθον τὸν καὶ πυρίτην λεγόμενον ἐὰν γλύψῃς φοινικόπτερον, παρὰ δὲ τοὺς
πόδας αὐτοῦ σκορπίον, καὶ ὑποβάλῃς τῷ λίθῳ ῥίζιον τοῦ φυτοῦ μικρόν, ἕξεις φυλακτήριον ἐκ πάντων
ζῴων ἰοβόλων. ἀποστρέφει δὲ καὶ ἰνδαλμοὺς νυκτερινούς. ποιεῖ δὲ καὶ ἐπὶ λιθιώντων. βασκανίαν δὲ
πᾶσαν ἀποστρέφει.

of hostile magic. A binding curse, for example, against a charioteer of the Blue Team in Apamea in Roman Syria asks in addition to dissolve (*lusate, apolusate*) any protective magics he may have had performed on his behalf; magical protection was as much a fact of life in this competitive world as the magical attacks against which they were to protect.[2]

While normal strategies of defense and protection against one's enemies and the ordinary perils of life in the ancient world could be employed in everyday problems, for extra-ordinary crises, extra-ordinary means with extra-ordinary efficacy were needed. Such means were needed not only to ward off potential harm but also to heal the damage already done. Special knowledge might be required to determine the necessary remedy for an unusual or serious problem, whether that knowledge was transmitted in the traditional lore about various plants and minerals or in systematic treatises that compiled the arcane lore for scholarly minded philosophers and doctors.

Either the traditional lore or the occult knowledge might be labeled as 'magic.' The former category appears as magic because of its social location; it is the knowledge and practices of certain kinds of marginal elements in the society—the old wives' tales, the rustic lore, and so forth.[3] Such practices are abnormal, not what ordinary people do, but this abnormality may either be substandard (the superstitions of the foolish) or supereffective (the lost secrets of the ancients). While the boundaries of this category change over time and in the different regions of the Greco-Roman world, anything that was considered 'superstition' or 'secret wisdom' might be labeled 'magic.'[4] The latter category of occult knowledge really only appears with the systematization of traditional lore in the Hellenistic period, but it is from the texts produced by that systematization that we have the bulk of our evidence for what Gordon calls 'natural magic,' the magical

---

[2] DT 15 = Gager 4. Other charms against magical attack appear in GMA #36.15, #52.12; PGM XIII.253 (ἐὰν πρὸς λύσιν φαρμάκων); XXXVI.256–264 (λύσατε πᾶν φάρμακον); Bonner 156 (πρός πέτ(α)λα); the agate from Anapa analyzed in Faraone 2010; cp. PGM IV.2176–2178 (Homeric verses); VIII.32–35; XXXVI.221–223.

[3] Of course, what is regarded as superstition in the big city may be considered sensible standard practice in the country. Within the social circles in which such practices were considered 'normal,' they are therefore not classified as magical; only outsiders looking at such communities may consider their practices to be magic, often under some specifically derogatory term like 'superstition.'

[4] Gordon 1999a: 248 describes this category in terms of Bourdieu's idea of objective profanation (see Bourdieu 1971: 308–309). That is, the knowledge or practices in question are profane/abnormal/extra-ordinary simply because they are practiced by certain people, whose social location is outside the mainstream of society, whether as old wives (i.e., not male and not mature adults) or as other kinds of outsiders. See the discussion in ch. 1, pp. 9–10, nn. 15–17.

effects of certain plants, animals, and mineral substances. Magic, in accounts that systematically rationalize the order of the cosmos, becomes the occult knowledge of those things that escape the rational pattern, the exceptions to the increasingly detailed sets of rules.[5] Such knowledge is hidden from all but a select few, who again stand outside the mainstream of society because of their access to this extra-ordinary understanding of how to transcend the normal rules. The rationalizing author Pliny argues that magic must be regarded as false and deceptive, precisely because it promises a level of efficacy beyond that which normal medical procedures can achieve.[6] Such promises, whether resulting from the ignorance of superstitious rustics or the charlatanry of professional magicians, violate the ordinary rules of the cosmos and thus cannot be fulfilled. In either case, the knowledge and practices of such curative or protective magics are suspect because of their social location, their distance from the ordinary.

This very distance from the ordinary, however, is the reason that people in the ancient Greco-Roman world turned to magic in times of extra-ordinary troubles. Depending upon which of the myriad possible dangers was concerned, protective or curative magic might take a variety of different forms—application of special material substances, ritual procedures, or even just verbal incantations—but such magic addressing extra-ordinary crises differed both from ordinary practical means of handling the dangers of the world and from the appeals for divine aid found in votive dedications made at temples. Protective and curative magic channeled divine power in special ways to achieve its extra-ordinary effects, and so, like other forms of magic in the ancient Greco-Roman world, it was at times viewed askance as superstition and at other times eagerly sought as the only solution to otherwise insuperable problems.

---

[5] Gordon 1997: 137 describes the way that the systematization of traditional lore in the Hellenistic period creates a place for a new conception of magic as secret, occult knowledge of the exceptions to the rational system: "the redescription of selected natural facts as marvels strung together on an occult string had the effect of clearing a space between the tacit, incoherent quality of traditional belief on the one hand, and those trends in Hellenistic cosmology, particularly Epicureanism and scepticism, which tended toward rationalism and agnosticism on the other. That space the occultists attempted to fill with a demonstration of the superabundant strangeness of nature."

[6] Pliny, *HN* 37.54: *sed etiam maiore utilitate vitae coarguemus Magorum infandam vanitatem, quando vel plurima illi prodidere de gemmis ab medicinae blandissima specie ad prodigia transgressi*. "But to the greater profit of mankind I shall incidentally confute the abominable falsehoods of the Magi, since in very many of their statements about gems they have gone far beyond providing an alluring substitute for medical science into the realms of the supernatural." Cp. *HN* 26.20, 30.2. As Dickie 1999: 172 comments, "In his view, magic is medicine overreaching itself and promising to do more than it can justly hope to do."

WHAT KINDS OF PROTECTIVE AND
HEALING MAGICS ARE FOUND?

A wide variety of rituals, substances, and materials appear in the evidence for protective and healing magic in the ancient Greco-Roman world, but there is no simple and useful set of ancient terminology to describe them. The English word 'amulet' is perhaps the best suited to cover a range of devices employed for their protective and healing effects, whether they are engraved stones carried loose in a pouch or set into jewelry, or inscribed lamellae of precious metals rolled up and carried in amulet cases or strapped directly onto the body (*periapta*), or even scraps of papyrus with magical writing. (A 'phylactery' is specifically a protective charm, while other words such as 'talisman' can also apply to magical amulets in general.) While the form—ring or necklace or armband or loose stone—is one way to categorize the range of such amulets, the final form receives less attention in the ancient sources than the medium (stone, metal, papyrus, etc.), the iconography, and the text. All of these forms serve the important function of keeping the amulet close to the body of the bearer, whether visibly displayed or hidden beneath clothing.

The form of protective or healing magic employed would clearly depend on the needs of the situation, since some applications would be more appropriate for a given threat or problem than others. Pindar, in relating the marvelous healing powers of the semidivine Asclepius, pupil of the centaur Chiron, describes the range of methods he employs.

> Now all who came to him afflicted with natural sores or with limbs wounded by gray bronze or by a far-flung stone, or with bodies wracked by summer fever or winter chill, he relieved of their various ills and restored them; some he tended with calming incantations, while others drank soothing potions, or he applied remedies to all parts of their bodies; still others he raised up with surgery.[7]

In addition to the rather harsh treatment of surgery (literally, 'cuttings,' *tomais*), Pindar specifies verbal incantations chanted over the patients, concoctions for them to drink, and *pharmaka*, remedies or magical substances, that were wrapped around the afflicted parts. A large number of the physical amulets survive from antiquity in the form of engraved gems and inscribed metal amulets. Verbal charms and potions, on the other hand, leave no trace in the archaeological record, but we have literary accounts of their use, such as Pindar's, as well as recipes and instructions preserved in various kinds of sources, ranging from the scientific studies

[7] Pindar, *Pythian* 3.47–54.

of the Aristotelian philosopher Theophrastus, through the traces that remain of systematic treatises on stones and plants from the Hellenistic period, to recipes in the Greek Magical Papyri.

Indeed, the record of verbal incantations goes back all the way to the oldest Greek sources, the Homeric epics. In the famous digression on how Odysseus acquired his crucially recognizable scar, Homer recounts that, when he was young, Odysseus went boar hunting with his uncles, who bound up the wound caused by the boar's tusks and sang incantations over it so that it would heal.[8] More than a thousand years later, the fifth-century CE Marcellus of Bordeaux records some incantations to stop nosebleeds (*sirmio sirmio* or *soksokam sukuma*).[9] Such evidence suggests that the tradition of healing incantations and protective charms persisted through the centuries, despite the invisibility of oral traditions in the material record.

In addition to incantations, the textual record preserves other kinds of written texts used in protective and healing magic, from the literary descriptions of the uses of such magic to the magical names, invocations, and adjurations used on amulets. Although, as with the curse tablets, the earliest evidence contains much less writing, there is a veritable explosion of written evidence by the time of the Roman period, when the 'epigraphic habit' has become so much more securely entrenched in the cultures of the ancient Mediterranean. Many of the late amulets have extensive and complex texts, even if recipe books such as the Greek Magical Papyri show that oral incantations still accompanied many of the inscribed amulets. Earlier amulets may just have a single name or image on them, and it is only by reference to recipe books and learned treatises on the powers of stones (*Lithika*) that we can even suspect that they might have been used as magic amulets.[10]

Such *Lithika* collect and to some extent systematize the traditional lore about the powers of stones, just as similar systematic treatises were written about the powers of plants and various animals. Although the Hellenistic period seems to have been the time for the efflorescence of such systematic collections of lore, with the exception of Theophrastus's work, most of the Hellenistic material has been lost, preserved only in later collections or

---

[8] Homer, *Odyssey* 19.455–458; cp. Renehan 1992. In the Homeric Hymn to Demeter (227–230), the goddess, in her disguise as an old nursemaid, claims to know incantations that would protect her nursling. See Faraone 2001.

[9] Marcellus, *De medicamentis* X.34, 56, 69 = #97, 187, 188 Heim. Heim 1893 still remains the best collection of such incantations. See Faraone 2012b: 7 on the possible derivation of *sukuma* from the Greek word for 'wave.'

[10] Cp. Faraone 2011c: 50 on the distortions in scholarly interpretations caused by this explosion of textual material and the problems with identifying amulets without textual parallels.

quotations. Other treatises, like the *Lithika* of Socrates and Dionysos or the catalog couched as a letter from the magician Damigeron or King Evax of Arabia, to the Emperor Tiberius, seem to come from the Roman imperial period, as do the enormous collections of natural lore in Dioscorides's *Medical Materials* and Pliny's *Natural History*.[11] Other texts, like *Kyranides* or the medical collection of Marcellus of Bordeaux, come from the fourth century CE or later, but often preserve earlier materials that can help scholars interpret the symbolic significance of the materials or the images in the amulets from earlier periods.

Images engraved on stone amulets represent a large store of iconographic evidence for our analysis, and recent scholarship has begun to make exciting progress in this field. Although Bonner's 1950 study brought a great collection of evidence together with exemplary analyses of the uses and contexts, his pathbreaking study has remained without a successor for over half a century. Recent publications of the gem collections from museums around Europe have shown the enormous potential for further work, especially with the advances in color digital photography over the primitive means available to Bonner, but scholarly analysis is just beginning to make use of this vast trove of material.[12]

Bonner already identified certain types of iconography, such as the figure of a reaper in a grain field (figure 11), whose image was carved into a gem carried as an amulet to protect against sciatica (since a life of reaping grain tends to wear on the sciatic nerve, causing crippling pains). More recently, Faraone has discussed sore throat amulets with the image of a bunch of grapes, designed to cure infections of the uvula, which hangs at the back of the throat like a bunch of grapes.[13] One amulet, a ring from the second or third century CE set with an engraved lapis lazuli stone, has an image of a bunch of grapes on one side and the word *staphyle* (bunch of grapes) on the reverse, set in a diminishing triangle form known as the *staphyle* (figure 12). Such word images provide another source of understanding for the function of these amulets, since they may illustrate the desired effect of shrinking the inflamed part or work in other, more complex, ways to achieve the purpose of the magic.

The materials from which the amulets are made can often provide important information about the magical function of the item, although the material items must often be analyzed in conjunction with treatises on the

[11] See the introductions in Halleux and Schamp 1985 for the issues of dating these texts.

[12] Cp. Phillipp 1986; Mastrocinque 2004, 2008, and 2014; as well as Michel 2001 and 2004. The Campbell Bonner Magical Gems Database (http://classics.mfab.hu/talismans/visitatori_salutem) provides an excellent resource, including recent color images and references to publications since Bonner's work.

[13] Faraone 2012b: 9, with fig. 1.3.

Figure 11. Carnelian amulet, Mich. 26123; Ann Arbor, Kelsey Museum of Archaeology. © Genevra Kornbluth. (See plate 7a.)

power of stones and plants that often present conflicting or even contradictory interpretations. The dark blue color of the lapis lazuli amulet may be related to the grape imagery, just as the yellow-brown stones engraved with scorpions reflect the color of the most dangerous variety of scorpion in the Mediterranean basin.[14] While such symbolic connections are observable, the use of light green jasper for amulets protecting the stomach is less obvious, although it happens to be amply attested in the few treatises on the power of stones that have survived from antiquity.[15]

In general, one difference may be noted between the materials used for protective and healing magic and those used for curses. Although amulets made from papyrus, ostraka, lead, or other such substances do appear, far more precious metals and gems are used in the manufacture of amulets than of curses. Exceptions occur, of course, but, whereas curses are designed to be disposed of, amulets are kept, often on one's person, and sometimes even for generations.[16] The resources necessary to purchase the

[14] Cp. Faraone 2011c: 55; Faraone 2012b: 9.

[15] Cp. Faraone 2011c: 50–52.

[16] Bonner notes that a stone (#156) engraved on one side with a charm against curse tablets was repurposed as an erotic charm by the inscription on the other side that follows the formulae for an *agōgē* obtaining spell, asking to either bring Achillas back or to lay him

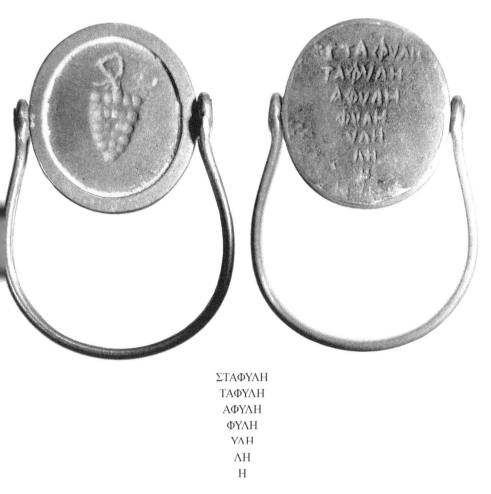

ΣΤΑΦΥΛΗ
ΤΑΦΥΛΗ
ΑΦΥΛΗ
ΦΥΛΗ
ΥΛΗ
ΛΗ
Η

Figure 12. Lapis amulet with grape cluster. Bibliothèque nationale,
département des Monnaies, médailles et antiques, Froehner.
XIV.36 (cliché Attilio Mastrocinque-DR). (See plate 7b.)

precious metals or engraved gems are more likely to be expended on an
item designed for long-term personal use (and possibly display) than one
manufactured for one-time use and disposal.

---

low. As Bonner comments, "A point of technical interest to the student of amulets is the fact
that the Newell stone, originally made and inscribed for one purpose, namely as a prophylactic against enchantment, was adapted upon a buyer's demand to serve as a love charm. It
is a useful warning against the temptation to find a consistent system in the manufacture and
use of such objects" (Bonner 1950: 118).

The precious nature of such amulets, however, creates a different problem for their preservation from antiquity for modern scholars. Whereas lead curse tablets were discarded and ignored until their excavation, colorful engraved gems and gold tablets have been much more apt to be taken away from their original findspots and put into museum collections (or traded illicitly in private collections). The valuable information about the context of the magical item that careful archaeological excavation can uncover is lost for the vast majority of these amulets, and scholars must rely on problematic methods such as the dating of letter forms and analysis of image styles to form hypotheses about from where and when these amulets come.

Thousands of engraved gems are now in museum collections, but they have only recently been the objects of systematic study. There is, however, an inherent problem in the task of analyzing these items within only a museum context. How can one tell if a gem with an image is magical rather than just decorative? Even from an emic point of view, this is a tricky question, since one man's jewel may be another man's amulet. From our etic point of view, we can postulate that a gem is magical if we can reconstruct an emic theory of how it would work and what it would work for. This criterion is obviously a messy one, however, since there were undoubtedly images that had magical significance to which we have no key, while some that seem 'magical' to us, may have been taken merely as exotic but not esoteric images. The apparent 'explosion' of amulets in the Roman period may simply stem from the fact that the textual evidence is richer from that period onward, leaving us unable to recognize earlier amulets without textual markers or the parallels in written treatises.[17] The evidence over all the periods of Greco-Roman antiquity suggests, however, that people were using magical rituals and items for protection and healing from the earliest witnesses to our latest evidence, in the form of verbal incantations, ritual practices, written texts, and physical amulets of various kinds.

WHY EMPLOY PROTECTIVE MAGICS?

The reasons why someone might choose to employ protective or healing magic are as obvious and as varied as the many obvious sources of harm

---

[17] As Faraone 2011c: 57 argues, "It is, I suggest, only in the Roman period when the written text takes on any importance at all. Indeed, as we have seen, there were probably a number of powerful stones and powerful images circulating independently around the Mediterranean basin long before the advent of the Roman Empire. The 'big-bang' approach to magical gems, therefore, misreads the texts on these gems as evidence for an historic rise of superstition or magic, when we would do better to see these texts as additional evidence for the rise in Roman epigraphic habits and the increasing scribalisation of magic."

and danger in the world. While every individual and every society has a normal set of means to handle the manifold perils of the world, those ordinary means at times seem insufficient for dealing with the crisis at hand. Of course, this perceived insufficiency of normal means depends not only on the situation but upon the temperment of the person involved, so some people were far more inclined to turn to protective magic than others.[18] Some protective magic was tailored to very specific threats, whereas others were more general, a prophylactic against all possible harm.

A first- or second-century CE gold amulet from Segontium, the Roman outpost in North Wales, invokes a number of magical names to ask for protection for the Roman soldier stationed out on the barbaric frontier.

> *Adōnai Elōaie Sabaōth, Eie Esar Eie, Soura Arbatiaō*, being, being, being, living excellently, *Elliōn Hannōra Hagibbōr Baillalaamōth Barouch Aththa Oubarouz Houdēcha* ever *Ōlam-leōlam Akkramarachamari Amorim Phabzana Thouth* [magic signs]. Protect me, Alphianus.[19]

This gold amulet, with Hebrew invocations (*Barouch Aththa, Adōnai*) and Egyptian gods (*Thouth*) inscribed in Greek characters for a Roman soldier on the borders of Britannia, perfectly encapsulates the cosmopolitan world in which the magic of the ancient Greco-Roman world operated. Poor Alf must have had a lot of things to worry about out there, more than could be easily articulated in a list, so he opted for a general prayer for protection rather than to carry an amulet protecting himself against venomous beasts, nightmares, or digestive troubles. It is worth noting that amulets were not usually inscribed to protect specifically against any particular sort of wound that a military man might expect; the amulets were more general, against all the mischances that might occur in battle.

Other amulets might specify protection for more than one individual. A second-century CE gold amulet from Renania in Germany lists a series of people to be preserved from any loss, probably in a law court context.

> OYDAEAGANFOZL . . . UNI Ia Ia Iai Sabaōth [Adōnai A]blanathana-lba Akra[machari] Semeseilam Sēsēngem[barphara]ngēs, io io io, preserve Te[rtullum], whom Leib[ia the mothe]r bore, from any risk of loss; [preserve] Chilon; preserve Luciolus; preserve Mercussa.[20]

Whereas Alf probably carried his own amulet with him, it is less clear who might have held this one or whether it might have been deposited somewhere, perhaps the family home, to protect the group. Sometimes the

---

[18] Cp. the caricature of the superstitious man in Theophrastus (*Char.* 16), who throws three stones to take away the bad luck if a weasel crosses his path and who spits into his chest if he even sees a madman.

[19] GMA #2.

[20] GMA #7.

function of the amulet clearly suggests where it might have been placed. Two second-century CE bronze amulets designed to protect a vineyard in Avignon from weather damage were probably affixed to stones at the boundaries of the property.

> * *Thōsouderkyō* * vineyard *oumixonthei*, divert from this property all hail and all snow, and whatever might injure the land. The god, Oamoutha, orders it, and you Abrasax, assist! *Iaē Iaō*. (Julius Pervincus)[21]

The vineyard owner's name, Julius Pervincus, appears on one of the inscriptions, and both tablets clearly mark the concerns that he had in trying to protect his livelihood from the unpredictable and uncontrollable vagaries of the weather. However hard and well he might labor in his vineyard, an untimely hailstorm could destroy the crop for the year, leaving him in serious economic troubles, so such extra-ordinary measures as these lamellae might well have seemed a reasonable investment for insuring his property. The fact that a later Roman law specifically exempts such protective amulets for vineyards from prosecution as magic indicates that enough people at the time must have considered them magic for the exemption clause to be needed.[22]

Another circumstance in which a protective amulet might have seemed a worthwhile insurance strategy was in the dangerous business of sea travel. The poet Hesiod warns of the dangers of seafaring, and the epic tales of Odysseus recount his multiple shipwrecks.[23] A late treatise on the power of stones provides instructions for creating an amulet to protect against shipwreck by carving the figure of Poseidon, god of the seas, holding his trident and with a dolphin under his foot.[24] A number of gems with such iconography have been discovered, and it is likely that they were used, by at least some of their owners, as amulets protecting them against peril upon the sea. (figure 13)

While natural threats like the weather and the seas are certainly the kind of uncontrollable dangers that would encourage the use of protective magic, some amulets were designed to protect against the use of harmful

---

[21] GMA #11.

[22] Constantine in the Theodosian Code (*CTh* 9.16.3).

[23] Hesiod, *Works and Days* 618–695.

[24] See *Orphic Lithika kerygmata* 27. Γλύφεται ἐν τούτῳ τῷ λίθῳ τῷ καθαρῷ Ποσειδῶν ἔχων δελφῖνα . . . τῷ δεξιῷ ποδὶ καὶ τρίαιναν τῇ δεξιᾷ χειρί· τελέσας οὖν οὕτως ἔχε φορῶν τῷ δακτυλίῳ, καὶ ποιεῖ πάντα ὅσα καὶ ὁ σμάραγδος. Ἀλλὰ καὶ τοὺς διὰ θαλάσσης ἐμπορευομένους ἀπὸ κλύδωνος ῥύεται. "On this purified stone is engraved Poseidon holding a dolphin, [with a prow under] his right foot and a trident in his right hand. Therefore, having thus hallowed it, keep hold of it, wearing it as a ring, and it will do all the things that an emerald does. And it also saves those venturing through the sea from the rough wave."

Figure 13. Ring with carved figure of Poseidon. Ashmolean 40004552, Marlborough, 138, by permission. (See plate 7c.)

magic itself. A long fourth-century CE silver amulet from Roman Beirut begins with the plea to protect the bearer from all kinds of demonic attack or other magical harm.

> I adjure you by the one above heaven, Sabaōth, by the one who comes above the Elaōth, by the one above the Chthothai. Protect Alexandra whom Zoē bore from every demon and from every compulsion of demons, and from demons and sorceries and binding spells.[25]

Alexandra presumably wore this amulet rolled up inside the bronze tubular amulet case in which it was found. The remainder of the text contains a long series of invocations to a fascinating hierarchy of divine beings, ending with a reaffirmation of the plea to protect Alexandra, the

[25] GMA #52.1–12.

daughter of Zoē. Other such antimagic amulets have been found, as well as recipes for producing charms to dissolve any enchantments.[26] Of course, when dealing in the world of hostile demons and harmful magic, a protective amulet might be needed for protection during the performance of a magic ritual to ensure that the dangerous forces with whom the magician is dealing would not lash out at the magician instead of the target. One formulary warns,

> Do not therefore perform the rite rashly, and do not perform it unless some dire necessity arises for you. It also possesses a protective charm against your falling, for the goddess is accustomed to make airborne those who perform this rite unprotected by a charm and to hurl them from aloft down to the ground. So consequently I have thought it necessary to take the precaution of a protective charm so that you may perform the rite without hesitation. Keep it secret.
>
> Take a hieratic papyrus roll and wear it around your right arm with which you make the offering. And these are the things written on it: "MOULATHI CHERNOUTH AMARŌ MOULIANDRON, guard me from every daimon, whether an evil male or female." Keep it secret, son.[27]

The inscribed papyrus phylactery is a necessary precaution for performing this erotic spell, which calls upon the dangerous moon goddess Aktiōphis (identified with Hekate and the Babylonian underworld goddess Ereškigal) to punish the target for slandering the goddess by inflicting *eros* upon her. The strategy, however, of telling the goddess all the terrible things the target has said about her is intended to get the goddess angry, but a protective amulet is required so that the anger of Aktiōphis is channeled at the target and not at the magician recounting all the dreadful things she said.[28]

It is not clear whether the papyrus phylactery is a specific anti-Aktiōphis amulet or a more general protection against being made airborne and hurled off a roof, but it is clear that an amulet's efficacy was imagined to be confined to certain areas. An exchange in an Aristophanic comedy emphasizes the importance of having the right amulet for the situation.

---

[26] Cp. PGM XXXVI.256–264. "Taking a Three-Cornered Sherd from a Fork in the Road—pick it up with your Left Hand—inscribe it with Myrrhed Ink and hide it. [Write:] 'ASS-TRAELOS CHRAELOS, dissolve every Enchantment against me, NN, for I conjure You by the Great and Terrible Names which the Winds fear and the Rocks split when they hear it.'" Cp. Anapa stone (πρὸς φαρμάκων ἀποπομπάς), GMA #36.15, #52.12; PGM XIII.253 (ἐὰν πρὸς λύσιν φαρμάκων); XXXVI.256–264 (λύσατε πᾶν φάρμακον); cp. PGM IV.2176–2178 (Homeric verses); VIII.32–35; XXXVI.221–223; also Bonner 156 πρὸς πέτ(α)λα—against *defixiones*.

[27] PGM IV.2505–2520.

[28] "For she said that you slew a man and ate his flesh, and she says that your headband is his entrails, that you took all his skin and put it in your vagina" (PGM IV.2594–2599).

DIKAIOS: I don't care a hang for you; I am wearing this ring, bought
    of Eudamus for a drachma.
CARION: But it is not inscribed "for an informer's bite."[29]

Dikaios ('just man') has a ring that he thinks will protect him, but the wily
Carion jokes that something designed 'for a snake's bite' or the like will
not defend him against the perils of an unjust lawsuit brought by an informer. Whereas Alphianus in Segontium carries a general protective amulet to defend himself against an unknown host of perils, a more specifically
targeted amulet might be more effective against the specific problem it
was designed to counteract.

Beyond the general versus specific focus of the amulet, another important distinction is beween the preventative and curative scope. Many amulets and phylacteries are designed to ward off or prevent the harm done
by some attack or misfortune, that is, they are designed for a future problem. Others, however, are aimed rather at a present problem, to stop the
harm currently being done and to cure the bad effects already suffered,
but both future and present problems are addressed in similar ways. A
fragment of Attic comedy refers to another drachma amulet designed to
ward off possible stomach problems.

There's nothing wrong with me and I hope there won't be; but if after
all I get a twist about the stomach or the navel, I have a ring, bought
of Phertatus for a drachma.[30]

The *Kyranides* has a recipe for making a protective device against the onset
of cataracts and other eye problems by engraving the figure of a long-
sighted vulture on a piece of amber, while a scrap of papyrus from Egypt
calls on angels to protect a certain Sophia, daughter of Theonilla, from all
fever and shivering.[31]

While cataracts are something one might worry about for a long time
before their onset, fever often comes on suddenly, and so a fever amulet
might really be aimed at a current rather than a future problem. Another
papyrus amulet (third or fourth century CE from Tebtunis in Egypt) has
variants of two palindromes, *ablanathanalba* and *charamarach*, together in
a reducing triangle form, together with a plea to save Tais from every kind
of fever.

---

[29] Aristophanes, *Plutus* 883–885 (trans. Bonner 1950: 4).

[30] Antiphanes, fr. 177 Kock (trans. Bonner 1950: 4).

[31] *Kyranides* I.11.20–22. Engrave a vulture onto an amber stone and put a little frankincense underneath and the wingtip of the bird and wear it. For it will help against dim-
sightedness and cataract of the eyes. PGM XLIII. Michael, Sabaōth Iapapa Gabriel, Souriel,
Raphael, protect Sophia, whom Theonilla bore, from every shivering and fever, quickly, now.

ABLANATHANABLANAMACHARAMARACHARAMARACH
BLANATHANABLANAMACHARAMARACHARAMARA
LANATHANABLANAMACHARAMARACHARAMAR
ANATHANABLANAMACHARAMARACHARAMA
NATHANABLANAMACHARAMARACHARAM
ATHANABLANAMACHARAMARACHARA
THANABLANAMACHARAMARACHAR
ANABLANAMACHARAMARACHA
NABLANAMACHARAMARACH
ABLANAMACHARAMARA
BLANAMACHARAMAR
LANAMACHARAMA
ANAMACHARAM
NAMACHARA
AMACHAR
MACHA
ACH
A

O Tireless One, KOK KOUK KOUL, save Tais whom Taraus bore from every Shivering Fit, whether Tertian or Quartan or Quotidian Fever, or an Every-other-day Fever, or one by Night, or even a Mild Fever, because I am the ancestral, tireless God, KOK KOUK KOUL! Immediately, immediately! Quickly, quickly![32]

This amulet lists all the different kinds of fever that might afflict the sufferer, divided according to the categories of contemporary medical science, which divided up fevers according to their cycles of return (daily, every third or fourth day, etc.). This propensity toward listing the contingencies, which appears in the curses as well, shows up in an unusual gem found in the Black Sea region near the Greek colony of Gorgippa, probably from the second or third century CE.[33] Engraved on this large agate sphere is a plea for knowledge, healing, and health for various parts of the head: brain, ears, eardrum, uvula, throat, forehead, nostril, polyp, teeth, mouth. As Faraone notes, the list moves from general to specific, from the ears to the eardrum, from the nostril to the polyp growth within, and so forth. Moreover, this list corresponds neatly with the list of parts of the head in

---

[32] PGM XXXIII.1–25. While some scholars, e.g., ad loc in Betz 1992, have understood KOK KOUK KOUL as coming from the Egyptian *kky*, meaning darkness and related to CHOOCH, Faraone 2012b: 20n59, notes that the name (or an abbreviation KKK) appears frequently in conjunction with an image of Herakles wrestling the Nemean Lion and suggests that the name may be an epithet or 'secret name' of Herakles.

[33] Gordon 1999b, "What's in a List?" analyzes the phenomenon of listing in curses and other magical procedures.

a Hippocratic medical treatise, suggesting a shared systematic view of the parts of the body.[34] Next to each part is a magical name or symbol, presumably the power invoked to protect and heal the afflicted part. The amulet might thus be used to protect the entirety of the head, carefully outlined part by part to ensure sufficient specificity, or the stone might be used as a reference point so that one could invoke the power associated with the single afflicted part.

Some problems, of course, are recurrent, making the use of an amulet both curative for the present trouble and preventative for the next recurrence. One of the most common images on amulets, the lion-headed serpent, seems to be for digestive troubles (figure 14). Instructions for making an amulet in a treatise on the power of stones correspond with allusions in medical writers such as Galen and Marcellus of Bordeaux. "Engrave on it a serpent coil with the upper part of head of a lion with rays. Worn thus it prevents pain in the stomach; you will easily digest every kind of food."[35] This image is often referred to by the name of Chnoubis or Chnoumis, and Bonner calls attention to a lion-headed snake with the name of Chnoumos, whom a hermetic treatise identifies as a decan of Leo, suggesting an astrological influence on the healing power.[36] While digestive troubles are common and painful, some maladies, such as migraine headaches, are not just recurrent, but debilitating, seeming to come at irregular intervals like an attack from outside. While various remedies can be found in the ancient evidence, one interesting amulet takes the form of a historiola, a mythic narrative that narrates the solution to the problem.[37] The text consists of a dialogue between the demon responsible for the headache and the powerful goddess, Artemis of Ephesus.

For the 'Half-Head' [hemi-kranon = migraine]: Antaura came out the sea. She shouted like a hind. She cried out like a cow.

[34] Faraone 2010: 94–104.
[35] Orphic Lithika Kerygmata 35–36. Cp. Galen, De simpl. 10.19, citing the Hellenistic treatise attributed to the Egyptian magician Nechepso; Marcellus, De medicamentis XX.98.
[36] Bonner 1950: 54, citing (17.105–109) the Hermetic treatise on the decans published in Ruelle 1908. He also notes that Hephaestion's astrological treatise (Apotelesmatica 11.15, 12. 20–23 Pingree) lists Chnoumis as the third decan of Cancer, a power that serves as a phylactery for the stomach. μὴ λαθέτω δὲ ὡς εἰκότως εἰς φυλακτήριον τοῦ στομάχου παραδέχονται τὸν Χνουμὶν ὡς κύριον ὄντα τοῦ στήθους τοῦ κόσμου καθὼς ἡ διαίρεσις τῶν ζῳδίων περιέχει. Let it not be omitted how reasonably they provide Chnoubis for the protection of the stomach, since he is ruler of the order of the chest, just as the division of the zodiac supplies. The later Latin Liber Hermetis lists the first decan of Leo as "the lord of the stomach. It is a great serpent with the form of a lion having solar rays encircling its head," but the name given is Zaloias.
[37] Cp. the mini-historiola in the formulary recipe PGM VII.199–201: "Take oil in your hands and utter the spell: 'Zeus sowed a grape seed: it parts the soil; he does not sow it; it does not sprout.'"

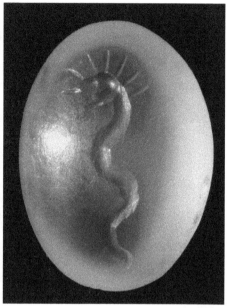

Figure 14. Chnoubis amulet from Lewis Collection, Fitzwilliam Museum;
Chnoubis amulet BM G173. © Genevra Kornbluth, by permission.
(See plate 81.)

> Artemis of Ephesos met her (saying): "Antaura, where are you going?"
>
> (*Antaura*): "Into the half-part of the head."
>
> (*Artemis*): No, do not [go] into the [half-part of the head.][38]

While the text of this silver amulet breaks off here, we can reconstruct the pattern of its missing part from a medieval prayer that follows the same pattern, substituting Jesus Christ for Artemis of Ephesus.

MIGRAINE PRAYER AGAINST THE HEADACHE:

> Migraine came out from the sea rioting and roaring, and our Lord Jesus Christ came to meet it and said to it: "Where are you going, O headache and migraine and pain in the skull and in the eyes and inflammation and tears and leukoma and dizziness?"
>
> And the Headache answered our Lord Jesus Christ: "We are going to sit down in the head of the servant of God, NN."

[38] GMA #13.

And our Lord Jesus Christ said to it: "Look here, do not go into my servant, but be off altogether and go into the mountains and settle in a bull's head. There you may eat flesh, there drink blood, there ruin the eyes, there darken the head, seethe and wriggle. But if you do not obey me, I shall destroy you there on the mountain where no dog barks and cock does not crow."

You who have set a limit to the sea stop headache and migraine and the pain in the skull and between the eyes and on the lids and from the marrow from the servant of the Lord, NN.[39]

In both spells, the headache is personified as a demon who is told to depart from the half-part of the head of the sufferer and go off, in the later spell into a remote part of the mountains where it can find the head of a wild bull to torment. In the story, the divine power exerts its authority over the demon, forcing it to obey, exactly the effect that the sufferer wishes for his own headache. Since migraines often recur in family lines, it is interesting to note that, although the text of the silver amulet comes from the first or second century CE, the grave in Austria in which it was found dates to the third century, suggesting that the amulet may have been passed down in the family to ward off an affliction that was likewise passed down.

How Do Amulets and Other Protective and Healing Magics Work?

The historiola in the Antaura amulet raises the question of how these protective magics work. Why should narrating a story of how one headache demon was expelled serve to relieve the headache of the person wearing the text in a case around her neck? There seems no obvious connection between a stone engraved with a lion-headed snake and the amelioration of one's digestive troubles. Yet thousands of such amulets, in all shapes and sizes, appear in the material evidence, along with countless references to protective and healing magics in the textual sources. People in the ancient Greco-Roman world clearly acted as if these amulets worked, passing down the Antaura amulet from one generation to the next, continuing to buy protective rings for a drachma, and having gemstones engraved with increasingly complex texts and images.

Once again, we must be careful to distinguish an etic from an emic perspective when attempting to answer these questions, since the assumptions about the nature of the world that modern observers bring to the study of these materials are different from those of the people in Greco-

---

[39] For this text and several parallels, see the discussion in GMA.

Roman antiquity who made use of these things. Both perspectives can help us understand the phenomenon, providing insights into why people used amulets and other protective and healing magics, as well as why they made them in the forms that they did.

It is easy, for example, to provide an etic rationalizing explanation of an ancient procedure that Cato the Elder records in his treatise on agriculture for setting a broken bone.

> Any kind of dislocation may be cured by the following charm: Take a green reed four or five feet long and split it down the middle, and let two men hold it to your hips. Begin to chant: "motas uaeta daries dardares astataries dissunapiter" and continue until they meet. Brandish a knife over them, and when the reeds meet so that one touches the other, grasp with the hand and cut right and left. If the pieces are applied to the dislocation or the fracture, it will heal. And none the less chant every day, and, in the case of a dislocation, in this manner, if you wish: "huat haut haut istasis tarsis ardannabou dannaustra."[40]

Putting a splint on a broken bone is a medically proven way to help heal the fracture, immobilizing the broken pieces so that they can grow back together again properly. Even if the rest of the procedure, with the strange *voces magicae* and ritual manipulations of the reed, has no medical effect, the splinting would serve to speed proper healing.

The recipes for magical healing have particularly interested historians of science, who have sought to identify the elements with the magical materials whose effects can be described in modern scientific terms. Scholars such as Scarborough have analyzed the chemical properties of some of the remedies described in the collections of herbal lore such as Theophrastus, Dioscorides, and Pliny, pinpointing the chemical compounds that might produce the kinds of effects sought in the healing process. Scarborough notes that cyclamen, which Theophrastus recommends for treating wounds, contains "cyclamin [triacetyloleandromycin] employed in modern medicine as an antibacterial, emetic, purgative, and hemolytic agent." He notes that "with the mild antibiotic character of honey added to the cyclamen, this dressing would be quite beneficial."[41] In some recipes, he finds chemically potent materials among other magical ingredients he would dismiss as useless. In a contraceptive recipe from the Greek Magical Papyri, for example, he identifies bitter vetch and henbane among the ingredients as "pharmacologically potent herbs." The henbane contains hyoscyamine, while the vetch contains xanthine, guanidine, and vicianin, a cyanogenetic glycoside, an overdose of which would resemble cyanide

---

[40] Cato, *On Agriculture* 160; cp. the discussions in Graf 1997: 43 and Luck 2006 ad loc #5.
[41] Scarborough 1979 (2010): 365.

poisoning. "Muffled among the earwax, blood, milk, and nasal mucus [of the recipe] is a record of the potency of two drugs."[42] In this kind of etic approach, the explanation of how the magical procedures worked is found in the traces of 'pharmacologically potent' materials buried among the weird magical ingredients that have no actual power or effect.

As Scarborough and other scholars have noted, the remedies in the learned collections of Theophrastus and his successors undoubtedly stem from a systematization of the herbal lore of the traditional 'root-cutters,' who gathered plant materials (as well as animal and mineral substances) for use in healing procedures. The implicit argument that these remedies must have had some observable success in order to be preserved and passed on in the tradition is not entirely without merit, and so the empirical and experimental tradition can, at least to some degree, be projected back onto the nameless root-cutters and healers who tried to cure the ailments of the unrecorded patients based on their experience with previous cases. Such retrojection must be done cautiously, however, to avoid imposing models of modern scientific empiricism upon practitioners whose logical systems of operation may have been quite different. The fascination with magical herbs and substances cannot be explained simply by the chemical effects that the compounds might have had (either accidentally or through careful experimentation); such manipulations of magical material go back to the earliest depictions of magicians, the potion of Circe in the *Odyssey* or plays entitled *Rootcutters* that recounted the story of Medea.

This etic account of the pharmacological properties of various magical recipes is sometimes supplemented with reference to the 'placebo effect,' since modern scientific studies have amply demonstrated that sometimes patients will get better when given remedies of no pharmacological effect that they nevertheless *believe* will help them heal. Such explanations shift the ground from physiological to psychological, a mode of etic explanation that helps explain a wider variety of protective and healing magics that do not involve pharmacological substances, such as the majority of amulets and phylacteries. Gager, for example, discusses the protective amulets as "a counterstrategy of individual action, undergirded by feelings of self-confidence, optimism, and the ability to formulate and achieve goals."[43] Making reference to Roheim's Freudian idea of the 'counterphobic attitude,' he explains the efficacy of amulets in terms of their power to encourage the bearer to overcome the potentially paralyzing fears of danger and harm. The individual who feels protected by an amulet can act, even in the tense, agonistic social environment where he knows that his rivals are actively seeking his downfall, since he feels protected from their malice

---

[42] Scarborough 1991 (2010): 158 on PGM XXXVI.320–332.
[43] Gager 1992: 221–222.

and covert attempts to harm him. Their efforts in the ordinary sphere of social interactions can be countered by ordinary means, but even if they are using extra-ordinary, magical means, the individual feels protected. Regardless of the validity of Roheim's Freudian concepts of conflicting superego and ego, this explanation has the merit of locating the user of protective and healing magics within a social context and seeing the use of these magics as strategies adapted for such contexts.

A similar approach is suggested by Tambiah's emphasis on ritual as performative acts.[44] From such a perspective, acts such as the wearing of an amulet or the performance of a healing ritual appear as acts of communication, even if the audience is merely the individual him or herself. By choosing to wear the amulet, the individual sends a message to himself that he is protected, that he can safely engage in his regular business. By performing a healing ritual, with incantations, magical substances, and so forth, the healer tells the patient that she will be healed. Such acts can be analyzed rhetorically, like the rites involved in curses, to see the ways in which the act is authorized, how it appeals to its audience as valid and convincing. Of course, the etic point of view concerns only the horizontal axis of communication, the ways in which the performer addresses the human audience in the social context, whether that audience be the self or others. Nevertheless, we can analyze the ways such rituals appeal to traditional authorities, make use of familiar patterns of ritual or familiar pieces of knowledge, and incorporate unfamiliar elements to enhance the authority of the performance beyond the normal level by raising its 'coefficient of weirdness.' Richard Gordon, drawing on the narratological work of Todorov, has investigated a number of the healing rituals from the Greco-Roman world in such terms, analyzing their rhetorical and narratological structures and strategies to shed light on the traditions and social contexts underlying such acts.[45]

Emic theories are always harder to find, since most of the people who used healing and protective magics did so without theorizing how they worked or preserving such theories in texts. Moreover, those who did choose to theorize may have devised systematic theories that serve their own philosophical or religious agendas and have little to do with the implicit understandings of their contemporaries who used the magic.[46] Nev-

---

[44] Cp. Tambiah 1979a.

[45] Gordon 1995. Cp. Haluszka 2008, who, drawing on the anthropologist Gell for the concept of statues as social actors, makes use of Peircean semiotic theory to discuss the relation of statue and deity, a concept that could be applied as well to the images on amulets as miniaturized images or other kinds of symbols of the divine powers.

[46] Gordon 2011a: 44: "It would however be over simple to think only in terms of the explicit intentions of designers. In my view, it is quite implausible to suppose that all practitioners could have provided the type of commentary to individual designs that one finds in

ertheless, some of the theories surviving from antiquity of how healing and protective magic worked can help elucidate the way the vertical axis was understood, the connection between the mortal and divine power, and thus illuminate the materials that have come down to us.

One of the most basic is a simple kind of symbolism that is refined by later thinkers into an elaborate system of correspondences, sometimes called the 'doctrine of signatures.' At its most fundamental level, this theory involves the idea that the visual form of a substance, be it animal, vegetable, or mineral, corresponds in some way with its power. Thus, the milky-white stone known as galactite (from the Greek *galaktos*, of milk) is thought to help with lactation in animal or human mothers, while the wine-colored amethyst (whose name comes from the Greek *a-methys*, not drunk) protects against overindulgence in wine. The names attached to these stones provide the implicit theorization of their powers, as does the name of hematite, the blood-red iron ore whose name derives from the Greek *haima*, blood, and which was thought to help with various problems relating to the flow of blood. Similar connections, ranging from simple indexical links of visual correspondences to more complex symbolisms, can be found in the names of plants and even some animals.[47]

The ideas of such correspondences are further developed in the systematic treatises that collect the traditional lore about stones, plants, and animals. While the symbolic links may no longer be clear to the outside observer (or even to the ancient systematizers), the works of Theophrastus and his Hellenistic contemporaries theorize that certain substances are more suited to certain functions than others, and they prescribe remedies and protective amulets on the basis of those connections. Later philosophers, especially among the Stoics and Neoplatonists, develop theories of cosmic sympathy in which all the elements of the cosmos are linked to each other in various degrees and it is possible to manipulate the correspondences within the chains of related materials to achieve certain effects.[48] These Neoplatonic philosophers represent the idea of correspondences between materials and their special powers taken to the extreme of theorization. The rituals of consecration they discuss that purify matter to receive divine power are unlikely to have been part of every process of creating magical amulets, but the idea of correspondence that underlies

---

modern catalogues. The extent of routinisation, as well as the probable existence of receptaries for common designs, surely excludes this. Routinisation also implies that most amulets were not elaborately consecrated. Such considerations lead us on to considering magical gems as an aspect of culturally specific consumption."

[47] Cp. the extension of Jakobson's ideas of metaphor and metonymy in ch. 3, p. 84, n. 70.

[48] Cp., e.g., Proclus, *de sacr.* 150.26–30 and Hermias, *in Plat. Phaedrum* 87.4. For further discussion of these theories within Neoplatonic theurgy, see ch. 9 .

their theories helps modern scholars understand the implicit logic of less elaborate ideas.[49]

A different kind of emic theory appears, particularly in the medical material, that arises from the systematization of the traditional lore about animals, plants, and stones. While not perhaps as similar to modern empirical methods as historians of science and medicine in the nineteenth and twentieth centuries were inclined to believe, the practitioners of medicine associated with the Hippocratic school and natural philosophers associated with the Aristotelian Peripatetic school sought explanations for the efficacy of certain remedies and treatments through a systematic understanding of the nature of the plants and animals involved. Drawing on theories of the basic elements of the cosmos like Empedokles's four elements (fire, air, earth, and water), the Hippocratic thinkers postulated a system of 'humors,' elements within the body that needed to be kept in appropriate balance. The Hippocratic treatise *On the Nature of Man* describes four humors: phlegm, blood, black bile, and yellow bile. Each humor is associated with hot or cold and wet or dry, as well as being linked to the seasons of the earth when such conditions apply. Phlegm, for instance, is moist and cold, linked to the cold wet season of winter, while blood is warm and moist, like the season of spring.[50] This theory of a balance of elements within the body is linked to a systematization of experience in altering the balance of elements to restore health to a system whose composition has become out of balance. The Hippocratic doctors indeed insist upon the importance of experience to their art, arguing that their systematic application of their principles leads to treatment that is targeted to the problem, rather than merely haphazard.

> Some practitioners are poor, others very excellent; this would not be the case if an art of medicine did not exist at all, and had not been the product of any research and discovery, but all would be equally inexperienced and unlearned therein, and the treatment of the sick would be in all respects haphazard.[51]

These theories grounded in elements and humors also includes a different concept of the nature and action of divine beings than is operative in the

---

[49] Gordon 2011a: 49n81 argues that we should careful about presuming that elaborate consecration rituals lie behind most of the extant amulets. "In my view elaborate consecration was an ideal associated with 'high' ritual magical practice, a theoretical norm that was usually not followed (cf. Damigeron-Evax 46.3: *'hunc antem de qua vis consecratione consecras'*; Socrates and Dionysius 39.7, where 'consecration' involves simply the act of engraving and fitting into a ring)."

[50] Hippocrates, *de natura hominis* 7. The precise dates and authorship of the Hippocratic treatises have been much debated.

[51] Hippocrates, *de prisca medicina* 1.1.

ideas of their competitors, and some of the early Hippocratic treatises provide the best evidence for the emic ideas of magical practitioners, even if the polemical context must be taken into account. In the treatise *On the Sacred Disease* (i.e., epilepsy), the Hippocratic author argues that this disease is no more sacred or divinely caused than any other, but "being at a loss and having no treatment that would help, they [the rival healers] concealed and sheltered themselves behind superstition, and called this illness sacred in order that their utter ignorance might not be manifest."[52] One of the fundamental assumptions at issue in the dispute is the role of the gods in causing illness, and the Hippocratic doctors vehemently claim that the idea of gods causing disease is contrary to the nature of divinity. "A god is more likely to purify and to sanctify than he is to cause defilement." Disease is an impurity and a defilement of the normal human condition, but the gods are superlatively pure and holy, so it makes no sense that the gods could cause this kind of defilement.

This Hippocratic idea about the gods finds parallels in various philosophical schools, from Plato's Academy and Aristotle's Peripatetic school to the Stoics, but, as the polemic context of the treatise indicates, it runs directly counter to other contemporary emic ideas about the role of divine beings in disease. The Hippocratic author mocks the ridiculous methods of his rivals:

> [Men put] the blame for each form of the affliction on a particular god. If the patient imitate a goat, if he roar, or suffer convulsions on the right side, they say that the Mother of the Gods is to blame. If he utter a loud and piercing cry, they liken him to a horse and blame Poseidon.[53]

He taunts these rivals as charlatans and quacks, with crazy ideas about the causes of disease, but we can see the underlying logic of these other healers—the symptoms of the patient are symbolic indicators of the divinity responsible for the condition. If the patient makes a sound like a horse, that indicates that Poseidon, father of horses, has acted, whereas goat sounds are rather associated with the Mother of the Gods.

The underlying assumption in all these cases is that a personal agent is responsible for all these abnormal conditions, and this theory appears to have been far more prevalent and mainstream than the elemental/humoral theories of the Hippocratics or even the sympathetic theories of other schools. While the adherents to such theories were less inclined to write systematic treatises than the Hippocratics or philosophers, the surviving evidence more often points to an underlying theory of personal agency

[52] Hippocrates, *de morbo sacro* I.
[53] Hippocrates, *de morbo sacro* IV.

than to some other emic theory. If some abnormal harm or affliction besets an individual that cannot be attributed to the agency of another person or observable normal agent, then some extra-ordinary power must be at work.[54] To counteract this extra-ordinary power, extra-ordinary means are necessary, which is to say, magic.

Many amulets reveal this underlying assumption with their plea for protection against unspecified or unknown demonic forces. Indeed, the term *daimon* in Greek, in the earliest attested usages in Homer and other early poetry, simply means some unknown divine power. Such an entity might be a spirit of a dead person, a minor divinity of the trees or streams, or even a major Olympian god, but its identity is unknown to the one using the term. Later, the term *daimon* comes to designate particular classes of divine or supernatural entities, most often spirits of the dead and minor divinities whose benevolence is not to be taken for granted, but they remain entities of more than human power.[55]

In times of crisis, then, the agency of such a being may be suspected, as in this amulet designed to ward off fever from a child.

> I, Abrasax, shall deliver. Abrasax am I! ABRASAX ABRASICHO'OU, help little Sophia-Priskilla. Get hold of and do away with what comes to little Sophia-Priskilla, whether it is a Shivering Fit—get hold of it! Whether a Phantom—get hold of it! Whether a Daimon—get hold of it! I, Abrasax, shall deliver. Abrasax am I! ABRASAX ABRASICHO'OU. Get hold of, get hold of and do away with . . . what comes to little Sophia-Priskilla on this very day, whether it is a Shivering Fit—do away with it! Whether a Daimon—do away with it![56]

Little Sophia-Priskilla is afflicted with fever and chills, perhaps even hallucinations, and the amulet is intended to drive away whatever entity is inflicting such suffering upon her. In fact, two divine entities are imagined here: the *daimon* or personified fever and the supremely powerful god, Abrasax, who can ward off the attacking demon and deliver the poor little girl from her sufferings. Most protective and healing magics that work with the underlying theory of personal agency in fact operate with either or both of these kinds of agents. Some merely address the demonic force that is causing (or might come to cause) the harm, whereas others just address the deity who has the power to relieve the suffering.

While Sophia-Priskilla's amulet acts through the rhetorical device of claiming the power of Abrasax, other such devices invoke the divinity

---

[54] Murdock 1980 discusses the widespread appearance of such 'spirit aggression theories' in cultures studied by anthropologists.

[55] For more on the history of daimones, see Brenk 1986, as well as ch. 10, pp. 323–328.

[56] PGM LXXXIX.1–27.

whose aid is desired, such as a second- or third-century CE gold lamella from Amphipolis in Thrace.

> *Barouch Adōnai Iaō Sabaōth Elōaie Ouriēl Michaēl Raphaēl Anaēl Phanaēl Saraphil Istraēl Ailam, Semesilam, Thobarrabau Abrasax Ablathanalba Panchouchi Thassouth, Iarbatha Gramme Phibaō Chnēmēoch Akramma-chamari Sesengenbarpharangēs,* protect from every male and female demon, Phaeinos who Paramona bore, *Melchias, Melchias,* O holy god of the holy [ones], only guard of the Aions, *E.IBGACHRSATAN.*[57]

The holy god of the holy is invoked by a wide variety of names to protect Phaeinos from any possible kind of demon, be it male or female. Different gods may be invoked by name or by one of the many special epithets or even secret magical names that are associated with the god. These names and invocations may be inscribed on amulets of papyrus or precious metal or even engraved minutely on precious stones.

On the tiny surfaces of these materials, images often take the place of words, and a god may be invoked by its image rather than (or in addition to) the inscription of its name. An image of Poseidon may serve to ward off shipwreck, whereas Hekate may be preferred for an amulet against magical or demonic attack. For unusual problems, unusual gods may be sought out, and the figures of Egyptianizing gods such as Harpokrates appear with increasing frequency in the Roman imperial period, for the alien wisdom of Egypt and its traditional associations with magic provide these deities with extra cachet. Other even stranger figures appear, including the cock-headed anguipede often labeled Abrasax, whose rooster head and snake feet signify his solar and chthonic powers. Often we cannot be sure of the intended purpose of an amulet, but the presence of *voces magicae* or other kinds of invocation suggests a magical use, such as an amulet from Aquileia in the Museo Archeologico Nazionale museum depicting Hermes with his caduceus and several stars, with Abrasax engraved on the back.[58] In other cases, the inscription assists our interpretation, as in an amulet engraved with a picture of Perseus holding the gorgon's head, inscribed with the words, "Flee, gout, Perseus pursues you!" The power of Perseus and the terrifying gorgon's head are deployed to repel the gout from the sufferer's foot.[59]

While some amulets depict the power invoked to help, others depict also the power that threatens. Numerous amulets depict a rider trampling and spearing a female figure; the rider is sometimes identified as Solomon, legendary for his control of demons, and the target is one of the demons

---

[57] GMA #38.
[58] Inv. R.C.1219 = SGGII Aq 18.
[59] Heim 1893: 481 #59.

Figure 15. Abrasax amulet Kelsey 26054 rev, © Genevra Kornbluth, by permission; Scorpion amulet GB-BM-MMEu_G 180, EA 56180 = CBd 719 (image by Christopher Faraone, by permission). (See plate 8b.)

that preys on pregnant women and infants (Gello, Mormo, Lilith, Abyzou, Obyzouth, etc.).[60] Other amulets simply have the threatening form. Numerous amulets of yellow-brown stone bear the image of a scorpion, the very venomous beast that they are intended to repel (figure 15).[61] The sore-throat amulet with the grape cluster likewise depicts the problem, the swollen uvula, rather than the power called upon to bring relief. The diminishing word triangle on the other side of the gem serves to illustrate the shrinking of the swelling, performing the desired effect of the magic, the *deletio morbi*, the removal of the disease (figure 12).

The name of the demonic power responsible for the affliction may likewise be diminished through ritual inscription, like the name of Gorgophonos, which is written out in a wing-formation that is surrounded by an exorcistic prayer, "I adjure you by the sacred name to heal Dionysius, whom Herakleia bore from every shivering fit and fever," banishing the demonic fever demon from the sufferer.[62] Faraone has argued that a similar

---

[60] Cp. *Testament of Solomon* 58. See Dasen 2015: 181–184 for this type of amulet; Johnston 1995 for the type of demon.

[61] GB-BM-MMEu_G 180, EA 56180 = CBd 719 in figure 15.

[62] Faraone 2012b: 29–30. He suggests an earlier stage of oral performance behind this tradition, "the wing- and heart-formations on amulets are written versions of earlier disap-

effect is at work with the amulets that diminish the word 'Ablanathanalba,' a palindromic name for a solar power associated with the burning of fevers. As the name of Ablanathanalba is erased, character by character, so his heating power is removed from the sufferer.[63]

Faraone suggests that such a strategy may be a textualization of an earlier (and probably persisting) oral tradition of verbal incantations such as are preserved only in literary depictions and late manuals. However, with the growth of the epigraphic habit and the increasing textualization of the Greco-Roman world, the significance of such word triangles may have altered. Rather than being perceived as a diminishment of the power, the repeated writing of the name becomes instead an emphasis added to the invocation. Thus, the name of Ablanathanalba might be written in a triangle form to add the power of this solar deity to a curse, repeating the name many times to increase the effect.[64]

The transformations of the names and invocations inscribed on the amulets in the process of retranscription over time can lead to the production of incomprehensible *voces magicae* of the *hocus-pocus* type. An invocation to the eternally thirsty Tantalus to drink up the flow of blood in an amulet for bleeding appears as a diminishing triangle of the nonsense letters *dipstnalamepie*, transforming the Greek for "thirsty Tantalus, drink the blood" (*dipsas Tantale haima pie*).[65] The most spectacular transformation uncovered by scholars is the set of *hocus-pocus* words known as the *ephesia grammata*, which turn out to derive from early hexametrical verses in which the god Paian (Apollo) promises protection from dangers on earth or sea or sky.

Paieon, for in every direction you send averting charms,| and you spoke these immortal verses to mortal men:| "As down the shady mountains in a dark-and-glittering land| a child leads out of Persephone's garden by necessity for milking| that four-footed holy attendant of Demeter,| a she-goat with an untiring stream of rich milk."[66]

The first few words of Paian's averting charm, 'As down the shadowy mountain' (*hossa kata skiarōn oreōn*) become *aski kataski*, while the 'goat' (*aix*) and 'four-footed one' (*tetrabēmona*) become *lix* and *tetrax*.

---

pearing 'speech-acts'—oral performances in which the demon's name was gradually reduced in speech and then finally replaced by complete silence" (Faraone 2012b: 6).

[63] Faraone 2012b: 31–33. Note that Greek θ is a single letter represented by 'th' in English at the center of the palindrome.

[64] Faraone 2012b: 67–78.

[65] δίψας Τάνταλε αἷμα πίε into διψτναλαμεπιε, as Faraone 2012b: 35–49 argues; cp. Faraone 2009.

[66] The text and translation, along with several interpretive essays, may be found in Faraone and Obbink 2013.

These meaningless words, collected together as *aski, kataski, lix, tetrax, aision,* and *damnameneus,* are known as the *ephesia grammata,* probably originally meaning "averting words" (taking *ephesia* from *ephiemi,* to avert), but later understood to mean "words from Ephesus." The late lexicon of Photius describes them as incomprehensible charms that brought invincibility to an Ephesian wrestler, but also as warding magics (*alexipharmaka*).

> Ephesia Grammata: Some charms hard to understand, which Kroisos also spoke on the pyre. And in the Olympics, when a Milesian and Ephesian were wrestling, the Milesian could not defeat his opponent in wrestling because that other one had the Ephesian letters on a knucklebone. When this was revealed and they were removed from him, the Ephesian fell thirty times in a row. Ephesian incomprehensibles: some Ephesian charms which are hard to understand, as was said before. Ephesian letters: also Ephesian warding magics, some names and phrases having an innate remedy for suffering.[67]

The *ephesia grammata* appear, either as these words or in various forms of evolution from the hexameters to the words, in a number of magical spells over an astonishingly long period, from a fifth-century BCE lead tablet in Crete to a fourth-century CE spell book in the collection of the Greco-Egyptian Greek Magical Papyri. In all these uses, however, the formula in whatever form retains its protective power, showing that the original significance was never entirely lost.[68]

CONCLUSIONS

The incomprehensibility of the *ephesia grammata,* what in modern etic terms we might call the coefficient of weirdness, clearly mark the performance of these words as something beyond the ordinary, and the tales of their extra-ordinary efficacy likewise reinforce their classification as magic. Although originally channeling the protective power of the god, this *hocus-pocus* formula derives its authority from its place in the ongoing tradition, rather than a comprehensible appeal to divine power. Other amulets function in different ways, calling on divine power through their materials, their texts, or their images—or the combination of those things. The boundary, however, between magical incantations that harness the power of the gods and other forms of accessing divine power remains difficult to discern. Does calling on a god to ward off enchantments or cure a fever count as magic or religion, or is there no significant difference that can be

---

[67] Photius, *Lexicon, s.v. Ephesia Grammata.*
[68] As I have argued in detail in Edmonds 2013 in Faraone and Obbink 2013.

drawn, either by the ancient Greeks and Romans themselves or by us as modern scholars?

J. Z. Smith's distinction between the religion of *here*, the religion of *there*, and the religion of *anywhere* provides a useful way of approaching the question.[69] The place *where* interactions with the divine take place is crucial to the classification of the ritual performance within the social order. Setting aside the category of *here* (which mostly pertains to domestic rites), we may contrast the requests for help and protection from the gods that take place at their normatively marked places, the temples and sanctuaries, with the kind of interactions involved in the use of magical amulets and healing rituals. To obtain the first kind of interactions, the mortal must go *there*, to the place of the gods. By contrast, the amulets function *anywhere*, regardless of which divine power they rely upon. They protect the bearers, who carry them on their persons anywhere and everywhere they go, from the myriad possible dangers of the world.

The contrast in *what* is involved is less significant. Healing rituals took place in the sanctuaries of healing gods such as Asclepius, and miraculous cures were recorded in the temple grounds. Often the sufferer would undertake a ritual incubation, sleeping within the temple to receive a visitation from the god.[70] As with magical healing, the visit to such a temple might be an extra-ordinary measure, undertaken when other kinds of remedies had failed, but the non-normative nature of the extra-ordinary efficacy of a miraculous cure is mitigated by the normative performance and social location. One inscription at Asclepius's temple at Epidaurus records the miraculous healing of a man whose wound continued to ooze pus.

> Gorgias of Heracleia with pus. In a battle he had been wounded by an arrow in the lung and for a year and a half had suppurated so badly that he filled sixty-seven basins with pus. While sleeping in the temple he saw a vision. It seemed to him the god extracted the arrow point from his lung. When day came he walked well, holding the point of the arrow in his hands.[71]

The god himself removes the arrow from Gorgias's lung and stops the oozing that had been going on for a year and a half. At other times, the god not only cures the affliction but brings additional help to the patient. Another Epidaurian inscription was erected by an athlete whose career was turned around by the god's intervention.

[69] J. Smith 2003, see the discussion in ch. 2, p. 40, n. 7, as well as ch. 6, p. 169, n. 46.

[70] The ritual of incubation involved various preliminary sacrifices and purifications, as well as special rites afterward to help preserve the memory of the dream. See now Ahearne-Kroll 2014 for a study of the role of Mnemosyne in such rites.

[71] B10 LiDonnici 1995 (Testimony 423 #30 Edelstein) (trans. from Edelstein and Edelstein 1945).

Hagestratus with headaches. He suffered from insomnia on account of headaches. When he came to the sanctuary he fell asleep and saw a dream. It seemed to him that the god cured him of his headaches and, making him stand up naked, taught him the lunge used in the pancratium. When day came he departed well, and not long afterwards he won in the pancratium at the Nemean games.[72]

Such inscriptions praising the god's power are one form of dedication in thanks to the god for the god's help, but other forms are less explicit, some mere tokens of gratitude like a silver cup or a crystal ring. Others are more symbolic; huge numbers of models of various body parts have been uncovered in the excavations of healing sanctuaries around the Mediterranean, tokens of the afflicted part the god has been asked to heal. Many were clearly mass produced in the vicinity for the use of visitors to the healing shrine, but it is not clear whether such symbols of healing were gifts made in thanks for the healing or tokens offered as part of the request. Like an amulet with the image of a grape-cluster designed to relieve an infected uvula, the terracotta arms, legs, wombs, toes, and the rest served as symbols of the afflicted part in need of divine power to cure.

Such votives that either give thanks to a god for help or request it are not confined to healing sanctuaries. Numerous votives were deposited in the temples of Poseidon either commemorating a successful rescue from shipwreck or requesting Poseidon's protection from shipwreck during an upcoming voyage. Like the shipwreck amulet made from an emerald engraved with the figure of Poseidon holding his trident, these votives symbolize the request for Poseidon's power and protection.

The most significant difference between these symbols of the power of the divine is not what kinds of thing they are (*what*), the sorts of dangers and afflictions for which the divine power is invoked (*why*), or even *how* the power of the god is brought to the mortal through symbolic representations. All those elements involve the vertical axis of communication, the interaction between mortal and divine—what the mortal gives the god, why the mortal makes the offering, and how the mortal gets the god to respond. The differences appear rather in the horizontal axis, the mortal audience for the performance, the context *where* the act occurs. The votive offerings for the gods are publicly displayed in a particular place, the sanctuary or temple of the god, while the magical amulets are kept private on the person. The public display of the votive serves in itself as an added gift to the god, since it proclaims the god's power to all passersby, whereas the power of the amulet resides wholly in its mode of creation, whether it is seen by others or not.

[72] B9 LiDonnici 1995 (29 Edelstein).

Evidence for the social reception of such amulets adds to the distinction drawn here in the normativity of the performance, and Gordon, making use of the anthropologist Bourdieu's concept of 'objective profanation,' draws attention to the element of the social location of such magic.[73] While the use of amulets was rarely prohibited by law in Greek or Roman contexts, there are suggestions that the wearing of amulets was not really within the bounds of normative behavior, but rather the province of marginal people—the rustics, the old wives and children, those too ignorant or backward to know any better. A fragment of comedy includes the wearing of *ephesia grammata* amulets as part of the description of the backward rustic who tries to show his sophistication in town:

> oiling his skin with golden perfumes, trailing cloaks, dragging slippers, eating hyacinth bulbs, gobbling cheeses, gulping down eggs, having whelks, drinking Chian wine, and on top of all that wearing lovely Ephesian letters in scraps of stitched leather.[74]

Pliny likewise marks the wearing of amulets as something that is not quite normative behavior, noting as part of a general decline of morals the new fashion of *even* men (*viri quoque*) wearing rings and amulets with the figures of Egyptian gods upon them.[75] That women should indulge in such superstitious behavior is one thing; that it should have spread to men is quite another! Such references attest at the same time to the ubiquity of protective amulets and to their status as not quite normative. Even if they were not, like curse tablets, considered a form of cheating within the agonistic contexts of the ancient Greco-Roman world, they were nonetheless not the ordinary mode of behavior. To hedge oneself about in daily life with these extra-ordinary means for protection might seem to be superfluous caution, a disproportionately anxious response to the perils of normal life. Likewise, to avail oneself of the remedies of the country folk and the old wives opens one to the suspicion of superstitiousness, of indulging in useless activities with no practical effect.

[73] See ch. 1, p. 19, n. 35, as well as ch. 5, p. 117, n. 4, and ch. 7, p. 189, n. 4 , and especially Gordon 1999a.

[74] Anaxilas, *The Harp-Maker* (II 268 K) from Athenaeus, *Deipnosophistae* 12.14.12–18 548C.

[75] Pliny, *HN* 33.12; cp. Bonner 1950: 7. The association between amulets and superstitious women also appears in Plutarch's account of the deathbed of the fifth-century BCE Athenian statesman Perikles, where the fact that he has permitted his anxious womenfolk to bedeck him with protective amulets shows the extent of his weakness and deterioration (Plutarch, *Vit. Per.* 38.2). Children, too, were often seen as in special need of amulets; cp. the common *bulla* amulet worn by free-born boys in Roman culture. Such simple amulets, however, have a much lower coefficient of weirdness than the amulets with Egyptian figures about which Pliny complains.

Alternatively, of course, the use of such extra-ordinary protective and healing measures could be seen as the sign of specialized occult knowledge, an understanding of the exceptions to the cosmic rules that govern the normal mortal order. Such arcane wisdom might signal a sage and benevolent person, close to the gods in his extra-ordinary understanding of the cosmic order, but such knowledge could likewise indicate a person with the ability to break mortal rules and the inclination to do so whenever he or she so chose. Whether seen as superstition or the occult, extra-ordinary protective and curative procedures could thus fall into the suspicious category of magic, indicated by the cues of the weirdness of the performance or the non-normative social location of the performer. Despite such suspicions, however, the evidence from both the material record and the texts indicates that many people of both genders, at all times and throughout the ancient Mediterranean world, made use of protective and curative magics, wore amulets, and chanted healing charms. Such protections and cures were not only for the threats of curses and other forms of hostile magic, a defense against the dark arts, but for all the perils of life, from venomous beasts to shipwrecks, from demonic attacks to sore throats. These protective and curative magics tapped into divine power, either directly through the gods or indirectly through the special powers of the plants, animal parts, or stones that comprised the amulets. These extra-ordinary, magical powers might be invoked through verbal incantations or by inscribed texts or even in the images engraved upon the amulets, but, rather than deriving from contact made with a divine power in a temple or holy sanctuary, the power reached the recipient anywhere he or she might be, focused through the amulet worn on the person or the charm uttered at the sickbed. In their various forms and applications, protective and healing magic provided extra-ordinary solutions for the crises of life, the problems or threats that seemed too great to handle by normal means.

6

Relationships with the Divine: Prayer and Magic

Why do the gods trouble to heed these spells and herbs, and fear to despise them? What mutual bond puts constraint upon them? Must they obey, or do they take pleasure in obedience? Is this subservience the reward of some piety unknown to us, or is it extorted by unuttered threats? Has witchcraft power over all the gods, or are these tyrannical spells addressed to one special deity who can inflict upon the world all the compulsion that he suffers himself?—By these witches the stars were first brought down from the swiftly-moving sky; and the clear moon, beset by dread incantations, grew dim and burned with a dark and earthy light.
(Lucan, *Pharsalia* 6.492–502)[1]

INTRODUCTION: THE PROBLEM OF MAGICAL PRAYER AND SACRIFICE

In reflecting on the power of the superwitch Erictho, Lucan points to the problem debated both in the ancient and modern considerations of magic. If magic is taken as non-normative religious activity, why should the gods respond to it? Prayer and supplication are often taken to be the most significant defining characteristic of religion in contrast to magic, so how can magical prayer exist? Invocations of various deities are, as we have seen

---

[1] *Quis labor hic superis, cantus herbasque sequendi,*| *Spernendique timor? cuius commercia pacti*| *Obstrictos habuere deos? Parere necesse est,*| *An iuvat? Ignota tantum pietate merentur,*| *An tacitis valuere minis? Hoc iuris in omnes*| *Est illis superos, an habent haec carmina certum*| *Imperiosa deum, qui mundum cogere, quidquid*| *Cogitur ipse, potest? Illic et sidera primum*| *Praecipiti deducta polo: Phoebeque serena*| *Non aliter, diris verborum obsessa venenis,*| *Palluit, et nigris terrenisque ignibus arsit.*

in the study of both curses and amulets, an important part of magical practices, but making claims for divine assistance is also part of normal religion. The question, as always, is how we can find the boundaries between the categories of normative religion and what gets labeled 'magic'; what cues are most significant in that labeling? It is worth taking a look at the general dynamics of the relationships between mortal and divine to understand what, if anything, falls into the category of magic, since the same basic structures and patterns of divine and mortal interactions underlie both ordinary and extra-ordinary acts of prayer and sacrifice.

Why make prayers and sacrifices? Mortals pray to the gods for an infinite variety of reasons; anything that is beyond the power of mortals may prompt an appeal to the gods who have power beyond that of mortals.[2] Even if some mortal wishes are more socially acceptable than others, a mortal may petition a deity in private or in public for help for self and friends or harm to enemies or anything in between. Such petitions to gods, just like appeals made to fellow mortals, consist of an address to the entity petitioned, an argument for why the petitioned should help the petitioner, and a description of what is desired. The one who offers the prayer or performs the ritual offering may be anyone who wants the prayer fulfilled, but some mortals are more qualified to contact the gods than others. It is worth noting, however, that there is no profession of priest in Greek religion, no priestly class as in the contemporary empires of the Near East or group of experts qualified by their expertise to perform the rituals.[3] Rather, the rites are performed by the one who is most appropriate in the circumstance, the one with the highest status to represent the community, or the one with the best relation with the deity in question and thus most likely to win a favorable response. The relationship with the deity is envisioned as a reciprocal relation of favors, not unlike the social relationships between mortals, and, like the mortal relationships, the dynamics of such a relation must be negotiated with care.

---

[2] Lucian, *Icaromenippus* 25 provides a humorous list of all the petitions Zeus has to listen to daily, ranging from the ridiculous to the sublime and endlessly contradicting and conflicting with one another. Although Versnel 1991b: 178–180 points to 'intention' as one of the categories by which modern scholars have distinguished magic from religion, he notes that the evidence from the Greco-Roman world does not support such a distinction and points to the roots of the criterion in the intra-Christian debates about the appropriateness of concrete, rather than abstract, aims for prayer.

[3] As Johnston 2008a: 177 notes, "In Greece there were very few 'professional' priests or priestesses, very few who kept the job for their whole lives or depended on it for their living. Instead, the priesthoods of most cults rotated among members of the elite class (or members of elite sub-groups, such as certain noble families)—every Greek knew how to perform basic priestly duties." In Rome, various priestly organizations did exist, but see Rüpke 2007: 216 on the "part-time" nature of their duties; most were still people who performed priestly duties in addition to other offices and honors.

If prayer is seen as a form of communication between mortal and divinity, an analysis of the rhetorical strategies that communication involves reveals the assumptions the one performing that communication makes about both himself (or herself) and the entity to whom he (or she) is communicating. As previously noted, Graf draws a useful distinction in his analysis of such acts. Any ritual of prayer or sacrifice involves not only a communication between the mortal worshipper and the deity, along a vertical axis from earth to heaven, but also a communication along a horizontal axis within the world of mortals.[4] Although modern scholars, with an etic perspective, can only observe the horizontal axis, the vertical axis is actually the most significant in the emic point of view of the performers of the ritual. They are making the prayers and sacrifices to contact the gods, even if the modern scholar can only observe the ways the performance of such rituals has impact upon the community and the status of the performers within it.

In addition to observing who is involved on the horizontal axis, the modern scholar can also note the times and places where and when these ritual acts of communication are performed. However, we can also analyze the texts of the prayers to see the ways in which the interrelation of the parties along the vertical axis is constructed, that is, how the one making the prayer depicts the relationship between the mortal and divine parties in the communication. The arguments in the prayers explain why the deity should grant the favor that the mortal requests, so those arguments reveal the way the mortal making the prayer imagines his own (or her own) relation with the deity addressed. The offerings, including animal sacrifices, that accompany prayers are further symbolic arguments to win the god's favor, so analysis of the sacrificial rituals also illuminates the relationship between mortal and immortal.

Earlier scholars, following the model of Frazer's distinction between magic and religion (itself grounded in much older theological disputes), have often differentiated magic from religion with regard to the attitude by which the mortal addresses the god, as well as by the types of aims sought in those addresses. While religion supplicates submissively, it is imagined, magic hubristically commands the gods, uttering coercive threats and expecting

---

[4] "Even if we admit that the communication conveying messages functions only at the horizontal level and that the gods are only symbolic objects making it possible for the communication to exist, it is still no less true that in the fiction of the ritual—theatrical, if you will—action there is another, vertical communicative axis. . . . This vertical communication is played out differently from the horizontal one and is conscious and carefully staged by the human actors: it is this communication that is spoken about by the indigenous people. The chance observer from outside, uninformed about theology and mythology, perceives only the interaction of the horizontal ritual messages whose signifiers are determined by an ancestral cultural tradition" (Graf 1997: 214). See the discussion in ch. 2, p. 50, n. 22.

automatic fulfillment of the demands.[5] Such a distinction, however, fails to fit with the actual evidence for prayers in the ancient Greco-Roman world, both those that might be labeled 'magic' and those that would not. The aims sought by all kinds of prayer span the range of possibilities, from the most selfish, concrete, and destructive to the most benevolent, abstract, and helpful. Likewise, supplication and coercion are not the only two choices, but instead extreme strategies on a spectrum of rhetorical strategies in prayer, and both are grounded in theological assumptions about the nature of the divine hierarchy that governs the cosmos. The available evidence presents a wide range of rhetorical strategies, and the choice of strategy in prayer and sacrifice is much more complex and nuanced than the simple grand dichotomy of supplication/coercion would suggest.

The most useful way of distinguishing magical prayer lies in the analysis of some of these strategies for performance, since the prayers found in such magical sources as the Greek Magical Papyri, the curse tablets, and the amulets all share a peculiar focus on the immediately present moment of contact with the divinity, in contrast to other prayers, which more often employ rhetorical strategies that emphasize the past history of the mortal and the god or make promises for the future of such a relation. The magical prayers, however, base their arguments for divine favor upon the present actions of the one praying—the offerings being made, the pure status of the ritual performer, the secret names being recited, and so forth. Moreover, it is the status of the performer that counts above all in magical prayer, not when or where the ritual of communication is performed. Whereas traditional religious prayers and sacrifices tend to be performed in traditionally sanctioned spaces and at traditionally hallowed times, magical rites may take place anywhere and at any moment when the present necessity becomes pressing.

A general overview of the mechanics of prayer in the polytheistic religions of the Greco-Roman world provides a context in which to see how distinctions may be drawn. A survey of the way prayer is performed in ordinary religious contexts helps distinguish what might have appeared as extra-ordinary within that religious context and hence labeled as 'magic.' A comparison with sources such as the Greek Magical Papyri helps to

---

[5] As Graf 1991: 188 describes it, "The most widespread theory about the difference between magic and religion (at least among classicists), [is] the one made famous by Sir James Frazer, namely, that the magician constrains, coerces, and forces the divinity to do his will, whereas religious man meekly submits himself to God's overpowering will. (The slight denigration of religion is Sir James's.) Among anthropologists, this Frazerian dichotomy is long dead and buried. In classical scholarship however, it loomed very large and still is among us, explicitly or, more often nowadays, implicitly." Versnel 1991b and Braarvig 1999 discuss the history of the coercive/submissive dichotomy, suggesting (albeit in different ways) that it may at least retain a use within a modern, etic, scholarly approach.

highlight the differences that exist within the strategies for negotiating the relationships with the divine.

MECHANICS OF PRAYER

The two most essential concepts in understanding the complex networks of reciprocal relations between gods and humans in ancient Greek thought are *euchē* and *charis*, words that may be translated into English as 'prayer' and 'favor,' although both terms imply a different set of meanings than the English words.[6] Relationships with the divine consist in the reciprocal exchange of favors in the same way that social relationships among humans do, and the prayers addressed by humans to the gods are an essential part of shaping this exchange.

The word for prayer, *euchē*, derives from the verb *euchesthai*, a verb that means to make some sort of claim for oneself within a social context. Homeric heroes boast of their superiority, in martial prowess or in distinguished lineage, with this verb, but they also use *euchesthai* to describe the place and community from which they come. By contrast, mortals asking for divine favor use *euchesthai* to make a request of the gods for help or benefit. As a number of scholarly studies have shown, the various meanings of 'boast' and 'pray' come together in this underlying sense of making a claim.[7] As Depew notes,

> The verb denotes an interactive process of guiding another in assessing one's status and thus one's due. The purpose is not to "boast" or "declare" something about one's past, but to make a claim on someone in the present, whether in terms of an actual request or of recognition and acknowledgement of status. . . . When Homeric heroes εὔχονται, what they are doing is asserting their identity and their value in the society they inhabit, and by means of this assertion creating a context in which the claim they are making on another member of that society will be appropriate and compelling.[8]

Homeric heroes on the battlefield make claims of prowess and ancestry to guide one another in assessing how much of a threat they are on the battlefield; someone with enormous military prowess and divine ancestry should

---

[6] As Pulleyn 1997: 64 notes, *euchē* can serve as a general term for various types of prayers that can be further specified, such as *ara, lita, hiketeia*, etc. For the general mentality underlying Greek and Roman prayer, see Versnel 1981: esp. 42–50 on *charis* as 'favor' rather than simply 'thanks.'

[7] Cp. Adkins 1969; Depew 1997; contra Muellner 1976. See also Aubriot-Sévin 1992: 199–253.

[8] Depew 1997: 232.

be avoided or treated with immense respect, rather than contemptuously assaulted.[9]

When a mortal prays to a god, however, the aim of the claim is usually somewhat different. The mortal generally stresses his or her own inferiority in relation to the god's greatness but often reminds the god of existing ties of obligation between them. The nature of these ties may differ greatly, but the point of the claim being made is always that the god now has some obligation to grant favor to the mortal, and the logic of the prayer always depends on this process of establishing the nature of the obligation.

This logic is best understood in terms of the dynamics of a reciprocal exchange of favors, *charis*, between the mortal and the divinity.[10] Reciprocity does not imply equality, however; what each party contributes depends upon the relative status of the party. A mortal gives the sort of things mortals can give, in proportion to his or her status as a mortal, while a divinity provides the sort of things that a god can provide, as befits the divinity's status as a deity. As Mauss noted in his classic essay on the gift, in such systems of reciprocal exchange, the gift functions as a symbol of the giver, his identity, status, and place in society, but also as a symbol of the receiver and indeed of the relationship between the parties.[11] The lower-status mortal offers to the god a token of his respect, be it a hymn of praise or the slaughter of a hundred oxen, and this token at the same time marks the mortal's place in the relationship as the inferior and indicates that the bond of the relationship between them obligates the god to provide some return.

The prayer of Pelops to Poseidon in Pindar's *Olympian 1* again helps illustrate the dynamic here. Pelops, when he wants aid in winning Hippodameia, calls upon Poseidon, reminding him of their previous relationship (in this case, an intimate sexual one). "If the loving gifts of Cyprian Aphrodite result in any gratitude [*charis*], Poseidon, then restrain the bronze spear of Oenomaus, and speed me in the swiftest chariot to Elis, and bring me to victory."[12] Pelops refers to the *charis* he provided for Poseidon and asks for *charis* in return, in this case the binding back of

---

[9] Of course, it may turn out that the identities revealed in this exchange of identity claims indicate that another kind of interaction is appropriate, as in the famous case of Glaucus and Diomedes (Homer, *Iliad* 6.235–236) where they discover that they are familial guest-friends and part to seek other opponents after ceremoniously exchanging armor with one another as a token of their continuing *xenia* relationship.

[10] Cp. Pulleyn 1997: 37: "One can see that the relationship of the Greeks with their gods in prayer as in all other respects can best be thought of as a continuum of reciprocal χάρις extending both forwards and backwards in time."

[11] See Mauss 1967 for the general anthropological theory.

[12] Φίλια δῶρα Κυπρίας| ἄγ᾽ εἴ τι, Ποσείδαον, ἐς χάριν| τέλλεται, πέδασον ἔγχος Οἰνομάου χάλκεον,| ἐμὲ δ᾽ ἐπὶ ταχυτάτων πόρευσον ἁρμάτων| ἐς Ἆλιν, κράτει δὲ πέλασον.

Oenomaus's deadly spear and a chariot swift enough to win the race. The favors they exchange are not the same or even equal in value, but each provides something within his capacity to give to the other.

THE FORM OF THE PRAYER

Prayers in Greek religion, as scholars have noted, generally have a tripartite form, consisting in a preliminary invocation, some sort of argument or narrative that explains why the divinity should grant the prayer, and the actual wish itself.[13] The invocation serves to get the god's attention and request the god's presence, often invoking the god by a variety of epithets and titles that identify the god. Such addresses are not so much to make sure that the prayer reaches the right entity as to begin the process of establishing the identities of the participants in the prayer relation. Often these invocations enumerate the many places where the god has power and the many epithets that indicate the special powers and functions of the god. The process of identifying the participants in the relationship continues in the argument section, which often sets out a narrative of the god's past deeds or of the previous relationship, the history of the interactions and exchanges of favors between god and mortal. The actual wish of the prayer may come at the very beginning, but often comes at the end of the prayer, following all the descriptions of the status of the god and the mortal and their relationship that provide the reasons why the god should grant the mortal's request.

The classic example of this sort of prayer is Chryses's plea to Apollo in the first book of the *Iliad*. The old priest, having been spurned by Agamemnon when he sought to ransom his captured daughter, calls upon Apollo to punish the Greeks.

> He went forth in silence along the shore of the loud-resounding sea, and earnestly then, when he had gone apart, the old man prayed to the lord Apollo, whom fair-haired Leto bore: "Hear me, god of the silver bow, who stand over Chryse and holy Cilla, and rule mightily over Tenedos, Sminthian god, if ever I roofed over a temple to your

---

[13] The central part is described differently by various scholars: *argumentum, pars epica, eulogia, mnematio.* Furley and Bremer 2001: 50–64 provide a good discussion of the parts; cp. Aubriot-Sévin 1992: 199–200; Graf 1991: 189, etc. Ausfeld's fundamental study simply defines it as the part that is neither invocation nor the wish itself. "Plerumque sunt divisae preces in tres partes, quarum una comprehendit invocationem, altera semper fere media, si modo ab ceteris partibus, accuratius secerni potest, omnia continet, ut generaliter dicam, quae neque ad invocationem neque ad tertiam partem, preces ipsas, pertinent" (Ausfeld 1903: 514–515).

pleasing, or if ever I burned to you fat thigh-pieces of bulls and goats, fulfill this prayer for me: let the Danaans pay for my tears by your arrows."[14]

Chryses begins with the simple call, 'hear me,' followed by the descriptive epithet 'god of the silver bow,' and then mentions the various places in which Apollo wields power. He reminds the god of the many favors he has done for the god, building temples and making sacrifices, and then makes his request for harm to the Greeks.

Chryses's claim is a strong one: not only has the relationship between god and mortal been in existence for some time, but Chryses has done a number of favors that obligate some return. Pulleyn, in his typology of prayer requests, calls this form of prayer the *da quia dedi*, 'give because I have given,' and it is the strongest kind of claim one can make in a prayer. Gods, of course, can refuse to fulfill their obligations just as humans can, but Chryses has, as it were, racked up some credit, and it is the god's turn to provide the favors.[15]

The analogy of a credit line is perhaps useful for understanding another kind of prayer strategy, the *da quia dedisti*, 'give because you have given previously.' Here the mortal relies on the fact that the relationship has been established and that reciprocal exchanges of favors have taken place in the past. Like someone borrowing on an established line of credit, the mortal can ask the god for a favor, with the understanding that the relationship will continue.

Such a relationship is depicted in Sappho's charming poem, where she adapts the prayer form to call on Aphrodite for help in her latest love affair.

Ornate-throned immortal Aphrodite, wile-weaving daughter of Zeus, I entreat you: do not overpower my heart, mistress, with ache and anguish, but come here, if ever in the past you heard my voice from afar and acquiesced and came, leaving your father's golden house, with chariot yoked: beautiful swift sparrows whirring fast-beating wings brought you above the dark earth down from heaven through the mid-air, and soon they arrived; and you, blessed one, with a smile on your immortal face asked what was the matter with me this time and why was I calling this time and what in my maddened heart I most wished to happen for myself: "Whom am I to persuade this time to lead you back to her love? Who wrongs you, Sappho? If she runs away, soon she shall pursue; if she does not accept gifts, why, she shall give them instead; if she does not love, soon she shall love even

---

[14] Homer, *Iliad* 1.34–40.
[15] Cp. Naiden 2013: 131–182 on the various reasons for failed sacrifices.

against her will." Come to me now again and deliver me from oppressive anxieties; fulfil all that my heart longs to fulfil, and you yourself be my fellow-fighter.[16]

Sappho's poem not only includes the formulaic invocation and epithets, but imagines the response of the goddess. The repeated reference to 'this time' emphasizes the longstanding nature of the relationship between the goddess of love and her worshipper. Even though there is no reference to what Sappho has done for Aphrodite, the very fact that Aphrodite has helped her in previous situations shows their ongoing relationship and establishes the pattern for this new situation.

It is worth noting that the relationship between god and mortal need not be as direct and personal as Sappho's; mortals can appeal to a relationship that has been set up by some other mortal, especially someone closely linked to them. The logic of the prayer is thus *da quia dedit*: give because he (or, less frequently, she) gave previously. In the *Odyssey*, Penelope prays to Athena, making reference to the many sacrifices and honors her husband, Odysseus, made to the goddess and the longstanding relationship between them. Even Odysseus's swineherd Eumaeus can draw on the credit Odysseus established with the local divinities through his past sacrifices when he invokes the nymphs and prays for Odysseus's return. The best analogy here is with the relationship of hospitality, *xenia*, where the guest-host obligations between two individuals extend to their families, even for generations.[17] Telemachus makes such claims upon Nestor and Menelaus, praying in the same formulaic words to both, "I beseech thee, if ever my father, noble Odysseus, promised aught to thee of word or deed and fulfilled it in the land of the Trojans, where you Achaeans suffered woes, be mindful of it now, I pray thee, and tell me the very truth."[18] Such a plea is not as compelling as one made on the basis of favors previously rendered by the one praying, but it nevertheless makes a strong claim from the previous relationship.

Another kind of indirect relationship appears particularly in later sources, when the divine hierarchies become more elaborate. Rather than appealing directly to a powerful god for a favor, the prayer might be directed at a lesser entity, who might be imagined to be more ready to respond to a minor request. Rather than mentioning a past relationship with this power, the one praying nevertheless may invoke the authority of the

[16] Sappho, fr. 1.

[17] Cp. Homer, *Odyssey* 4.758, 17.239. The guest-friendship relation of Glaucus and Diomedes (*Iliad* 6.235–236) goes back to their respective grandfathers.

[18] Homer, *Odyssey* 3.98–101 = 4.328–331. λίσσομαι, εἴ ποτέ τοί τι πατὴρ ἐμός, ἐσθλὸς Ὀδυσσεύς,| ἢ ἔπος ἠέ τι ἔργον ὑποστὰς ἐξετέλεσσε| δήμῳ ἔνι Τρώων, ὅθι πάσχετε πήματ' Ἀχαιοί,| τῶν νῦν μοι μνῆσαι, καί μοι νημερτὲς ἐνίσπες.

higher divine power to ensure that the lesser divinity carries out the request. The previous choice of the higher deity to grant a favor to the petitioner provides sufficient cause for the lesser power to do what the petitioner asks. A Roman prayer addressed to the powers within herbs illustrates this dynamic; the petitioner asks the herbs to yield their potency, since the goddess Terra herself has granted permission to gather the herbs and the deity of medicine has also shown his favor. "Hither, hither come with your powers, because the one who gave you birth, she herself has given me leave to gather you, and he also to whom medicine is entrusted has bestowed his favor."[19] The prayer is not directly addressed to Mother Earth, but her previously granted favor underlies the request.

All of these forms of prayer depend upon the relationship established in the past, but other forms of prayer look more to the future than the past. One of the most common forms of prayer is the simple *do ut des*: I give so that you might give. No real history of relationship between mortal and divinity is implied. Rather, the mortal is initiating a relationship by offering some favor—a gift offering, a sacrifice, or even simply praises in the prayer, in hopes that the god will reciprocate. The mortal's gift in the present is intended to make the deity feel obliged to respond with a favor in the future. While such a claim is not as strong as a reference to a long history of offerings to the god, the mortal nevertheless does make the request from the position of the one who has already provided a favor, rather than one already in debt for previous favors. Such a prayer may well be offered by those who do have a longstanding relation with the divinity, but the emphasis is on the present gift and the new reciprocation that is expected, rather than on the past.[20]

A more presumptuous and daring (or desperate) request is *da ut dem*: give so that I will give. Rather than offering something in hopes of a future return, the one praying asks for a favor and promises reciprocation in the future. Again, such a prayer does not preclude a previous relationship between mortal and deity, but the emphasis is on the promises for the future instead of the interactions of the past. This strategy underlies the common practice of votive dedications, offerings made in return after the deity grants the request for some favor. Such a request is weaker than other

---

[19] *huc huc adeste cum vestris virtutibus, quia, quae creavit, ipsa permisit mihi, ut colligam vos; favit hic etiam, cui medicina tradita est* (Anon., *Precatio omnium herbarum*, vol. 1 of *Minor Latin Poets* in the Loeb Classical Library, translated by J. Wight Duff and Arnold M. Duff). Cp. the invocation in PGM IV.2967–3006, which likewise asks the daimon of the herbs to increase their efficacy by reference to the more powerful deities who were responsible for their creation.

[20] Cp., e.g., Hippolytus's prayer to Artemis in Euripides (*Hippolytus* 115ff.), where he offers a garland and asks for a happy end to his life. Even here, however, he makes reference to his special ongoing relationship with the goddess.

forms of prayer, since the divinity has no past precedent or present gift that might motivate reciprocation but is rather being asked to initiate the reciprocal exchange. This weakness is recognized in the scene in Aristophanes's *Peace*, when Trygaeus tries to induce Hermes to help them rescue Peace with the promise of future honors, comically transferred from other gods.

> And so, my dear Hermes, lend us an eager hand, and help us pull her out, and in your honor we'll celebrate the Great Panathenaea and all the other rites of the gods—the Mysteries, the Dipolieia, the Adonia, all for Hermes; and when the other cities are rid of their troubles, they'll sacrifice to you everywhere as Hermes Averter of Trouble. And you'll get other benefits too; to begin with, I'm giving you this as a gift [*gives him a golden bowl*], to use for libations.[21]

Hermes is swayed more by a drink right away than by the promise that the great festival of the Panathenaia will in the future be celebrated in his honor rather than Athena's; the situation is Aristophanic comedy, but the point is that future promises (or even past gifts) are less convincing than presents in the present.

At times, however, such a promise of future payback is the only available strategy, as in the case of a mortal in dire and immediate peril, such as a shipwreck. In such situations, the *da ut dare possim*: give so that I shall be able to give, type of prayer is most appropriate, since the mortal is emphasizing the fact that, if the deity does not provide help right away, there will be no ongoing reciprocal relationship, no chance of the mortal providing offerings at some later point in time. This form of prayer underlies the deposit of many votive offerings, since a mortal might vow to make a certain offering to a god as a return for the granting of the mortal's prayer. Shipwrecks are not the only occasion for such distressed and desperate pleas; more metaphorical SOS calls might be made for illnesses or other kinds of danger. In Aeschylus, Orestes and Electra pray to Zeus for help against Clytemnestra and Aegisthus on the grounds that, if they are destroyed, then no one will be left to continue the relationship that their father and family had with the god.

> Zeus, Zeus, look down on these things! Behold the orphan brood of the eagle father, of him who died in the twisting coils of the fearsome viper! The bereaved children are hard pressed by ravenous hunger, for they are not yet full-grown so as to be able to bring home to the nest the prey their father hunted. So too you can see this woman, Electra, and me, children robbed of their father, both alike in banish-

---

[21] Aristophanes, *Peace* 385–425. Note that the chorus refers to previous sacrifices of pigs as well as promising more in the future.

ment from their home. And if you allow us nestlings to perish, whose father was the great sacrificer who greatly glorified you, from whence will you get the honour of a fine feast given with comparable generosity? If you let the brood of the eagle perish, you would never again be able to send mortals signs that they would readily believe; and if this ruling stock is allowed to shrivel away entirely, it cannot minister to your altars on days when oxen are sacrificed. Take care of us, and you can raise this house from littleness to greatness, a house that to all appearance is now utterly fallen.[22]

Orestes even raises the possibility that, if Zeus refuses to help them now, mortals in the future will not trust in the gods to help them; the emphasis is on the choice between positive or negative future consequences, rather than on the past. The one praying stresses his helplessness, his complete inability to provide something in the present that would oblige a favorable return; instead, the prayer relies on the divinity's abundance of power to take care of someone who is so helpless. Rather than relying on credit built up in the past or the offering of a present favor, the one praying asks the divinity to open a relation that may involve reciprocity in the future. Such a prayer resembles the ritual of supplication more often found in human contexts, where one mortal supplicates (*lissesthai*) another by completely abasing himself and praising the power of the one being supplicated rather than by making a claim to a particular kind of treatment on the basis of his own honors (*euchesthai*). While such an appeal is weak by comparison with other kinds of appeals, it relies on evoking the idea of the whole reciprocal system, pleading that the god's action in the present will enable the reciprocal relations between mortals and divinities to continue.[23]

Mortals, however, continue to make prayers to the gods in hopes of having them answered, even despite the abundant examples of failed prayers and sacrifices.[24] Sanctuaries, especially those of protective and

[22] Aeschylus, *Choe* 246–263. Note that Orestes also refers to the past relationship of his father (*da quia dedit*), but the emphasis is on the danger that there will be no future relationship.

[23] Gould 1973: 92–95 points out that supplication (ἱκετεία) also takes place within a reciprocal system that creates obligations between the parties. "Supplication involves a form of self-abasement which constitutes an inversion of the normal patterns of behaviour. A normal face to face encounter between two men who are not φίλοι involves, in ancient Greek society, a transaction of challenge and counter-challenge in a context of competing claims to τιμή. The ritual of supplication, on the other hand, puts the new arrival 'out of play' in terms of the normal 'game' of competition, precisely because the suppliant's behaviour is an inversion of normal expected behaviour. Before the game of challenge and counter-challenge can commence the suppliant 'surrenders': the match is now a 'walk-over' and the other 'competitor' must now play according to a new set of rules" (Gould 1973: 95).

[24] Naiden 2013: 131–182 devotes a whole chapter to discussing failed sacrifices.

salvific gods such as the Great Gods at Samothrace, were crowded with votive offerings made by those thanking the gods for exercising their power, but it was observed even in antiquity that the number of those whose prayers were not granted must have far outnumbered those who wishes were fulfilled.

> When someone expressed astonishment at the votive offerings in Samothrace, his comment was, "There would have been far more, if those who were not saved had set up offerings."[25]

This cynical remark, attributed to Diogenes the Cynic as well as to the notorious atheist Diagoras of Melos, shows just how prevalent the custom was.

In all these forms of prayer, the mortal praying articulates some form of reciprocal relationship, actual or potential, between the mortal and the divinity. This relationship is often reinforced by conditional curses, by which the mortal calls down divine punishment upon himself and his community if he should violate the good faith of the relationship.[26] The mortal refers to the gifts to the god (either given in the past, being given at the moment, or promised in the future), while specifying the gifts to be given by the god in exchange.

The *preces*, the final part of the prayer, is, in fact, the articulation of the wish, whatever it is that the one praying is asking of the divinity. The nature of such requests varies wildly, depending on the particular circumstances; the petitioner may ask the god to grant safety to ships, to bring peace and prosperity, to send forth the earth's fruits, or simply to provide a favorable divine presence for the one praying. In the ritual handbooks of the Greek Magical Papyri, the particular request is often left as a blank to be filled in, "grant me success in the NN matter" or even "the usual."[27] In some form or other, minutely specified or broadly general, the mortal asks the god for *charis*, divine favor.

GIFTS FOR THE GODS

In the reciprocal system of such *charis* relations, favor implies favor; any divine *charis* must be linked with the favors offered by the mortal. The

---

[25] Diogenes Laertius 6.59 (2). Θαυμάζοντός τινος τὰ ἐν Σαμοθράκη ἀναθήματα, ἔφη, "πολλῷ ἂν ἦν πλείω εἰ καὶ οἱ μὴ σωθέντες ἀνετίθεσαν."

[26] Such a curse actually involves a continuation of the reciprocity, substituting negative 'giving' for positive, an exchange of harm instead of favors. Cp. Demosthenes 18.141; Aristophanes, *Thesmophoriazeusae* 295ff., 1136ff.

[27] E.g., *Orphic Hymn* 17, 30, 41; and PGM IV.1331–1389; VII.528–539. For 'the usual,' see, e.g., PGM III.1–164; IV.1390–1495; VII.390–393, etc.

favors mortals offer are limited by their limited power to give, but a mortal must always offer something to the deity, even if it is only words of praise. The more elaborately crafted the hymn, the more beautiful the poetry, the more exhaustive the praises of the deity, the more of a favor it provides for the god.[28] Of course, such praise and honor is ultimately what the gods are thought to desire; what else can a god want but honors? Those honors may be symbolized by words, in hymns and prayers, but also by material offerings that stand in the temples to attest to the worship of the god or even by the erection of shrines and temples themselves.[29] Chryses's prayer in the *Iliad* provides a picture of all the possibilities; he praises the god by his epithets and then describes the sacrificial offerings he has made, as well as the shrines he has created for the god.

Temple inventories record some of the kinds of gifts presented to the gods: a ribbon with a couple of drachmas attached to it, a small crystal ring, a cup made of silver, as well as more massive and impressive offerings of the kind recorded by visitors to major sanctuaries such as Herodotus or Pausanias.[30] Small tokens such as knucklebones or cheap little pots might form the bulk of offerings, while plaques, reliefs, friezes, and even sculptures supplement the smaller gifts. Statues dedicated to gods are often called *agalmata*, literally 'things that bring joy,' but all such gifts to the gods are intended as favors, extending *charis* to the god.[31] Offerings were put on display in the temples; the most impressive were left on permanent display, while the lesser offerings were cleared out regularly to make room for new ones. The very magnificence of the offerings serves as a testimony to the greatness of the god—the value of the materials, their artistic quality, the sheer size and quantity of offerings. Moreover, in addition to the things themselves, any inscriptions on the offerings might provide further force to the offering, as an inscribed petition literally re-presents the offering to the god (and the wish for a return) each time the inscription is read, whether the object is thought to be speaking or whether the prayer is imagined as performed by the one reading the inscription.[32]

[28] Furley and Bremer 2001: 2–4 discuss the history of the distinction between prayer and hymn, but modern scholars tend to emphasize the more elaborate and artistic nature of the hymn (whether in poetic meter or not). Ancient definitions of hymns stress the point that the hymn remains in the memory as a lasting offering of praise to the god. See Furley and Bremer 2001: 8–14, citing esp. *Etymologicum Magnum* s.v. *hymnos*.

[29] Jim 2012 summarizes the range of terms used for different types of offerings found in literary and epigraphic evidence.

[30] Cp., e.g., Herodotus's description of Croesus's dedications at Delphi (1.51) or the lengthy descriptions by Pausanias of the offerings at Olympia throughout book 5. For a discussion of different types of dedications, see van Straten 1981.

[31] See van Straten 1981: 75 on the term *agalmata* applied to other offerings intended to delight the gods.

[32] Depew 1997: 237–247 discusses the impact of the technology of writing on the way prayers were imagined to work.

While making offerings at an established temple is one way of providing favors to the god, creating a new shrine goes even further. Chryses boasts of the many temples he roofed for Apollo, and whole communities might dedicate a monumental temple to a deity, but private individuals might do the same thing on a much smaller scale. One of the most interesting of such private creations is the shrine of Archedamos the Nympholept. Archedamos transformed a small cave in Attica into a sanctuary for the Nymphs, by whom he claimed to have been divinely inspired (*nympholeptos* means 'seized by the nymphs'). He decorated the walls of this cave with some carved reliefs and some inscribed verses, all of such amateur quality as to guarantee that they were his own personal work. He appears to have tended this shrine, adding new dedications over the years, as an act of honor for these divinities, although it is not clear whether other worshippers came to make sacrifices while he was taking care of the cave sanctuary.[33] Archedamos's cave shrine attests to the private dedications of temples along the same lines as the ones sponsored by the whole community; regardless of the scale, the pattern of reciprocal exchange of favors underlies the activity.[34]

Sacrifice

Words are evanescent offerings, disappearing as soon as they are said, while offerings of stone or precious metals may last through the ages. In between, however, are other kinds of offerings, more substantive than words but more transitory than stone, offerings of food, drink, and incense. These consumable offerings constitute a significant part of the favors provided by mortals for the gods, but they also illuminate another aspect of the reciprocal relationship in the ways in which they are shared (or not) between the gods to whom they are offered and the mortals who offer them.

Offerings of incense are a common part of rituals that bring mortals into contact with the gods. The good smells from the burnt fragrant materials rise up into the heavens, bringing pleasure to the gods, and the offering of precious materials such as the incense is a token of respect for the god, a valuable gift or favor peformed by the worshipper to win the return favor of the god. While the smoke of incense is nearly as transient as the words of prayer, incense burning does leave tangible traces behind, in the form of *thumiateria*, incense burners, either in the material record or in the depictions of such vessels in artwork.[35] Burnt remains of the

---

[33] For nympholepsy, see Connor 1988b; Larson 2001; Jim 2012; and Fabiano 2013.

[34] Plato's prohibition in the *Laws* (909d–910d) likewise shows the prevalence of such private shrines.

[35] Cp. the discussion of Mehl 2008, with figures of such depictions, as well as Naiden 2013: 70–75.

incense itself linger in places, confirming the evidence of texts that describe its use in many kinds of ritual. The selection of the incense depends on the god being contacted, and the collection of texts known as the *Orphic Hymns* contains a series of hymns to a variety of different gods, each with a prescription for the type of incense to be burned during the recitation of the hymn.[36]

Libations are among the simplest and most common offerings to the gods, a quick dollop of liquid poured out for the god before the rest is consumed or otherwise employed by the mortals. Such libations are so common before symposia and other gatherings that they are hardly even mentioned, and they are so integral to the practice of military treaties that such pacts are usually just called *spondai*, libations, for the libations that signal the participants' invocations of the gods to guarantee that agreement.[37] In addition to their value as gifts offered to the deity, the different liquids offered have their own symbolic resonance—wine, oil, water, milk, honey, and so forth. Offering the divinity a sip provides a symbolic sharing with the god, both giving a favor and reinforcing the sense of relationship between god and mortal.

The same is true for simple offerings of grain or other vegetal matter, either in plain form or cooked into cakes; such offerings have a value in themselves as gifts, but they also have a further symbolic value.[38] Such offerings might symbolize the past harvest for which the mortal is thanking the god, or they might indicate the future prosperity for which the mortal is asking, but the choice of a food offering also introduces the symbolism of a shared meal, another important way of articulating a reciprocal relationship. Just as in the guest-friendship relation of *xenia* the bond between the participants is strengthened by sharing a meal (regardless of who provides the food eaten by both parties), so too in the relations between gods and mortals, the sharing of food enhances the bond, thus increasing the obligation to reciprocate for favors given.

Animal sacrifice probably provides the most symbolically charged offering to the gods, and it is found at every level of mortal-divine interaction, from the private offering of a small bird to the epic-scale offering of hekatombs, the hundred head of cattle favored by the Homeric heroes (and their imitators). The choice of the scale, the offering, the attendant ceremonies, and so forth, all depend on the particular circumstance, and a hier-

---

[36] Cp. Graf 2009 for a discussion of the *Orphic Hymns* as ritual texts.

[37] Note the way Plato refers to these rituals in passing in *Symposium* 176a, merely indicating that the real business of the evening's symposium got underway after these customary preliminaries had been attended to. Thucydides, who goes out of his way to avoid mentioning religious rituals, nevertheless refers to all the truces and treaties in the Peloponnesian war as *spondai*.

[38] Cp. Naiden 2013: 75–76.

archy of means determines how elaborate the ritual will be. That is, a request of lesser importance that pertains only to an individual may be accompanied with a smaller sacrifice, perhaps even only a libation or offering of a grain-cake, whereas a more significant request that affects the welfare of a larger community may involve the sacrifice of several large animals, accompanied by libations and incense, along with many prayers and hymns composed and performed by professional musicians. The larger the favor requested, the larger and more elaborate the offerings made in the ritual; the more significant the favor, the more valuable the offerings; the more people affected, the more people involved in the ceremony.

Just as the *euchesthai* of the prayer speech-act serves to articulate the status relations between the one praying and the divinity addressed, so too the act of sacrifice can articulate the status relations of all the parties involved. A larger offering not only marks a greater honor to the god but also the higher status of the one who can afford to make such an offering.[39] The division of the sacrifice also marks the relative positions of all those who are taking part. Sometimes the entirety of the sacrifice is burned in a holocaust sacrifice, rendering it all into smoke, but at other times the emphasis is on the sharing of the food from the sacrifice. Hesiod's tale of the foundation of sacrifice puts at the heart of the act the division between the mortals' edible portions and the gods' smoke from the fat and bones, and Vernant has pointed out how mortals are thus marked as the ones who need to eat, in contrast to the gods who do not need to eat but merely enjoy the savory smoke that rises to the heavens.[40] The division is not just on the vertical axis between god and mortal, but along the horizontal axis as well, among the various human participants who may be involved. Although sacrifice may be done by a single person, one person often performs the rite (and the attendant prayers) on behalf of himself and others. As is typical in Greek religion, there is no sort of ritual manual that provides instructions for the procedures, but literary texts provide descriptions that fill in details, such as Homer's description of the sacrifice performed by the swineherd Eumaeus.

> So saying he split wood with the pitiless bronze, and the others brought in a fatted boar five years old, and set him by the hearth.

[39] In some cases, however, a relative scale may be involved, as when a poor man makes a sacrifice that represents a large portion of his income; it is valued by the gods, even if the offering is actually smaller than that of a rich man for whom it represents only a miniscule portion. Porphyry recounts several stories with this point in *de abst.* II.15–16.

[40] Hesiod, *Theogony* 535–557. See Vernant 1989 for a structural analysis of the various kinds of positive and negative giving, as well as the repercussions of the division. Only in comic authors such as Aristophanes do the gods depend on the smoke of sacrifices as mortals do upon food. Cp. the blockade of sacrifices in Aristophanes's *Birds* as well as Plato's allusion to the idea in Aristophanes's speech in the *Symposium* (190c).

Nor did the swineherd forget the immortals, for he had an understanding heart, but as a first offering he cast into the fire bristles from the head of the white-tusked boar, and made prayer to all the gods that wise Odysseus might return to his own house. Then he raised himself up, and struck the boar with a billet of oak, which he had left when splitting the wood, and the boar's life left him. And the others cut the boar's throat, and singed him, and quickly cut him up, and the swineherd took as first offerings bits of raw flesh from all the limbs, barley meal, but the rest they cut up and spitted, and roasted it carefully, and drew it all off the spits, and threw it in a heap on platters. Then the swineherd stood up to carve, for well did his heart know what was fair, and he cut up the meat and divided it into seven portions. One he set aside for the nymphs and for Hermes, son of Maia, making his prayer, and the rest he distributed to each. And Odysseus he honored with the long chine of the white-tusked boar.[41]

It is worth noting the careful distribution of portions, with certain bits reserved for the gods and for the guest; for larger-scale public festivals, the distribution of sacrificial portions is designated by decree, and, after the specially assigned portions for the gods, the most important officials receive portions relative to their importance in the community that is sacrificing.[42] Sacrifice can thus become a way to mark out community, since all those who belong receive a share, and the order of precedence articulates the relative positions within the group.[43]

Sacrificers and Priests: Who Has the Authority for Prayer and Sacrifice?

In the hut of Eumaeus, there are no priests or officials, but Eumaeus performs the rite as the person of the highest rank—even though he is the lowliest of swineherds on the margins of Odysseus's estate, he still has

---

[41] Homer, *Odyssey* 14.418–438. Compare the systematic and theoretical instructions provided by Apollo in an oracle cited by Eusebius from Porphyry's *Philosophy Drawn from Oracles* (Porphyry, *Philos. Ex Orac.* frr. 314 & 315 = Eus., *PE* IV 8.4–9.7), with the discussion in Johnston 2010b.

[42] For the prerogatives reserved for priests and other public officials, see Naiden 2013: 204–209; cp. also Lupu 2005: 266–268. Ekroth 2011 discusses the whole practice of dividing portions of sacrificial meat.

[43] So important is this participation in sacrifice that it can be used to prove membership in a family, as in the inheritance case for which Isaeus 8 is written. The plaintiffs claiming to be the grandsons of the deceased adduce as evidence for their acknowledged family status their regular participation in the sacrifices conducted by their grandfather (Isaeus 8.15–16).

more social honor than his assistants or the beggar who comes to his door. The authority to perform prayer and sacrifice in Greco-Roman polytheism is relative, not absolute, and the choice of who should perform depends upon the simple logic of who seems most likely to win a favorable response from the deity being petitioned. A priest, with an official and longstanding relationship with the divinity, naturally has a better chance of getting a favorable response in a public festival than a slave without status, but, in a family ceremony, the head of the family is the most appropriate to appeal to the gods of the household, even if someone of higher status (or even holding the position of a priest at a temple) should happen to be present. Professional expertise might be recognized as a factor, but the established relation with the god and the status as a representative of the community making the petition play the largest part in such determinations.[44]

The individual performing the ritual wants to do everything to enhance his worthiness to address the deity, so many rituals involve preliminary purifications that prepare the mortal to draw nearer to the divine. Such rites remove the taint of mortal impurity from the worshipper, an effect complemented by donning fresh, clean garments and adorning oneself with a wreath or other such ornaments that mark the special occasion. Like 'dressing up' to pay a visit to a respected person in the community, such preparations are a token of respect to the deity and an acknowledgment of the divinity's divine status, but the rituals of purification, even those as simple as an aspersion with water from the *perirrhanteria* basins standing outside a sanctuary, also serve to shift the worshipper from the normal status of a mortal into a worthier state more appropriate for contact with a god.

Home Territory or Sacred Space: Where and When Do Prayer and Sacrifice Take Place?

Not only must the person who is making the prayers and sacrifices be as appropriate as possible, purified for the occasion and having the best claim to authority in the situation, but the place and time when and where the rite takes place must also be carefully selected. The choice of place and time depends on which deity is being petitioned, and some places and times are better than others. In a crisis, of course, one can appeal to the gods anywhere—on a sinking ship or in the midst of a battle, but if one has the opportunity to choose, it is better to approach the god in a place specially consecrated to that god, whether that space be a

---

[44] Auffarth 2005 discusses how everyone in Greek society learned the practices of sacrificial ritual without instruction manuals, comparing it with learning to cook or to make love. Cp. also Chaniotis 2008 on professional expertise among diviners and priests.

domestic altar or a monumental public temple.[45] A prayer requesting the god's appearance or favorable intervention has a better chance of attracting the god's notice when performed in a space that has been made sacred, set apart from normal, profane life, and reserved for contact with the divine. Likewise, the customarily appointed time for a certain ritual is a better time, and some days (and even times of day) are more propitious for contacting the gods than others, as Hesiod's catalog of days in the *Works and Days* attests. Hesiod recommends sunrise and sunset as propitious times:

> According to your capability, make holy sacrifice to the immortal gods in a hallowed and pure manner, and burn splendid thigh-pieces on the altar; at other times, seek propitiation with libations and burnt-offerings, both when you go to bed and when the holy light returns, so that their heart and spirit will be propitious to you, so that you may barter for other people's allotment, not someone else for yours.[46]

The economic incentive for proper sacrificial behavior is characteristically Hesiodic, but the idea that periodic contact with the gods is the key to favorable relations underlies the whole religious system.

Again, the concept of a hierarchy of means helps make the distinctions; some spaces are more sacred than others, and some times are more holy than others. The great pan-Hellenic sanctuaries of Olympia or Delphi are more important than the temples of a particular city, for example, the temple of Apollo in Corinth or the temple of Hera at Argos, while these in turn are more significant than small local shrines like the cave of Archedamos the Nympholept. The special festivals dedicated to the god mark the most propitious times to honor the deity, whether on a large scale, like the Karneia for Apollo or the Thesmophoria for Demeter celebrated in many cities across Greece, or on a smaller scale, like the Spartan Hyacinthia or the Athenian Skirophoria. Depending on the circumstance, it may be worth waiting for the best time or traveling to the most holy site in order to make a really important and unusual petition to the god. A more routine request of lesser importance, on the other hand, may be made at a more convenient place and time, stopping at the local shrine on the way back from the fields in the evening, while a desperate plea in an emergency may be made wherever and whenever it is necessary.

---

[45] As Damascius comments, "We prefer to appear before the gods in holy places, even though they are everywhere." καὶ μᾶλλον ἐν ἱεροῖς τόποις βουλόμεθα προσιέναι τοῖς θεοῖς, καίτοι πανταχοῦ εἰσιν (Damascius, *in Phaed.* I.499 [on 108b3–4]).

[46] Hesiod, *Works and Days* 335–341. Cp. the designation of various days as appropriate or inappropriate in Roman calendars, as explained, e.g., in Michels 1967.

Prayer and Sacrifice: Magic or Religion?

With all these variations in who, how, why, where, and when, how then can we distinguish magical prayer or sacrifice? The Greek Magical Papyri include a large number of prayers and hymns, as well as directions for sacrifices and other offerings, among the various recipes for rituals, and prayers are also found inscribed on lead tablets and other epigraphic sources. These prayers all tend to follow the same basic patterns found among prayer throughout the evidence for prayer in Greco-Roman antiquity, but a few significant differences can be traced. Although earlier scholars have often seen magical prayer as different from religion in its aims (*why*) or in the attitude with which the petitioner approaches the deity (*how*), such criteria rooted in Judaeo-Christian models of religion prove less valid than other differences that better reflect the distinctions drawn in the ancient sources. In sources that are labeled as 'magic' in antiquity or that are marked with a high coefficient of weirdness, distinguishing them as extra-ordinary religious acts, the prayers focus on the present moment of contact with the divinity, rather than the past or future of a reciprocal relationship. The acts of prayer and sacrifice likewise pay less attention to places and times sanctioned by the religious tradition of the community, making the contact with the gods whenever and wherever the present necessity demands.

Here, There, or Anywhere

As I noted in chapter 2, the historian of religion Jonathan Z. Smith proposes a distinction between three different kinds of religious activity involving their orientation to kinds of space. Drawing on the well-known formulation of Dr. Seuss, he distinguishes between the religion of here, the religion of there, and the religion of anywhere.[47] Religious activity that is focused on a public place, marked by the community as sacred, differs from religion centered on the private domestic space of the household. Rather than going 'there' to the temple to contact the god, one might remain 'here' to worship at the household altars or family tombs. There is a temporal element as well, since public festivals are at publicly determined times, in contrast to the domestic rituals whose rhythms are conditioned by the dynamics of the family's life in the household. The religion of 'anywhere,' by contrast, takes place at any time and in any space, and the traditionally sanctioned times and places (be they public or private) are of less significance than the identity of the performer, whose privileged connection with

---

[47] "I will not eat green eggs and ham. . . . I will not eat them here or there, I will not eat them anywhere." Cp. J. Smith 2003: 22. See ch. 2, p. 40, n. 7.

divinity does not depend on being in the right place or at the right time. While scholars working in the Durkheimian anthropological tradition of Mauss have often distinguished private and personal magic from the public and community activity of religion, Smith suggests that the activities most often labeled as 'magic' fall into this class of the religion of 'anywhere.'[48] Even though the activities of the religion of 'here' are private and hidden from the view of the community, they are nonetheless a sanctioned part of the community's tradition, and their validity depends on their performance in the proper spaces and at the proper times.

Graf's distinction between the vertical and horizontal axis of ritual action helps explain the differences. While both the religion of 'here' and the religion of 'there' involve similar kinds of contact between mortal and deity along the vertical axis, the horizontal axis shows the differences. A religious act performed in private minimizes the effects along the horizontal axis, since only the worshipper alone (or perhaps the small circle of intimates present within the household) is a witness to the activities. Eumaeus marks his own status as master of the house (or hut), as well as showing honor to the strange beggar, through his private act. By contrast, a public sacrifice is a public articulation of the identity of the performer, an assertion perhaps of the priest's authority to make sacrifice and offer prayers on behalf of the larger community. The magnitude of the offerings, the elaborate preparations for the festival, the beauty and artistry of the prayers and hymns, all illustrate the status of the performer whose act of *euchesthai*, of prayer, serves to make a claim to status before the whole community on the horizontal axis as well as to the god addressed along the vertical axis.[49]

Like the religion of 'here,' religion of 'anywhere' often involves a very limited horizontal axis, but the secret rites of the magician share a deemphasis on the established place and time with the public miracles of the wonderworker, whose performances have a very large audience along the horizontal axis. Both can take place when and where the performer wishes, rather than when traditional observances dictate.[50] In this regard, crisis appeals such as those made on a sinking ship or other moments of imminent peril fall into the category of 'anywhere' rather than 'here' or 'there,'

---

[48] J. Smith 2003: 35. Cp. Mauss 1972: 90, who sees religion as the collective idea of the society and claims that, in magic, "these individuals have merely appropriated to themselves the collective forces of society."

[49] Chaniotis 1997: 245–248 discusses the 'theatrical' aspects of religious aspects and their impact upon the community, while Chaniotis 1995 provides details of the epigraphic evidence for festival preparations in the Hellenistic period.

[50] Cp. Smith 1995: 26. "The sacrality of the place is established, temporarily, through ritual activities, and by virtue of the direct experience of a mobile, professional ritualist (the 'magician') with an equally mobile deity."

but further consideration of the strategies for how the relation between mortal and deity are negotiated helps distingish them from prayers and sacrifices that might best be termed 'magical.'

Present and Pressing Necessity: The Past, Present, and Future of Relations with the Divine

Such a crisis appeal usually takes the form of a vow to provide an offering in the future should the deity grant the appeal in the present, and the common practice of the dedication of votives attests to the employment of this strategy in all times and places throughout the Greco-Roman world. If the god agrees to help at the present moment, the mortal promises to reciprocate with favors in the future. This focus on future action helps distinguish such activities from magic, which tends to concentrate on the present situation rather than the past or the future relation with the deity.[51] Rather than rely on a place consecrated by past tradition, the magician creates his own temporary sacred space for ritual performance. Rather than wait for a traditionally appointed festival, the magician acts when the need arises—and expects quick results from the divine powers he petitions. The magician still makes offerings and prayers to divine powers, but, rather than rely on a relationship with the divinity built up by a longstanding reciprocity in the past or even by promises for such a relation in the future, the magician stresses his credentials for the immediate present of the interaction.

The collections of ritual prescriptions in the Greek Magical Papyri provide useful insights into this focus on the immediate present, since they contain not only the recipes for the rituals, including all the prayers and sacrifices to be made, but they also provide explanatory notes, extolling the virtues of the particular spells. The spell books repeatedly emphasize the fact that the spells can be used whenever, wherever, and for whatever purpose the caster might desire. Rather than go to a temple and wait upon the schedule of divinatory consultations, one recipe proclaims, "You will observe through bowl divination on whatever day or night you want, in whatever place you want."[52] Most recipes indeed specify no time or place for the performance of the ritual, while some merely suggest that it be

---

[51] The establishment of shrines and other new places of worship not sanctioned by tradition (often on the site of some divine manifestation or epiphany) likewise sets up a relation for the future. Because the god has appeared or provided a wondrous gift to the mortal, the mortal will, from henceforth, provide honor and worship to the deity in that place, even if it had not been a place of worship before. Cp. Archedamos the Nympholept (see ch. 6, p. 163, n. 33) or Plato's complaints about the establishment of new private shrines in the *Laws* (909d–910d).

[52] PGM IV.154–285.

performed at night on the rooftop of the house, a private place unlikely to be observed. The significant time frame for these rituals is now; the ritual is performed the moment when it is needed, and the performer often specifies that he wants results immediately. One spell exhorts a variety of divine powers: "May the [NN deed] come about for me immediately, immediately; quickly, quickly; because I conjure you, at this place and at this time."[53] The desired result is a fill-in-the-blank, but, whatever it is that the magician wants, he wants it now.

Some spell recipes do specify a place or time that is necessary for the proper performance of the ritual to ask a favor from the divinities, but such times and places are neither the public temples and festival times of the religion of 'there,' nor the personal spaces and times of the religion of 'here,' the household altars and the burial monuments of the kin group. Rather, the spaces are made sacred temporarily for the purpose of the ritual, the brief moment of communication or contact with the deity. One spell requires the magician to perform a sacrifice in "a place from which the Nile has recently receded, before anyone walks on the area that was flooded," that is, in a liminal space that is neither the river nor normal dry land. The magician builds a temporary altar of bricks, digs a trench around it, lights a fire of olive wood, and sacrifices a chicken, before immersing himself in the nearby river.[54]

Such a construction of a temporary altar appears in other spells, often with instructions for the particular sacrifices. "Build a pure altar," instructs one recipe, "that is, take two unbaked bricks and form them into four horn-shaped objects, on which you lay fruit-bearing branches."[55] Others have more elaborate instructions:

The consecration [requires] the following equipment: Making a pit in a holy place open to the sky, [or] if [you have none] in a clean, sanctified tomb looking toward the east, and making over the pit an altar of wood from fruit trees, sacrifice an unblemished goose, and three roosters and three pigeons. Make these whole burnt offerings and burn, with the birds, all sorts of incense. Then, standing by the pit, look to the east and, pouring on a libation of wine, honey, milk, [and]

---

[53] PGM III.1–164 (36–37). This demand for results "quickly, quickly" is an extremely common feature of such spells, found not just in the formularies but also in the texts of executed examples. Cp., among others, PGM XIXa.1–54; PGM XXXII.1–19; XXXIIa.1–25; IV.1227–1264; I.247–262; III.1–164; IV.94–153; IV.930–1114; IV.2006–2125; VII.222–249; VII.250–254; VII.319–334; as well as the examples in Gager 1992 (6, 9, 11, 12, 15, 29, 30, 35, 36, 106, 107, 112, 115, 125).

[54] PGM IV.26–51. See also Johnston 2002: 353–354.

[55] PGM XII.14–95. Cp. the construction of an altar of unburnt clay with a lamp set upon a wolf's head for invoking Apollo in PGM I.262–347.

saffron, and holding over the smoke, while you pray, [the stone] in which are engraved the inscriptions, say.[56]

This ritual takes over a previously sanctified space for its own purposes, digging a pit for the sacrifices and building an altar, but even a commonplace space like one's bed can be consecrated for the purpose of a magical ritual.

> In the evening, just before retiring, purify your bed with ass's milk, and then, holding in your hands twigs of laurel (the preparation for which is given below), speak the invocation given below. Let your bed be on the ground, either upon clean rushes or upon a rush mat, and lie on your right side, on the ground and in the open air.[57]

In all these cases, the space is prepared before the god can be invoked with prayers and gratified with sacrifices and other kinds of offerings. Most of these preparations are fairly brief, even if it would naturally take a while to dig a pit and build an altar, but a few spells require advance preparation so that the ritual may be performed at a particular time—at the new moon, on the third day of the month, or at a particular astrological configuration. Perhaps the most elaborate setup is found in the formulary that entitles itself the "Eighth Book of Moses."

> Remain pure forty-one days, having calculated in advance so that your completion of them will coincide with the dark of the moon which occurs in Aries. Have a house on ground level, in which no one has died during the past year. The door should face west. Now set up in the middle of the house an earthen altar and have ready cypress wood, ten pinecones full of seed, two white roosters uninjured and without blemish, and two lamps each holding an eighth of a pint, filled with good oil. And don't pour in any more, for when the god comes in they will burn more fiercely. Have the table prepared with these following kinds of incense, which are cognate to the god.[58]

The space, while not already sanctified, must be free from the taint of death pollution so that it may be more easily transformed into a suffi-

---

[56] PGM XII.201–269.

[57] PGM II.1–64.

[58] PGM XIII.1–343 (4–14). The papyrus contains several versions of the elaborate rituals, with some variations between the versions. It has been noted that the preliminary period of purification of forty-one days ending at the new moon in Aries corresponds interestingly to the Lenten purification period before Easter, the date of which is also tied to the lunar cycle around the spring equinox in Aries.

ciently sacred space for the ritual. The time must be carefully calculated in advance, and the last seven days involve further rituals of greeting the gods of the hour and the day, whose identities must be worked out with precision.[59] The magician still marks his own sacred time, however, rather than working by festival calendars or the rhythms of domestic religion.

It is worth noting the emphasis on the purification, not just of the place, but of the ritual performer. While some level of purification is always part of initiating contact with the divine, the personal purity of the practitioner is even more significant in the absence of a ritual status that is defined by the community. Eumaeus presides over the sacrifice in his hut and the Hierophant at the Eleusinian Mysteries because they are the most appropriate persons in the ritual community to perform the rites, and their status is acknowledged as such by the other participants. The magician must define his own ritual status, his worthiness to address the god, so the purifications serve to mark the magician (to himself, if no one else on the horizontal axis) as someone who is appropriately prepared to approach the god. Many prayers in the Greek Magical Papyri are preceded by instructions to purify oneself or to keep pure for a specified time in advance.[60] This pure status is not, however, mentioned in the prayers as part of the petitioner's credentials; the performer of the rite, whether magical or not, must rely on other strategies to assert his worthiness in his communication with the deity on the vertical axis.

In contrast to the references in other prayers to past favors given to the god or other evidence of an ongoing reciprocal relationship, the emphasis on current status in the magical prayers is striking. A few prayers in the magical papyri do make reference to a previous ritual preparation or even provide instructions for a preliminary ritual to which the magician then makes reference in his prayer to the god, but even these exceptions do not place these references to qualifications from the past in the center of the rhetorical strategy of the prayer.[61] The magician may claim in passing to be sanctified or pious, but the emphasis in the prayer is on the magician's other credentials.

---

[59] PGM XIII.1–343 (114–122).

[60] E.g., PGM II.1–64; III.282–409; IV.26–51; IV.52–85; IV.930–1114; IV.3209–3254; VII.319–334; VII.359–369; VII.664–685; VII.703–726; VII.740–755; VII.981–993; IV.1265–1274; XXIIb.27–31; XXXVIII.1–26; LXXVII.1–24. Most of these instructions simply direct the practitioner to be pure, without further instructions, but a few provide specific instructions, such as to abstain from meat and bathing (PGM IV.475–829) or to remain pure from intercourse (PGM IV.850–929). Perhaps the most intriguing is the instruction to abstain from pork in PGM IV.3007–3086, for "this charm is Hebraic."

[61] Cp. the reference to a previous ritual of *thronosis* in PGM VII.740–755, or the claim to have been sanctified by holy consecrations (ἁγίοις ἁγιασθεὶς ἁγιάσμασι) in PGM IV.475–829 (522). On the initiation of the magician, see, e.g., PGM IV.154–285 and Graf 1994.

What's the Magic Word? Voces Magicae
and the Magician's Credentials

As Graf has shown, the prayers from the magical papyri characteristically substitute claims to special knowledge for the descriptions of past or future reciprocal relations in the *argumentum* section of the prayer.[62] The name of the god, along with epithets and places of power, is a standard part of any Greek prayer, but the prayers and hymns in the magical papyri tend to include long strings of obscure, arcane, and even incomprehensible epithets in place of the descriptions of the god's traditional places of worship or the past deeds of the god found in other kinds of hymns and prayers.[63] It is the incomprehensible words, the so-called *voces magicae* or *nomina barbara*, that seem to mark the prayer as magical, raising the coefficient of weirdness beyond that of ordinary religious prayer. Graf argues, "They are not used, as some have claimed, to force the divinity: they take the place of, and serve as, the credentials, an ample display of knowledge."[64] Despite their weirdness, these magical words are not 'magic' in the sense that they are automatically efficacious; rather, they serve as special passwords to the god's favor, a potent rhetorical strategy that replaces other kinds of arguments for winning the favor of the god. Although earlier scholars have often assumed that the magical words must operate in the *ex opere operato* mode of performative speech that makes the desired effect occur automatically, the contingency plans in the spells themselves for what to do if the god does not respond positively the first time indicate that the performers did not believe that the magical words were infallible.[65] Graf's examination of the *voces magicae* in the prayers of the magical papyri shows clearly that they supplement or substitute for the other elements of the prayer that seek to win the favor of the god.

[62] Graf 1991.

[63] To some extent, this feature is simply characteristic of hymns of the Roman Imperial period and later, and we find hymns composed almost entirely of strings of epithets in the collection of the *Orphic Hymns* or Proclus's Hymns or even the model of the hymn in the rhetorical manual of Menander Rhetor (2.445.25–446.13). However, while literary hymns also have a diminished focus on the content of the wish itself, the magical prayers are very clearly practical, aiming not just to praise the god but to persuade him to do something specific.

[64] Graf 1991: 192.

[65] Various spells provide backup procedures, in case the god does not hearken to the prayer, e.g., PGM IV.3209–3254 (3229) "but if she does not listen, say." Some include coercive prayers for use when the *da quia do* argument doesn't work after a few days of trying (usually three), e.g., IV.1331–1389 (1295) "the charm of compulsion for the third day"; IV.1390–1496 (1435) "when you have done these things for 3 days and accomplish nothing"; etc. By contrast, IV.2006–2125 (2074) notes that a backup procedure may not be necessary. Some spells even have multiple layers of contingency plans, e.g., II.1–64 (45) "if he does not appear," followed by (55) "if even after this he does not hearken."

Rather than citing the long history of a reciprocal relation between mortal and divinity, the magician uses the *voces magicae* to prove that he has a special connection to the god that entitles him to a favor from the god. In one spell, a magician invokes the sun god to grant his wish: "Grant all the [petitions] of my prayer, because I know your signs, [symbols and] forms, who you are at each hour, and what your name is." The special knowledge of the names and forms of the sun god at each hour substitute in this prayer for the kind of longstanding reciprocal relationship found in the arguments of other prayers.[66] Another spell invokes Hermes and then recites a catalog of special names and other attributes that the magician knows of the god.

> Your names in heaven: LAMPHTHEN OUOTHI OUASTHEN OUOTHI OAMENOTH ENTHOMOUCH. These are the [names] in the 4 quarters of heaven. I also know what your forms are: in the east you have the form of an ibis, in the west you have the form of a dog-faced baboon, in the north you have the form of a serpent, and in the south you have the form of a wolf. Your plant is *the grape which is the olive.* I also know your wood: ebony. I know you, Hermes, who you are and where you come from and what your city is: Hermopolis. . . . Your true name has been inscribed on the sacred stele in the shrine at Hermopolis where your birth is. Your true name: OSERGARIACH NOMAPHI. This is your name with fifteen letters, a number corresponding to the days of the rising moon; and the second name with the number 7, corresponding to those who rule the world, with the exact number 365, corresponding to the days of the year. Truly: ABRASAX. I know you, Hermes, and you know me. I am you, and you are I. And so, do everything for me, and may you turn to me with Good Fortune and Good Daimon, immediately, immediately; quickly, quickly.[67]

The petition itself, whatever it might be, can be added with the usual formula, so commonplace that it need not even be recorded in the spell book, but the invocation with the special names and symbols is the crucial information for the magician to perform the spell successfully and win the favor of the deity to fulfill the wish in the petition.

Why should these weird and incomprehensible utterances be taken as a good strategy for winning the favor of a god? These names and symbols are often described as secrets, so the magician's knowledge of them marks

---

[66] PGM III.494–611; the list of the forms, names, plants, animals, etc. of the sun appears following the invocation, e.g., "In the third hour you have the form of a cat; the tree you produce is the fig tree; the stone, the *samouchos*; the bird, the parrot; on land, the frog; your name is AKRAMMACHAMAREI" (507–509).

[67] PGM VIII.1–63 (6–15, 41–52). The italicized phrase is Coptic written in Greek letters.

him as one with a privileged relationship to the god, in the same way that a long history of sacrifices or undergoing a special ritual of initiation for the god would mark a special relationship. Knowing the secret name of Aphrodite is the key to winning a beautiful woman; the magician must simply say "Nepheriēri" in his soul seven times while gazing at her for seven days in a row and the power of Aphrodite will inspire love in her.[68] The most powerful and important names are those that are secret and hidden from general knowledge, not to be spoken without authorization, "the hidden and unspeakable name" whose utterance marks the speaker as one privileged in his association with the god whose secret name he knows.[69]

At times, the one praying even notes that the special name was provided by the divinity itself as a way for mortals to make special contact.[70] A text cited in Porphyry describes Hekate responding to an invocation. Although she asks, "Why then have you summoned me, goddess Hekate, from purest heaven by means of god-taming constraints?" she also makes it clear that the summons is not a hubristic coercion by a mortal of a god, but rather a special prayer that the gods themselves helped mortals discover. "I have come in response to your eloquent prayer, which was invented by mortals in accordance with divine counsels."[71] The gods have arranged that certain mortals should know the special ways of summoning them, and the magician proves himself to be one of the privileged by his knowledge of the secret names and prayers.

One aspect of the privileged status conferred by the special knowledge is the power to make use of the great divine name to get lesser divine powers to comply with the magician's wishes. The authority of the higher divinity is vested in the one who speaks in its name, and the lesser powers must obey the one who defines himself as the representative of the higher authority. Some prayers make this power explicit, as in the spell that calls upon a daimonic spirit of the dead to torment the object of an erotic spell,

> because I adjure you by the name that causes fear and trembling, the
> name at whose sound the earth opens, the name at whose terrifying

---

[68] PGM IV.1265–1274.

[69] PGM XII.240; XIII.763. Cp. Proclus, *in Alc.* 150.

[70] And be not angry at my potent chants, For you yourself arranged these things among Mankind for them to learn about the threads Of the Moirai, and this with your advice. I call your name, Horus, which is in number Equivalent to those of the Moirai, ACHAIPHŌ THŌTHŌ PHIACHA AIĒ ĒIA ĒIA THŌTHŌ PHIACHA. PGM IV.296–466 (453–456), μηδὲ σὺ μηνίσῃς κρατεραῖς ἐπ᾽ ἐμαῖς ἐπαοιδαῖς· ταῦτα γὰρ αὐτὸς ἔταξας ἐν ἀνθρώποισι δαῆναι νήματα Μοιράων, καὶ σαῖς ὑποθημοσύνῃσι. κλῄζω δ᾽ οὔνομα σόν, Ὧρ,᾽ ὃν Μοιρῶν ἰσάριθμον· αχαϊφω θωθω φιαχα αϊη ηϊα ιαη· ηϊα θωθω φιαχα· Cp. PGM IV.1980.

[71] Porphyry, *Philos. ex Orac.* fr. 347 Smith = Philoponus, *op. mundi* 202. τίπτε δ᾽ ἀεὶ θείοντος ἀπ᾽ αἰθέρος ὧδε χατίζων θειοδάμοις Ἑκάτην με θεὴν ἐκάλεσσας ἀνάγκαις; . . . καὶ ἑξῆς· ἤλυθον εἰσαΐουσα τεῆς πολυφράδμονος εὐχῆς, ἣν θνητῶν φύσις εὗρε θεῶν ὑποθημοσύνῃσι.

sound the daimons are terrified, the name at whose sound rivers and rocks burst asunder. I adjure you, god of the dead, whether male or female, by BARBARITHA CHENMBRA BAROUCHAMBRA and by the ABRAT ABRASAX SESENGEN BARPHARANGGĒS and by the glorious AŌIA MARI and by the MARMAREŌTH MARMARAUŌTH MAR-MARAŌTH MARECHTHANA AMARZA MARIBEŌTH; do not fail, god of the dead, to heed my commands and names.[72]

The magician adjures (*exorkizō*) the *nekydaimon*, the spirit of a dead person, calling upon the secret names of the high god, and daimons must obey someone who claims such an authority. Adjuration, the Latinate form of the Greek exorcism, appears frequently in the prayers of the Greek Magical Papyri as a way for the magician to get a lesser divine power to obey his commands.[73] Exorcism or adjuration is not, as in modern parlance, simply compelling a demon to stop possessing someone; it is specifically making use of the name of the higher power to command the lesser, whether the command is to depart from a body or to go forth and prevent a woman from resting until she comes to sleep with the one issuing the commands.[74]

The process makes use of an implicit cosmic hierarchy, a worldview in which the divine powers are arranged in carefully organized ranks. The lower ranks must obey the higher, and the whole structure is governed by a supreme leader, rather as the Roman Empire was led by an emperor, under whom, in hierarchical order, were the various levels of imperial bureaucracy and government—provincial, regional, local, and so forth. Rather than appeal directly for a favor from a divinity on the basis of one's personal relationship, the petitioner makes use of the divine hierarchies to obtain the desired result from a figure lower down in the hierarchy on

---

[72] PGM IV.296–466 (356–368). ὅτι σε ἐξορκίζω κατὰ τοῦ ὀνόματος τοῦ φοβεροῦ καὶ τρομεροῦ, οὗ ἡ γῆ ἀκούσα[σ]α τοῦ ὀνόματος ἀνοιγήσεται, οὗ οἱ δαίμονες ἀκούσαντες τοῦ ὀνόματος ἐνφόβου φοβηθήσονται, οὗ οἱ ποταμοὶ καὶ αἱ πέτραι ἀκούσαντες τὸ ὄνομα ῥήσσονται. ὁρκίζω σε, νεκύδαιμον, εἴτε ἄρρης, εἴτε θῆλυς, κατὰ τοῦ Βαρβαριθα χενμβρα βαρουχαμβρα καὶ κατὰ τοῦ Ἀβρατ Ἀβρασὰξ σεσενγεν βαρφαραγγης καὶ κατὰ τοῦ αωια μαρι ἐνδόξου καὶ κατὰ τοῦ Μαρμα<ρ>εωθ Μαρμαραυωθ Μαρμαραωθ μαρεχθανα αμαρζα· μαριβεωθ· μή μου παρακούσῃς, νεκύδαιμον, τῶν ἐντολῶν καὶ τῶν ὀνομάτων.

[73] ἐξορκίζω appears fifty-six times in the corpus of the Greek Magical Papyri, while the related ὁρκίζω appears sixty-seven times.

[74] The exorcisms of Jesus are certainly the most famous, e.g., Mark 5:1–20, 9:17–29; Luke 8:26–39, 4:31–41, 9:37–43; Matthew 4:23–25, 12:22–24, 15:22–29, 17:14–18. Such was his reputation that an exorcism in the Greek Magical Papyri, IV.3007–3086, begins the exorcism: "I adjure you by the god of the Hebrews, Jesus." There must have been many making use of the name of Jesus, since the story in Acts 19:13–17 recounts a demon rejecting the authority of an exorcist who calls on the name of Jesus, not because it doesn't recognize the authority of Jesus, but because it doesn't recognize the authority of the exorcist to claim the authority of Jesus.

the authority of one higher up. This strategy of mortal interactions with the divine becomes more common in the Greco-Roman world as the bureaucracy and hierarchical structure of the Roman Empire becomes more entrenched, but the same strategy can be found much earlier in Egyptian prayers, perhaps because the structure of Egyptian society (both human and divine) was hierarchically stratified and centrally organized millennia before the Roman Empire was established.

Such manipulations of the celestial hierarchy do not always use the terms of adjuration, but all the prayers that use coercive rhetoric to compel a divine entity make use of the same logical structure. As Graf has shown, coercion is not essentially characteristic of magical prayer, but merely one strategy that can be employed.[75] Some spells indeed only make use of coercion after more positive appeals have failed, since it is far preferable to have a pleased and benevolently disposed deity rather than a hostile one who only grants the request for fear of retribution from a higher power. A spell of attraction invokes the moon goddess, employing a hymn in dactylic hexameter that praises her by many names (Artemis, Persephone, Selene, Mene, and even Aphrodite), describing her many cosmic roles and terrifying powers. A fragrant offering accompanies the hymn to further propitiate the goddess and make her favorably inclined. If, after this procedure, she does not respond favorably, there is a coercive rite that can be performed. It comes, however, with a warning label. "Do not therefore perform the rite rashly, and do not perform it unless some dire necessity arises for you." The strategy of forcing the goddess should not be used lightly, because such treatment might cause the goddess to retaliate. "It also possesses a protective charm against your falling, since the goddess is accustomed to make airborne those who perform this rite unprotected by a charm and to hurl them from aloft down to the ground."[76] The magician must have the special names that supply his credentials to wield the authority, and, even still, making this goddess angry is a dangerous business. To make use of the political analogy again, an imperial envoy in the Roman Empire would far rather get the provincial governor to do what he wants with some flattery and gifts, leaving the emperor's name diplomatically implicit, than by threatening him explicitly with punishment from the emperor far off in the capitol.

A less risky strategy, then, is to try to please the divinity, reserving a strategy of coercion for the last resort. Here again the magician's special knowledge of names and symbols can serve, since the gods are at times even said to be pleased, that is, to receive *charis*, at hearing these special names. "I appeal to you, imploring and supplicating that you may do the

[75] Graf 1991: 194.
[76] PGM IV.2441–2621 (2505–2509).

NN thing, because I call upon you with your holy names at which your deity rejoices, names which you are not able to ignore: BRIMÕ, earth-breaker, etc."[77] An invocation by such a name is less likely to be ignored or rejected, and the mere fact that the invoker calls the god by that name counts as a favor done for the god that obliges repayment.

Magical Sacrifices

Such verbal favors of calling on the god by secret and special names supplement the usual offerings of *charis* in prayers constituted by the invocations of the god by names, places of power, and so forth. As in other interactions with the gods, verbal prayers are often accompanied by physical offerings, and the various kinds of sacrifices offered with the prayers play an even more important role in magical rituals because of the immediate nature of the interaction. Whereas Chryses can make use of a *da quia dedi* strategy, recounting all the great gifts he has made to Apollo in the past, the magician makes his argument for divine favor neither from past actions nor promises of the future, but from his special knowledge and his actions in the present moment. The rhetorical strategy might be called *da quia do* (give because I give) or the more familiar *do ut des* (I give so that you may give), but the emphasis is always on the present act of giving, whether the 'gifts' are sacrificial offerings or simply pleasing the god by using his secret name. The prayers are full of first-person singular present indicative verbs—I call upon you, I know your names, I adjure you, etc.—marking the magician's actions at the current moment and almost never making promises for future offerings or reminding the god of favors past.[78] Such first-person singular present indicative verbs appear not only in the formularies of the Greek Magical Papyri, but also in the epigraphic evidence of curse tablets and other inscribed magical prayers that lack the framing descriptions of the formularies to help us understand the ritual context.[79]

---

[77] PGM VII.686–702. Cp. the Orphic *Lithika* 726–727: "For they [the blessed gods] rejoice, whenever someone in the rites chants the mystic name of the heavenly ones." τέρπονται γάρ, ἐπεί κέ τις ἐν τελετῆσι μυστικὸν ἀείδησιν ἐπώνυμον οὐρανιώνων.

[78] Cp., e.g, PGM I.216; II.8; III.36; III.499; IV.2241–2358. Of particular note is the use of the verb ἐπικαλοῦμαι, I call upon, which occurs 115 times in various forms within the corpus of the Greek Magical Papyri, although not always in the first-person singular. Although the verb appears in other texts for the invocation of a god, the middle voice is unusual elsewhere but overwhelmingly common in the papyri. Perhaps the middle voice calls attention to the magician calling upon the god for his own benefit. (I thank Andrew Mihailoff for drawing my attention to the use of this verb.)

[79] The verb ὁρκίζω (I adjure) and its cognates appear frequently, e.g., Gager 45 = DT 22, a legal curse from Amathous in Cyprus and Gager 13, a chariot race curse from Rome; both

The sacrifices prescribed for magical rituals in the Greek Magical Papyri often reflect the spur of the moment nature of the magical ritual. Smith has noted the miniaturization and domestication of ritual elements in these rituals.[80] Rather than offering a whole animal, some symbolically representative element may be substituted.[81] In a love spell, for example, the offering to (the star of) Aphrodite, rather than the sacrifice of her characteristic doves, consists of burning small pills of incense composed of dove fat and other ingredients. "A white dove's blood and fat, untreated myrrh and parched wormwood. Make this up together as pills and offer them to the star on pieces of vine wood or on coals."[82] Once the materials have been prepared, the rite can be performed on a small altar, burning the tiny fragrant pills on a little brazier on the rooftop of the house whenever the magician desires. The contents of the pills vary for the different uses; one recipe calls for one pill made of sweet-smelling incenses (cinnamon, frankincense, and bay) for a beneficent offering, but another pill composed of a variety of ingredients that include wormwood, garlic, and vinegar (not to mention the fat of a virgin dappled goat) for the coercive rite. The sweet odor of the incense provides *charis* to the goddess, while the bitter smells of the other pills reinforce the compulsive element of the coercive rite that is used if the beneficent one is not successful, and the magician can have this second type of offering right at hand in case the first prayer does not induce the goddess to act. The handiness of ready-made pills is even more important for offerings that involve more complex ingredients, each one of which has a symbolic resonance.

Take a field mouse and deify it in spring water. And take two moon beetles and deify them in river water, and take a river crab and fat

---

use ὁρκίζω repeatedly, while Gager 9 = DT 237, a chariot curse from Carthage, uses ἐξορκίζω. Gager 10 = DT 242, another Carthaginian curse, uses ὁρκίζω, ἐξορκίζω, and even προσεξορκίζω repeatedly through the spell. ὁρκίζω appears (both in Latin and Greek characters) in Gager 36 = DT 36, an erotic spell from the Roman cemetery in Hadrumentum. Cp. Faraone 1991a: 4–5 on the first-person singular forms in binding spells on curse tablets. All these performative verbs describe the current actions of the one performing the rite, rather than making reference to his past actions or promising something in the future.

[80] "They are not only highly portable, but appear to be miniaturized. The table, the throne, the tripod, and the censer seem, themselves, to be small and to hold relatively small objects. The sacrificial altar—most often constructed of two or more (unbaked) bricks, but never more than seven—seems especially so. What must be the scale of an altar on which is sacrificed 'on grapevine charcoal, one sesame seed and (one) black cumin seed' (IV.919)?" (J. Smith 1995: 24).

[81] LiDonnici 2001 surveys some ingredients in the recipes of the magical papyri, particularly incense, pinecones, and wormwood. LiDonnici 2002 looks at the strangest types, as well as the list of more commonplace equivalences in PGM XII.401–444.

[82] PGM IV.2891–2942.

of a dappled goat that is virgin and dung of a dog-faced baboon, two eggs of an ibis, two drams of storax, two drams of myrrh, two drams of crocus, four drams of Italian galingale, four drams of uncut frankincense, a single onion. Put all these things onto a mortar with the mouse and the remaining items and, after pounding thoroughly, place in a lead box and keep for use. And whenever you want to perform a rite, take a little, make a charcoal fire, go up on a lofty roof, and make the offering as you say this spell at moonrise, and at once she comes.[83]

The complexity and specificity of the ingredient list provide this ritual with a high coefficient of weirdness, marking it as an exceptional ritual that thus logically must be exceptionally efficacious. Apart from the strange ingredients, however, the actual process of making offerings is familiar. As scholars have pointed out, the sacrifices found in the Greek Magical Papyri operate in the same basic mode as normal sacrifices and offerings in the Greek religious tradition. The ritual performers engage in a bit more creative improvising than appears in the evidence for normal sacrificial rituals, but they are still working with the same procedures and underlying ritual logic.[84] Most often, they miniaturize the ritual actions, condensing them into representative symbolic actions, offering a token piece of the animal blended in with incense instead of slaughtering a whole beast and offering incense along with it.

As Smith has noted, one form this miniaturization can take is the substitution of writing for doing: "the chief ritual activity within the Greek Magical Papyri appears to be the act of writing itself."[85] Rather than a sacrifice involving burning ingredients along with a chanted prayer, the magician may inscribe the prayer on a piece of purified papyrus using an ink composed of a variety of strange and symbolic elements.

This is also the composition of the ink: myrrh troglitis, four drams; three karian figs, seven pits of Nikolaus dates, seven dried pinecones, seven piths of the single-stemmed wormwood, seven wings of the Hermaic ibis, spring water. When you have burned the ingredients, prepare them and write.[86]

---

[83] PGM IV.2441–2621 (2456–2470). To "deify" something in this context means to drown it (like Osiris).

[84] Cp. Johnston 2002. Petrovic 2012 analyzes all the different rites involving animals in the corpus, pointing out that most of the animal killings follow standard sacrificial procedure. A few do involve more symbolic action, e.g., strangling birds to preserve the breath-spirit, but most of those still do not simply reverse the standard operating procedure of sacrifice. See also the study of magical sacrifice in Zografou 2013a.

[85] J. Smith 1995: 26.

[86] PGM I.232–247 (244–247).

The whole symbolic process is shifted away from the ritual action of sacrifice and into the ritual of writing, making the process even less dependent upon a particular time and place. The ink can be used now, whenever the magician wants and anywhere he happens to be, but the symbolic offerings to the deity remain, even in the token traces of the ink.

CONCLUSIONS

The rituals for contacting the gods, the prayers and sacrifices and other kinds of offerings, work according to the same kinds of logical structures in the evidence labeled 'magic' as in nonmagical evidence. At the heart of the process is an idea of a reciprocal relation between mortal and deity, in which the mortal offers tokens of respect and honor that please the god, while the god supplies some aid that is beyond human capacity. The formularies in the Greek Magical Papyri, because of their recipe-book format, provide an insight into the underlying logic of the rituals unavailable in most other magical evidence, but the forms of the prayers inscribed on tablets seem consistent with the evidence of the papyri. The most notable differences in the magical materials lie not in the attitude with which the mortal approaches the deity or even in the ends for which the mortal is pleading, but rather in the dynamics of the relationship—the emphasis on the present moment and the deployment of strange elements to reinforce the extra-ordinary nature of the rite.

The rhetorical strategies of the magical prayers focus on the present moment, rather than on the history of the relationship established in the past or even on promises for the future. The magician makes his argument for divine favor on the basis of the offerings being made at the present moment, and he expects the gods to respond immediately. The magician may have contacted the god in the past or may plan to do so again, but such contact is not the grounds on which the magician asks for divine assistance. On the vertical axis of communication between mortal and divine, then, one may note the shift in magical prayers to a concentration on the present need.

This shift of emphasis also has implications on the horizontal axis, for the way that the magician defines his own identity in the prayers. Rather than defining himself as one who has given past favors or who vows offerings in the future, the magician stresses his current special knowledge of the deity, particularly the secret names by which the divinity likes to be addressed. These magical names fill the prayers in the magical rituals, marking them as extra-ordinary despite the ordinary nature of the underlying process of contacting the god (invocation, argument, and wish).

The Greek Magical Papyri provide further evidence of the importance of this marking the prayers and rites as extra-ordinary, with the 'advertisements' that appear in the rubrics of many of the spells: "The charm is marvelous"; "I have not found a greater spell than this"; "the world has had nothing greater than this"; "no charm is greater"; and so forth.[87] Some of the spells even have what might be called 'celebrity endorsements,' references to the famous people who used the spell: "The spell of Pnouthis," "King Pitys's spell of attraction," "Pythagoras's request for a dream oracle," "Lunar spell of Klaudianos," "Zminis of Tentyra's spell for sending dreams," and so forth.[88] Occasionally, the advertisement is extensive.

> Pachrates, the prophet of Heliopolis, revealed it to the emperor Hadrian, revealing the power of his own divine magic. For it attracted in one hour; it made someone sick in two hours; it destroyed in seven hours, sent the emperor himself dreams as he thoroughly tested the whole truth of the magic within his power. And marveling at the prophet, he ordered double fees to be given to him.[89]

Not only does the spell have the endorsement of a famous magician but even of a famous client, the Emperor Hadrian himself, and the story points out the moral clearly: the spell was so good that the emperor gave the magician a doubled fee. This story raises the question of the audience for these advertisements—are they just to convince the magician himself of the efficacy of the spell, or do they serve to impress the magician's client? In either case, the horizontal axis of the rite is limited to those parties (or just to the one performing the rites for his own benefit), and so the rhetoric of the performance must serve to persuade that audience that the performer has the proper authority to perform the rite. From a modern, etic, perspective, modern scholars can analyze the coefficients of weirdness and intelligibility in the spells as a way of reinforcing their extra-ordinary nature coupled with their familiar and traditional ritual patterns.

---

[87] Betz 1992:248 calls attention to this phenomenon. Cp., e.g., PGM IV.2373–2440; IV.475–829; XII.270–350; XXXVI.35–68; cp. also PGM XXXVI.69–101 "Love spell of attraction, excellent divination by fire, than which none is greater"; PGM XXXVI.134–60 "Marvelous love spell of attraction, than which none is greater"; PGM XXXVI.161–177 "No charm is greater." Note the series of spells in the same papyrus, each of which claims that "no charm is greater."

[88] PGM I.42–195; IV.1928–2005; VII.795–845; VII.862–918; XII.121–143; and many others. These titles tend to be concentrated in particular papyri (esp. PGM IV, VII, and XII), but examples do appear in some others, whereas some papyri, e.g., PGM XXXVI, have no such titles.

[89] PGM IV.2441–2621. Cp. III.424–466: "A procedure greater than this one does not exist. It has been tested by Manethon, [who] received [it] as a gift from god Osiris the greatest." This advertisement stresses the divine origin of the spell.

Previous scholars have often differentiated magical prayer in terms of its coercive attitude, in contrast to a supplicative attitude of 'real' religious prayer, but such a distinction ignores the subtleties of the rhetorical strategies of all of these prayers. Both coercion and supplication are rare, extreme strategies in the relationship of god and mortal, to be used only when other methods fail or are not available. Coercion is a dangerous business that relies on claiming the authorization of a higher divine authority to command a lesser one, making use of a theological understanding of the divine hierarchies that undergird the entire cosmos. Supplication, by contrast, involves giving up any favor that the mortal might offer to the god and relying entirely on the god's unprompted benevolence. Both strategies may be effective in certain circumstances, but neither is the normal or essential mode of prayer of any type.

The distinction, however, is not merely a modern anachronism, but has its roots in theological disputes that go back to antiquity. In a theology that stresses divine omnipotence and perfection, the idea of offering favors to the gods in return for other benefits seems to undermine the idea of divine perfection. What could the gods need from mortals? Why would they bargain with mortals, if they need nothing and can do anything? The perfect gods cannot enter into reciprocal relations with mortals; the gap between mortals and gods is too great. This kind of theology appears first in the Classical philosophers, but it has a long life in the Western theological tradition. In the *Republic*, Plato attacks the line in Homer that articulates the idea that the gods can be moved by prayers and offerings: "The gods themselves are moved by prayers| And men by sacrifice and soothing vows| And incense and libation turn their wills| Praying, whenever they have sinned and made transgression."[90] This attack portrays the whole Homeric system of reciprocity as a mercantile *quid pro quo* that simply tries to bribe the gods. Moreover, any assumption that such a ritual will be effective constrains the gods to act according to human wishes, so the spectrum of prayers between complete supplication and coercion is obliterated.

From such a perspective, the only kind of prayer that can appropriately address the gods is one that leaves all the decisions of what is best to happen in the hands of the gods. Xenophon tells us that Socrates always just prayed to the gods to give him good things, since they know what sort of things are good, and the Platonic *Alcibiades II* discusses a prayer with a similar idea.[91]

---

[90] Plato, *Republic* 364a, citing Homer, *Iliad* 9.497.
[91] Xenophon, *Mem.* 1.3.2; Platonic *Alc.* 2 143a = *Anth. Pal.* 10.108. Ζεῦ βασιλεῦ, τὰ μὲν ἐσθλὰ καὶ εὐχομένοις καὶ ἀνεύκτοις| ἄμμι δίδου, τὰ δὲ δειλὰ καὶ εὐχομένοις ἀπαλέξειν. Cp. Socrates's prayer at the end of Plato's *Phaedrus*, 279b–c.

> King Zeus, give unto us what is good, whether we pray or pray not;
> But what is grievous, even if we pray for it, do thou avert.

This theological assumption predominates also in early Christian theology, where the proper form of prayer follows the model of Jesus's prayer in the Garden of Gethsemane: "Father, let thy will, not mine, be done."[92] Early Christian critiques of pagan polytheism in the first few centuries of the Common Era pick up the philosophical critiques of prayer as coercive ritual, and the attack returns in the same form when Protestant theologians attack Catholic ritualism. Any ritual that operates automatically constrains the deity to do the mortal's will; any offering that is made constitutes an attempt to bribe the deity who, by definition, needs nothing. These theological fights lie in the background of the influential distinction between magic and religion made by Frazer, and Frazer's influence continues to lurk behind scholarly definitions even in the twenty-first century. When taken to their logical conclusions, such assumptions either render all of ancient polytheistic ritual magical in nature or fail to distinguish the kinds of prayers found in the magical papyri from those found in Homer or other literary and epigraphic sources.[93]

The other criterion often used in modern scholarship, the aim of the prayer, is even more problematic, since many prayers in the magical papyri ask only for divine favor or benevolent contact, whereas many prayers from more normative religious sources ask for concrete harm to someone else. Chryses asks Apollo to bring a plague upon the Greeks, whereas some of the prayers in the Greek Magical Papyri call on the god for whatever aid he might provide: "I call upon you, lord of the universe, in an hour of need; hear me, for my soul is [distressed], and I am perplexed and in want of [everything]."[94] Even those prayers that do ask for a result that might not be something that one could boast of publicly, such as the curses against competitors or the erotic spells that drag an unwilling woman out of her house for sex, still operate in the same way that more publicly acceptable prayers do. The same kind of hierarchy of means applies to all kinds of relations with the gods; the request is made to the divinity most likely to fulfill it, either because of the powers and functions of the deity or because of the relation that the one praying has with the

---

[92] Luke 22:42; Matthew 26:39; Mark 14:36.

[93] This solution of regarding all ritual action as essentially magical particularly troubles older scholarship on Roman religion, which is often characterized as a set of ritualized actions performed for automatic effect but without real belief. Cp. Thomassen 1997 on the problem of classifying all instrumental ritual action as magical; all ritual is performative action, so performative speech and action cannot be the essential defining feature of magic.

[94] Homer, *Iliad* 1.34–40; PGM I.195–222.

deity. The performance of magical prayer includes more extra-ordinary elements, more symbolically charged offerings, but the main difference is the focus on the immediate need and the momentary contact with the god, instead of the reciprocal relationship established in the past and promised for the future.

7

Through a Glass Darkly:
Divination and Magic

And when he comes, ask him about what you wish, about the art
of prophecy, about divination with epic verses, about the sending
of dreams, about obtaining revelations in dreams, about interpretations of dreams, about causing disease, about everything that is
a part of magical knowledge.
(PGM I.327–331)[1]

INTRODUCTION: DIVINATION AND MAGIC

The various forms of divination listed in this spell are collected together
as parts of magical knowledge, and Apollo's arrival provides the magician
the opportunity to inquire into each of them. What then is the relation
between magic and divination? Divination consists of soliciting and receiving messages from the gods; it is in some sense the reverse of prayer, since
it is communication from gods to mortals. If the reciprocal relationships
envisaged in prayers are the normal mode of religion, then how can the
communication from gods to mortals be considered magic?

As with prayer, divination is an area in which the definition of magic
as an extra-ordinary form of ritualized action becomes particularly useful.
Apuleius, in his trial on charges of magic, says that the common definition
of the magician is one who, through communication with the gods, has
the power to do whatever marvels he wishes.[2] The fact of such commu-

---

[1] καὶαδααν εἰν εθν εὲν εα αετόν, περὶ οὗ θέλεις, περὶ μαντείας, περὶ ἐποποιίας, περὶ ὀνειροπομπείας,
περὶ ὀνειραιτησίας, περὶ ὀνειροκριτίας, περὶ κατακλίσεως, περὶ πάντων, ὅ[σ]ων ἐστὶν ἐν τῇ μαγικῇ
ἐμπει[ρίᾳ].

[2] Apul., *Apol.* 26 *Magus est qui communione loquendi cum dis immortalibus ad omnia, quae
velit, incredibili quadam vi cantaminum polleat.* On this definition of magic, see Graf 1999.

nication with the divine is not in itself something to be labeled 'magic,' but certain extra-ordinary forms of divination, performed by extra-ordinary individuals or in extra-ordinary circumstances and producing extra-ordinary results, might well merit the label. The term 'divination' covers a broad range of activities, and a full exploration of the place of divination in the ancient Greco-Roman world is far beyond the scope of this study, but it is worth exploring what extra-ordinary forms of divination are categorized as magic, and in what circumstances.[3] Like prayer and sacrifice, divination forms a large part of the order of normal religion in the Greco-Roman world, so divination is only labeled 'magic' when it makes claims to authority far outside this normal order, either as a superlatively efficacious procedure that depends on specialized arcane knowledge or, conversely, as a bit of traditional superstition that seems ineffective in comparison with the normally accepted procedures.[4]

The variety of ancient terms for divination is nearly as confusing as the plethora of modern terms, since different forms of divination might be called by specific names or lumped together under general terms. Cicero, the first-century BCE Roman politician and philosopher, in his treatise on divination, notes that the Greek and Roman words for divination come from different roots. The Greek word *mantike* comes from *mania*, madness, whereas the Roman *divinatio* comes from *divi*, the gods. The madness associated with the mantic art refers to the ecstatic trances of some diviners, who receive messages from the gods.[5] One who engages in *mantike* is a *mantis*, a term often rendered in English as 'seer,' but 'diviner' is probably the best translation for this general term, since it can cover one who engages in all sorts of divination, from 'seeing' visions to hearing the words of the god to reading the signs in a sheep liver.[6] The English word 'prophet' derives from the Greek *prophetes*, which literally means one who

---

[3] Bouché-Leclercq's four-volume study (1879) remains the most comprehensive, but a number of excellent recent studies treat the subject. Flower 2008b focuses on the figure of the diviner, while Johnston 2008a provides a broader survey, including a discussion of the issue of magic within divination. Struck 2004 grapples with the essential issue of how the interpretive process in divination works, and Struck 2016 approaches the nature of divination through a cognitive perspective.

[4] Gordon 1999a: 178 makes use of Bourdieu's terminology of 'objective profanation' to refer to those practices that are marginalized because of the marginal identities of their practitioners—the old wives' superstitions or the exotic foreign rites—in contrast to the 'intentional profanation' of practices that deliberately distort the normal practices to mark themselves as extra-ordinary.

[5] Modern scholars dismiss this etymology, preferring to derive the word from –men, an Indo-Europena verb stem having to do with mental activity, but as with so many ancient etymologies, it is useful to see what the ancients themselves thought of the word. Roth 1982: 9–18 discusses the etymology, and this (unpublished) dissertation on the mantis remains an important resource.

[6] Contra Flower 2008b: 23, who prefers the word 'seer' for *mantis*. Cicero, *de div.* 1.1.

speaks for another, in this case, a mortal who speaks for the god. 'Prophet' is a useful term to indicate a diviner who communicates (prophesies) the words of the god (prophecy), rather than reads the message through some other means.[7] The Roman *vates* corresponds more nearly with prophet, since it usually refers to one who speaks poetically and prophetically, while the *augur* is a term for an official who divines through signs in the sky. The *haruspex* is a specialized term for an Etruscan diviner, who specializes in the interpretation of livers and lightning. All of these terms are often used interchangeably in the ancient sources, so it seems best to refer in the analysis to divination and diviners.

The divination of diviners may be described as magic in certain cases, but the label of 'magic' applies less to particular forms of divination than to certain diviners, those who make extra-ordinary claims to authority from their divinatory activities, especially when those claims bring them into conflict with more ordinary authorities in the community. The claim to receive special communications from the gods always has the potential to disrupt the social order and win the label of 'magic,' but forms of divination practiced by diviners of the lowest social prestige making the weakest claims to authority may also be labeled 'magic' in the sense of a useless superstition. Magical divination thus appears as a limited subset of divination, abnormal in either a positive or negative sense.

WHY USE DIVINATION?

Mortals may turn to divination whenever a difficult decision needs to be made in a crisis situation.[8] Divination is thus always to some extent an extra-ordinary measure, but some crises are more difficult than others, and some means of seeking the solutions are more extra-ordinary than others. A survey of questions asked at oracular shrines such as Dodona, where the questions were written on small lead tablets, provides a snapshot of the sorts of problems for which the Greeks sought divinatory guidance. Not surprisingly, the queries center around issues of travel, marriage and chil-

---

[7] The most confusing English term is undoubtedly 'oracle,' which can be used to mean the words spoken by a divine entity, the person who conveys those words, or even the sacred place where the prophecy is spoken. The Oracle of Delphi can proclaim the oracles at the Oracle in Delphi. To avoid such confusion, it is preferable to confine the term 'oracle' to the words and refer to the person or place with other terms, e.g., the Pythian priestess who speaks oracles at the temple of Apollo.

[8] As Park 1963: 195 comments in his study of the social contexts of African divination, "Divination is always, I think, associated with a situation which, from the point of view of the client or instigator, seems to call for decision upon some plan of action which is not easily taken." Parker 2000: 78 explains, "Divination helps the consultant to move from doubt to action by providing counsel that is apparently objective and uniquely authoritative."

dren, illness, unsolved crimes, and military and business ventures—precisely the sort of issues the outcome of which is most difficult to control.[9] In any case, divination allows the one consulting to transcend his or her own resources of knowledge or authority in making the difficult decision, and such an expansion of resources provides reassurance and security to the one faced with the choice.[10]

Divination can be a way to remove the onus of decision-making from the individual mortal and displace it to the realm of the divine. From an emic point of view, the divine has greater knowledge and understanding with which to advise a decision, and any advice thus comes weighted with greater authority. From an etic point of view, anthropological studies of divination have pointed to the ways divinatory practices distribute the burden of the choice among the members of the community engaged in the divination.[11] Collins argues that the divinatory process can be analyzed, from the etic point of view, as a performance:

> When divination is conceived as a performed rhetoric that reshapes events as the diviners intended them to have been, we can also see how oracular (re)interpretation moves both forward and backward in time. Divination allows past events to be reconfigured to present communal intentions and aims, while present events can be recalibrated in the light of past experience and made pregnant with future intentions.[12]

---

[9] See the catalog of Dodona responses in Eidinow 2007: 72–124, also categorized in Raphals 2013: 233–239.

[10] Gordon 1997: 150 compares divinatory procedures to hedging one's bets with risk insurance. "In fact, we might see catarchic astrology, analogous to the Hellenistic dice oracle, as a thoroughly 'modern' phenomenon in the Hellenistic world, and in particular as an early form of that archetypal expression of capitalist rationality, risk-insurance." Cp. Eidinow 2007: 16–25 on risk management. Struck approaches divination from a cognitive perspective, comparing it with the modern concept of intuition. "Both are widely accepted, socially authorized placeholders to mark those things we know without quite knowing how we know them. Neither is fully understood, when used in the common parlance of their respective times, and this undertheorized nature is likely to be part of their point and usefulness for the general audiences that put the categories to use" (Struck 2016: 16).

[11] Cp. Abbink 1993: 722: "It is a kind of problem-solving. I have argued that this form of indirect discourse reveals itself as an effective but subtle social tactic, to express and convey personal and community concerns in a veiled, non-direct way. Although acknowledged experts take the lead in interpreting the entrails, they cannot claim any firm authority on the basis of their expertise. Instead, they let the inferential process run its course. Entrail-reading is thus a running commentary on pertinent problems in the community, urging people to take these problems seriously, to be prepared for them and, if necessary, to take redressive action." See also, for the Greek situation, Parker 2000.

[12] Collins 2002: 22. He analyzes the way Odysseus restages the oracular interpretation of the mantis Calchas, recalling the omen seen at the start of the war and reminding the Greeks how it foretold their eventual victory. "Odysseus has the rhetorical and performative author-

The emic and etic perspectives both show divination as a way to make sense of a problematic situation and to provide a way to take action to handle it.

While divination is often thought by modern observers to pertain exclusively to 'seeing the future,' the necessary information to make a decision in the present often has less to do with the future than it does with the past. To resolve a crisis, it is often most important to know what caused that crisis situation, for only then can the proper steps be taken to redress it. In the Greco-Roman world, divinatory inquiries very often seek to discover which deity has been so offended that it caused the crisis situation. The divination tries to identify the event in the past that created the offense and to identity the offended party so that the deity can be propitiated and remove the problem.

At the beginning of the *Iliad*, after Chryses's prayer to Apollo for revenge against the Greeks who have refused to return his daughter has been answered by a plague that has struck down the men and animals in the Greek army, the distressed Greeks gather in assembly to figure out how to deal with this sudden and mysterious illness. Achilles speaks:

> But come, let us ask some seer or priest, or some reader of dreams—
> for a dream too is from Zeus—who might say why Phoebus Apollo
> is so angry, whether he finds fault with a vow or a hecatomb; in hope
> that he may accept the savor of lambs and unblemished goats, and
> be willing to ward off the pestilence from us.[13]

Phoebus Apollo is the god who sends plagues, but Achilles realizes that the Greeks need to discover what might have angered him so much. He suggests several different kinds of divination to identify the cause and expects that the remedy discovered will be propitiatory sacrifices to the god.[14]

When a plague struck the regions of Asia Minor around 160 CE, several cities consulted the oracle of Apollo at Claros to uncover the source of the

---

ity at this moment to enable the Achaeans to envision themselves in the omen (the switch to the nonnormal mode of cognition) at Aulis, and then to emerge from that recollection back into the world of the here and now (the synthesis or mediation) on the Trojan shores, nine years in to battle, invested with a new significance. The prophecy allows them to see themselves as they would ideally like to be, which means to see themselves engaged in an ultimately successful mission that has been confirmed by Zeus himself" (Collins 2002: 25).

[13] Homer, *Iliad* 1.62–67.

[14] Likewise, the people of Thera consulted the oracle at Delphi after a seven-year drought had brought famine and pestilence to the island. "For seven years after this there was no rain in Thera; all the trees in the island except one withered. The Theraeans inquired at Delphi again, and the priestess mentioned the colony they should send to Libya" (Herodotus 4.151.1). It turned out that the cause of the trouble was the neglect of Apollo's earlier instructions to send out a colony to the coast of Africa, so the Theraeans were able to take action to redress the current problem by sending out the founders of Cyrene.

problem. Inscriptions from these cities record the (different) causes and solutions proposed by the oracle for each city.[15] The advice from the oracle might be about what future action to take, but the crucial piece of information in each case was the identification of the past error. The famous diviner Epimenides the Cretan claimed that such knowledge of the past was the special art of the diviner. Aristotle tells us, "For he used to divine, not the future, but only things that were past but obscure."[16] The "best of diviners," Calchas in the *Iliad*, is the one "who knows the things that are, the things that will be, and the things that have been," and this description becomes a standard way to describe the mantic art.[17]

At times, however, the impetus for divination is not some life-threatening problem but merely an unusual occurrence that might betoken some problem in the future. Such omens likewise demand interpretation so that preventative action can be taken. Of course, different people find different things unusual enough to count as significant omens. The superstitious man caricatured by Theophrastus consults a whole series of diviners whenever he has a dream, and if a mouse nibbles through one of his bags of grain, he takes it as an omen and consults a religious specialist to see which god he should propitiate.[18] Some signs, however, appear significant enough to the whole community that the community sanctions divinatory consultation. Demosthenes quotes a response from the oracle at Delphi when the Athenians decided to consult the oracle about some sign that appeared in the sky.

> May good fortune attend you. The people of the Athenians make inquiry about the sign which has appeared in the heavens, asking

[15] Várhelyi 2001 discusses the collection of different responses, which range from attributing the plague to magical attacks, to unpropitiated spirits of the earth, to a need for public festivals (involving all the youths of the city) to the major Olympian deities. Cp. Johnston 2008a: 79–80, who points to the ways the oracular responses were tailored to the cities' ideas about the problem.

[16] Aristotle, *Rhet.* 3.17. Ἐπιμενίδης ὁ Κρής - ἐκεῖνος γὰρ περὶ τῶν ἐσομένων οὐκ ἐμαντεύετο, ἀλλὰ περὶ τῶν γεγονότων μὲν ἀδήλων δέ.

[17] Homer, *Iliad* 1.69–70. Cp. Hesiod, *Theogony* 38; and the collection of parallels in Pease (1920) 1979: 204–205 [i.366–367]), with the addenda on 596 (ii.414). A similar skill is recommended for the Hippocratic doctor: "Knowing beforehand and telling beforehand, in the presence of the patients, what is, what has been, and what will be, and mentioning details which the patients do not mention, he will more easily be believed to know about the patients' condition, so that people dare to entrust themselves to the physician" (Hippocrates, *Progn.* 1.1).

[18] Theophrastus, *Char.* 16. "If a mouse nibbles through a bag of barley, he goes to the expounder of sacred law and asks what he should do; and if the answer is that he should give it to the tanner to sew up he disregards the advice and performs an apotropaic sacrifice. . . . When he has a dream he visits not only dream-analysts but also seers and bird-watchers to ask which god or goddess he should pray to."

what the Athenians should do, or to what god they should offer sacrifice or make prayer, in order that the issue of the sign may be for their advantage. It will be well for the Athenians with reference to the sign which has appeared in the heavens that they sacrifice with happy auspices to Zeus most high, to Athena most high, to Heracles, to Apollo the deliverer, and that they send due offerings to the Amphiones; that they sacrifice for good fortune to Apollo, god of the ways, to Leto and to Artemis, and that they make the streets steam with the savour of sacrifice; that they set forth bowls of wine and institute choruses and wreathe themselves with garlands after the custom of their fathers, in honor of all the Olympian gods and goddesses, lifting up the right hand and the left, and that they be mindful to bring gifts of thanksgiving after the custom of their fathers. And ye shall offer sacrificial gifts after the custom of your fathers to the hero-founder after whom ye are named; and for the dead their relatives shall make offerings on the appointed day according to established custom.[19]

The Romans likewise would consult their most authoritative source of divinatory wisdom, the Sibylline Books, when some strange event occurred. Phlegon of Tralles, in his collection of *Mirabilia* (amazing things), records the oracle that was brought forth at the birth of a hermaphrodite, instructing the Romans to perform sacrifices to Demeter and Persephone.

And indeed I say that one day a woman will give birth to a hermaphrodite having all the male parts and as many of those as infant female women show. I shall no longer keep hidden but indeed I shall tell out openly the sacrifices to Demeter and holy Persephone, through my loom, I myself a queenly goddess, those things, if you obey me, for most venerable Demeter and holy Persephone.[20]

The oracle goes on to prescribe specific sacrifices and festival celebrations, all to be performed by groups of women in the city, maidens, matrons, and old women each performing different rites. The abnormal birth thus seems to signal the anger of the goddesses most concerned with the lives of women in the community, and so the women must redress the problem by paying further honors to these divinities.

What is seen as significant enough to warrant divination depends on the individuals and their circumstances, but the more startlingly abnormal

[19] Demosthenes 43.66.
[20] Phlegon of Tralles, *Mirabilia* 10. καί τοί ποτέ φημι γυναῖκα| Ἀνδρόγυνον τέξεσθαι ἔχοντά περ ἄρσενα πάντα| Νηπίαχοί θ᾽ ὅσα θηλύτεραι φαίνουσι γυναῖκες.| Οὐκ ἔτι δὴ κρύψω, θυσίας δέ τοι ἐξαγορεύσω| Προφρονέως Δήμητρι καὶ ἁγνῇ Περσεφονείῃ,| Ἱστῷ δ᾽ αὐτὴ ἄνασσα θεά, τὰ μὲν εἴ κε πίθηαι| Σεμνοτάτῃ Δήμητρι καὶ ἁγνῇ Περσεφονείῃ (my trans.).

the phenomenon and the more dire the situation, the more likely people are to turn to divination. A very strange occurrence like an abnormal birth is less likely to be treated as a significant omen from the gods if life is in general unproblematic, while in times of trouble even a small anomaly is apt to be taken as some sort of sign that could provide guidance if properly interpreted. Such circumstances also inform the methods of divination chosen, since the ancient Greeks and Romans had a wide variety of divinatory practices to which they could turn in times of tribulation.

HOW DOES DIVINATION WORK?

All forms of divination in the ancient Greco-Roman world seek special information from the divine to deal with some kind of extra-ordinary crisis, but the actual means could differ widely, from reading meaning in a chance sneeze or twitch of the eye to receiving the information directly from a god. There are various ways in which this range of methods may be categorized, and there is an unusual amount of evidence from antiquity about the ways the kinds of divination were imagined to work. All of the major philosophical schools propounded theories about divination, abstracting and systematizing the principles by which the unphilosophical practiced divination. Some divination is understood on the model of speech as interpersonal communication between deity and mortal, while other kinds are seen on the model of writing as impersonal communication that involves the decipherment of signs. In the *Phaedrus*, Plato draws the fundamental distinction between inspired prophecy and other forms of divination through signs, and this dichotomy remains basic to all subsequent discussions, whether described as direct and indirect, natural and technical, interpersonal and textual, or otherwise. Plato connects the art of the *mantis* with *mania*, madness, arguing that the inspired diviners of the oracular shrines at Delphi and Dodona do their divinatory work while out of their minds.[21] By contrast, those who read the signs of birds or other omens work rationally to interpret the meanings.[22]

---

[21] Plato, *Phaedrus* 244a–b. "In reality the greatest of blessings come to us through madness, when it is sent as a gift of the gods. For the prophetess at Delphi and the priestesses at Dodona when they have been mad have conferred many splendid benefits upon Greece both in private and in public affairs, but few or none when they have been in their right minds."

[22] In *Phaedrus* 244c–d, Plato plays off the name, deriving οἰωνιστική, augury, from οἰονοΐστική, since it provides mental activity and information (οἰήσει νοῦν τε καὶ ἱστορίαν). "And so, when they gave a name to the investigation of the future which rational persons conduct through observation of birds and by other signs, since they furnish mind [*nous*] and information [*historia*] to human thought [*oiesis*] from the intellect [*dianoia*] they called it the oionoistic [*oionoistike*] art, which modern folk now call *oiōnistic* making it more high-sounding by introducing the long O."

In the *Phaedrus,* Plato privileges the divine communications that come through prophetic madness (just as he privileges oral communication over textual), and the inspired prophet continues to present the more exceptional figure throughout the tradition, as the proverb attests, "Many are the lot throwers [*thrioboloi*], but the diviners [*manteis*] are few."[23] Inspired prophecy requires direct contact and communication between the divine and the mortal, a rare and special event that requires either the god to reach out to the mortal or the mortal to the god. In either case, a mortal who comes into proximity with the divine must be unusually pure or extraordinarily favored by the deity, and the strain of the contact may be extreme, as in the depictions of the raving diviner Cassandra.[24] Some theories of prophetic divination imagine the connection between god and mortal only in the most immortal and divine part of the mortal, the soul. The soul, when the diviner is in a trance or asleep, may be freer to establish contact with the divine, and Platonic philosophers such as Plutarch and Iamblichus devote no little effort to working out how such a process might operate in accordance with their ideas of the soul and the nature of the cosmic order.[25] Those whose souls are better able to make contact with the divine are the best diviners, whether they communicate with the god in a dream or in an ecstatic trance.

If the inspired prophets capable of making such direct contacts with the divine are few and far between, indirect communication may still happen through a number of means. The gods make signs in the phenomenal world that indicate their messages, and divination becomes the art of interpreting such signs. The movement of a bird in the sky, a flash of lightning and thunder, or even the shape of the liver of a sacrificial animal may be a message sent from a god to the mortal who observes it. In some cases, the divine act of signification is in the particular sign or omen, but some philosophical theories generalize this idea into a systematic view of the cos-

[23] Steph. Byz. s.v. θρία. Cp. the (probably older) proverb in Plato's *Phaedo* 69c: "Many are the narthex-bearers, but the *bacchoi* are few." Plato is less complimentary to inspired prophecy in other dialogues, but the same distinction between communication to the inspired and rational interpretation of signs appears in, e.g., *Timaeus* 71e–72a, where the seat of irrational divination is located in the liver.

[24] Cp. Aeschylus, *Ag.* 1035–1330. As Ustinova 2013: 32–33, points out, the descriptions of the Sibyl in Vergil, *Aeneid* 6.45–50 and Heraclitus, fr. 92 = (Plutarch, *de Pyth. orac.* 397a), as well as those of the Pythia in Lucan, *Pharsalia* 5. 147–196 and Plutarch, *de def. orac.* 438a–b provide the same kind of image, and the Delphic Pythia only gave oracles nine times a year.

[25] Cp. Plutarch, *de def. orac.* 431e–432e. Iamblichus, *de myst.* 3.4–6 describes the prophetic trance in Neoplatonic terms of the soul's participation in the higher ontological levels of the cosmos. The third book of Iamblichus's *de mysteriis* indeed represents the most extensive theorization of inspired divination from antiquity. See further Johnston 2008a: 40–47.

mos—the whole natural order is a sign system that can be read.[26] In his treatise on divination, Cicero describes the Stoic idea.

> In the beginning, the universe was so created that certain results would be preceded by certain signs, which are given sometimes by entrails and by birds, sometimes by lightnings, by portents, and by stars, sometimes by dreams, and sometimes by utterances of persons in a frenzy.[27]

The benevolence of the gods assures us that they must want to provide us with help; therefore, divination of the signs that they leave must be possible. While the Stoics perhaps developed this view of divination most elaborately, the idea that the gods have left signs in the world for mortals to decipher underlies the ancient explanations of most forms of indirect divination. Aristotle, in his treatise on dream interpretation, suggests that the sleeping mind may pick up mental stimuli, the sort of thing Demokritos describes as *eidola*, images of existing things, and figure out the pattern of future events.[28] Plutarch's character Theon suggests that the events of the past, present, and future fit together in a logical pattern, which may be deduced, as in a logical proof.

> The god, moreover, is a prophet, and the prophetic art concerns the future that is to result from things present and past. For there is nothing of which either the origin is without cause or the foreknowledge thereof without reason; but since all present events follow in close conjunction with past events, and all future events follow in close conjunction with present events, in accordance with a regular procedure which brings them to fulfilment from beginning to end, he who understands, in consonance with Nature, how to fathom the connexions and interrelations of the causes one with another knows and can declare "What now is, and in future shall be, and has been of aforetime." Very excellently did Homer place first in order the present, then the future and the past, for the syllogism based on hypothesis has its source in what is.[29]

---

[26] The implications of this idea for literary interpretation and the development of semiotic theories in the ancient world far exceed the scope of this inquiry. For the best treatment of this idea, see Struck 2004. Manetti 1993 explores theories of the sign in antiquity, including divination.

[27] Cicero, *de div.* 1.52 (118).

[28] Cp. Aristotle, *div. somn.* 464a. Cp. Cicero (*de div.* 1.131 = Demokritos, *test.* 138), who informs us that Demokritos argued for the validity of liver divination based on the correlations between the health of the liver and the conditions of the animals, fields, and environment.

[29] Plutarch, *de E* 6 387b.

The fundamental order of the cosmos, arranged by the divine intelligence, provides a way for mortals to use their reason to understand the signs provided by the gods, linking cause to effect, past to future.[30]

Not all the ancients shared the philosophical assumption of a rationally ordered cosmos for which a diviner might deduce the future. A line from a lost play of Euripides, "the best prophet is the good guesser," is often quoted by skeptics of divination.[31] Even those thinkers who believed in an ordered cosmos might not accept the validity of divination, and the second book of Cicero's treatise on divination contains a sustained attack on the Stoic ideas of divination. Fraudulent diviners were a favorite subject of comedy, and the third-century CE Christian apologist Hippolytus devotes a section of his treatise *The Refutation of All Heresies* to debunking various divination procedures.[32] The satirist Lucian devotes a whole treatise to the exposure of the extremely popular and successful prophet Alexander of Abonoteichos, whose oracular shrine provided direct revelations from the mouth of a human-headed serpent named Glycon in the second century CE (around 150–170 CE). Coins with the image of Glycon and other material evidence attest to the widespread appeal and acceptance of Alexander's oracle, but Lucian provides explanations of the ways in which the tricks were worked much in the same manner as Hippolytus does a few decades later. It is open to question, however, whether these elaborate explanations of fraud are any more reliable than the descriptions of divinatory procedures that take their validity for granted, since many of these rationalized procedures are quite implausible as successful frauds and may simply be the imaginative constructs of those convinced that the divinations must have been fake. In any case, despite an abundance of claims to the falsity of particular diviners or procedures, the validity of divination as a system seems to have been accepted by the vast majority of people in the ancient Greco-Roman world, and the arguments for its validity and the specific ways divination worked outweigh both in quantity and quality the arguments against it.

Modern scholars, approaching the topic from an etic perspective, need not accept the validity of the divinatory process in the same ways that the ancients did from their own emic perspective within the cultural system.

---

[30] Cp. Plutarch, *de Pyth. orac.* 398f for a similar idea.

[31] μάντις δ᾽ ἄριστος ὅστις εἰκάζει καλῶς. Euripides, fr. 973 Nauck. This proverbial line is quoted not only in Plutarch, *de Pyth. orac.* 399a, but also *de def. orac.* 432c. Cicero, *de div.* 2.5 (12) renders it *bene qui coniciet, vatem hunc perhibeto optimum.* Cp. Menander, fr. 225 Kock, Com. Att. Frag. iii.65.

[32] Hippolytus, *Haer.* 4.28–42 contains, in addition to the explanation of drawing down the moon (see above, ch. 1), debunkings of sealed letter questions, bowl divination (lecanomancy), fire apparitions, and many other tricks. See Kelhoffer 2008 for an analysis of similarities between Hippolytus's descriptions and the recipes in the PGM.

Nevertheless, taking as given the fact that those who participated in divination accepted its validity, modern scholars can analyze how divination worked in the ancient world.

One feature common to all means of divination is the dynamic interplay between the fixed elements of the system and the more or less random variables. The fixed elements are determined by the religious tradition, just as the fixed elements of a linguistic system are determined by the cultural tradition, while the variation of the variable elements creates meaning.[33] As Gordon explains,

> Most systems of divination, from reading tea-leaves or coffee-grounds to the trigram of the I Ching, consist of a limited (albeit sometimes very large) set of meanings linked to a fixed matrix, crossed by an element of chance. Thus tea-leaves, "makeshift ideograms," are the matrix, the meanings are stored in the memory of the practitioner, chance enters in the outfall of the gesture of emptying the cup.[34]

The fixed matrix provides the range of possible responses to any divinatory query, while the variable elements mean that the answer is not predetermined by the inquirer.[35] To take a simple modern example, the popular Magic 8-Ball toy has a twenty-sided object floating in liquid, and each side provides a different answer. The range of answers is limited by the number of sides, and the shaking of the ball to make one side float to the top provides the randomization. Some divinatory systems are far more complex than others, with much larger and complicated fixed matrices of responses, while others involve very little complexity.

The relation between the fixed and variable elements is much easier to perceive in technical forms of divination that involve the reading of signs, but even natural or inspired forms involve the same kind of interplay. Even

---

[33] Cp. Frankfurter 2005: 236: "Divination always involves the creative use of tradition: that is, some degree of *authority*, of recognizability, that can be brought to bear on the situation at hand. This tradition may comprise the performative style of a medium, the identity of the speaking god, the divination materials themselves, the expertise of the diviner, or simply the shrine at which divination occurs. Tradition provides the framework, the fixed and sacred theater, for the 'chance' occurrence in the materials that signals the god's own communication." Maurizio 1995: 81 notes, "An important aspect of divination as institutionalized procedure is just this—that it provides 'resistance' in its own right to any client's proposal. Without such resistance, real or imagined, the diviner or the divinatory institution would lose its credibility and appear merely as a slavish accessory to whomever it served. By establishing resistance, randomizing devices insure that divination is an 'objective' system of access to divine knowledge."

[34] Gordon 1997: 141. The idea of randomization in divination is explored in the introduction and several of the essays in Johnston and Struck 2005.

[35] Park 1963 discusses the "resistance" built into every divinatory system, the element that convinces the participants of the objectivity of the oracle.

when the god communicates directly with the mortal inquirer, the communication from the divinity in inspired divination never comes unambiguously but still always requires some sort of interpretation.[36] Maurizio points out that "in the case of spirit possession, the human body becomes the randomizing device. The spirit may speak through the human body by means of twitches, pains, dreams, automatic writing, or it may employ the voice of the individual."[37] Even if the communication comes in the form of a voice, the words may be unintelligible sounds or, as so often in the case of the famous oracles like the oracle of Apollo at Delphi, the utterances of the divine voice may be ambiguous, riddling, or confusing. The Delphic oracle's response to Croesus's inquiry whether he should attack Persia, "If you cross the river Halys, you will destroy a great kingdom," leaves ambiguous whether that great kingdom is that of the Persians or of Croesus's own Lydia.[38] Whether the variable elements are the sounds of the human voice or the fall of the dice, the divinatory practice produces some configuration of those elements that can be read against the traditional fixed matrix to produce meaning. Like any semiotic system, the interplay of the specific signs variably produced on each occasion with the traditional patterns of signification produces the message.

As scholars have pointed out, not all systems of divination are equally authoritative in the cultural tradition; rather, there is always a hierarchy of means that ranks some above others.[39] Four factors affect the position of any given means of divination within this hierarchy: the level of complexity, the level of difficulty of access, the level of expense, and the level of social prestige. A divinatory procedure, like consulting the oracle at Delphi, that requires a long journey, involves many complicated and expensive preliminaries, and carries the weight of authority from a long and widespread tradition, will naturally be valued more highly than a passerby's simple reading of a bird's flight across the sky from left to right. The complexities and expenses seem to guarantee the significance of the former, while the commonplace occurrence of the bird's flight makes it seem more likely to be an insignificant chance occurrence. On the other hand,

---

[36] As Parker 2000: 79 notes, "The brusque contemptuous tone that the Pythia sometimes adopted towards persons of rank (P /W, ii. xxv), so different from anything possible for her as a humble peasant woman of Delphi, was a sure sign that through her spoke the god. Her riddling speech too provided a kind of resistance to the understanding." Johnston 2001: 109–111 discusses the way that the interpretation of what a medium says actually functions as another randomizing factor in the process, even as the interpretation appears to derandomize the enigmatic answer.

[37] Maurizio 1995: 81.

[38] Herodotus 1.53.

[39] Gordon usefully applies this concept from Evans-Pritchard 1937 in a number of his studies of Greek magic and divination; see especially Gordon 1997 and Gordon 1999a.

if the bird omen is observed by an officially appointed augur at a specially designated sacred time, this simple procedure is invested with more social prestige, while even a complex procedure may rank lower in the hierarchy of means if performed by someone of dubious authority.

This hierarchy of means also sustains the viability of the whole divinatory system, since if one means disappoints, there is always a better method that might provide satisfaction.[40] Access to the privileged information from divination, it would seem, increases with the level of complexity, expense, and so forth of the methods used to obtain it, so if the answers provided by one type of divination seem inaccurate or unhelpful, perhaps a more complicated or expensive procedure would provide (or at least would have provided) a better answer. Moreover, because there are many factors that go into this hierarchy of means within the traditional system, new variations and methods can always be devised that improve upon other means in terms of complexity, access, expense, or prestige.[41] The historical record indeed shows a bewildering variety of forms of divination that range all over the hierarchy of means, from the simplest folk prognostications to the most elaborate rituals for obtaining direct contact with a god. While none of these methods are inevitably labeled as 'magic,' it is worth noting that the extreme ends of the spectrum, both the peasant superstitions and the arcane rituals, tend more often to be classified as magic, while the middle ranges fit more comfortably into the category of normative religious practice. Once again, the cue of *efficacy* proves most valid, as those methods whose efficacy appears extra-ordinary, either non-normatively high or non-normatively low, more often receive the label of 'magic.'

WHAT ARE THE VARIETIES OF DIVINATION?

In analyzing the various methods of divination in classical antiquity, most modern scholars of the subject, starting with the monumental study of Bouché-Leclercq in 1879, have followed the lead of the most comprehensive

[40] Cp. Park 1963: 202: "these various forms of trial should be conceived as ranging along a gradient of increasing unimpeachability; and that each item of procedure should be understood as essentially contributing toward that end—the dramatic establishment of an ostensibly irrevocable judgment."

[41] As Gordon 1997: 147 notes, "This hierarchy of means has two effects relevant in the present context: on the one hand it helps to prevent scepticism relating to individual incidents (i.e. disconfirmation) from corroding belief in the system as a whole; on the other, by leaving plenty of room for innovation especially in low-level practices, it permits the system to adapt to new circumstances and perceptions."

analysis of the topic from antiquity, Cicero's dialogue *On Divination*. Following Plato's distinction, Cicero's interlocutors agree that divination may be divided into two types, the technical or artificial kind and the natural or interpersonal kind.

> You divided divination into two kinds, one artificial [*artificiosum*] and the other natural [*natural*]. The artificial consists in part of conjecture and in part of long-continued observation; while the natural is that which the soul has seized, or, rather, has obtained, from a source outside itself—that is, from the divine, whence all human souls have been drawn off, received, or poured out.[42]

Technical, indirect, or artificial divination consists in the observation of significant phenomena and the puzzling out of the significance, whereas natural or inspired divination does not rely on such interpretive techniques but rather on interpersonal communication with the divine. Of course, these lines may be blurred at times, since the signs that are read in technical divination may be understood as indirect communications from the divine, whereas most forms of communication from the gods involve some sort of mediation and interpretation.[43] Nevertheless, the distinction between more and less direct communication with the divine is a useful one, with the added benefit of being an ancient as well as modern scholarly categorical division.

TECHNICAL DIVINATION: READING THE DIVINE SIGNS

Technical or artificial divination involves reading and interpreting significant phenomena, but there is a huge variety in the kinds of phenomena that may be considered significant, ranging from the sights and sounds of various animals and people to more arbitrary systems like the fall of dice and lots or the movement of flames or oil on water. In each method, however, the random element is linked to a fixed matrix of meanings, which may be either items of traditional lore or a fixed set of texts.

[42] Cicero, de div. 2.26 XI. *Duo enim genera divinandi esse dicebas, unum 'artificiosum,' alterum 'naturale.' Artificiosum constare partim ex coniectura, partim ex observatione diuturna. Naturale quod animus arriperet aut exciperet extrinsecus ex divinitate, unde omnes animos haustos aut acceptos aut libatos haberemus.*

[43] Ustinova 2013 argues for the continuing validity of this emic distinction, despite recent scholarship (e.g., Flower 2008b: 84–91 and the essays in Georgoudi, Koch Piettre, and Schmidt 2012) that prefers to see a spectrum of different methods without a clear divide. Nissinen 2010: 345 argues that prophecy and omen divination belong to the same "symbolic universe," even if they are diffent kinds of procedures, requiring different qualifications and expertise.

Kleromancy: Lots, Dice, and Knucklebones

This relation of fixed matrix and random element can be seen most easily in the various forms of kleromancy. There are many different types of divination by lots (*kleroi*), dice (*kuboi*), or knucklebones (*astragaloi*, the knucklebones of sheep or goats, which serve as four-sided dice), and the fall of the lots or dice provides the random element influenced by the divine to be matched with the fixed set of meanings to determine the significance.

Dice oracles could provide a way to contact a god in his own shrine. Pausanias tells of a small cave shrine to Heracles Buraicus, where the worshipper throws a set of four dice lying on the table in the sanctuary and reads out the answer to his inquiry from a set of answers written on a tablet nearby. This procedure seems akin to that of a number of dice oracles in Asia Minor, where some of the tablets have been uncovered in excavations, showing the list of answers that correspond to each combination of the roll of five knucklebones.

> If three fours and two ones are cast: the daimon will lead you on the way that you undertake, and the lover of smiling, Aphrodite, will lead you toward good things. You will return with rich fruit and an untroubled Fate.[44]

The inscribed stone tablets preserve the matrices of meaning for these public oracles, but such divination could also be performed privately. At the beginning of one of the Greek Magical Papyri is an elaborate dice oracle where the random element of the three dice is keyed to a selection of 216 verses from the Homeric epics, for example, "6-2-5 But hurry into battle, and rouse the other soldiers [Homer, *Iliad* 19.139]." Of course, the Homeric verses themselves require further interpretation in order to apply them to the question asked, but such a negotiation of meaning is part of the ritual of oracular consultation.[45] The beginning of PGM VII is lost, but another papyrus codex with a Homer oracle preserves the preliminary ritual:

> First, you must know the day on which to use the Oracle; second, you must pray and speak the incantation of the god and pray inwardly for what you want; third, you must take the die and throw it three

---

[44] Graf 2005: 87. Graf provides a translation of the set of answers from the oracles at Kremna and Perge, with an excellent discussion of dice oracles in general. Cp. Pausanias 7.25.10 for Heracles Buraicus.

[45] PGM VII.1–221. Cp. the single text that the charlatan priests in Apuleius, *Met.* 9.8 provide to all divinatory queries, adapting the interpretation to the situation, with Grottanelli 2005: 133–135.

times and having thrown consult the Oracle according to the number of the three throws of the die, as it is composed.

> Hear, Lord, that art in Lycia's fertile land
> Or yet in Troy, that hearest in every place
> His voice who suffers, as I suffer now
> Tell me this truth, that I may come to know
> What most I wish and is my heart's desire.[46]

A listing of propitious days to consult the Homer oracle follows, providing further ritual instructions, but the process has the advantage of being easily performed almost anywhere.[47]

A more complex system of lot divination, known as the *sortes Astrampsychi* after the famous magician Astrampsychos, provides a similar set of fixed answers, but in a complicated relation to a fixed set of questions. The inquirer would select one of ninety-two questions, and for each question there were ten possible answers. This oracle procedure, first attested in the second century CE, survived through Christianizing adaptations into the Late Antique era.[48]

Another mode of divination with a fixed matrix is the alphabet oracle, where a board is inscribed with the letters of the alphabet (or some other set of signs), and a random motion, such as a ring suspended by a thread, picks out a sequence of letters to answer the divinatory question. The historian Ammianus Marcellinus provides details of such a divination by a group of conspirators in fourth-century CE Rome, who want to know who will become emperor after Valentinian.

> The tripod was placed in the middle of a house purified thoroughly with Arabic perfumes; on it was placed a perfectly round plate made of various metallic substances. Around its outer rim the written forms of the twenty-four letters of the alphabet were skillfully engraved, separated from one another by carefully measured spaces. Then a man clad in linen garments, shod also in linen sandals and having a fillet wound about his head, carrying twigs from a tree of good omen,

---

[46] P. Oxy. 3831 in Parsons 1989: 46. As Parsons notes, the first three lines of the incantation are adapted from *Iliad* 16.514–516, the following line from *Odyssey* 1.174, and the next from *Odyssey* 18.113. See especially Martín-Hernández 2014 for the comparison of the Homeromanteia in the PGM and other papyri, P.Bon. 3 (= SM 77) and P. Oxy. 3831. For the PGM VII Homeromanteion, see Karanika 2011 and Zografou 2013c.

[47] The Homeromanteion in PGM VII likewise has a list of propitious times and days following the verses (VII.155–167), although a recipe for repelling insects from the house intervenes (VII.149–154).

[48] For an introduction to the *sortes Astrampsychi* and an English translation, see Stewart and Morrell in Hansen 1998.

after propitiating in a set formula the divine power from whom predictions come, having full knowledge of the ceremonial, stood over
the tripod as priest and set swinging a hanging ring fitted to a very
fine linen thread and consecrated with mystic arts. This ring, passing
over the designated intervals in a series of jumps, and falling upon
this and that letter which detained it, made hexameters corresponding with the questions and completely finished in feet and rhythm,
like the Pythian verses which we read, or those given out from the
oracles of the Branchidae.[49]

The conspirators are too hasty, however, for when the ring starts to spell out
Theo . . . , they assume that it is validating their choice of a usurper, Theodorus, and break off the session. Theodorus is put to death with the rest
of the conspirators, but Valentinian's eventual successor is Theodosius.

A curious device was excavated near Pergamon, which may have had
a similar function, since it includes a metal disk inscribed with three outer
circles with eight sets of characters, as well as a center circle with seven
sets. But the three sets of eight characters do not correspond to the twenty-
four letters of the Greek alphabet, nor would it be easy to set up a method
of using them to spell out words even if they did. Modern scholars do not
agree on how it might have been used, but the strange characters and
complex design, as well as the three images of Hekate on the base of the
stand, suggest that it would have been labeled a magical device by the
ancients as well as by modern scholars.[50]

Augury in the Flight of Birds

Many forms of divination are much less complex than the Late Antique
device from Pergamon. One of the most basic and widespread forms of
divination involves observation of the movement of birds, *oionomanteia*.[51]
Indeed, the term, like the Roman name of augury, is often used in ancient
texts to refer to divination in general, regardless of the form. As the poet
Hesiod claims, "That man is happy and lucky in them who knows all these
things and does his work without offending the deathless gods, who dis-
cerns the omens of birds and avoids transgression."[52] Such ornithomancy
may simply involve observing an unusual motion and interpreting its significance, or it may involve a more complex procedure, noting the number

[49] Amm. Marc. 29.1.30–31.
[50] See now Mastrocinque 2002 and Gordon 2002a for discussions of this curious item;
Gordon suggests it may have been used for captromancy or lecanomancy.
[51] Cp. M. Dillon 1996 for an overview of the evidence.
[52] Hesiod, *Works and Days* 825–828. τάων εὐδαίμων τε καὶ ὄλβιος, ὃς τάδε πάντα| εἰδὼς
ἐργάζηται ἀναίτιος ἀθανάτοισιν,| ὄρνιθας κρίνων καὶ ὑπερβασίας ἀλεείνων.

and timing of birds moving through a particular space in the sky at a particular time. Homer provides some dramatic examples of the simplest form.

> So spoke Telemachus, and in answer far-seeing Zeus sent forth two eagles, flying from on high, from a mountain peak. For a time they flew in the stream of the wind side by side with wings outspread; but when they reached the middle of the many-voiced assembly, then they wheeled about, flapping their wings rapidly, and down on the heads of all they looked, and death was in their glance. Then they tore with their talons one another's cheeks and necks on either side, and darted away to the right across the houses and the city of those who stood there. The people were seized with wonder at the birds when their eyes beheld them, and pondered in their hearts what was to come to pass. Then among them spoke the old hero Halitherses, son of Mastor, for he surpassed all men of his day in knowledge of birds and in uttering words of fate. He with good intent addressed their assembly and spoke among them: "Hearken now to me, men of Ithaca, to the word that I shall say; and to the suitors especially do I declare and announce these things, since on them a great woe is rolling. For Odysseus shall not long be away from his friends, but even now, I doubt not, he is near, and is sowing slaughter and death for these men, one and all. Yes, and to many others of us also who dwell in clear-seen Ithaca will he be an evil. But long before that let us take thought how we may make an end of this—or rather let them of themselves make an end, for this is without doubt their better course. Not as one untried do I prophesy, but with sure knowledge.[53]

The fighting eagles are a striking sight, but the community turns to the individual who has proved himself a skillful interpreter in the past to determine the meaning of the omen. It is worth noting that the suitors, for whom Halitherses prophesies doom, brutally reject his interpretation and authority, threatening him and arguing that not all the movements of birds are significant, but, in epic literature, as in tragedy, the diviner is almost always correct, and the suitors meet the doom prophesied for them.[54]

The founding of Rome is linked to a story of simple bird divination, as the twin brothers Romulus and Remus seated themselves on the hills of what was to become Rome and looked for the flight of birds. Remus saw six, while his twin saw twelve, so the Romulus became the founder of the

[53] Homer, *Odyssey* 2.146–170.

[54] As a number of scholars have noted; cp. Parker 1983: 15; Flower 2008b: 19; Smith 1989.

city he named after himself.[55] Such simple omens could be easily interpreted by any observer, but other more elaborate systems of deriving meaning from birds were also devised, increasing the complexity and the need for an expert, especially in the official auguries of the Roman state.[56] Although Plutarch mentions that some people have an art of divining with fish in the way that Greeks do with birds, the movements of other animals were less often interpreted than those of birds.[57]

Extispicy: Divination through Entrails

While the movements of living birds and other animals might provide significant omens to be read, their carcasses could also provide even better fodder for divination. Extispicy, the reading of entrails, was performed nearly every time an animal sacrifice was made to the gods. As the animal was butchered on the altar and the portions distributed, the condition of certain parts was examined. Some looked to the entrails (*splanchna*), while others noted the way that the tailbone (*osphys*) curled as it was roasted, but the liver was the most important element of the sacrificed animal for divinatory purposes.[58] Sheep and goats seem to have been the preferred animals for such divination, but in grander circumstances, cattle might be used, and likewise other animals in other cases.[59]

[55] Plutarch, *Vit. Rom.* 9.4.

[56] Collins 2002: 28–29 discusses a late sixth- or early fifth-century BCE inscription from Ephesus (LSAM 30) that elaborates a basic right-favorable vs. left-unfavorable binary distinction with other binaries, such as whether the bird has its wing tips lifted or not.

[57] Plutarch, *de soll.* 976c. καὶ περὶ Σούραν πυνθάνομαι, κώμην ἐν τῇ Λυκίᾳ Φελλοῦ μεταξὺ καὶ Μύρων, καθεζομένους ἐπ᾽ ἰχθύσιν ὥσπερ οἰωνοῖς διαμαντεύεσθαι τέχνῃ τινὶ καὶ λόγῳ ἑλίξεις καὶ φυγὰς καὶ διώξεις αὐτῶν ἐπισκοποῦντας. "Indeed, I have heard that near Sura, a village in Lycia between Phellus and Myra, men sit and watch the gyrations and flights and pursuits of fish and divine from them by a professional and rational system, as others do with birds." Birds remained a favored source of omens to be interpreted throughout the Greco-Roman world, and Plutarch attributes the significance of bird movements and cries to the gods. "It is, in fact, no small or ignoble division of divination, but a great and very ancient one, which takes its name from birds; for their quickness of apprehension and their habit of responding to any manifestation, so easily are they diverted, serves as an instrument for the god, who directs their movements, their calls or cries, and their formations which are sometimes contrary, sometimes favouring, as winds are; so that he uses some birds to cut short, others to speed enterprises and inceptions to the destined end." οὐ γάρ τι μικρὸν οὐδ᾽ ἄδοξον, ἀλλὰ πολὺ καὶ παμπάλαιον μαντικῆς μόριον οἰωνιστικὴ κέκληται· τὸ γὰρ ὀξὺ καὶ νοερὸν αὐτῶν καὶ δι᾽ εὐστροφίαν ὑπήκοον ἁπάσης φαντασίας ὥσπερ ὀργάνῳ τῷ θεῷ παρέχει χρῆσθαι καὶ τρέπειν ἐπί τε κίνησιν ἐπί τε φωνὰς καὶ γηρύματα καὶ σχήματα νῦν μὲν ἐνστατικὰ νῦν δὲ φορὰ καθάπερ πνεύματα τὰς μὲν ἐπικόπτοντα τὰς δ᾽ ἐπευθύνοντα πράξεις καὶ ὁρμὰς εἰς τὸ τέλος (Plutarch, *de soll.* 975a–b).

[58] On the osphys, see van Straten 1988, as well as S. Peirce 1993 and Ekroth 2009.

[59] Ogden 2001: 197–201 discusses cases in which human entrails are said to be used for perverse or magical divinations, but all the cases seem clearly to be slanderous polemics where the person is accused of perverting normal practice.

Such sacrificial divinations seem to have been performed regularly be-fore battle, since the onset of fighting is one of the most high-risk activities possible, and the participants are naturally anxious to assess their chances before the fight begins. Numerous stories in the Greek historians recount that a battle is delayed because one side or the other is waiting to obtain favorable omens before the charge.[60] Xenophon tells of how a continuing series of unfavorable readings of the sacrificial entrails prevent him from leading his mercenaries off on a raid for provisions. When his men com-plain and begin to accuse him of deliberate stalling, he invites anyone who wishes to come see the sacrifices for themselves.[61] Not only does this epi-sode underscore the seriousness with which the Greeks took their liver divinations, but it also shows that everyone was expected to have a certain basic level of understanding of how to interpret signs from the liver of a sacrificial animal.

The technical art of divining through the liver seems to have come to the Greeks from Mesopotamian culture, but, while the elite priestly class of Mesopotamian diviners worked from elaborate ritual manuals that traced the significance of each spot or discoloration on each section of the liver, Greek practice seems to have been much simpler.[62] The usual avoid-ance of ritual texts in Greek religion means that the expertise was passed down in performance, just as with the rest of the sacrificial procedure. Every one of Xenophon's soldiers, then, would have seen countless sacri-ficial divinations and interpretations, and Xenophon sees no need to ex-plain to his readers what made the sacrifices seem unfavorable. Modern scholars, without the benefit of such practical experience, must rely on allusions in various texts, such as the description of the sacrifice made by Aegisthus in Euripides's play *Electra*. Aegisthus, about to be killed by Or-estes, finds that the liver of his sacrificial animal is missing the important lobe, and the portal vein and gall bladder likewise bode ill.[63] Those same three parts of the liver, Collins has shown, are also significant in the Meso-potamian divination systems.[64] In the Roman context, liver divination,

[60] For discussions of the diviner on the battlefield, see Johnston 2008a: 116–117; Flower 2008b: 153–187; as well as Jameson 1991; and Dillery 2005: 200–209.

[61] Xenophon, *Anabasis* VI.4.13–22.

[62] For a detailed discussion, see Collins 2008b, who argues that Greek liver divination worked on a simple binary system. Struck 2016: 18–19 points to the contrast of the simpler forms of Greek interpretation with the complex sets of alternatives in the Mesopotamian. Furley and Gysembergh 2015 provide more discussion, with comparisons to the Mesopota-mian evidence.

[63] Euripides, *Electra* 826–829. Taking in his hands the sacrifice, Aegisthus inspected it. The lobe was not there among the entrails, and the portal vein and the gall bladder made clear to him as he looked that evil afflictions were near.

[64] Collins 2008b: 322–323, who also notes that Prometheus, in *Prometheus Bound* 493–495, refers to the lobe and the gall bladder in his boast that he had taught liver divination to

called 'haruspicy,' was connected with the Etruscans, whose techniques were likewise said to be derived from the Near East. A bronze model of a liver, dating to the second century BCE, was found at Piacenza in Italy. The different portions of the liver are inscribed with the names of Etruscan deities, and it seems to serve as a template for liver divinations, so the Etruscan haruspicy seems to involve more technical expertise than the basic mode of Greek hepatoscopy.[65]

Twitches, Sneezes, and Other Bodily Omens

Other forms of divination show the same range of levels of complexity. Forms of divination from bodily twitches or sneezes might be the simple interpretation of good luck to come when a sneeze is heard on the right side or might involve a complex set of correspondences such as those found in the treatise on palmomancy (twitch divination) attributed to the legendary mantis Melampous. Penelope may take heart at the omen when her son sneezes just when she has spoken about the return of Odysseus, and she can expect that the swineherd Eumaeus will understand its meaning as well as she does.[66] The omens preserved in a third-century CE treatise on palmomancy are less obvious.

> A quiver of the left buttock signals joy; for a slave, a fine thing; for a maiden, blame; for a widow, quarrels, for a soldier, a promotion. Propitiate Hekate.
>
> A shaking of the right leg signals pain; for a slave, freedom; for a maiden, marriage; for a widow, profit; for a soldier, a fright. Propitiate Zeus.[67]

Such treatises resemble medical treatises in their systematic movement through the human body, as do the descriptions of symptoms coupled with diagnoses of the problem and prescriptions for a solution.[68] The solutions,

---

mankind. Cp. also Burkert 1992: 46–52 for the transmission of technical knowledge from Mesopotamian contexts. Bachvarova 2012, by contrast, argues for a Hittite intermediary, pointing to the differences between the Greek and Mesopotamian systems, while Furley and Gysembergh 2015 adduce papyrological evidence to suggest more similarities of terminology.

[65] Similar models (although not as clearly labeled) have been found from Mesopotamia. See Burkert 1992: 46–48 for a comparison of the Piacenza liver with Assyrian models. On the place of haruspicy in Rome, see, e.g., Briquel 1999 and 2014; Santangelo 2013.

[66] Homer, *Odyssey* 17.537–547.

[67] P. Flor. III.391 in Costanza 2009: 45. For this text, see further Dasen and Wilgaux 2013: 114–116.

[68] Cp. the injunction in Hippocrates, *Epid.* 1.2.5: ὅ τι δὲ τούτων ἔσται μάλιστα, σκεπτέον ἐξ ἄλλων. λέγειν τὰ προγενόμενα, γινώσκειν τὰ παρεόντα, προλέγειν τὰ ἐσόμενα: μελετᾶν ταῦτα. "But it is by a consideration of other signs that one must decide which of these results will be most

however, tend to be ritual propitiations of a god who has been angered or who might be able to help, rather than a letting of blood or purgation of bile with an emetic, since the dominant explanatory model is divine causation rather than an imbalance of humors. The systematic nature of these palmomantic manuals also recalls Babylonian divinatory manuals from nearly a millennium earlier; the mantic technology may have entered the Greek tradition earlier, but the textual systematization again comes only in the late Hellenistic and Roman periods.[69]

Divination through Other Natural Phenomena

A similar process may have occurred with other modes of divination, shifting from unsystematic oral tradition to textual arcana, but the evidence is scarce. Nevertheless, it is clear that various forms of divination interpreted signs in all the elements of the natural world, not just the shapes, sounds, and movements of animals. The idea of foretelling through signs in the heavens, such as clouds, lightning, and winds, appears in the lore recounted in didactic works like Hesiod's *Works & Days*, but much of this lore must have been passed down in the oral tradition before its systematization in the Hellenistic period, when it moved from the province of marginal superstition to arcane knowledge.[70] At either extreme of the hierarchy of means, superstition, or arcana, such a divinatory process might be considered magic, but much of the knowledge would simply be considered a normal part of a farmer's business.

By the Roman period, the diverse modes of divination from natural phenomena were categorized systematically by the learned, such as Varro's classification of divination by the four elements: geomancy (earth), hydromancy (water), aeromancy (air), and pyromancy (fire).[71] If divination from rocks or weather might be considered geomancy or aeromancy, the forms of hydromancy and pyromancy were often more complex. Omens were read in the flames of the sacrificial fires at the shrines of Zeus at

---

likely. Declare the past, diagnose the present, foretell the future: practise these acts." Cp. Langholf 1990: 248–251 for parallels in the structure of medical and divinatory treatises.

[69] For the Babylonian texts, see Böck 2000.

[70] Cp. Hesiod, *Works and Days*, as well as the Peripatetic treatise attributed to Theophrastus, *On Weather Signs*. Sider and Brunschön 2007 provide a useful introduction to the history of weather signs. A text purporting to be the collection of Etruscan brontoscopic (thunder-divination) lore by the first-century BCE Roman Nigidius Figulus survives in a late text by Johannes Lydus. The format is standardized and systematic, like the Mesopotamian divinatory manuals, listing the significance if it should thunder on any given day in a given month. See Turfa 2012.

[71] Varro apud Isidore, *Etymologies* VIII.9.13. The same division appears credited to Varro in Servius on Verg., *Aen.* 3.359.

Olympia and Apollo Ismenios at Thebes, but pyromancy could also be done in private contexts.[72] Ritual directions for lychnomancy, or divination by the flame of a lamp, appear in several of the Greek Magical Papyri, and, in Apuleius's novel *The Golden Ass*, a witch, Pamphile, predicts a coming storm by the flickering of the lamp's flame.[73] The witch's clueless husband scoffs at her prediction as an old wives' tale, but the (scarcely less clueless) protagonist, Lucius, pedantically explains the flickerings of the lamp as the flame's sympathetic response to the celestial fires, whose movements in the heavens do indeed create storms on earth. Both explanations mark the divination as extra-ordinary, either as useless superstition or as the reading of the arcane cosmic sympathies that govern the universe.

In such private contexts, hydromancy often takes the form of lecano-mancy, bowl divination.[74] The diviner puts a little oil on the surface of a bowl of water and makes contact with the divine through its movements, not by deciphering the patterns of the oil's movements, but by direct com-munication with the divinity.[75] A recipe in one of the Greek Magical Pa-pyri explains the use of different types of water in the bowl to contact different divinities.

> Whenever you want to inquire about matters, take a bronze vessel, either a bowl or a saucer, whatever kind you wish. Pour water: rain water if you are calling upon heavenly gods, sea water if gods of the earth, river water if Osiris or Sarapis, springwater if the dead. Hold-ing the vessel on your knees, pour out green olive oil, bend over the vessel and speak the prescribed spell. And address whatever god you want and ask about whatever you wish, and he will reply to you and

[72] Cp. Johnston 2008a: 98. For empyromancy at Olympia, see Pindar, *Olympian* 6.68–74, with Scholiast on 111; *Olympian* 8.1–7. Herodotus claims (8.134) that the mode of divination for Apollo Ismenios is the same as at Olympia; cp. also Sophocles, *OT* 21, Scholiast on Eurip-ides, *Phoin.* 1255. Cp. Euripides, *Phoin.* 1254–1258 for a description of reading omens in the fire.

[73] Apuleius, *Met.* 2.12.2; cp. Vergil, *Georg.* 1.390–392. In the PGM, cp. PGM IV.1103; V.1–53; VII.430–578; XXIIb.27–31. Note that all of the lychnomancy spells in the PGM in-volve either a direct vision or use a medium (for which see ch. 7, p. 214, n. 84). See Zografou 2010 on lychnomancy in the PGM.

[74] Such divination seems less common in public contexts, although Pausanias 7.21.12 describes a rite at a sanctuary of Demeter where a mirror is lowered into a pool and then used to divine if a sick man will live or die. See Hopfner 1983 II §272 for more on catoptro-mancy, as well as the study of catoptromancy through the ages in Delatte 1932.

[75] Graf 1999: 288 notes this point. "Lecanomancy, we might think, would work like a Rorschach test: the fine oil film on the surface of the water would yield any form the inter-preter could imagine. But, surprisingly enough to our modern mind, it did not quite work this way. . . . [T]he ancient magician does not rely on his own power of intuition when in-terpreting signs on a surface: he meets the divinity in person whose superior knowledge will help."

tell you about anything. And if he has spoken dismiss him with the spell of dismissal, and you who have used this spell will be amazed.[76]

Other bowl divinations in the spell books likewise provide communication with the deity, and a discussion of lecanomancy attributed to the Byzantine Psellos explains that certain demons are attracted to the water in the bowl that has been ritually prepared.[77] Similar processes may be imagined in divination with mirrors (catoptromancy) or in reflective or translucent stones, such as a ball of crystal. Such procedures move out of the realm of indirect or artificial divination and into natural divination that seeks direct communication with the divine.

NATURAL DIVINATION: INTERPERSONAL COMMUNICATION WITH THE DIVINE

Although the signs of birds or lots are often understood as messages left by some divine entity, natural divination seeks to engage in more direct communication. The rituals for lecanomancy seek to produce an appearance of the god in the waters, such as the saucer-divination of Aphrodite in which the goddess stretches out her hand to the diviner.[78] Likewise, a lychnomantic ritual produces, not random flickerings of fire, but a complete vision of Harpokrates.

> Signs of the lamp: After saying the light-bringing spell, open your eyes and you will see the light of the lamp becoming like a vault. Then while closing your eyes say (differently: three . . . after saying three times), and after opening your eyes you will see all things wide-open and the greatest brightness within, but the lamp shining no-where. Then you will see the god seated on a lotus, decorated with rays, his right hand raised in greeting and left [holding] a flail, while being carried in the hands of two angels with twelve rays around them.[79]

Such a direct vision of the god is the ultimate form of divination, in which the deity can communicate directly with the diviner, and their revelations

[76] PGM IV.222–233 in IV.154–285, a longer spell that prepares the magician for divine contact.

[77] Ps. Psellos, *Graecorum Opiniones de Daemonibus* 7. For a discussion of the history of this text, see Gautier 1988.

[78] PGM IV.3209–3254. Ogden 2001: 191 treats nearly all lecanomancy and lychnomancy as necromantic evocation of ghosts, although he admits that "sometimes the prophesying power behind bowl and lamp divination was a ghost or ghosts, although gods and demons, too could be consulted by this method."

[79] PGM IV.1102–1114.

carry the most authority.[80] Such procedures tend to be at the highest end of the hierarchy of means, requiring the most complex procedures, the most arcane knowledge of divine names for summoning, and so forth. The Greek Magical Papyri contain a number of recipes to obtain this direct vision (*autopsis*) or meeting with the god (*systasis*), and such an encounter becomes the goal of the philosophical practice known as theurgy.[81]

The recipes for a direct vision in the Greek Magical Papyri show the blending, in Greco-Roman Egypt, of the Greek and Egyptian traditions, since divinatory rituals for a direct vision of a god have a long history in the Egyptian temple religion. The story of a certain Thessalos of Tralles shows how such traditional *ph̲-ntr* spells could be put into the category of magic. In the first century CE, Thessalos visited Egypt in search of miraculous wisdom and persuaded an old Egyptian priest to perform a special Egyptian divination for him. Thessalos triumphantly relates that he got the reluctant priest to provide a direct vision of Asclepius, rather than the mediated one through bowl divination he had planned. Moyer has analyzed the ways in which Thessalos regards this traditional Egyptian *ph̲-ntr* as an extra-ordinary magical ritual, providing the opportunity for the Egyptian priest to repackage his tradition as an exotic and extra-ordinary procedure, something even higher on the hierarchy of means—and therefore something even more valuable.[82]

More common than direct visions of the god are the procedures that involve a medium, that is, some other person who acts as an intermediary between the diviner and the divine. Most often in the ancient sources, the medium is a young child, since children, especially those too young for sexual experience, were considered to be more pure—and thus more fit to meet with the gods—than adults. However, they were also considered to be simpler and less prone to imagining things on their own, and thus they served as better, more transparent intermediaries with the divine.[83] The diviner invokes the deity into the medium: "Come to me, spirit that flies in the air, called with secret codes and unutterable names, at this lamp divination which I perform, and enter into the boy's soul, that he may

---

[80] Priam, in *Iliad* 24.221–224, claims that only the direct vision of the goddess would have induced him to go talk to Achilles, not any other kind of omen or pronouncement of diviners.

[81] See ch. 10. For direct vision charms in the PGM, see, e.g., I.1–41; I.262–347; III.187–262; IV.930–1114; IV.3086–3124; VII.319–334; VII.335–347; VII.727–739; etc. Johnston 2010a surveys the ways the magicians imagined such divine encounters.

[82] Moyer 2003, drawing on the previous studies of J. Smith 1978a and Ritner 1995, along with the work of Frankfurter 1998 regarding 'stereotype appropriation' by Egyptians in Roman Egypt. See further, ch. 11, p. 415, n. 76.

[83] Cp. Johnston 2001, who also notes how this assumption of childhood innocence and inability to fabricate imagined experiences lingers in contemporary court cases. For ancient testimony, cp. Iamblichus, *de myst.* 3.24; Olympiodorus, *in Alc.* 8

receive the immortal form in mighty and incorruptible light, because while chanting, I call, IAŌ, etc."[84] The divine spirit enters the medium's soul, and the boy is able to speak prophetically. Such direct communications from the gods to individuals are the sort of extra-ordinary divination more likely to be labeled as 'magic.'

The Delphic Oracle and Hexameter Verse Oracles

A medium in a sacred space whose authority is sanctioned by the community's religious tradition is less likely to receive such a label. The most famous medium in the Greek religious tradition, of course, was the Pythia, the priestess of Apollo's oracular shrine at Delphi, whose oracles chanted in hexameter verse were the most authoritative in the culture.[85] City-states would send delegations to consult the oracle, and the sanctuary was filled with the lavish gifts to the god, testifying to his greatness. The Pythia's answers, however, were notoriously enigmatic; as Heraclitus famously says, "The ruler whose oracle is at Delphi, neither speaks, nor conceals, but signifies."[86] Apollo's message, channeled through the medium of the Pythia, comes in comprehensible words, rather than meaningless gibberish, but those words still require interpretation.

The Pythia was imagined to be inspired by the god: the words she spoke were breathed into her from the divine. How precisely this process worked, for the Pythia or for other types of medium, has been the subject of some debate, in antiquity as well as in modern scholarship.[87] Whether the divine force was imagined to take the form of vapors or light or an invisible intermediary daimon or the power of the god himself, the Pythia was said to be filled by the divine power. Despite the supposed derivation of *mantike* from *mania*, however, the mediumistic trance or altered state produced by the god's presence does not appear as ecstatic madness. At the Delphic Oracle, at any rate, the result of this inspiration, enthusiasm, or possession was that the medium spoke in a way different from her normal mode, not in hysterical and meaningless ravings but in poetic verse. Some literary depictions portray a much wilder ecstatic trance, however, where the di-

---

[84] For other such medium divinations in the PGM, cp. VII.348–358; V.1–53; IV.850–929. Hopfner 1932 discusses such mediums in lecanomancy, lynchnomancy, catopromancy, and onychomancy (divination by reflections of light off the medium's fingernails).

[85] The status of Delphi from the Archaic through the Classical period is confirmed by many testimonies, but the story (Herodotus 1.46–54) of Croesus testing the oracular shrines of Greece and choosing Delphi as the best illustrates its prominence. For studies of the collected oracles from Delphi, see Fontenrose 1978 and Parke and Wormell 1956.

[86] ὁ ἄναξ, οὗ τὸ μαντεῖόν ἐστι τὸ ἐν Δελφοῖς, οὔτε λέγει οὔτε κρύπτει ἀλλὰ σημαίνει. Heraclitus, fr. 93 ap. Plutarch, *de Pyth. orac.* 404d.

[87] Cp. Johnston 2008a: 33–58 for the best recent overview of the Delphic oracle, summing up controversies in Bowden 2005; Maurizio 1995, 1997, and 2001; and earlier scholarship.

vine possession is more violent or even sexualized as a rape, an image that early Christian authors fastened upon gleefully in their critiques of pagan religion as comprised of depraved rituals.[88]

Rather than ecstatic rants, the prophecies were traditionally spoken by the Pythia in dactylic hexameter poetic verses, a form of speech that is linguistically marked as different from normal conversation. Some modern scholars, however, have doubted that the Pythia, a woman who the historical sources recount was often an uneducated peasant girl, could spontaneously have produced such poetry.[89] The traditional meter of epic, however, is as close to the rhythms of normal Greek speech as the iambic pentameters of Shakespeare are to English, and recent scholarship has shown the plausibility of a Pythia raised in a tradition of oral poetry producing such verses, even in a trance-state.[90] The fact that, at a certain point in time, the Delphic oracle stopped producing hexameter oracles and began substituting prose may thus stem from the shift away from the oral tradition in Greek culture, rather than from the departure of an intermediary daimon or the cessation of the vapors that arose from a crack beneath the Pythia's tripod, as Plutarch suggests in his dialogue on *Why the Pythia No Longer Gives Oracles in Verse*.[91]

The Delphic Pythia was not the only medium inspired by a god to speak verse oracles; similar oracles are associated with the names of Bakis and the Sibyl. Bakis, a man from Boeotia who claimed to be inspired by the nymphs to speak their oracles, produced many verse oracles, and Herodo-

---

[88] Cp. Origen, *Contra Celsum* 7.3–4; John Chrysostom, *Homilies on the First Epistle to the Corinthians* 29.12.1. The ancient images often owe much to Aeschylus's depiction of Cassandra in the *Agamemnon* (1200–1212), but Lucan is the only source to really blatantly sexualize the encounter (*Pharsalia* 5.86–224, although cp. Longinus 1.13.2).

[89] Bowden 2005: 33–38 argues that the Pythia always gave clear prose responses, which were later versified by professional poets at the sanctuary. While this theory is more plausible than earlier ideas of the Delphic priests who manipulated the process by turning the incoherent female ravings into masculine Apollonian verse, it still fails to account for the continuing importance of orality through the Classical period. Significantly, the testimonies that do suggest prose oracles and subsequent versification come from the Roman Imperial period. Plutarch (*de Pyth. orac.* 403e–405c) suggests that an uneducated, unmusical girl could not produce verses, but he also notes that, in previous times, people were more accustomed to expressing important ideas in poetry, a practice that has died out in his own era, which prizes philosophical clarity over poetic effect.

[90] Cp. Maurizio 1995.

[91] Plutarch, *de def. orac.* 394c. Cp. Cicero, *de div.* 1.38, 1.79; cf. Aristotle, *de mund.* 395b26–29; Diod. Sic. 16.26; Pliny, *HN* 2.208. Modern scholars seeking to explain away the religious experience of the oracular consultation with reference to hallucinogenic drugs have often turned to Plutarch's vapors explanation as one congenial to a modern, etic perspective. The most recent attempts by Hale et al. 2003 and Spiller, Hale, and De Boer 2002 to argue for hallucinogenic vapors produced by the geological conditions of Delphi have been convincingly refuted by Lehoux 2007.

tus vigorously defends the validity of these oracles against skeptics, even if Bakis may actually have been a name claimed by a number of different individuals in a particular prophetic tradition.[92] The Sibyl likewise seems a title applied to a number of women who spoke inspired verse, and, unlike Bakis, whose prime prestige seems to have been in the Archaic and Classical periods, the fame of the Sibyl increased into Late Antiquity. Various lists of different Sibyls circulated, and even the Delphic Pythia was later enrolled in their number.[93] The oracles of the Sibyl were collected into written form, and the Roman Sibylline Books were consulted on the most serious of state occasions. Although the Roman Sibylline books perished in the flames, later collections purporting to be the Sibylline books continued to circulate, accumulating new prophecies and reworking old ones for new purposes, including Jewish and Christian prophecies that foretold the coming of the Messiah and the judgment at the end of the world. So effective was this process of Christianization that the Sibylline Oracles were considered by some Christian apologists to be authentic and divinely pre-Christian prophecies of Christian salvation, on a par with the Old Testament prophets, and Michaelangelo includes several Sibyls along with other prophets on the Sistine Chapel ceiling.

The collection of oracles into written form seems to have started very early, however, since Herodotus mentions that the Spartan Kleomenes, when he took the Athenian Acropolis in his expulsion of the Pisistratid tyrants from Athens in 510 BCE, brought back the Pisistratids' collection of oracles to Sparta, to augment the Spartan kings' collection.[94] Whose oracles were in these collections at the end of the sixth century BCE remains obscure, although the Pisistratids' diviner, Onomacritus, was known for his collection of the oracles of Musaeus. The Roman era Pausanias claims to have read the oracles of Euclus of Cyprus, Musaeus of Athens, and Bakis of Boeotia, and Aristophanes, several centuries earlier, depicts characters referring to collections of oracles by Bakis and others. Like the Roman Sibylline books, these oracle collections seem to have been consulted in times of need by various interpreters who claimed that a given

---

[92] Hdt. 8.77. "Considering this, I dare to say nothing against Bacis concerning oracles when he speaks so plainly, nor will I consent to it by others." Cp. Hdt. 8.20, 96; 9.43; Pausanias 4.27.4. Connor 1988b: 162 argues for Bakis as a generic title. "It is not the name of a single individual, but of various persons who claimed prophetic powers. It may be thought of as a role or identity adopted by certain individuals and closely associated with possession by the nymphs. This does not exclude the use of the name as a literary persona and hence as a way of referring to collections of hexameter oracles that circulated through much of antiquity."

[93] The fundamental study of Sibylline prophecy is still Parke 1988.

[94] Hdt. 5.90.2 on the Pisistratid collection taken by Kleomenes 6.57.4 for the Spartan collection.

oracle was relevant to the situation. Aristophanes parodies this process in his *Knights*, when two rival rogues pull out oracle after oracle, offering outlandish interpretations to flatter and win the approval of Demos, the old man who represents the Athenian people (*demos*).[95] Verse oracle collections remain a significant mode of divination for individuals and communities from the Archaic period onward, increasing in importance with the spread of textualization from the Hellenistic period through Late Antiquity.

Other Oracular Shrines and Methods

Although the Pythia of Delphi produced verse oracles, it is likely that lot oracles were used in Delphi as well (perhaps in the Corycian Cave of the Nymphs), and other oracles in important sanctuaries provided other ways of communication with the god. At the sanctuary of Zeus in Dodona, divination occurred in a number of different modes to provide answers to the queries of the pilgrims to the shrine, from divine inspiration to the priestesses interpreting the rustling of leaves in the sacred oak trees (or perhaps the calls of the doves in those trees) to the sacred oak itself speaking, while at Klaros, Didyma, and other oracular shrines, a lot divination seems to have been employed as well as a priest who gave prophecies.[96] More direct and personal communication with the divine always ranked higher in the hierarchy of means, however, and the oracle shrine of Trophonius at Lebadea provided a special opportunity to consult the god directly. Pausanias, who consulted the oracle himself in the second century CE, describes the ritual in detail, from the days of preliminary purifications to the descent into the oracular shrine itself.

> The descender lies with his back on the ground, holding barley-cakes kneaded with honey, thrusts his feet into the hole and himself follows, trying hard to get his knees into the hole. After his knees the rest of his body is at once swiftly drawn in, just as the largest and most rapid river will catch a man in its eddy and carry him under. After this those who have entered the shrine learn the future, not in one and the same way in all cases, but by sight sometimes and at other times by hearing. The return upwards is by the same mouth, the feet darting out first.[97]

[95] Pausanias 10.12.11; cp. Aristophanes, who in *Peace* mentions Bakis and the Sibyl (1070, 1095); for Bakis, also *Birds*. 961–963; *Knights* 1003; etc. See N. Smith 1989 for discussion of the role of diviners in Aristophanes.

[96] For detailed discussions of these oracles, see Johnston 2008a, chs. 3 and 4; as well as Bonnechere 2007.

[97] Pausanias 9.39. For a detailed study of the Trophonius oracle, see Bonnechere 2003.

After this ordeal of being sucked into the earth and spat back out again, the one consulting Trophonius is led by the priests of the shrine to the Throne of Memory, where he must recount his experiences. Pausanias does not tell his own experience, but it was probably not as elaborate as the vision of Timarchus described in Plutarch, since that vision of the cosmic order is tailored to the topic of Plutarch's philosophical dialogue.[98] Nevertheless, the legend (mentioned also by Pausanias) that those who consult the Trophonius oracle lose (at least for a while) the ability to laugh testifies to the awe-inspiring effect such a consultation would have.

What Dreams May Come . . . : Dream Divination

The preparations for the encounter with the god at the Trophonius shrine resemble to some extent one of the most popular ways for individuals to directly contact a divinity, sleeping at a sanctuary in hopes of receiving a revelation in a dream. Many healing shrines used this process of ritual incubation (sleeping in) to produce cures or revelations that might lead to a cure. The inscriptions at the temple of Asclepius in Epidaurus provide a number of descriptions of dreams in which Asclepius appears to the sufferer.[99] Revelations for healing were not, however, the only reason that ritual incubation was practiced; one of the inscriptions at Epidaurus records the case of a woman who sought to discover where the gold left by her deceased husband was buried and received a dream from Asclepius.[100] A court case from fourth-century BCE Athens involves a certain Euxenippus, who had been authorized by the Athenians (with two other men) to sleep in the temple of Amphiaraus to receive a dream that might help settle a property dispute.[101] We do not know how often a city like Athens might have turned to this form of divination, but it is not presented as anything

---

[98] In Plutarch, *de genio Soc.* 22 590a–592e, Timarchus disappears into the Trophonius shrine for two whole days, during which his disembodied spirit tours the cosmos, from the celestial regions to the depths of the underworld.

[99] See ch. 5, p. 145, n. 71. For a recent discussion and edition of the texts, see LiDonnici 1995, as well as the older Edelstein and Edelstein 1945. The Hippocratic treatise *On Regimen* devotes several sections (book IV, sections 86–93) to a discussion of the role of dreams in diagnosing and curing illnesses within the Hippocratic medical tradition.

[100] LiDonnici 1995 C 3 (46). The god's message, "In the month Thargelion in the noontime, within the lion lies the gold," was too enigmatic, and, after searching fruitlessly inside the stone lion nearby, she consulted a mantis, who advised her to dig where the shadow of the lion fell at noon in Thargelion, and found the treasure. See now the comprehensive study of ritual incubation in Renberg 2017.

[101] Hyperides 4.14–15. Euxenippus is being prosecuted for falsifying the oracle's response. It is worth noting that Hyperides suggests that, if the prosecutors were dubious of the validity of the dream oracle, they should have consulted the oracle at Delphi, that is, selected a form of divination higher up on the hierarchy of means.

out of the ordinary. Dreams were a familiar way of making contact with the divine.

Since everyone dreams, anyone could engage in dream divination, regardless of social position or expertise.[102] Such open access, of course, means that dream divination can rank very low on the hierarchy of means, especially since it is notoriously difficult to tell whether a dream is significant or not. A dream might be a communication from a god or it might be a meaningless jumble of images, and Artemidorus of Daldis, the author of the only surviving complete manual of dream interpretation from antiquity, carefully distinguishes in his introduction between significant (*oneiroi*) and insignificant dreams (*enhypnioi*).[103] To further complicate matters, even a significant dream might be a false one, like the misleading dream Zeus sends to Agamemnon in the *Iliad*.[104] Penelope in the *Odyssey* speaks of the two gates, of horn and of ivory, through which true and false dreams come to mortals, an image that has had a long reception tradition in Western literature, notably in Vergil's *Aeneid*.[105]

Some dream revelations come unprompted, without any ritual incubation or other divinatory ritual. An inscription records the case of a certain Athenaios, who after suffering a number of (unspecified) troubles, has a dream in which he learns that he has unwittingly committed a transgression against Zeus, for which he must atone by erecting the stele with the inscription to tell of Zeus's power.[106] In other cases, however, the dream revelation is sought, whether by incubation at a temple or by a more per-

[102] Synesius comments, "It makes no difference to the god if someone is an Eteoboutad aristocrat or Manes the newly freed slave. And this democratic nature of it is very beneficial to humans" (*de insomn.* 12.21 [my trans.]). διαφέρει δὲ οὐδὲν τῷ θεῷ, τίς ὁ Ἐτεοβουτάδης καὶ τίς ὁ Μανῆς ὁ νεώνητος· καὶ τὸ δημοτικὸν αὐτῆς μάλα φιλάνθρωπον

[103] Artemidorus, *Oneirocriticon* 1.2. Dodds 1951: 107, drawing on other ancient sources, further distinguishes the enigmatic significant dream from the more straightforward vision and the oracular dream in which an authoritative personage (god or mortal) appears to the dreamer.

[104] Johnston 2010c: 68 calls attention to spells in the PGM designed to send dreams. "But although, arguably, a human practitioner *might* send you a shape-shifting dream in order to advise you kindly of an important matter ... we have no indication that such was ever the intention of any practitioner; the assumption seems to be that when human practitioners send shape-shifting dreams they mean to serve their own selfish purposes." She discusses the dream sent by Nectanebo in the Alexander Romance to Alexander's mother Olympias to convince her to sleep with him, but she further notes that people seemed not to worry much about the possibility of false dreams being sent at them. "The average person did not usually connect the dreams he or she had with oneiropompic incursions" (Johnston 2010c: 77).

[105] Homer, *Odyssey* 19.560–567; cp. Vergil, *Aeneid* 6.895–896; for a similar idea, see Plato, *Republic* 572a. In Agamemnon's false dream in *Iliad* 2.1–36, Sleep personified appears to Agamemnon in the form of the wise old man, Nestor, but it is devised by Zeus to bring destruction to the Greeks.

[106] Renberg 2010: 40–41 discusses such cases, including this inscription from the sanctuary of Zeus of the Twin Oaks in Lydia (Petzl 11 = SEG 33.1013). While such inscriptions are

sonal method not dependent on a traditionally recognized sacred space, that is, in Smith's terms, by the mode of the religion of "anywhere" as well as the religion of "there."[107] The Greek Magical Papyri furnish instructions for over thirty different rituals to obtain a dream, many of which seem to create a sacred space for incubation in the magician's own bedchamber.[108] The one performing the rite must be ritually pure and must set up the inquiry by writing the question for the god.

> [Write] on a strip of tinfoil, and after crowning the strip of foil with myrtle, set up the censer. Then make a burnt offering of frankincense and carry the leaf of metal around the vapor while saying: "Lords, gods, reveal to me concerning the NN matter tonight, in the coming hours. Emphatically I beg, I supplicate, I your servant and enthroned by you." Then place the piece of foil under your pillow, and, without giving answer to anyone, go to sleep after having kept yourself pure for three days.[109]

In this spell, the magician stresses his ritual credentials as having undergone the rite of enthronement (*thronismos*) as well as his specialized knowledge of the magical words to be written on the metal foil. Some spells put even more emphasis on the purification of the space as well as the magician, and different spells require varying levels of complex preparations and invocations to make contact with the god.[110]

While some dreams seem to provide a direct communication from a divinity to the dreamer (and the spells in the Greek Magical Papyri often specifically request that the god appear in his recognizable form), often the imagery of a dream is confusing and unclear, more of an indirect communication through signification than a direct revelation. Just as with other indirect forms of divination, such dreams must be interpreted, and expertise at such interpretation is one of the skills of the diviner. Achilles suggests getting a dream interpreter to respond to the crisis at the beginning of the *Iliad*, and the sophist Antiphon was said to have set up a stall in the marketplace in Corinth in the fifth century BCE where he interpreted

---

later, Plato mentions shrines and other dedications founded because of dream omens; see *Laws* 909e–910a; cp. *Epinomis* 985c.

[107] J. Smith 2003. Cp. ch. 2, p. 40, n. 7, as well as ch. 6, p. 169, n. 46.

[108] Cp. Johnston 2010c: 69–75. Johnston lists thirty-four dream-obtaining spells in her appendix on p. 79. See Zografou 2013b for the involvement of lamps, incense, and other ritual preparations in such spells.

[109] PGM VII.740–755. For *thronismos* or *thronosis* rituals, see Edmonds 2006.

[110] Cp. PGM VII.795–845, which involves elaborately inscribing a branch of laurel leaves with names and characters linked to the Zodiac and performing a long invocation to the angel Zizaubio, and which specifies, "You must have [the place] where you perform absolutely pure" (843). The attribution of this spell to Pythagoras and Demokritos adds to its authority and cachet.

the dreams of his clients. Antiphon is credited with producing a book on dream interpretation, but the second-century CE dreambook (*Oneirocriticon*) of Artemidorus is the earliest to survive. It provides a wealth of interpretations for various signs, as well as discussions of the principles of interpretation, and Artemidorus's work inspired Freud in his own psychological studies of dreams.[111]

The similarities of the dreambook to other kinds of systematic divination manuals, both from Hellenistic and Roman Greece and from older Mesopotamian sources, is striking; they all employ the same basic format: if you see X, it signifies Y for person Z. "To observe a lion that is tame and simpering and approaches harmlessly is good and delivers assistance to a soldier from a king, and to an athlete from the good condition of his body, and to a citizen from a ruler and to a slave from his master."[112] The benevolence of the powerful lion indicates help from a powerful source, but that source and that help differ depending on the circumstances of the dreamer. Some of the dream symbolism seems fairly transparent, while other significances are based on complex word plays, traditional cultural associations, and even numerical equivalences between the spellings of words.[113] All these types of signification are embedded in the cultural vocabulary of the dreamers, and the process of interpretation thus reinforces the cultural system of meaning—from the emic perspective, the shared language by which mortals and gods communicate.[114] The divinity communicating might be Asclepius or Delphic Apollo or the Egyptian deity

---

[111] See Harris-McCoy 2012 for a recent commentary on the text, as well as White 1975. Freud was especially excited by section 1.79, interpreting the various meanings of having sex with one's mother, and this section remains one of the most often commented upon in modern scholarship. For Antiphon and his dreambook, see Artemidorus 2.14 and Cicero, *de div.* 1.39 (20), as well as Fulgentius, *Myth.* 1.14; Tertullian, *de anima* 46.10. Ps. Plutarch, *Vit. X Orat.* I.18.8 33c–d claims that Antiphon set up shop near the marketplace in Corinth, promising to cure woes through words by discovering the causes. This description, while historically dubious, would fit the divinatory interpretation of dreams. See further Laín Entralgo 1970: 97–107.

[112] Artemidorus 2.102 (trans. Harris-McCoy). Cp. the palmomantic treatise, ch. 7, p. 209, n. 67.

[113] E.g., a weasel (γαλῆ) signifies a lawsuit (δίκη) since the numerical equivalents of both words = 42 = 3 (γ) + 1 (α) + 30 (λ) + 8 (η) = 4 (δ) + 10 (ι) + 20 (κ) + 8 (η). Artemidorus 3.28.

[114] As Dodds 1951: 104 argues, "Not only the choice of this or that symbol, but the nature of the dream itself, seems to conform to a rigid traditional pattern." Cp. Noegel 2007: 195 on the culturally conditioned semiotic structures. "The appearance of puns connecting apodoses to protases in the omen materials permits us to see the oneirocritic process as one link in a series of performative 'rituals,' one that was designed to inscribe the dreamer's fate by activating the illocutionary power of words. At the same time, punning encapsulated the process of divine judgment inherent in divinatory activity, by underscoring the direct relationship between the divine sign and its meaning."

Bes or the angel Zizaubio or some unnamed divine force, but dreams provide a means for this communication, whether unsought and unexpected by the mortal or carefully engineered through ritual.

Divination from the Dead: Necromancy

The gods are not the only entities who may communicate with mortals through dreams; at times the dead appear, like the Homeric Patrokles who makes a heart-rending appeal for burial in Achilles's dream. Such apparitions were not merely in the literary imagination; a grieving wife set up an imperial-period inscription on a cenotaph in Lydia for her husband who was lost at sea in response to his appearance to her in a dream. "Sekoutilla made this according to a dream: 'I, Kallinikos, lie in watery depths, but unconquered by the briny multitude.' "[115] The dead can bring messages to the living, communicating things that the living do not know.

As a result, the living may prefer not to wait in the hopes of a spontaneous dream communication but decide to seek out contact with the dead. Such contact is, however, always beyond the bounds of normal practice, which keeps the boundaries between living and dead intact. Herodotus tells of the tyrant Periander, who sends to the oracle of the dead in Thesprotia to consult the spirit of his dead wife, Melissa, to discover where some money had been buried. She refuses to tell him until he provides her with honors in recompense for his neglect of burning funeral garments for her, so he assembles all the matrons of Corinth in their best finery, strips them publicly, and burns all the clothing as an offering to Melissa. Such behavior is cited as the outrageous conduct of a tyrant, especially since Periander is convinced of the validity of Melissa's message when she mentions that he had engaged in necrophilia with her corpse, another egregious violation of the proper boundaries between the living and the dead.[116]

Not all necromancy is presented as quite so perverse an act. Acting on the instructions of the enchantress Circe, Odysseus calls up the shade of Teiresias with libations of milk and honey, followed by wine, water, and barley, into a pit he has dug at the edge of the world, beyond the stream of Ocean. After prayers to all the spirits of the dead and to Hades and Persephone as rulers of the dead, he makes a sacrifice of a ram and ewe, burns the bodies, and guards the pit, which is now filled with the blood of

---

[115] TAM V.1, 661; see Renberg 2010: 56, who compares the Ovidian story (*Met.* 11.573–709) of Alcyone, who received a dream from Juno about the death of her husband Ceyx. Cp. Homer, *Iliad* 23.65–93; cp. Aeschylus, *Choe.* 21–41 for the ghost of Agamemnon haunting his murderous wife, Clytemnestra, in her dreams.

[116] Herodotus 5.92; cp. the discussions in Johnston 1999: vii–viii; and Ogden 2001: 53–60.

the sacrifices. Teiresias comes to the blood, along with many other dead spirits, whom Odysseus has to prevent from drinking the blood before Teiresias. Although all the later literary examples of necromancy clearly draw on this model of filling a pit with blood and calling up the spirits, Odysseus's ritual seems in many ways more like a sacrifice to the dead than an evocation, and the fact that he performs the rite at the borders of the underworld (and then seems to roam about, meeting other shades) has prompted many to deny that the epic hero is actually practicing necromancy.[117] Even in antiquity, it appears, the rite seemed insufficiently weird to be necromancy, and one fragment of the *Kestoi* of Julius Africanus (second to third century CE) includes what purports to be the 'real' invocation used by Odysseus. He claims that this lengthy invocation, which calls upon Anoubis, Ptha, Phre, and Ablanatha, was suppressed from the official recension of the Homeric poems by the Pisistratids, who thought it unsuitable for epic.[118]

The evidence for necromancy in Archaic and Classical Greece is slim, but the necromantic evocation of the Persian King Darius in Aeschylus's *Persians* or the fragments surviving of Aeschylus's *Psychagogoi*, a play treating Odysseus's evocation (and an Aristophanic parody featuring Socrates and his pupil Chaerophon), indicate that necromancy remained a divinatory option in the Greek imaginary, even if so outrageous a procedure was seldom actually performed. A fragment of Euripides, preserved in Clement, refers to calling spirits of the dead up to explain the cause of a crisis.

> Send to the light the souls of those below for those who wish to learn in advance from where the struggles began to grow, what was the root of evils, which of the blessed gods we must propitiate with sacrifice to find a cessation from toils.[119]

Plutarch tells us that the Spartan general Pausanias, corrupted by luxuries after his victory over the Persians in the battle of Plataea in the Persian war, consulted an oracle of the dead (*nekymanteion*) to find out how to rid himself of hauntings by the ghost of a young woman he had murdered. The ghost informed him that he would be free of his troubles when he

---

[117] Homer, *Odyssey* 10.516–529, 11.24–35. See Edmonds 2010. Rohde 1925: 24 claims that "Homer knows nothing of necromancy," and Johnston 2005: 288 argues, "This isn't really necromancy." Ogden 2001: 43–53 sees it as a consultation of a *nekuomanteion*, a necromantic oracle shrine.

[118] Sextus Julius Africanus, *Kestoi* 18 = P. Oxy. 412 = PGM XXIII.

[119] *Strom.* 5.11.70.6 = Euripides, fr. 912 Nauck. πέμψον δ' ἐς φῶς ψυχὰς ἐνέρων| τοῖς βουλομένοις ἄθλους προμαθεῖν| πόθεν ἔβλαστον, τίς ῥίζα κακῶν,| τίνα δεῖ μακάρων ἐκθυσαμένους| εὑρεῖν μόχθων ἀνάπαυλαν (my trans.). See Ogden 2001: 233–236 for an overview of ghosts revealing how they perished or other causes for restlessness.

returned to Sparta, which he was, after a fashion, since he perished there shortly after his return.[120]

It is worth noting that all these consultations concern matters that the particular dead spirit might have knowledge of; the dead are not thought of as having the broader knowledge of the gods. Most of the consultations with the dead are indeed about how a restless ghost might be pacified and laid to rest, although other dead spirits are at times consulted with regard to matters pertaining to their lives or those of their families. Just as a family member, making offerings at a tomb or during an annual festival of the dead, such as the Athenian Anthesteria or the Roman Parentalia, might pray to the spirits of the dead to be benevolent, granting prosperity and fertility to their living family, so too those consulting the dead often limit their requests to matters pertaining to that same sphere of influence.[121] The Odyssean Teiresias may have special knowledge after death, just as he did in his life as a diviner, but the rest of the dead, while not completely mindless shadows, still have little more knowledge than they did in life.[122]

Sometimes, of course, a particular dead spirit is sought. Several stories tell of the evocation of Homer or the heroes of the Trojan war, and the Late Antique Aeneas of Gaza complains of the charlatans who make a living with promises to call up the spirits of famous people.

> And yet those among the Chaldaeans, the Egyptians, and the Greeks who go about touting mystery rites, and who promise to conjure up

---

[120] Plutarch, *Vit. Cimon* 6.4–6 claims he consulted at the nekymanteion at Heracleia near Byzantium. Cp. Pausanias 3.17.7–9, who recounts that he consulted *psychagogoi*, spirit leaders or necromancers, at Phigelia. Cp. Thucydides 1.133 for his death by starvation after fleeing for asylum to a temple when the Spartan Ephors tried to arrest him.

[121] Plato, *Laws* 927a–b remarks on the way the dead were thought to care for their living relatives. "The souls of the dead have a certain power of caring for human affairs after death, . . . the souls of the dead, whose natural instinct it is to care especially for their own offspring, and to be kindly disposed to those who respect them and hostile to those who disrespect them." Johnston 2005: 292 perhaps goes too far in claiming, "The Greeks, in other words, had trouble conceiving of contact with the dead as beneficial except insofar as it provided additional information about when and how to avert their dangerous anger." She is certainly correct, however, to note that consultation of the dead was not as common or normal for the Greeks as it was for their Mesopotamian or Egyptian contemporaries. Cp. the famous Biblical example of Saul's necromantic consultation of Samuel in 1 Samuel 28.

[122] Cp. Bouché-Leclercq 1879 vol. 1: 334. Ogden 2001: 242 points out that the dead may have more knowledge about the nature of life, death, and the cosmos simply by virtue of having died and experienced the afterlife. The dead, even in Homer, retain awareness of the world of the living to the extent that they can know of and respond to the actions of the living such as tomb rites and sacrifices. A few passages in Homer stress the idea that the dead are completely mindless and that there is no meaningful afterlife except the immortal glory provided by epic verse, but such passages are exceptional, even in the Homeric epics, and do not reflect the general understanding. See Edmonds 2015.

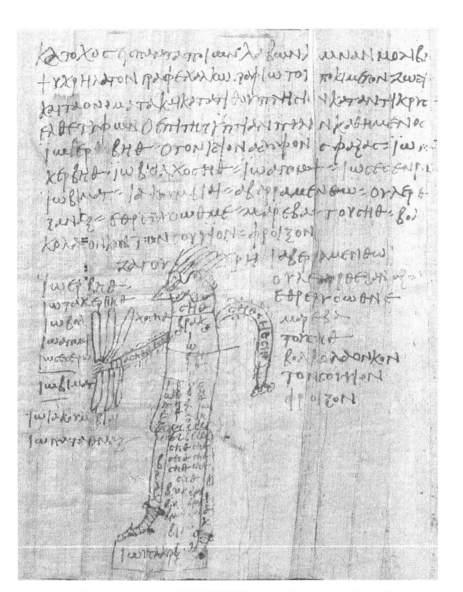

Plate 1 (fig. 2). P. Oslo 1 (PGM XXXVI.1–34), Courtesy of the University of Oslo Library Papyrus Collection.

Plate 2a (fig. 2). DTAP 475561, Museo Nazionale Romano at the Baths of Diocletian, room of the fountain of Anna Perenna, from Piranomonte 2012 (fig. 10, p.165).

Plate 2b (fig. 3). DTAP 500189 Museo Nazionale Romano at the Baths of Diocletian. Room of the fountain of Anna Perenna, from Piranomonte 2012 (fig. 14, p. 166).

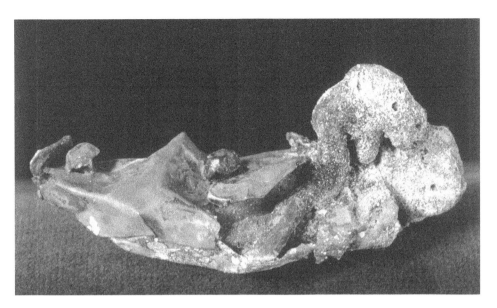

Plates 3a and b (figs. 4a and 4b). DTAP 500189 Baths of Diocletian, room of the fountain of Anna Perenna, from Piranomonte 2012 (fig. 35, p. 172; fig. 2, p.162).

Plates 4 (figs. 4c, d, and e). DTAP 475550, 47549, 475552, and 475567 Baths of Diocletian, room of the fountain of Anna Perenna, from Piranomonte 2012. Left: fig. 32, p. 171; right: fig. 14, p. 166.

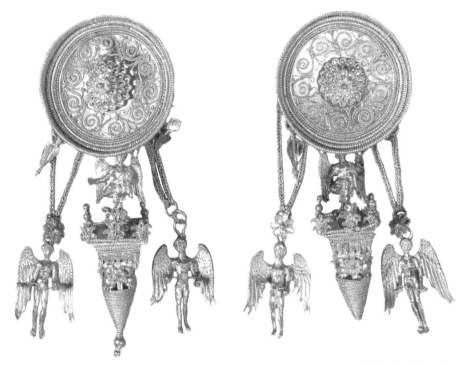

Plate 5a (fig. 5). Iunx earring BM 1877,0910.17, by permission of the British Museum, © Trustees of the British Museum.

Plate 5b (fig. 6). Attic Pyxis (London E774), Eretria Painter 499–415 BCE, by permission of the British Museum, © Trustees of the British Museum.

Plate 5c (fig 7). Apulian Red Figure Loutrophoros (Malibu 86.AE.680), Louvre MNB Painter, 350–340 BCE. Digital image courtesy of the Getty's Open Content Program.

Plate 6a (fig. 8). Perugia Inv. 1526; collezione Guardabassi. Image courtesy of Attilio Mastrocinque.

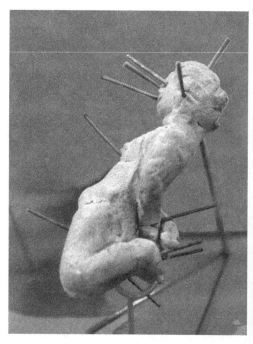

Plate 6b (fig. 9). Clay figurine Louvre E27145b © Marie-Lan Nguyen /Wikimedia Commons / CC-BY 2.5.

Plate 6c (fig. 10). Clay figurine Louvre E27145b. © Genevra Kornbluth, by permission.

Plate 7a (fig. 11). Carnelian amulet, Mich. 26123; Ann Arbor, Kelsey Museum of Archaeology. © Genevra Kornbluth, by permission.

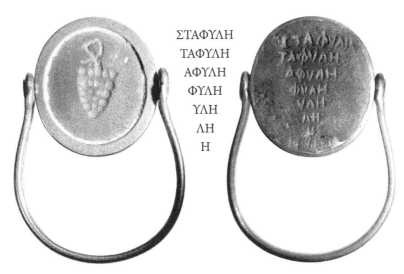

ΣΤΑΦΥΛΗ
ΤΑΦΥΛΗ
ΑΦΥΛΗ
ΦΥΛΗ
ΥΛΗ
ΛΗ
Η

Plate 7b (fig. 12). Lapis amulet with grape cluster. Bibliothèque nationale, départment des Monnaies, médailles et antiques, Froehner. XIV.36 (cliché Attilio Mastrocinquie-DR).

Plate 7c (fig.13). Ring with carved figure of Poseidon. Ashmoleon 40004552, Marlborough, 38, by permission.

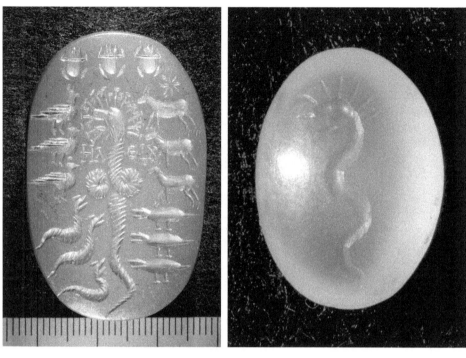

Plate 8a (fig. 14). Left: Chnoubis amulet from Lewis Collection, Fitzwilliam Museum; right: Chnoubis amulet BM G173, © Genevra Kornbluth, by permission.

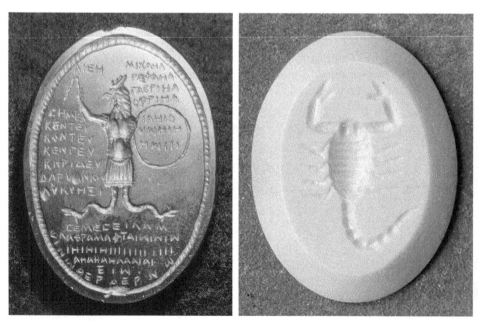

Plate 8b (fig 15). Left: Abrasax amulet Kelsey 26054 rev, © Genevra Kornbluth, by permission; right: Scorpion amulet GB-BM-MMEu_G 180, EA 56180 = Cbd 719, image by Christopher Faraone, by permission.

the souls of persons who have died long ago and who by incantations promise to drag them along wherever they wish, say that, if they should wish to summon up the soul of Homer, or of Orpheus, or of Phoroneus, or the soul of Cecrops, by sacrificing cocks and inscribing mystical characters, they claim to be able to call them up and exhibit them.[123]

Such necromantic rites seek revelation from those of the dead whose fame in life provides the authority for their pronouncements after death. The performers of such rites are marked as strangers with strange rites, but the sacrifices of chickens and inscription of strange characters are weird but not necessarily terrible.

In the Roman period, the literary depictions of necromancy become suddenly much more horrific.[124] Instead of just summoning shades to provide revelations, the necromancers in sources such as Lucan and Heliodorus actually reanimate corpses, creating a truly gruesome and uncanny scene in which the boundaries of life and death are blatantly violated. Most horrific is the rite performed by Lucan's Erictho, who forces a recently dead corpse to reanimate and prophesy. Lucan piles up the gruesome details throughout the scene, as the witch pours boiling blood into the corpse and lashes it with a live snake to make it speak; the coefficient of weirdness could not be higher, and the witch herself emphasizes how this outrageous mode of divination is far more effective than the ordinary consultation of an oracle like Delphi. "From the tripod [of Delphi] and the prophets of the gods one expects an ambiguous answer, but whoever seeks the truth from the shades and has the nerve to approach the oracles of grim death must leave with clear information."[125] Necromancy may be an extra-ordinary means of divination, beyond the bounds of acceptable religious behavior,

---

[123] Aeneas of Gaza, *Theophrastus* 18.21–19.1. Καὶ μὴν παρὰ Χαλδαίοις καὶ Αἰγυπτίοις καὶ Ἕλλησιν οἱ τὰς τελετὰς ἀγείροντες καὶ γοητεύειν τῶν πάλαι τελευτησάντων τὰς ψυχὰς ἐπαγγελλόμενοι καὶ ταῖς ἐπῳδαῖς ἄγειν τε καὶ ἕλκειν ὅποι ἂν ἐθέλωσιν, εἰ τὴν Ὁμήρου ψυχὴν ἐθέλοις καλεῖν, εἰ τὴν Ὀρφέως, εἰ τὴν Φορωνέως, εἰ τὴν τοῦ Κέκροπος, ἀλεκτρυόνας θύοντες καὶ χαρακτῆρας ὑπογράφοντες, λέγουσι προκαλεῖσθαι καὶ δεικνύναι (trans. from Gertz, Dillon, and Russell 2014). Cp. Pliny, *HN* 30.18, where Apion claims to have evoked the shade of Homer.

[124] Seneca, *Oedipus* 530–626 includes a necromantic scene full of the trappings of horror, where Laius is brought up from the dead to confirm that Oedipus was his killer. It is unclear whether Laius is a reanimated corpse or a spirit, but the disgusting nature of his body is emphasized: "his body horribly covered with gore, his hair dirty, disgusting, and covered with filth." The gruesome witches of Roman elegy often make use of corpses; cp., e.g., Horace, *Satires* 1.8; and Tibullus 1.2.43–50. Gordon 1999a: 206–208 provides the best discussion of this necromantic "night-witch." Claudian, *in Ruf.* 1.154–156 mentions bringing spirits back into bodies among a list of magical powers.

[125] Lucan, *Pharsalia* 6.770–773. *Tripodas vatesque deorum| Sors obscura decet; certus discedat, ab umbris| Quisquis vera petit duraeque oracula mortis| Fortis adit* (trans. Luck 2006).

but the revelation provided by the dead in these extreme methods contains the clearest truth.[126]

The Late Antique rituals of the Greek Magical Papyri provide surprisingly few examples of necromancy, despite the number of rituals in which the dead are invoked to provide other services. The spirits of the dead are more often coerced to torment a woman with *eros* to bring her to the magician's door than they are invoked to provide divinatory revelation. The spells that do involve necromancy, as Faraone has shown, often disguise the use of corpses for divination by speaking of the skull as a *skyphos* (cup) or the body as a *skenos* (tent).[127] One spell involves inscribing three Homeric verses on a metal lamella and attaching it to a recently executed criminal: "speak the verses in his ear, and he will tell you everything you wish."[128] But the spell books provide many other sources for divinatory revelations, and the sun god, who proverbially sees and knows all, seems a better source for divinatory knowledge than a dead spirit. Necromancy in the Greek Magical Papyri is not as horrific as the necromancy depicted in Roman poetry, even if it remains a practice that warrants careful handling with coded terminology and labeling.

Who Performs Divination?

One difference in the treatment of necromancy may lie in the performers: the scribal magicians who compiled the Greek Magical Papyri in Roman Egypt are a far cry from the monstrous superwitches of Roman poetry. As Ogden comments, "Necromancy was as good or bad as the person practicing it," and the same might be said of other modes of divination as well.[129] The social evaluation of divination in the ancient Greco-Roman world depends greatly on who is performing it, and the range of possible performers spans the entire society. Anyone, from the lowliest slave to the greatest emperor, might have a significant dream or observe the flight of birds in the sky. Like prayer and sacrifice, divination may be performed by anyone,

[126] Cp. Statius, *Thebaid* 4.409–414. Apuleius mocks such an idea in the scene of necromancy in the *Golden Ass*, where, after an Egyptian sorcerer reanimates the corpse of a murdered man to name his wife as his murderer, the watching crowd is divided between those who want to lynch the wife and those who argue you can't trust a corpse. *Populus aestuat diversa tendentes: hi pessimam feminam viventem statim cum corpore mariti sepeliendam, alii mendacio cadaveris fidem non habendam* (*Met.* 2.29).

[127] See Faraone 2005, who also traces the practice of skull divination back to earlier Mesopotamian models. For more examples of skull divinations, see Ogden 2001: 208–216.

[128] PGM IV.2145–2240, at 2165.

[129] Ogden 2001: 264. On the night-witch of Roman poetry, see Gordon 1999a: 204–210, along with 192, where he describes Lucan's Erictho as the imaginary negative pole at the extreme end of the spectrum of religious behavior. On Erictho, see also Gordon 1987b.

but some people are more qualified, through their position in society or their personal expertise, than others. It is a mark of their curious relationship that, when the bird omen appears to Telemachus as he is parting from Menelaus and Helen, Helen steps forward to make the interpretation while Menelaus is still pondering its significance; she is better at this than he is.[130] While Helen, the daughter of Zeus, is an exceptional figure in many regards, skill in divination seems to have been regarded as something that could be both an inborn talent and a learned craft. Certainly, we hear of craftsmen in divination throughout the sources, starting with Homer, whose inclusion of *manteis* among other *demiourgoi*, like healers and carpenters, prompted Burkert's classic study of the transmission of such crafts to Greece from the societies of the Near East.[131] The authors of the Greek Magical Papyri, which include so many different forms of divination among their recipes, certainly were professionals in their craft.

Like other crafts, divination seems to have been passed down in families, and a few very famous families of diviners appear repeatedly in the historical record: the Melampids, the Iamids, the Clytiads, and the Telliads. Each of these families traced its lineage to a legendary diviner, just as the family of doctors known as the Ascelpiads traced its lineage to the divine hero Asclepius. Pindar sings of how Iamus received the gift of divination from Zeus and Apollo, and the famous diviner Tisamenos of Elis, who was so exceptional that the Spartans granted him citizen status (an unheard-of honor in xenophobic Sparta), traced his lineage to Iamus. Tisamenos's grandson, Agias, was honored in Sparta for enabling the Spartan general Lysander to win the decisive battle of Aegospotami against the Athenians to win the Peloponnesian War.[132]

As in other crafts, the family name was valuable, and craftsmen were often adopted into the line (or pretended to be).[133] A fourth-century BCE

---

[130] Homer, *Odyssey* 15.160–178.

[131] Homer, *Odyssey* 17.384–386. Cp. *Odyssey* 1.415–416, where Telemachus mentions the diviner (*theopropos*) whom Penelope entertained in hopes of hearing news of her long-lost Odysseus. For the migrations of craftsmen, see Burkert 1992. For inborn talent, the evidence is less clear, since many of the references to diviners stress their abilities without mention of craft, but some of these nonetheless also refer to the diviner's expertise acquired over many occasions. In addition to myths about diviners such as Teiresias or Melampus, Herodotus's story of Evenus (9.92–94) shows that some diviners were imagined to get their powers straight from divine gifts. Cp. Grottanelli 2003 on Evenus's acquisition of his mantic powers.

[132] Cp. Pindar, *Olympian* 6 for Iamus. Herodotus 9.33–35 tells the story of Tisamenos and the prophecy that he will win five victories (not in the Olympics, it turns out, but in military divination contexts). Pausanias 3.11.5 tells of the monument for Agias at Sparta, referring to another monument set up at Delphi in 10.9.7. Flower 2008a provides the best recent look at the Iamid family; see also Flower 2008b: 37–50 for discussions of divinatory families.

[133] Membership in a mantic lineage was an important element of self-presentation, the

lawcourt speech of Isocrates tells of a diviner Polemainetos, who passed his books of divination on to a certain Thrasyllos so that Thrasyllos could make his living in the profession.

> Thrasyllus, with these books as his capital, practised the art of divination. He became an itinerant soothsayer, lived in many cities, and was intimate with several women, some of whom had children whom he never even recognized as legitimate, and, in particular, during this period he lived with the mother of the complainant.[134]

The books, perhaps oracle collections, are not sufficient to make Thrasyllos a diviner, but they provide him with some tools of the trade, and his association with Polemainetos no doubt provided him with training in the craft. Thrasyllos was successful enough in his trade that his various offspring might engage in lawsuits over his estate, but his status was clearly not on the level of the Iamid Agias or one of the Pythias at Delphi. Not all diviners had the patronage of the Spartan kings or the prestige of a Panhellenic oracular shrine, and itinerant diviners like the promiscuous Thrasyllos must often have been viewed with suspicion as people claiming expert authority outside the established power structures.[135]

Plato provides a contemptuous picture of such itinerant mantic practitioners, lumping the diviners together with magicians who perform binding curses and ritual experts who promise to purify clients from the consequences of previous misdeeds.

> Wandering priests and prophets approach the doors of the wealthy and persuade them that they have a power from the gods conveyed through sacrifices and incantations, and any wrong committed against someone either by an individual or his ancestors can be expiated with pleasure and feasting. Or if he wishes to injure any enemy of his, for a small outlay he will be able to harm just and unjust alike with certain spells and incantations through which they can persuade the gods, they say, to serve their ends.[136]

Such a collocation of divination with magical binding spells shows exactly how divination can be considered magic on the basis of who is performing

---

sort of thing one might put on one's tombstone, as, e.g. SEG 23.161. Herodotus 9.95 denies that the diviner Deiphonos is a descendent of Evenius, although he claims to be.

[134] Isocrates 19.6.

[135] As Eidinow 2011: 23 notes, "As Thrasyllos' somewhat busy personal life suggests, we need to be careful that we do not confuse a theoretical liminality with actual physical and social isolation. Here was a man who seems to have lived and practiced successfully from within a community, indeed, within several different communities, before he finally returned to Siphnos."

[136] Plato, *Republic* 364a–b. See Burkert 1983, as well as Serafini 2016 for a recent study of such itinerant practitioners.

it; the immoral charlatans who claim to be able to annul the consequences of injustice also perform curses on innocent victims and claim to foretell the future. The extreme of such a characterization appears in the super-witches of Roman poetry, like Lucan's Erictho, who in these exaggerated literary portraits engage in every form of immoral action imaginable.

Such is the negative side of the extra-ordinary nature of divination, the social liminality and suspicions of wrongdoing or fakery. On the other hand, however, the very fact that the diviner claims authority outside the normal social structures can be important for resolving crises within the normal order, which is why divination is used in such circumstances. The diviner can provide apparently neutral arbitration to help settle a dispute, since the diviner or oracle stands outside the dispute in society and can thus make an impartial decision, speaking with the authority of the divine that lies outside the normal human social structures.[137] It is no accident that the most prestigious oracular shrines of Delphi and Dodona were sites for pilgrimage, far off from communities and individuals who came to consult them.[138]

The elaborate precautions taken in a particular Athenian consultation show the importance of an arbitrary outside decision to a split community. A mid-fourth-century BCE inscription concerns the resolution of a dispute over whether to cultivate a certain plot of land sacred to the goddesses Demeter and Kore.

> [The alternatives are to be engraved on tin plates and the appropriate official] is to wrap each plate in wool and put them in a bronze jar in the presence of the people. The presiding officers are to prepare these things, and the treasurers of the goddess [Athena] are imme-diately to bring a gold jar and a silver jar into the midst of the people. The *epistates* is to shake up the bronze jar and draw out each tin plate in turn, and to put the first one into the gold jar and the other into the silver jar, then to tie them up. The *epistates* is to mark it with the public seal, and any other Athenian who wishes may put his own seal on besides. Then the treasurers are to carry the jars to the Acropolis. Next the people are to choose three men, one from the council and two from the whole citizen body, to go to Delphi and ask the god which of the written plans the Athenians should follow in regard to

[137] Studies of contemporary African divination in action have shown the ways in which a diviner, even if a highly regarded insider in the community himself, can help resolve tensions within that community with this appeal to the outside power. Cp. P. Peek 1991; Abbink 1993; and Turner 1975.

[138] "The most influential shrine lay outside the territory of the great Classical city-states not because these had no use for it, but because the most convincing prophecy comes from afar" (Parker 2000: 79). See Parker 2000 for an account of the relations between oracles (especially Delphi) and city-states.

the sacred land, that in the gold jar or that in the silver. When they come back from consulting the god, they are to deliver the jars and both the prophecy and the writing on both tin plates are to be read to the people: whichever writing the god indicates is more advantageous to the Athenian people, so shall it be done.[139]

The multiple levels of precautions show the distrust the Athenians have for the partisans of each side who might try to fix the consultation, but they also show the potential for the corruption to be at the level of the diviner. The Delphic oracle might be the most authoritative and prestigious form of divination in the Greek world, but the Greeks knew that the Pythian priestesses were human and corruptible. Herodotus recounts the scandal that arose when the Spartan Kleomenes got the Pythia Perialla to proclaim that his rival, Demaratus, was not the legitimate heir to the kingship, opening the way for Kleomenes to become king of Sparta.[140] Even though Perialla was deposed from her position, the authority of the Delphic oracle continued to be preeminent. Individual diviners might be discredited, but the system of divination remains intact.

The conflict often arises between the extra-ordinary authority of the diviner and the ordinary authority of the leader of the community. The holder of one form of authority in the community naturally resents the claims of another, especially when their interests and advice conflict.[141] In the Roman Empire, various emperors sought to prohibit divination, especially about their own lives and the stability of their power, and their prohibitions became part of the legal regulation of religious activity characteristic of the later Roman state, whereas earlier Greek legal codes rarely touch on such matters.[142]

In tragedy, the blind diviner Teiresias often represents mantic authority in conflict with the political power of the king. Pentheus in the *Bacchae*

---

[139] IG II.204 = SIG I.204, lines 31–51 (from 352/351 BCE) (trans. Rice and Stambaugh 2009).

[140] Herodotus 6.66; cp. 6.84, where Herodotus opines that it was this crime that lead to Kleomenes's horrible death through maddened self-mutilation. Herodotus also alleges (5.63) that the Alcmaionids of Athens, after being exiled by the Pisistratid tyrants, bribed the Pythia to urge the Spartans, every time they came to consult the oracle to free Athens from tyranny. Plutarch (*de Malign. Herod.* 23) regards this claim as false and an example of the malignity of Herodotus.

[141] See Burkert 2005: 43–48. Calchas, at the beginning of the *Iliad*, takes the precaution of securing the support of the most powerful warrior, Achilles, before he proclaims that actions of the king, Agamemnon, are responsible for the plague from Apollo, and Agamemnon rages at this alliance between the diviner, whose authority comes from his connection to divinity, and the headstrong young warrior, whose prowess in battle threatens the authority of Agamemnon as the military commander (*Iliad* 1.57–120). Likewise, the suitors in the *Odyssey* reject the bird omen of Halitherses, and they laugh at Theoclymenos's predictions of doom (*Odyssey* 2.146–168; 20.351–370).

[142] Graf 1999: 286 provides a brief summary of Roman legislation against divination.

accuses Teiresias of encouraging the worship of Dionysos in the city in order to gain more authority and more sacrificial portions from this strange new religion.[143] The most striking example comes in the interaction between Oedipus and Teiresias in Sophocles's *Oedipus Tyrannos*. Oedipus at first welcomes Teiresias as the only man with sufficient divine connection to discover the problem at the root of the plague afflicting Thebes.

> Teiresias, you who dispose all things, those that can be explained and those unspeakable, things in heaven and things that move on earth, even though you cannot see you know the nature of the sickness that besets the city; and you are the only champion and protector, lord, whom we can find.[144]

When, however, Teiresias tries to avoid prophesying and then proclaims that Oedipus himself is the guilty party, Oedipus accuses him of being fraud and a magician conspiring with Prince Creon to overthrow Oedipus.

> Creon the trusty, my friend from the first, has crept up to me and longs to throw me out, setting upon me this wizard [*magos*] hatcher of plots, this crafty beggar, who has sight only when it comes to profit, but in his art is blind! Why, come, tell me, how can you be a true prophet?[145]

This dramatic shift between Teiresias as the city's only savior and a corrupt magician takes place in one brief scene of less than a hundred lines, pointing to the inherent instability of the extra-ordinary authority of divination. Teiresias's divination falls from the highest point on the hierarchy of means to the lowest for Oedipus, and so he uses the label of 'magic,' one of the earliest such uses in extant Greek.

In Greek tragedy, the diviner is always correct and never heeded, whereas in Attic comedy, diviners are inevitably the charlatans Oedipus accuses Teiresias of being. Aristophanes presents as disreputable itinerant quacks several diviners whom other evidence shows to have been prominent and authoritative figures in Athenian society. The extra-ordinary claims to divine authority by diviners such as Hierocles and Lampon provoke the attacks of Aristophanes, but both seem to have been honored in inscriptions with various responsibilities and even granted the highest honor of the city of meals in the Prytaneion.[146] Their expertise in the man-

---

[143] Euripides, *Bacchae* 215–369. See Roth 1982 and Carastro 2007.
[144] Sophocles, *OT* 300–304.
[145] Sophocles, *OT* 385–395.
[146] See especially Dillery 2005: 196–197. Lampon is undoubtedly the Thuriomantis to whom Aristophanes refers in *Nub.* 332, and he was a prominent figure in Athens at the time, an associate of Pericles (cp. Plutarch, *Vit. Per.* 6.2) who was one of the founders of the colony of Thurii (Diod. Sic. 12.10.3–4; cp. Scholiast on *Nub.* 332). For Hierocles, cp. *Nub.* 332; *Av.*

tic craft provides them with great authority and influence in the city, the ability to shape both domestic and foreign policy through their interpretations of signs from the divine.

The importance of the interpretive process is clear in the famous 'wooden walls' oracle reported by Herodotus when the Athenians consulted of the oracle at Delphi before the Persian invasion. After the Athenians got an oracle prophesying defeat and despair, they refused to take it and asked for a better one. The Pythia provided a second answer.

> Vainly doth Pallas strive to appease great Zeus of Olympus;
> Words of entreaty are vain, and cunning counsels of wisdom.
> Natheless a rede I will give thee again, of strength adamantine.
> All shall be taken and lost that the sacred border of Cecrops
> Holds in keeping to-day, and the dales divine of Cithaeron;
> Yet shall a wood-built wall by Zeus all-seeing be granted
> Unto the Trito-born, a stronghold for thee and thy children.
> Bide not still in thy place for the host that cometh from landward,
> Cometh with horsemen and foot; but rather withdraw at his
>   coming,
> Turning thy back to the foe; thou yet shalt meet him in battle.
> Salamis, isle divine! 'tis writ that children of women
> Thou shalt destroy one day, in the season of seedtime or harvest.[147]

When this oracle was presented to the people of Athens, they debated what it meant for how they could save themselves. What were the wooden walls that the oracle claimed could save the city? Despite some oracles-experts (*chresmologoi*) who claimed that they referred to an old fence around the acropolis, the Athenians were persuaded by the interpretation of Themistokles that the 'wooden wall' meant ships. Themistokles was an important politician, on whose advice Athens had recently built up its navy, and his advice to abandon the city and attack the Persian fleet at Salamis provided Athens with one of the biggest Greek victories in the Persian Wars.[148]

987–988; *Pax* 1043–1047. IG I² 39 (IG I³ 40) lines 65–69 mentions Hierocles as an expert; in Aristophanes, *Pax* 1084, Trygaeus threatens Hierocles with losing his privilege of dining in the Prytaneum.

[147] Herodotus 7.141.3–4. Judging from the responses recorded in Herodotus, Delphi revealed itself to be (from the point of view of a modern historian looking back at the evidence) fairly pro-Persian, giving oracles that warned of the futility of resisting the invasion and counseling submission to the Persian empire, but as Parker 2000: 98 comments on the oracles in Herodotus, "If one merely accepts them as reported in Herodotus the pattern seems to be one of confirming the consultants in their own inclinations."

[148] On this wooden walls oracle, see the discussions in Struck 2003 and Dillery 2005. Note how the interpretation hinges on the significance of a single word, 'divine,' to describe Salamis, since Themistokles argues that it must indicate good fortune for the Athenians. As Struck 2003: 185 comments, "In practice, a divine sign comes to mean precisely what the best of

CONCLUSIONS: DIVINATION AND MAGIC

Obviously, the Athenians did not view the future as an absolutely fixed and unchangeable thing; they could ask for a better oracle, and they felt that Athena was lobbying Zeus on their behalf. Divination, for the Greeks of the Archaic and Classical periods, can provide insight into the plans of the gods for the future or into the events of the past that have shaped the actions of the gods in the present. Divination receives, directly or indirectly, the personal communications of the gods, the particular expressions of their individual or collective will. Whether the god speaks to an inspired prophet, to a dreamer, or sends a message through the movement of birds or in the liver of an animal, the act of communication is personal and particular, from the god to the mortal. In this model, divinatory questions about a specific course of action—is it better to do one thing or another?—are asking for help in judgment from a source that is wiser than humans, since the gods are more experienced as well as more knowledgeable than mortals.

With the systematization of lore in the Hellenistic period and later, the model shifts from an interpersonal (oral) communication toward a more generalized (textual) communication. The gods write, in the ordered patterns of the cosmos, their messages for mankind, and those messages are available for all who have the skill to read them. The consequence of a cosmos ordered by the rational activity of the gods is a world in which the future is increasingly seen as preordained; everything must be part of the unalterable plan of the gods. Divination becomes a way of reading this text, but the end of the story is already written.

While a general shift over time between these two models may be seen, both ideas are in tension with one another at any given point in the history of the Greco-Roman world. The idea of an ordered cosmos goes back to the 'Pre-Socratic' thinkers of the Archaic period, and even the Homeric epics occasionally present Zeus as an all-powerful distributor of fate.[149] Conversely, even as the cosmos came to be seen as more ordered and its patterns as predetermined, people sought for the marvelous exceptions to the increasingly stringent rules, leading, as Gordon has argued, to the rise of collections of occult lore.[150] The aim of divination then becomes to find the way out of the predetermined pattern, the exception to the rules, for

---

the men who read it say it means. The correct reading of it is, by definition, that which is delivered by the hero who is best equipped, with the tools of persuasive speech, to press his case on his peers."

[149] The idea of Zeus dealing out the fates of all is perhaps best captured in the image of the urns of Zeus (Homer, *Iliad* 24.527–528).

[150] See Gordon 1987a and Gordon 1997, as well as the longer treatment in Gordon 1999a.

what is the use of knowing the future if nothing can be done to avoid it?[151] A divinatory spell in the Greek Magical Papyri brings an encounter with a supreme god who will tell your fate, but the instructions direct: "And if you hear something bad, do not cry out or weep, but ask that he may wash it off or circumvent it, for this god can do everything."[152]

The attempt to subvert fate indeed becomes the mark of magic in these later periods, distinguishing extra-ordinary divination from more normative practices. Philostratus, trying to defend the miracle-worker and Neopythagorean philosopher Apollonius of Tyana from the charge of being a magician (*goēs*), does so on the grounds that Apollonius only foretold through his divine insight, but never tried to alter the divine plan.

> Magicians [*goētes*], who are in my opinion the greatest scoundrels on earth, resort to questioning ghosts or to barbaric sacrifices, or to forms of incantation or unction, and thus profess to alter fate. Many of them have been induced by accusations to admit their skill in such matters. Apollonius, however, followed the warnings of the Fates, and foretold the way they had to be fulfilled, and his clairvoyance was due not to magic [*goēteuōn*] but to divine revelation.[153]

Philostratus's definition of magic as the practice of trying to influence the future, rather than just foretelling it, is echoed in Bouché-Leclerq's monumental study, which provided the foundation for the modern scholarly study of ancient divination.[154] This formulation, while appropriate for the Roman Imperial context of Philostratus or the Greek Magical Papyri, fails to make sense of the earlier evidence, in which there was always the possibility of appealing to a god to intervene in the course of events. In this context, we find that label of 'magic' attached to the extra-ordinary claims of practitioners whose social location does not match the level of authority

---

[151] Some philosophical schools maintained that divinatory foreknowledge could help one prepare oneself to face a coming disaster, but few were able to sustain such resignation as expressed by a character in the novel *Leucippe and Clitophon* by Achilles Tatius. "The divine power often wishes to show the future to human beings in the night, not in order to protect them from a tragic event (because fate cannot be controlled), but to help them accept such an event when it occurs. For when disasters come in a row, unexpectedly, they produce a sudden shock and overwhelm people totally, but if people are prepared for them and can think about them beforehand, it averts a little the sharp edge of pain" (1.3.2).

[152] PGM XIII.714–715. J. Z. Smith (e.g., 1978b) has described the difference between a worldview in which one seeks to know and improve one's place in the world order and one in which one seeks to escape entirely the oppressions of the cosmic order as the contrast between locative and utopian models of the world.

[153] Philostratus, *VA* 5.12.

[154] "On pourrait dire que la divination est la magie contemplative, substituant l'exercice de l'intelligence à celui de la volonté agissante" (Bouché-Leclercq 1879 vol. 1: 10). Cp. Graf 1999: 283–284 on the influence of the Frazerian paradigm on the scholarship.

and efficacy they claim for their practice, whether because they are socially marginal figures or because they are in conflict with more prominent
authorities. So too, if the diviner's authority is not tied to a traditionally
sanctioned place *where* and traditionally sanctioned times *when* the divination takes place, then the divination is more likely to be deemed magical.
Smith's characterization of the magician as the practitioner of the religion
of anywhere makes more sense of the diviner who gets labeled a 'magician'
than Bouché-Leclerq's active versus contemplative dichotomy.

   In distinguishing a category of magical divination, then, the *social location* of the one *who* is performing it plays a role, as well as *where* and *when*
the divination is performed. *What* sort of divinations is performed makes
less of a difference, although certain forms of divination, such as necromancy, are always more apt to be seen as magic. The level of *efficacy*
claimed for the divination can also play a role. In general, the forms of
divination most likely to be considered extra-ordinary enough for magic
are those at either end of the hierarchy of means, either the low prestige
and low authority superstitions or the exceptional and marginal means
whose high prestige and authority stem from the very stamp of strangeness
that marks them.

8

Mysteries of the Heavenly Spheres: Astrology and Magic

> [Incorporating medicine and religion, magic] made a further addition of astrology, because there is nobody who is not eager to learn his destiny, or who does not believe that the truest account of it is that gained by watching the skies. Accordingly, holding men's emotions in a three-fold bond, magic rose to such a height that even today it has sway over a great part of mankind.
>
> (Pliny, *HN* 30.1.1–2)[1]

INTRODUCTION: THE MAGIC OF THE ASTROLOGICAL SYSTEM

Astrology is perhaps the best known of the divinatory practices of the ancient Greco-Roman world, and its afterlife in Western culture has been remarkable, from the Renaissance up through its modern revival in the twentieth century.[2] But astrology was also disproportionately significant in antiquity as well, as Pliny's reference suggests. Its practice was widespread, and its authority as a means to obtaining special knowledge remained high. Pliny classifies astrology as one part of his broader category of magical arts, and, although like other forms of divination, astrology is

---

[1] ... *miscuisse artes mathematicas, nullo non avido futura de sese sciendi atque ea e caelo verissime peti credente. ita possessis hominum sensibus triplici vinculo in tantum fastigii adolevit ut hodieque etiam in magna parte gentium praevaleat.*

[2] Cp. Barton 1994: 1–8. The standard modern study of ancient astrology is Bouché-Leclercq 1899, a companion to his broader study of divination and, as Gordon 2013a: 103 comments, it is "a work that no modern scholar would be capable of writing, or perhaps even wish to write." The brief volumes of Barton 1994 and Beck 2007 provide good overviews of the subject, while Greenbaum 2016: 399–414 provides a concise introduction to the mechanics.

not always and automatically considered magic, astrology always potentially can receive this label because of the extra-ordinary efficacy it promises—astrology provides a model of the rational ordering of the cosmos that can guide individual choice and action.

This rational order, laid out in a systematic fashion, brings astrology close to the modern category of science, and some of its ancient practitioners certainly claimed it as a science alongside medicine, mathematics, and physics (or that combination of astronomy, physics, and chemistry called *physika*). At the same time, the personification of the planets, stars, and other celestial entities as divinities who could favor or harm mortals (and who could be called upon by mortals to do so) means that astrology cannot be entirely separated from the modern category of religion. Magic, religion, and science all appear as labels for astrology in different contexts, and ancient astrology is thus worth investigating in detail, precisely because of the ways in which it fails to fit neatly into the categories, ancient or modern.

The astronomical model of the cosmos described in astrology, with the divinities of the heavens proceeding in systematic and observable paths as they preside over the world of mortals, becomes one of the most important and widespread models for understanding the cosmos in the Greco-Roman world, starting with the Hellenistic period and increasingly so during the Roman Empire.[3] Some form of this cosmological model appears almost everywhere in the Greco-Roman world in this time period, ranging from the most basic identification of traditional Greek and Roman gods with the visible planets to the most sophisticated and complicated systems detailed in the astrological manuals or Gnostic theologies.

The most outstanding features of astrology that distinguish it from other forms of divination are its extreme complexity and systematicity. All forms of divination operate with a fixed matrix of signs and a random element of chance, but, whereas the Magic 8-Ball has a limited number of possible signs and a large element of chance determining which will turn up, astrology works with a vast array of celestial signs, and the element of chance is limited to the moment of birth (or some other significant moment that is chosen). The sign system in astrology is not limited to the simple placement of individual elements (the planets, constellations, etc.) but includes the complex layers of the interrelation of these signs to one another that

[3] Cp. Pingree 2014: 9: "ancient Greek astrology in its strictest interpretation was the most comprehensive scientific theory of antiquity, providing through the application of the mathematical models appropriate to it predictions of all changes that take place in a world of cause and effect." Although ancient terminology did not often distinguish between 'astronomy' and 'astrology,' I here use 'astronomy' to mean the description of the cosmic motions, while I use 'astrology' to refer to the interpretations of the effects of those cosmic movements.

determine their meaning, just as letters or even words in linguistic sign systems derive their meaning from their positioning with regard to one another.

In addition to the complexity of its sign system, astrology is distinguished by the extent to which these complexities are systematized within a rational order. Gordon sees ancient Greco-Roman astrology as a type of what Weber calls *Planmäßigkeit*, "the application of systematisation and ordered procedures to specific areas of human experience." More than any other form of divination, astrology makes use of systematic ordering to create meaningful predictions. He argues, "Despite its modern reputation as pure irrationalism, it seems clear to me that ancient astrology represented a form of *Planmäßigkeit*, the systematic application of explicit ideas based upon a rationalised account of the cosmos, to the uncertainties of human experience."[4] Astrology in this way defines itself as a science, a rational and systematic discourse of knowledge for dealing with the observable world, but astrology also appears with the label of 'magic,' not just labels applied by external observers like Pliny but in the self-classifications of practitioners who use astrology for extra-ordinary aims, like the magicians of the Greek Magical Papyri.

The complexities of the astrological systems explain *how*, in emic terms, astrology worked in the ancient Greco-Roman world, both in terms of the actual practice and the cosmological models that underlie it. This same complexity and systematicity also explain *why* the ancient Greeks and Romans turned to astrology in such numbers to deal with the uncertainties of life. Although the evidence for astrology (*what*) is perhaps somewhat skewed by the astrological treatises that elaborate their systems in enormous detail, the authors of these manuals are not the only ones *who* made use of astrology, but the ideas and iconography of astrology appear all over the Greco-Roman world. While some of this multitude of uses of astrological ideas and images don't appear to be marked as abnormal or extra-ordinary, others bear the familiar stamp of strangeness that marks the practice as extra-ordinary, beyond the bounds of normal—magical.

WHAT: THE SOURCES OF EVIDENCE FOR ASTROLOGY

Our evidence for understanding ancient astrology comes not only from the manuals written by theoretically minded practitioners (and the theoretical

---

[4] Gordon 2013c: 95. As Pingree 2014: 8 argues, this brings astrology under the category of science for a historian of science. "What is the proper definition of science for a historian of science? I would offer this as the simplest, broadest, and most useful: science is a systematic explanation of perceived or imaginary phenomena, or else is based on such an explanation."

critiques of both philosophical and religious thinkers), but also from a plethora of other kinds of sources, from horoscope charts drawn by practitioners to poems detailing the celestial phenomena to reports of legal prosecutions of astrological divination to widespread astrological iconography throughout the Roman Empire. The theoretical treatises (and critiques) provide the best evidence for reconstructing the ideas behind the practices, as well as the development of these ideas over time, but the other evidence helps reconstruct the place of astrological practices within the cultural contexts of Greek and Roman society.

Although a massive collection of texts from the manuscripts containing astrological treatises, the *Catalogus Codicum Astrologorum Graecorum*, was put together under the direction of Franz Cumont and Franz Boll at the end of the nineteenth century, remarkably little has been done by scholars with this trove of texts in the last century. This collection nonetheless provides a glimpse of the vast history of astrological writings in Greek from the Hellenistic period to the Byzantine Empire. The earliest texts from the Hellenistic period have disappeared along with the majority of texts from that era, but traces and fragments remain of these earliest works in quotations by later authors. Many of these earliest surviving texts, perhaps from the first century BCE, bear the names of mythical personages, as innovative astrologers sought to validate their ideas with the names of mythical ancient Egyptian kings and priests such as Nechepso or Petosiris or of Hellenized Egyptian deities such as Hermes Trismegistus or Asclepius.

These pseudepigraphic texts bear the names of Egyptian authorities, most likely because they were produced in the Greek cultural environment of Ptolemaic Egypt, but the astrological material of which they make use seems to derive in the main from the Hellenistic Greek astronomical tradition, of which Kallipos of Kyzikos and Eudoxos of Knidos are the most important representatives in the fourth century BCE. Aratus's *Phainomena*, a third-century BCE poetic version of Eudoxos's treatise on celestial phenomena, was hugely important in popularizing the ideas of the planets and constellations and their rotations that formed the basis for astrological calculations, and Aratus's work was imitated and copied by many later thinkers (including Latin versions by Cicero and Germanicus, adopted son of the Emperor Tiberius).

The astronomical works of Eudoxos and Kallipos were, in part, systematizations of traditional Greek star lore, since references to constellations appear as early as the earliest Greek epics of Homer and Hesiod (eighth century BCE). However, the impetus for much of their development seems to have come from the influx of astronomical lore from the Persian Empire, where the Babylonian tradition of astronomical observations can be traced to the second millenium BCE. Some of this influence can be seen already in the Classical period, with Meton's attempt to reform the Athenian calendar in 432 BCE and in the cosmological models in Plato (especially the *Timaeus*), but the flow increased after the conquests of Alexander brought new levels of interaction between the cultures.[5]

The Babylonian base-60 number system, which had a place value component that still survives in our modern divisions into 360 degrees, 60 minutes, 60 seconds, and so forth, was certainly better suited for the cataloging of numerical data than the cumbersome Greek number system, and the earliest text with such data about the appearances of the planet Venus goes back to 1646 BCE.[6] It remains unclear how much of this tradition of observational data was transmitted directly to the Greeks, but the shapes and natures of many of the constellations, especially in the Zodiac, seem to come directly from the Babylonian ones without any indication of earlier names in Greek. Even though the planets are identified with Greek gods and acquire many of the mythological traits of those deities, the basis of the identifications of the planets with deities seems to come through the Babylonian tradition—for example, the planet Venus is identified as the star of Aphrodite because of its earlier Babylonian association with Ishtar, a goddess who is regularly identified as Aphrodite in Greek sources. The data were used for predictions of eclipses and other celestial phenomena, as well as in lists of omens and their meanings, and the casting of genethlialogical horoscopes seems to have begun by the fifth century BCE. Aristotle's pupil Theophrastus may provide the first Greek witness to such Babylonian horoscopes when he mentions contemporary Chaldaeans who forecast not just seasons and storms but the whole life and death of individuals by the stars (mentioned in Proclus, *in Tim.* III.151), but the diffusion of Babylonian data is clear by the second century BCE, when Hipparchus of Rhodes uses it to calculate the precession of the equinoxes.[7]

Some influence of Egyptian traditions does appear in this Hellenistic astrology, especially with the importance of Sirius (the Egyptian Sothis, whose rising was used for millennia to predict the flooding of the Nile) and in the appearance of the decans. The decans appear to be derived from the thirty-six constellations (the first of which included Sothis) whose risings before sunrise (heliacal rising) were taken as the last hour of the night. The number of constellations that rose between sunset and sunrise determined the number of hours in the night, and this becomes a way of divid-

---

[5] Barton 1994: 21–22.

[6] Greek numbers, like the Roman, were represented by letters, and larger numbers were created by adding together smallers ones. 372 and 365 would thus be TOB and TΞE or 300 + 70 + 2 and 300 + 60 + 5, rather than, in the Babylonian equivalent 1 1′ 12″ and 1 1′ 5″. The place value system makes complex computations with the numbers very much simpler.

[7] Barton 1994: 12–16. On the Mesopotamian systems, see Rochberg 2004.

ing up time into small chunks to measure the appearance of other celestial phenomena. This system, which appears in second-millennium BCE Egyptian evidence, seems to have been adapted, along with many of the decan names, into the Greek systems in Hellenistic Ptolemaic Egypt, but, despite the appeals to authorities of Egyptian antiquity, most of the astronomical system underlying Greco-Roman astrology seems to derive from Hellenistic Greek ideas based on ancient Babylonian astronomy.

Most of the evidence for Greco-Roman astrology comes from the Roman Empire, but astrology began to be popular in Rome by at least the first century BCE. An associate of Cicero's, Publius Nigidius Figulus, who was also associated with the rise of Neopythagoreanism in Rome, earned his sobriquet, Figulus (the potter), because of a demonstration he did to quell the critics of astrology who raised the standard question of why twins don't have the same fate. Figulus spun a potter's wheel and likened it to the rotation of the heavens, showing that trying to hit the same spot twice with inky fingers was just as impossible as two people being born at precisely the same configuration of the heavens.[8] The popularity of astrology at Rome appears in the Latin translations of Aratus's *Phainomena*, as well as other Latin works such as a lost treatise by Varro and, most importantly, the didactic epic of Manilius, entitled the *Astronomica*.

One of the earliest treatises we have on astrology seems to come from the first-century CE Roman Empire, a text by Dorotheus of Sidon, who probably lived around 25–75 CE. His treatise, which refers to earlier Hermetic astrological texts, survived for modern scholars only in quotations of the original Greek in later authors, until an eighth-century Arabic text was recently identified as a translation of Dorotheus from a fifth-century Pahlavi (Persian) translation of the original. In the second century CE, the principles of astrology were systematized by Claudius Ptolemaeus, whose *Tetrabiblos* (four books) supplement his treatises on geography and astronomy with astrology. Ptolemy's cosmological system is incredibly detailed and mathematically complex, and the Ptolemaic model, passing through the Arabic tradition into the Latin medieval one, remained the standard until the time of Copernicus (Ptolemy's astronomical treatise was known as *Al-magest*, the Great Book, in Arabic). His younger contemporary, Vettius Valens of Antioch, produced a compendious *Anthologiae* of astrological lore, which includes numerous practical examples of horoscopes and their interpretation, something the more theoretical Ptolemy avoids. His work is full of arabesques, complications, and nuances that show how his system is superior to that of other astrologers (whom he often helpfully cites).

[8] Augustine, *Civ. Dei* 5.3.

Later treatises continue the elaboration of the tradition. In the fourth century, Julius Firmicus Maternus (possibly the same as the Christian author of a treatise *On the Errors of Profane Religions*) provides a detailed and systematic treatise in Latin, while Maximus of Ephesus (the Neoplatonist teacher of the emperor Julian the Apostate) presents a poem in Greek hexameter on the significance of the Moon in katarchic astrology. The fifth-century CE Hephaistion of (Egyptian) Thebes provides excerpts from earlier astrologers such as Ptolemy and Dorotheus in his *Apotelesmatica*. In addition to these systematic expositions of astrological theory, we have systematic refutations of astrological ideas, such as the attack of the Skeptic Sextus Empiricus, and arguments by philosophers such as the Neoplatonist Plotinus and the Christian Origen against the validity of astrological ideas.[9]

WHO: ASTROLOGY IN PRACTICE

These authors, however, are clearly railing against widely accepted ideas, for astrology was everywhere in the world of the Roman Empire. Astrological cosmology informed the latest developments in science and religion, while the imagery of astrology was ubiquitous. Everyone had at least some sense of the cosmological model underlying astrology, of planetary influences and fate written in the stars. Even if most people in the Roman Empire could no better read the messages in the stars than they could read Greek or Latin, everyone knew that there were literate experts who could decipher the mysterious messages. Those in need of guidance when starting a new venture might turn to one of these experts for a katarchic horoscope, while others might consult about the birth of a new relative—or check on the birth signs of a rival.

A limited number of actual horoscopes furnish some additional information about the practice of astrology in the Greco-Roman world. Some of these appear as examples within the manuals of certain astrologers (particularly Vettius Valens), but others have been uncovered on papyrus or other materials. These executed examples of horoscopes provide surprisingly little interpretive detail, however, being mostly rough sketches of the positions of the planets without any of the complex arabesques and elaborations of the manuals. They are generally presumed to be birth charts, but many could have been used for katarchic consultations, and the dearth of information about the circumstances makes it difficult to determine who

---

[9] Long 1982 reviews these refutations.

produced these charts and for whom.[10] The production of the charts would generally require some expertise, but not nearly as much as demanded in the manuals of Ptolemy, Vettius Valens, or even Firmicus Maternus, while the clientele could come from any walk of life—although presumably more often from those who could more easily afford the services.

Astrology thus reached into every level of society, providing a cosmological model and a set of associated terms, entities, and images everyone could recognize. As an extreme example of the ubiquity of astrological imagery, the Roman novelist Petronius describes the astrological designs on a platter at an absurdly extravagant banquet.

> There was a round plate with the twelve signs of the Zodiac set in a circle, and on each one the artist had laid some food fit and proper to the symbol; over the Ram ram's-head chick-pea, a piece of beef on the Bull, testicles and kidneys over the Twins, over the Crab a wreath of flowers, an African fig over the Lion, a barren sow's paunch over Virgo, over Libra a pair of scales with a muffin on one side and a cake on the other, over Scorpio a small sea-fish, over Sagittarius an oblade, over Capricornus a crawfish, over Aquarius a goose, over Pisces two mullets.[11]

The gauche and nouveau riche ex-slave Trimalchio hopes to impress his guests with this clever concoction, showing off his erudition as well as his opulence with this symbolic platter. The signs of astrology, as Beck has argued, became so familiar that they could serve as something of a secondary symbolic system to communicate meanings to those who could read them.[12] Perhaps the most famous example is the Emperor Augustus, who put Capricorn, the ruling sign of his horoscope, on his coinage to proudly proclaim his association with the start of a bright new order, like the return of the sun after the winter solstice in Capricorn see (figure 16).[13]

---

[10] The best collection of these texts remains Neugebauer and Van Hoesen 1959, who note (162), "Were it not for an extensive astrological literature, the original horoscopes alone would hardly reveal their purpose to foresee events from the initial configuration of the planets."

[11] Petronius, *Satyricon* 35. *Rotundum enim repositorium duodecim habebat signa in orbe disposita, super quae proprium convenientemque materiae structor imposuerat cibum: super arietem cicer arietinum, super taurum bubulae frustum, super geminos testiculos ac rienes, super cancrum coronam, super leonem ficum Africanam, super virginem steriliculam, super libram stateram in cuius altera parte scriblita erat, in altera placenta, super scorpionem pisciculum marinum, super sagittarium oclopetam, super capricornum locustam marinam, super aquarium anserem, super pisces duos mullos.*

[12] Cp. Beck's discussion of the 'star-talk' in Mithraic monuments in Beck 2006.

[13] Cassius Dio 56.25.5. As Barton 1995: 47 remarks, "It would nicely symbolize the shift from the older style of omen lore to the new."

Figure 16. Silver denarius of Augustus, 18–16 BCE; British Museum
R.6080 ©Trustees of the British Museum.

HOW: THEORIES OF CELESTIAL INFLUENCE

In contrast to other types of divination, where we have little evidence for
the specific details of the way the process works, the astrological treatises
provide, in their systematic expositions, an overwhelming abundance of
technical details. The underlying assumption of astrology is that the movements and positions of the observable celestial phenomena correlate to the
workings of the divine powers. Some ancient thinkers see this correlation
as causal (that is, the stars cause things to happen to people on earth),
whereas others see the correlation as merely symbolic (that is, the stars
indicate things that the gods are making happen on earth), but divination
through astrology always involves interpreting the message encoded in the
celestial phenomena, figuring out the significance of each of the things
that appear in the heavens.

The observable effects of the sun and the moon on earthly life provide
the model for the influence of all the other celestial forces.[14] As Ptolemy
notes, both the daily and the yearly cycles of the sun affect all life on earth,
from the alternations of sunlight and darkness that provide a blend of heat,
moisture, dryness, and cold, to the seasonal changes of temperature and

[14] For example, Hesiod, *Works and Days* 383–387, 564–573, 609–623. Indeed, the term
'influence' is at root an astrological metaphor, referring to the power of the stars that flows
in and affects earthly life. Influenza, the 'flu,' takes its name from such a theory of celestial
influence, so the yearly flu shots may be imagined as inoculating oneself against the malign
influence of the stars!

weather that enable plants and animals to grow and flourish. The tides clearly correlate with the motions of the moon, and lunar cycles seem to play a role in the lives of various animals, including humans. From these easily observable effects of the sun and moon, the influence of all the other bodies in the heavens can be extrapolated, and this influence is reinforced by the connection between the appearance of certain stars and the change of seasons, connections noted in Greek lore as early as Hesiod's *Works and Days*.[15]

This influence of heavenly bodies on earthly ones occurs because of a fundamental connection between all things in the cosmos, an idea that is often expressed in the ancient sources in some form of the notion of *sympatheia*.[16] The rational order of the cosmos involves a link between all of the different parts of the cosmic order, so, just as earthly things affect one another, so too heavenly things affect earthly things.[17] Manilius expresses this idea of cosmic interconnection, along with the idea of an organizing divine principle that governs all.

> Thus everything is organized throughout the whole world and follows a master. This god, and the reason that controls everything, brings down from the heavenly stars the creatures of the earth. Though the stars are very distant and remote, he makes us feel their influence, as they give to the peoples their ways of life and destinies

[15] Ptolemy, *Tetrabiblos* I.2. "A very few considerations would make it apparent to all that a certain power emanating from the eternal ethereal substance is dispersed through and permeates the whole region about the earth, which throughout is subject to change, since, of the primary sublunar elements, fire and air are encompassed and changed by the motions in the ether, and in turn encompass and change all else, earth and water and the plants and animals therein. For the sun, together with the ambient, is always in some way affecting everything on the earth, not only by the changes that accompany the seasons of the year to bring about the generation of animals, the productiveness of plants, the flowing of waters, and the changes of bodies, but also by its daily revolutions furnishing heat, moisture, dryness, and cold in regular order and in correspondence with its positions relative to the zenith. The moon, too, as the heavenly body nearest the earth, bestows her effluence most abundantly upon mundane things, for most of them, animate or inanimate, are sympathetic to her and change in company with her; the rivers increase and diminish their streams with her light, the seas turn their own tides with her rising and setting, and plants and animals in whole or in some part wax and wane with her. Moreover, the passages of the fixed stars and the planets through the sky often signify hot, windy, and snowy conditions of the air, and mundane things are affected accordingly." Cp. Cicero, *de div.* 2.89.

[16] Luck 2006: 395–406 collects a series of passages from Manilius that illustrate the notion of *sympatheia* in an astrological context (particularly 2.60–149 and 1.149–254). While the concept of *sympatheia* is elaborated in many Stoic sources, it is by no means confined to them; the idea of like affecting like appears as a physical theory as early as the Pre-Socratics.

[17] It is worth noting that arguments against the validity of astrology, especially among the Epicureans, often take the form of a denial of this premise, claiming to the contrary that the heavenly realm is so far removed from the earthly that there is no effect of the one upon the other.

and to every person a character of his own. We do not have to look far for proof: this is why the sky affects the farmland, why it gives and takes away various crops, why it moves the sea by ebb and tide. This constant motion of the sea is sometimes caused by the moon, sometimes provoked by her withdrawal to another part and sometimes depends on the yearly course of the sun through the year.[18]

Again, the sun and the moon are the model for the whole system, the proof of the validity of the idea that the remote stars could have any effect on mortal life.

Although the sun seems clearly to cause the effects of the light and heat it provides, many ancient thinkers were uncomfortable with the idea that the stars could be causes of the things they signify. The Platonist Plotinus critiques the idea that divine powers such as the stars could be so unjust as to provide good and bad things for mortals regardless of whether they deserve them or not.

They say that the planets in their courses do not only cause everything else, poverty and riches, sickness and health, but also ugliness and beauty and, what is most important of all, virtue and vice, and even the actions which result from them in each particular case on each particular occasion; just as if they were angry with men over things in which men have done them no wrong, since it was the planets which made the men what they are; and that they give benefits (so-called), not because they feel kindly towards those who receive them but because they themselves are either pleasantly or unpleasantly affected according to the point they have reached on their course, and again are in a different state of mind when they are at their zeniths and when they are declining.[19]

For Plotinus, the divine stars cannot possibly be such changeable and emotional entities, inflicting harm on mortals who have done bad things merely because they were already disposed to do so by astral influence.[20]

---

[18] Manilius 2.80–149.

[19] Plotinus, *Enneads* 2.3.1.

[20] Cp. Plotinus, *Enneads* 3.1.6. "Admitted that the universal circuit co-operates (conceding the main part to the parents), and admitted that the stars contribute a great deal corporeally to the constituents of the body, heat and cooling and the consequent bodily temperaments; how, then, are they responsible for characters and ways of life, and especially for what is not obviously dominated by bodily temperament—becoming a man of letters, for instance, or a geometer, or a dice-player, and a discoverer in these fields? And how could a wicked character be given by the stars, who are gods? And in general, how could all the evils be given by them which they are said to give when they are brought into an evil state because they are setting and passing under the earth—as if anything extraordinary happened to them if they set from our point of view, and they were not always moving in the heavenly sphere

While other philosophers make similar arguments, most astrological writers discuss the influence of the stars in straightforwardly causal terms.[21]

How: The Mechanics of Astrological Divination

If the heavenly bodies influence the lives of mortals, how can their influences be known? In addition to the sun and the moon, the most important figures are the planets, the so-called wandering stars that look like tiny points of light just as the other stars but that do not move in the same simple rotation that all the other stars do. The sun, moon, and the other planets (Mercury, Venus, Mars, Jupiter, and Saturn) move across the backdrop of the 'fixed stars,' providing a variety of positions relative both to the fixed stars and to each other, and these changing positions indicate the changing influences that these entities have on earthly life, just as the changing position of the sun indicates the change of the seasons.

The astrologer calculates these relative positions from the perspective of the earth, imagining the sphere of the heavens rotating around a spherical earth in the center. From this perspective, just as the sun appears to rise in the east, travel across the sky, and set in the west, so too all the other heavenly bodies appear to travel from east to west, the fixed stars all together but the planets in their own patterns. Although the entire sphere of the heavens is covered with stars, the sun and all the other planets appear to travel only in a narrow path across the sky, just 8° around the line of the sun's path, which is known as the *ecliptic*.

---

and holding the same position in relation to the earth? Nor must it be said that when one of the gods sees another in this or that position he becomes better or worse so that when they are in a good state they do good to us, but harm us when the opposite. We must rather say that the movement of the stars is for the preservation of the universe, but that they perform in addition another service; this is that those who know how to read this sort of writing can, by looking at them as if they were letters, read the future from their patterns, discovering what is signified by the systematic use of analogy—for instance, if one said that when the bird flies high it signifies some high heroic deeds." Cp. Origen, *Philocalia* 23.1–21.

[21] E.g., Hephaestion *Apotelesmatica* 160.18–20 (2.18) discusses which planet caused a man to marry only one wife. Τὸν δὲ τοιοῦτον συνέβη μιᾷ γυναικὶ συζευχθῆναι ἀπὸ παρθενίας οὐ διὰ τὴν Ἀφροδίτην ἐνταῦθα, ἀλλὰ διὰ τὴν Σελήνην ὑπὸ τὰς αὐγὰς τοῦ Ἡλίου φερομένην. "That such a one was joined to one woman from maidenhood did not here result from Aphrodite, but from the Moon being carried under the beams of the Sun" (trans. Schmidt 1998). Sextus Empiricus, *Adv. Math.* 5.5 claims that the 'Chaldaeans' "declare that the seven stars stand in the relation of efficient causes for the bringing about of everything which occurs in life, and that with them the parts of the zodiac co-operate." δραστικῶν μὲν αἰτιῶν λόγον ἐπέχειν φασὶν εἰς τὸ ἕκαστον τῶν κατὰ τὸν βίον συμβαινόντων ἐκβαίνειν τοὺς ἑπτὰ ἀστέρας, συνεργεῖν δὲ τὰ τοῦ ζῳδιακοῦ μέρη. Ptolemy is often more circumspect in his phrasing, leaving the issue open. Long 1982 distinguishes between 'hard' astrology and 'soft,' which does not attribute a causal role to the stars.

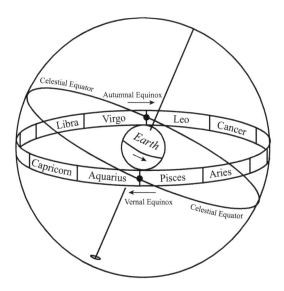

Figure 17. The Celestial Sphere with the Zodiac and the Ecliptic.

THE ZODIAC

The stars in this band around the ecliptic are the constellations of the Zodiac (the belt stars), twelve sets of stars within the celestial sphere that provide the backdrop for the planets' courses. While some of these groups of stars were noted by the Babylonian astronomers centuries earlier, the Latinate names are commonly used, along with a set of conventional symbols (which appear as shorthand in the manuscripts): Aries the Ram, Taurus the Bull, Gemini the Twins, Cancer the Crab, Leo the Lion, Virgo the Maiden, Libra the Scales, Scorpio the Scorpion, Sagittarius the Archer, Capricorn the Goat, Aquarius the Water Carrier, and Pisces the Fish.

Aries	♈		Libra	♎
Taurus	♉		Scorpio	♏
Gemini	♊		Sagittarius	♐
Cancer	♋		Capricorn	♑
Leo	♌		Aquarius	♒
Virgo	♍		Pisces	♓

Planets are said to be 'in' a sign of the Zodiac when they are in the same region of the ecliptic as that constellation (or rather the 30° section in which the constellation appears, since the arrays of stars are not actually evenly distributed across the ecliptic). The entire celestial sphere rotates, so all the stars rise and set each day, but the orbits of the planets make them appear to shift position relative to the backdrop of the fixed stars. Because the planets actually orbit around the sun, rather than the earth, their motions from a geocentric perspective appear to go sometimes with the movement of the celestial sphere (either faster or slower than the other stars), but also sometimes against the motion (this is called 'retrograde'). Even the sun shifts slowly through the constellations of the Zodiac, as the rotation of the celestial sphere is four minutes shorter (23 hours, 56 minutes) than the daily 24-hour circuit of the sun. The sun thus appears to move slowly backward through the constellations of the Zodiac, counterclockwise from Aries through Taurus and so on until Pisces and then Aries again in about a year's time. The path of the ecliptic is at a roughly 23° angle from the celestial equator (because of the tilt of the earth on its own axis of rotation), which accounts for the varying lengths of day and night as the sun moves along throughout the year. The equinoxes (where night, *nox*, is equal to the day) occur when the sun's ecliptic path intersects with the celestial equator. When the sun reaches the furthest point away from the equator line, this is either the summer or winter solstice, and the turning point (tropic) is either in Cancer (midsummer) or in Capricorn (midwinter).

THE CHART

An astrological chart, in modern parlance usually called a 'horoscope,' is simply an image of the relative positions of all the planets and stars at a given moment, enabling the diviner to see the variety of influences that these celestial divinities exert at that particular moment. The chart shows the location of each planet in the sky relative to the observer's perspective, whether it has risen above the horizon, is sinking below it, or even traveling below the horizon. The planet's position relative to the fixed stars, as well as their relative positions to each other, all have significance, and the diviner must figure out the way that all these influences combine.

One moment generally taken as significant is of course the moment of birth, and the branch of astrology known as *natal* or *genethlialogical* concerns itself with determining the influence of the stars upon an individual at the moment that the individual enters the earthly world. Other moments, such as a wedding, the start of a journey, or the beginning of some new business venture, might likewise be taken as significant moments in which the stars exert their influence on the outcome of the events. *Katarchic* astrology is the kind having to do with the beginnings of things, and, although it may actually have been the more commonly employed form of astrology on a daily, practical basis, the astrological manuals from antiquity attend far more to genethlialogical astrology than katarchic.[22] The start of an individual's life provides the moment at which that individual's nature and character can be shaped by the forces of the cosmos, with each planetary power furnishing some influence. The late Roman writer Macrobius describes the journey of the soul into birth as a passage through the layers of the heavens, with each planet having a sphere of its own below the fixed stars.

> The soul, having started on its downward movement from the intersection of the zodiac and the Milky Way to the successive spheres lying beneath, as it passes through these spheres, not only takes on the . . . wrapping in each sphere by approaching a luminous body, but also acquires each of the attributes which it will exercise later, as follows: in the sphere of Saturn it obtains reason and understanding, called *logistikon* and *theoretikon*; in Jupiter's sphere, the power to act, called *praktikon*; in Mars' sphere, a bold spirit or *thymikon*; in the Sun's sphere, sense perception and imagination, *aisthetikon* and *phantastikon*; in Venus' sphere, the impulse of passion, *epithymetikon*; in Mercury's sphere, the ability to speak and interpret, *hermeneutikon*; and in the sphere of the Moon, the power of sowing and growing bodies, *phytikon*.[23]

[22] "Although the technical manuals are almost all devoted to genethlialogical astrology, because it was held to be more difficult and prestigious, in my view the main pragmatic value of the art lay in katarchic astrology ('interrogations'), which offered the authority of the stars in helping individuals to take decisions regarding imminent projects, such as going on a sea-journey, buying land, erecting a house, marrying off a daughter, quarrels with a wife, buying or freeing a slave, debts" (Gordon 2013a: 105–106).

[23] Macrobius, *Commentary on the Somnium Scipionis* 1.12 (trans. Stahl 1952). A Hermetic treatise likewise imagines the ascent of the soul as a reverse process. *Corpus Hermeticum* I.24–26. "Poimandres said: 'First, in releasing the material body you give the body itself over to alteration, and the form that you used to have vanishes. To the demon you give over your temperament, now inactive. The body's senses rise up and flow back to their particular sources, becoming separate parts and mingling again with the energies. And feeling and longing go on toward irrational nature. Thence the human being rushes up through the cosmic framework, at the first zone surrendering the energy of increase and decrease; at the second evil machination, a device now inactive; at the third the illusion of longing; at the fourth the ruler's arrogance, now freed of excess; at the fifth unholy presumption and daring recklessness; at the sixth the evil impulses that come from wealth, now inactive; and at the seventh zone the deceit that lies in ambush. And then, stripped of the effects of the cosmic framework, the human enters the region of the ogdoad; he has his own proper power, and along with the blessed he hymns the father.'" The traits shed at each sphere match those acquired on the way down in Macrobius's account.

The various attributes of the individual thus derive from the influence picked up as the descending soul makes its way through each sphere, so the amount and nature of the influence must depend upon the position and condition of the planet of that sphere at the time.

THE WANDERING STARS: THE PLANETS

It is notable that the influence of each planetary sphere resembles the character of the divinity for whom the planet is named. The star of Saturn infuses the soul with the cunning reasoning characteristic of Kronos of the crooked counsel (the Greek equivalent of Saturn); Jupiter provides the ruling power of Jupiter/Zeus, the king of the gods; the warlike spirit of Greek Ares (or his Roman counterpart, Mars) comes from the next sphere; the desires inspired by the goddess of love, Aphrodite/Venus, come from the star of Venus; and the star of smooth-tongued Hermes/Mercury provides the ability to speak and interpret. In specific circumstances, the influence of these planets often has something to do with the special nature of the deity as it appears in the Greco-Roman mythological tradition.[24]

The characters of the gods from the vast and complicated traditions of the myths tend, however, to be flattened out and simplified for the purposes of astrological interpretation, and the natures of the planets are (characteristically) systematized into a set of pairs of opposites: masculine/feminine; beneficent/maleficent; hot/cold; wet/dry; and so forth. Thus, the planets are identified as male or female on the basis of their mythological equivalents (Venus and the Moon are female, the rest male), but some are perceived as beneficent (Jupiter, Sun, Venus, Moon, and sometimes Mercury), some maleficent (Saturn, Mars, and sometimes Mercury). The character of Mars/Ares and Saturn/Kronos in myth can account for the selection in this regard, but many astrological writers, including Ptolemy, also assign a balance of elements to each planet, so that every one is some combination of hot/cold and wet/dry. Saturn is predominantly cold, but also dry, while Jupiter is primarily hot, but also wet. The Sun, by contrast, is both hot and dry, but more hot than dry, whereas Mars is more dry than hot. Venus and the Moon are both wet, but Venus is also hot, while the Moon is cold. Mercury partakes of all these traits together, perhaps because of his role as a boundary crosser in the mythic tradition.[25] It is worth noting the conflation of different systems of explanation here. The gods have

---

[24] The association of planets with gods appears also in the Babylonian tradition and may account for the Greeks' identification of particular planets with certain gods rather than others. The planet Venus, for example, is linked to the Babylonian Ishtar, whom the Greeks identified with Aphrodite, while Jupiter is linked with Marduk, the ruling deity of Babylon, who exercises the same kind of supreme authority as Zeus.

[25] Cp. Ptolemy, *Tetrabiblos* I.4–7, who sets out all these oppositions.

TABLE 8.1.

Planet	Beneficent	Maleficent	Masculine	Feminine	Hot	Cold	Dry	Wet
Saturn ♄		*	*			**	*	
Jupiter ♃	*		*		**			*
Mars ♂		*	*		*		**	
Sun ☉	*		*		**		*	
Venus ♀	*			*	*			**
Mercury ☿	*	*	*	*	*	*	*	*
Moon ☾				*		*		**

personalities, and therefore they have certain kinds of characteristics, but the cosmos is composed of opposing pairs of elements, the balance of which produces the observable world—physics and mythology blend to produce a systematized set of influences from the planets.

THE POSITION OF THE PLANETS

The influence of the planets is determined by their position in three different respects: first, in the sky with respect to the observer on earth; second, with respect to the background of the fixed stars; and third, with respect to each other. Each kind of position affects the quality and quantity of influence that the planet exerts upon the individual, whether at the time of birth in a genethlialogical reading or at some other significant beginning point in a katarchic one.

Four places on the celestial sphere, the *cardines* (*kentra* or angles) have special significance, and any planet in those places has a greater effect than elsewhere. The most important is the *ascendant,* the portion of the sky that is just beginning to ascend over the horizon at the particular moment. A celestial body that is thus just starting to appear has the greatest influence over the thing that is just starting; it is known as the *watcher of the hour,* the *horoskopos,* and from this name comes the term most often used for any astrological chart. The *descendant,* that portion of the sky just beginning to disappear over the horizon, is likewise significant. The other two cardines are *midheaven* and the *nadir,* the highest point of the heavens and the lowest. The midheaven (often referred to as the *zenith*) is usually taken to be 90° from the ascendant, even though, due to the shifting path of the sun, that would technically only be true for an observer at the latitude of the earthly equator at the time of an equinox. Some astrologers, such as

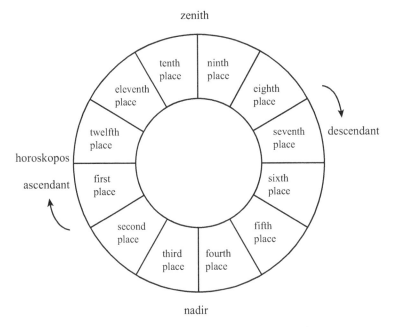

Figure 18. The Places on the Horoscope Chart.

Ptolemy, engage in the complex trigonometrical calculations to pinpoint the actual midheaven and the corresponding low point of the *nadir* to the precise degree, minute, and second, depending on the exact latitude of the observer and time of the year, but such precision was beyond the means (or interest) of most astrologers. In the two-dimensional circle (or even square) used to represent the heavens on most horoscope charts, the ascendant, nadir, descendant, and midheaven are marked 90° apart, starting from the left and going counterclockwise, like east, south, west, and north (respectively) on a modern map.[26]

In addition to the cardines, the celestial sphere (or, rather, the Zodiac band of the ecliptic) is divided equally into parts, usually twelve, starting from the ascendant and moving counterclockwise around. Because the celestial sphere rotates from east to west in a clockwise motion, the first of these parts to move over the horizon will be the section just below the horizon, the second to cross the horizon will be the one further back and

[26] Gordon 2013a: 110 points to the importance of these cardines or kentra in marking the significant features of a chart for katarchic predictions. "Ultimately, the kentric schemes served to underwrite the non-arbitrariness of advice given on the basis of a complex set of data. This was precisely what traditional institutionalised oracles lacked: they had no means of showing they appreciated the complexity of projects and situations."

below, and so on in succession until the section that is already just over the horizon at the moment becomes the twelfth to rise over the horizon. These twelve sections, known in the ancient sources as *topoi* or *places*, each provide a special area of focus for the influence of the celestial bodies. The significance varies somewhat in different authors, but the most common scheme has the following set of places: life, money, friends, parents, children, disease, marriage, death, journeys, honors, accomplishments, enemies.[27] The influence of the stars in the eleventh place, for example, pertains most to issues of money, while one would look to the seventh place to see which influences are most significant to marriage.[28] These places (confusingly called 'houses' in modern astrology) are one of the ways the position of a given planet might be described in a chart, providing a more precise description (within 30º) of the location of the planet in the sky than the four cardines.

The location of the planet with respect to the fixed stars also carries significance; every planet can be located within the scope of a sign of the Zodiac. These twelve constellations provide another way of dividing the circle of the heavens into twelve parts, and this division is usually into twelve equal segments of 30º, which do not correspond precisely with the actual space that the constellations take up in the sky. These constellation signs each have a particular character that affects the planets within it, although they are rarely personified as gods in the way the planets themselves are. The natures of the Zodiacal signs are set up in various authors as systematic oppositions, as single-formed or bicorporeal, as fiery or watery, as airy or earthy, and so forth, and these characteristics have an impact depending on their location. The position of a planet within a sign is often the most important factor in determining its influence. The location in the sky of the sign and the planet within it will depend on the time of day the chart describes, but the relation between the sign and the planet endures longer. The sun stays within a sign for a whole month, moving slowly back day by day toward the next sign, but different planets move through the signs at different paces, with the outer planets remaining at times for very long stretches in a single sign.

Certain signs are more congenial to certain planets than others, and the influence of a planet is increased when it is in the right place in the Zodiac. Each planet was thought to have its own proper domicile (*oikos* or *domus*) for day or for night, except the sun and moon, which have only day or night domiciles or houses. The allotment of these domiciles is in a systematic pattern around the Zodiac, with Saturn having the adjoining signs of

---

[27] See the discussion in Riley 1987: 241–242 about the systems.
[28] Some authors, e.g., Firmicus Maternus (2.14) or Manilius have eight-place systems (2.808–840) alongside the twelve-place one (2.856–970).

NOCTURNAL			DIURNAL	
Planet	*Domicile*		*Domicile*	*Planet*
Saturn ♄	Aquarius ♒		Capricorn ♑	Saturn ♄
Jupiter ♃	Pisces ♓		Sagittarius ♐	Jupiter ♃
Mars ♂	Aries ♈		Scorpio ♏	Mars ♂
Venus ♀	Taurus ♉		Libra ♎	Venus ♀
Mercury ☿	Gemini ♊		Virgo ♍	Mercury ☿
Moon ☾	Cancer ♋		Leo ♌	Sun ☉

Figure 19. Planets and Their Domiciles.

Aquarius and Capricorn as its domiciles for night and day respectively, Jupiter with Pisces and Sagittarius, Mars with Aries and Scorpio, Venus with Taurus and Libra, and Mercury with Gemini and Virgo. The Moon has its nocturnal domicile in Cancer, while the Sun has a diurnal domicile in Leo. A planet in its diurnal domicile during the day, or its nocturnal one during the night, has far more influence than in another position. In some authors, these domiciles were the positions of the planets at the creation of the world, so they in some sense represent the right and proper place to be.[29]

In addition to these domiciles where they feel at home, the planets are exalted in certain locations and dejected in others (180° opposite the exaltation). Firmicus Maternus claims that these exaltations (*hypsomata*) were what the ancient Babylonian astrologers called the true houses of the planets, and they are thus even more important than the domiciles, but neither ancient astrologers nor modern scholars can provide any explanation of why these planets have their exaltations where they do.[30]

The idea that certain spots are more favorable than others can be carried to much greater lengths, since each of the signs can be broken up into

[29] Firmicus Maternus 3.1–19 claims that, although the cosmos was never created at any moment, the ancient, wise Egyptian astrologers Nechepso and Petosiris, along with Aesculapius, devised this schema as an allegory for later astrologers to follow in making charts for mortals.

[30] Firmicus Maternus 2.3.4–6; cp. Dorotheus 1.1.2 and Vettius Valens, *Anth.* III.4, who provide the specific degrees of the location of the exaltations but no explanation. Rochberg-Halton 1988 and others have argued that the Babylonian cuneiform evidence for the *bit niṣirti* or 'secret houses' of the planets corroborates the idea that the Greek *hypsomata* derive from the Babylonian tradition.

smaller sections, and each section could then be associated specially with a planet. Some authors use dodecatemories (twelve 2.5º divisions of each sign) or 1º or even .5º divisions, while others divide up each sign unevenly, allotting different planets to sections.[31]

The most important subdivision, however, especially in later texts, are the decans, the division of each sign into three sections of 10º each. The thirty-six decans are sometimes simply assigned to the powers of the Zodiac constellations, but they are at times (more often than the Zodiac constellations themselves) thought of as independent powers, who could be appealed to for help or even commanded for control.[32] Lists of the names of decans appear in various sources, and many of these names appear to derive from ancient Egyptian names of constellations whose risings marked thirty-six significant periods in the year.[33] Some of these names appear in invocations in the Greek Magical Papyri, apparently referring to divine powers whose aid the magician is seeking. The decans may also appear as images; some at least of the mysterious *charakteres* in the Greek Magical Papyri and epigraphic sources may be symbols of decan divinities, and the later medieval tradition preserves catalogs of the peculiar appearance of each decan, while figures matching these descriptions show up in the visual arts as late as the Renaissance.

A Hermetic treatise describes the decans as the intermediary powers between the fixed stars of the Zodiac and the planetary deities, governing the whole class of in-between powers, the *daimones* (demons or angels).

> I told you, my son, that there is a body which encloses all things. You must conceive the shape of that body as circular, for such is the shape of the universe. . . . And you must understand that below the circle of this body are placed the thirty-six Decans, between the circle of the universe and that of the zodiac, separating the one circle from the other; on the one hand they bear up, as it were, the circle of the universe, and on the other hand they circumscribe the zodiac, moving in a circle with the planets; they have the same force as the movement of the All, by turns with the Seven. . . . And subject to the Decans is the constellation called the Bear, which is centrally situated with regard to the zodiac. The Bear is composed of seven stars, and

---

[31] Cp. Firmicus Maternus 2.6 for the uneven divisions; he refers to duodecatemoria in 2.13. For 1º divisions, see Dorotheus 1.8.7; for .5º, see Manilius 2.738–748.

[32] Cp. the list of decan demons in the *Testament of Solomon* 18, where each decan has a name, a kind of affliction it creates, and another divine power that can be invoked to neutralize it.

[33] Cp. the charts in Gundel 1936: 77–81, which provide only a glimpse of the complexities and inconsistencies in the sources. For a recent discussion of decans, see Greenbaum 2016: 213–235.

has overhead another Bear to match it. The function of the Bear resembles that of the axle of a wheel; it never sets nor rises, but abides in one place, revolving about a fixed point, and making the zodiacal circle revolve. . . . The force which works in all events that befall men collectively comes from the Decans; for instance, overthrows of kingdoms, revolts of cities, famines, pestilences, overflowings of the sea, earthquakes—none of these things, my son, take place without the working of the Decans. And those things also which befall men individually result from the workings of the Decans; for if the Decans rule over the seven planets, and we are subject to the planets, do you not see that the force set in action by the Decans reaches us also, whether it is worked by the Decans themselves or by means of the planets? And besides this, my son, you must know that there is yet another sort of work that the Decans do: they sow upon the earth the seeds of certain forces, some salutary and others most pernicious, which the many call daemons.[34]

It is worth noting the prominence of the Bear constellations (Ursa Major and Minor) in this passage. The Bears are imagined as entities positioned at the center of the celestial sphere, around the axis upon which the whole sphere turns, and so they become the power responsible for the turning of this celestial axis. A number of spells in the Greek Magical Papyri contain invocations to the Bear as the *polokrator*, the divine entity that rules the celestial pole and makes the entire cosmos go round.[35] This control of the cosmic revolution means control over all fate, and the ruling celestial pole becomes an attribute of the supreme deity of the universe under many different names.

The relations between the planets make up the final type of position significant to calculating their influence, since one planet may enhance or diminish the effects of another or perhaps even create a peculiar variation of the effects. These relations are calculated in terms of the angular distance between the signs that they are in, and they are imagined as the two planets looking at each other (*aspect*, from *ad-specto*). Planets that are in the same sign are in *conjunction*, while those 180° apart from each other are said to be in *opposition*, since they appear at opposite sides of the celestial sphere. Halfway in between, in either direction, the two planets are 90° apart, which is called a *quartile* or square aspect. Both opposition and quartile are considered hostile aspects, and the planets affect each other's influence in a negative way. By contrast, planets that are 120° apart (in *trine*) or even 60° apart (in *sextile*) are considered to be in a friendly aspect

---

[34] Hermetica, Stobaeus 6 1.21.9 (trans. Scott 1924).
[35] See ch. 8, p. 265, n. 58.

to one another, which creates positive effects upon their influences. Conjunction, opposition, and trine are the most significant aspects, and some astrologers do not take quartile or sextile aspects into account. Others, however, also include *antiscia*, the sideways glances between planets in signs that are in parallel lines across the circle of the Zodiac from one another. The glances that the planets cast at each other in the different aspects are at times imagined, in accordance with ancient theories of vision, as rays that emanate from the eyes of one to strike the object of the gaze, with either hostile or beneficent force. The aspects thus involve active relations between the celestial entities that affect their influence, not merely passive positions in the sky.

In addition to calculating the aspects of the planets, many astrologers also calculate the positions of special Lots (*kleroi*), which were specific points on the celestial chart that could also have significance from their position and interrelations. Most important of these is the Lot of Fortune, which could indicate the good (or bad) things in store. The position of the Lot of Fortune is calculated by measuring the distance between the sun and the moon on the chart and then determining the point that is the same distance away from the Ascendant, the horoscopic point at the horizon. The Lot of Daimon is found the same distance away in the other direction, and the direction away from the Ascendant depends on whether it is day or night (i.e., if the sun is above or below the horizon). Some astrologers, such as Dorotheus, calculate other Lots: Father ($\odot$-$\hbar$), Mother ($\female$-$\mathbb{C}$), Brothers ($\hbar$-$\mathfrak{2}$), Marriage ($\female$-$\hbar$), Children ($\mathfrak{2}$-$\hbar$), Friendship ($\mathbb{C}$-$\female$), but others, like Ptolemy, pay little heed to such calculations. Each Lot marks a spot on the chart, like the position of a planet, which carries potential meanings that must be factored into the overall understanding of the chart.[36]

The combinations of these different relations between planets, along with the meaning of the positions within the Zodiac constellations and the position in the sky, all create an almost infinite number of significant relations that shape the total celestial influences affecting the individual at the moment of the horoscope chart. The key to successful astrological divination is thus figuring out the outcome of all the conflicting influences and applying them to the situation, whether it be the birth of a new individual or the start of some particular undertaking. The choice of which factors to include in the calculations, as well as the relative weight to place on each

[36] See Riley 1987: 238–240 for a brief overview of the Lots, relying on Dorotheus 1.13, 1.14, 1.19, 2.4, 2.10. Greenbaum 2016: 303–338 provides an extensive study of the Lot of Fortune and the Lot of Daimon, as well as appendices discussing the use of lots in Vettius Valens, Antiochus of Athens, Rhetorius, Paulus Alexandrinus, and Firmicus Maternus (446–467).

factor, differs greatly among the astrological authorities, and each argues the superior merits of his own system for the best understanding of the message the gods provide through the stars.

Barton has shown the ways that, within the ancient texts about astrology, scientific precision becomes a kind of rhetorical device, used to signal the author's superior authority. Introducing further complications to the calculations provides the opportunity for the astrological expert to demonstrate how far his expertise goes beyond that of other experts, and such "arabesques," as Barton calls them, create procedures within the astrological manuals that are far more complicated than seem ever to have been used in practice.[37] As Gordon comments of the astrological manuals,

> They display all the typical features of a discourse driven by the need to compete in a market-place. The discourses needed to establish two things: the authority to speak, and its capacity to deliver reliable information. Now the basic material, the cosmos, was complicated enough; the major means of establishing authority to speak was the elaboration and presentation of individual, at least partly personal schemes.[38]

The complexities revealed in the manuals, then, do not represent the factors taken into account by every astrologer in each horoscope, but rather a theoretical elaboration designed to reinforce the authority of the text in competition with its rivals.

WHY: ASTROLOGY AND RISK MANAGEMENT

In a world of uncertainties and risks, astrology presents itself as a system by which the unknown factors influencing events could be identified and thereby controlled, at least with some degree of certainty. The systematicity and complexity of astrology provides a rational model for understanding the cosmos and acting within it.[39] As Pliny suggests, everyone wants to know what will happen to him, and the movements of the heavens seem to provide an orderly set of signs that could be interpreted by the astrolo-

---

[37] Cp. Barton 1994: 134–142. Gordon 1997: 143 notes, "We may roughly distinguish between two functions of complexity, which we might term 'extrinsic' and 'intrinsic.' The first is the 'arabesque syndrome,' by which I mean the invention of new distinctions by means of which the writer's authority is validated. The discussion of the zodiac at Manilius, 2.150–692 may serve to illustrate this type."

[38] Gordon 2013a: 104.

[39] Cp. Gordon 2013c: 110: "Uncertainty is inescapable but requires to be managed. What they needed was a means of objectifying, naming, discriminating, uncertainties alongside a method of putting the risks involved into a relatively formal hierarchy of acceptability."

gers' art to reveal what fortune lay in store, not just in general but in particular circumstances of importance or crisis. Gordon points out that this kind of astrological divination, the katarchic, was the most valuable in practice.

> Although the technical manuals are almost all devoted to genethli-alogical astrology, because it was held to be more difficult and prestigious, in my view the main pragmatic value of the art lay in katarchic astrology ("interrogations"), which offered the authority of the stars in helping individuals to make decisions regarding imminent projects, such as going on a sea-journey, buying land, erecting a house, marrying off a daughter, quarrels with a wife, buying or freeing a slave, debts.[40]

An astrological consultation may not provide a perfect and clear picture of the future, since there are always more variables that might be taken into account, but it can nonetheless provide a basis for making choices in a world that, despite its apparent confusion, has an underlying divine order. Astrology provides insight into the order of the cosmos, creating a rationalized schema of the influence of divine powers upon human affairs.[41]

The astrologers themselves, especially the most philosophically minded, celebrated this divine order and the insights that their art provided. "I know that I am mortal, the creature of one day," says Ptolemy. "But when I explore the winding courses of the stars I no longer touch with my feet the earth: I am standing near Zeus himself, drinking my fill of Ambrosia, the food of the gods."[42] Firmicus Maternus proclaimed that astrology prompts humans to contemplate the divine heavens, turning their souls from the corrupt mortal world to the perfection of the divine, and Vettius

---

[40] Gordon 2013a: 105–106.

[41] This rational order of astrology is not the same as Cumont's claim that astrology was actually a scientific theology, combining good Greek science with mystical Oriental religion. "Astrology was really the first scientific theology. Hellenistic logic arranged the Oriental doctrines properly, combined them with the Stoic philosophy and built them up into a system of indisputable grandeur, an ideal reconstruction of the universe" (Cumont 1911: 178).

[42] Ptolemy, *Anthologia Palatina* 9.577. Cp. Vettius Valens, *Anth.* VI.1 (= p. 242 Kroll). "I never got carried away by the various kinds of horse races or by the sharp crack of the whip, or by the rhythmic movements of dancers, nor did I enjoy the superficial charm of flutes and poetry and melodious songs or anything else that attracts an audience by a certain art or by jokes. I never took part in any harmful or useful occupations that were divided between pleasure and pain. I had nothing to do with disgraceful and troublesome. . . . But once I had experienced the divine and reverent contemplation of celestial phenomena, I wished to cleanse my character of every kind of vice and pollution and leave my soul immortal. I felt that I was communicating with divine beings, and I acquired a sober mind for research."

Valens repeatedly asserts the divine origin of the astrological science, describing those just learning astrology as those "who are just entering the heavenly places, who are surveying for a time the dancing places and the mysteries of the gods, and who are gaining god-like glory."[43]

At the same time, astrology could not deliver on the promise of perfect godlike knowledge for anyone who attempted it. Many astrologers, like Vettius Valens or Firmicus Maternus, blame these failures on the imperfection of the would-be astrologers, immoral cheats or incompetent impostors.[44] Others, like Ptolemy, however, pointed to the overwhelming number of factors involved, the practical impossibility of obtaining sufficiently precise data, and the fallibility of human observations.[45] Barton points to the similarities in these regards between astrology and medicine, and Komorowska and Greenbaum discuss astrology as a stochastic art, one that, like medicine, proceeds systematically to obtain successful results but whose general validity is not determined by its individual successes or failures.[46] To judge astrology by the success or failure of a particular prediction is to treat it as a productive art, like house-building, where the art is successful if a solid house is produced, rather than like medicine, where the art may have been successfully applied even if the patient ends up dying. The individual consulting an astrologer about a decision is thus in some ways less concerned about the ultimate accuracy of the prediction (which will only become clear later, if ever), than about the skill and authority of the astrologer to help in the immediate crisis of decision-making. As Gordon puts it,

> The individual facing the need to make choices regarding specific alternatives in situations of marked uncertainty—the uncertainty-marking being itself part of the frame—saw in katarchic astrology not a set of intellectual propositions but precisely one possible means of managing uncertainty, a means that combined a high-prestige

---

[43] Vettius Valens, *Anth.* IV.11.7; cp. V.6.16; VI.1.7. Cp. Firmicus Maternus 8.1.6: "Look with wide open eyes at the heavens and let your soul contemplate the most beautiful fabric of the divine creation. This is the way to free our souls from the depraved snares of the body and to put off the dangers of mortality. They will then hasten to their maker with an accelerated pace, seeking nothing other than divine things through all the moments of all the hours."

[44] Vettius Valens, *Anth.* V.8.109; and Firmicus Maternus 1.8.

[45] Ptolemy, *Tetrabiblos* I.2.17–19. Cp. Barton 1995: 70: "From the point of view of astrological theory, a complete codification involved an almost infinite number of permutations of determining factors. Ptolemy, who argued for physical causation in terms of the four elements as an explanation of astrological influence, was careful to spell out the complexity."

[46] Barton 1995 explores astrology, medicine, and physiognomy in the Roman Empire. For the stochastic nature of astrology, cp. Komorowska 2009 and Greenbaum 2010. The term 'stochastic' comes from Greek στοχάζεσθαι, meaning to aim at, since the art aims at certain results, rather than simply creating products.

cosmological model with the production of negotiable project-narratives. To my mind, it did not matter that many—most, all even—such prognoses were "objectively" disconfirmed. The point lay in the production of usable stories.[47]

Such 'usable stories' enabled people to act among the uncertainties of the world, to navigate among the necessary choices, and to handle the vagaries of fortune, retaining a sense of agency without surrendering to a sense that everything was predetermined by fate.

The impersonal and rational order of the cosmos was increasingly argued by philosophical schools from the Hellenistic period onward, finding particular expression in the ideas of the Stoics. The Stoic Cleanthes compares mortal life to a dog hitched to a horse cart; if the dog follows the path that the cart is taking, its life goes by relatively smoothly, but if it tries to deviate from the path, it will be knocked down and dragged along unwillingly.[48] Best to be a good dog and resign oneself to the course of life mapped out in the cosmic order. Not everyone could adopt such Stoic resignation to the decrees of Fate, however, and katarchic astrology provides a way of reconciling a rational cosmos with individual agency.[49] The elaborations of the astrological system in the manuals provide the models of the rational cosmos that underlie this system of astrological practice, as well as the techniques for interpreting the signs by which the workings of the cosmos can be understood in any given case.

CONCLUSIONS: MAGIC AND ASTROLOGY

If astrological imagery and ideas are so prevalent and familiar, how can astrology be considered magic? As with other forms of divination, astrology becomes labeled 'magic' when there is some discrepancy between the *social location* of the practitioner (real or imagined) and the extra-ordinary claims to *efficacy*—authority, wisdom, and power—for their practice. Astrology as magic thus appears both above and below more normal and acceptable practices of astrology; it is characterized as magic when it is considered either as a useless superstition or as a nearly omnipotent means

[47] Gordon 2013c: 119–120.

[48] Hippolytus, *Haer* 1.21.2.

[49] As Cumont 1911: 181 remarks, "The masses, however, never reached that height of resignation." Cp. Barton 1995: 71: "Astrologers, if they could not achieve omniscience, or indeed the total power to control afforded by magic, attempted to mediate between the two poles of Fate and free will in such a manner as afforded them maximum power." Greenbaum 2016 provides a study in the ways that fate and chance could be mediated in the philosophical and astrological traditions.

to knowledge, rather than when it is simply used as a regular means of managing risk.[50]

While the treatises of the astrologers that praise the power of their art and the critiques of the skeptics that condemn it as useless show these two sides separately, an episode in Apuleius (*Met.* 2.12–13) illustrates this familiar bipolar nature of astrology as magic in a single scene. The narrator Lucius praises the extra-ordinary wisdom of the Assyrian astrologer, Diophanes, whom he consulted before his journey. His host, Milo, however, recounts how Diophanes was exposed as being incapable of predicting the misfortunes that befell him on his own journey and ridiculed as a charlatan. Milo mocks Lucius because he believes that Diophanes had extraordinary insight through his astrological predictions (which, incidentally, all turn out to be true for Lucius), whereas Milo's account shows that Diophanes cannot even use his wisdom to avoid misfortunes for himself. The activity is the same, the common katarchic astrological divination about the fortune of a journey, but the evaluations are polar opposites, both sub- and supranormal.

Supranormal insight can be a dangerous thing, especially to those in control of the political order, and it is not a coincidence that crackdowns on astrology come periodically in the rule of the Roman emperors. One of the ways in which astrology becomes magic is through the legal system, which classifies certain uses of the practice as contrary to law. Astrological predictions about the life of the emperor in particular are construed as treason, and some of the charges of magic that Tacitus recounts in his history of the early Empire involve accusations of using astrology to inquire about the emperor's predicted lifespan.[51] In certain circumstances, any astrological consultation may be seen as usurping authority from the sovereign and prosecuted, and historians record several mass expulsions of all the astrologers from Rome.[52] The fact that these purges needed to be

---

[50] As Gordon 2013a: 106 notes, "Consultation of a competent mathematicus should be seen as a relatively rational form of uncertainty-resolution, by comparison with innumerable types of inductive divination, where the client had to rely on the mere assertion of the practitioner, let alone the response provided by an institutionalised oracle. Moreover, each such consultation reaffirmed faith in the 'new standard' cosmology."

[51] Cp., e.g., the convictions of Aemilia Lepida (Tacitus, *Annals* 3.22) and Lollia Paulina (12.22). See Cramer 1954: 248–270 for discussion of various cases that seem to have been prosecuted under the decree of Augustus in 11 CE against the use of astrology to inquire about the emperor. Firmicus Maternus 2.30.4–7 has stern words for anyone who tried to ask an astrologer about the emperor and declares that the emperor alone is not subject to the power of the stars but only directly to the highest god, so astrological consultations are doomed to failure.

[52] Cramer 1954: 233–248 discusses the expulsions, starting with an edict in the Republic (139 BCE) up to the time of Marcus Aurelius.

repeated eight times between the death of Julius Caesar (44 BCE) and that of Marcus Aurelius (180 CE) suggests that, in the interim, astrologers found a ready clientele for their services, who considered their practices more or less normal.[53]

Augustus may have published his own horoscope, but he was also the first to make astrological consultations about the emperor illegal, and his successor, Tiberius, was obsessed with the power of astrology. Tacitus recounts how he forbade others to use astrology but also sought to retain the services of the best astrologers for himself.[54] Tiberius is said to have used astrologers to locate noblemen in whose horoscopes imperial power was predicted and then killed them off as a precaution against usurpation, and the same story is attached to later 'bad' emperors like Domitian. The strategy could backfire, however. As Dio Cassius tells the story, Emperor Caracalla (188–217 CE) sought information from astrologers about his own death and about those who might take imperial power. One of his agents was sending back a report from an astrologer, warning that the stars suggested that Caracalla's prefect, Macrinus, was a threat and should be executed. Unfortunately for Caracalla, Macrinus intercepted the letter and, on the strength of his horoscope predicting imperial power, set up a coup and assassinated Caracalla.[55]

Astrology was well positioned to claim extra-ordinary authority in the Roman Empire, to place itself high up on the hierarchy of means. First of all, the complexity of its system could be expanded nearly without limit, meaning that it could always best rival means in terms of systematicity and complexity, *Planmäßigkeit*. So too, astrology's own genealogy as the ancient lore of the Egyptians and the Chaldaeans provided it with the exoticism of alien wisdom.[56] The mythical antecedents of Nechepso and

---

[53] Ripat 2011, however, makes the point that to avoid expulsion, the astrologer need only stop practicing his trade, although some may well have capitalized on the advantages of being labeled an 'expellable astrologer' potent enough to cause anxiety among the authorities. See further below, ch. 11, p. 388, n. 21.

[54] Compare the story in Tacitus 6.20 of how Tiberius tested astrologers and had those he suspected of fraud thrown off a cliff, until Thrasyllus proved his validity by not only predicting imperial power for Tiberius but near-fatal danger for himself when he was leaving. Gordon 2013a: 105 remarks, "As far as emperors were concerned, above all in the third and fourth centuries, the more reliable their own astrologers, the more dangerous the astrologers of potential rivals. The cultural authority of genethlialogical astrology in the Roman world was a by-product of this paradox."

[55] Cassius Dio 79.4.1–5. See Cramer 1954: 215; as well as Barton 1994: 44–49.

[56] "The accounts, such as they are, suggest that the 'Orient' was a device to legitimate a claim about the marvellous powers inherent in Nature" (Gordon 2013a: 108) Vettius Valens refers to coming to Egypt to learn special aspects of the craft (e.g., *Anth.* IV.11.4–9), just as Thessalos of Tralles comes to Egypt to learn arcane magical secrets and discovers the special astrological components of the virtues of healing herbs. See Moyer 2003 for the cultural

Petosiris, Zoroaster and Hermes, may have obscured the actual sources of the astronomical data that provided the complexities of the system, but the authority of those names, their antiquity, and alien origin bolstered the authority of astrology as a system for obtaining the most privileged information about the workings of the cosmos, from the highest divinities to the basest of mortals.

This cosmological model underlying astrology, widely accepted in various forms throughout the Roman Empire, provides an orderly system of divine powers ruling the world, a hierarchy that can be manipulated by those with sufficient understanding of the astrological cosmic model. Such manipulations enabled by extra-ordinary knowledge are not confined to divinatory predictions, and the Greek Magical Papyri show a number of ways in which astrology was used in magic beyond divination. Among the invocations to myriad deities in these compendious spell books is an invocation to the Star of Aphrodite (that is, the planet Venus) in a love spell of attraction. Another spell instructs the practitioner to inscribe the constellations of the Zodiac (with their secret names) on laurel leaves, to be used in Pythagoras's dream oracle, where the angel Zizaubio comes from the Pleiades to provide a revelation—hardly standard astrological divinatory procedure. The planets and constellations are not the only astrological powers invoked; a number of spells invoke the names of decans within their *voces magicae*, and one spell not only invokes the decans Biou and Erō, but has a full set of thirty-six *charakteres* to represent the whole set of decans to be invoked to carry out the *agōgē* love charm.[57]

The constellation of the Bear appears more often in the Greek Magical Papyri than any other astrological power because of its pivotal role in the rotations of the celestial sphere. The "Bear charm that accomplishes everything" begins with an invocation to the Bear as the ruler of the celestial axis. "I call upon you, the greatest power in heaven, appointed by the lord god to turn with a strong hand the holy pole." By controlling the rotation of the heavens, the Bear can control all destinies under the influence of the power of the stars and planets.[58]

---

exchange in the Thessalos story; it is worth noting that both Thessalos and Valens complain of the high prices for Egyptian wisdom.

[57] Star of Aphrodite PGM IV.2891–2942; Zodiac PGM VII.795–845. PGM CVII.1–19, with the commentary in Daniel 1975; cf., e.g., PGM V.483; XVI.63; XIII.1058; II.123; XIII.325; and XII.81 for other such uses of decans. A careful study of the use of decan names in the PGM has yet to be undertaken, but the complexity of the task, given the alternate lists of decan names and the varying modes of transliteration of Egyptian names into Greek, is daunting. Cp. the charts of names in Gundel 1936: 77–81. For a discussion of astrological elements in the PGM, see Greenbaum 2016: 195–209.

[58] PGM IV.1275–1322. Cp. PGM IV.1323–1330; PGM IV.1331–1389; PGM VII.478–490; PGM VII.686–702; PGM XII.190–192; PGM LXXII.1–36, for other Bear invocations. The Egyp-

The Bear itself, however, is merely a tool used by the supreme lord of the universe to move the celestial pole, an idea most vividly portrayed in the so-called Mithras Liturgy, where the magician ascends to meet the supreme god Mithras.

> You will see lightning-bolts going down, and lights flashing, and the earth shaking, and a god descending, a god immensely great, having a bright appearance youthful, golden-haired, with a white tunic and a golden crown and trousers, and holding in his right hand a golden shoulder of a young bull: this is the Bear which moves and turns heaven around, moving upward and downward in accordance with the hour.[59]

This supreme ruler of the cosmos is the ultimate astrological power, who controls all the other lesser powers of the heavens, not just the visible stars and planets that rotate around the pole, but even the invisible decans.[60] This deity can transcend the calculations of the astrologers and arrange the influences of the celestial powers to suit his own will.[61] He must be appeased in some rituals lest he alter the stars unfavorably, but he can be petitioned to provide good things in one's horoscope.[62]

> You, then, ask, "Master, what is fated for me?" And he will tell you even about your star, and what kind of daimon you have, and your horoscope and where you may live and where you will die. And if

---

tian name for the Bear constellation is the Shoulder of the Bull, which was identified with Set-Typhon, as Plutarch notes in *de Is. et Os.* 21 359d. Cp. Beck 1976 and Beck 1977b, as well as my discussion in Edmonds 2003.

[59] PGM IV.694–705. ὄψῃ κατερχομένας ἀστραπὰς καὶ φῶτα (695) μαρμαίροντα καὶ σειομένην τὴν γῆν καὶ κατερχόμενον θεὸν ὑπερμεγέθη, φωτινὴν ἔχοντα τὴν ὄψιν, νεώτερον, χρυσοκόμαν, ἐν χιτῶνι λευκῷ καὶ χρυσῷ στεφάνῳ καὶ ἀναξυρίσι, κατέχοντα τῇ δεξιᾷ χειρὶ μόσχου (700) ὦμον χρύσεον, ὅς ἐστιν Ἄρκτος ἡ κινοῦσα καὶ ἀντιστρέφουσα τὸν οὐρανόν, κατὰ ὥραν ἀναπολεύουσα καὶ καταπολεύουσα. ἔπειτα ὄψῃ αὐτοῦ ἐκ τῶν ὀμμάτων ἀστραπὰς καὶ ἐκ τοῦ σώματος ἀστέρας ἁλλομένους. The whole spell is PGM IV.475–829.

[60] PGM I.195–222 and PGM IV.1167–1226 both contain invocations to the supreme god as the one who established the decans.

[61] Such an idea appears in the Gnostic *Pistis Sophia* 1.13–23, where Jesus Christ, in his ascent after his resurrection, reverses the rotation of one of the astrological spheres, throwing off the calculations of the astrologers and freeing humans from the domination of the evil celestial archons. Cp. also Lucius's appeal to Isis, in Apuleius's *Metamorphoses* 11.2, to save him from the persecutions of Fortuna.

[62] Cp. the instruction in PGM LVII.1–37 at 30–31: "And immediately say these words, [lest] there occur a removal of the stars and your lucky day." In an invocation in the so-called Eighth Book of Moses, the magician pleads, "Protect me from all my own astrological destiny; destroy my foul fate; apportion good things for me in my horoscope; increase my life even in the midst of many goods, for I am your slave and petitioner and have hymned your valid and holy name, lord, glorious one, ruler of the cosmos" (PGM XIII. 634–649).

you hear something bad, do not cry out or weep, but ask that he may wash it off or circumvent it, for this god can do everything.[63]

This god can do anything and everything, and therefore the one who can communicate with this god and win favors from him can also do anything. The spell indeed lists a variety of things one can do by invoking the special name of this god, from fetching a lover or breaking another spell to resurrecting a dead body or crossing the Nile on a crocodile.

Such extra-ordinary power qualifies as magic, but to meet with this supreme ruler of the universe requires, among other things, specialized astrological knowledge, not just the incense and flowers appropriate to each of the planetary powers but the astrological rulers of the particular hour, day, and week.

> Say [the names of] the gods of the hours, with [the prayer on] the stele, and [those of] the gods of the days and of those set over the weeks, and the compulsive formula for these; for without these the god will not listen but will refuse to receive you as uninitiated, unless you emphatically say in advance the [names of] the lord of the day and of the hour.[64]

Specialized astrological calculations are needed to determine which celestial power rules the particular moment of the magician's rite, and the magician must show himself initiated into the mysteries of astrology or the god will refuse to come at his invocation. Extra-ordinary understanding of the science of astrology, the variables and complexities of the astrological cosmological system, enables the magician to perform his magic.

Astrology, then, is not magic, but some astrological divination may be labeled 'magic,' and astrological ideas may play an important role in other kinds of magical rituals, further blurring the categories. The systematic cosmic model of astrology, with its infinite complexities and its authoritative pedigree, fits easily into the kinds of claims to extra-ordinary efficacy that characterize things labeled 'magic,' both by those practicing it themselves and by others who fear or revere the power of the practitioners. As with other forms of divination, such grandiose claims may be scorned by doubters, but their classifications of astrological divination as a useless superstition nevertheless end up lumping astrology with magic, imagined as extra-ordinary in the negative sense as below normal efficacy and authority. Astrology often appears, however, as one of the most erudite and

---

[63] PGM XIII.709–715.

[64] PGM XII.53–58. πρόλεγε τοὺς ὡρογενεῖς σὺν τῇ στήλῃ καὶ τοὺς ἡμερεσίους <καὶ> τοὺς ἐφεβδοματικοὺς τεταγ<μ>ένους καὶ τούτων τὸν ἐπάναγκον. ἄτερ γὰρ τούτων ὁ <θ>εὸς οὐκ ἐπακούσεται, ἀλλ᾽ ὡς ἀμυστηρίαστον οὐ παραδέξεταί <σε>, εἰ μὴ τὸν κύριον τῆς ἡμέρας προείπῃς καὶ τῆς ὥρας πυκνότερον.

specialized forms of systematic occult knowledge about the cosmos, the work of the most learned magicians and most scientific thinkers of the ancient Greco-Roman world.[65]

[65] "If we can talk about a strategy here, it might be to establish the claim that there exists an objective hierarchy of means to occult power, knowledge of which distinguishes true—and essentially literate and learned—magicians from quacks and wise women. Quacks and wise women know only a praxis; the true magus, equipped with a demanding theory of intentionality in Nature, can give reasons" (Gordon 2013a: 108–109).

9

Transmutations of Quality: Alchemy and Magic

> Receive the stone that is not a stone, that is without value and much-valued, multiformed and formless, unknown and known to all, many-named and nameless, which I call moon-foam [*aphroselenon*].
>
> (Zosimus, *On Excellence and Interpretation 6* = CAAG II.122.5–7)

INTRODUCTION: THE NATURE OF ALCHEMY

Alchemy is one of the best-known, yet most misunderstood, forms of arcane magical lore. Its practice in the Middle Ages through the early modern period has left a residue in the popular imagination of grey-bearded wizards hunched over bubbling alembics seeking to turn lead into gold or to find the elixir of life. Yet it was also a practice that drew the zealous attention of such thinkers as Sir Isaac Newton, the discoverer of the law of gravity and inventor of modern mathematical calculus, who spent hours in his laboratory (no doubt hunched over bubbling alembics) trying to probe the nature of the physical world. The ambiguity between alchemy as legitimate arcane knowledge and magic persists; it is telling that the title of J. K. Rowling's first Harry Potter book was changed (for ignorant American audiences) from *Harry Potter and the **Philosopher's** Stone* to *Harry Potter and the **Sorcerer's** Stone*. The idea of magic associated with a substance that enables one to transmute lead to gold or to attain immortality is conveyed by the label of 'sorcerer's stone' better than by the traditional association with philosophers.

The term 'alchemy' comes into our language from the Greek term *chemeia*, filtered through the Arabic reception of Greco-Egyptian texts that passed into Latin at the end of the Middle Ages. Various plausible origins of the term have been suggested, including Plutarch's *chēmia* referring to the 'black land' of dark-earthed Egypt (found also in the Coptic word *kheme*) and a derivation from *chemeia* or *chumeia* from the verb *cheō*, to melt or fuse, but Latin *alchemia* is simply the Greek term *chemeia* preceded by the Arabic definite article *al*.[1] The medieval Latin sources from which the early modern alchemical tradition developed drew upon the rich Arabic tradition, which preserved more of the original Greek texts than survived in the Byzantine Greek tradition. Both the Byzantine and Arabic cultures developed and altered the ideas from the earlier Greek tradition, so the alchemy taken up by the Latin tradition was already much different from the Greek and was transformed still more by the later alchemical tradition of Renaissance and early modern Europe.

Alchemy in the ancient Greco-Roman world may be defined as the art or craft of the transmutation of the qualities of matter. Such a definition hinges on the theoretical aspect, stressing the importance of considering qualities as transferrable in the abstract, but it encompasses a range of practices, from procedures to change the color of metals to rituals to purify and perfect the soul. There are, of course, rituals to perfect the soul that do not involve alchemical transmutation of qualities, just as operations exist for changing the color of metals that do not rely on such a theory, but it is procedures with such a shared theoretical underpinning that are labeled as 'alchemy' (*chemeia*) in the ancient evidence, and such procedures of various kinds are discussed together by alchemical authors.

Alchemy as such seems to appear in the first centuries BCE or CE in Greco-Roman Egypt, developing in such flourishing centers of learning as Alexandria, where the intellectual products of the Hellenistic age were collected and concentrated. The traditional lore of nature, systematized and recorded starting with the Peripatetics in the early Hellenistic period, was further refined and developed by later Hellenistic authors of whom only traces remain. Although the accounts that trace the origins of Greek alchemy back to the alien wisdom of the Persian *magi* and the Egyptian sages are essentially a familiar kind of mythic tale of origin designed to reinforce the authority of the discourse, much of the technical knowledge that supports this lore for the manipulation of physical substances can nevertheless be clearly traced to very ancient metallurgical practices in Mesopotamia and Egypt. The technical traditions that underlie the alchemical practices must have developed within the Mediterranean world even before the conquests of Alexander linked even more closely the Persian Empire (including not just Mesopotamia but Egypt and the Levant)

---

[1] Plutarch, *de Is. et Os.* 33 364c. Compare the similar origin of important words in later alchemy such as alembic (*al-'anbīq* from Greek *ambix*) and elixir (*al-'iksīr* from Greek *xērion*). See Principe 2013: 23–24 for a brief summary.

with the Greek. As these traditions of knowledge are systematized into arcane lore that derives its authority from the alien wisdom of the Egyptians and the *magi*, the practices of alchemy shift into the realm of things that can be labeled as 'magic.'

WHAT: THE SOURCES OF EVIDENCE FOR ALCHEMY

The evidence for the practices and theories of alchemy in the Greco-Roman world is limited, since alchemical practices, like other kinds of magical rituals, leave little in the way of material evidence, and the bulk of the textual evidence comes down to modernity through a few collections of alchemical texts that seem to have been made in the early Byzantine period (perhaps seventh century CE). Nevertheless, the texts preserve recipes and ideas that seem to go back to the third century BCE and the flourishing of systematic inquiry in the Hellenistic period, while the underpinnings of alchemical theory come from Plato and Aristotle and their reworking of the physical theories of the so-called Pre-Socratic thinkers centuries earlier.

As with the technical traditions of astrology, and indeed healing magic and divination, the systemization of the traditional lore seems to be the product of Hellenistic authors, whose works have for the most part been lost.[2] In the Roman period, however, various authors draw upon these Hellenistic treatises for their encyclopedic works, and the catalogs of marvels of the natural world that they record from these sources provide a glimpse of the material collected. The most important of these is Pliny's first-century CE *Natural History*, but the *Kestoi* of Sextus Julius Africanus, although it survives only in fragments itself, attests to the distribution of this kind of knowledge in the second and third centuries CE. Through these treatises, we can catch glimpses of some of their Hellenistic sources, particularly the collection of lore attributed to the fifth-century BCE thinker, Demokritos of Abdera.[3]

---

[2] As Gordon 1997: 131 notes, "The occult writings on Nature and the books of early astrologers were essentially compilations of reference material, lists of reported facts and procedures whose significance was not so much individual as cumulative. These materials required to be written down in systematic order, whether alphabetic, topical or schematic, because their inherent connections were extremely meagre. Both kinds of text depended upon the prior existence of a tradition of natural-scientific enquiry and of an audience able to place their claims and procedures in context. There can for example be little doubt that the facts and supposed facts ('factoids') listed by the occult writers were mainly drawn from work put in hand by the Peripatetic tradition, above all Theophrastus' works on nature; from geographies of the Orient, such as the works of Ctesias, Callisthenes, and Onesicrates; and from the characteristically Hellenistic genre of the agricultural manual."

[3] As Gordon 1997: 138 comments, "Magical beliefs were redescribed under the rubric of

The real Demokritos is perhaps best known as the inventor of atomic theory, that is, the idea that all matter is composed of tiny, indivisible (*a-tomos*, un-cuttable) particles, but the marvels later associated with the name of Demokritos seem to have little to do with the figure who emerges from the small number of authentic fragments still extant of his work. While modern scholars' knowledge of the ideas of the real Demokritos is lamentably sparse, the materials that were attributed to him in the Hellenistic period and later are certainly for the most part the creations of Hellenistic authors making use of the name of the respected and authoritative ancient thinker. Even in Pliny and other Roman sources, the authenticity of Demokritos's works was disputed, and various names were mentioned as the real author of works under his name.[4] Bolos of Mendes is perhaps the figure for whom the most evidence exists that he created a Demokritean work, but the origin of all the Hellenistic and later Demokritean works is unlikely to be as tidy as a single pseudepigrapher, and so little is known about the figure of Bolos that assigning works to him provides little insight.[5] Similar material is credited to figures such as Anaxilaus of Larisa and Nigidius Figulus, who flourished in the first century BCE. At this time, Demokritos is being credited with Pythagorean connections, as well as journeys to the sources of alien wisdom: the Chaldaeans, the Persian magi, and even the gymnosophists (naked philosophers) of India.[6] Both Anaxilaus and Nigidius were associated with the revival of Pythagorean wisdom and the Neopythagorean fashion that swept Rome in that period, and both were said to have been expelled from Rome as magicians, so they are likely channels for this Demokritean tradition, even if they are not composing Demokritean works themselves.[7]

---

marvels, free from the messy and tedious practicalities of collection, preparation, and application. The 'Democritean' tradition was not primarily, if at all, practical in intention. But it does form an essential part of an emergent Hellenistic concept of magic far removed from the actual practice of root-cutters and wise women."

[4] About the works attributed to Demokritos, Pliny argues, "So utterly are they lacking in credibility and decency that those who like the other works of Democritus deny that the magical books are his. But it is all to no purpose, for it is certain that Democritus especially instilled into men's minds the sweets of magic" (*HN* 30.10 [2]). By contrast, Columella, *Rust.* 7.5.17 claims Bolos of Mendes wrote the *Cheirokmekta* under name of Demokritos, and the *Suda* mentions a Bolos Demokritos (s.v. Βῶλος β481).

[5] Despite the attempts of Wellmann 1928 and Bidez and Cumont 1938: vol. 1, 117–118, 169–174, to assign everything Demokritean to Bolos, more recent studies, such as Dickie 1999, Hershbell 1987, and Martelli 2013, more reasonably argue for a multitude of pseudepigraphers using the name of Demokritos.

[6] Demokritos visiting the Persian magi is mentioned in a number of sources, e.g., Cicero, *de fin.* 5.50; Pliny, *HN* 24.156, 160, 25.13, 30.9, while Aelian, *VH* 4.20 and Diogenes Laertius 9.3 describe his tour to the Chaldaeans, Magi, and gymnosophistae. Diodorus Siculus (1.96–98) claimed that Demokritos, like Pythagoras, visited Egypt to learn his sacred lore.

[7] Jerome, *Chron. Tab.* 188.1 refers to Anaxilaus of Larisa as a magus, expelled in 28 BCE

Out of this Hellenistic systematization of traditional lore that is attributed to various sources of ancient and alien wisdom come the earliest
witnesses to alchemical procedures, techniques that are placed firmly outside the norm but that illustrate by contrast the boundaries of normality
within the natural world. Among the extra-ordinary curiosities that the
encyclopedic treatise of Pliny and the learned collection of Africanus attribute to Demokritos or Anaxilaus are included a number of alchemical
procedures.[8] The tricks for coloring precious stones or creating verdigris
or metal plating on a plate of another metal resemble those found, for
example, in the Leiden and Stockholm papyri.[9]

The oldest surviving alchemical texts appear in two papyrus codices,
now preserved in Leiden and Stockholm, which date from around the third
century CE (P. Leid. J397 and P. Holm.). Ancient classifications put these
texts clearly in the category of magic, for they appear to come from the
same cache of papyrus texts that form the collection of the Greek Magical
Papyri, and indeed these two codices were written by the same scribal
hand that wrote the text of PGM XIII.[10] Because of their alchemical content, however, modern scholars have treated them separately, and they
have not been included in the editions and translations of the Greek Magical Papyri but rather studied by historians of science interested in their
place in the origins of chemistry. Nothing, not even the separation by Preisendanz and other editors of Christian magical formularies from contemporary non-Christian ones, shows so clearly the impact of modern scholarly
categorizations on the study of the ancient materials for magic than this
segregation of the alchemical texts from other magical texts written in the
same hand.

Both codices are collections of alchemical recipes and procedures, with
a few references to earlier authorities such as Demokritos and Anaxilaus

---

(188th Olympiad), *Anaxilaus Larisaeus Pythagoricus et Magus ab Augusto urbe Italiaque pellitur*,
while he claims Nigidius was expelled earlier (183.4), *Nigidius Figulus pythagoricus et magus
in exsilio moritur.*

[8] Gordon 1997: 137 comments on "the occult discourse on nature typified by the work of
Bolus. I would urge that the redescription of selected natural facts as marvels strung together
on an occult string had the effect of clearing a space between the tacit, incoherent quality of
traditional belief on the one hand, and those trends in Hellenistic cosmology, particularly
Epicureanism and scepticism, which tended towards rationalism and agnosticism on the
other. That space the occultists attempted to fill with a demonstration of the superabundant
strangeness of nature."

[9] Pliny on coloring stones, cp. *HN* 37.51 (12), 83 (22), 98 (26), 197 (75). For metals, see
HN 33.100 (32), 33.125 (42), 34.110–113 (26). Cp. the list of tricks from Africanus preserved
in Psellos, *Opusc.* 32.

[10] As Brashear 1995: 3402–3404 notes. Another magical papyrus, PGM Va, which contains
a single page with a spell for a direct vision from Helios, was found among the leaves of P.
Holm., further corroborating the intertwining of alchemical and other magical practices.

of Larisa. The procedures are relatively uncomplicated, although they make use of technical terminology.

MANUFACTURE OF FUSIBLE ASEM.

> Copper of Cyprus, 1 mina; tin in sticks, 1 mina; stone of Magnesia, 16 drachmas; mercury, 8 drachmas, stone of Paros, 20 drachmas. Having melted the copper, throw the tin on it, then the stone of Magnesia in powdered form, then the stone of Paros, and finally the mercury; stir with an iron rod and pour at the desired time.[11]

This recipe from the Leiden papyrus provides instructions for making *asemos*, literally metal that is unmarked for coinage, but most often referring to a whitish metal-like silver, out of a combination of copper, tin, and other ingredients. Likewise, a recipe in PGM XII, inscribed between a prayer for a dream oracle and instructions for making a magic ring, provides technical instructions for making a tincture of gold.

> [To make] a tincture of gold: Take thickened pungent vinegar and also have ready 8 drachmas of ordinary salt, 2 drachmas of rock alum that has clear cleavage, 4 drachmas of massicot, and triturate them [together] with the vinegar for 3 days, and strain off [and] use. Then add one drachma blue vitriol [cupric sulfate] to the vinegar, 1/2 obol in weight of chalcopyrite, 8 obols of rock alum, 1/2 obol in weight of melanterite, a carat of ordinary salt, 2 [carats] of Cappadocian [salt]. Make a leaf [of metal] of 2 fourths by weight, dip [it] 3 times into fire until the leaf [breaks up] into fragments. Then take up the pieces [and] assume them as "reduced" to the metallic state of gold. Treatment: Take [2] fourths by weight of gold, make a leaf and [purify it in] fire, dip it in blue vitriol triturated with water. And another [treatment]: Pound dry vitriol and dip [it] in the vinegar. (Yet another [treatment]: with the compound): Pour off the verdigris and throw it in.[12]

The recipes in the Stockholm papyrus are focused less on the manipulation of metals than in the coloring of stones and other substances, especially producing purple dyes. Most of the procedures in these texts have a technical focus, with little rhetoric about the origin or authority of the recipes, but one recipe from the Stockholm papyrus traces the process for whiten-

[11] P. Leid. 9 (trans. Caley 1926). A drachma was six obols, where an obol was a coin weight (about .025 oz.). Larger measures include the mina (100 drachmas) and the talent (60 minas).
[12] PGM XII.193–201.

ing copper back to fifth-century BCE philosopher Demokritos, through the Hellenistic thinker Anaxilaus of Larisa.

> Anaxilaus traces back to Democritus also the following recipe. He rubbed common salt together with lamellose alum in vinegar and formed very fine small cones from these and let them dry for three days in the bath chamber. Then he ground them small, cast copper together with them three times and cooled, quenching in sea water. Experience will prove the result.[13]

Many of the procedures in these papyri resemble the recipes that are attributed to Demokritos in other sources.

The Byzantine and later manuscripts that preserve the bulk of the corpus of Greek alchemical texts include a variety of material attributed to Demokritos, in epitomized excerpts from his famous *Four Books on Natural and Mystical Things* as well as quotations in other authors. However, the name of the famous fifth-century BCE philosopher from Abdera was probably only attached to these ideas and procedures in the Hellenistic period, and the *Four Books*, in the form from which they were epitomized, were probably only composed in the Neronian period (first century CE). Nevertheless, these works represent the oldest strand of alchemical material preserved in the manuscripts.[14] The other materials in the alchemical manuscripts may be divided into three chronological groups. The first is materials attributed to other pseudepigraphic authors from the first few centuries CE such as Hermes, Agathodaimon, Maria the Jewess, Kleopatra, and Isis. There is also a large collection of technical and theoretical texts by Zosimus of Panopolis from the third century CE, some of which comment on the earlier material. Finally, there are various commentators on earlier materials, ranging from Synesius in the fourth century CE and Olympiodorus in the sixth to Stephanos of Alexandria and the so-called Christian and Anonymous commentators in the seventh century and later.

The preservation of the Greek alchemical corpus rests on remarkably few strands, a few significant early manuscripts that have received a certain amount of scholarly attention, as well as other materials in Syriac and Arabic that have hardly been studied at all.[15] The oldest manuscript (M—

---

[13] P. Holm. 2 (trans. Martelli).

[14] Martelli 2013: 29–31 provides the best overview of the discussion surrounding the dating of the Demokritean material; see also Letrouit 1995: 74–80.

[15] The monumental nineteenth-century work of Berthelot and his collaborators provided editions of the Greek texts, along with French translations, but little more is available for the Syriac and Arabic material than French translations (whose accuracy has been critiqued by the few scholars who have ventured to look at the texts themselves). The unpublished dissertation of Hallum 2008 does augur well for new studies of the Arabic receptions of the

Marcianus graecus 299) seems to have been written in a neat hand with elegant diagrams in the Byzantine period, perhaps somewhere in the ninth to eleventh century, although the materials themselves may have been first collected as early as the seventh century. The table of contents with fifty-two entries does not actually match the order of the contents, leading scholars to argue that the pages of the manuscript were shuffled around at some point.[16] Many of those same texts appear in a fifteenth-century manuscript (A—Parisinus graecus 2327), which contains a few additional texts not in M (including one of the important 'Visions' of Zosimus). A few other manuscripts from the thirteenth through fifteenth centuries provide further witnesses to the same sets of texts, and traces of the alchemical tradition appear as quotations and references in other kinds of sources, including the works of the Byzantine Michael Psellos, but the channels through which the Greek alchemical texts were passed down to modern scholars (and to the alchemists of the Renaissance and early modern periods) are extremely limited.

While the encyclopedias of Pliny or Africanus provide parallels for the technical processes, some of the same theoretical ideas that appear in alchemical texts also crop up in the Hermetica, texts from the first few centuries CE that are attributed to Hermes Trismegistus. While technical alchemical texts also appear under the name of Hermes, some of the texts, especially from the collection of excerpts preserved in the Anthology of Stobaeus, take a more theoretical approach, providing insights into the cosmological and philosophical underpinnings of the alchemical practices.

HOW: COSMOLOGY AND ALCHEMY

At the root of alchemy lies the process of transformation of matter, so any alchemical procedure must be informed by a theory, explicit or more often implicit, of the nature of matter and the cosmic order of which it is a part. Ancient Greek alchemical works trace their own art back to the physical theories of the Greek philosophical tradition, invoking figures such as Empedokles and Demokritos, as well as Plato and Aristotle. The technical procedures by which they produced the results they sought seem to have

---

Greek materials, and Martelli 2014a heralds future work on the Syriac alchemical material. Some of the Greek texts have received more recent editions in the Budé series, notably some of the works of Zosimus edited by Mertens, but the series' ambitious goal to edit all the texts remains as yet incomplete.

[16] Mertens 1995: xx–xlii provides an overview of the contents of all the major manuscripts (M, A, B, and L) with discussion of the ideas of Saffrey 1995 on the reshuffling of the sections of M. Letrouit 2002 provides a new discussion, correcting some of Saffrey's assumptions.

been built up from centuries of technical expertise garnered not just within the Greek tradition, but importantly from older traditions in Mesopotamia and Egypt, but the theories they used to explain their effects are for the most part derived from the Greek philosophical tradition.[17]

The so-called Pre-Socratic philosophers, who were often referred to as *physikoi*—investigators into nature (*physis*)—sought the fundamental principles of the cosmos, trying to figure out where the phenomenal world came from, what it was composed of, and the order that regulated it. While thinkers such as Thales or Anaximenes posited that all things came from a single principle (*archē*) such as water or air, the four-element theory of Empedokles proved most influential to later thinkers.

> Hear first of all the four roots of all things: Zeus the gleaming, Hera who gives life, Aidoneus, and Nēstis, who moistens with her tears the mortal fountain.[18]

Empedokles identified earth, fire, air, and water with the names of traditional deities of mythology and argued that everything is composed of varying combinations of these four fundamental roots, mingled and dispersed through the action of the principles of Love and Strife that guide the cosmos.[19]

The most influential theory for alchemy, however, was undoubtedly Plato's vision in his *Timaeus* of a divine craftsman (demiurge) working with the physical elements to form a cosmos on a divinely perfect model. The four Empedoklean elements are particular forms of the basic stuff with which the demiurge works, but this matter itself is not reducible to any one of these elements. Plato uses the analogy of gold, which can be worked into any number of different shapes but always remains gold.

> For it is laid down by nature as a molding-stuff for everything, being moved and marked by the entering figures, and because of them it appears different at different times. And the figures that enter and

---

[17] Festugière 1944: 218–219 famously describes Greco-Egyptian alchemy as being born of metallurgical practices, in the Egyptian tradition, together with Greek philosophy from Plato and Aristotle, blended with some mystic imaginings. "L'alchimie gréco-égyptienne, d'où ont dérivé toutes les autres, est née de la recontre d'un fait et d'un doctrine. Le fait est la pratique, traditionelle en Égypte, des arts de l'orfèvrerie. La doctrine est un mélange de philosophie grecque, empruntée surtout à Platon et à Aristote, et des rêveries mystiques."

[18] Fr. D57 = DK31 B6. Nestis is here probably a name for Persephone.

[19] The equations seem to have been: Zeus = air, Hera = earth, Hades = fire, Nestis = water. Later thinkers and some modern scholars claim Zeus = fire, Hera = air, Hades = earth, Nestis = water, relying on an etymological play of the name of Hera (HPA) with air (AHP), and identifying Zeus with celestial fire. Empedokles, however, conceived of fire at the center of the earth not, as Stoics and others later, in the heavens. See Kingsley 1995: 13–48.

depart are copies of those that are always existent, being stamped from them in a fashion marvellous and hard to describe.[20]

This basic material of the cosmos is itself without qualities, the better to take on the qualities of the various forms into which it is modeled by the creator.[21] The most fundamental of these forms are indeed the four familiar elements, imagined as invisibly small shapes with particular properties. Plato's *Timaeus* connects these elements with the regular geometric solids built up in mathematical proportions from triangles: fire is a tetrahedral pyramid with four triangular sides, air forms as an octahedron with eight triangular sides, water as an icosahedron, which has twenty triangular sides, while earth brings its triangular components together to form a cube. The demiurge uses the final regular solid, the dodecahedron, which is not made up of triangular sides, for the whole cosmos.[22] These four elements can combine and interact with one another to produce the variety of materials found in the cosmos.

More significantly for the theory of alchemy, these four elements can convert into one another as their qualities change. Plato takes the example of the multiple forms of water—liquid water, solid ice, gaseous air, and so forth.

> First of all, we see that which we now call "water" becoming by condensation, as we believe, stones and earth; and again, this same substance, by dissolving and dilating, becoming breath and air; and air through combustion becoming fire; and conversely, fire when contracted and quenched returning back to the form of air and air once more uniting and condensing into cloud and mist; and issuing from these, when still further compressed, flowing water; and from water earth and stones again: thus we see the elements passing on to one another, as it would seem, in an unbroken circle the gift of birth.[23]

Materials that contain different proportions of the elements exhibit different qualities, as liquid water becomes like air when fire is applied to it. Plato attributes the fusible quality of metals to the presence of water within them, so that they become liquid in form when fire is applied to them, in

---

[20] Plato, *Timaeus* 50c–d.

[21] Cp. Plato, *Timaeus* 50e. "Wherefore it is right that the substance which is to receive within itself all the kinds should be void of all forms; just as with all fragrant ointments, men bring about this condition by artistic contrivance and make the liquids which are to receive the odors as odorless as possible; and all who essay to mold figures in any soft material utterly refuse to allow any previous figure to remain visible therein, and begin by making it even and as smooth as possible before they execute the work."

[22] Plato, *Timaeus* 55a–56b.

[23] Plato, *Timaeus* 49c–d.

contrast to earthy solids without such liquid components that simply burn into ash and smoke. Different metals have varying proportions and qualities, and gold is the most perfect.

> Of all the kinds of water which we have termed "fusible," the densest is produced from the finest and most uniform particles: this is a kind of unique form, tinged with a glittering and yellow hue, even that most precious of possessions, "gold," which has been strained through stones and solidified. And the off-shoot of gold, which is very hard because of its density and black in color, is called "adamant." And the kind which closely resembles gold in its particles but has more forms than one, and in density is more dense than gold, and partakes of small and fine portions of earth so that it is harder, while it is also lighter owing to its having large interstices within it—this particular kind of the bright and solid waters, being compounded thus, is termed "bronze." And the portion of earth that is mixed therewith becomes distinct by itself, when both grow old and separate again— each from the other; and then it is named "rust."[24]

Not only does this theory explain the differences between gold and other metals, but it also accounts for the formation of 'rust' (ἰός), the general term for any different material created on the surface of a metal through the interactions with air or water. The 'rust' is thus the metallic material with its watery element removed, no longer fusible or malleable like a metal, and this dry substance takes on a greater significance in later alchemical thought as the transformative elixir (from Greek *xērion*, another word for the 'dry' element left behind when the moist vapor is extracted).

Aristotle develops these physical theories in greater detail, specifically defining metals as earthy materials that can provide moist exhalations when heated in contrast to nonmetals that only produce dry exhalations.

> For there are, we maintain, two exhalations, one vaporous and one smoky; and there are two corresponding kinds of body produced within the earth, "fossiles" and metals. The dry exhalation by the action of its heat produces all the "fossiles," for example, all kinds of stones that are infusible—realgar, ochre, ruddle, sulphur and all other substances of this kind. Most "fossiles" are coloured dust or stone formed of a similar composition, for instance cinnabar. Metals are the product of the vaporous exhalation, and are all fusible or ductile, for example, iron, gold, copper. These are all produced by the enclosure of the vaporous exhalation, particularly within stones, whose dryness compresses it together and solidifies it, just as dew

[24] Plato, *Timaeus* 59b–c.

and frost solidify when they have been separated—only metals are produced before separation has taken place. So they are in a sense water and in another sense not: it was possible for their material to turn into water, but it can no longer do so, nor are they, like tastes, the result of some change of quality in water that has already formed. For this is not the way in which copper or gold is produced, but each is the result of the solidification of the exhalation before it turns to water. So all metals are affected by fire and contain earth, for they contain dry exhalation. The only exception is gold, which is not affected by fire.[25]

Aristotle's distinctions here remain fundamental to the entire alchemical tradition. Aristotle prefers to talk in terms of qualities of hot, cold, dry, and moist, rather than elements that embody such properties, although fire may be seen as hot and dry, air as hot and moist, earth as cold and dry, and water as cold and moist.

Aristotle also develops further the idea of the featureless underlying substance of all things, a prime matter in contrast to the variety of forms that matter can take.[26] While Plato's example of the sort of thing that can be shaped into all sorts of different forms is gold, Aristotle's word for such matter (*hylē*) literally means 'wood'; a more modern analogy might be 'plastic,' a word that literally means 'that which can be molded.' Aristotle's terminology, however, remains dominant in the later tradition, and the quest to identify the prime matter (*prōtē hylē*) of the cosmos continues to drive scientific research.

As Viano points out, however, practicing alchemists are looking less to isolate this prime matter in itself than to manipulate the qualities of the forms in which the matter appears.[27] Any metal manifests various qualities, from the color or shine to its weight or its malleability or fusibility, that mark its identity as gold or copper or iron, even if the underlying substratum of metallic substance is imagined to remain the same, so the transformation of one metal into another becomes a process of manipulat-

[25] Aristotle, *Meteor.* III.6 378a–b.

[26] Cp. Aristotle, *Phys.* 1.7 191a. "The underlying nature is an object of scientific knowledge, by an analogy. For as the bronze is to the statue, the wood to the bed, or the matter and the formless before receiving form to any thing which has form, so is the underlying nature to substance, i.e. the 'this' or existent."

[27] Viano 1995: 128. "Mais la πρώτη ὕλη aristotélicienne prise absolument, c'est-à-dire séparée des qualités dont elle est le support, est empiriquement insaisissable. Cette séparation relève uniquement de l'abstraction intellectuelle. En revanche, la matière première métallique doit être une nature que l'on peut isoler et à laquelle on peut appliquer des qualités, en lui donnant ainsi l'εἶδος du métal que l'on veut obtenir. L'alchimiste ne vise pas la séparation totale des qualités du substrat dans la matière physique en général, mais dans une matière déjà déterminée: le métal. C'est alors le substrat métallique pur qu'il faut isoler, c'est-à-dire la liquidité."

ing the qualities with which the substrate is imbued. Whereas modern chemistry defines the identity of a material in terms of irreducible atoms of a particular substance—gold, copper, iron, and so forth—the ancient Greek theories deriving from Plato and Aristotle define the identity of the material empirically by its qualities. Therefore, insofar as a material manifests the qualities of gold—the color, shine, weight, fusibility, and so forth—to that extent it *is* gold, since gold is only the manifestation of the prime material that possesses those certain qualities. It is therefore possible, in theory, to transmute one material into another by changing its qualities.

The Aristotelian idea of exhalations (*anathumiaseis*) within solid materials that impart certain qualities to the material is crucial, since many alchemical operations involve releasing such vapors or condensing them back into a liquid or solid state. Plutarch discusses the Stoic idea that airy vapors provide form to inert matter.

> The physical states are nothing else but spirits, because the bodies are made cohesive by them. And the binding air is the cause for those bound into such a state being imbued with a certain property which is called hardness in iron, solidity in stone, brightness in silver. . . . Matter, being inert, by itself and sluggish, is the substratum of the properties, which are pneumata and air-like tensions giving definite form to those parts of matter in which they reside.[28]

These airy spirits (*pneumata*) serve to provide qualities to the featureless matter, so the manipulation of these spirits works to alter the qualities of the materials.[29] As Principe has commented,

> The spirit seems to carry the color and the other particular properties of the metal. The body seems to be the same substance in all metals. . . . Thus, the identity of the metal is dependent on its spirit, not its body. Accordingly, Zosimos uses fire—in distillation, sublimation, volatilization, and so on—to separate the spirits from the bodies. Joining separated spirits to other bodies would then bring about transmutation into a new metal.[30]

The process of separating a particular kind of spirit from its body and altering the quality of the spirit that is put back into the body enables one type

---

[28] Plutarch, *de stoic. Repugn.* 43 1053f–1054a (trans. Lindsay 1970).

[29] Although many scholars have taken the references to *pneuma* in alchemical treatises to indicate specifically Stoic ideas, Viano 2005: 92n6 points out that, even if ideas similar to Stoic and Epicurean ones are found, Stoics and Epicureans are not cited in the alchemical corpus, and the authorities cited for the theories are Plato and Aristotle.

[30] Principe 2013: 16.

of metal (or other material) to be transformed into another type, from lead to gold or from copper to silver or from emerald to amethyst.

Admittedly, both Plato and Aristotle deny that such fundamental transformations are within human capacity to effect, reserving such changes only for the power of the gods, but later alchemists have a greater degree of confidence in their abilities to manipulate the qualities of substances.[31] Zosimus of Panopolis indeed responds that Aristotle, while a master of the knowledge of the physical world, was insufficiently spiritual to appreciate the true power and mysteries of the alchemical art.

> [Aristotle] was not [united with] the Divine Mind, but was rather a mortal man, a mortal intelligence and a mortal body. He was the most brilliant of the nonluminous beings, in contrast to the incorporeal beings. . . . But since he was mortal, he could not elevate himself as far as the heavenly sphere; nor did he know how to render himself worthy. This is why his science and his deeds stayed in the lower region of this sphere.[32]

Zosimus and other alchemists see the potential to act in concert with the divine Demiurge to effect demiurgic transformations within the material world. Such transformations of qualities need not be limited to metallic substances, however, but operate analogously in all things within the material world, including the human body and the spirit or soul that provides it with individual qualities.

One of the other fundamental principles that the alchemists take from Plato is indeed the concept of the unity of all nature. Even if the slogan "All is one," quoted in many later alchemical texts, does not actually appear in Plato's *Timaeus*, the idea of the cosmos as a rationally ordered and unified whole is most influentially articulated in that dialogue. As it is expressed in the late alchemical text known as the *Emerald Tablet of Thrice-Great Hermes*, "What is below is like that which is above, and what is above is like that which is below": the heavenly realms reflect the mortal realms and vice versa.[33] Various particular sets of correspondences were imag-

---

[31] Cp. Viano 2005: 202. "Cette application impropre de l'entéléchie marque le point de rupture avec la philosophie d'Aristote: le refus du principe de la fixité des espèces dans le domaine des métaux, qui sont considérés comme les états provisoires d'une espèce unique, sera la source principale des perplexités des philosophes et de leurs attaques contre les alchimistes."

[32] Zosimus, *On Electrum* CMA Syr. II.12.4 (trans. Grimes 2006).

[33] The image of the ouroboros, the snake biting its own tail, appears in manuscript M, with the slogan "All is one" inside; another image includes the label, "All is One, and All is through One, and All is for One, and if One does not contain All then the All is Nothing." Plato, *Sophist* 244b6 refers to earlier thinkers who claim that all is one; cp. Aristotle, *Physics* 188a20, who attributes the idea to Parmenides. Zosimus, *On What Is Substance and Nonsubstance*, CAAG II.169.9–11 attributes the slogan to Chymes. Χύμης δὲ καλῶς ἀπεφήνατο· Ἕν

TABLE 9.1.

Saturn ♄	Jupiter ♃	Mars ♂	Sun ☉	Venus ♀	Mercury ☿	Moon ☾
lead	tin	iron	gold	copper	mercury	silver

ined, but the most significant were undoubtedly the connections made between the planetary powers of astrology and the most important metals in alchemical processes.[34]

The influences of these astrological powers could thus affect their corresponding materials on earth, and the movements of the planets in the heavens might impact the alchemical operations performed upon their counterparts on earth. Insofar as alchemical operations involve such additional symbolic resonances, they function not simply as instrumental processes, but as ritualized actions, where the significance of any given operation may not be its instrumental effect but its symbolic meaning.

The notion that similar parts of the whole resonate with one another leads to the ideas of cosmic sympathy and antipathy: like goes to like while unlike things repel or counteract one another. Perhaps the most often quoted slogan of the alchemical texts that encapsulates the alchemical ideas about the physical cosmos is the line attributed to Demokritos: "Nature delights in nature, and nature conquers nature, and nature masters nature."[35]

WHY: THE ALCHEMICAL PERFECTION OF MATTER

Alchemy is often dismissed as nothing more than the fruitless pursuit of making gold out of lead, but such a view ignores the evidence for the many kinds of ways in which alchemists were engaged in manipulating nature, exploiting the relations of different substances to one another—complementary, counteractive, or cooptative—to produce a variety of effects. Although alchemists often sought to produce gold, other recipes in the surviving texts are for producing other materials, some precious, like silver

γὰρ τὸ πᾶν· καὶ δι' αὐτοῦ τὸ πᾶν γέγονεν· ἐν τὸ πᾶν· καὶ εἰ μὴ πᾶν ἔχοι τὸ πᾶν, οὐ γέγονε τὸ πᾶν· δεῖ σε οὖν τοῦτο βάλλειν τὸ πᾶν, ἵνα ποιήσῃς τὸ πᾶν. Cp. Zosimus, *On the Necessity of Round Alum*, CAAG II.171.17 and Olympiodorus, CAAG I.84.12–14, commenting on Zosimus, who calls Chēmes a follower of Parmenides. Plass 1982 discusses the formula.

[34] Cp., e.g., Origen, *Contra Celsum* 6.22.

[35] Demokritos, PM 3.61–63 Martelli. The slogan appears in many places, e.g., CAAG I.20.5–6, I.22.4–7, III.359.3; Isis, CAAG I.30.17–18; Zosimus, *On the Four Elements as Nourishment of the Tinctures*, CAAG II.171.5–6; Synesius, *To Dioscorus*, CAAG I.57.13–15 = 1.15–17 Martelli; Moses, CAAG II.307.16f.; Stephanos 200.36–37, 215.6–7, 240.6–7 Ideler; Philos. Christ. Alch. CAAG III.395.9–10, III.416.20–21.

or gemstones or purple dye, but others less obviously so, like the rust of copper or the water of sulphur. All these recipes, however, share the common goal of mastering nature, of acting in the manner of the demiurge to shape the form and quality of physical substances. What might be called 'mystical alchemy' focused on the human individual, while practical alchemy worked on inanimate material substances, but the procedures of both involved the same kinds of manipulating natures to effect transmutations in the qualities of the materials.

Practical Alchemy

The technical or practical aspect of alchemy is concerned with the physical manipulation of material substances, and the bulk of the texts that provide evidence for alchemy in the ancient Greco-Roman world focus on these technical details. The vocabulary is often very specialized, employing obscure technical terminology for materials and processes that make it difficult for scholars to reconstruct what the ancient alchemists are doing. Among these processes, however, we may distinguish two rough groupings, one set often associated with the name of Demokritos and the other with the name of Maria the Jewess. Demokritean alchemy is found in sources such as the Stockholm and Leiden papyri as well as the later collections of Demokritean material, while Marian alchemy is represented most of all in the extensive works of Zosimus of Panopolis.

The alchemical procedures that appear in the Demokritean tradition bear close resemblances to the technical procedures for metallurgy or dyeing from the Hellenistic tradition in works like those of Aristotle's pupil Theophrastus or preserved in encyclopedic works like those of Pliny, Dioscurides, or Sextus Julius Africanus and presented there as marvelous manipulations of nature.

DEMOKRITEAN ALCHEMY

The alchemical works of Demokritos are often referred to as *The Four Books,* and it seems that at some point the alchemical lore attributed to the philosopher was collected into four different books with processes pertaining to gold, silver, purple (and other dyes), and the coloring of stones.[36] The procedures that seem to come from these works are, like the recipes in the Leiden and Stockholm papyri, relatively short and simple in form, and they often operate explicitly through the application of the Demokritean slogan regarding the manipulation of nature, working with sub-

---

[36] Martelli 2013: 29–31 provides the best overview.

stances whose qualities complement, counteract, or co-opt those of the substance being worked upon, so that nature rejoices in, conquers, or masters nature.

The recipes for making gold thus work to bring the qualities of gold to another substance. One recipe preserved in the *Natural and Mystical Things* describes how to make silver golden.

> Whiten Cyprian cadmia as is customary; I mean the cadmia that has been forced out [of its ores]. Then make it yellow: you shall yellow it with the bile of a calf, or terebinth resin, or castor oil, or radish oil, or egg yolks, which substances can make it yellow. Then lay it on silver; it will be gold by means of the gold and of the ferment of gold. For nature conquers nature.[37]

The procedure focuses on the yellowish color of gold that silver lacks, even if silver does possess many of the other qualities of gold (malleability, weightiness, etc.). Through the application of other substances with yellow coloring, the silver can take on the desired yellow quality, as the yellow nature of the applications conquers the whitish nature of the silver.

Sulphur is another popular ingredient for bringing the desired yellowish quality to a metal, and the preparation of 'sulphur water' becomes an important step in many processes. One of the recipes from the Leiden Papyrus provides the earliest attestation of this substance, which acquires an important symbolic value in later alchemy because of the double meaning of the word for sulphur (*theion*), which also means 'divine.' This divine sulphur water has remarkable properties in the process of transmutation.

> The discovery of sulfur water: mix one drachma of lime and the same quantity of sulfur that has been crumbled in a vessel containing strong vinegar or the urine of a virgin boy. The liquid is then burnt by applying fire below so as to make it like blood; filter to remove sediment and employ it neat.[38]

The modern scholar Lawrence Principe has demonstrated how such a process might work, translating it into a modern recipe: 5 g of calcium hydroxide (CaOH) and 5 g of sulfur boiled gently in 100 ml of distilled white vinegar for an hour and filtered while hot.[39] A blood-colored solution

---

[37] PM 10 (trans. Martelli 2013).

[38] P. Leid. 87 (trans. Martelli 2009).

[39] See Principe 2013: 10–11, where he notes that urine does actually work better than vinegar, along with n. 4. Principe explains the result in terms of modern chemistry: "The color changes result from the formation of extremely thin layers of sulfides on the metal surface, owing to the action of calcium polysulfides present in this 'water of sulfur.' "

results, which, if a silver object is dipped into it, produces a gold coloring of the silver. Principe's photo of a silver coin treated in such a way is impressive and shows that the techniques for the transfer of qualities could produce empirical results.

Since the silver has not actually *become* gold, however, many modern scholars have drawn the distinction between processes of aurifiction (the actual production of gold) and aurifaction (making something like gold) and see ancient alchemy as a process of aurifaction masked as aurifiction, either through intentional greedy deceit or through a primitive and unscientific inability to tell the difference. Such condemnation, however, overlooks the scientific and philosophical background of these texts, the Platonic and Aristotelian theories that posit a featureless substrate of material on which various qualities rest. In such a context, making something enough like gold that it has all of the essential properties of gold is in fact to make it gold. Transmuting the color of a metal from that of silver to that of gold is thus only one step of such a process, but the resulting material is *more* gold than the original silver was, since it shares more of gold's qualities (and fewer of silver's). The nature of the metal is not defined by sharp and simple boundaries (such as the atomic structure used in modern chemistry) but rather along a spectrum of qualities, and the question of whether something is seen as silver or gold thus depends on the criteria selected: Is it colored like gold? Does it shine like gold? Does it weigh as much as gold? Does it melt like gold? Is it as malleable as gold? The qualities in question range from easily observable to perceptible only through careful testing.

A modern parallel might be the various types of gold used in jewelry, none of which are pure gold as a chemist would define it but rather various alloys of gold and other materials. 22-karat gold has a color and luster and weight closer to pure (24-karat) gold than 18-karat or 14-karat, but even 10-karat gold can still be used (and sold) as gold for jewelry, because it has enough of the qualitative features of gold to satisfy the customer. Some of the ancient recipes indeed refer to creating gold that will pass the tests of the touchstone or other methods used to determine the value of precious metals in antiquity.

FOR GIVING TO COPPER OBJECTS THE APPEARANCE OF GOLD.

And neither fire nor rubbing against the touchstone will detect them, but they can serve especially for a ring. Here is the preparation for this. Gold and lead are ground to a fine powder like flour, 2 parts of lead for 1 of gold, then having mixed them, knead them up well with gum, and one coats the ring with this mixture; then it is fired. One repeats this several times until it takes the color. It is difficult to detect, because rubbing gives the mark of a gold object, and the heat consumes the lead but not the gold.[40]

This recipe is often held up as proof that the ancient alchemists were no more than counterfeiters, seeking to deceive a gullible public, but the recipe is designed to produce a substance that serves for all intents and purposes as gold—or at least for the purposes of use in a ring. A higher standard can perhaps be seen in another recipe for the production of silver *asem*, where tin is mixed with copper and silver, and the resulting metal is said to be of such fine quality that even artisans using it will notice nothing amiss when they hammer it and make whatever is wished out of it.[41]

Many of the recipes for silver indeed are simply for the process of doubling (*diplosis*), whereby a certain weight amount of unstamped silver (*asem*) is combined with other ingredients to produce double the weight of a metal with the same appearance and other properties.

> Doubling of *Asem*. Take refined copper of Cyprus, throw upon it equal parts, that is, 4 drachmas of salt of Ammon and 4 drachmas of alum; melt and add equal parts of *asem*.[42]

The resulting copper-silver alloy has enough of the qualities of silver that it can function as silver.

While the precise mechanisms by which these processes were imagined to work is never spelled out in these recipes of the Demokritean tradition, the basic Demokritean idea of nature is often cited.

> < Take > the mercury that comes from orpiment, or from realgar, or according to your knowledge, and make it solid as is customary; lay it on the copper < or > on the iron which have been purified with sulphur, and they will turn white. . . . You will melt iron by adding magnesia, or the half of sulphur, or a pinch of magnetite. For magnetite has affinity with iron. Nature delights in nature.[43]

This recipe from the treatise attributed to Demokritos on the making of silver describes a process by which copper or iron might be transmuted to silver, noting that magnetite has a special affinity with iron and thus, by the principle that nature delights in nature, is particularly effective at influencing iron.

---

[40] P. Leid. 37 (trans. Caley 1926). The 'touchstone' was a stone on which a substance being tested would leave a mark that could be used to determine the purity of the gold (hence the modern metaphor).

[41] P. Leid. 39 (trans. Caley 1926).

[42] P. Leid. 10. Recipes 3–11 in P. Leid. deal with the manufacture of *asem*; cp. also 18–22, 29–30, etc.

[43] AP 1 (trans. Martelli 2013).

The aim of transmuting the qualities of various substances also appears in the recipes that deal with the dyeing of fabrics and the coloring of stones. The coloring of precious stones seems to work in much the same way as the transmutation of colors in metals; the existing quality of color must be removed and a new quality infused into the stone. Crystals are imagined to be materials formed from the hardening of purified water that can take on various colors when dyed by vapors, so the material substrate is provided with qualities from the *pneuma* (spirit) with which it is imbued.[44] One recipe from the Stockholm papyrus describes the preliminary purification of a crystal to prepare it for coloring.

> The purification of a smoky crystal. Put it in a willow basket, place the basket in the boiler of the bath and leave the crystal there 7 days. Take it out when it is purified, and mix warm lime with vinegar. Stick the stone therein and let it be etched. Finally, color it as you wish.[45]

Once the stone's coloration has been wiped clean, a new color can be applied, and the codex contains a variety of recipes for producing emeralds and other gemstones. This recipe appears twice:

> Mix and put together in a small jar ½ a drachma of copper green, ½ a drachma of Armenian blue, ½ a cup of the urine of an uncorrupted youth, and two-thirds of the fluid of a steer's gall. Put entire stones therein, indeed (about) 24 pieces, so that they weigh about ½ an obolus. Lay the cover upon the pot, lute the cover all around with clay, and boil it with a gentle fire for six hours, at which olive wood is to be burned. But if this sign appears, namely, that the cover becomes green, then heat no more, but cool off and take the stones out. Thus you will find that they have become emeralds. The stones are of crystal; all crystal, however, changes its color by boiling.[46]

If the stones are boiled with another set of substances, different colors may be produced, and different qualities thus identify different stones. To obtain amethyst, for example, the stones must be boiled in a particular substance that imparts its wine-purple quality.

> Corrode the stones beforehand with three times as much alum as stone. Cook them in it until it boils thrice, and let them cool down.

[44] Cp. Diodorus Siculus 2.52. τοὺς γὰρ κρυστάλλους λίθους ἔχειν τὴν σύστασιν ἐξ ὕδατος καθαροῦ παγέντος οὐχ ὑπὸ ψύχους, ἀλλ᾽ ὑπὸ θείου πυρὸς δυνάμεως, δι᾽ ἣν ἀσήπτους μὲν αὐτοὺς διαμένειν, βαφῆναι δὲ πολυμόρφως ἀναθυμιάσει πνεύματος. "For the rock-crystals, so we are informed, are composed of pure water which has been hardened, not by the action of cold, but by the influence of a divine fire, and for this reason they are never subject to corruption and are dyed in many forms by the exhalations of spirit."

[45] P. Holm. 16 (trans. Caley 1927).

[46] P. Holm. 88 (trans. as #83 in Caley 1927), cp. P. Holm 43.

Take and soften *krimnos* with vinegar. Then take and boil the stones in it as long as you like.[47]

Unfortunately, it is unclear what precisely *krimnos* might be, but it is clearly the material that imparts the desired quality of purpleness to the stones.

Purple was indeed a desirable quality, not just for stones but even more so for fabrics. As precious as gems or gold and silver might be, the special Tyrian purple dye that produced the deep crimson cloaks of the Spartans or the purple stripe of the Roman toga praetexta was perhaps even more costly.[48] Ten thousand little murex shellfish were needed to make an obol's weight of purple dye, and the processes by which the dye was rendered from the murex were lengthy and complex.[49] As a result, there was great demand for other substances that might serve to impart the same qualities as the Tyrian purple dye, and the *Natural and Mystical Things* attributed to Demokritos contains a number of recipes for making purple. One recipe, which survives only in a Syriac translation, replaces the rare shellfish with seaweed, specially processed.

Take seaweed and throw it into quicklime, or vinegar, or alum for three days. Filter this water [i.e. solution] and boil it; mix 'srṭws [perhaps a type of clay?] with this water. As soon as it boils, plunge in wool or white woolen cloth. Take them out and wash with seawater. You will find a beautiful purple.[50]

The Stockholm papyrus, which seems to draw from the same tradition, likewise has a large number of recipes for purple that involve ingredients that are easier to obtain.

Dyeing in purple with herbs. Take and put the wool in the juice of henbane and lupines boiled sour in water. This is the preliminary mordant. Then take the fruit clusters of buckthorn, put water in a kettle and boil. Put the wool in and it will become a good purple. Lift the wool out, rinse it with water from a forge, let it dry in the sun and it will be first quality.[51]

The fabric must first be prepared to receive the dye with the preliminary mordant, literally, a biting substance that opens up the fabric to receive

[47] P. Holm. 44 (trans. Caley 1927).
[48] Theopompus reports that the dye cost its weight in silver, in Athenaeus, *Deipnosophistae* 12.526. Bélis 1999 explores the resonances of the purple-producing murex shellfish in the Greco-Roman world.
[49] Cp. Vitruvius VII.13 for processes of rendering the shellfish.
[50] Demokritos, PM 3SyrC #6 (trans. Martelli 2013).
[51] P. Holm. 118 (trans. Caley 1927).

new qualities. Then the fabric must be exposed to the dye itself that imparts the quality of the desired color.[52]

The idea of a substance that has the power of imparting some one of its qualities to another is the key to all of these recipes in the Demokritean tradition, and this alchemical art is often referred to simply as dyeing or tincturing (*baphika*), since color is the most significant of the qualities the alchemists sought to impart.

THE MARIAN ALCHEMY OF ZOSIMUS AND LATER ALCHEMISTS

While the Demokritean tradition works to transmute the qualities of substances through contact with other substances, the alchemical tradition that traces itself to the ideas of Maria the Jewess develops more complex and sophisticated means of transmutation. Maria, like Demokritos and many of the early names in the alchemical tradition (Hermes, Agathodaimon, Kleopatra, et al.), is probably not a real person but rather a name attached to a set of ideas and practices.[53] She is at times identified with Miriam the sister of Moses, but her ideas seem to come from the context of the Jewish communities in Alexandria in first couple of centuries CE. Maria is credited with a variety of inventions and discoveries, and the double boiler, which allows substances to be heated without direct application of flame, is still often referred to as the *bain-marie* or *Marienbad*, Maria's bath, in her honor. Most of what we know of this tradition comes through references in the texts of Zosimus, the third-century CE alchemist from Panopolis in Egypt, who takes many of the ideas and innovations of this Marian tradition and develops them still further.

This tradition picks up the crucial idea from Aristotle of the kinds of vaporous exhalations that distinguish metals from other solids and develops procedures for separating the vapors or spirits within materials from the solid substrates. Sulphur is particularly important in this tradition, since the exhalation of malodorous sulphur gas from a solid is a particularly noticeable phenomenon, and there are a number of well-known substances that yield a metal when the substance is burned and the sulphuric component escapes as a gas. Galena, for example, is a common ore of lead composed of lead and sulphur (PbS), while pyrite is an iron sulphide (FeS_2) whose shiny golden appearance earns it the name of 'fool's gold.' Two

---

[52] For an exhaustive survey of the chemical processes of ancient dyeing, see Pfister 1925.

[53] It is worth noting, however, the prominent place of female authors within the Greco-Egyptian alchemical tradition. Not only do Maria and Kleopatra appear as early authorities, but Zosimus's exchanges with Theosebeia indicate the she too was a practicing alchemist. This prominent place for women in alchemy stands in contrast with, e.g., astrology, but authoritative female figures appear also in theurgy.

forms of arsenic sulphide were well known in the ancient Greco-Roman world, red realgar or *sandaracha* (As_4S_4), and yellow orpiment (As_2S_3), as was the brilliant red sulphide of mercury, cinnabar (HgS). Any of these nonmetallic materials, if ground to a powder and heated properly, will produce sulphuric gas and a metallic residue, and these two components were seen as the vapor or spirit that is released from the substrate or body of the substance. As Zosimus explains, "Orpiment has a body and a soul; its soul is the cloud that rises from it, when it is liquefied and distilled; its body is the heavy and dense part."[54]

Sulphides are not the only materials with which the alchemists worked; other substances give off vapors when treated. Limestone ($CaCO_3$), for example, breaks down when burned properly, giving off carbon dioxide (CO_2) gas and leaving behind a residue of quicklime (CaO), an ingredient found often in alchemical recipes. Mercury can be vaporized directly from compounds, moving from solid state to gas and only returning to its liquid quicksilver form when the heated gas condenses, and so vapors extracted from solids and then condensed back into liquid forms were often referred to as mercury. Synesius claims that Demokritos mentions both the mercury that comes from cinnabar and that which comes from orpiment or realgar, and he compares this mercury to wax as a substance that takes on the qualities to which it is exposed: "for as wax takes on any color it receives, in the same way mercury does also, O philosopher; it whitens all substances, draws to itself and absorbs their souls."[55]

The later alchemist Stephanos compares copper to a human being, composed of body and spirit.

> Copper (♀) like a man has a soul and a body; it is necessary to make orphaned the matter of its body, so that its spirit [*pneuma*] remains, that is, its tincturing element. . . . What is its soul? And of what sort is its body? The soul is the subtle part within it, that which is extracted through treatment, that is, the tincturing spirit [*to baptikon pneuma*].[56]

The *pneuma*, the spirit of the material, is that which provides its qualities, described as the dyeing or tincturing element because the colors are the

[54] Syriac text from CMA Syr. II.42.2–4. The idea is attributed in the text to Hippocrates, which may be an error for Demokritos.

[55] Synesius, *To Dioscorus*, CAAG I.62.9–12 = 9.135–138 Martelli (trans. Martelli 2013). With regard to the different types of mercury, Synesius also helpfully notes, "Mercury is of many kinds but is only one." Modern chemists would distinguish between actual mercury that comes from cinnabar (HgS) and various arsenic-sulphur compounds that might result from condensing the vapors that come from realgar (As_4S_4) or orpiment (As_2S_3). Martelli 2014b surveys the significance of mercury in the tradition.

[56] Stephanos 241.13–18 Ideler.

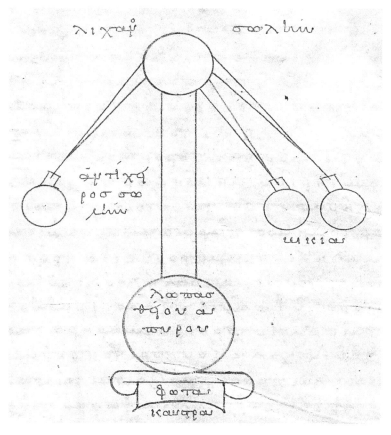

Figure 20. Tribikos apparatus, figure from manuscript M, fol. 194v.

most notable of the qualities involved. The alchemical procedures then have the aim of separating out the spiritual element from the underlying substance.

In order to achieve such separations of vapors from solid substances, the alchemists develop sophisticated technical equipment, starting with the basic stills and double boilers credited to Maria and other figures in first- or second-century CE Greco-Roman Egypt and expanding to complex, multi-armed stills and furnaces designed for the specialized procedures of separating the spirits from the bodies of the materials. The modern term 'alembic' derives from the ancient Greek word for the glass or pottery vessel used in such procedures, the *ambix* (through the Arabic, *al-'anbîq*), but such a vessel was only part of the complicated double and triple stills that appear in the alchemical manuscripts.

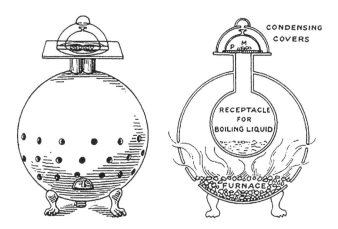

Figure 21. Illustrations of Alchemical Furnaces.

The *tribikos* was an apparatus with a heating element underneath the vessel, from which a tube led to another vessel on top. When materials were heated in the bottom vessel, the vapors would rise to the upper vessel and condense on its surface. Three tubes leading from the upper vessel to smaller containers would prevent the distillate from falling back into the heat below (see figure 20 from manuscript M, fol. 194v). While the upper vessel might be round, the texts at times refer to the 'breast-shaped' vessel, whose peculiar shape would help ensure that the condensed liquids would run off into the arms rather than fall straight back down.

Another important piece of specialized equipment was the *kerotakis*, an elaborate furnace designed to bring substances into contact with vaporized elements. The *kerotakis* is described in detail in a text of Zosimus, but its exact operation remains unclear.[57] The *kerotakis* apparatus seems to consist of a furnace under a *phiale* vessel with an *oxybaphon* (literally, vinegar saucer), a little holder for the materials being heated; on top of the *phiale* is the *kerotakis* itself, a metal plate that does not cover the entirety of the *phiale* opening, thus allowing the vapors to rise from the substances heated below and to come into contact with other substances on the *kerotakis* plate or with pieces of metal somehow affixed to the *kerotakis*. On top is another terracotta piece and a glass or bronze cap, preventing the vapors from escaping. (see figure 21)

Substances that vaporize easily, such as mercury, sulphur, or orpiment, were placed in the *oxybaphon*, heated, and vaporized so that the vapors would interact with the substances on the *kerotakis*, condense on the upper

---

[57] Zosimus, *On Apparatus and Furnaces*, MA 7.17–30. The discussion of Mertens 1995: cxxx–clii provides the best overview of the evidence and the scholarly debates.

terracotta and return below to be reheated and revaporized. Such treatments of metals resembles the process Pliny describes of forming verdigris on copper by hanging the copper over vinegar for several days, but the apparatus makes the whole process much more efficient and effective.[58]

Zosimus and other alchemists often distinguish four different phases of the transmutation of substances in general, described by the terminology of colors. In the treatise *On the Philosophers' Stone*, the stone of the philosophers is described as the substance with the property of inducing all these changes of quality.

> The philosophers divide all the works of the stone into four: first is the blackening [*melanosis*], second the whitening [*leukosis*], third the yellowing [*xanthosis*], and fourth the rusting [*iosis*]. Between the blackening and whitening and yellowing is the earth-making, which is truly the preservation, and the washing of the forms. It is impossible for these things come to be except through the operation of the breast-shaped implement and the unification of the pieces.[59]

The sequence of colors is noteworthy, since first the ordinary color of the material is removed, leaving only black. Upon this blank slate of qualities, the whitish color of silver may be imposed and likewise the yellowish color of gold. The final phase is the formation of the *ios*, the rust, reddish or purplish in color, that contains the property of imbuing or tincturing other substances with its qualities.[60] As the reference to the breast-shaped vessel indicates, these processes must involve repeated distillations of the sublimates from the substances heated in the furnace. The transmutation of color in these processes stands for the general idea of transformation of qualities in a substance by the removal and replacement of the quality-bearing spirit through the alchemical process.

Such a process captures the *ios*, the 'rust' that forms when the liquid, water-like component of a metal is drawn out and the nonmetallic substrate remains to lend its properties to the substance to which it is at-

---

[58] Pliny, *HN* 34.110 [26]; the process is not a new one; cp. Dioscorides 5.79; Theophrastus, *de Lap.* 57.

[59] Zosimus, *On the Philosophers' Stone* = CAAG II.199.1–6.

[60] Taylor 1930: 133–135 has suggested that this sequence can been seen in the treatment of copper with mercury. First, the copper blackens from oxidation in the heat of the furnace, then forms a white amalgam with the mercury; more heating volatilizes some mercury from the compound, producing a yellow, gold-like alloy. Of *iosis*, Taylor claims, "no reasonable explanation can be given." He suggests that perhaps it simply means removing the tarnish (*ios*) from the final golden product. His empiricist explanation seems to miss the general nature of the alchemical process of transmutation of qualities, but it has proved influential—see, for example, Keyser 1990: 336, who compares the purpled gold found in the tomb of Tutankhamon.

tached.[61] The term *ios* can also mean the color violet or the venom of a serpent, and alchemists play in various ways with the interconnected ideas of color, poison, and the extracted essence of a metal, often using the term *pharmakon* to refer to the magical/medical/poisonous substance.[62] This magic substance that contains the transferable qualities of the body from which it was extracted can then be used to transmute other bodies, and the later term 'elixir,' which could transmute lead to gold, provide immortality, or any other miraculous result, develops out of this idea of *ios*, the residue from the sublimation process.

Zosimus describes a procedure that makes use of the *kerotakis* to produce a sublimate that transmutes copper into gold.

> Beautiful it is to see the transformations of the four metals—lead, copper, silver, tin—into becoming perfected gold. Having taken salt, moisten the brilliant sulphur, that which is like a honeycomb. Having bound the force of each, add in vitriol and make from them vinegar, the prime-fermented of the work [and of the vitriol]. Step by step in these things you will overpower the white appearing copper by necessity and you will find it after the fifth procedure. Under the three sublimates in succession it becomes what is called gold. See, in conquering matter you receive in full the single-formed out of the multiformed.[63]

The Demokritean idea of one nature conquering another appears as the sublimate overpowers the white appearance of the copper and transfers its goldness. Zosimus is characteristically concerned with careful methodology in this process; everything must be done step by step, and it takes

[61] As Stephanos explains in his letter to Theodore (208.19–22 Ideler), "The truth is that there is a certain moist sublimate and a dry sublimate. And the moist sublimate is torn up in the stills, those having the breast-shaped vessels; the dry sublimate in the pots and the bronze cover, like the white sublimate from cinnabar."

[62] The function of the 'rust' in transferring qualities can be seen in another passage of Zosimus preserved only in the Arabic as a dialogue between Theosebeia and Zosimus. Theosebeia asks, "Tell me, why did the sages name the rust the poison of honey?" Zosimus replies, "When the water is cooked with the bodies it takes their taste, in the same way that water takes the taste of honey when mixed with it. Like that, the sages extracted the dye from the bodies with moisture. Then they added it to whatever they wanted" (*Muṣḥaf aṣ-ṣuwar* fol. 189b, 10–14, [trans. in Abt 2007: 49]). Here taste serves instead of color as a synecdoche for all qualities; water takes the taste of the honey with which it is mixed, just as the divine water takes the 'taste,' the qualities of the material substances. When the tincturing 'rust,' the dye, is extracted from material bodies that contain moisture (i.e., fusible metals), it can be added to another substance to pass on the 'taste' taken from the first substance. The 'rust' (ὁ ἰὸς) is called the 'poison of honey' (φάρμακον μελιτῶδες) in a surviving Greek text from manuscript M (Zosimus, *To Theodorus*, CAAG II.216.10–15).

[63] Zosimus, *On Excellence*, CAAG II.112.19–113.7 = MA 10.137–148 M.

five repetitions of the procedure and three formations and reformations of the sublimate to produce the desired result.

Zosimus stresses the critical importance of the systematic methodology of the procedures; the essence of true alchemy for him is indeed the manipulation of nature in a systematic way.

> And all things are woven together and all things are unraveled; and all things are mixed together and all things combined; and all things are mingled together and all things separated; and all things are drenched and all things are dried off; and all things flower and all things fade in the bowl altar. For each thing happens by method and by weighing and measurement of the four elements. The weaving together and unraveling of all things and the whole binding together of things does not occur without method. The method is natural [physikē], breathing in [physōsa] and breathing back out [ekphysōsa] and preserving the organizations, increasing and decreasing. And everything, to put it briefly, produces nature, when it is harmonious with its separation and unification, as long as nothing of the method is left out. For nature turned upon itself transforms nature. And this is the nature of the excellence of the whole cosmos and what binds it all together.[64]

Nothing of the method must be neglected in order for the manipulation of the natural processes to work; eveything must be measured and weighed correctly, and all the procedures for separating and combining different elements must be done methodically.

By working within the system of nature, the alchemist thus participates in the work of the cosmic demiurge, shaping and fashioning the elements of the world to his wishes. Pseudo-Demokritos rhapsodizes on the blessed state of those who thus participate in the interactions of natures. "O natures, artificers [demiourgoi] of natures! O greatest natures that conquer natures with your transformations! O natures above nature, which delight in natures!"[65] The seventh-century CE alchemist Stephanos describes such a figure.

> Then such a man, who is contemplative and comprehends the workings of nature, in examining each nature and mixing their mixtures according to reason [logos], and analyzing intelligently their interweavings and myriad compositions, he prepares the aforesaid interlacing scientifically, and he brings about the contact into a single-formed unity.[66]

[64] Zosimus, *On Excellence*, CAAG II.110.15–111.7 = MA 10.85–99 M (my trans.).
[65] PM 15 (trans. Martelli).
[66] Stephanos 224.25 Ideler (my trans.).

As in the Platonic worldview of the *Timaeus*, all things are ordered through reason (*logos*), and making use of this reason enables the mortal alchemist to take part in the demiurgic process. As Stephanos puts it, "The mystic demiurgic work handles the cosmos methodically through reason [*logos*], so that the man of divine thinking and divine kind understands through the direct works of the theological and mystical reasonings [*logoi*]."[67]

One of the Hermetic treatises urges that one must explore the manifold aspects of the cosmos, understanding all the physical elements and the processes of coming into being and destruction.

> Thus, unless you make yourself equal to god, you cannot understand god; like is understood by like. . . . Collect in yourself all the sensations of what has been made, of fire and water, dry and wet; be everywhere at once, on land, in the sea, in heaven; be not born, be in the womb, be young, old, dead, beyond death. And when you have understood all these at once—times, places, things qualities, quantities—then you can understand god.[68]

To be like the divine is to understand the divine, and understanding the divine involves understanding the work of the divine creator. Physical alchemy thus involves a craftsman working like the divine craftsman with the same kinds of physical elements to produce the same kinds of processes found in nature.

MYSTICAL ALCHEMY

What might be termed 'mystical' alchemy operates on the same principles as practical alchemy, but the focus of the procedures is upon the human individual, its body and spirit, rather than the physical substances that appear in the recipes of practical alchemy. Since these physical substances are themselves often described in terms of bodies and spirits, the gap between the two types of alchemy is small and often indistinguishable, and the processes of manipulating the combinations of body and spirit are always imagined as analogous. None of the evidence, however, ever explains precisely how the analogy works, and the connection between physical processes and mystical purification of the soul is never made explicitly.[69]

---

[67] 208.19–33 Ideler (my trans.).

[68] *Corpus Hermeticum* XI.20 4–6, 12–18 (trans. Copenhaver 1992).

[69] Various scholars have imagined how the connection might function, usually drawing parallels from later alchemy or some other religious tradition, e.g., Grimes 2006: 55–87, who examines Zosimus's texts on the model of the kind of 'spiritual exercises' described by Hadot 1995. Her explanation is more plausible than many, but still has no firm grounding in the

If the aim of practical alchemy is the transmutation of the qualities of some substance by altering the nature of the spirit that imbues the material substrate with those qualities, then the aim of mystical alchemy may be described as similarly altering the nature of the spirit within the body to produce a transformation of qualities. Such a transformation may be described in philosophical terms as a purification of the soul from the corrupting elements of the body, as well as a perfection and sanctification of the spirit that brings it closer to the divine. These are both concepts with a firm grounding in the Platonic philosophical tradition, even if the language used to describe these processes is very different in the alchemical texts.[70]

The demiurgic activity of practical alchemy provides the analogy for mystical alchemy. Zosimus, who provides the most theoretical accounts of this process, proclaims that "the allegory [*symbolon*] of alchemy is drawn from the creation of the cosmos for those who save and purify the divine soul chained in the elements, or rather the divine spirit kneaded in with flesh."[71] The procedure for this purificatory or even salvific action likewise involves the transformation of qualities, described as an act of dyeing or tincturing.[72] Zosimus relies on Aristotle's *Physics* to argue that the qualities carried by the spirits effect all the transformations in a person. "For the qualities alone take action. For it is impossible for bodies to go through bodies (Aristotle); the qualities go through each other. . . . For every vapor is spirit and the qualities themselves are tincturing."[73] Bodies of humans, as well as of other physical substances, are thus imagined as passive and inert, subject to the actions of the spirits within them that produce their actions as well as the quality of their actions.

These spirits or vapors that infuse the bodies arise from the formation of the body out of its original constituitive elements, as a manifestation of the proportions of these combinations. In one of the Hermetic texts preserved in the anthology of Stobaeus, Isis explains the nature of the mingled mass that is the human being.

---

evidence itself. Jung 1967 likewise explains the alchemical texts in terms of his own psychoanalytic theories.

[70] For purification of the soul from the corruptions and confusions of the body, see, e.g., Plato, *Phaedo* 65a, 66b–67b. The idea that philosophy may be described as an assimilation to the divine as far as possible may be found in *Theaetetus* 176b; cp. *Timaeus* 90b–d. Olympiodorus, *in Phd.* 1.2 simply defines philosophy as the assimilation to the divine, ὁμοίωσις γὰρ θεῷ ἡ φιλοσοφία.

[71] Zosimus, *True Book of Sophe*, CAAG II.213.15–18 (my trans.).

[72] Zosimus quoted by Pelagius, CAAG II.258.20. Ὅτι γὰρ αὐτὸ τὸ μυστήριον τὸ τῆς χρυσοβαφῆς· σώματα ὄντα πνεῦμα γίνεται, ἵνα ἐν ταῖς καταγραφαῖς πνευματικῶς βάψῃ. "For this is the mystery of the gold tincture. Being bodies they become spirit, so that it may tincture spiritually in the diagrams."

[73] Zosimus, *On Substances and the Four Elements*, CAAG II.150.4–7, 12.

It is a combination and mixture of the four elements; and from it there is exhaled a vapor, which envelops the soul, and is diffused in the body, imparting to both, that is to the body and to the soul, something of its own quality; and thus are produced both the differences between one soul and another and the differences between one body and another. . . . As long as the soul continues to be in its original condition, it maintains its good order unimpaired; but when either the kneaded mass as a whole, or some one part of it, receives by subsequent addition from without, a portion of one of the elements larger than that which was originally assigned, then there is an alteration in the vapour thence produced, and the altered vapour alters the condition of the soul.[74]

This ingenious explanation provides one account for the way that the corporeal body can affect the incorporeal soul, a longstanding philosophical problem. Changes in the composition of the material elements of the body produce changes in the vapors that envelop the soul, which in turn affect the soul itself.

Often this change in the composition of the body is described in terms of a dissolution and reformation of the elements, and the process is thus analogous to the breaking down of physical materials in the processes of practical alchemy. After describing an elaborate procedure attributed to Demokritos that involves cutting up materials, mixing them with mercury, roasting them in a *kerotakis*, and collecting the sublimate in a breast-shaped distilling apparatus, Synesius speaks of this distillate as the divine liquid that breaks down the material components to enable the transformation. "This is called the divine water. The transmutation is this, you bring out by that process the thing hidden inside; this is called the dissolution of bodies."[75] The substance that serves to break down the existing structures of the body need only be a tiny amount to catalyze the process, transforming the qualities of a large mass. Zosimus compares it to the leaven that makes bread rise.

It is necessary that this liquid, in the manner of leaven, breaks down with the like element that like element in the body that is about to be tinctured. For just as leaven in bread, being a small amount, leavens a great mass, so too a tiny golden bit will leaven the entire dry matter.[76]

[74] *Stob. Herm.* 26.13, 28–29 (trans. Copenhaver 1992), alt.

[75] Synesius, *To Dioscorus*, CAAG I.61.1–3 = 7.102–104 Martelli (my trans.). For the procedure, see the notes in Martelli 2013: 242–244.

[76] Zosimus, *Useful Advice for Those Undertaking the Craft*, Παραινέσεις συστατικαὶ τῶν ἐγχειρούντων τὴν τέχνην CAAG II.145, 7–11 (my trans.).

This liquid carries the quality of goldness or some other quality (such as silverness or purpleness or perhaps even purity or holiness), and so it can transform another body so that it manifests the same quality throughout, working according to the principles of nature to alter through its like elements. Like yeast or some other leaven that transforms a dense matter into one that is filled with air or spirit, this divine liquid infuses a spirit throughout the body on which it acts; like a tiny quantity of purple dye, it tinctures a larger mass of material. This remarkable substance that can create such transmutations is often known in later alchemical texts as the philosophers' stone or as the elixir, but a wider variety of terms is used in the earlier evidence.

Zosimus describes the aim of the alchemical tincture, the dyeing process that imparts qualities to the person, as a separation of the spirit from the body, just as vapors are released from material substances in the alchemical furnaces.

> The spirit, having been purified and assimilated to it through fire, saves the soul, if it is taken care of with craft. This is the beneficial tincture, and in such it is necessary for a man to be subtle in mind, so that he may understand the spirit going out from the body and that he may experience this thing, and out of this, taking care thoroughly, he may accomplish his aim, when the body is manifestly destroyed, and the spirit is destroyed with it. But it is not destroyed, but slips through the solid matter, when he performs the operation.[77]

The spirit is released when the elements of the body are loosened, and, like a sublimate released from material substances in the furnace and then distilled and purified, it becomes a potent agent for the care of the immortal soul, imbuing it with the most pure and virtuous qualities. An intelligent and subtle-minded man, claims Zosimus, can understand this process and accomplish his aim of the perfection of himself, so long as he observes the method carefully.

Zosimus describes other processes of dissolution in graphic and memorable images from a series of dreams he had about the alchemical processes.[78]

> I fell asleep, and I saw a sacrificer standing before me, high up on an altar, which was in the shape of a *phialē*. There were fifteen steps leading up to the altar. And the priest stood there, and I heard a voice

---

[77] Zosimus, *On Substances and the Four Elements*, CAAG II.151.3–10 (my trans.).

[78] These 'Visions of Zosimus' attracted the attention of the psychoanalyst Carl Jung, who saw the dreams as images of the process of the composition of the self. See especially Jung 1967.

from above saying to me: "I have fulfilled the act of my descending the fifteen dark-gleaming steps, and of ascending the light-glowing steps. And he who makes me anew is the sacrificer, by casting away the grossness of the body; and out of necessity I am sanctified as a priest and now am perfected as spirit." And on hearing the voice of him who stood upon the altar, I asked to know who he was. And he answered me in a feeble voice, saying: "I am Ion, the priest of the inner sanctuary, and I submit myself to an unbearable torment. For there came one in haste at daybreak, who overpowered me, and cut me open with the sword, and dismembered me in accordance with the composition of harmony. And he drew off the skin of my whole head with the sword, which he wielded with strength, and he mingled the bones with the pieces of flesh, and caused them to be burned upon the fire he had on hand, until I perceived by the transformation of the body that I had become spirit. And that is my unbearable torment." And even as he spoke thus, and I held him by force to converse with me, his eyes became as blood, and he spewed forth all his own flesh.[79]

All of these dreams are filled with allegorical images of alchemical processes, where the body of some person is torn apart or burned or otherwise subjected to the kinds of treatments that the alchemist might use upon physical substances in the furnaces or vials. This one proclaims that he has stripped away the grossness of the body and become sanctified like a priest, transforming his body into spirit.

Zosimus provides other kinds of imagery of the alchemical processes applied to the body and spirit of the human being. In his treatise *On the Letter Omega*, Zosimus recounts a myth of the creation of the human being as a spirit imprisoned within a body fashioned out the four elements by the evil ruling powers (*archons*) of the world. Zosimus identifies this first man as the Biblical Adam, as well as the Egyptian Thoth, and he interprets the four letters of Adam's name allegorically to indicate the four elements—the initial A with air, D with earth, A with water, and M with fire.[80] This Adam, however, is merely the outer man, the material prison in which the inner man is bound by the deception of the archons; the inner

---

[79] Zosimus, *On Excellence*, CAAG II.108.2–21 = MA 10.17–38 M.

[80] "With respect to the body the name they refer to him by is symbolic, composed of four elements from the whole sphere. For the letter A of his name signifies the ascendant east, and air; the letter D of his name signifies the descendant west, and the earth, which sinks down because of its weight; . . . and the letter M of his name signifies the meridian south, and the ripening fire in the midst of these bodies, the fire belonging to the middle, fourth planetary zone" (Zosimus, *On the Letter Omega* 9 = MA 1.87–96 M [trans. Jackson 1978]). The text has a lacuna where the explanation of the second A would be, but it must surely have been connected with water and the north (*arktos*), since the letters are linked more

man he calls Phōs, playing on the double sense of the Greek word to mean both 'man' and 'light.'

> When Phōs was in the Garden, spirited along on the wind, at the instigation of Fate they persuaded him, since he was innocent and unactivated, to clothe himself with their Adam, who comes from Fate, who comes from the four elements. But Phōs, for his innocence, did not refuse, and they began to exult to think that he had been made their slave.[81]

This inner light of the soul is bound, Zosimus tells us, like Prometheus, while its material prison of the body is like Prometheus's foolish brother, Epimetheus, who accepted the gift of the first woman, Pandora, whom Zosimus then identifies with Eve.[82] The spiritual inner man is thus imprisoned by the body, as Adam was bound by Eve to a fallen life of imperfection. Salvation can only come by the transcendance of this material bondage, when the soul, through knowing god, is drawn up out of its mortal clay into the divine realms from which it came before it was born into corporeality.[83] Zosimus's myth here has been called 'Gnostic' by modern scholars, because of the cosmological background of evil archons who trap the souls of men in the foul world of material creation, but, whatever its precise origins, it displays a fascinating blend of ancient Greek, Jewish, Christian, Zoroastrian, and Hermetic influences as it depicts the crafting of the human being as a body of material elements and a spirit.[84]

Zosimus is not the only figure to employ alchemical allegories for the purpose of explaining the relations of body and soul, the imprisonment of the soul in the body and its process of liberation. In his commentary on Socrates's prohibition of suicide in Plato's *Phaedo*, the sixth-century CE Neoplatonic commentator Olympiodorus provides an alchemical reading of one of the Neoplatonists' favorite myths, the Titans' dismemberment of Dionysos. The Neoplatonists frequently explain this story as an allegory of

---

directly with the compass points (*anatolē* = east; *dusin* = the setting of the sun in the west; *mesēmbrian* = south).

[81] Zosimus, *On the Letter Omega* 11 = MA 1.104–109 M (trans. Jackson 1978).

[82] "Hesiod called the outer man 'fetter,' with which Zeus bound Prometheus. Then, after this fetter, Zeus set yet another fetter upon him, Pandora, whom the Hebrews call Eve. For Prometheus and Epimetheus are by the allegorical method, a single man that is, soul and body" (Zosimus, *On the Letter Omega* 12 = MA 1.110–115 M [trans. Jackson 1978]).

[83] See Zosimus, *On the Letter Omega* 7 = MA 1.57, where he is referring to a Hermetic text.

[84] Cp. the commentary in Jackson 1978 and Mertens 1995, as well as Jung 1967. Stolzenberg 1999 contextualizes Zosimus's ideas within various 'Gnostic' ideas. Cp. also Fowden 1986: 120–126; and the discussions in Festugière 1944: 275–281. See also the unpublished dissertation of Grimes 2006.

the movement from the one to the many, the essential process of the formation of the existing cosmos in the Platonic tradition, but Olympiodorus tacks on an explanation of the formation of human beings, which he depicts in alchemical terms.

> Then Dionysus succeeds Zeus. Through the scheme of Hera, they say, his retainers, the Titans, tear him to pieces and eat his flesh. Zeus, angered by the deed, blasts them with his thunderbolts, and from the sublimate of the vapors that rise from them comes the matter from which men are created. Therefore we must not kill ourselves, not because, as the text appears to say, we are in the body as a kind of shackle, for that is obvious, and Socrates would not call this a mystery; but we must not kill ourselves because our bodies are Dionysiac; we are, in fact, a part of him, if indeed we come about from the sublimate of the Titans who ate his flesh.[85]

As Brisson has argued, Olympiodorus uses alchemical terms to describe the creation of man from the sublimate produced from the vaporization of the Titans by Zeus's lightning, and the participants in the story are identified with various materials used in alchemical operations.[86] The word *titanos* is a term used for whitish stones, such as marble or limestone, but the word naturally suggests the Titans. Quicklime (CaO), which is produced by burning marble or limestone ($CaCO_3$), is called *asbestos*, which literally means 'unquenched.'[87] This *asbestos* is also identified in alchemical lexica as the stone of Dionysos.[88] The burning of the *titanos* produces a vapor (*atmos*) with a sublimate (*aithalē*), and this sublimate is identified, through another wordplay, with the ever-flourishing (*aeithales*) spirit that runs through the body.[89] The lightning of Zeus thus represents the alchemical process that, through the burning of the Titanic and Dionysiac matter, generates the spirit that flows through the human body, and the whole myth thus explains how individual humans came about,

---

[85] Olympiodorus, *in Phd.* 1.3 (my trans.).

[86] "En définitive, en foudroyant les Titans, Zeus aurait procédé à une opération alchimique, dont aurait résulté l'être humain" (Brisson 1992: 493–494). Although Westerink 1976 has claimed that the Neoplatonist Olympiodorus cannot be the same as the alchemist of that name, Viano 1995: 99–102 provides good arguments to accept the identity.

[87] Quicklime, when water is added, gives off great heat, an exothermic reaction still used today, for example, in MREs to heat the food without fire, just by adding water. Thus, quicklime without water is unquenched; its heat has not been released but is still potentially in there: unquenched, *asbestos*.

[88] According to the lexicon preserved in manuscript M, *titanos* is the lime of the egg (τίτανός ἐστι ἄσβεστος ᾠοῦ), and the stone of Dionysos is lime (λίθος Διονύσου ἐστὶν ἄσβεστος) (*Lexicon Alchemicum*, CAAG I.14.2, 10.2).

[89] As Zosimus notes, "Sublimate is spirit, by spirit through the body" (Zosimus, *On Substances and the Four Elements*, CAAG II.151.1).

instead of the divine perfection remaining whole and unseparated into many individuals.

These alchemical processes in mythic form are not easy to understand, as comments from the ancient alchemists themselves indicate. As Stephanos notes, "The mythic alchemy is one thing and the mystic and hidden alchemy another. The mythic is poured together with a great quantity of words, but the mystic demiurgic work handles the cosmos methodically through reason."[90] The great quantity of words poured together in the mythic versions contrasts with the direct and methodical operations of physical alchemy, but word and deed work through the same principles for the same ends. Demokritos warns against those who disregard the deeper mystical significance in their haste to obtain practical results.

> But those who with ill-judged and irrational haste want to prepare a remedy for the soul and for relieving any distress do not perceive that they will go wrong.[91] For they believe that we are presenting a mythical rather than a mystical discourse, so they do not carry out any close examination of the images.[92]

Systematic method remains essential to the alchemical process, whether the aim is combining two substances or healing the soul.

Conclusion: The Aims of Practical and Mystical Alchemy

It would be erroneous, however, to conclude that there were two types of alchemists in antiquity, those who aimed at purifying the soul through mystical alchemy and those who employed the techniques of practical alchemy to produce material results that could be sold for material gain. No doubt there were some practitioners who were little better than con men and counterfeiters, who sought to deceive ignorant buyers with their cheaply faked substances, but most of the recipes are too complicated and involved to appeal to such charlatans; there are too many easier cons. Likewise, there were doubtless some who spent little time in the workshop, preferring simply to contemplate the mysteries of matter, but again many religious options were open for one so inclined to contemplation that did not involve such technical language of furnaces and stills. Alchemy is characterized by the combination of the practical and mystical, in varying

---

[90] Stephanos 208.29 Ideler (my trans.).

[91] Fowden 1986: 90 sees this going wrong (βλαβησόμενοι) as a reference to suicide, either accidental or intentional, in attempts to separate through material means the soul from the body by those who were "over-literal in this alchemization of the spiritual life." He compares the death of the magus Ostanes, teacher of Demokritos, who according to some used poison to separate his soul from his body (Demokritos, CAAG I.43.5–6 = PM 3.47–48 Martelli).

[92] Demokritos, CAAG I.47.12 = PM 16.166–170 Martelli (my trans.).

proportions in different authors to be sure, and the aims of alchemy seem likewise twofold.

Nothing sums up such an attitude better than the saying attributed to Demokritos and quoted in many variations throughout the alchemical corpus: "If you are mindful and operate according to what has been written, you will be blessed, for through method you will conquer poverty, the incurable disease."[93] The alchemist certainly has the practical aim of overcoming the dreadful affliction of poverty through his successful application of the alchemical procedures, but he also seeks to become blessed (*makarios*), a word that does not suggest simple material satisfaction or even a happy emotional state, but rather the well-being of one who is favored by the gods. It is worth noting that such success comes through method and the systematic application of the procedures specified in the alchemical writings, not from a miraculous divine intervention, even if material wealth has often been taken as the sign of divine favor.

Janowitz has argued that alchemy may be seen as "the harnessing of Late Antique τέχναι (arts/practical instructions) for religious goals," but the reverse may be equally true; the cosmological and theological ideas (stemming largely from the Platonic tradition) provided a theoretical underpinning for the technical processes, leading them in directions, such as the refinement of techniques for distilling the sublimates of burned materials, that practical aims might never have taken them.[94] The practical and mystical aims of alchemy intertwine in the sources, despite all the efforts of modern scholars to disentangle them.

WHERE AND WHEN: THE PRACTICE OF ALCHEMY

Given that alchemy takes each individual human and the entirety of the material cosmos as its object, it is perhaps not surprising to find that little attention is paid to *where* the alchemical procedures are performed. In contrast to other kinds of magical recipes, the alchemical recipes never provide specifications for where the procedure must take place. The practitioner must, however, be somewhere that all the technical apparatus of furnace, glassware, and other materials are available for use, which does in fact greatly limit the places alchemy can be performed to the specialized workshops of craftsmen who have such apparatus.[95] The placement of the

---

[93] Synesius, *To Dioscurus*, CAAG I.59.6–8 = 5.57–58 Martelli; cp. Zosimus, *On the Letter Omega* 18 = MA 1.187–188 M; and other versions in CAAG I.67.24–68.1; II.211.10–11; II.285.3; II.414.9.

[94] Janowitz 2002: 111.

[95] Little evidence remains of such workshops, but Psellos (*Chronographia* 6.64) preserves the story of a Byzantine princess who was accused of having a lab in the palace, making her

workshops themselves does not seem to have any significance, and alchemy can thus be done anywhere the alchemist decides to set up shop.

The timing of alchemical procedures, by contrast, does matter to some practitioners. Although we do not receive specific instructions in the recipes for particular times of day or even seasons of the year in which a procedure should be performed, some practitioners do seem to take into account the astrological configurations of the heavens to find the most propitious times for certain operations. Zosimus of Panopolis provides the best evidence for such a practice in his polemic against it, where he complains to his sister alchemist, Theosebeia, that other alchemists have mocked his careful and systematic technical procedures in his (lost) treatise *On Furnaces*, since they believe that the favorable influences of the astrological powers at the propitious times suffice for the procedure's success.

> The propitious tinctures have brought ridicule upon the book *On Furnaces*, lady. For many people, once they have acquired the favor from their personal demon to succeed with these tinctures, have ridiculed even the book *On Furnaces and Apparatus* as not being true. . . . And so, when their art and all their success are frustrated, and the same formulas by chance turn out first one way and then the opposite, then reluctantly, with clear proofs from their fate, they recognize that there is some truth to it.[96]

Zosimus maintains that the reliance upon astrological calculations and favor from a particular daimonic entity amounts to nothing better than submitting the operation to chance (*tuchē*) rather than his methodical processes. Chance here may refer simply to random happenstance, but it seems more likely to refer to the capricious whims of the malicious daimonic powers who can influence events on earth as it pleases them, since Zosimus elsewhere claims that daimonic *archons*, both astrological and terrestrial, have maliciously tricked mortals into providing them with sacrifices and honors to ensure the success of their operations by providing them with procedures that only work with their aid and by concealing the procedures that work without them.[97] While Zosimus urges Theosebeia to avoid procedures dependent upon such influences and rely instead

---

private chambers no more respectable than a craftsman's shop or a smithy, as servants ran around tending the braziers, mixing the materials, and so forth.

[96] Zosimus, *On the Letter Omega* 2 = MA 1.11–16, 20–23 (trans. adapted from Jackson 1978).

[97] Zosimus, *Final Reckoning* 6–7 = CAAG II.243.6–244.16. Stolzenberg 1999 explicates Zosimus's polemic against the reliance on 'propitious tinctures' here and contextualizes it within various 'Gnostic' ideas. See also Fowden 1986: 120–126; and the discussions in Festugière 1944: 275–281.

on his systematic methodology, his polemic here suggests that many other alchemists did in fact take calculations of the most propitious times into account as they sought to gain the aid of daimonic powers for their operations.

Conclusions: Alchemy as Magic, Science, or Religion

The conflict in alchemy between relying on systematic methodology or the intervention of divine powers may appear to the modern scholar as the conflict between science and religion. The modern categories of science and religion have certainly shaped the scholarship on ancient Greco-Roman alchemy, separating the alchemical codices of the Stockholm and Leiden papyri from the other Greek Magical Papyri despite the fact that they come from the same collection and were written by one of the same scribes. Much of the scholarship on the alchemical texts, from Berthelot onward, has been done by historians of science seeking to uncover the origins of modern chemistry and ignoring the religious contexts, but historians of religion have likewise ignored the technical aspects in their explorations of the theological ideas of alchemy. Both parties tend to dismiss the aspects of the other approach as 'magical' elements in alchemy, meaning either unscientific procedures incapable of producing real effects or unspiritual practices designed to produce concrete effects that have little or nothing to do with the real religious beliefs. Rather than, from a modern perspective, labeling the elements of the unwanted other as 'magic,' we should look to the ways the ideas and practices of alchemy were classified in the ancient sources to see how alchemy as a whole or in particular circumstances might be considered magic.

Science?

Scholars have seen Greco-Egyptian alchemy as the culmination of metallurgical practices from Egypt and Mesopotamia that date back to the third millennium BCE.[98] Archaeological evidence for processes such as cupellation (separating gold or silver from other elements by a special melting process) or creating alloys such as bronze or brass from copper and tin or zinc appears far earlier than any of the textual evidence. Zosimus provides an account in which the secrets of alchemy were known to the ancient Egyptians but the secrets, which were engraved in symbolic characters (hieroglyphics) on stelai buried in temples, were carefully guarded by the

---

[98] See, e.g., Keyser 1990, who cites many older works of scholarship.

Pharaohs and their associates as part of the state's regulation of the processes involved with precious metals.[99] Zosimus's attempt here to claim
the origin of alchemy for Egypt has sometimes been taken as historical fact,
but the Mesopotamian evidence shows that many of the techniques were
practiced far earlier in that region, and the work of Zosimus and the other
Greco-Egyptian alchemists seems rather to draw on and refine techniques
that had spread across the Mediterranean world, from Egypt and Mesopotamia to the Greece of Theophrastus and the Italy of Pliny.[100]

However, the insistence upon theory and systematic method in Zosimus
and other alchemists does certainly mark alchemical practice as something
out of the ordinary. The alchemist must do everything rationally and in
careful accord with the procedures laid down in the works of the experts
of the craft. Some modern scholars have seen this attitude as an indicator
of the essentially scientific nature of alchemy. "Alchemy can in truth be
called a science, for though its structure is not mathematical it describes,
classifies and draws conclusions from analogies. It combines both theoretical speculation and empirical techniques."[101] This systematicity, however,
is not simply an instrumental tool for achieving superior results; it is also
a discursive strategy for establishing the authority of the practitioner and
his ideas on the basis of his extra-ordinary *efficacy*.[102] Zosimus is superior
to his rivals because he is more methodical, more learned in the practices
of his predecessors, and more experienced in the techniques of the craft.
Those who mocked his treatise *On Furnaces* have learned to their dismay,
when their tinctures timed for propitious moments failed, that there is no
substitute for his systematic methods. The extra-ordinary complexity and
sophistication of this alchemy, like the extra-ordinary complexity and sophistication of certain astrological systems, might be classified as magic
by an ancient thinker because it so far outstrips what the ordinary practi-

---

[99] Fortunately, the secrets were revealed by Jews such as Maria and by others like Demokritos. Zosimus, *Final Reckoning*, CAAG II.239–246, with the edition and translation in
Festugière 1944: 363–368.

[100] Keyser 1990: 360–363 notes that Theophrastus mentions distilling (*de Odor.* 22) and
creating *ios* by exposing copper to vinegar (*de Lap.* 56–57), while Pliny refers to distilled
alcohol (*HN* 14.62–63 [6]) and the process for making *ios/aerugium* (*HN* 34.110 [26]).

[101] Forbes 1964: 125. Cp. Lindsay 1970: 390: "We may definitely claim that the alchemists
were the first scientists in the full sense of the word. . . . They sought to grasp the nature of
the process itself and to test out their ideas in the laboratory, to recreate and repeat phenomena under controlled conditions. That their controls were too often inadequate and crude is
beside the point. They did make the attempt to grasp and recreate processes, and that is the
crucial thing."

[102] Cp. the 'arabesques' in astrological treatises described by Barton 1994: 134–142. As
Gordon 1997: 144 notes, however, "not all complexity is solely rhetorical, serving to enhance
the impression of the writer's originality and knowledge. Some complications, the 'intrinsic'
type, serve to protect the system as a whole." See ch. 8, p. 259, n. 37.

tioner might achieve, and the rhetoric of systematicity in these practices marks the *performance* of these practices as non-normative and extra-ordinary.

Zosimus, however, explicitly refuses to consider his own practices as magic. In *On the Letter Omega*, he contrasts his own approach, based on the works of Hermes, to that of Zoroaster and the Magi.

> Now Zoroaster boastfully affirms that by the knowledge of all things supernal and by the Magian science of the efficacious use of corporeal speech one averts all the evils of Fate, both those of individual and those of universal application. Hermes, however, in his book *On the Inner Life* condemns even the Magian science, saying that the spiritual man, one who has come to know himself, need not rectify anything through the use of magic, not even if it is considered a good thing, nor must he use force upon Necessity, but rather allow Necessity to work in accordance with her own nature and decree. He must proceed through that one search to understand himself, and, when he has come to know God, he must hold fast to the ineffable Triad and leave Fate to work what she will upon the clay that belongs to her, that is, the body.[103]

For Zosimus, magic seeks to resist the workings of Fate and Necessity, rather than working philosophically within the systems of nature to know oneself and understand the nature of the divine. Whereas a Pliny might consider the extra-ordinary technical procedures as a form of magic, like the other marvelous tricks of Demokritos, Zosimus classifies his own activity as philosophy rather than magic.[104]

Religion?

Such an emphasis on contemplation of the divine has led other modern scholars to classify Zosimus and such alchemists as essentially religious thinkers, for whom the technical details were less important than the 'true end' of personal spiritual development.[105] Even if such a valorization of the interior, personal religious experience as the essential aim of religion imposes modern ideas of religion upon the ancient sources, other indicators of the religious nature of alchemy appear in the evidence. Various ancient texts describe the practices of alchemy as the product of divine revelation, usually from divine powers intermediate between mortals and

[103] Zosimus, *On the Letter Omega* 7 = MA 1.54–64 (trans. Jackson 1978).

[104] E.g., Pliny, *HN* 24.160 or 30.10, where the marvels recounted by Demokritos are explicitly linked with magic.

[105] Cp. Fowden 1986: 126: "Zosimus and his 'sister' Theosebeia clearly agreed that the true end of the alchemist's operations is spiritual purification and contemplation."

the supreme powers of the cosmos, that is to say daimonic or demonic powers. These encounters are never unproblematic, however, making these stories of the origins of alchemy less than straightforward endorsements of the normative religious nature of alchemy.

One of the most striking stories is the tale Isis recounts to her son, Horus, of how she obtained the secrets of alchemy. One of the angels from the first heavenly sphere (i.e., of the moon) spotted her and lusted after her, but she refused his advances, asking to know the secrets of making silver and gold. This lesser angel could not provide them, but the next day arrived a greater angel, Amnael, who likewise desired Isis and from whom she obtained certain secret recipes that she passes down to Horus in the text.[106] The story behind these divine secrets revealed only to one true son (and, of course, to all readers of the text) establishes the authority and validity of the recipes, grounding it in divine revelation (however dubiously obtained).

In his treatise *On Tin (and the Letter Eta)*, preserved only in Syriac, Zosimus attributes to Hermes a similar story of the origin of alchemy, in which the lust of divine beings for mortal women provides the opportunity for obtaining divine revelation. A race of daimons or angels, filled with desire for human women, descends to earth and teaches them the secret workings of nature. These secrets are recorded in a book, entitled *Chema*, from which, Zosimus claims, alchemy (*chemia*) takes its name.[107] This story resembles the account of the Watchers in the *Book of Enoch*, an apocryphal Biblical work that riffs on the passage in Genesis 6:1–4 that describes the sons of heaven descending to mate with the daughters of men to breed the race whom God will destroy in the Flood.[108] In all these accounts, special divine knowledge comes illicitly to mortals, rather than as an authorized revelation from the supreme deity, so, while its extra-ordinary efficacy is validated, its legitimacy is at the same time called into question.

Zosimus goes further, warning Theosebeia against further machinations of these lustful daimons and urging her to make protective sacrifices and undergo special purificatory rituals to ward them off.

> Offer sacrifices to them [the demons], not those that nourish and entice them, but rather the sacrifices that repel and destroy them, those of which Membres spoke to Solomon the king of Jerusalem, and especially those that Solomon himself wrote as the product of his own wisdom. So doing, you will obtain the genuine and natural propitious [tinctures]. Do these things until you perfect your soul.

---

[106] CAAG I.28–33, with another version in 33–35.

[107] CMA Syr. II.8.1.

[108] Cp. 1 Enoch 6–10. The Byzantine chronicler, George Syncellus, who preserves this story in his *Chronographia* (14.4–11), actually cites Zosimus as an authority for it.

When you recognize that you have been perfected; then realizing the natural tinctures, spit on matter, take refuge in Poimenandres, and once baptized [tinctured?] in the krater ascend quickly to your own race.[109]

Zosimus advocates using the rites of Mambres and Solomon for the control of demonic forces as a way to obtain the personal perfection and alchemical transformation that is sought; even if Zosimus himself did not consider these figures to be magicians, they are certainly so identified in many other sources.[110]

Magic?

Once again, the collocation, in the ancient evidence, of alchemy with other things that get classified as magic provides the best guide to understanding the ways in which alchemy may be understood as magic. In the account of the Watchers, the angels who descend to mate with the daughters of men provide their offspring with a whole collection of arcane arts, and alchemical tinctures (*baphika*) are listed among the secrets imparted alongside astrology, baneful incantations, root-cutting (the magical use of plant matter), *pharmakeia*, and even the art of drawing down the moon.[111] Within this tradition that Zosimus cites, alchemy is regarded as one form of magic.

This origin story is not the only one to place alchemy among the works of magic, since the legend associated with Demokritos attributes his arcane knowledge to the magus Ostanes. Ostanes, unfortunately, died before Demokritos had mastered the alchemical arts of combining natures, but that did not stop the enterprising Demokritos, who conjured his spirit from Hades. In this necromantic consultation, Ostanes could only indicate that the book with the secrets was in the temple, and when the book was miraculously found it revealed the formula that became the slogan of Demokritean alchemy: "nature delights in nature, nature conquers nature,

---

[109] Zosimus, *Final Reckoning* 8 CAAG II.244.24–245.7 (trans. adapted from Fowden 1986: 122–123). The final lines evoke two Hermetic texts, the *Poimandres* (*Corpus Hermeticum* I) and the *Krater* or *Mixing-Bowl* (*Corpus Hermeticum* IV), both of which provide a revelatory vision of the nature of the cosmos as the work of a demiurge along the lines of the cosmogony in Plato's *Timaeus*, including the mixing-bowl (*krater*) for soul-stuffs. For the parallels between these texts and the Platonic tradition, as well as various 'Gnostic' texts, see Festugière 1944, Fowden 1986, and more recently Fraser 2007 on the 'Gnostic' parallels.

[110] Membres or Mambres is another name for Jambres, identified in 2 Timothy 3:8 as one of the magicians who opposed Moses in Exodus 7:11–13. His partner Jannes is mentioned by Apuleius (*Apologia* 90) as a well-known magician (along with Moses). Jannes and Jambres appear in *Testament of Solomon* 25 as magicians who controlled the demon Azethibou. For discussions of this passage, see Fraser 2004 and Stolzenberg 1999, as well as Festugière 1944: 275–281.

[111] 1 Enoch 8:1–3.

nature masters nature."[112] The foundation of alchemy thus derives from the necromantic revelation of a Persian magus, layering magical origin upon magical origin.

Pliny frequently connects the marvelous tricks of Demokritos that involve the transformations of matter to his training with the Magi, even blaming Demokritos for transmitting all this alluring magic to the Greco-Roman world.[113] The little magic tricks (*paignia*) of Demokritos appear in the Greek Magical Papyri, while the two authors cited in the Stockholm papyrus, Anaxilaus of Larisa and Sextus Julius Africanus, are both credited with such little transformation tricks. Africanus, in addition to providing recipes for hair dye and curing snakebites, tells how to dye gemstones and to create a 'rust' of gold.[114] Such an alchemical magic trick is also firmly located among the magicians by Sextus Empiricus, who, in a discussion of how little things can affect vision, notes, "Magicians [*goetes*] also, by smearing lamp-wicks with rust [*ios*] of copper or cuttle-fish ink, make those standing by appear at times copper-colored or black."[115] The transfer of the quality of copper color to those within the light of the lamp through the alchemically produced *ios* is thus the work of magicians. The fact that the alchemical recipes of the Stockholm papyrus were written by the same scribe who transcribed the magical procedures in the various versions of the Eighth Book of Moses in PGM XIII indicates that one of the compilers of the Greek Magical Papyri brought together alchemical and magical materials in his work. Such recipes were also not collected as a technical manual for a professional dyer or metalworker. Even if such a professional technician might well have employed a process similar to one of these recipes, all these various recipes—for transmuting colors, hardness, and other qualities—are assembled as a collection that suits the needs of someone interested in the processes of transmutation, not of someone making a living from using a particular process.

Other kinds of collocation are even more telling for the classification of alchemy from a normative perspective. In the third century, the Emperor Diocletian ordered the burning of all books of alchemy (*peri chēmeias argurou kai chrusou*) in the Empire, along with the works of the astrologers. While the emperor may well have been partly moved by a desire to crack down on the counterfeiting of coinage, the banning of such magical arts as alchemy and astrology fits in with other Roman imperial attempts to keep control over these elements of the culture.[116]

---

[112] PM 3.35–64 Martelli = CAAG I.42.21–43.22.

[113] Pliny, *HN* 30.10 [2]: *hunc enim maxime adfixisse animis eam dulcedinem constat.*

[114] Africanus is summarized in Psellos, *Opusc.* 32.27, 42–43, 47–49. Anaxilaus in Pliny, *HN* 32.141 [52], 28.181 [49], 30.74 [32], 35.175 [50], 25.154 [95].

[115] Sextus Empiricus, *Pyrrhonian Outlines* 1.46.

[116] For the banning of alchemy, see John of Antioch, fr. 165 Müller; *Suda* δ 1156: s.v.

The rhetoric of systematicity and other extra-ordinary elements of the ritualized performances of alchemical procedures place alchemy within the discourse of magic, as do the claims to extra-ordinary efficacy and marvelous power over the world of nature. Zosimus himself may deny that what he practices is magic and draw a firm distinction between his practices and those of other alchemical practitioners, but the line between the tinctures that depend on propitious moments and those that rely only on the understanding of the nature of the cosmos must have been as obscure to most of Zosimus's contemporaries as it is to modern audiences. Moreover, the same combination of the systematization of knowledge to the most arcane degree and the grounding of the authority for the practice in divine revelation that characterizes the evidence for astrology, can be found to the greatest degree in Zosimus's works of all the alchemical corpus. Like his contemporary Iamblichus, whose attempts to distinguish his brand of theurgy from magic provide the most detailed accounts of theurgy, Zosimus doth protest too much. The nature of alchemy in the ancient Greco-Roman world, especially as it appears in the works of Zosimus, fits into the category of things that can be labeled with the discourse of magic, and the philosophers' stone, that can effect the transmutations of color and quality in substances, might well have been called 'the sorcerer's stone.'

Διοκλητιανός; χ 280: s.v. Χημεία; for the astrologers (*mathematici*) Codex Justinianus 9.18.2. Vlachou, McDonnell, and Janaway 2002 provide a fascinating account of coins discovered from that era that appear to have been silver-plated with a silver mercury amalgam of the kind that could be produced by contemporary alchemical methods.

10

The Illuminations of Theurgy: Philosophy and Magic

From this evidence of the eyes, the authorities on the priestly art have thus discovered how to gain the favor of powers above, mixing some things together and setting others apart in due order. They used mixing because they saw that each unmixed thing possesses some property of the god but is not enough to call that god forth. Therefore, by mixing many things they unified the aforementioned influences and made a unity generated from all of them similar to the whole that is prior to them all. And they often devised composite statues and fumigations, having blended separate signs together into one and, by unifying many powers, having made by artifice something embraced essentially by the divine, the dividing of which makes each one feeble, while mixing raises it up to the idea of the exemplar.

(Proclus, *de sacr.* 150.24–151.5)[1]

Proclus's description, in his treatise *On Sacrifice and Magic*, of what he calls the 'hieratic art' provides the best encapsulation of theurgic ritual from the ancient sources. The 'natural magic' of the Renaissance that forms

---

[1] οἱ τῆς ἱερατικῆς ἡγεμόνες ἀπὸ τῶν ἐν ὀφθαλμοῖς κειμένων τὴν τῶν ἀνωτέρω δυνάμεων θεραπείαν εὑρήκασι, τὰ μὲν μίξαντες, τὰ δὲ οἰκείως ἀναιρούμενοι· ἡ δὲ μῖξις διὰ τὸ βλέπειν τῶν ἀμίκτων ἕκαστόν τινα ἔχον ἰδιότητα τοῦ θεοῦ, οὐ μὴν ἐξαρκοῦν πρὸς τὴν ἐκείνου πρόκλησιν· διὸ τῇ μίξει τῶν πολλῶν ἐνίζουσι τὰς προειρημένας ἀπορροίας καὶ ἐξομοιοῦσι τὸ ἐκ πάντων ἓν γενόμενον πρὸς ἐκεῖνο τὸ πρὸ τῶν πάντων ὅλον· καὶ ἀγάλματα πολλάκις κατασκευάζουσι σύμμικτα καὶ θυμιάματα, φυράσαντες εἰς ἓν τὰ μερισθέντα συνθήματα καὶ ποιήσαντες τέχνῃ ὁποῖον κατ' οὐσίαν τὸ θεῖον περιληπτικὸν καθ' ἕνωσιν τῶν πλειόνων δυνάμεων, ὧν ὁ μὲν μερισμὸς ἡμύδρωσεν ἑκάστην, ἡ δὲ μῖξις ἐπανήγαγεν εἰς τὴν τοῦ παραδείγματος ἰδέαν. [trans. Copenhaver 2015]

the basis for much of the ideas of positive magic in the early modern and later periods comes from the reception of ancient ideas of theurgy, especially those of Proclus and his predecessor Iamblichus. From the uses of the term in the ancient evidence, 'theurgy' may be defined as the art or practice of ritually creating a connection between the mortal, material world that is before one's eyes and the unseen, immortal world of the gods. Such a practice may be a lifelong assimilation of the individual soul to the divine, or it may be a momentary activation of the connection with divine power to achieve some more immediate end on earth.[2] While theurgy, defined narrowly in modern scholarship, is often taken to be a particular set of ritual practices based in the revelations of the *Chaldaean Oracles*, the ancient evidence provides examples of theurgic practice that make no reference to this mysterious set of hexameter oracles.[3] Nevertheless, 'theurgy' is not simply a label for any kind of ritual that practitioners want to distinguish from nonritual theology or philosophy, on the one hand, or from unacceptable magic, on the other.[4] Although the ritual practices and the theological ideas underlying them shift from the time of the *Chaldaean Oracles* in the second century CE to the later Neoplatonists of the fourth and fifth centuries, theurgy always involves the activation of existing connections between mortal and immortal to bring the two together in some way or to some degree.[5]

The word 'theurgy' is composed of two Greek terms: *theos* (god) and *ergon* (work), but it remains a subject of debate whether 'theurgy' should mean 'the work of the gods' or 'working on the gods.' Some of its defenders insist that the essence of theurgy is the gods reaching down to help mortals, while others critique theurgy as an attempt by mortals to force the gods to do work. Theurgy in any case is work or action involving the gods as well as humans, that is to say a religious ritual with corresponding actions in both the mortal and divine worlds. However, whereas normative religious action in the Greco-Roman world tends to involve just the human

[2] Addey 2014: 24 stresses the ongoing aspect of theurgy. "Theurgy remains notoriously difficult to define, partly because ancient philosophers conceived of theurgy as *a way of life* or, strictly speaking, *a way of being*, as well as a nexus of ritual practices."

[3] Cp. Johnston 1997: 165, who defines theurgy as "an esoteric, revelatory religion that took as its authoritative basis the Chaldean Oracles, dactylic-hexameter poems that were divinely dictated to the sect's leaders in the mid-second century CE." As Tanaseanu-Döbler 2013: 14 notes, however, "the text and the rituals need not go together. . . . Discussing the development of theurgy requires us to differentiate between the reception of the *Chaldean Oracles* and their philosophical system on the one hand, and actual ritual practice on the other."

[4] As Janowitz 2002: 17 would seem to suggest.

[5] Tanaseanu-Döbler 2013 examines the shifting meanings of theurgy over this time period, noting however (13) that theurgy remains significant long afterwards, as it is adapted in the Byzantine and even Renaissance contexts.

worshipper and the divine god in a sequence of reciprocal responses, theurgy, as it appears in the ancient evidence, attempts to bring the divine and mortal together, uniting the divine power with the human worshipper. This process of unification involves connecting elements of the cosmos at every level of being, from the lowest dregs of inanimate matter through the animal and human living creatures and up to the various kinds of divinities, including the very highest. While the normative religion explored in the earlier chapter 6 on prayer involves a model of reciprocal gift exchange, theurgy is more like the creation of a circulatory system that lines up the connections between the various points in the system to allow the divine power to flow through. Although such a circulatory system was familiar in the ancient world from the famous Roman plumbing that created channels for the flow of water throughout the cities of the Greco-Roman world, the more modern analogy of an electric circuit is perhaps more apt for understanding theurgy, since it was often described as the flow of light, emanating down out the divine world and flowing back up through special channels to rejoin its source. The Byzantine commentator Psellos quotes one of the *Chaldaean Oracles* to describe such circulation. "Seek out the channel of the soul, from where it descended in a certain order to serve the body; and seek how you will raise it up again to its order by combining ritual action with a sacred word."[6] Like an engineer who seeks to line up all the wires and nodes of a circuit so that the power may flow through every part, the theurgist seeks to line up the mixture of materials, sacred words, and other parts of his or her ritual so that the divine power illuminates every element. Whereas alchemy is concerned primarily with the qualities of the material elements and astrology with the movements of the heavenly bodies, theurgy undertakes to bring them all together into one. Like astrology and alchemy, theurgy is closely connected with particular theorizations of the cosmos; these ideas of *how* it works mark the difference from normative religion, rather than *why* or even *what* things are done.

The *Chaldaean Oracles*, as well as other oracles of the sort cited in Porphyry's *Philosophy from Oracles*, provide a source of direct divine revelation, a way of immediate connection between the divine and mortals. The oracles thus supply an important authority for theurgical practice, and many of the proponents of theurgy cite them in their explanations. In addition to Proclus's work on sacrifice and magic, the treatise of Iamblichus

---

[6] *CO* 110 = Psellos, *in Chald. Orac.* 131 = PG 122 1129c–d. Other Chaldaean Oracles that mention the 'channels' (*oxetoi*) include *CO* 2 = Damascius, *de princ.* I.155 11–15; *CO* 65 = Proclus, *in Tim.* II.107 6–11; *CO* 66 = Proclus, *in Remp.* I.178 17–20. *CO* 60 refers to the sun as a channel of fire (= Proclus, *in Tim.* II.9 16).

responding to the questions of Porphyry about theurgy (known from the title given to it in the Renaissance, *On the Mysteries of the Egyptians* or *de mysteriis*) provides theoretical background for the practice of theurgy. The questions and critiques of Porphyry are taken up by later Christian critics, who likewise provide valuable evidence for understanding how theurgy was imagined in the ancient world. These thinkers, however, are primarily interested in how theurgy works, the shape of the whole system that undergirds it, rather than in the practical details of ritual performance. Evidence from some of the most complex spells of the Greek Magical Papyri provides insights into the ritual practice, illuminating the ideas of theurgy's proponents while at the same time confirming some of the critiques of its detractors. From any of these perspectives, however, theurgy appears as magic, labeled as an 'extra-ordinary ritual practice,' whether in a positive or negative sense.

WHO: THEURGY AMONG THE ELITE

More information survives about the individual practitioners of theurgy than any other form of magic, because many of them were important members of the elite classes of the Roman Empire in the first several centuries of the Common Era. Many of the names associated with theurgy are connected with Roman emperors, while others are leaders of schools of philosophy; theurgy is for the educated and elite. Because such educated elites are the ones who practice theurgy, the evidence for this form of magic shows it to be more complicated and more highly theorized than other forms of magical practice.

Chaldaean Oracles and Theurgy

The *Chaldaean Oracles*, which were cited as the most authoritative source for theurgical ideas and practices by the Neoplatonists, survive only in fragments in the quotations by those Neoplatonists. According to some of our later sources, the *Chaldaean Oracles* were produced through the inspiration of a certain Julian, called the Theurgist, who was the son of another Julian, called the Chaldaean. The younger Julian may have channeled the soul of Plato or have received the hexameter verse oracles directly from various gods, but his theurgical practices enabled him to receive the divine revelations that were collected, perhaps by his father, into the *Chaldaean Oracles*. The younger Julian is said to have gone with the Roman Emperor Marcus Aurelius on campaign in 172 CE, where he conjured up a rainstorm to save the troops from thirst and fabricated a magical figure that hurled lightning bolts at the enemy whenever they came near.[7] While the sources agree in placing Julian during the reign of Marcus Aurelius, it is much less clear where he and his father, the Chaldaean, came from. Athanassiadi speculates that the elder Julian may have been a priest at the famous temple of Bel in Apamea, a city in (current) Syria that would have been considered Chaldaean at the time. Apamea in the second century was the home of the Platonist philosopher Numenius, whose cosmology seems to resemble greatly that of the *Chaldaean Oracles*, as well as later of Iamblichus, the Neoplatonic philosopher whose (lost) commentary on the *Chaldaean Oracles* seems to have been the work that catapulted the *Chaldaean Oracles* into prominence among the Platonists.[8]

Iamblichus and his predecessors Porphyry and Plotinus represent the first set of Platonic thinkers who show an interest in what Iamblichus calls 'theurgy.' While the ideas of Middle Platonists such as Plutarch of Charoneia (46–120 CE), Apuleius of Madauros (c. 124–170 CE), and Numenius of Apamea (end of second century CE) provide parallels with the *Chaldaean Oracles*, the philosophy of Plotinus (205–269/270 CE) is generally taken to represent the shift from the understanding of Plato that characterized Middle Platonism to the complex systems of Neoplatonic thought. Plotinus shows an interest in ideas and techniques that resemble those of theurgy, although he never mentions the term, and modern scholars have debated whether he knew of the *Chaldaean Oracles* and theurgic practices.[9] Plotinus's pupil Porphyry (232–305 CE) wrote his master's biography and arranged his works, but he also wrote a large number of treatises himself, including a study of *Philosophy Drawn from Oracles*, in which he apparently argued that (his brand of) Platonic philosophy was embedded in oracles that provide revelations from the gods themselves. This lost work survives in copious quotations by the Christian apologist Eusebius, who attacks the revelations from pagan gods and the whole system Porphyry derives from them. Another work of Porphyry's, an attack on Christianity in fifteen books, was burned in 448 CE by order of Christian emperors, and almost nothing survives. Porphyry is said to have been the teacher of his younger contemporary Iamblichus (250–325 CE), and Iamblichus frames his *de*

---

[7] *Suda* s.v. Ἰουλιανός iota 433 and 434. Cp. the stories in Psellos, *Opusc.* 3.139–147 and 46.40–50.

[8] "When one considers everyday scenes in the courtyards and the prayer halls of mosques today one should have no great difficulty in visualizing how in Antonine times, in the shadow of the ancient trees of the temple of Bel at Apamea, philosophy mingled with religion, and tradition with new trends in an act of cross-fertilization, until, inspired by his conversations with Numenius and many other anonymous sages, a priest by the name of Julian, following an ancient practice, fell into a trance and pronounced hexameter verses in the theological idiom of the age and the region" (Athanassiadi 2005: 125).

[9] See Mazur 2003 and 2004 for the debates; Mazur argues controversially that Plotinus knew of theurgic practices and borrowed techniques for his own contemplative philosophy.

Mysteriis, the most important work on the theory of theurgy, as a response to Porphyry's questions about theurgy.[10]

Neoplatonists and Christians

Iamblichus's works provide the framework for the serious consideration of theurgy—and perhaps particularly the theurgical ideas of the *Chaldaean Oracles*—within the continuing Neoplatonic schools.[11] His own school at Apamea dissolves after his death, but his pupil Aedesius founds a school at Pergamon, where Neoplatonic theurgists such as Sosipatra and Maximus of Ephesus (c. 310–372 CE) study. Sosipatra, who also taught in Aedesius's school, is said to have been trained in all the theurgic arts in childhood by a pair of divine and mysterious strangers, and other miracles attended her life, as it is recounted in Eunapius (who provides much of the information for all these figures). Maximus becomes the advisor in matters theurgical of the Emperor Julian, who sees in Iamblichean theurgy a religious system to counter the encroachment of Christianity into the Roman Empire.

The Emperor Julian, Flavius Claudius Julianus (331–363 CE), is the nephew (son of the half-brother) of the Emperor Constantine, who officially converts himself (and thus the Roman Empire) to Christianity in 312 CE. After Constantine's death, Julian's father and several other members of his family are assassinated at the behest of some of Constantine's sons, one of whom, Constantius, eventually gains control of the Empire. Julian grows up in exile or under careful imperial supervision and is given a Christian education. Nevertheless, he studies Neoplatonic philosophy and, in 351, is initiated into theurgic mysteries by Maximus. Julian revolts against Constantius in 360, and his troops proclaim him emperor, creating a civil war in the Empire. Fortunately, Constantius dies of illness shortly thereafter, and on his deathbed he proclaims Julian emperor, averting further war. When he becomes emperor in 361 CE, Julian officially turns the Roman Empire back to traditional Hellenic religion and tries to formulate a coherent polytheistic religious system to counteract organized Christianity. He bans Christians from teaching Hellenic literature and philoso-

[10] Addey 2014: 135 argues that Porphyry's critiques, in his *Letter to Anebo* that Iamblichus quotes in his responses, are not actually a condemnation of theurgy, as they have often been understood, but rather his engagement in a philosophic debate with his colleague. "Rather than being a scathing attack on pagan religious practice, Porphyry's *Letter to Anebo* functions within the dialogue tradition of a constructive, philosophical inquiry" (cp. Addey 2014: 128).

[11] Tanaseanu-Döbler 2013: 129 notes the significance of Iamblichus's systematization of theurgy as a label for his philosophical ideas in its continuing authority. " 'Theurgy' can therefore be considered as one particular label for the ideal religious expertise taken from the Chaldean Oracles; its systematic develoment in *De mysteriis* in order to respond to Porphyry's attacks made it a useful tool for developing a philosophical ritual theory and thus ensured its success over others."

phy, saying that, if they wished to teach, they could preach the gospel in their churches, but he did not persecute Christians physically (in fact, some Christian bishops denounce him for not letting Christians achieve martyrdom). Saloustios's treatise *On the Gods and the World* seems to be an articulation of Julian's theological system, recounting in somewhat simplified terms the Iamblichan theurgical ideas he learns from Maximus.[12] Julian himself wrote a number of works, including a *Hymn to King Helios* and a *Hymn to the Mother of the Gods*, which make use of theurgic imagery.

Julian dies pretty much a failure in 363 CE, having tried to mount a massive invasion of Persia to expand Rome's power, during which he is killed in action. His troops appoint a Christian general, Jovian, to be emperor, and, although Jovian also only lasts around a year before dying, he is succeeded by the Emperors Valens and Valentinus I, who keep the Roman Empire firmly in the Christian camp, reversing the revolution Julian sought (hence he is called Julian the Apostate). After Julian's death, Maximus is prosecuted and tortured for financial improprieties and then finally executed in 370 CE by the Emperor Valens.

Theurgy, however, remains important to the Neoplatonists. The Neoplatonist Synesius (c. 373–414 CE), who was a pupil of the famous Hypatia of Alexandria, becomes the Christian bishop of Cyrene, but continues to write works that touch on theurgical themes, such as some hymns and his treatise on dreams (*de insomniis*). Proclus (412–485 CE) learns his theurgy from Asclepigeneia, the daughter of Plutarch of Athens, and eventually becomes head of the Platonic school in Athens. His commentary on the *Chaldaean Oracles* (now lost) was massively influential on later thinkers, and his other works provide much evidence for theurgy as well as many of the surviving fragments of the *Chaldaean Oracles*. His fragmentary treatise, dubbed *On Sacrifice and Magic* by its Renaissance commentators, provides the clearest picture of theurgic activity. Hermias (c. 410–450 CE), who was a fellow pupil along with Proclus of the Neoplatonist known as Syrianus, makes numerous references to theurgical matters in his commentary on Plato's *Phaedrus*. Their contemporary Hierocles of Alexandria blends Neoplatonism with Neopythagoreanism in his commentary on the *Golden Verses* of Pythagoras, which likewise engages with theurgical ideas and quotes the *Chaldaean Oracles*. Further evidence comes from Damascius (462–539 CE), who was the last head of Platonic Academy when Emperor Justinian shut down all pagan schools in 529 CE. Damascius also preserves many fragments of the *Chaldaean Oracles*, often, however, with markedly different interpretations than Proclus has. Proclus's ideas seem to predomi-

---

[12] This Saloustios may have been either Flavius Sallustius, a consul in 363, or, as Tanaseanu-Döbler 2013: 149–151 argues, Saturninus Salutius Secundus, the *praefectus praetorio Orientis* from 361 to 366.

nate, however, in the last major source for ancient theurgy, the Byzantine courtier and scholar Michael Psellos (c. 1019–1078 CE). Although a Christian, Psellos preserves much of the evidence for the *Chaldaean Oracles* in his comments on Proclus's lost commentary on the Oracles.

Other Elites: Lector-Priests and Magician Scribes

The doctrines of Neoplatonic theurgy thus seem to move in exalted circles, among the heads of the philosophical schools and the highest levels of the Roman Empire.[13] This elitism may well be an illusion from our limited resources for evidence, but the complexity of the arguments involved in the ideas of theurgy ensures that only a limited number would be able to follow them, and the rhetoric of the theurgical texts often differentiates the theurgist from the common 'herd.' As with astrology, however, there were probably plenty of people who made use of simplified versions of the complex theological doctrines, but, whereas we have references to common people using astrological ideas, such evidence seems lacking for theurgy. Even the other source for theurgical practices, the spells of the Greek Magical Papyri, show signs of coming from an intellectual elite, since the writers of the papyri that contain theurgical material clearly come from a select class of Egyptian scribes rather than the wide range of authors from every walk of life who inscribed curse tablets.

Not all the papyri in the collection of the Greek Magical Papyri contain spells that might be characterized as theurgic in nature, but those that do are no random scraps of papyrus but the careful productions of highly educated and expert scribes who seem to combine mastery of multiple languages (Demotic Egyptian, Coptic, and Greek) and scripts (Demotic, Hieratic, Coptic, and Greek) with an awareness of multiple ritual traditions. As Frankfurter has suggested and Dieleman recently argued, the authors of the large papyri from the so-called Theban Magical Library, such as PGM I, IV, XII, and XIII (the very ones that contain the most evidence of theurgical rites) were probably lector-priests, that is, Egyptian ritual experts with scribal training who used the traditional Egyptian temples as a base of operations for their work, both scribal and ritual.[14] They collated multiple manuscripts of the same spell recipe, carefully noting alternate readings in their source materials. They included glosses of technical terms in other languages, showing their mastery of languages and scripts that the majority

---

[13] As Johnston 1997: 178 has noted.

[14] Cp. Frankfurter 1998: 210–237; Dieleman 2005: 285–294. The former discusses the idea of 'stereo-type appropriation' among the Egyptian priests, while the latter discusses the phenomenon of 'code-switching' to understand the multiple languages in which the papyri are written, on which see also Love 2016.

of their countrymen at the time had little or no access to.[15] Some of the arrangements within the papyri, such as the multiple versions of the cosmogonic myth in PGM XIII or the divisions between sun and moon spells in PGM IV, suggest an awareness of and interest in broader theological and philosophical issues beyond the immediate practical aims of the spells themselves.

The practitioners of theurgy, then, whether they are Egyptian lector-priests, adapting traditional Egyptian rituals in the light of Greek philosophical ideas and ritual practices, or Greek Neoplatonic philosophers moving between the temples of Syria to the schools of Athens and Alexandria to the courts of Rome, all belong to a rarefied stratum of Greco-Roman society. It is worth noting the number of women among these theurgic figures, not just Sosipatra and Asclepigeneia in the Platonic schools but even the 'daughter' to whom the ritual of the Mithras Liturgy is to be handed down.[16] Although the scribes of the Greek Magical Papyri remain as anonymous as the authors of many other forms of magical texts, the Neoplatonic theorists are known by name and often even with a biographical tradition. Even if such biographical traditions can never be taken at face value as indicators of the real historical facts about the individuals, they nevertheless provide more insight into the ways the people who practiced theurgy were thought of by their contemporaries and successors, as intellectuals, as representatives of the most important values of Greek culture, and as performers of miraculous deeds through the powers of their theurgical contacts with the gods.

How: Philosophical Accounts of Theurgy

Because of the elite intellectual circles of the sources, the evidence for theurgy provides more theoretical explanations of how the process works than is the case for other forms of magic. The philosophical arguments for theurgy engage with the critiques in systematic and detailed ways, defending the efficacy of the practice through elaborate theoretical explanations of *how* it works. Since much of the debate takes place among philosophers of the Platonic schools, they all look to Plato to provide the basis for their arguments, but the disputes revolve around differing ideas of the nature of the cosmic hierarchy and the nature of the soul, since theurgy aims to bring together the individual soul with the highest powers of the cosmic hierarchy. The Platonic conception of the daimon as an intermediary between divine and human is fundamental to all these ideas, although the

[15] Cp. the study of Dieleman 2005: esp. 47–87, 103–110.
[16] Cp. the introduction to PGM IV.475–829.

nature of such daimons varies widely. Theurgy also depends upon the nature of the human being as a composite that includes both immortal soul and mortal body, as well as upon the nature of the divine with which the human soul seeks to meet.

Intermediary Daimons

The passage in Plato's *Symposium* where the wise woman Diotima explains the nature of Eros as a daimon to Socrates is basic for any understanding of the Platonic conception of the daimon. Daimons, she explains, are

> between a mortal and an immortal. . . . Interpreting and transporting human things to the gods and divine things to men; entreaties and sacrifices from below, and ordinances and requitals from above: being midway between, it makes each to supplement the other, so that the whole is combined in one. Through it are conveyed all divination and priestcraft concerning sacrifice and ritual and incantations, and all soothsaying and sorcery. God with man does not mingle: but the spiritual is the means of all society and converse of men with gods and of gods with men, whether waking or asleep. Whosoever has skill in these affairs is a spiritual man; to have it in other matters, as in common arts and crafts, is for the mechanical. Many and multifarious are these spirits, and one of them is Love.[17]

This conception of the daimon as the intermediary between a divine and a human entity that cannot mingle directly articulates the gap between mortal and immortal while at the same time providing a way to bridge it. Daimons can thus be imagined as something that partakes of the qualities both of gods and of humans, remaining betwixt and between, neither one nor the other. They are therefore not as perfect as the gods, but remain nevertheless superior to mortals. This intermediary position, however, raises the problem of evil daimons (demons): how can something superior to humans have the worst of human passions?

A SHORT HISTORY OF DEMONS

The Greek word *daimon* appears in Homer and other pre-Platonic sources as a term for a divine entity of unspecified type. When the Homeric heroes suspect divine intervention but, unlike the audience, are unaware which god has just acted, they attribute it to 'some daimon.'[18] Of course, unex-

---

[17] Plato, *Symposium* 203a.
[18] For a useful overview on daimons in Greek materials, see Brenk 1986. Greenbaum 2016 provides discussions of ideas of daimons throughout the tradition, particularly with respect

pected disasters are more likely to be blamed on some unknown force than successes that could be credited to one's own ability, so daimons are more often suspected at misfortunes. When a man's young son died unexpectedly, Plutarch tells us, he naturally suspected some daimonic intervention and consulted an oracle to determine what had happened. In that case, the oracle informed him that it wasn't a daimon, but, on another occasion when a mother noticed strange aberrations in her son's behavior, the miracle-worker Apollonius of Tyana was able to determine that the adolescent had been possessed by a demon and to expel the culprit, restoring her son to normal.[19] The amulet for the little Sophia-Priskilla who is struck by fever assumes that the affliction is caused by the attack of some daimon and seeks to drive it out.[20] Likewise, the premature deaths of children are at times blamed upon evil female demons who envy the mothers' achievement of bearing children.[21]

The betwixt and between status of daimons is often reflected in a monstrous appearance, especially for the evil daimons whose dreadful form betokens their dreadful deeds. In Polygnotus's fifth-century BCE painting of the Underworld at Delphi, there is a daimon, Eurynomos, who, Pausanias tells us, "is of a color between blue and black, like that of meat flies; he is showing his teeth and is seated, and under him is spread a vulture's skin."[22] Some demons, such as the Mormolukos or Mormohippos, seem to be partly bestial, while the Lamia sometimes appears with huge, sagging breasts, an erect phallus and large, filthy testicles.[23] Later sources, such

---

to their role in shaping an individual's life, in tension with the works of fortune (*tuchē*). For a study of the daimon in the Platonic tradition, see Timotin 2012.

[19] Plutarch, *Cons. Apoll.* 109a–d; Philostratus, *VA* 4.20.

[20] PGM LXXXIX.1–27. "I, Abrasax, shall deliver. Abrasax am I! ABRASAX ABRASICHO'OU, help little Sophia-Priskilla. Get hold of and do away with what comes to little Sophia-Priskilla, whether it is a Shivering Fit—get hold of it! Whether a Phantom—get hold of it! Whether a Daimon—get hold of it! I, Abrasax, shall deliver. Abrasax am I! ABRASAX ABRASICHO'OU. Get hold of, get hold of and do away with . . . what comes to little Sophia-Priskilla on this very day, whether it is a Shivering Fit—do away with it! Whether a Daimon—do away with it!"

[21] Cp. Sappho, fr. 178. "Zenobius, explaining a phrase used by Sappho, tells Gello's story: 'Fonder of children than Gello' is a saying used of those who died prematurely, or of those who are fond of children but ruin them by their upbringing. For Gello was a virgin, and because she died prematurely, the Lesbians say that her ghost haunts little children, and they attribute premature deaths to her." On the traditions of such demons, see further Johnston 1995 and Johnston 1999: 161–199.

[22] Pausanias 10.28.7. Cp. his description of the demonic ghost at Tmesa, 6.6.7–11: "Horribly black in color, and exceedingly dreadful in all his appearance, he had a wolf's skin thrown round him as a garment." Ovid provides a suitably grotesque image of a demonic Envy, *Met.* 2.775–782, but even this creature is predominantly anthropomorphic, rather than a *Mischwesen*, a combination of human and animal forms.

[23] See Johnston 1995 and Johnston 1999: 161–199 on these depictions, from a series of

as the *Testament of Solomon* and some of the so-called Gnostic texts, provide copious descriptions of such mixed monsters, including a demon with the body of a serpent with wings on its back but the face and feet of a man or another with the form of a horse in front and a fish behind.[24]

As Smith has pointed out, such hybrid creatures, representing violations of the categories that structure the world order, generally belong at the margins of the cosmic order, and so, whenever they intrude upon the normal order—to attack a small child with fever, for example—they must be relocated, sent back to the margins where they belong. Rituals of exorcism serve to expel these abnormal entities from normal space, restoring the normal order of which they have no part. Of course, other kinds of rituals of relocation can move such daimons from outside the normal world into it; the curse tablets that send spirits of the dead or other hostile and harmful entities provide ample examples of such rites.[25]

Such rites of relocation for demons presume a cosmic order in which normal mortals properly belong in the ordinary world, the gods in their heavenly world, and the demons outside either realm, what Smith calls a 'locative' cosmology. This kind of worldview, however, is often in tension with another, which Smith terms 'utopian,' in which the proper place of mankind is not actually the imperfect world we normally inhabit but more properly the perfect divine realm, from which we have fallen and to which we can return. Such a 'utopian' cosmology, which pervades the Platonic philosophical tradition, underlies the entire aim of theurgy to bring humans into contact with the gods. As Smith argues,

> Within a "utopian" world-view, it is man who is out of place, who is estranged from his true home "on high." The demons are "in place"—they have their spheres, their realms, their "houses." And thus the ritual adjustments are directed against the practitioner rather than the demon. It is the man who will daringly attempt his own redirection or relocation (frequently, as in theurgic materials, by reinterpreting the older rites).[26]

---

references in literature and images on vases, as illustrating the displacement of the demonic through the mixing of categorical taxa (human-animal, male-female, etc.).

[24] *Testament of Solomon* 14.1, 16.1; cp., e.g., the depiction of Ialtabaoth in the *Apocryphon of John* 10 as a lion-faced serpent.

[25] J. Smith 1978b: 428–429. Cp., e.g., PGM IV.3007–3086 and IV.1227–1264 for rites of exorcism. For curse tablets, see ch. 2, pp. 76–80.

[26] J. Smith 1978b: 438, who refers to PGM VIII.1–63 as an example. Recent scholars on theurgy have misconstrued Smith's important distinction between locative and utopian cosmologies, taking theurgy as an essentially locative system because of the elaborate celestial hierarchies involved. Cp. Addey 2014: 28–29 on theurgy in general, as well as Tanaseanu-Döbler 2013: 177 (on Salutius), 240 (on "Proclus' extremely static locative worldview"), and 282–283 (on Proclus and theurgy in general). Johnston 2004 argues for a mixed view, with

The demons thus have their places in the cosmic order, arranged in a hierarchy from the superior to the inferior, and such a hierarchy of daimonic entities enables the later Platonists to provide an answer to the problem of evil daimons—they merely fall somewhat lower on the hierarchy, and their overall ontological superiority to mortals is mitigated by their deficiencies in other regards. Iamblichus compares these daimons of limited capacity to a knife, which is supremely good at its one task of cutting; just so, certain entities have been allotted the task of one particular operation within the cosmic system, a task that may, like a knife's, seem to be entirely destructive.[27] Such an explanation of evil demons did not satisfy the Christian critics of theurgy or even many of the adherents of the tradition Hellenic polytheism, among whom the traditional locative ideas of evil demons often remained in tension with other, more utopian, cosmological ideas. Although the Platonic theurgists generally follow Plato's lead in assuming the benevolence of the divine, which was seen as actively cooperating in restoring human souls to the divine from which they descended, other more pessimistic cosmologies (often referred to as 'Gnostic') assume that many of the higher powers seek to keep human beings entrapped in the material world and prevent them from rising back to the divine realm. In such systems, the intermediary powers, whether the planetary gods and other astrological forces or other malevolent archons, appear as evil demons in contrast to the higher divinities who dwell in realms beyond the world.[28]

THE PERSONAL DAIMON

In some utopian systems, the souls of mortals return to their proper place only after death; the dead are 'coming home' to their rightful place as immortal beings. In a locative cosmology, by contrast, the spirits of the dead are in their proper place when they are safely tucked away in the underworld, but they are dangerous demons if they are in the normal world of humans, whether sent to attack a particular person or just roaming restlessly about. In the Greco-Roman tradition, the dead are often referred to

---

utopian aims in a locative system. However, a locative cosmology may have a rigid hierarchy of different ontological levels, such as the distinction between mortals and immortals in, e.g., the Homeric and Hesiodic poems, but Smith here explicitly gives the example of theurgy in discussing the movement through the cosmic hierarchy of a utopian cosmology.

[27] Iamblichus, de myst. 4.1. Cp. Plutarch, de facie 945a–d on certain souls dominated by their passionate elements. Iamblichus argues (de myst. 4.13) that what some people take for evil demons are actually disembodied human souls still stained with mortal passions.

[28] Cp. the accounts in Origen, Contra Celsum 6.30–31; Apocryphon of John 10–11, 15–19. Williams 1996 provides a useful warning about the term 'Gnostic' and the problems with that category in modern scholarship.

as daimons, starting with Hesiod, who transforms the earlier races of mortals into daimons who dwell on or below the earth. The dead are given offerings and prayers in funeral cults throughout the Greco-Roman world, especially by the family and descendants of the dead, but also by a wider community in the case of those dead whose memory is honored for their deeds.[29] Apuleius, in his essay *On the God of Socrates*, plays with the Latin terms for ancestral spirits (*Lares*) and for restless ghosts (*larvae*) to claim that they are all forms of the daimonic spirits the Romans call *genii*. Plato, in his *Cratylus*, has Socrates make the claim that, although the poets say that a good man becomes a daimon after he dies, any good man should be called a daimon even before he dies, since the term signifies his wise and knowing spirit.[30]

The prime example of a man with a wise and knowing spirit, for Plato and his followers, was of course Socrates himself, and much of the discussion of what that daimonic element actually means centers around the question of the *daimonion* of Socrates, the little daimon that Socrates claims helps direct him in making important decisions.[31] Not only Apuleius, but also Plutarch devoted a work to the issue of Socrates's daimon, and the way that Socrates's *daimonion* guided him serves as the model for later Platonic discussions of the personal guardian spirit of each person. Plato himself mentions the idea of a daimonic spirit that serves as a guardian and guide to each individual. In the myth of Er at the end of the *Republic*, he describes how each soul coming into incarnation receives (through a combination of lot and choice) a daimon that shapes his destiny, while in the myth of the *Phaedo* he describes how the guardian daimon conducts the soul of one who has died to the underworld for judgment, just as it had guided him in life.[32]

Plato is clearly adapting a previously existing idea of such a spirit, but the evidence for the traditional idea he is manipulating is scanty, with little beyond Heraclitus's famous dictum "Character is fate" (literally, character is the daimon of a person).[33] Later Platonists, however, develop the idea

[29] Hesiod, *Works and Days* 109–193; cp. Pausanias 1.32.3–4, who refers to the spirits of the fighters (and horses) at Marathon who are honored as daimons by the people of Marathon.

[30] Apuleius, *de deo Socratis* 152–154; Plato, *Cratylus* 398c, playing off the resemblance of the word δαήμονες (knowing) and δαίμονες.

[31] The key passages are Plato, *Phaedrus* 242b–c and *Apology* 40a–c, along with Xenophon, *Apology of Socrates* 10–13.

[32] Plato, *Republic* 617d. "Your daimon will not be allotted to you, but you choose your daimon; and let him who draws the first lot have the first choice, and the life which he chooses shall be his destiny." *Phaedo* 107e. "For after death, as they say, the daimon of each individual, to whom he belonged in life, leads him to a certain place in which the dead are gathered together for judgment."

[33] Heraclitus, fr. 121; cp. Menander, fr. 550: "A daimon is appointed as a mystagogue for

in detail, using the personal daimon as a way to talk about all the choices an individual makes in life. As Proclus comments on the reference to the daimon in the Platonic *Alcibiades I,*

> The guardian spirit alone moves, controls and orders all our affairs, since it perfects the reason, moderates the emotions, infuses nature, maintains the body, supplies accidentals, fulfils the decree of fate and bestows the gifts of providence; and this one being is ruler of all that lies in us and concerns us, steering our whole life.[34]

Proclus gives the daimon a maximal role in the guidance of human life, but other thinkers take pains to distinguish the daimon's limits in its participation with the human being. Plotinus in particular insists that the daimon, as a divine entity, rises superior to the mortal human life to which it is connected.

> This guardian spirit is not entirely outside but only in the sense that he is not bound to us, and is not active in us but is ours, to speak in terms of soul, but not ours if we are considered as men of a particular kind who have a life which is subject to him.[35]

Plotinus describes the daimon as something somehow within the individual and belonging to that individual's soul, but yet still somehow unsubordinated to the mortal existence.

The Psychology of Theurgy

How the relation of the personal daimon to the individual is imagined depends upon the way that the nature of the individual human is understood, and the relation of the daimon to the soul and the other elements that comprise the individual is thus described in different ways. The basic distinction between body (*soma*) and soul (*psyche*) is taken for granted, but some thinkers also distinguish an intellect or mind (*nous*) from the principle of life (*psyche*) that animates the inert material body (*soma*). Plutarch's image of the way mind and soul and body are related is particularly vivid.

> Every soul partakes of understanding; none is irrational or unintelligent. But the portion of the soul that mingles with flesh and passions suffers alteration and becomes in the pleasures and pains it undergoes

---

every person as soon as he is born." Both suggest the idea of a daimon guiding every individual, but details are lacking.

[34] Proclus on *Alcibiades* 78 (trans. O'Neill 1965).

[35] Plotinus, *Enneads* 3.4.5. See the discussion of Pachoumi 2013 for an overview of the philosophical ideas of the interrelation.

is irrational. Not every soul mingles to the same extent: some sink entirely into the body, and becoming disordered throughout, are during their life wholly distracted by passions; others mingle in part, but leave outside what is purest in them. This is not dragged in with the rest, but is like a buoy attached to the top, floating on the surface in contact with the man's head, while he is as it were submerged in the depths; and it supports as much of the soul, which is held upright about it, as is obedient and not overpowered by the passions. Now the part carried submerged in the body is called the soul, whereas the part left free from corruption is called by the multitude the understanding, who take it to be within themselves, as they take reflected objects to be in the mirrors that reflect them; but those who conceive the matter rightly call it a daemon, as being external.[36]

The soul is the portion of the divine and immortal intellect that is submerged in the body in the process of incarnation; the mind itself may appear to be in the body but really floats above it, at least for those individuals who are not so sunk in the affections of the body that they pay no heed to the guidance of this daimon.

Other philosophers describe the interaction of mind, body, and soul in different ways, mediating the mind-body problem (as it is called in modern philosophy) with the idea of a special vehicle that brings the soul down into the body. Drawing on images of a vehicle of the soul in Plato, most notably the soul-chariot in Plato's *Phaedrus*, the immaterial soul is imagined to be carried down into the material body in a vehicle (*ochēma*) that is neither immaterial nor entirely material. Combining Plato's reference to the visible vehicles of the divine stars and Aristotle's designation of the stuff of stars as the fifth element of *pneuma*, later thinkers saw the vehicle of the soul as made of *pneuma*, sometimes illuminated with light like the stars and sometimes clouded and murky with the stains of lower matter.[37] Like Plutarch's life-buoy, the pneumatic vehicle of the soul mediates between the two worlds in different ways for different souls, depending on how its pneumatic material is shaped and influenced in its descent into the body. As it descends into the material, the pneumatic vehicle passes through the various spheres of the heavens and thus receives the influences

---

[36] Plutarch, *de genio Soc.* 591d–e.

[37] As Kissling 1922: 318 puts it, "The theory of the ὄχημα-πνεῦμα, as met with in the Neo-Platonic writers, represents the reconciliation of Plato and Aristotle on a subject which the former never taught and the latter was incapable of defining intelligibly." The passages in question are Plato, *Timaeus* 41e, and Aristotle, *Gen. An.* 736b37–38. Cp. Damascius, *in Parm.* II.255.7–11: "Like a sponge, the soul [in embodiment] loses nothing of its being but simply becomes rarified or densified. Just so does the immortal body of the soul remain individually the same, but sometimes is made more spherical and sometimes less; sometimes it is filled with divine light and sometimes with the stains of generative acts."

of the various powers of each level, especially the influence of the astral and planetary divinities, so the configuration of the pneumatic vehicle is thus shaped by the astrological configurations during its descent.[38] Tanaseanu-Döbler explains Synesius's ideas, which rest in part upon his interpretations of the *Chaldaean Oracles*.

> During its descent, the soul gathers pneuma from the astral sphere which forms its first body and vehicle, the seat of the imaginative faculty. This vehicle then enables the soul to connect with a material body and mitigates the clash of extremes. Spellbound by nature and matter, the soul renounces its freedom and becomes a slave to matter, a situation from which deliverance is possible only with the hardest, truly Heraclean labours. Certain cathartic rituals (*teletai*) provide help toward the ascent.[39]

Synesius refers to ritual means of purifying the vehicle of the soul, which serve to enable things done in the material world to have an effect on the immaterial soul. Hierocles likewise mentions the importance of ritual purifications for the 'luminous body,' his term for what the *Chaldaean Oracles* call the 'fine vehicle of the soul.' The rational element of the soul can only be purified, argues this Neopythagorean Neoplatonist, by abstract mathematics and philosophical dialectic, but the pneumatic vehicle that brings the soul into the body requires ritual purification in order to rise back to communion with the gods.

> Surely then it is necessary that telestic purifications go along with mathematical purifications and that hieratic elevation accompany the deliverance wrought by dialectics. These practices in a special way purify and perfect the pneumatic vehicle of the rational soul: they separate it from the lifelessness of matter, and they also render it to be in a capable state for the fellowship of pure spirits. For it is not lawful for the impure to lay hold of the pure.[40]

[38] Porphyry, fr. 271, preserved in Stobaeus 2.8.42, discusses the relation between the descending soul and the horoscope, linking it to the choice of lives in Plato's myth of Er (*Rep.* 614b–621d). Cp. Proclus, *in Tim.* I.147–148, where the influence of the planetary spheres is linked to ethical qualities.

[39] Tanaseanu-Döbler 2013: 169, who discusses Synesius, *de insomn.* 6.2. Cp. Iamblichus apud Simplicius, *in Arist. Cat.* 374: "When the soul comes into each part of the cosmos, it accepts certain lives and powers, some of which it projects itself and others it receives from the cosmos. In each part of the universe, there are appropriate bodies; some it receives from the cosmos and other organic bodies it makes in accordance with its own *logoi*. These powers, lives, and bodies it puts aside whenever it changes to another allotment. From this, it is clear that all these are acquired for the soul and that the soul has them as different from its own essence."

[40] Hierocles, *in aurum pyth.* 26.22 (trans. Schibli 2002). Cp. 26.3–4 on the luminous body

The *Chaldaean Oracles* do warn against defiling the *pneuma*, and Psellos comments, "The Chaldaean says that we cannot be borne up to god, unless we strengthen the vehicle of the soul through material rites. For he believes that the soul is purified by stones, herbs, and conjurations in order to become well-wheeled for the ascent."[41] The soul-chariot needs good wheels to lift the soul back up into the company of the gods as it is described in Plato's *Phaedrus*, and theurgic rituals provide the means to fix up this pneumatic vehicle so that the immortal and divine soul can soar once more among the gods to which it is akin.

Assimilation to the Divine

Plato at various points in his dialogues defines virtuous and philosophical living as a process of assimilation to the divine as far as is humanly possible, and such a process involves tending to that personal daimon.[42]

> But he who has seriously devoted himself to learning and to true thoughts, and has exercised these qualities above all his others, must necessarily and inevitably think thoughts that are immortal and divine, if so be that he lays hold on truth, and in so far as it is possible for human nature to partake of immortality, he must fall short thereof in no degree; and inasmuch as he is for ever tending his divine part and duly magnifying that daimon who dwells along with him, he must be supremely blessed.[43]

Cultivating one's daimon well (*eu*) makes one blessedly happy (*eudaimon*) because the individual becomes more and more like the divine and thus more loved by the gods, who love what is like themselves.

Betz has pointed out the way the Delphic maxim, "Know thyself," was reinterpreted within the philosophical tradition to mean not simply 'know your human nature' but rather 'know the divine element within you that is most truly you.' Starting from the Platonic *Alcibiades*, in which the soul, immortal and divine, is identified as the true self, the admonition to know oneself is developed into a directive to seek understanding of the divine

---

and the Chaldaean vehicle (*CO* 120). Porphyry too thinks that theurgic ritual can only purify the pneumatic vehicle, not the soul itself, a position for which he is excoriated in Augustine, *Civ. Dei* 10.9 and 10.27 (Porphyry, fr. 288, 290, 287).

[41] Psellos, in *Chald. Orac.* 132 = PG 122 1132a; *CO* 104 = Psellos, *in Chald. Orac.* 137 = PG 122 1137c.

[42] Plato, *Theaetetus* 176b. ὁμοίωσις θεῷ κατὰ τὸ δυνατόν. Cp. *Republic* 613b; *Laws* 716c–d. This slogan becomes a standard definition of philosophy among the Neoplatonic authors, e.g., Olympiodorus, in *Phd.* 1.2: ὁμοίωσις γὰρ θεῷ ἡ φιλοσοφία.

[43] Plato, *Timaeus* 90c.

through and by means of the divine element within oneself.[44] Such an attempt to connect with the divine provides the basis for all theurgy.

Later Platonists develop this idea of assimilation to the divine through virtuous action to include ritual actions. As Saloustios argues,

> The truth simply is that, when we are good, we are joined to the gods by our likeness to them; when bad, we are separated from them by our unlikeness. And when we live according to virtue we cling to the gods, and when we become evil we make the gods our enemies—not because they are angered against us, but because our sins prevent the light of the gods from shining upon us, and put us in communion with spirits of punishment.[45]

The gods, being perfect and good according to this Platonist model, neither suffer anger nor demand gifts from mortals, but they simply radiate their goodwill to all things in the cosmos that are sufficiently attuned to their divinity to accept it. Drawing on the theurgical ideas of Iamblichus, Saloustios continues,

> The providence of the Gods reaches everywhere and needs only some congruity [epitēdeiotēs] for its reception. All congruity comes about by representation and likeness; for which reason the temples are made in representation of heaven, the altar of earth, the images of life—that is why they are made like living things—the prayers of the element of thought, the mystic letters of the unspeakable celestial forces, the herbs and stones of matter, and the sacrificial animals of the irrational life in us.[46]

[44] Cp. Betz 1990, who discusses *Alcibiades* 130e and *Corpus Hermeticum* I.18, where the divine *nous* of the individual is linked with divine *nous* of the cosmos. Cicero, *Tusc.* 5.70 interprets the Delphic maxim as that the mind should know its own self and feel its union with the divine mind, while in his Dream of Scipio he has the claim that only the body is mortal, whereas the individual is a god (*Rep.* 6.9–29).

[45] Saloustios, *de deis* 14.2. Ἡμεῖς δὲ ἀγαθοὶ μὲν ὄντες δι' ὁμοιότητα Θεοῖς συναπτόμεθα, κακοὶ δὲ γενόμενοι δι' ἀνομοιότητα χωριζόμεθα· καὶ κατ' ἀρετὰς μὲν ζῶντες ἐχόμεθα τῶν Θεῶν, κακοὶ δὲ γενόμενοι ἐχθροὺς ἡμῖν ποιοῦμεν ἐκείνους, οὐκ ἐκείνων ὀργιζομένων ἀλλὰ τῶν ἁμαρτημάτων Θεοὺς μὲν ἡμῖν οὐκ ἐώντων ἐλλάμπειν Δαίμοσι δὲ κολαστικοῖς συναπτόντων (trans. Murray 1925). For the same idea, cp., e.g., Iamblichus, *de myst.* 8.7.

[46] Saloustios, *de deis* 15.2. Καὶ ἡ μὲν Πρόνοια τῶν Θεῶν διατείνει πανταχῇ, ἐπιτηδειότητος δὲ μόνον πρὸς ὑποδοχὴν δεῖται· πᾶσα δὲ ἐπιτηδειότης μιμήσει καὶ ὁμοιότητι γίνεται, διὸ ὁ μὲν ναοὶ τὸν οὐρανόν, οἱ δὲ βωμοὶ μιμοῦνται τὴν γῆν, τὰ δὲ ἀγάλματα τὴν ζωήν—καὶ διὰ τοῦτο ζῴοις ἀπείκασται— αἱ δὲ εὐχαὶ τὸ νοερόν, οἱ δὲ χαρακτῆρες τὰς ἀρρήτους ἄνω δυνάμεις, βοτάναι δὲ καὶ λίθοι τὴν ὕλην, τὰ δὲ θυόμενα ζῷα τὴν ἐν ἡμῖν ἄλογον ζωήν (trans. Murray 1925). Cp. the idea in the Hermetic *Asclepius* 3, that nature manifests in images of the divine to please the divine. "God prepared matter as a receptacle for omniform forms, but nature, imaging matter with forms by means of the four elements, causes all things to reach as far as heaven so that they will be pleasing in the sight of god."

All virtuous worship of the gods, for Saloustios, thus requires bringing things into this congruity with the divine, both the worshipper and the material elements of the rituals, from the sacrificial animals and incense to the altars and temples themselves.

"Everything Is Full of Gods"

The omnipresence of the divine and divine providence is another crucial idea in this kind of cosmology deriving from the Platonic *Timaeus*; the divine stretches even to the lowest levels of created matter.[47] Iamblichus describes the universe as a single living being, whose parts all relate to one another like the parts of an animal.[48] Just as the human being is comprised of different elements of mind, soul, and body, so too this arrangement mirrors the elements of the cosmos itself, which has a material body (*hyle* or matter), an immaterial soul (sometimes called the 'World Soul'), and a divine Intellect that orders it all. The basic elements of this schema appear in Plato's *Timaeus*, but various developments of this triadic pattern appear in later sources.[49] The divine Intellect or *Nous* is referred to as the Paternal Intellect in the *Chaldaean Oracles*, but it is often identified with Zeus, the father of the gods, or with the Sun (as Helios, Apollo, Mithras, etc.). The feminine element of the soul (Psyche) may be equated with the element of life (Zoe) or nature (Physis) or with the providential care of the divine (Providentia/Pronoia) or even with particular goddesses, such as Hekate in the *Chaldaean Oracles* or Barbelo in certain so-called Gnostic texts. In the more elaborate cosmologies, this triadic pattern may be replicated on multiple levels of ontology; Proclus particularly loves to proliferate triads, articulating more levels in between the highest and lowest, while other thinkers prefer simpler systems.

Proclus quotes the slogan "Everything is full of gods."[50] Every portion of the universe thus has an element of divinity appropriate to it, more at the ontologically higher levels and less at the lower.

---

[47] Mazur 2004: 37 has characterized this idea as an 'axiom of continuous hierarchy,' "which entails that an ontologically-inferior principle can never control an ontologically-superior one, and, concomitantly, that no ethically-inferior entity could end up in a position of dominance over an ethically-superior one." Thus, the arrangement is hierarchical both ontologically, in that more divine entities are more powerful than less divine ones, and ethically, in that more divine entities are also more good than the less divine ones.

[48] Iamblichus, *de myst.* 4.12: ἓν ζῷόν ἐστι τὸ πᾶν; cp. the slogan ἓν τὸ πᾶν of the alchemists.

[49] See Edmonds 2004: 277–279 for a brief overview.

[50] Proclus, *Elem. Theol.* 145.20. μεστὰ δὲ πάντα θεῶν; cp. Iamblichus, *de myst.* 1.9. The idea seems to echo the claim of Thales, as quoted by Plato, *Laws* 899b; and Aristotle, *de anima* 1.5 411a8.

Things on earth are full of heavenly gods; things in heaven are full of supercelestials; and each chain continues abounding up to its final members. For what is in the One-before-all makes its appearance in all, in which are also communications between souls set beneath one god or another.[51]

These 'chains' are series of correspondences that link the parallel elements at every level of the universe, uniting the highest with the lowest. Proclus provides the example of a chain of the sun, which includes animals such as the rooster and the lion, as well as plants like the sunflower and minerals such as the sunstone, each of which partakes of some connection to the sun, just as the visible sun itself is connected to the higher solar powers that transcend the perceptible world. Some of these elements in the chain partake more thoroughly than others, with the result that the rooster, for example, is more closely linked to the sun than the lion (which causes, Proclus tells us, the lion to shrink back in fear at the sight of a rooster).[52] The lower elements reflect the divine illumination of the higher, as the sunstone glitters with golden rays or the sunflower follows the movement of the sun across the sky. Proclus describes this link as a form of worship.

> Why do heliotropes [*sunflowers*] move together with the Sun, selenotropes [*moonflowers*] with the Moon, moving around to the extent of their ability with the luminaries of the cosmos? All things pray according to their own order and sing hymns, either intellectually or rationally or naturally or sensibly, to heads of entire chains. And since the heliotrope is also moved toward that to which it readily opens, if anyone hears it striking the air as it moves about, he perceives in the sound that it offers to the King the kind of hymn that a plant can sing.[53]

Plutarch, by contrast, uses the metaphor of the rainbow, where the rays of the sun falling down upon the material world interact with the drops of water in a cloud or spray and refract the divine light into the colorful

---

[51] Proclus, *de sacr.* 149.28–150.2 (trans. Copenhaver 2015). Οὕτω μεστὰ πάντα θεῶν, τὰ μὲν ἐν γῇ τῶν οὐρανίων, τὰ δὲ ἐν οὐρανῷ τῶν ὑπὲρ τὸν οὐρανόν, καὶ πρόεισιν ἑκάστη πληθυομένη σειρὰ μέχρι τῶν ἐσχάτων· τὰ γὰρ ἐν ἑνὶ πρὸ τῶν πάντων, ταῦτα ἐν πᾶσιν ἐξεφάνη. Cp. the articulation of the same principle of the connections between levels in the chain in *Elem. Theol.* 145–146.

[52] Proclus, *de sacr.* 148.10; 149.19–22; 150.3–12.

[53] Proclus, *de sacr.* 148.10–18 (trans. Copenhaver 2015). ῍Η πόθεν ἡλιοτρόπια μὲν ἡλίῳ, σεληνοτρόπια δὲ σελήνη συγκινεῖται συμπεριπολοῦντα ἐς δύναμιν τοῖς τοῦ κόσμου φωστῆρσιν; Εὔχεται γὰρ πάντα κατὰ τὴν οἰκείαν τάξιν καὶ ὑμνεῖ τοὺς ἡγεμόνας τῶν σειρῶν ὅλων ἢ νοερῶς ἢ λογικῶς ἢ φυσικῶς ἢ αἰσθητῶς· ἐπεὶ καὶ τὸ ἡλιοτρόπιον ᾧ ἔστιν εὔλυτον, τούτῳ κινεῖται καί, εἰ δή τις αὐτοῦ κατὰ τὴν περιστροφὴν ἀκούειν τὸν ἀέρα πλήσσοντος οἷός τε ἦν, ὕμνον ἄν τινα διὰ τοῦ ἤχου τούτου συνῄσθετο τῷ Βασιλεῖ προσάγοντος, ὃν δύναται φυτὸν ὑμνεῖν.

rainbow.[54] The colors of the rainbow serve to indicate the light, which could not be clearly seen without its refraction; they provide traces or signs of the sunlight, tokens of its presence just like the movement of the sunflower or the glitter of the sunstone.

The Signs of the Gods: Symbola, Synthemata, Ichnē

These traces (*ichnē*) or tokens (*synthemata*) are referred to as symbols (*symbola*) of the divine, and each of these words denotes a thing (a footprint, a stamped image, or even a coin or stick broken in two, each half of which fits together with the other) that indicates some other thing beyond it. Peirce's distinction between types of signs may be useful here to show the range of ways in which a *synthema* may relate to the divine element higher in its chain. An *index* bears a causal relation to its signified, like a footprint to a foot or a rainbow to the sun, whereas an *icon* bears some qualitative similarity to its referent, like a sunflower with its golden petals to the sun. A Peircean symbol has a relation that is neither causal nor qualitative, but involves a more complex logical connection, like the rooster that crows at sunrise to the sun.[55] The *synthemata* mentioned by the ancient sources on theurgy bear all of these kinds of relations, and these sources do not distinguish between the types of relations as the modern semiotician Peirce does. The modern distinctions, however, can help remind us how wide the range of meaning for such *symbola/synthemata* is—they are not simply words or images or material substances, but may be any or all of these things.[56]

These signs appear throughout the universe through the providential plan of the highest divinity, a manifestation of his grace and favor. "For the Paternal Intellect has sown symbols throughout the cosmos," proclaims one of the *Chaldaean Oracles*, and Proclus elaborates upon this same idea.

> For as the fathers of all things brought everything into being, they sowed into everything tokens and traces. . . . In everything existent, down to the very last, there is a token of the ineffable cause itself that is beyond the intelligible, a token through which everything is connected back to it, some further and some nearer, depending on the clarity or vagueness of the token that is in them, and this is what

[54] Plutarch, *Amatorius* 765e–f; cp. *de Is. et Os.* 74 381e.

[55] Cp. Peirce 1991: 183. Proclus, *Theol. Plat.* VI.14, 68–69 notes that such relations can work through similiarity or dissimiliarity; cp. Proclus, *in Remp.* I.86.15–19.

[56] As Tanaseanu-Döbler 2013: 247 puts it, "*Symbolon* or *synthema* is anything which establishes and signifies correspondences between different entities in the ontological hierarchy." Cp. "συνθήματα of a divine class are its characteristic properties, τὰ ἴδια, or the symbolic expressions of those properties" (Tanaseanu-Döbler 2013: 237).

moves everything toward the desire of the good and instills into the existing things this inextinguishable love.[57]

These connecting tokens, which are generated by the highest for the lowest, motivate the lower entities to try to reach back to the higher, and they are enabled to do so to the extent that the signs are clear indicators of their origins. While beauty is, in the Platonic tradition, always the clearest sign of the divine, the range of tokens and symbols includes even things whose relation to the divine is less apparent, including the names that are the subject of discussion in Plato's *Cratylus* (the text upon which Proclus is commenting here).[58]

The names of gods and their traditional epithets provide one kind of connective symbol for the mortal worshipper, but theurgists make use of less traditional and well-known names that have an extra-ordinary power of connection with the divine, as well as other kinds of words and sounds, whose connection is less obvious to the uninitiate. Iamblichus defends at length the use of seemingly incomprehensible names and words, the *nomina barbara* that are sometimes referred to as *voces magicae*. These apparently meaningless words, he argues, signify things that are beyond ordinary human intelligibility: "thus, the symbolic character of divine similitude, which is intellectual and divine, has to be assumed in the names." In some cases, the words come from the languages of ancient peoples, such as the Assyrians or Egyptians, to whom the gods provided special revelation, and the very sounds of the words are significant and would lose their power if translated. "For the barbarian names possess weightiness and great precision, participating in less ambiguity, variability, and multitude of expression. For all these reasons, then, they are adapted to the superior beings."[59] Iamblichus further warns that any alteration of these symbolic names can disrupt their connective power, just like the breaking of a single string can disrupt the harmony of the whole intrument, and the *Chaldaean Oracles* likewise admonish, "Do not change the *nomina barbara*!"[60]

---

[57] Proclus, *in Crat.* 71.18–19, 29–35. πάντα γὰρ ὑφιστάνοντες οἱ πατέρες τῶν ὅλων, συνθήματα καὶ ἴχνη πᾶσιν ἐνέσπειραν· . . . ἀλλὰ αὐτῆς τῆς ἀρρήτου καὶ ἐπέκεινα τῶν νοητῶν αἰτίας ἐστὶν ἑκάστῳ τῶν ὄντων σύνθημα καὶ μέχρι τῶν ἐσχάτων, δι' οὗ πάντα εἰς ἐκείνην ἀνήρτηνται τὰ μὲν πορρώτερον τὰ δ' ἐγγύτερον κατὰ τὴν τρανότητα καὶ τὴν ἀμυδρότητα τοῦ ἐν αὐτοῖς συνθήματος, καὶ τοῦτό ἐστιν τὸ πάντα κινοῦν εἰς τὸν τοῦ ἀγαθοῦ πόθον καὶ ἄσβεστον τὸν ἔρωτα τοῦτον παρεχόμενον τοῖς οὖσιν (trans. Tanaseanu-Döbler 2013: 238). Cp. *CO* 108. Σύμβολα γὰρ πατρικὸς νόος ἔσπειρεν κατὰ κόσμον, quoted earlier in the treatise by Proclus, *in Crat.* 20.31.

[58] Cp. Plato, *Phaedrus* 250d–e.

[59] Iamblichus, *de myst.* 7.4.7–9; 7.5.11–13. Cp. Proclus, *in Crat.* 95 172, who takes Socrates's comments on the name of Persephone in the *Cratylus* as an exhortation to pay attention to the form of divine names.

[60] Iamblichus, *de myst.* 5.21; *CO* 150 = Psellos, *in Chald. Orac.* 132 = PG 122 1132 c1–3

Such *synthemata* need not even be words in a foreign tongue; the sacred tokens of the gods may be inarticulate sounds, strings of vowels or hissing and popping noises of the kind found often in the Greek Magical Papyri. Nicomachus of Gerasa (c. 60–c. 120 CE), in his treatise on music, links the seven vowels of the Greek alphabet with the seven planetary spheres and the sounds that they make as they revolve in the heavens, and, in what is perhaps the earliest extant use of the term 'theurgist,' he claims, "Thus, whenever the theurgists are conducting such acts of worship they make invocation symbolically with hissings and poppings, and inarticulate and discordant sounds."[61] The very incomprehensibility of such sounds to the ordinary listener indicates their extra-ordinary function as symbolic connectors to the divine.

Such hissings and poppings are not the only incomprehensible signs that the theurgists use to make contact with the divine; various sources make mention of *charakteres*, incomprehensible drawn figures that seem to resemble letters or images but without any clear iconic resemblance.[62] Again, such inexplicability adds to their power in connecting with the gods, as the Emperor Julian explains.

"For nature loves to hide," and the hidden core of the gods' substance does not bear to be thrown by naked words into impure ears. This is why the ineffable nature of the *charakteres* is by nature useful even if unknown; for it cures not only the souls, but also the bodies, and it brings about the presence of the gods.[63]

Saloustios describes such *charakteres* as images of the ineffable powers above, a way of symbolically representing heavenly powers that are impossible to represent through comprehensible words or iconic images.[64] In the Greek Magical Papyri, such *charakteres* are often found in conjunction with incomprehensible *voces magicae* as part of an invocation to a

---

(who explains, "that is, the names handed down by the gods to each race have ineffable power in the rites"). Cp. Simplicius, *in Enchiridion Epicteti* 94.42–46. "Just as in the case of a word, if letters are left off or added on, the form of the word is lost, so with divine works and words, if anything is left off or added on, or mixed up, the divine illumination will not take place."

[61] Nicomachus of Gerasa, *Excerpta* 6.276.12–18. διὸ δὴ ὅταν μάλιστα οἱ θεουργοὶ τὸ τοιοῦτον σεβάζωνται, σιγμοῖς τε καὶ ποππυσμοῖς καὶ ἀνάρθροις καὶ ἀσυμφώνοις ἤχοις συμβολικῶς ἐπικαλοῦνται. The reference to the vowels comes immediately before (8–12).

[62] Gordon 2011b provides the best discussion of these symbols. Dzwiza 2012 announces her new project on the *charakteres*, cataloging and classifying all the evidence.

[63] Julian, *Against the Cynic Heraclius* 11 216c–d (trans. Tanaseanu-Döbler 2013). «φιλεῖ γὰρ ἡ φύσις κρύπτεσθαι», καὶ τὸ ἀποκεκρυμμένον τῆς τῶν θεῶν οὐσίας οὐκ ἀνέχεται γυμνοῖς εἰς ἀκαθάρτους ἀκοὰς ῥίπτεσθαι ῥήμασιν. Ὅπερ δὲ δὴ τῶν χαρακτήρων ἡ ἀπόρρητος φύσις ὠφελεῖν πέφυκε καὶ ἀγνοουμένη· θεραπεύει γοῦν οὐ ψυχὰς μόνον, ἀλλὰ καὶ σώματα, καὶ θεῶν ποιεῖ παρουσίας.

[64] Saloustios, *De deis* 15.2 (see ch. 10, p. 332, n. 45).

particular god.[65] Iamblichus, in response to Porphyry's critique of diviners who stand upon *charakteres*, argues that, although there are indeed ordinary and easily accessible *charakteres* that deceptively leave the user open only to the influence of evil daimones, "but there is that type which truly connects with the gods, uncontaminated in all respects, pure, unwavering, true."[66] Such symbols, like the special words revealed by the gods, do enable the true theurgical practitioner to make contact with the divine, even if the difference between the truly efficacious *charakteres* and the deceptive ones may not be apparent to those who approach the procedure hastily and without sufficient philosophical training and purification.

Even physical substances, such as plants and stones, can serve as *synthemata* that connect mortals to the gods, like the sunstone and moonstone in Proclus's theory of 'chains.' The *Chaldaean Oracles* mention a mysterious *mnizouris* stone that is to be offered to an earthly daimon, for the reception of stones that correspond with them is pleasing to the gods, an idea that appears in the some of the treatises on the magical properties of stones.[67] For Iamblichus, it is important to note that all matter is potentially receptive of the gods, even if not everything to the same degree. This potential receptivity for divine power is described as congruity or fitness (*epitēdeiotēs*), the same term that might be used to describe the fitness of dry wood to produce fire.[68] Plotinus uses the image of light being received in clear or murky water to describe the varying levels of fitness (*epitēdeiotēs*) of an individual soul to receive divine illumination, but elsewhere he talks of the ways in which something might be made receptive by mirroring the image of the divine.[69] The *symbola* and *synthemata*, then, in all these theories of theurgical activity, serve as elements within the lower material world that provide the user with connections to the powers

[65] E.g. PGM II.154–155, among many others.

[66] Iamblichus, *de myst.* 3.13 130 (trans. E. C. Clarke, Dillon, and Hershbell 2003).

[67] Cp. *Orphic Lithika* 176: "No one denies that crystal makes the blessed ones happy." οὔτις τοι μακάρων ἀρνήσεται εὐχωλῇσι; cp. 195, 232, 244–246, etc. Tardieu 2010 argues that the *mnizouris* or *mnouziris* stone takes its name from its exotic place of origin, Mouziris, a trading port in southwest India (Kerala) and that it was used in ritual fumigations.

[68] As Shaw 1995: 86 notes, "Coined in the second century C.E. to describe the kind of Aristotelian 'potency' (*dunamis*) sufficient for 'actualization' (*energeia*) of a form, *epitēdeiotēs* came to be used by Neoplatonists to account for differences in mystical experiences. Just as 'dry wood' provided the capacity (*epitēdeiotēs*) for fire to be actualized, so, analogously, the purity of a soul provided the capacity for a god to become manifest." The example of dry wood appears in Sextus Empiricus, *Adv. Math.* 9.243.

[69] Plotinus, *Enneads* 6.4.11.3–10; cp. 4.3.1.1–7. "And I think that the wise men of old, who made temples and statues in the wish the gods should be present to them, looking to the nature of the All, had in mind that the nature of soul is everywhere easy to attract, but that if someone were able to construct something receptive [*prospathes*] to it and able to receive a part of it, it would of all things receive soul most easily. That which is receptive [*prospathes*] to it is what imitates it in some way, like a mirror is able to catch a form."

of the higher world, whether through a series within a chain (as in Proclus's view) or more directly, as a special name or figure revealed by the gods themselves.

Theoretical Critiques of Theurgy

The idea that manipulation of these symbols within the mortal world can create effects among the divine powers is not without resistance among some of the Neoplatonic philosophers. The systematic theory of theurgy that is outlined by Iamblichus in *de mysteriis* provides the response to the questions raised by his colleague Porphyry, and, although Iamblichus dismisses some of the critiques as based upon misunderstandings of theurgic practice, there are nevertheless some substantive philosophical and theological points of controversy. These controversies have been analyzed in detail in the scholarship, but a couple of key points are worth outlining here, since they bear upon the distinctions the critics (and their respondents) draw between theurgy (as true philosophy and/or religion) and magic (*goēteia*). The biggest issue is how the theurgist can, as a lowly mortal, manipulate the higher divine powers, since such entitities must be (according to the Neoplatonic 'axiom of continuous hierarchy') both ontologically and ethically superior.[70] This issue involves both the limits of the power of theurgy and the way that it operates.

Plotinus, for example, claims that, although sympathetic connections between material substances such as stones and plants may indeed produce effects inside the material world, to harm or heal the body, their effects are limited to their own lower ontological levels; the soul and the intellect are immune to such things, as are the spiritual entitities that exist at such higher levels. Plotinus labels as 'deception' and 'magic' (*goēteia*) the attempts to claim effects beyond the material level and even claims that someone who is perfectly directed by his higher elements of soul and mind can shrug off the effects of magic spells (although they may affect his body).[71] The Christian Neoplatonist Synesius praises the wisdom of those who can manipulate the correspondences within the cosmos, but he too limits their effects to the material realm; whatever divinity lies outside the

[70] In the phrase of Mazur 2004. For analyses of the Neoplatonic debates, the most recent treatments are Tanaseanu-Döbler 2013 and Addey 2014, both of whom go through the variety of sources in detail.

[71] Plotinus, *Enneads* 4.4.40–44. Porphyry's story, *Vit. Plot.* 10, of Plotinus repelling the attack of another philosopher, Olympius of Alexandria, who attempted to bring a star-strike on him, serves to illustrate Plotinus's idea. Plotinus admits that his body is affected by the attack, using the image from Plato's *Symposium* of a moneybag whose drawstrings are drawn tight, but even these somatic effects seem to have rebounded upon Olympius, who refrains from further attacks.

material cosmos is immune.[72] For Iamblichus, however, and for Proclus after him, the effects of theurgical operations are not limited, because the connections between the material world and the higher realms are uninterrupted and continuous; the Proclan chains are unbroken. Iamblichus argues that even the lowest things retain a connection to the highest within them. "Earthly things, possessing their being in virtue of the totalities of the gods, whenever they become ready [epitēdeia] for participation in the divine, straight away find the gods pre-existing in it prior to their own proper essence."[73] Such a theological viewpoint, as Shaw and others have shown, places greater value on the material world, emphasizing the divine participation of all levels of the demiurge's creation, but it also extends the power of theurgic ritual beyond the material realm, enabling the theurgist to contact the highest levels of the ontological hierarchy.[74]

The other objection raised by Plotinus, Porphyry, and others (especially hostile Christian authors like Eusebius and Augustine) is that the mortal theurgists claim to control divine powers; even evil daimons are ontologically superior to human beings, and yet the invocations of the theurgists command even the greatest gods to appear and do their will. "A thing that very much troubles me is this: how does it come about that we invoke the gods as our superiors, but then give them orders as if they were our inferiors?"[75] Either such commands impiously violate the ontological hierarchy that places divinities above humans, or they are merely delusions and deceptions, since the hierarchy cannot in actuality be violated. Iamblichus's answer is central to the nature of his conception of theurgy as a work by the gods, rather than a working upon the gods.

> The whole of theurgy presents a double aspect. On the one hand, it is performed by men, and as such observes our natural rank in the universe; but on the other, it controls divine symbols [synthemata], and in virtue of them is raised up to union with the higher powers, and directs itself harmoniously in accordance with their dispensation, which enables it quite properly to assume the mantle [schema] of the gods. It is in virtue of this distinction, then, that the art both naturally invokes the powers from the universe as superiors, inasmuch as the

[72] Synesius, de insomn. 2–3 132c, 133b. "The man who knows the kinship of the parts of the kosmos is wise, for he can attract one by means of another, having what is at hand as a pledge of what is far away, be it voice or matter or form. . . . Whatever divinity there is outside the kosmos is immune to magic: 'he sits apart and neither heeds nor cares' " (Homer, Iliad 15.106). By contrast, Eusebius, PE IV.1 dismisses all such manipulations as trickery and magic.

[73] Iamblichus, de myst. 1.8 29 (trans. E. C. Clarke, Dillon, and Hershbell 2003).

[74] Cp. Shaw 1995: esp. 19–58. See also Johnston 2008b.

[75] Articulated here most clearly in Iamblichus, de myst. 4.1 181, but responding to ideas found in, e.g., Plotinus, Enneads 2.9.14; Eusebius, PE V.8–10; Augustine, Civ. Dei 10.11.

invoker is a man, and yet on the other hand gives them orders, since it invests itself, by virtue of the ineffable symbols, with the hieratic role of the gods.[76]

The *synthemata*, provided by the gods themselves, enable the theurgist to assume the mantle of the gods, that is, to make commands on the basis of their authority, even taking on their self-presentation (*schēma*). The theurgist thus acts like an official in the Roman Empire, issuing commands to regional governors or other officials of higher rank than his own and bearing the seal of the Emperor to validate the authority behind his commands. The theurgist might even make threats to daimonic or divine entities, not (Iamblichus hastens to add) because he would really do terrible things but as a way of representing the higher level of divine power that he has access to through the *synthemata*.

> The theurgist, through the power of arcane symbols, commands cosmic entities no longer as a human being or employing a human soul but, existing above them in the order of the gods, uses threats that are greater than are consistent with his own proper essence—not, however, with the implication that he would perform that which he asserts, but using such words to instruct them how much, how great and what sort of power he holds through his unification with the gods, which he gains through knowledge of the ineffable symbols.[77]

Such an argument, grounded in the systematic theory of Iamblichean theology, jibes with the evidence of the much less theoretically inclined magical texts. In some of the spells in the Greek Magical Papyri, the magician asks the god not to be angry at being invoked, since the magician is only making use of incantations that the god himself arranged for mortals to learn in order to invoke him. "And be not angry at my potent chants; for you yourself arranged these things among mankind for them to learn."[78] Likewise, in an oracle cited by Porphyry, Hekate claims to appear in response to a summons that was devised by gods for mortals to discover. "I have come in response to your eloquent prayer, which was invented by mortals in accordance with divine counsels."[79] The theurgic magician can com-

---

[76] Iamblichus, *de myst.* 4.2 184 (trans. E. C. Clarke, Dillon, and Hershbell 2003).

[77] Iamblichus, *de myst.* 6.6 246–247 (trans. E. C. Clarke, Dillon, and Hershbell 2003).

[78] PGM IV.296–466 (453–456). μηδὲ σὺ μηνίσῃς κρατεραῖς ἐπ᾽ ἐμαῖς ἐπαοιδαῖς· ταῦτα γὰρ αὐτὸς ἔταξας ἐν ἀνθρώποισι δαῆναι. Cp. PGM I.324; IV.1980, which have the same line.

[79] Eusebius, *PE* V.8.5 = Porph. *Philos. ex Orac.* fr. 347 Smith = *CO* 222. This oracle is one of several cited by Eusebius in V.8.5–8 to describe how the magicians compel the gods, but scholars have disagreed whether these oracles come from the collection of the *Chaldaean Oracles* or from some other source. For the purposes of this argument, however, the precise source of the oracle is irrelevant, since Porphyry's citation of it indicates that he regarded it as a divine revelation authorizing ritual practice of a theurgic kind.

mand divinities with greater power than himself because the gods themselves arranged for the tokens that could validate those commands to be discovered by mortals.

The System of Theurgy

The philosophical texts of Neoplatonic thinkers such as Iamblichus and Proclus thus articulate explanations of *how* theurgy works, providing elaborate and systematic accounts of the cosmological and theological structures that underlie the ritual actions. Of course, these accounts differ in their details, and it is often these details that matter most to the authors themselves in their philosophical disputes with one another. So, too, it is worth remembering that any given practitioner of a theurgic ritual would not necessarily have the entire systematic theology in mind while undertaking the ritual, any more than a musician would be contemplating harmonic theory while performing. Nevertheless, the theory underpins the performance, and the systematic explanations of the theory can help outside observers like modern scholars understand how such rituals work, their internal logic and consistency as well as their ends and means.

WHAT: THE EVIDENCE FOR THEURGY

The theoretical texts also provide some evidence for the actual practices of theurgy, although this evidence is often frustratingly vague, in contrast to the careful and systematic descriptions of the philosophical systems.[80] Such texts, even Iamblichus's *de mysteriis* or Proclus's *de sacrificio*, were not written to provide instructions for theurgic ritual in the way that the recipes in the Greek Magical Papyri were, so the modern scholar must read them against the grain, as it were, to uncover evidence for what is to be done, rather than how the whole system works. Nevertheless, because the Greek Magical Papyri provide only one limited perspective on such rituals, it is necessary to cull evidence from these other sources to provide a more complete picture of the range of theurgic ritual activity.

If all theurgy is intended to activate a connection between mortal and divine, bringing the two together, then such a meeting (*systasis*—literally, standing together) can occur either by bringing the divine into the world

---

[80] Tanaseanu-Döbler 2013: 199 points to the vague references to rituals in Proclus and notes that "the fact that such references can be used freely in his rigorous philosophical argumentation and that he uses brief allusions that are not always fully intelligible to us, show that the rituals in question are part of a common background Proclus shares with his students, that he can rely on their comprehension and on their basic acceptance of such practices."

of the mortal or by transporting the mortal into the realm of the divine. We can use the terms *telestikē* and *anagogē* for these practices; the former refers to the perfection or purification of mortal and material things, while the latter is a 'leading up' of the individual. Although, philosophically speaking, the realm of the gods does not exist in a physically higher space than the mortal realm but transcends it, the metaphors of ascent and descent dominate the descriptions of all these procedures—the magician can ascend to the gods or bring the gods down to earth.[81] In either case, as the theoretical texts have made clear, like must be drawn to like, so either the material things must be made particularly fitting (*epitēdeia*) of the divine in order to receive it, or the magician must be assimilated as much as possible to the divine. This theoretical principle fits with the range of theurgical practices mentioned in the sources, particularly the hostile critiques—the making of statues and other material objects infused with divine power, the invocation of daimonic and divine powers to provide special revelations, and the elevation of the theurgist's soul to the divine.

Telestikē: Bringing the Divine into the Material World

The aim of the telestic art is to ritually consecrate matter in such a way as to make it a fit receptacle for the divine and thereby to draw the divine power down into the earthly realm. The *synthemata* and *symbola* of the theurgists provide the key to this activity, since such tokens of the divine have the most congruity or fitness (*epitēdeiotēs*) for receiving divine illumination. Proclus provides an analogy to explain how the similarity between the material and divine things works to bridge the ontological gap between mortal and divine: the *symbola* are like the preheated wick of a lamp, which bursts into flame when brought near another lit lamp wick, even though it is never touched by the flame.

> So by observing such things and connecting them to the appropriate heavenly beings, the ancient wise men brought divine powers into the region of mortals, attracting them through likeness. For likeness is sufficient to join beings to one another. If, for example, one first heats up a wick and then holds it under the light of a lamp not far from the flame, he will see it lighted though it be untouched by the flame, and the lighting comes up from below. By analogy, then, un-

---

[81] As Johnston 2008b: 460 notes, "This practice of building a home for the god out of elements akin to him nicely inverts the theurgist's practice of inhaling sunlight to lighten his soul: in that case, the traveler changes himself to suit his destination, in this case, the destination is changed to suit the traveler."

derstand the preparatory heating as like the sympathy of lower things for those above; the bringing-near and the proper placement as like the use made of material things in the priestly art, at the right moment and in the appropriate manner.[82]

The correspondences within the Proclan chains provide the similarities, whether the likenesses involve visible qualitative resemblances (like the sunflower to the sun) or less obvious connections (like the rooster and the rising sun). Since every chain includes multiple links of all kinds of materials and beings, the congruities are strengthened by the presence of multiple elements in the same chain. The theurgist must assemble appropriate materials in such a way as to enhance their inherent congruities so as to create a better receptacle for the divine. As Iamblichus explains,

> Observing this, and discovering in general, in accordance with the properties of each of the gods, the receptacles adapted to them, the theurgic art in many cases links together stones, plants, animals, aromatic substances and other such things that are sacred, perfect and godlike, and then from all these composes an integrated and pure receptacle.[83]

This receptacle may be of various forms, depending on the aim and purpose of the theurgist who assembles it, and the collection of *symbola* gathered depends upon which divine power the theurgist intends to contact.[84]

---

[82] Proclus, *de sacr.* 148.21–149.7 (trans. Copenhaver 2015). οἱ πάλαι σοφοί, τὰ μὲν ἄλλοις, τὰ δὲ ἄλλοις προσάγοντες τῶν οὐρανίων, ἐπήγοντο θείας δυνάμεις εἰς τὸν θνητὸν τόπον καὶ διὰ τῆς ὁμοιότητος ἐφειλκύσαντο· ἱκανὴ γὰρ ἡ ὁμοιότης συνάπτειν τὰ ὄντα ἀλλήλοις· ἐπεὶ καί, εἴ τις θρυαλλίδα προθερμήνας ὑπόσχοι τῷ λυχναίῳ φωτὶ μὴ πόρρω τοῦ πυρός, ἴδοι ἂν αὐτὴν ἐξαπτομένην μὴ ψαύουσαν τοῦ πυρός, καὶ τὴν ἔξαψιν ἄνωθεν τοῦ κατωτέρω γινομένην. Ἀναλόγως οὖν ἡ μὲν προθέρμανσις νοείσθω σοι τῇ συμπαθείᾳ τῶν τῇδε πρὸς ἐκεῖνα, ἡ δὲ προσαγωγὴ καὶ ἐν καλῷ θέσις τῇ τῆς ἱερατικῆς τέχνης κατά τε καιρὸν τὸν πρέποντα καὶ τρόπον τὸν οἰκεῖον προσχρήσει τῶν ὑλῶν. Cp. Apuleius, *Met.* 2.12.2, where Lucius puts forth a theory of *sympatheia* between the lamp wick and celestial flame.

[83] Iamblichus, *de myst.* 5.23 [233.9–13] (trans. E. C. Clarke, Dillon, and Hershbell 2003). Cp. Proclus, *de sacr.* 150. "They used mixing because they saw that each unmixed thing possesses some property of the god but is not enough to call that god forth. Therefore, by mixing many things they unified the aforementioned influences and made a unity generated from all of them similar to the whole that is prior to them all" (trans. Copenhaver 2015).

[84] The Renaissance Neoplatonist Ficino, developing the ideas of Proclus, provides an example of such a collection of symbola connected with Zeus (Jove) to help in dealing with a stomachache. "Move your body on the day and in an hour when Jove is reigning, and use Jovial things, like silver, amethyst, topaz, coral, crystal, beryl, spode, sapphire, green and airy colors, wine, white sugar, honey, and thoughts and feelings that are very Jovial, too: constant ones, balanced ones, religious and law-abiding ones. Associate with men of this kind, sanguine and handsome, venerable and versatile. . . . The Jovial animals are the lamb and the peacock, the eagle and the calf" (Ficino, *Three Books on Life* 3.1.110–118 [trans. Kaske and Clark 2002, modified in Johnston 2008b]).

MAGIC RINGS

The Greek Magical Papyri provide a number of examples of recipes for creating such consecrated objects that channel divine power, particularly rings or consecrated stones that can be set in rings. One spell (PGM XII.201–269) produces a ring that is touted as being "useful for every operation" and "very effective." An "air colored" (either blue or gray) jasper stone is carved with the ourobouros snake surrounding a moon with stars on its points and the figure of Helios the sun, with the name Abrasax, while the name of the supreme god Iao Sabaoth is engraved around the border. This combination of material substances with drawn figures and written names thus combines a particular set of *symbola* that draw in divine power, but the magician must do more to activate it. The magician must sacrifice a pure white goose, along with three roosters and three pigeons, over a fire of fruit wood in a holy place, pouring libations of wine with honey, milk, and saffron, while burning all sorts of incense, and then hold the stone over the smoke while invoking the god. The life force of the birds, as Saloustios tells us, provides a symbol on the level of the irrational life, the incense and other materials of the material element, while the prayer functions at the level of thought, providing further tokens of the god in the form of special names and epithets.[85]

Not all such recipes require animal sacrifices; others place more emphasis on the tokens of the god recited in the prayer. One spell for the consecration of a ring consists largely of a list of the different forms and names of the sun god Helios at the twelve different hours of the day. For example, "In the eighth hour you have the form of a bull; your name is DIATIPHE, who becomes visible everywhere. Let all things done by the use of this stone be accomplished."[86] The end of the spell provides the familiar fill-in-the-blank, "especially in the NN matter," to allow the magician to direct the divine power channeled by the spell to whatever ends he chooses. Another ring consecration spell provides a list of possible uses, and it is worth noting that such uses range from the beneficent (strengthening friendships and expelling demons) to the maleficent (subjecting legal opponents and causing physical harm); the power of the supreme divinity invoked here is at the disposal of the magician for whatever purpose he may desire.[87]

---

[85] Cp. Saloustios, *de deis* 15. Even if the magician of the PGM might not have such an exegetical interpretation in mind while performing the spell, Saloustios articulates a logical schema that underlies the spell's construction.

[86] PGM IV.1596–1715 (1675–1680). Such lists of the names and forms of the sun at different hours undoubtedly derive from older Egyptian models, prayers to the sun god adapted for this magical procedure.

[87] PGM XII.270–350 (303–306, 277–282). ψυχὰς μετατρέπειν, πνεύματα κινεῖν, ἀντιδίκους ὑποτάσσειν, φιλίας στηρίζειν, πόρους πάντας περιποιεῖν, ὀνείρους ἐπιφέρειν, χρησμοδοτεῖν, πάθη τε

MAGIC STATUES

This spell for consecrating a ring contains a curious slip late in the recipe, referring to the consecrated object as a *xoanon*, a statue, rather than a ring or a stone. As Moyer and Dieleman have pointed out, this slip shows that the consecrated ring is being imagined like a consecrated statue, one of the forms of receptacle that is most often mentioned in descriptions of theurgic *telestikē*.[88] Augustine and Eusebius both inveigh against the practice of creating magical statues, citing pagan philosophers such as Apuleius and Porphyry in order to refute their explanations of the process.[89] Augustine quotes the Hermetic *Asclepius*, which describes

> statues endowed with life, pregnant with sensation and inspiration, and performing so many wonderful things, statues that have foreknowledge of the future and can predict it by sortition, by prophecy, by dreams, and by many other methods, statues that can bring maladies upon men and heal them again, allotting them sadness or joy according to their deserts.[90]

The dialogue between Hermes Trismegistos and Asclepius privileges Egypt as the place where such magical statues are made, an idea to which the ancient Egyptian rituals involving cult statues (such as "the Opening of the Mouth") no doubt contributes.[91] Statues of the gods with special divine

---

ψυχικὰ καὶ σωματικὰ καὶ ἀσθένειαν ἐμποδισμόν τε ποιεῖν, φίλτρα ἐρωτικὰ πάντα ἀποτελεῖν. ... τούτου μεῖζον οὐδὲν ἔσχεν ὁ κόσμος· ἔχων γὰρ αὐτὸ μεθ' ἑαυτοῦ, ὃ ἂν παρά τινος αἰ[τ]ήσῃς, πάντως λήμψει. ἔτι δὲ βασιλέων ὀργὰς καὶ δεσποτῶν παύει. φορῶν αὐτό, ὃ ἄν τινι εἴπῃς, πιστευθήσῃ ἐπίχαρίς τε πᾶσιν ἔσει. ἀνοίξει δὲ θύρας καὶ δεσμὰ δια<ρ>ρήξει καὶ λίθους ὁ προσάγων τὸν λίθον, τοῦτ' ἔστιν ψῆφον, καὶ λέγων τὸ ὄνομα τὸ ὑπογεγραμμένον. ποιεῖ δὲ καὶ πρὸς δαιμονοπλήκτους· δὸς γὰρ φορεῖν αὐτό, καὶ παραυτὰ φεύξεται τὸ δαιμόνιον. "To call back souls, move spirits, subject legal opponents, strengthen friendships, produce all [sorts of] profits, bring dreams, give prophecies, cause psychological passions and bodily sufferings and incapacitating illness, and perfect all erotic philters. ... The world has had nothing greater than this. For when you have it with you, you will always get whatever you ask from anybody. Besides, it calms the angers of masters and kings. Wearing it, whatever you may say to anyone, you will be believed, and you will be pleasing to everybody. Anyone can open doors and break chains and rocks if he touches them with the stone, that is, the gem, and says the name written below. It also works for demoniacs. Just give it [to one] to wear, and the daimon will immediately flee."

[88] Moyer and Dieleman 2003: 55.

[89] Cp. Augustine, *Civ. Dei* 8.23, which quotes, as a text of Apuleius, a chunk of the Hermetic text *Asclepius*. Eusebius, *PE* III quotes chunks of Porphyry's lost work *On Images*, of which little beyond his quotations survives. The Christian authors aim their attacks against pagan worship involving cult statues in general, but they make clear that they consider the telestic animation of statues as the extreme case of the more general phenomenon.

[90] Augustine, *Civ. Dei* 8.23.

[91] Moyer and Dieleman 2003 point out the ways in which such rituals adapt the traditional Egyptian ritual of "the Opening of the Mouth," *wp.t-r3*, which appears in the text of this spell transliterated into Greek as *Ouphōr*. The Egyptian opening of the mouth ritual served to ani-

powers, however, appear in the Greek religious tradition from early on as well, and the telestic creation of statues with magical powers seems to draw on both traditions.[92] Stories abound of theurgists who miraculously make certain statues smile or move, like the Neoplatonic philosopher Maximus, whose feat of making a statue of Hekate smile and laugh and then causing the torches in the statue's hand to burst into flame impelled the future emperor Julian to forsake his more contemplative teachers and try to learn the theurgic secrets of Maximus.[93]

Maximus's miracle is intended to show how superior he is to the common herd, his ability to make special connections with the divine. In theurgy, a statue serves as a special symbol of a particular god that contains a collection of the *synthemata* of that divinity to provide an extra-ordinary link with the divine.[94] As Proclus says,

> The establishment of telestic art and oracles and statues of gods on earth through certain *symbola* makes them fitting [*epitēdeia*] to partake of the god, since they are made of portions of the material and corruptible world.[95]

The Neoplatonist Hermias explains how such an extra-ordinary connection is made between the divine and inanimate matter; the matter is first animated so that it can receive divine illumination in the way that a soul does.

> We have told, then, how the soul is inspired. But how can an image also be said to be inspired? Perhaps the thing itself cannot respond actively to the divine, inasmuch as it is without life; but the telestic art of consecration purifies matter, and, by attaching certain *charakteres* and *symbola* to the image, first gives it a soul by these means, and makes it capable of receiving a kind of life from the universe, thereafter preparing it to receive illumination from divinity.[96]

---

mate statues of the gods in the Egyptian temples by opening the mouths of the statues so that the divine power could enter in. While the spell in the PGM operates differently, as Haluszka 2008: 487 and Johnston 2008b: 474 both point out, the composer of the spell has clearly adapted Egyptian ritual elements to suit the similar aim of infusing the stone with divine power in the manner of the Greek theurgical *telestikē*. For the Egyptian elements, see further Dieleman 2005: 170–182.

[92] Cp. Johnston 2008b, as well as Faraone 1992b.

[93] Eunapius, *Vit. Soph.* 475. Maximus burns incense and recites a hymn in order to perform his magic.

[94] The best discussion of these statues remains Johnston 2008b.

[95] Proclus, *in Tim.* III.155.18–21 (my trans.). τὸ τὴν μὲν τελεστικὴν καὶ χρηστήρια καὶ ἀγάλματα θεῶν ἱδρῦσθαι ἐπὶ γῆς καὶ διά τινων συμβόλων ἐπιτήδεια ποιεῖν τὰ ἐκ μερικῆς ὕλης γενόμενα καὶ φθαρτῆς εἰς τὸ μετέχειν θεοῦ·

[96] Hermias, *in Plat. Phaedrum* 87.4–9 (trans. Bonner 1950, adapted). Πῶς μὲν οὖν ἡ ψυχὴ ἐνθουσιᾷ, εἴρηται. Πῶς δὲ καὶ ἄγαλμα λέγεται ἐνθουσιᾶν· Ἢ αὐτὸ μὲν οὐκ ἐνεργεῖ περὶ τὸ θεῖον, ὅ γε ἄψυχόν ἐστιν, ἀλλὰ τὴν ὕλην ἡ τελεστικὴ διακαθήρασα καί τινας χαρακτῆρας καὶ σύμβολα περιθεῖσα

Proclus describes this process of animation as one in which the statue "has received reflections of vitality from the universe which cause us to say it is ensouled." The statue does not become a fully animate mortal being with a soul but rather receives, through the power of the *symbola*, receptivity to divine power on the psychic as well as the material level. "For a telestic priest who sets up a statue as a likeness of a certain divine order perfects the *symbola* of its identity with reference to that order."[97]

As usual, our theoretical texts do not provide any practical specifics, but such details do appear in other sources, both the recipe books of the Greek Magical Papyri and certain divine revelations preserved in Porphyry's *Philosophy from Oracles*. In one such oracle, Hekate provides instructions for the creation of a statue to be used in invoking her power.

> But consecrate a statue, having purified it in the manner I shall teach you. Make the body of wild rue and adorn it with little animals, with domestic lizards, and when you have crushed a mixture of myrrh, styrax, and frankincense, blend it with these creatures, go out into the open air under a waxing moon and perform the rite by saying this prayer.[98]

The lizards and the incense, along with the special material of which the statue is made, provide one kind of *symbolon*, a material token, while the prayer (not included in Eusebius's quotation) would provide another.

In the Greek Magical Papyri, the instructions for the construction of the statue may be supplemented with the appropriate prayers and other ritual actions.[99] One spell calls for an elaborate ritual in order to create a statue

τῷ ἀγάλματι πρῶτον μὲν ἔμψυχον αὐτὸ διὰ τούτων ἐποίησε καὶ <οἷόν τε> ζωήν τινα ἐκ τοῦ κόσμου καταδέξασθαι, ἔπειτα μετὰ τοῦτο ἐλλαμφθῆναι παρὰ τοῦ θείου αὐτὸ παρεσκεύασεν· Cp. Proclus, *Theol. Plat.* I.28: "The telestic art, by thoroughly purifying *charactēres* and *symbola* and putting them around a statue, makes the statue ensouled."

[97] Proclus, *in Parm.* 847.23–24, 24–29. Καὶ τὸ ἄγαλμα μὲν τὸ ἔμψυχον μετέλαβε μὲν τυπικῶς, εἰ τύχοι, καὶ τῆς τέχνης τοιῶσδε μεμορφωμένον τορνευούσης αὐτὸ καὶ ξεούσης καὶ ἐκτυπούσης, ἐμφάσεις δὲ ἔσχε ζωτικὰς ἀπὸ τοῦ παντὸς δι' ἃς καὶ ψυχοῦσθαι λέγεται, ὡμοίωται δὲ ὅλον πρὸς τὸν θεὸν οὗ ἐστιν ἄγαλμα· τὰ γὰρ σύμβολα, δι' ὧν ὁ τελεστὴς ᾤκισεν αὐτὸ πρὸς τήνδε τὴν τάξιν ὅμοιον, πρὸς ἐκείνην ἀπεργάζεται τεταγμένος ἀνάλογον τῷ δημιουργοῦντι τὴν εἰκόνα πρὸς τὸ παράδειγμα τὸ οἰκεῖον.

[98] Porphyry, *Philos. ex Orac.* fr. 317 Smith = Eusebius, *PE* V.12 = *CO* 224. ἀλλὰ τέλει ξόανον, κεκαθαρμένον ὥς σε διδάξω·| πηγάνου ἐξ ἀγρίοιο δέμας ποίει ἠδ' ἐπικόσμει| ζώοισιν λεπτοῖσι, κατοικιδίοις σκαλαβώταις·| σμύρνης καὶ στύρακος λιβάνοιό τε μίγματα τρίψας| σὺν κείνοις ζώοισι καὶ αἰθριάσας ὑπὸ μήνην| αὔξουσαν, τέλει αὐτὸς ἐπευχόμενος τήνδ' εὐχήν (my trans.). Scholars disagree whether this oracle should be considered one of those drawn from the collection of *Chaldaean Oracles*.

[99] Cp., e.g., PGM IV.2359–2372: "Take orange beeswax and the juice of the aeria plant and of ground ivy and mix them and fashion a figure of Hermes having a hollow bottom, grasping in his left hand a herald's wand and in his right a small bag." Scraps of papyrus with *voces magicae* are inserted into the wax statue, and the ritual is completed with the sacrifice

of Eros that will do the magician's bidding. The statue is again made of wax (eight fingers high), carrying a torch and bow and arrows, and the Etrurian wax must be mixed with "every kind of aromatic plant." Once the statue is constructed (along with a similar figurine of Psyche, who disappears from the recipe thereafter), the magician must engage in a three-day ritual of consecration, involving symbolic offerings to the statue, the special sacrifice of a variety of birds, and a series of prayers to be said on the successive days of the ritual. The offerings include "fresh fruits of every kind and 7 cakes, 7 pinecones, every kind of sweetmeat, 7 lamps not colored red," presumably special materials designed to symbolically connect with Eros. The most unusual feature of the spell is the offering of a specified set of seven birds ("one cock, a partridge, a wren, a pigeon, a turtledove, and any two nestlings you can get hold of"), which are not to be made into a regular burnt offering but carefully strangled.

> Do not make a burnt offering of any of these; instead, you are to take them in hand and choke them, all the while holding them up to your Eros, until each of the creatures is suffocated and their breath enters him.[100]

This transfer of life-breath from the birds to the statue is a highly unusual procedure, although its purpose is clear enough. In subsequent days, other birds are strangled and burnt as offerings or consumed by the magician himself. On each day, the magician recites an invocation to the god, involving both comprehensible epithets and incomprehensible *voces magicae*. The magician claims to be the special initiate of the god, "to whom you gave the knowledge of your most great [name], which knowledge will I even keep in sanctity, imparting it to no one save the very initiates into your own holy mysteries." Along with the variety of types of *symbola* involved in the ritual, we see the idea of the divine origin for the key token that enables the magician to command the divinity to "submit to this service and be my assistant." The magician can command the services of the deity, "the one who overturned all things and set them up again," and even threaten that "if you disobey me, the sun's orb will burn out and darkness will cover the whole world," because he has the secret knowledge of the

---

of a rooster and a libation of Egyptian wine. Again, the various types of *symbola* in the procedure, from symbolic materials like orange beeswax and plants to special *synthemata* of incomprehensible words to the life of a bird, all serve to make the receptacle more appropriate or congruent for the divine power that is being called into it. Cp. the following spell, IV.2373–2440, for another set of instructions for making a statue of Hermes. Both of these statues are intended to bring the power and favor of Hermes to improve business and bring wealth.

[100] PGM XII.14–95. On the strangulation of the birds, see Zografou 2011 (expanded in Zografou 2013a).

divine *symbola* authorized and imbued with divine power by the god himself. Such compulsions and threats are the sort of things that Iamblichus goes to great pains to defend against the critiques of the opponents of theurgy, and the spell in the Greek Magical Papyri makes use of the same idea that the magician has been granted higher divine power by the favor of the gods, tokens of which enable him to issue commands and threats to divine powers despite his lower ontological status.

Magical Assistants and Personal Daimons

The magician can command the god Eros to go to the house of any person, taking the form of the god she worships and bid the target come to the magician at once. Lucian parodies such a procedure in his *Lover of Lies* (*Philopseudes*), relating the story of Hyperborean magician employed by a lovesick young man to win the affections of his neighbor's wife. The magician, after consulting with the shade of the youth's father, invoking Hekate and drawing down the moon, creates a little Eros figurine out of clay, which flies off to the lady next door to bring her to the youth's bed.[101] Lucian's tale draws on the same ideas that appear in the Greek Magical Papyri of the magician bringing down the power of the gods into a statue and making that statue into a divinely powered assistant who does the magician's bidding. Other spells in the Greek Magical Papyri provide instructions for summoning such an assistant, often called a *paredros*, even without the creation of a statue. This personal assistant is at times identified as the personal daimon of the magician himself, the particular spirit from higher realms who is linked with the magician.

One spell is entitled "the meeting [*systasis*] with your own daimon," and the magician invokes the powers of the universe each day for a week, writing a magical name on two eggs and then licking it off one and eating the other. This recipe lacks the elaborate details of another spell that makes use of a collection of *symbola* to cause the magician's own shadow to serve as his assistant.

> If you make an offering of wheaten meal and ripe mulberries and unsoftened sesame and uncooked *thrion* and throw into this a beet, you will gain control of your own shadow so that it will serve you. Go at the sixth hour of the day, toward the rising sun, to a deserted place, girt about with a new dark-colored palm-fiber basket, and on

[101] Lucian, *Philops.* 13–15. The punchline of Lucian's joke is of course that the youth paid the wizard twenty minas for his magical services, while the woman is the sort who would sleep with anyone for a mere twenty drachmas—the magic is a useless sham; cp. ch. 1, p. 21, n. 42; ch. 4, p. 109, n. 39.

your head a scarlet cord as a headband, behind your right ear the feather of a falcon, behind your left that of an ibis.[102]

The magician calls upon Helios to give him control over his shadow, citing his knowledge of the sacred names, signs, and symbols of the god, including his appearance at each hour. The previous recipe in the papyrus in fact provides in an invocation to Helios a list of the signs, symbols, and forms of Helios at each hour, similar to (but differing in detail from) the list in the spell for the consecration of the stone in PGM IV.1596–1715, discussed above. Here, rather than asking the god to bring down the divine power into an object, the magician seeks to get the god's authority to control an element of himself, his shadow.

The most elaborate spell for acquiring a personal divine assistant is the Spell of Pnouthis (PGM I.42–195), which involves extensive purifications and preliminaries in preparation for the arrival of the god. The arrival, however, is more spectacular than the appearance of the magician's shadow behind him as he faces the sun. A blazing star shoots down from the sky onto the rooftop and appears as an angel to the magician. After adjuring this divine entity with an oath to reveal his name and to remain with the magician forever, the magician takes him by the hand (the right hand) and brings him down to the dining room to be entertained at dinner with wine and foods that the magician himself is consuming. Having thus established a bond of hospitality and friendship with this divine being, even after he departs after dinner the assistant will remain available to the magician, invisible and inaudible to any but the magician himself. This divine spirit can perform any task imaginable:

If you give him a command, straightway he performs the task: he sends dreams, he brings women, men without the use of magical material, he kills, he destroys, he stirs up winds from the earth, he carries gold, silver, bronze, and he gives them to you whenever the need arises. . . . He will carry you into the air, and again hurl you into the billows of the sea's current and into the waves of the sea; he will quickly freeze rivers and seas and in such a way that you can run over them firmly, as you want. And especially will he stop, if ever you wish it, the sea-running foam, and whenever you wish to bring down stars.[103]

---

[102] PGM III.612–632. Systasis in PGM VII.505–528.

[103] PGM I.42–195 (97–100, 119–124). ἐὰν ἐπιτάξῃς, παραυτὰ τὸ ἔργον ἐπιτελεῖ· ὀνειροπομπεῖ, ἄγει γυναῖκας, ἄνδρας δίχα οὐσίας, ἀναιρεῖ, καταστ[ρ]έφει, ἀναρίπτει ἀνέμους ἐκ γῆς, βαστάζει χρυσόν, ἄργυρον, χαλκόν, καὶ δίδωσί σοι, ὅταν χρεία γένηται· . . . βαστάξει σ[ε εἰς] ἀέρα καὶ πάλιν ῥίψει σε εἰς κλύδωνα ποντίων ποταμ[ῶν καὶ] εἰς ῥ<ύ>ακας θαλασσίων, πήξει δὲ ποταμοὺς καὶ θάλασσα[ν συντ] ὅμως καὶ, ὅπως ἐνδιατρέχῃς σταδίως, ὡς βούλει· μά[λιστα] δὲ καθέξει σοῦ θελήσαντός ποτε τὸν ἀφρὸν ἁλί[δρομ]ον, καὶ ὅταν θέλῃς ἄστρα κατενεγκεῖν.

This powerful entity is linked with the magician throughout life and even after death, for "when you are dead, he will wrap up your body as befits a god, but he will take your spirit and carry it into the air with him. For no aerial spirit which is joined with a mighty assistant will go into Hades." The *pneuma* of the magician will thus be raised up to the level of this divinity after the magician's death, rather than sinking down further into the underworld.

Many features of these spells, and the Spell of Pnouthis in particular, are reminiscent of Iamblichus's discussion of the personal daimon in *de mysteriis*. There, Iamblichus argues that "the invocation of daimons is made in the name of the single god who is their ruler," who appears in these spells most often as the sun god, with various names and epithets. "For it is always the case, in the theurgic hierarchy, that secondary entities are summoned through the intermediacy of their superiors." The Spell of Pnouthis uses an adjuration of Helios, a complex set of *synthemata* in the form of *voces magicae*, to compel the daimon to reveal the name by which it can be summoned and commanded. So too, Iamblichus recounts, "when the personal daimon comes to be with each person, then he reveals the mode of worship proper to him and his name, and imparts the particular manner in which he should be summoned."[104] The magician too makes offerings of wine after the spirit departs, acknowledging the divine power of his assistant.

Whether the assistant summoned by the spell of Pnouthis is the personal daimon assigned to the individual at his birth or a superior power drawn down to replace that daimon in guiding the magician's life remains unclear; it is described as a *paredros*, an angel, an aerial spirit, and a god, so its ontological status is uncertain. Iamblichus mentions that theurgical practice can enable the theurgist to replace his personal daimon with a more powerful deity, and such may be the intent here.[105] On the other hand, some individuals were imagined to have greater gods as their personal daimons. Porphyry recounts the episode in which Plotinus was persuaded to visit an Egyptian temple, where the priest conjured up his personal daimon. As the divinity manifested, however, it appeared to be such a great god that one of those present panicked and strangled the chickens, causing the spirit to depart, but the episode provoked the wonder and amazement of Plotinus's followers.[106]

---

[104] Iamblichus, *de myst.* 9.9. Cp. PGM I.42–195 (133–142). The spell also involves a gem carved with the sun god and an invocation to Selene.

[105] Iamblichus, *de myst.* 9.6. "Until, through sacred theurgy, we establish a god as the overseer and leader of our soul; for then it either withdraws in deference to the superior principle, or surrenders its administrative role, or subordinates itself so as to contribute to the god's direction of the soul, or in some other way comes to serve it as master."

[106] Porphyry, *Vit. Plot.* 10. Porphyry unfortunately does not explain why the friend was

EPIPHANIES OF THE GODS

Plotinus's 'séance at the Iseum' shows that minor personal daimons are not the only kind of divinity that can be brought down and made manifest on earth by theurgic operations. Making use of the same hierarchical principles of commanding the lesser divinities by the authority of the higher, a theurgist could call down daimons and divinities of all kinds, from every level of the cosmos, and have them manifest on the earth.

A spell in the Greek Magical Papyri that entitles itself the *Eighth Book of Moses* provides an unusual example of an invocation that attempts to contact the supreme deity directly, rather than one of the lower levels of divinity.[107] The magician must undergo a period of purification for forty-one days, ending when the new moon appears in the zodiac sign of Aries.[108] After an elaborate set of sacrifices to the gods of the hours of the day and the days of the week (i.e., the planets), the magician performs a lengthy invocation, which includes a recitation of a cosmogonic myth where the creator brings the primordial deities into being through laughter.[109]

> I call on you, who are greater than all, the creator of all, you, the self-begotten, who see all and are not seen. For you gave Helios the glory and all the power, Selene the privilege to wax and wane and have fixed courses, yet you took nothing from the earlier-born darkness, but apportioned things so that they should be equal. For when you appeared, both order arose and light appeared. All things are subject to you, whose true form none of the gods can see; who change

---

holding chickens or why their strangulation should cause the invoked deity to disappear. Much scholarly speculation has swirled around "the séance at the Iseum," as Dodds called it, but the episode does clearly show the connections between the debates around the personal daimon among the Neoplatonic philosophers and the magical practices like those found in the PGM. See Dodds 1951, Merlan 1953, Armstrong 1955, and Mazur 2003. Ammianus Marcellinus 1.21.14 indeed recounts that three marvelous individuals had gods for their personal daimons: Hermes Trismegistos, Apollonius of Tyana, and Plotinus; the superior form of their personal daimonic spirits indicated the superior nature of these men.

[107] The structure of the papyrus is complicated, since it contains three different versions of the same spell, each more or less fragmentary, with several sections that are mostly parallel and others that are not replicated in the other versions. The best analysis of the structure remains Smith's "The Eighth Book of Moses and How It Grew" (M. Smith 1996), but some of his analysis is included in the notes to his translation in Betz 1986.

[108] While the similarity of this period to the forty-day purificatory period of Lent before Easter, which falls on the first Sunday after the full moon following the vernal equinox (i.e., when the sun is in Aries) is notable, no real conclusions can be drawn from the parallel.

[109] Much of the scholarship on this text has focused on the myth, which appears in different versions in the papyrus, but an analysis of this fascinating myth is beyond the scope of this study. See M. Smith 1996a and 1996b, as well as Zago 2008, Merkelbach and Totti-Gemünd 1990 (vol 3., 1992), and the textual study of Daniel 1991.

into all forms. You are invisible, Aion of Aion. I call on you, lord, to appear to me in a good form.[110]

The magician asks for this supreme god to appear in a good form in the special canopy (*skēnē*) the magician has set up and purified for the encounter. The god will reveal "the things that concern you"; that is the fate of the magician, as well as the god's special Name, which the magician can then use to perform all sorts of magical feats. This Name gives the magician the authority of the supreme god to command all the other powers of the cosmos; the possession of this special *synthema* makes the magician equivalent to the god.

> For you are I, and I, you. Whatever I say must happen, for I have your Name as a unique phylactery in my heart, and no flesh, although moved, will overpower me; no spirit will stand against me—neither daimon nor visitation nor any other of the evil beings of Hades, because of your name, which I have in my soul and invoke.[111]

With the power of this Name, the magician can fetch a lover, kill a snake, resurrect a dead body, or even cross the Nile on a crocodile, among the many other uses listed for this token of the supreme ruler of the universe.[112]

While the highest supreme deity is generally only called upon to authorize the commands given to the lower divinities, the sources show that deities such as Apollo or Asclepius might be summoned to manifest themselves or even the potentially dangerous goddess Hekate, whether as the mistress of demons or as the manifestation of the World Soul, the Psyche of the cosmos. A whole demonological literature seems to have appeared providing the necessary *symbola* to control a whole host of demons and lesser divine powers. The *Testament of Solomon* provides one of the earliest and most detailed examples of such texts in Greek. This work recounts how the Biblical king Solomon, when one of his workers was plagued by a demon, received from the supreme god a seal (*sphragis*) that enabled him to summon a variety of demons and demand to know their names, their forms, and the divine entities who were specially empowered to prevent them from doing harm. Like the Name of the supreme deity in the *Eighth Book of Moses*, this seal from God represents a token of the authority of the highest divinity, which enables a mere mortal to command other divinities. Solomon interrogates the first demon about his name and identity.

> The demon replied, "I am called Ornias." I said to him, "Tell me, in which sign of the zodiac do you reside?" The demon replied, "In

[110] PGM XIII.63–72 ≈ 568–581.
[111] PGM XIII.796–800.
[112] PGM XIII.235–340.

Aquarius; I strangle those who reside in Aquarius because of their passion for women whose zodiacal sign is Virgo. Moreover, while in a trance I undergo three transformations. Sometimes I am a man who craves the bodies of effeminate boys and when I touch them, they suffer great pain. Sometimes I become a creature with wings (flying) up to the heavenly regions. Finally, I assume the appearance of a lion. In addition, I am descended from an archangel of the power of God, but I am thwarted by Ouriel, the archangel."[113]

After interrogating a whole host of demons (including the thirty-six decans), Solomon binds them all to work on building his temple and writes his *Testament*, so that the knowledge of how to control such demons can be given to the people of Israel. Solomon's reputation as a magician is very high among the Greeks of Late Antiquity; he is mentioned as an authority, for example, both in the Greek Magical Papyri and by Zosimus of Panopolis.

While the *Testament of Solomon* names Beezebul and Asmodeus as the rulers of demons, that role in the Greek Magical Papyri and the oracles cited by Porphyry is taken by Hekate as the goddess of the Moon. Hekate manifests herself in response to the invocations of the magicians, describing her own epiphany in one fragment.

And here am I, the many-formed maid, heaven-wandering, bull-faced and three-headed, ruthless and armed with golden arrrows, unbedded Phoebe, Eilythuia shining to mortals, bearing the triple sign of the three elements of nature, manifest in aither with fiery images, in the air I am carried around with gleaming chariot wheels, and earth holds the reins on my dark brood of pups.[114]

Hekate here apears in her moon chariot, in her triple form representing the phases of the moon, ruling over her brood of demons. An even more elaborate description appears in some of the spells in the Greek Magical Papyri, such as an incantation of over one hundred lines of iambic trimeters that invokes Hekate as the Moon (PGM IV.2241–2358) or another hymn that invokes the moon in nearly one hundred dactylic hexameters (PGM IV.2785–2890). Another spell invokes the moon, not by her visual appearance, but by her symbols.

---

[113] *Testament of Solomon* 2.2–4, 13.7–14.8 (trans. Durling 1983). Cp. the Charm of Solomon, PGM IV.850–929; Zosimus, *Final Reckoning* 8 CAAG II.244.24–245.7.

[114] Porphyry, *Philos. ex Orac.* fr. 328 Smith = Eusebius, *PE* IV.23. Cp. the conjuration of Hekate in Lucian, *Philops.* 14, as well as the exposé of an invocation of Hekate by Hippolytus, *Haer.* 4.35–36, who describes a fraudulent performance where a burning bird is thrown into the air by an accomplice of the supposed magician.

And the first companion of your name is silence, the second a popping sound, the third groaning, the fourth hissing, the fifth a cry of
joy, the sixth moaning, the seventh barking, the eighth bellowing,
the ninth neighing, the tenth a musical sound, the eleventh a sound-
ing wind, the twelfth a wind-creating sound, the thirteenth a coercive
sound, the fourteenth a coercive emanation from perfection. Ox, vulture, bull, beetle, falcon, crab, dog, wolf, serpent, horse, she-goat,
asp, goat, he-goat, baboon, cat, lion, leopard, field mouse, deer, mul-
tiform, virgin, torch, lightning, garland, a herald's wand, child, key.
I have said your signs and symbols of your name so that you might
hear me, because I pray to you, mistress of the whole world. Hear
me, you, the stable one, the mighty one, APHEIBOĒO MINTĒR
OCHAŌ PIZEPHYDŌR CHANTHAR CHADĒROZO MOCHTHION
EOTNEU PHĒRZON AINDĒS LACHABOŌ PITTŌ RIPHTHAMER
ZMOMOCHŌLEIE TIĒDRANTEIA OISOZOCHABĒDŌPHRA (add the
usual).[115]

Note the hissing and popping sounds characteristic of theurgic incantations, as well as the differing sets of *symbola* used. Like the catalog of the
forms of the sun at each hour of the day, the fourteen sounds and twenty-
eight symbols correspond to the forms of the goddess across the twenty-
eight day lunar cycle, while the final *voces magicae* provide ineffable tokens
that cannot be rendered in comprehensible speech. All these *symbola* represent the special knowledge of the magician that authorizes him to draw
the moon goddess down from her place in the sky and get her to accomplish the magician's will.

Apollo too makes his appearance in the Greek Magical Papyri conjurations, usually as a form of the sun god. In one spell requesting a *systasis*
with the god, after the magician has ground up fruit and honey with a
magnet and recited a hymn, "then the deity will come to you, shaking the
whole house and the tripod before you."[116] The oracles cited by Porphyry
provide another set of evidence for such manifestations of deities. Apollo
provides instructions for his invocation in one oracle, demanding sacrifices
of incense, wine, and milk, and in another he tells how to invoke a series
of other gods using the silent prayer of the Magi.[117] An Apollonian invocation in the Greek Magical Papyri provides an elaborate set of instructions

[115] PGM VII.756–794 (766–794). The tag, 'add the usual,' is a common feature of the recipes in the PGM, enabling the magician to add whatever further *voces magicae* or ritual components experience has shown to be efficacious.

[116] PGM III.187–262. Apollo was apparently a popular choice; Eunapius, *Vit. Soph.* 473
relates the story of how a certain Egyptian conjured up a supposed epiphany of Apollo, but
Iamblichus was able to perceive that the apparition was merely the ghost pretending to be
the god.

[117] Porphyry, *Philos. ex Orac.* fr. 329 Smith = Eusebius, *PE* IV.20; Porphyry, fr. 330 Smith

for assembling a collection of the *symbola* of the god, ranging from laurel leaves inscribed with *charakteres* to the head of a wolf, in order to summon the god. The magician must purify himself before making the sacrifice of a wolf's eye burned with various spices, a libation, and two sets of seven cakes (round and flat), "so that you may bring the god into the greatest desire toward you." The collection of *symbola* creates the greatest congruence for the god's appearance, a congruence that is heightened by the pure state of the magician, so that like may be drawn to like.

Another spell for a direct vision (*autoptos*) of and *systasis* with the god involves a series of hymns and incantations that summon the god, culminating in a vision of the god himself. "Then you will see the god seated on a lotus, decorated with rays, his right hand raised in greeting and left holding a flail, while being carried in the hands of 2 angels with 12 rays around them."[118] This spell includes procedures for compelling the god to come if the first set of invocations does not work.

> Charm of compulsion: If somehow he delays, say in addition this following incantation (say the incantation one or 3 times): "The great, living god commands you, he who lives for eons of eons, who shakes together, who thunders, who created every soul and race, IAŌ AŌI ŌIA AIŌ IŌA ŌAI. Enter in, appear to me, lord, happy, kind, gentle, glorious, not angry, because I conjure you by the lord, IAŌ AŌI ŌIA AIŌ IŌA ŌAI APTA PHŌIRA ZAZOU I CHAMĒ. Enter in, lord, appear to me happy, kind, gentle, not angry" (repeat).[119]

Even once the god arrives, however, special measures must be taken to ensure that he does not depart too soon. The 'charm to retain the god' specifies, "When he comes in, after greeting him, step with your left heel on the big toe of his right foot, and he will not go away unless you raise your heel from his toe and at the same time say the dismissal."[120]

= Eusebius, *PE* V.14. Cp. the oracles that provide the responses of Asclepius, Hermes, and Pan to such invocations; Eusebius, *PE* III.14 = Porphyry, fr. 312, 313, 318.

[118] PGM IV.930–1114 (1109–114). τὸν δὲ θεὸν ὄψῃ ἐπὶ κιβωρίου καθήμενον, ἀκτινωτόν, τὴν δεξιὰν ἀνατεταμένην ἀσπαζόμενον, τῇ δὲ ἀριστερᾷ κρατοῦντα σκῦτος, βασταζόμενον ὑπὸ β΄ ἀγγέλων ταῖς χερσὶν καὶ κύκλῳ αὐτῶν ἀκτῖνας ιβ. This iconography appears frequently for Harpokrates, especially on gems; for the lotus as a symbolon of the sun, see Proclus, *de sacr.* 12–18.

[119] PGM IV.930–1114 (1035–1046). ἐπάναγκος· ἐάν πως βραδύνῃ, συνεπίλεγε τὸν λόγον τοῦτον ὕστε-ρον τῆς θεολογίας, λέγων ἅπαξ ἢ γ΄ τὸν λόγον· 'ἐπιτάσσει σοι ὁ μέγας ζῶν θεός, ὁ εἰς τοὺς αἰῶνας τῶν αἰώνων, ὁ συνσείων, ὁ βροντάζων, ὁ πᾶσαν ψυχὴν καὶ γένεσιν κτίσας· Ἰάω αωῒ ωῒα αῖω· ἰωα· ωαῒ· εἴσελθε, φάνηθί μοι, κύριε, ἱλαρός, εὐμενής, πρᾷος, ἐπίδοξος, ἀμήνιτος, ὅτι σε ἐφορκίζω κατὰ τοῦ κυρίου Ἰάω αωι ωια αιω ιωα· ωαι απτα φωῖρα ζαζου χαμη· εἴσελθε, κύριε, φάνηθί μοι ἱλαρός, εὐμενής, πρᾷος, <ἐπίδοξος,> ἀμήνιτος.'

[120] PGM IV.930–1114 (1053–1057). κάτοχος τοῦ θεοῦ· εἰσελθόντος αὐτοῦ μετὰ τὸ χαιρετίσαι τῇ ἀριστερᾷ πτέρνῃ πάτει τὸν μέγαν δάκτυλον τοῦ δεξιοῦ ποδός, καὶ οὐ μὴ ἀποχωρήσει, μὴ βαστάξας τὴν πτέρναν ἀπὸ τοῦ δακτύλου, ἅμα εὐθὺ λέγων ἀπόλυσιν.

Christian critics like Eusebius wax sarcastic about such procedures, mocking the nature of any divinities that can be constrained in such a fashion. Nevertheless, procedures for compelling the god's epiphany, retaining its presence, and dismissing it when the rite is finished appear in a number of the spells in the Greek Magical Papyri as well as the divine revelations Eusebius cites from Porphyry in which a god complains about being constrained or asks to be released.[121] One particular form of compulsion that appears in invocations of the Moon in the Greek Magical Papyri also seems to play a role in the theurgy of the *Chaldaean Oracles*, the whirling of the *iunx* or the spinner (*rhombos* or *strophalos*) of Hekate. In the invocation to the Moon in PGM IV.2241–2358, the *rhombos* is one of the *symbola* of Hekate that the magician recites to prove his special credentials for summoning her, but he also claims to "whirl the wheel" for the goddess. In the Chaldaean context, the wheel of Hekate seems to have been called a *strophalos*, and Proclus is said to have employed the "divine and ineffable spinners [*strophaloi*] in his ritual *systaseis* and encounters with the gods," perhaps specifically for producing the epiphany of Hekate in luminous form that he wrote about in a lost work.[122] Psellos informs us that the Chaldaean Hekatic whirligigs were of gold and sapphire, inscribed with *charakteres*, and spun on a bull's hide cord. These devices, also called *iunges*, which might be round or triangular in shape, produced indistinct sounds when they were spun around by the theurgists while laughing and whipping the air to produce the ineffable power of the rite.[123] Such an instrument or entity may seem a far cry from the simple whirligig device used in love magic or even the rite of Theocritus's Simaetha to draw down

---

[121] The magician in PGM IV.2241–2358 seems to be retaining the moon goddess by holding onto her thumb, "with awesome compulsion I hold fast your thumb" (2323). Cp. PGM I.262–347 (335–347); III.187–262 (259–262) release of Apollo; VII.319–334 (333–334) release of Anubis; spells of compulsion: PGM II.1–64 (59) for Apollo; IV.1275–1322 (1296) for the Bear; V.370–446 (436) for Hermes. Likewise, in *PE* V Eusebius cites a series of examples of compulsion in chapter 8, along with examples of retention and the need for ritual dismissal in chapter 9.

[122] Marinus, *Vit. Procl.* 28 677–679. ταῖς γὰρ τῶν Χαλδαίων συστάσεσι καὶ ἐντυχίαις καὶ τοῖς θείοις καὶ ἀφθέγκτοις στροφάλοις ἐκέχρητο. 684–686. ὁ φιλόσοφος τοῖς Χαλδαϊκοῖς καθαρμοῖς καθαιρόμενος, φάσμασι μὲν Ἑκατικοῖς φωτοειδέσιν αὐτοπτουμένοις ὡμίλησεν, ὡς καὶ αὐτός που μέμνηται ἐν ἰδίῳ συγγράμματι. Proclus in any case was said to have used the *iunx* to bring rain during a drought in Attica: ὄμβρους τε ἐκίνησεν, ἴυγγά τινα προσφόρως κινήσας, καὶ αὐχμῶν ἐξαισίων τὴν Ἀττικὴν ἠλευθέρωσεν (686–688). Cp. ch. 1, p. 30, n. 59. See Johnston 1990: 90–110 for this spinner in the Neoplatonic tradition.

[123] Psellos, *in Chald. Orac.* 132.16–23 = PG 122 1133a. Χαλδαϊκὸν λόγιον. ἐνέργει περὶ τὸν Ἑκατικὸν στρόφαλον. Ἐξήγησις. ὁ Ἑκατικὸς στρόφαλος σφαῖρά ἐστι χρυσῆ, μέσον σάπφειρον περικλείουσα, διὰ ταυρείου στρεφομένη ἱμάντος, δι' ὅλης αὐτῆς ἔχουσα χαρακτῆρας· ἣν δὴ στρέφοντες ἐποιοῦντο τὰς ἐπικλήσεις. καὶ τὰ τοιαῦτα καλεῖν εἰώθασιν ἴυγγας, εἴτε σφαιρικὸν ἔχοιεν εἴτε τρίγωνον εἴτε ἄλλο τι σχῆμα. ἃ δὴ δονοῦντες τοὺς ἀσήμους ἢ κτηνώδεις ἐξεφώνουν ἤχους, γελῶντες καὶ τὸν ἀέρα μαστίζοντες. διδάσκει οὖν τὴν τελετὴν ἐνεργεῖν τὴν κίνησιν τοῦ τοιούτου στροφάλου ὡς δύναμιν ἀπόρρητον ἔχουσαν.

the moon to bring back her lover, but the essential elements of the whirling device and the buzzing sound with an attractive force remain the same.[124] The sound of the spinning *iunx, rhoizos*, was identified by Iamblichus with the music of the celestial spheres turning round in their orbits as well as the sound that a divine spirit makes when entering the soul to purify it.[125] The effect of these *iunges* was to draw down the divine powers from on high, as one of the oracles quoted by Porphyry indicates, "drawing them down from the aither with the ineffable *iunges*, you brought them easily to this earth here against their will."[126] Like other compulsive powers within theurgy, the *iunges* were authorized at the highest level of the cosmological hierarchy for the purpose of allowing the lower levels to connect to the higher. The *iunges* seem at times to have been imagined as daimonic intermediaries or as the personified thoughts of the highest Father, providing connections like the *synthemata* from the highest levels to the lowest.[127]

The spells in the Greek Magical Papyri for evoking the epiphany of a god thus seem to resemble many of the practices mentioned in the *Chaldaean Oracles* and in the Neoplatonic texts that discuss theurgy. The use of a variety of *symbola*, from material substances to verbal utterances, in order to increase the attraction for the god provides one striking parallel, as does the attention to the cosmic hierarchy. The emphasis on visual apparitions, especially ones glowing with light, likewise seems to resemble the descriptions in Porphyry's oracles and the *Chaldaean Oracles*. As one of the Oracles preserved by Proclus explains,

> After this invocation, you will either see a fire, similar to a child, extended by bounds over the billow of air, or you will see a formless fire, from which a voice is sent forth, or you will see a sumptuous light, rushing like a spiral around the field. But you may even see a horse, more dazzling than light, or even a child mounted on the nimble back of a horse, a child of fire or covered with gold, or, again, naked or shooting a bow and standing on the back of the horse.[128]

[124] Theocritus, *Idyll* 2; see also ch. 1, p. 22, n. 45; ch. 4, p. 91, n. 1.

[125] Iamblichus, *de myst.* 3.2 104; 3.9 119. For the sounds of the celestial spheres, cp. Proclus, *in Remp.* II.76.20–21; Manetho, *Apotelesm.* 2.66; and Iamblichus, *Vit. Pyth.* XV 65, where Pythagoras invents musical charms after hearing the sounds of the celestial spheres. Iamblichus, *de myst.* 3.2 contrasts this divine sound with the human-produced music that accompanies Corybantic or Metroac rites.

[126] Porphyry, *Philos. ex Orac.* fr. 347.31–32 Smith = Eusebius, *PE* V.8.

[127] As Majercik 1989: 10 summarizes, "The Iynges play both a cosmic and a theurgic role in the Chaldean system: identified with the Platonic Ideas and Intellectual Supports they both inform and participate in ruling the Universe; identified with magic wheels and *voces mysticae*, they aid the theurgic act."

[128] *CO* 146 = Proclus, *in Remp.* I.111.1–12 (trans. Majercik 1989). See Johnston 1992 for analysis of this text, including suggestions that the child on the horse might be an epiphany of Harpocrates, Mithras, or other cavalier figures of the period.

The references to what "you will see" indicate an emphasis on the visualization of the divine epiphany that some scholars have compared to the contemplative exercises of the Neoplatonic philosophical tradition, such as Plotinus's visualization of the cosmic whole stripped of matter and subsequent invocation of the divine. While the dearth of evidence prevents significant comparisons from our modern scholarly standpoint, it is worth noting that such similarities might well have provoked ancient critics to conflate Plotinian contemplation with magical practice, however much others might have stressed the differences and rejected any such classification.[129]

These rites for commanding the presence of a god also resemble the ritual found in Egyptian sources known as the 'god's arrival' (*pḥ ntr*), and this Egyptian tradition undoubtedly contributed to the formation of the spells in the *Greek Magical Papyri* and possibly to the theurgic rituals associated with the *Chaldaean Oracles* and the Neoplatonic philosophers as well. Charting the cross-cultural influences is complicated, however, especially given the gaps in the evidence, and any models of simple translation or appropriation are to be rejected.[130]

The rites in the Greek Magical Papyri, then, like the epiphanies in the Chaldaean and other Oracles, take part in a complex tradition, where theurgical magical practice is formed by the process of bricolage from a variety of earlier practices. Proclus comments on the complex nature of theurgical practice, including the multiple sources from which the ability to make contact with the gods may come.

> For consecrations and other divine services they search out appropriate animals as well as other things. Starting with these and others like them, they gained knowledge of the demonic powers, how closely connected they are in substance to natural and corporeal energy, and through these very substances they achieved association with the demons, from whom they returned forthwith to actual works

---

[129] Mazur 2004: esp. 43–53 suggests that Plotinus, *Enneads* 5.8.9.1–15, 15–28 may be seen as a kind of "inner ritual" that Plotinus indeed adapted from contemporary magical rituals. See also Addey 2014: 199–205; Shaw 1999. Mazur 2003 and Mazur 2004: 29–43 acutely discusses the resistance in modern scholarship to the idea that Plotinus might have practiced mystical rituals.

[130] The quest for divine revelation recounted by Thessalos of Tralles perhaps best illustrates the complexities of the cultural interactions; see ch. 11, p. 411, n. 65, as well as ch. 7, p. 213, n. 82. See Moyer 2003 for a thorough analysis, making use of the earlier studies of Festugiere, Ritner, and J. Z. Smith. The 'god's arrival' spells in the PDM, the demotic texts that have been translated along with the Greek Magical Papyri in Betz 1986, exhibit some differences with the divine epiphany spells analyzed above, but they are nevertheless also products of the ongoing cultural blending and differ in certain respects from the evidence for *pḥ ntr* rituals in earlier Egyptian evidence. Cp. Ritner 1993: 214–220.

of the gods, learning some things from the gods, for other things being moved by themselves toward accurate consideration of the appropriate symbols. And then, leaving nature and natural energies below, they had dealings with the primary and divine powers.[131]

Anagōgē: Leading the Mortal up to the Divine

The direct experience of the divine powers, of course, might occur by a mortal raising himself or herself up into the realm of the divine, rather than by bringing the divine down into the material world. Iamblichus refers to this possibility for a soul that preserves the mystic *symbola* within it in order to elevate itself to meeting with the gods, but he characteristically puts more emphasis on the role of the gods in assisting mortals to rise.

> The gods in their benevolence and graciousness unstintingly shed their light upon theurgists, summoning up their souls to themselves and orchestrating their union with them, accustoming them, even while still in the body, to detach themselves from their bodies, and to turn themselves towards their eternal and intelligible first principle.[132]

Although some of his followers preserved stories about Iamblichus literally levitating, hovering up in the air when he engaged in contemplation, such an ascension seems only a token of the real ascent all the way up to the divine.[133]

As scholars of theurgy from Lewy to Johnston have noted, the peculiar spell in the Greek Magical Papyri known as the 'Mithras Liturgy' provides the best model for understanding what sort of procedure a theurgic anagogical elevation ritual might have been.[134] This spell provides the instructions for a ritual of immortalization (*apathanatismos*) that involves an ascent through the heavens to a meeting with the supreme deity of the universe, who is identified as Mithras by his appearance in Persian trousers (among other cues).[135] After some preliminary purifications, the magician

---

[131] Proclus, *de sacr.* 151.14–23 (trans. Copenhaver 2015).

[132] Iamblichus, *de myst* 1.12 (41.9–13) (trans. E. C. Clarke, Dillon, and Hershbell 2003). Cf. Iamblichus, *de myst.* 7.4 (255.13–256.2).

[133] Eunapius, *Vit. Soph.* 458; cp. Philostratus, *VA* 3.15, on the levitation of the Indian Gymnosophistae.

[134] Johnston 1997 remains the best treatment, although see also Edmonds 2003 for some details. Lewy 1956 provides the fundamental study of theurgic ritual, although his starting assumption that the Mithras Liturgy reflects the practices of Chaldaean theurgy means that his reconstruction of Chaldaean ritual ends up resembling the Mithras Liturgy quite closely.

[135] The name Mithras Liturgy comes from Dieterich's 1903 groundbreaking study of the text, in which he argues that the ritual represents the actual secret rituals of the Mithras cult found throughout the Roman Empire. The leading scholar of Mithraism at the time, Franz Cumont, famously retorted that the Mithras Liturgy was neither Mithraic nor a liturgy, that

begins with a prayer to transform all of the elements comprising the material body, airy spirit, fire, water, and earth, into immortal elements through a new birth into immortality. This new immortal birth is strictly temporary, however paradoxical that might seem, but the magician asks to be released for a short time only from the "present bitter and relentless necessity which is pressing down upon me."[136] The replacement of the mixture of elements in the body with immortal elements serves as part of the process of the assimilation to the divine in Platonic thinking, since the magician needs to become as like the gods as possible to ascend into their realm.

However, the primary technique by which the magician ascends is through the incorporation of divine light as it streams down from the heavens on the rays of the sun.

> Draw in breath from the rays, drawing up three times as much as you can, and you will see yourself being lifted up [anakouphizomenon] and ascending to the height, so that you seem to be in mid-air. You will hear nothing either of man or of any other living thing, nor in that hour will you see anything of mortal affairs on earth, but rather you will see all immortal things.[137]

This peculiar breathing in of sunlight recalls the words of some of the Chaldaean Oracles, which describe the ascent of the souls of theurgists. "They rest in god, drawing in the flowering flames which come down from the Father. From these flames, as they are descending, the soul plucks the soul-nourished flower of fiery fruits."[138] These flowering flames are the pneumatic equivalent of the material sun's rays. The Emperor Julian explains the analogy in his Hymn to the Mother of the Gods:

---

is, a communal ritual. ("La Mithrasliturgie n'est pas une liturgie et n'est pas mithraique," in A. Harnack, *Die Mission u. Ausbreitung des Christentums in den ersten drei Jahrhunderten II* (Leipzig, 1924), p. 941.) As subsequent scholars have noted, however, the text does involve elements attested in Mithraic cult, so some Mithraic connection must exist, even if the rite could not be the ritual practiced by Mithraic communities. See Edmonds 2003 on the Mithraic connections.

[136] PGM IV.475–829 (486–539). See Edmonds 2014 for an exploration of the paradox of temporary immortality. The replacement of the four elements of the bodily mixture is reminiscent of alchemical imagery, especially, e.g., Zosimus, *On the Letter Omega* 9; MA 1.87–96; and the *Corpus Hermeticum* (Stob. Herm. 26.13, 28–29), but such parallels must await further investigations.

[137] PGM IV.537–544. ἕλκε ἀπὸ τῶν ἀκτίνων πνεῦμα γʹ ἀνασπῶν, ὃ δύνα[σ]αι, καὶ ὄψῃ σεαυτὸν ἀνακουφιζόμενον [κ]αὶ ὑπερβαίνοντα εἰς ὕψος, ὥστε σε δοκεῖ[ν μ]έσον τοῦ ἀέρος εἶναι. οὐδενὸς δὲ ἀκούσει [ο]ὔτε ἀνθρώπου οὔτε ζῴου ἀλλ<ου>, οὐδὲ ὄψῃ οὐδὲν τῶν ἐπὶ γῆς θνητῶν ἐν ἐκείνῃ τῇ ὥρᾳ, πάντα δὲ ὄψῃ ἀθάνατα·

[138] CO 130 = Proclus, *in Tim.* III 266.18–23.

Consider it clearly: the sun, by his vivifying and marvellous heat, draws up all things from the earth and calls them forth and makes them grow; and he separates, I think, all corporeal things to the utmost degree of tenuity, and makes things weigh light [*kouphizei*] that naturally have a tendency to sink. We ought then to make these visible things proofs of his unseen powers. For if among corporeal things he can bring this about through his material heat, how should he not draw and lead upwards the souls of the blessed by the agency of the invisible, wholly immaterial, divine and pure substance which resides in his rays?[139]

The *Chaldaean Oracles* likewise refer to the idea that the soul is made light by breathing in warm *pneuma*, "lightening [*kouphizousa*] the soul with a warm breath," while another Oracle notes that "those who, by inhaling, drive out the soul, are free."[140]

When the magician has reached the heavens by lightening his soul through inhaling the light, he will see the other powers of the celestial realm within the cosmos, the visible gods who are the planets and stars, who rush at this intruder in a menacing fashion. The magician must recite a *symbolon*, the knowledge of which proves his right to ascend into the realm: "Silence, symbol of the living incorruptible god, . . . I am a star, wandering about with you, and shining forth out of the deep."[141] The *symbolon* from the supreme god enables the magician to prevent the celestial deities from destroying the mortal interloper into the heavenly world and to move the borders of the cosmic realm, the doors of the sun, where the

---

[139] Julian, *Hymn to the Mother of the Gods* 172b. σκόπει δὲ ἐναργῶς ἕλκει μὲν ἀπὸ τῆς γῆς πάντα καὶ προκαλεῖται καὶ βλαστάνειν ποιεῖ τῇ ζωπυρίδι καὶ θαυμαστῇ θέρμῃ, διακρίνων οἶμαι πρὸς ἄκραν λεπτότητα τὰ σώματα, καὶ τὰ φύσει φερόμενα κάτω κουφίζει. τὰ δὴ τοιαῦτα τῶν ἀφανῶν αὐτοῦ δυνάμεων ποιητέον τεκμήρια. ὁ γὰρ ἐν τοῖς σώμασι διὰ τῆς σωματοειδοῦς θέρμης οὕτω τοῦτο ἀπεργαζόμενος πῶς οὐ διὰ τῆς ἀφανοῦς καὶ ἀσωμάτου πάντῃ καὶ θείας καὶ καθαρᾶς ἐν ταῖς ἀκτῖσιν ἱδρυμένης οὐσίας ἕλξει καὶ ἀνάξει τὰς εὐτυχεῖς ψυχάς;

[140] *CO* 123 = Proclus, *Ex. Chald.* I.192.17–19 Pitra (fr. 1 Des Places); *CO* 124 = Psellos, *in Chald. Orac.* 142 = PG 122 1144c4.

[141] PGM IV.559, 574–575. σιγῇ, σύμβολον θεοῦ ζῶντος ἀφθάρτου· . . . ἐγώ εἰμι σύμπλανος ὑμῖν ἀστήρ, καὶ ἐκ τοῦ βάθους ἀναλάμπων. Cp. Synesius, *Hymn* I.622–645, which describes the special sphragis seal of the soul as "an object of awe for the hostile daimones, who spring up from the hollows of the earth and breath impious impulses into mortals, a token of recognition for your pure servants, who serve as key-bearers of the fiery ascent paths all along the depths of the glorious universe, so that they may open wide for me the gates of light, and so that, even while I crawl upon the vain earth, I do not belong to earth. Of my fiery works, grant me already here fruit as testimony, unerring words, and everything that warms in the soul immortal hope." Johnston 1997: 186–187 points out that such passwords are not a feature of the apocalyptic genre of texts that describe the ascent of some privileged visionary, since the aim of those texts is to describe the cosmic order, and the visionary has already been authorized.

magician meets the sun god, Helios.[142] Like the encounter with the planetary gods, this vision of the doors of the sun is elaborately described, as is the encounter with the sun god himself: "you will see a youthful god, beautiful in appeance, with fiery hair, and in a white tunic and a scarlet cloak, and wearing a fiery crown."[143]

The final epiphany of the supreme god is preceded by the manifestation of the seven Fates as asp-faced maidens and the seven Pole Lords as bull-headed youths, who line up on either side as the supreme lord of the cosmos appears.

> Now when they take their place, here and there in order, look in the air and you will see lightning-bolts going down, and lights flashing, and the earth shaking, and a god descending, a god immensely great, having a bright appearance youthful, golden-haired, with a white tunic and a golden crown and trousers, and holding in his right hand a golden shoulder of a young bull: this is the Bear which moves and turns heaven around, moving upward and downward in accordance with the hour. Then you will see lightning-bolts leaping from his eyes and stars from his body.[144]

The god resembles the image of Mithras on countless Mithraic monuments throughout the Roman Empire, while the flashes of lightning recall the imagery of a Chaldaean Oracle: "you will perceive all things growing dark. . . . The light of the moon is hidden and the earth does not stand steady, but everything is seen with flashes of lightning."[145] Again, the focus on the visual imagery reinforces the similarities between the theurgies of the *Chaldaean Oracles* and the spells of the Greek Magical Papyri; the performer of the ritual has raised his soul out of the mortal realm into

[142] The magician here does not pass through each of the planetary spheres individually, as some commentators have assumed, following the model of Celsus's description of the seven planetary spheres in Origen, *Contra Celsum* 6.30–31. See Edmonds 2004 and Edmonds 2003, contra Betz 2003: 134–141, who follows Dieterich 1903 in dividing the magician's ascent into seven scenarios.

[143] PGM IV.635–639; cp. 545–556 and 576–584.

[144] PGM IV.693–704. The seven Fates and Pole-Lords may be the powers of the Bear constellations that encircle the celestial pole and thus provide the power behind the entire celestial rotation, that is, the workings of astrological fate. The shoulder of a bull is the Egyptian image for the constellation of the Bear (Ursa Major), and Mithras appears holding this object in a number of Mithraic monuments as a symbol of his power as the supreme deity to turn the heavenly vault and generate astrological fate. See Beck 1977b and Edmonds 2003 for further discussions.

[145] *CO* 147 = Psellos, *in Chald. Orac.* 134 = PG 122 1133b5–8. The first line of text reads, ἀθρήσεις πάντα λέοντα, which would mean "you will perceive everything as a lion," but Johnston 1990: 112–114 plausibly argues for Lobeck's emendation, πάντ' ἀχλύοντα, all things growing dark.

the divine, and the divine power manifests itself in overwhelming flashes of light.

The ritual of immortalization in the Mithras Liturgy thus provides a model for the kind of assimilation to the divine that might be entailed in the theurgic *anagōgē* mentioned in the *Chaldaean Oracles* and the Neoplatonic commentaries. The magician removes his soul from the constraints of his mortal body, temporarily while still living, and rises up on the rays of the sun, following a reverse course from these divine emanations coming from the supreme deity. The rite culminates in a face-to-face meeting between the theurgist and the supreme lord of the cosmos at the boundaries of the supracelestial realm, for the magician waits at the doors of the sun for the great god to make his appearance. Rather than lining up *synthemata* in the form of material and verbal symbols of the gods' power to draw the gods down into the material world, as in the telestic art, the anagogic theurgist takes the *symbola* as tokens of divine authority, passwords to allow him to ascend up to the realms of those divine powers of which his tokens provide the symbolic likeness. Raising up or drawing down, however, the theurgic rituals serve to bring together through such *symbola* the mortal and immortal realms.

WHEN: CHOOSING THE PROPITIOUS TIMES

The immortalization in the Mithras Liturgy can be performed three times a year, as the instructions declare, although a later redaction claims that the god instructed the magician to use the ritual once a month, at full moon, instead of three times a year. This revision of timing has implications for the cosmological assumptions of the spell, particularly the role of the moon, since the preparatory instructions must begin at the 'seizure of the moon,' which is the time before the new moon appears.[146] This emphasis on the appropriate time stands in contrast to the absence of any discussion of where the rite must take place. Theurgic rituals for *systasis* with the divine powers do not need to take place in certain hallowed locations, like the famous oracular consultations at Delphi or Claros, but rather, in the terminology of Smith, theurgy is part of the religion of anywhere. The theurgist may consecrate a particular space for the divine power to descend to, but the place is made special by his actions, rather than his actions by the nature of the place.[147]

[146] PGM IV.748–749, 798–799, 754. See Edmonds 2003 and 2004 for discussions of the significance of the moon's absence and the general underlying cosmology of the spell.

[147] J. Smith 2003. Cp. Iamblichus, *de myst.* 3.12 128 on the divine power that inspires the oracles at Claros, Delphi, and Branchidae actually being free from any boundary of place or time.

The magician in the Eighth Book of Moses, for example, purifies himself for forty days in a house that must be free from the impurities of death, and he creates a special canopy (skēnē) as a particular spot to which the god will descend to meet with him. The text pays far more attention, however, to determining the precise rulers of the day and hour, the astrological powers that rule over the specific time. The text of the spell has a little appendix with a chart for figuring out the ruler of the day, making the conversion from the Greek reckoning of planetary ruler for the days of the week to the Seven-Zoned reckoning; the former pattern follows the order of the days still in use (Sunday, Monday, etc.), while the latter takes the planets in reverse order of their distance: "For if the day be subject to Helios in the Greek reckoning, Selene rules the pole."[148] (see table 10.1)

In addition to this chart, the text instructs the magician to take the names of the gods of the days, hours, and weeks from the list given in another work, entitled the *Key*. Proper attention to the exact time and the ruling divinities is essential,

> for without these the god will not listen but will refuse to receive you as uninitiated, unless you emphatically say in advance the names of the lord of the day and of the hour, which information you will find at the end of this tractate; for without these you will not accomplish even one of the things you find in the *Key*.[149]

Likewise, the preparations for an associated ritual using the Name must be timed for propitious astrological configurations.

> Try to prepare this when the moon is in the east and in conjunction with a beneficent planet, either Zeus or Aphrodite, and when no maleficent one, Kronos or Ares, is in aspect. You may do it best when one of the three beneficent planets is in its own house, while the moon is taking the position of conjunction or aspect or diametrical opposition and when the planet, too, is in the east, for then the rite will be effectual for you.[150]

In the theurgical oracles mentioned in Porphyry, such attention to the timing and the astrological configurations is essential for success. In one oracle, Hekate refuses to respond to the theurgist's queries: "I do not speak,

---

[148] PGM XIII.215–225 ≈ 720–734. Although the chart is in this order on the papyrus, the instructions are to work backward from the bottom of the seven-zoned column to find the equivalent. The English names for the days of the week are built upon the names of the Germanic gods equated with the Greco-Roman ones, so Tiu for Mars, Woden for Mercury, Thor for Jupiter, and Freya for Venus; the equivalents are closer in the modern Romance languages. For the planetary powers, see further ch. 8, p. 251, "The Wandering Stars."

[149] PGM XIII.55–60.

[150] PGM XIII.1027–1039.

TABLE 10.1

GREEK	SEVEN ZONED
Helios (Sunday)	Kronos (Saturn)
Selene (Monday)	Zeus (Jupiter)
Ares (Tuesday)	Ares (Mars)
Hermes (Wednesday)	Helios (Sun)
Zeus (Thursday)	Aphrodite (Venus)
Aphrodite (Friday)	Hermes (Mercury)
Kronos (Saturday)	Selene (Moon)

I shall shut the gates of the long throat, for in the night the horned goddess Titania drives towards the most unpropitious goads of night, looking at malignant Ares."[151] The unfavorable aspect between Mars and the Moon (the horned Titania) makes the timing unpropitious for the goddess to respond to the theurgist. Iamblichus notes that the Egyptian theurgists, making use of the astrological material in the Hermetic books, base their theurgical rituals on the critical time rather than any other kind of connection with the gods.

> They recommend that we ascend through the practices of sacred theurgy to the regions that are higher, more universal and superior to fate, towards the god who is the creator, without calling in the aid of matter or bringing to bear anything other than the observation of the criticial time for action.[152]

Iamblichus takes pains to differentiate what is under the control of astrological fate from that which is linked directly to the higher divine powers, and he insists that it is through the principle of the soul that is higher than nature and fate that the theurgist unites with the gods.[153] The Hermetic practitioners are not wrong to pay attention to the propitious times, but Iamblichus does not place as much importance on when the theurgic rite takes place as other sources do.

[151] Porphyry, *Philos. ex Orac.* fr. 342, lines 3–5 = Philoponus, *De Opificio Mundi* 201.20–22. Οὐ λαλέω, κλείσω δὲ πύλας δολιχοῖο φάρυγγος·| Νυκτὸς γὰρ κέντροις ἀχρειοτάτοις προσελαύνει| Τιτηνὶς κερόεσσα θεὴ κακὸν Ἄρη ἰδοῦσα. As Addey 2014: 121 notes, "There also seems to be a pun based on the word κέντρον, the ancient astrological term for the 'angles' of the horoscope, which has a more generic meaning in Greek of 'stinging goad.' "

[152] Iamblichus, *de myst.* 8.4 267 (trans. E. C. Clarke, Dillon, and Hershbell 2003). Cp. the importance of the καιρός in the alchemists criticized by Zosimus, *On the Letter Omega* 2–3 = MA 1.11–33.

[153] Iamblichus, *de myst.* 8.5–8 (268–272).

WHY: THE PURPOSE OF THEURGIC RITUALS

Iamblichus proudly proclaims that "theurgists do not address the divine Intellect over trifling matters but only concerning things that pertain to the purification, liberation, and salvation of the soul."[154] Iamblichus has to protest so vehemently because of the critics of theurgy who complain that theurgists harness the powers of the gods for unworthy purposes—satisfaction of bodily needs or greeds, unphilosophical attempts to get out of the consequences of their unjust actions, or simply trivial displays of marvels just for the sake of creating amazement among their audience. Although Iamblichus in de mysteriis insists that theurgy is not really about such things, the theories he articulates for bringing the individual soul into contact with the power of the gods apply perfectly well to exactly the kinds of aims that the critics cite. While the ultimate end might always be the communion with the gods, a whole range of shorter-term goals appear in the evidence—not just in the Greek Magical Papyri, but also in the evidence for the Neoplatonist philosophers who practiced theurgy.

The two most elaborate theurgical rites in the Greek Magical Papyri, the so-called Mithras Liturgy and the Eighth Book of Moses, both exhibit this apparent tension between ultimate and proximate aims, which has led some previous scholars to imagine a history of revisions that altered these texts from 'religious' texts with aims of which Iamblichus would approve to 'magical' texts with less worthy aims. The immortalization (apathanatismos) ritual in the Mithras Liturgy, for example, culminates in a face-to-face meeting with the supreme god, who then provides the magician with oracular revelations in verse.

> After you have said these things, he will immediately respond with a revelation. Now you will grow weak in soul and will not be in yourself, when he answers you. He speaks the oracle to you in verse, and after speaking he will depart. But you remain silent, since you will be able to comprehend all these matters by yourself; for at a later time you will remember infallibly the things spoken by the great god, even if the oracle contained myriads of verses.[155]

We may well imagine such verse oracles as the same kind that Porphyry preserves in his Philosophy Drawn from Oracles, direct divine revelations

---

[154] Iamblichus, de myst. 10.7 (293.5–8).

[155] PGM IV.725–733. ταῦτά σου εἰπόντος εὐθέως χρησμῳδήσει. ὑπέκλυτος δὲ ἔσει τῇ ψυχῇ καὶ οὐκ ἐν σεαυτῷ ἔσει, ὅταν σοι ἀποκρίνηται. λέγει δέ σοι διὰ στίχων τὸν χρησμὸν καὶ εἰπὼν ἀπελεύσεται, σὺ δὲ στήκεις ἐνεός, ὡς ταῦτα πάντα χωρήσεις αὐτομάτως, καὶ τότε μνημονεύσεις ἀπαραβάτως τὰ ὑπὸ τοῦ μεγάλου θεοῦ ῥηθέντα, κἂν ἦν μυρίων στίχων ὁ χρησμός. Cp. the story in Eunapius, Vit. Soph. 464 about Aedesius, who receives a verse oracle from a god and, when he fears that the verses are slipping from his memory, realizes that the words have been written on his hand.

with specially authoritative instructions for living life or, perhaps like the *Chaldaean Oracles*, with privileged insights into the structure of the cosmos.

The immortalization itself is only temporary, an extreme form of purification or consecration that enables the magician to meet with the supreme deity of the cosmos, like Iamblichus's reference to those who accustom themselves, while still in mortal incarnation, to rise up out of their bodies to the gods.[156] Nevertheless, many scholars, following Lewy's groundbreaking study, imagine that such a ritual immortalization was the whole aim of theurgical practice, perhaps even of a Chaldaean theurgical community. Proclus refers to a theurgic immortalization (*apathanatismos*) in his interpretation of the Homeric description of the funeral rites Achilles performs for Patroclus. "The whole of Achilles' ritual practice concerning that funereal pyre imitates the immortalization of the soul practiced by the theurgists, leading Patroclus' soul upwards toward the life that is separated [i.e., from the body]."[157] Proclus interprets various elements in Homer's description as symbolic representations of the lifting up of the soul; exposing the pyre to the winds is a token of having the vehicles of the soul purified "and . . . restored to its proper allotted place, drawn upward by the aereal and seleniac and heliac rays." Likewise, the libations poured signify the fount of the soul, and the pyre itself "the immaculate purity which is able to turn around the soul from the body to the invisible." Although Lewy imagined a Chaldaean theurgic community practicing such funereal rites as a kind of sacrament of *anagōgē*, Proclus here is using the Homeric description as an allegory for an anagogic ritual that, with its descriptions of the soul being drawn upward by the sun's rays, seems to resemble the Mithras Liturgy's ascent more than the sequential stripping away of bodily passions in the rebirth account of *Corpus Hermeticum* XIII.[158] More importantly, Proclus's allegorical interpretation, aimed as it is at freeing Homer from the charge of "contempt for gods and men" by his description of Achilles's behavior, makes no claims about the purpose of the immortalization ritual of the theurgists, which may have been as temporary as the immortalization in the Mithras Liturgy or the contemplative union with the One that Porphyry claims his master Plotinus achieved four times during his life.[159]

---

[156] Cp. Edmonds 2014; Iamblichus, *de myst.* 1.12 (41.9–13).

[157] Proclus, *in Remp.* I.152. See the discussion of Tanaseanu-Döbler 2013: 207–214.

[158] Cp. *Corpus Hermeticum* XIII; the other parallel that is adduced is the experience of Lucius in Apuleius, *Metamorphoses* 11. Lewy discusses the Proclus passage at length in Lewy 1956: 204–211.

[159] Porphyry, *Vit. Plot.* 23.15. Plotinus, Porphyry tells us, achieved this *systasis* four times by means of the methods Plato teaches in the *Symposium*, while Porphyry himself only managed it once.

The *systasis* with the supreme deity in the Eighth Book of Moses provides the magician with the divine Name, which has a plethora of practical applications, but the magician can also take the opportunity to ask the god about his fate.

> You, then, ask, "Master, what is fated for me?" And he will tell you even about your star, and what kind of daimon you have, and your horoscope and where you may live and where you will die. And if you hear something bad, do not cry out or weep, but ask that he may wash it off or circumvent it, for this god can do everything.[160]

The ruler of the universe is superior to the astrological powers that control fate, so he can both know what those powers intend and command them to change it. This attempt to alter fate is taken by some ancient sources as the very definition of a magician, someone who, through dubious rituals, claims to be able to dominate the established order of the world.[161] Iamblichus by contrast argues that we should all worship the gods as powers higher than fate; since they can "dominate necessity by means of rational persuasion, they may free us from the evils that lie in wait for us from fate."[162] The alteration of fate thus appears as an accepted aim of theurgical ritual, even though such operations were considered magic (*goēteia*) by others.

While the alteration of fate might fall under the Iamblichean aims of purification, liberation, and salvation of the soul, theurgy seems to have been used for less lofty purposes, even by Iamblichus himself. In addition to the stories of his levitation, Iamblichus is said to have evoked the spirits of two springs (in the form of Eros and Anteros) to the amazement of his followers, while Porphyry, by contrast, is said to have expelled a daimon from a bathing place.[163] Iamblichus discusses walking on water or over hot coals as a sign of true divine inspiration, just like being cut with knives or axes and not feeling it, "because at this time they are not living the life of an animate being," that is, their souls have been separated from the body and joined with the divine.[164] Other such miracles are attributed to theur-

---

[160] PGM XIII.709–715; cp. 634–639. "Protect me from all my own astrological destiny; destroy my foul fate; apportion good things for me in my horoscope; increase my life even in the midst of many goods, for I am your slave and petitioner and have hymned your valid and holy name, lord, glorious one, ruler of the cosmos."

[161] Cp. Hierocles's arguments that Apollonius of Tyana should not be considered a magician because he always stayed within the dictates of fate. Eusebius, *contra Hier.* 27.

[162] Iamblichus, *de myst.* 8.7 (269.10–270.5).

[163] Eunapius, *Vit. Soph.* 458 (levitation); 459 (evocation, as well as the ability to sense impurity when he turns aside from a road along which a funeral procession is coming); 457 (Porphyry's exorcism, which Eunapius claims to have heard about in a book by Porphyry himself). Iamblichus himself mentions levitation in *de myst.* 3.5 112.

[164] Iamblichus, *de myst.* 3.4 110.

gists; Nestorius prevented an earthquake in Attica by fashioning a statue of Achilles and placing it in the Parthenon, and Proclus, in addition to being able to predict earthquakes, stopped a drought in Athens by bringing the rain with his *iunx*.[165] Julian the theurgist is also credited with bringing rain, and one story even tells of him creating special masks for the Roman army that shoot lightning bolts at the enemy.[166] Such miracle stories resemble the ones told of Apollonius of Tyana and Jesus of Nazareth, whose expulsions of demons and raising spirits from the dead seem comparable to the feats the magician of the Eighth Book of Moses might do with the great Name or even to what the magician can do who has used the Spell of Pnouthis to obtain a divine assistant.[167]

CONCLUSIONS: THEURGY AS MAGIC OR RELIGION OR PHILOSOPHY

Of course, such extra-ordinary performances incur the risk of being labeled 'magic' by hostile audiences, and Eunapius indeed reports that several Neoplatonic philosophers suffered from charges of magic. Sopator is executed after a rival philosopher accused him of using his powers to charm the winds to prevent the grain ships from getting into Rome, while Eustathius is accused of using *goēteia* to enhance his persuasive power during his embassy to the Persian court (by, ironically, the magi at the court).[168] Other Neoplatonic theurgists are more circumspect in their use of power; Sosipatra performs only minor miracles for her close circle, despite the marvelous story of her theurgic training, while her son, Antoninus, lives quietly teaching philosophy in Egypt and only manifests his power by predicting the destruction of the great temple of Serapis.[169] Such extraordinary power from the gods, with efficacy beyond that of mortal kind, can always be classified as magic in certain kinds of circumstances, particularly in the midst of high-stakes power struggles at court.

[165] Zosimus of Constantinople IV.18 (Nestorius); Marinus, *Vit Procl.* 28.

[166] *Suda* s.v. Ἰουλιανός iota 433 and 434. Cp. the stories in Psellos, *Opusc.* 3.139–147 and 46.40–50.

[167] For the miracles of Apollonius of Tyana, cp. raising a girl from dead in Philostratus, *VA* 4.45, expelling a lamia daimon in 4.25, and other exorcisms in 4.10 and 3.38. Cp. the list of things the magician can do in PGM I.42–195 (97–124); XII.270–350 (303–306, 277–282); and XIII.1–343 (245–340).

[168] Eunapius, *Vit. Soph.* 466 (Eustathius).

[169] Eunapius, *Vit. Soph.* 466–471. The miraculous life of Sosipatra has been analyzed in detail by Johnston 2012 and Lewis 2014, both of whom point out the way the female theurgist is treated by Eunapius as a model woman, in ways similar to the lives of the Christian saints, to avoid assimilations to the witch stereotype.

Courtly settings were not the only arenas in which the status of theurgical practices were contested, however; the preeminence of a number of the sources for theurgy within the Platonic schools made them targets for rival claimants to wisdom, both within the schools and between the Platonic schools and other schools of thought. Eusebius's and Augustine's attacks on Porphyry and Apuleius show the contestation with emergent Christianity, and the condemnation of the rival's practices as *goēteia*, magic, could be a potent way to discredit them. Likewise, in the contests for authority within the Platonic schools, the claim to be the legitimate heir to the teachings of Plato could be bolstered by attacking the validity of a rival's approach as relying too much on material concerns or the powers of the mortal world.

It is worth noting the differences between the ways these disputes are framed in the ancient sources and in the modern scholarly analyses. Modern scholars tend to use familiar modern criteria for distinguishing legitimate religious or philosophical activity from magic, specifically the differences in attitude, intention, and action.[170] Religion takes a passive attitude toward the divine powers, while magic is active and coercive; religion has intentions for abstract goals such as salvation of the soul, while magic aims at concrete and selfish ends; religious action depends upon personal interactions, while magic involves impersonal manipulation. Ancient sources, by contrast, focus on different issues. While there is some concern about ends, the focus is more on whether the results play out in the material world or in the higher realms. More important for the ancient sources is the question of whether the activity actually works, that is, its objective validity or efficacy.[171] The critiques of theurgy as magic come in two forms, familiar in other circumstances of the labeling of 'magic'; either the activity fails to accomplish what it claims, or it is too successful for comfort.

The prosecution of Sopator for using his ritual power to hold back the grain ships and the praise of Nestorius for preventing an earthquake are both examples of the evaluation of the theurgic practice as extra-ordinarily efficacious, either in a negative or in a positive sense. By contrast, the critiques of theurgy as a contact with deceptive demons who cannot deliver on their promises treat theurgy as magic in the other sense, as false or ineffective religious action. When Plotinus argues that the magicians can only create effects through cosmic sympathy on the material plane, he dismisses the claims of theurgists (whether or not they called themselves that in his day) to be tapping into the higher divine levels, labeling their actions as

[170] Versnel 1991b articulates most clearly these categories that usually remain implicit in the scholarship. See ch. 1, p. 15, n. 25.

[171] For the Weberian criteria of legitimate religious action (performance, social location, objectivity, and ends) applied to the definition of magic, see Gordon 1999a, especially 191ff. See ch. 1, p. 19, n. 35.

false magic. Porphyry adds the idea of deceptive demons who masquerade as higher powers to discredit any objective success that a practioner might be able to claim. Like Zosimus in his polemic against the alchemists who rely on 'propitious tinctures' that depend on the cooperation of daimonic entities, Porphyry warns of daimons who provide some results just to gain the worship and trust of the deluded ritual practitioner.[172]

Iamblichus cleverly responds to Porphyry, not by denying the existence of such deceptive demons, but by distinguishing his true theurgy from that false practice. He turns the tables on Porphyry and Plotinus by critiquing contemplative philosophical theology as limited to the mortal realm in just the same way that they critiqued magical practice based in cosmic *sympatheia*. Because such intellectual contemplation depends on the mortal intellect, it cannot go beyond the mortal level to reach the gods.

> It is not pure thought that unites theurgists to the gods. Indeed what, then, would hinder those who are theoretical philosophers from enjoying a theurgic union with the gods? But the situation is not so: it is the accomplishment of acts not to be divulged and beyond all conception, and the power of the unutterable symbols, understood solely by the gods, which establishes theurgic union. Hence, we do not bring about these things by intellection alone; for thus their efficacy would be intellectual, and dependent upon us. But neither assumption is true. For even when we are not engaged in intellection, the symbols themselves, by themselves, perform their appropriate work, and the ineffable power of the gods, to whom these symbols relate, itself recognises the proper images of itself, not through being aroused by our thought.[173]

Mortal intellection is insufficient, so any philosopher who depends solely upon it is limited to the mortal realm, just like the magicians Plotinus critiques. Theurgic practice is thus validated for its objective efficacy; it provides a theoretically possible way to transcend the mortal realm and contact the gods, so it cannot be magic in the way that Plotinus and Porphyry have alleged. As the truly divine form of religious practice, theurgy may be magical for Iamblichus in the sense of abnormally efficacious ritual, but he does not make such an argument, nor does he evaluate the claims to magical power of practices such as those found in the Greek Magical Papyri.[174]

---

[172] Cp. Zosimus, *On the Letter Omega* 17–18; MA 1.160–188 M; Porphyry, *de abst.* II.38–41.

[173] Iamblichus, *de myst.* 2.11 96.13–97.2 (trans. E. C. Clarke, Dillon, and Hershbell 2003).

[174] Addey 2014: 38 speculates, "Certain texts contained therein, such as the so-called 'Mithras Liturgy,' an elaborate text setting out instructions for the immortalisation of the soul, bear similarities to the nature of theurgy as expounded by Iamblichus and the latter

When Augustine and Eusebius pick up the attack, they make use of many of the same arguments as Porphyry, but they condemn all religious interactions with divinities other than the Christian god as false and ineffective. Any other power is a form of deceptive demon, promising more than it can deliver even if it can deliver some objective results. The Christian authors berate Porphyry for his inconsistency and incoherent theology, repeatedly using his own arguments to Iamblichus against him. This Christian challenge to the coherence of theurgical ideas is met, in different ways, by the responses of later pagan philosophers.[175] Saloustios distills Neoplatonic theology into a simple and easily communicated set of doctrines, whereas Proclus creates a vastly complex but rigorously systematic theology, laid out in the form of Euclidean propositions in his *Elements of Theology* and developed throughout his other works. Again, the dispute in the ancient sources revolves around the objective validity of the system: can it work, or is it incoherent and ineffective?

Modern scholars have portrayed the disputes in different terms, opposing the passive attitude of religion, with personal interactions aimed at salvific goals, to the coercive attitude of magic, with impersonal manipulations aimed at concrete and selfish goals. In her introduction to her edition of the *Chaldaean Oracles*, Majercik distinguishes theurgy from magic.

> Theurgy certainly appropriates many of the techniques familiar to the magician, but its purpose is quite different: whereas "common" magic has a "profane" goal (e.g., in its "white" form, influencing a lover or affecting the weather), theurgy has a specific religious or salvific end, namely, the purification and salvation of the soul (see, e.g., Iamblichus, *De myst.* I.12: τῆς ψυχῆς σωτήριον). In addition, and most importantly, theurgy emphasizes a passive attitude towards the gods (with the gods taking the initiative), whereas magic involves coercing or forcing the gods against their will.[176]

---

may well have approved of such practices and classified them as theurgy. . . . With his great respect for Egyptian religious tradition, Iamblichus was presumably well aware of this situation: thus, some practices attested in the PGM may well have been considered by the philosopher as theurgical rather than 'magical' because of their basis in religious tradition."

[175] It is worth noting that some Christian authors, such as Dionysius the Areopagite, co-opted the language of theurgy to describe (and validate the authority of) Christian ritual practices, including the Eucharist, and the miracles of Jesus (cp. *Ecclesiastical Hierarchy* 432b). See Struck 2001.

[176] Majercik 1989: 22–23. Cp. Tanaseanu-Döbler 2013: 110n330, on the arguments of van Liefferinge 1999. "Van Liefferinge's attempt to demonstrate that Iamblichus' theurgy is not magic is futile from the outset: she does not recognize the fluidity, flexibilty and polemical context of the notion, does not pay heed to the modern debate and therefore takes up the criteria which older scholarship had developed to distinguish magic and religion as separate fields and applies them to the *De mysteriis* in order to prove that it is not really about magic."

Dillon makes use of the same criteria, but places theurgy in the opposite camp of magic, which he classifies together with science in opposition to religion.

> The distinction commonly made between magic and theurgy is in fact, in my view, basically an unreal one. The real distinction is between magic/theurgy—and its remote descendant, the modern scientific world-view—and religion. Behind the latter is the impulse to abase oneself before some force alien to oneself that is infinitely powerful and mysterious; behind the former is the impulse to come to terms with that force, and the physical world it has created, to ferret out what makes it tick, and to manipulate it for one's own ends. These are two very different impulses in man.[177]

For both of these scholars, the distinguishing characteristics of religion are its spiritual aims and the supplicative attitude the practitioner takes to the personal interactions with the superior powers, in contrast to the magician's active manipulation of impersonal elements to serve his material aims. Some modern scholars emphasize the Iamblichean insistence on theurgy as the action that the gods take, rather than as the product of human effort, to characterize theurgy as religion, while others focus on the manipulation of efficacious *symbola* and the systematic hierarchy of the theurgic cosmology to liken it to magic.

Some of these debates have their root in disputes about the place of ritual within modern religion, a debate in which Protestant critiques of Catholic ritualism as magic have historically played an important role. The divide cited by Damascius between the philosophers who saw contemplation as the highest form of philosophy and those who valued telestic ritual more highly is understood in terms of the conflict between pure religion focused on internal and personal relations with the divine and debased religion that relies on outward and impersonal actions in the manner of magic.[178] More recent scholars have begun to transcend this model by looking to religious traditions, such as Tantric Buddhism, that place a high

---

[177] J. Dillon 2007: 40. "I would go so far as to suggest that theurgy is really no more than magic with a 'rational account,' or *logos*, to back it up. The vulgar magician knows, perhaps, what is to be done to achieve a certain, usually rather trivial, result; the theurgist knows in addition *why* such procedures are to be followed, and how they really work. He does not flatter himself that he is in any way superior to divinities (except perhaps, stretching a point, to little local daemons), and he will avoid any suggestion of arrogance when addressing his superiors, but deep down he knows this great truth: that if he presses the right buttons, *they will come*."

[178] Damascius, *in Phaed.* I.172 divides the Neoplatonists who honor philosophy (Plotinus and Porphyry) over hieratic (Iamblichus, Syrianus, and Proclus), but, as Addey 2014: 181–183 notes, this passage has often been used to set up a sharp opposition between contemplation and theurgy; cp. Tanaseanu-Döbler 2013: 268–273; Mazur 2004: 39.

value on ritual performance, which enables them to take theurgy seriously as a form of ritual religion.[179] This approach, however, while it does away with the modern criterion of action, still emphasizes the crucial importance of intention and attitude in evaluating religious performance, as in Addey's recent definition of theurgy.

> Theurgy (θεουργία) designates a lifelong endeavour incorporating a set of ritual practices alongside the development of ethical and intellectual capacities, which aimed to use symbols (σύμβολα) to reawaken the soul's pre-ontological, causal connection with the gods, operating primarily through divine love (θεία φιλία) and, subordinately, through cosmic sympathy (συμπάθεια). The goal of theurgy was the cumulative contact, assimilation and, ultimately, union with the divine and thereby the divinisation of the theurgist; in other words, the ascent of the soul to the divine, intelligible realm (ἀναγωγή) and the manifestation of the divine in embodied life.[180]

Theurgy is defined by its goal and its nature as a lifelong practice of cultivating a relation with the gods. Such an etic definition does have its uses in understanding theurgy, particularly in relation to modern religious and philosophical movements, but attention to the criteria that are significant to the emic sources provides a different level of insight into theurgy.

The ancient debates over theurgy show that the nature of the soul and its place in the cosmic hierarchy lie at the center of the disputes. If some part of the soul remains undescended in the divine realm, then theurgy is ineffective posturing that neglects the attention due to accessing that divine element, but if its complete descent requires divine intervention to rise back into the divine realm, then theurgy is an effective means of cultivating that divine aid.[181] If the cosmos consists of a continuous chain of correspondences linking the highest entities to the lowest, then theurgy is a valid way of interacting with the higher powers, but if the ontological division between the material world of Becoming and the divine realm of Being is unbridgeable, then it is merely a delusional activity that is confined to the mortal world.

[179] Shaw 1995 and subsequent studies have been important in this development, and his lead has been followed by scholars such as Mazur and Addey and even Dillon. It is worth contrasting this Tantric model with the model of spiritualism used by Dodds 1951 to explain theurgy or even the parallels with hallucinogenic shamanism and ESP cited by Luck 2000.

[180] Addey 2014: 25. Cp. the excellent analysis in Tanaseanu-Döbler 2013: 187–188, with n. 6, of the modern scholarship that tries to divide theurgy into two or three 'levels,' ranging from lower, practical, and magical to higher, contemplative, and religious. She cites A. Smith 1974 and Majercik 1989 for the two-level version, as well as Sheppard 1982 and van den Berg 2001 for the three-level one.

[181] Addey 2014: 205 stresses the importance of the dispute over the complete or incomplete descent of the soul to the varying theories of theurgy.

For the ancient advocates of theurgy, its efficacy as a religious performance is authorized by the direct divine revelations that underlie its practices. The *Chaldaean Oracles* and other oracles that Porphyry cites provide immediate connections with the divine, something that was in high demand during the first several centuries of the Common Era. Theurgy's authority is reflected not only in its importance to the elite philosophers and imperial courtiers who practiced and commented upon it, but also in the fact that it became the target for Christian polemicists like Eusebius and Augustine, who saw in theurgy a formidable opponent to their own claims of religious authority. Both those who claimed the title of theurgists and those who attacked theurgy regarded theurgy as an extra-ordinary form of religious practice, either as an empty and deceptive demonic fraud or as the ultimate form of philosophical religion. From the perspective of the modern scholar of magic, however, the very controversies over the label of 'magic' show that theurgy should be analyzed among the types of magic in the ancient Greco-Roman world. The Neoplatonic theurgists rejected the label of 'magic' (*goēteia*) that their opponents so strenuously tried to apply to their practices, but the ritual practitioners of the Greek Magical Papyri are more willing to accept the label of 'magic,' to refer to themselves like the practitioner in the Spell of Pnouthis as a "blessed initiate of the sacred magic."[182]

[182] PGM I.127. ὦ μακάριε μύστα τῆς ἱερᾶς μαγείας.

11

The Label of 'Magic' in the Ancient Greco-Roman World

He will serve you suitably for whatever you have in mind, O
blessed initiate of the sacred magic, and will accomplish it for you,
this most powerful assistant, who is also the only lord of the air.
And the gods will agree to everything, for without him nothing
happens. Share this great mystery with no one else, but conceal
it, by Helios, since you have been deemed worthy by the lord god.
(PGM I.125–131)[1]

This spell in the Greek Magical Papyri explicitly labels the performer as
a 'magician,' an initiate in the great mystery that is sacred magic; that
is, both the person and the ritual are grouped within the discourse of
magic. Through his performance of a magical ritual, the performer of the
rite uses the text to label himself performatively as 'magical.' Such explicit
self-labelings are one of the most fascinating aspects of the evidence for
magic in the ancient Greco-Roman world, since they provide direct insight
into the emic category of magic and, in particular, into the positive sense
that magic might have for one who sought the extra-ordinary. Only a small
part of the evidence for the discourse of magic, however, comes from self-
labeling; far more comes from the labeling of someone else. In either case,
however, it is worth exploring the reasons why such a label is applied, as
well as how the one applying the label, to himself or to another, validates
the use of the discourse of magic in the circumstances.

This attention to why the label is applied, by whom, to whom, and in
what circumstances, helps to resolve the problems that occur if the bound-

---

[1] δουλεύσει σοι ἱκανῶς εἰς [ἃ] ἂν ἐπινοήσῃς, ὦ μα[κάρι]ε μύστα τῆς ἱερᾶς μαγείας, καὶ ἐπι– τελέσει
σοι ὁ κράτιστος πάρεδρος οὗτος, ὁ καὶ μόνος κύριος τοῦ ἀέρος, καὶ συνφων[ή]σουσι πάντα οἱ θεοί·
δίχα γὰρ τούτου οὐδέν ἐστιν. μηδενὶ [ἄλλῳ με]ταδῷς, ἀλλὰ κρύβε, πρὸς Ἡλίου, ἀξιωθεὶς ὑπὸ τοῦ
κυρί[ου θεοῦ], τὸ μέγα τοῦτο μυστήριον.

aries of the category of magic are solely determined by substantive questions of *what* is done, that is, if magic is treated as a thing, rather than a way of talking about things. Many of the things labeled as 'magic'—curses or prayers or divinatory rituals—may, depending on the circumstances, be regarded as perfectly normative: the curses on the enemies of the community that begin the assembly, a votive prayer made hurriedly to the god as the ship starts to go down, the examination of entrails before battle, and so forth. But these ritual acts may also be considered non-normative if the same things are done by different people in different contexts (*social location*) or with different claims to power and authority (*efficacy*). Claims to extra-ordinary efficacy in the positive sense tend to characterize examples of self-labeling, since such a claim can be a useful strategy in the contests for authority in the various agonistic social arenas of the ancient world. By contrast, the non-normative social location of the accused tends to be the crucial factor in the use of magic as a label for someone else. In this final chapter, I examine the ways these cues of social location and efficacy are used in the discourse of magic, both for the labeling of the self and of others. For other-labeling, the dynamics are especially clear in the legal arena, where the community or its representative are deciding where that person fits within the community. In such evidence, claims of extra-ordinary efficacy remain secondary to the cue of the social location of the performer. By contrast, self-labeling is much rarer and appears only in limited kinds of evidence, such as the Greek Magical Papyri, but the cue of extra-ordinary efficacy is the most important, and claims to extra-ordinary social location tend to be secondary to it. The appearance of such self-labeling, however, is unusual in the discourse of magic found in other cultures, so these examples are particularly revealing for the nature of the discourse of magic in the ancient Greco-Roman world.

OTHER-LABELING: ACCUSATIONS OF MAGIC

> How do you *know* she's a witch?
> She looks like one! . . .
> What makes you think she is a witch?
> Well, she turned me into a *newt*!
> A newt?
> I got better. . . .
>
> (*Monty Python & the Holy Grail*)

This parody of a medieval witch trial highlights the dynamics of the labeling an other as 'magic' in a legal context, absurdly bringing out two of the key features in any such situation—the social location of the accused figure and the actions of which she (or occasionally he) is accused. The accused is marked as objectively profane, in a marginal social location—an old, ugly peasant woman dressed in strange clothes (even if such markers have to be imposed in this case by the crowd). The specific cues that mark such a social location may differ from context to context, but such markers nonetheless often play a primary role in the legal contexts. What the magician does is often a secondary consideration, its significance shaped by the evaluation of the social location. The cues of weird performance and socially unacceptable ends may affect the way the accused is evaluated, but the extra-ordinary efficacy of the acts tends to draw the most focus, whether such acts are miraculous reversals of nature (she turned me into a newt!) or are revealed to be a sham (I got better . . .). In the evidence for accusations in the ancient Greco-Roman world that seem to involve the discourse of magic, these same factors appear; the laws under which magical activity is prosecuted address the harm done to another individual or the community by that activity, but the dynamics of the trial center upon the social location of the accused, even more than her extra-ordinarily efficacious acts.

The Legal Context for Magic in Greece

The evidence from ancient Greece is scanty, but no city seems to have had any specific law that specifically addressed magic as a non-normative ritual activity. There is no evidence of any law code that banned *mageia* or *goētia*, and, while there are some mentions of *pharmaka*, such laws are including *pharmaka* among other ways of doing harm (*blabē*), rather than singling out their use as a particularly problematic and prosecutable offense. In the Classical period, fifth or fourth century BCE, the community of the Teans recited their communal curses against the enemies of the community, those who use harmful *pharmaka*, those who block the importation of grain, those who engage in robbery, piracy, or civil strife; the collocation of *pharmaka* with these other acts indicates that it is the harm that they may do that is the focus of attention. An even more extensive collocation occurs in a later (first-century BCE) inscription of rules for conduct within a cult association in Lydia.

> Upon entering this house men and women, free and slave, must swear an oath by all the gods not to use trickery against men or women, not to devise or perform a wicked spell [*pharmakon*] against people, nor wicked charms [*epōidai*], nor a love charm [*philtron*], nor an abortifacient, nor a contraceptive, nor themselves to commit robbery/rape or murder, nor to incite another person to do so, nor to be an accessory after the fact to these crimes.[2]

[2] TAM V.3 1539 = LSAM 20.14-22. [πορευ]-|όμενοι εἰς τὸν οἶκον τοῦτον ἄνδρε[ς καὶ γυναῖκες]||

The use of *pharmaka* and *epōidai* are lumped together with fraud, assault, and murder as criminal acts, whether the *pharmaka* cause bodily harm or have some sort of impact on the erotic sphere.

From Classical Athens we have evidence from lawcourt speeches of trials involving *pharmaka*, some of which seem to be focused on the deadly harm caused by introducing strange substances into the food or drink of the victim, but others of which refer more broadly to the effects of the *pharmaka* as affecting the victim's mind. The orator Isaeus, who specializes in inheritance cases, twice mentions the idea that a man might have been bewitched by *pharmaka* to change his will, while Demosthenes claims that the laws ordain that a man who is mad or diseased or bewitched by *pharmaka* (or persuaded by a woman) may not freely change his will.[3] Antiphon's speech in the case *Against the Stepmother* describes a scenario in which two women gave *pharmaka* to their lovers in order to retain their affections. Whether by accident or, as the prosecutor alleges, through malice aforethought, the men died, and the wife of one man (the stepmother of the prosecutor) faces a charge of murder, while the slave concubine of the other man has already been summarily tortured and killed. Since we have only the prosecutor's speech, we cannot know the outcome of the trial (which may, as with other of Antiphon's speeches, be simply a rhetorical exercise), but later testimonies describing similar scenarios report both acquittal on the grounds that the death was unintended and conviction on the grounds that the death was a result of the woman's actions.[4] By contrast, another speech of Antiphon's deals with a case in which a *pharmakon* is blamed in the death of a chorus boy, but the defendant claims that he never gave the boy a *pharmakon* and was not even present when the boy drank it. Here, as in the case of the stepmother, the *pharmakon* is clearly imagined as a substance added to a drink, but there is no suggestion that it could do anything but kill. The defendant claims that the prosecutors have trumped up this charge merely to prevent him from prosecuting their friends for embezzlement and other improprieties, but he never tries to argue that the boy did not die from drinking a lethal *pharmakon*.

Plato draws a distinction between those pharmaka that work as a material body on a material body (*sōmasi sōmata*) and those that work by

---

ἐλεύθεροι καὶ οἰκέται τοὺς θεοὺς [πάντας ὀρκοῦσ]]-θωσαν δόλον μηθένα μήτε ἀνδρὶ μή[τε γυναικὶ εἰδό]]-τες μὴ φάρμακον πονηρὸν πρὸς ἀνθ[ρώπους, μὴ ἐπωι]]-δὰς πονηρὰς μήτε γινώσκειν μή[τε ἐπιτελεῖν, μὴ]] φίλτρον, μὴ φθορεῖον, μὴ [ἀτ]οκεῖον, μ[ὴ] ἄλλο τι παιδο]]-φόνον μήτε αὐτοὺς ἐπιτελεῖν μήτε [ἑτέρωι συμβου]]-λεύειν μηδὲ συνιστορεῖν (trans. Ogden 2009).

[3] Isaeus 6.21, 9.37; Demosthenes 46.14.

[4] Antiphon 1.14–20. The *Magna Moralia* attributed to Aristotle mentions a woman tried in the Areopagus and acquitted because she had not intended murder (1188b), whereas the fourth-century CE Basil of Caesarea argues in a letter (*Letters* 188.8) that the extra-ordinary and illicit nature of erotic *pharmaka* incurs guilt for the woman even if she did not intend to kill. See the discussion in Faraone 1999: 110–119.

enchantments (*magganeiais te tisin kai epōidais kai katadesesi*), but he treats both as modes of doing harm by various means. He admits uncertainty as to the efficacy of such enchantments, but in the absence of a clear philosophical explanation of how or even if these nonmaterial *pharmaka* work, he notes that both the perpetrators and victims believe in their efficacy, and the punishments should thus depend on the harm that it is thought that the *pharmakon* has done. He also distinguishes between the expert (*mantis* or doctor), who knows the full implications of what he is doing, and the layman (*idiotēs*), who merely makes use of something prepared by another. Plato's emphasis on intention here stems from his philosophical position that the true danger in wrongdoing is the harm done to the soul of the wrongdoer, which is more important even than the harm done to the body of the victim. Such a position is not, however, representative of the legal or even ethical ideas of his contemporaries, where the result generally outweighs any consideration of intent, and Plato's proposal to institute such a law in his imagined ideal city indicates pretty clearly that no such law existed in his world.[5]

There are references to other trials in Classical Athens that involved *pharmaka*, but some of these seem to have revolved around, not the harm done to individual bodies, but rather the harm to the community through the impious activities (*asebeia*) of the accused. Most famous is the case of Theoris of Lemnos, who was put to death, a Demosthenic speech tells us, because of her use of *pharmaka*. A late encyclopedia entry, however, cites the third-century BCE religious expert, Philochorus, as claiming that Theoris was convicted of impiety, that is, of performing religious rituals that were found to be contrary to the norms of the community.[6] A similar case is that of Ninon, whom a Demosthenic speech mentions as a priestess who performed private rituals and was executed. A scholiast claims she made love potions (*philtra*) for young men, but the first-century CE historian Josephus relates that she was prosecuted for the impiety of introducing new gods.[7] As Eidinow has recently shown, this confusion of charges arises from the complex social situations in which such trials took place.[8]

---

[5] Plato, *Laws* 992e–993e. See Collins 2008a: 139–141; and Gordon 1999a: 248–252, but cp. also the discussion of this passage in Saunders 1991: 318–323, with the background in Plato's ethical theology (300–318).

[6] Demosthenes 25.79–80; Philochorus FGrH 382 F60 apud Harpocration s.v. Theoris.

[7] Demosthenes 19.281. The scholia identify the priestess as Ninon and her activity as making *philtra* (495a) or bringing ridicule and abuse on the real mysteries (495b). Ninon and her prosecutor, Menecles, are also mentioned in Demosthenes 39.2 and 40.9 (cp. Dionysius of Halicarnassus, *Dinarchus* 11). Josephus, *contra Apionem* 2.267–268 claims that Ninon was executed for initiating people into the mysteries of foreign gods.

[8] Eidinow 2016 provides a detailed and nuanced analysis of the cases of Theoris and Ninon, as well as others such as Socrates and the courtesan Phryne. She focuses on the ancient textual evidence (11–37).

The contestive, personal trials of the Athenian legal system meant that the particular charge was often less important to the trial's outcome than the personal victory of one of the litigants, who managed to sway the jury in his own favor, rather than his opponent's. A charge of harm through *pharmaka*, like that brought against the defendant in the poisoning of the chorus boy, could be a convenient way to bring the accused into court, where the community's disapproval of the accused's conduct within society could result in a negative judgment.

References to the impiety (*asebeia*) of the accused, then, need not imply that individuals like Theoris or Ninon were actually charged with impiety, but they do indicate the nature of the prosecution's strategy in such cases. Although there was no law against magic as such, the accusers made use of what, from an etic perspective, we would call a discourse of magic to attack their targets, focusing on their non-normative performance and social location. Women must have been particularly vulnerable to such marginalizing attacks, particularly non-Athenian women like Theoris of Lemnos, but any outsider to the community might likewise be attacked. The philosopher Anaxagoras from Klazomenai in Asia Minor, who was an advisor of the controversial politician Pericles, is said to have been prosecuted for impiety by Pericles's enemies, and a particular decree by a certain Diopeithes against impiety is associated with him. Pericles's mistress, Aspasia, who was from Miletus, may also have been attacked in this way, since she was more vulnerable than Pericles himself, a native citizen of Athens who came from a prominent aristocratic family.[9]

Plato calls attention to the significance of social location in such accusations when he has Meno, who has just been befuddled by Socrates's arguments, tell Socrates that, if he were a foreigner, he would be accused of being a sorcerer (*goēs*).

> And now, as it seems to me, you are ensorcelling me and bewitching me and completely enchanting me, so that I am filled with perplexity. And you totally seem to me, if I can joke about it, most like a flat stingray in the ocean, both in your appearance and in other ways too. For the stingray benumbs whoever comes near and touches it, and you seem now to have done the same to me. For truly I am numb in my soul and in my tongue, and I am unable to answer you. And yet I have spoken thousands of times about excellence, many speeches and for many people—and totally great speeches too, as they seemed to me. Now, however, I am completely unable to say what it is. And

[9] The limited evidence for the decree of Diopeithes in Plutarch's *Life of Pericles* (32.1) does not specify what the charge might have been, and the fact that the decree is said to be aimed at creating suspicion of Pericles through an attack on Anaxagoras suggests that even this piece of legislation did not create a legal definition of *asebeia*.

it seems to me you would be well advised not to sail away from here or travel away from this city, for if you did such things as a foreigner in another city, you would swiftly be arrested as a sorcerer.[10]

Socrates's bewitching words have such an extra-ordinary effect that, if his social location were equally non-normative, someone would certainly use the discourse of magic to attack him. Of course, as Plato and his readers well knew, Socrates was indeed accused of engaging in non-normative religious practices, both in the satires of comedians such as Aristophanes (in his *Clouds*) and in the lawsuit in which he was convicted and punished with death. His trial took place after restoration of the Athenian democracy following the fall of the Thirty Tyrants, the junta installed by the Spartans at the end of Peloponnesian war, and it is Socrates's association with the notorious Critias, leader of the Thirty, that is mentioned by Aeschines in a later speech as the reason for his execution.[11]

Eidinow's analysis shows how the networks of gossip, rumor, and slander, operating in the agonistic context of Athenian political life, blend together accusations of political and religious wrongdoing with those of personal harm as part of the strategies for besting rivals and enemies. While there was no law against *mageia* or *goētia*, or even the use of *pharmaka* or *epaoidai*, opponents could use what appears from an etic standpoint as a discourse of magic to slander one another, to locate their enemies outside the normal social order and thus subject to the retributive action by the Athenian community. The charge of non-normative ritual activity, however, was only one of a complex of such marginalizing attacks deployed in such struggles, rather than the primary factor that triggered a witch-hunt.

The Legal Context for Magic in Rome

The situation in Rome was, mutatis mutandis, quite similar, although the Roman legal system was more codified and professional than the personal agonism of Classical Athens. The legal codes themselves focus on the aspect of harm in defining criminal acts, and it is only in later commentary that the discourse of magic is explicitly brought into the discussion of such

---

[10] Plato, *Meno* 80a–b. καὶ νῦν, ὥς γέ μοι δοκεῖς, γοητεύεις με καὶ φαρμάττεις καὶ ἀτεχνῶς κατεπᾴδεις, ὥστε μεστὸν ἀπορίας γεγονέναι. καὶ δοκεῖς μοι παντελῶς, εἰ δεῖ τι καὶ σκῶψαι, ὁμοιότατος εἶναι τό τε εἶδος καὶ τἆλλα ταύτῃ τῇ πλατείᾳ νάρκῃ τῇ θαλαττίᾳ· καὶ γὰρ αὕτη τὸν ἀεὶ πλησιάζοντα καὶ ἁπτόμενον ναρκᾶν ποιεῖ, καὶ σὺ δοκεῖς μοι νῦν ἐμὲ τοιοῦτόν τι πεποιηκέναι, [ναρκᾶν]· ἀληθῶς γὰρ ἔγωγε καὶ τὴν ψυχὴν καὶ τὸ στόμα ναρκῶ, καὶ οὐκ ἔχω ὅτι ἀποκρίνωμαί σοι. καίτοι μυριάκις γε περὶ ἀρετῆς παμπόλλους λόγους εἴρηκα καὶ πρὸς πολλούς, καὶ πάνυ εὖ, ὥς γε ἐμαυτῷ ἐδόκουν· νῦν δὲ οὐδ' ὅτι ἐστὶν τὸ παράπαν ἔχω εἰπεῖν. καί μοι δοκεῖς εὖ βουλεύεσθαι οὐκ ἐκπλέων ἐνθένδε οὐδ' ἀποδημῶν· εἰ γὰρ ξένος ἐν ἄλλῃ πόλει τοιαῦτα ποιοῖς, τάχ' ἂν ὡς γόης ἀπαχθείης (my trans.).

[11] Aeschines, *Against Timarchus* 1.173.

acts. The reports we have of trials reinforce the importance of the social dynamics of each case; social location often appears as the determining factor in judgments, from the earliest reports in the Roman Republic to the later Roman Empire.

The earliest Roman lawcode, the Twelve Tables, survives only in fragmentary references, but two sections have often been discussed in terms of magic, the prohibition against *mala carmina* and the prohibition against enchanting away someone's crops from their fields. In addition, a prohibition on secret nocturnal meetings may also have been brought in for cases that involve the discourse of magic as non-normative ritual activity.[12] Evil songs, *mala carmina*, may be understood as harmful incantations but also as slanderous verbal attacks that damage the social standing of their target. As Rives points out,

> A *malum carmen* was a chant that had a bad effect on a person or thing. *Incantare* and *occentare* both have the etymological sense of "to chant against," and so presumably described different ways of using a *carmen* against someone or something, that is, with a bad effect; a *carmen* that would create *infamia* and *flagitium* for someone, if indeed those terms existed in the original text of the law, was yet another example of the same sort of thing. In short, we may suppose that the action condemned by this law was the use of *carmina* to harm people or things in various ways; although we might distinguish these as very different sorts of actions, for example slander and magic, for the early Romans they may have instead been variants of the same general action, "malediction."[13]

The difference between the boundaries of the emic Roman categories and our modern, etic ones can create confusion in understanding how the law from the Twelve Tables played out in the Roman social arena, but the situation here is very like the networks of jealous gossip and slander that surround the Athenian law cases; words, like poisons, may create harm in mysterious and unseen ways. In any case, however, the harm inflicted is again the focus of the legal text, rather than the means by which it is inflicted.

Another kind of harm mentioned in the Twelve Tables is the financial and property damage caused by incanting away the crops from one field into another.[14] Our sources do not lead us to imagine sheaves of grain

---

[12] See Kippenberg 1997: 153–154. "The equation of 'illegal' with 'secret' can be called a genuine Roman tradition. It first appeared in a Roman statute on meetings. The XII Tables had laid down (VIII 26): 'No person shall have nocturnal meetings in the city.'"

[13] Rives 2002: 286. As he notes, the term *incantassit* refers to slander in two discussions by Cicero, *Rep.* 4.12 (apud Augustine, *Civ. Dei* 2.9) and *Tusc. Disp.* 4.4.

[14] While there are no clear cases of property damage through *pharmaka* in the Greek

marching solemnly in procession from one field to another, charmed by some Pied Piper or Orpheus to get up and move; rather, it is the fertile potential of the field that seems to be at issue. If crop harvests are seen, like so many other things in the ancient Greco-Roman world, as a zero-sum game, then any increase in one man's yield will be seen as a decrease in someone else's. A farmer whose crop yield was unusually bad might well look with envy and suspicion at his neighbor's unusually good harvest, and that envy might well lead to the use of the discourse of magic to describe the abnormal situation. Pliny tells us of precisely such a case, dating probably to around the first half of the second century CE. "Gaius Furius Cresimus, a liberated slave, was held in great envy because from a rather small farm he got much larger yields than the neighbors obtained from very large estates, as if he had lured away other people's crops by magic spells [*veneficiis*]." [15] The newcomer, his neighbors thought, had no right to outperform them, so something must be amiss; Cresimus must be cheating somehow.

It is worth noting the term here for magic spells, *veneficia*, since *venenum* is the Latin equivalent of the Greek *pharmakon*, something that produces an effect in a mysterious way, whether as (in Plato's distinction) one material body to another or in a nonmaterial way. The *Lex Cornelia de sicariis et veneficiis*, enacted in the dictatorship of Sulla in 81/82 BCE, in addition to stipulating prosecution of assassins and others who make assaults with a deadly weapon (*sicarii*), proclaimed that whosoever has made, sold, bought, owned, or administered a noxious drug (*venenum*) shall be tried on a criminal charge. As Rives argues, the law treats wrongful death caused by any of these means, be it a dagger (*sica*), a poison (*venenum*), or magic spell (*venenum*).[16]

It is only later that the scope of the law was explicitly expanded to address a broader range of activities within the discourse of magic. A passage in the *Sententiae* attributed to the third-century CE Roman legal expert Julius Paulus provides an expanded interpretation of the *Lex Cornelia*, spelling out in detail the kinds of things that may be considered as *veneficia* and associating them explicitly with the craft of magic.

---

evidence, Plato does include damage to flocks and hives, as well as dependents, in his discussion of cases of punishments for the use of *pharmaka* and *epaoidai* in *Laws* 933d.

[15] Pliny, *HN* 18.41. *C. Furius Cresimus e servitute liberatus, cum in parvo admodum agello largiores multo fructus perciperet quam ex amplissimis vicinitas, in invidia erat magna, ceu fruges alienas perliceret veneficiis.*

[16] Rives 2003: 320. "Within this conceptual framework, the word *venenum*, far from being ambiguous, denoted a consistent and fairly simple concept, namely, any natural substance that had an occult or uncanny power to affect something else. On an emic level, therefore, i.e., in Roman terms, it would be better to describe the law on *veneficium* as dealing not with both magic and poisoning, but rather with wrongful death effected through occult and uncanny means."

If they give someone a love potion or an abortifacient, even if they do not do it deceitfully, nonetheless, because it sets a bad example, the lower classes are relegated to the mines, the upper ones to an island, with a portion of their property forfeit. But if either a woman or a man dies as a result of this, they pay the ultimate penalty. Those who perform or direct the performance of impious or nocturnal rites, in order to bewitch, bind, or tie a person, are either crucified or thrown to the beasts. Those who sacrifice a human being, make offerings of human blood, or pollute a sanctuary or temple, are thrown to the beasts or, if they are of the upper classes, executed. It is resolved to subject those who know the craft of magic to the ultimate punishment, that is, to throw them to the beasts or crucify them. Actual mages, however, are burned alive. No one may have books on the craft of magic in his house. If they are found in someone's house, they are burned in public and their owner has his property confiscated; upper classes are deported to an island, lower classes are executed. Even the mere knowledge of this craft, let alone its pursuit as a trade, is forbidden. If a man dies as a result of a drug given to him as a cure or a palliative, the one that gave it him is relegated to an island, if he is of the upper class, but executed if of the lower one.[17]

Under such a construal of the law, one may be prosecuted not merely for the harm done by *venenum* but even for possessing books on magic, as well as engaging in ritual practices from them. Paulus's judicial opinions were decreed authoritative in 327/328 CE and incorporated into the legal statutes, thus codifying the development in the idea. The focus has shifted from harm to knowledge of non-normative ritual practice; magic itself is subject to prosecution, not just its effects.[18]

---

[17] *Pauli Sententiae* 5.23.14–19. *14. Qui abortionis aut amatorium poculum dant, etsi id dolo non faciant, tamen quia mali exempli res est, humiliores in metallum, honestiores in insulam amissa parte bonorum relegantur: quod si ex hoc mulier aut homo perierit, summo supplicio adficiuntur. 15. Qui sacra impia nocturnave, ut quem obcantarent defigerent obligarent, fecerint faciendave curaverint, aut cruci suffiguntur aut bestiis obiciuntur. 16. Qui hominem immolaverint exve eius sanguine litaverint, fanum templumve, polluerint, bestiis obiciuntur, vel si honestiores sint, capite puniuntur. 17. Magicae artis conscios summo supplicio adfici placuit, idest bestiis obici aut cruci suffigi. Ipsi autem magi vivi exuruntur. 18. Libros magicae artis apud se neminem habere licet: et penes quoscumque reperti sint, bonis ademptis, ambustis his publice, in insulam deportantur, humiliores capite puniuntur. Non tantum huius artis professio, sed etiam scientia prohibita est. 19. Si ex eo medicamine, quod ad salutem hominis vel ad remedium datum erat, homo perierit, is qui dederit, si honestior sit, in insulam relegatur, humilior autem capite punitur* (trans. Ogden 2009).

[18] Cp. Rives 2003: 335. "With the development of a 'strong view' of magic, certain acts that were already punishable because they were uncanny and malicious, such as *veneficium*, began to be viewed as acts of religious deviance as well; in other words, they were brought into an association with religion that evidently did not exist before. I would suggest that this

The prosecution of non-normative ritual practice also appears in the prohibition of nocturnal rituals that goes back to the Twelve Tables. What sorts of rituals might be barred by such a law, however, is unclear from the fragments of the text, but the occasions such as the famous repression of the Bacchanalian rites in 186 BCE suggest that groups suspected of politically subversive activities were targeted.[19] Such groups later included the Christians, whose associations were seen as rejecting the divine authority of the Roman emperor, but not, for example, the devotees of Mithras, whose secret ceremonies never seem to have been the target of repression by the Roman state. Certain forms of divination were banned from being performed in private; both the emperor Augustus and his successor Tiberius tried to control unauthorized divinatory practices, and Tiberius specifically banned the consultation of diviners (*haruspices*) without witnesses present.[20]

One group that seems to have been targeted repeatedly are the astrologers; decrees expelling astrologers from Rome first appear in 189 BCE and recur frequently during the first two centuries of the Roman Empire.[21] Marcus Vipsanius Agrippa, a supporter of Octavian Caesar who helped him become the first emperor Augustus, expelled the astrologers and magicians (*tous astrologous tous te magous*) from Rome in 33 BCE as part of his program to clean up Rome, a project that also involved reworking the sewer system and providing baths and barbers free of charge to the populace.

---

new association is a byproduct of the emerging discourse of religion, which necessarily involved a discussion of what did or did not fall within its parameters." See further thoughts on the nature of this development in the updated version in Rives 2011.

[19] The official decree, the *Senatus Consultum de bacchanalibus*, survives on a bronze tablet (ILS 18). See the lurid tale of debaucheries and conspiracies in Livy 39.8–14, who relates in 39.41.6–7 and 40.43.2–3 that five thousand people were executed for *veneficium* in the years following the decree.

[20] Suetonius, *Tiberius* 63.1. Cp. Cassius Dio 56.23 on Augustus's ban on divination for individuals. The *Sententiae* attributed to Paulus focus on the prohibition of inquiring about the death of the emperor (5.21.3), but the emperors were not just suspicious of those inquiring about their deaths, but anyone who sought special access to extra-ordinary information.

[21] The most thorough presentation of the evidence is still Cramer 1954: 232–248. Ripat 2011: 118 argues that the primary motive in such expulsions was not a particular anxiety about political elites getting special knowledge from astrologers and overthrowing the regime, but rather a general anxiety about unregulated ritual activity undermining social stability. "Most damning is the observation that none of the eight reasonably well-attested mass expulsions of astrologers can be definitively tied to the treasonous astrological activity of the elite. The earliest expulsions, for example, are recorded as driven not by the astrological activities of ambitious individuals, but rather from a desire to rid Rome of un-Roman habits. Valerius Maximus (1.3.3) relates that 'Chaldaeans' were expelled by praetorian edict from Italy in 139 BCE lest they mislead the Romans by selling them foreign knowledge; Jews were expelled at the same time for the same reason."

The historian Cassius Dio recounts that Agrippa justified his expulsions to Augustus by warning that such astrologers and magicians, by introducing foreign and non-normative rituals, foment conspiracies and rebellions that could destabilize the new emperor's rule.

> Such men, by bringing in new divinities in place of the old, persuade many to adopt foreign practices, from which spring up conspiracies, factions, and cabals, which are far from profitable to a monarchy. . . . There ought to be no workers in magic at all. For such men, by speaking the truth sometimes, but generally falsehood, often encourage a great many to attempt revolutions.[22]

Dio's Agrippa here explicitly draws the link between non-normative religious practice and social subversion that seems to underlie many of the Roman repressions of particular religious practices. It is notable that many of these repressive measures are enacted in times of particular social turbulence, such as the transition from the Republic to the rule of the emperors or the vicissitudes that accompanied the adoption of Christianity as the official religion of the Empire (especially after the reversion under Julian). The historian Ammianus Marcellinus paints a picture of the climate of fear and suspicion that lead to accusations of subversive activity for the indulgence in even the most innocuous of superstitious beliefs.

> If anyone consulted a soothsayer about the squeaking of a shrew-mouse, the meeting with a weasel on the way, or any like portent, or used some old wife's charm to relieve pain (a thing which even medical authority allows), he was indicted (from what source he could not guess), was haled into court, and suffered death as the penalty. . . . Anyone who wore round his neck a charm against quartan ague or some other complaint, or was accused by his ill-wishers of visiting a grave in the evening, was found guilty and executed as a sorcerer or as an inquirer into the horrors of men's tombs and the empty phantoms of the spirits which haunt them.[23]

---

[22] Cassius Dio 52.36.2–4. καινά τινα δαιμόνια οἱ τοιοῦτοι ἀντεσφέροντες πολλοὺς ἀναπείθουσιν ἀλλοτριονομεῖν, κἀκ τούτου καὶ συνωμοσίαι καὶ συστάσεις ἑταιρεῖαί τε γίγνονται, ἅπερ ἥκιστα μοναρχίᾳ συμφέρει. . . . τοὺς δὲ δὴ μαγευτὰς πάνυ οὐκ εἶναι προσήκει. πολλοὺς γὰρ πολλάκις οἱ τοιοῦτοι, τὰ μέν τινα ἀληθῆ τὰ δὲ δὴ πλείω ψευδῆ λέγοντες, νεοχμοῦν ἐπαίρουσι. For Agrippa's reforms, see Cassius Dio 49.43.1–5.

[23] Ammianus Marcellinus 16.8.2, 19.12.14. *Nam si super occentu soricis vel occursu mustelae, vel similis signi gratia consuluisset quisquam peritum, aut anile incantamentum ad leniendum adhibuisset dolorem, quod medicinae quoque admittit auctoritas, reus unde non poterat opinari delatus, raptusque in iudicium, poenaliter interibat. . . . Nam siqui remedia quartanae vel doloris alterius collo gestaret, sive per monumentum transisse vesperi, malivolorum argueretur indiciis, ut veneficus, sepulchrorumque horrores, et errantium ibidem animarum ludibria colligens vana, pronuntiatus reus capitis interibat.*

Non-normative ritual activity, no matter how little or how harmlessly it deviated from the norm, could be, in this circumstance, met with the penalty of death. Even things usually dismissed as being of extra-ordinarily low efficacy, the superstitions of old wives and peasants, were treated as attempts to exercise extra-ordinary power, a threatening move in such a charged political atmosphere.

Social Dynamics of Legal Trials: The Cases of Cresimus and Apuleius

The evidence for actual trials likewise indicates that the social location of the accused is the key point in the dynamics of the legal action; the focus rests on *who* the person is, and *what* the person is supposed to have done tends to be the sort of thing that such a person as the defendant is accused of being would do—the objectively profane members of society perform objectively profane acts. Success in such trial thus depends on the accused redefining his identity as something more acceptable, not a marginal person who would engage in non-normative acts, but an upstanding member of the community.

Pliny's tale of Cresimus provides the clearest example of such dynamics.[24] Because he is a freedman on the margins of society accused by his more well-established neighbors of a crime where no material proofs are possible, his strategy must be to prove himself as someone who is not on the dubious fringes of *Romanitas* but rather firmly entrenched in Roman traditional values. As Pliny relates,

> When the time came for the tribes to vote their verdict, he brought all his agricultural implements into court and produced his farm servants, sturdy people and also according to Piso's description well looked after and well clad, his iron tools of excellent make, heavy mattocks, ponderous ploughshares, and well-fed oxen. Then he said: "These are my magic spells, citizens, and I am not able to exhibit to you or to produce in court my midnight labours and early risings and my sweat and toil." This procured his acquittal by a unanimous verdict.[25]

---

[24] See the analysis in Graf 1997: 62–65; as well as Gordon 1999a: 253–254; and Rives 2002: 275–279.

[25] Pliny, *HN* 18.42–43. *cum in suffragium tribus oporteret ire, instrumentum rusticum omne in forum attulit et adduxit familiam suam validam atque, ut ait Piso, bene curatam ac vestitam, ferramenta egregie facta, graves ligones, vomeres ponderosos, boves saturos. postea dixit: 'Veneficia mea, Quirites, haec sunt, nec possum vobis ostendere aut in forum adducere lucubrationes meas vigiliasque et sudores.' omnium sententiis absolutus itaque est.*

Cresimus out-Romans the Romans by showing himself to be an exemplar of all the traditional values of hard work and careful management that the community imagines to be the essence of Roman culture. The former slave with a Greek name and a small property becomes the target of envy and resentment in a situation of agricultural trouble for the community; the community's woes are projected on the outsider.[26] Cresimus, however, shows how, rather than cheating in the agricultural rivalry with his neighbors with non-normative practices characteristic of an outsider, he outperformed them by simply taking the normative practices more seriously. His strategy of redefining his social location as normative by redefining his identity as a real Roman brings him success and a unanimous acquittal.

A similar, although more complex, strategy appears in the defense speech of Apuleius, who was charged at the court in Sabratha (near modern Tripoli in Libya) in 158 or 159 CE of using magic to win the affections of a wealthy widow, Aemilia Pudentilla, in the nearby town of Oea. Apuleius was an outsider in the community, having arrived in town on his journey to Alexandria in Egypt to stay with a friend of his from Athens, Sicinius Pontianus, the older son of Pudentilla. Apuleius, who had studied along with Pontianus at the Platonic Academy in Athens, stayed for a while to tutor the younger child, Sicinius Pudens, as well as to help Pudentilla with her own studies. Pontianus asked his friend to marry his widowed mother, who was coming under increasing and unwelcome pressure from her husband's relatives to marry again within the family to ensure that her sizeable estate (around four million sesterces) stayed in the family.

The marriage caused an uproar among the family of the Sicinii, and the social conflict culminated in a charge being brought against Apuleius by Sicinius Aemilianus (the brother of Pudentilla's deceased husband) and his ally Herenius Rufinus (the father-in-law of the now deceased Pontianus), probably on behalf of Pudens, who was still a minor. Citing a letter by Pudentilla in which she sarcastically commented on her relatives' reactions to her marriage, "Oh, so Apuleius is a magician, and I am bewitched by him and in love," they accuse Apuleius of using magic to induce Pudentilla to marry him and bolster their case with a series of other accusations of non-normative behavior characteristic of an outsider and a magician. Although

---

[26] Cp. Rives 2002: 278–279. "The central issue in the trial of Cresimus was not so much damage to property as the feeling that some people had more than they were entitled to. This, I would suggest, illustrates the key issues at stake in this law: not the actual removal of crops, but rather the feelings of suspicion, envy, and hostility connected with agricultural production. . . . We can analyse the function of this law as allowing for the creation of scapegoats: people who could act as lightning-rods for the feelings of suspicion, envy, and hostility that arose over agricultural production, and whose condemnation and punishment could provide some outlet for the social tensions that threatened to destabilize the community."

we have only the speech for the defense, which Apuleius seems to have published after his acquittal, Apuleius goes through each of the points his opponents raise in detail, so the speech provides the most lengthy and elaborate evidence for this kind of collocation of non-normative practices associated with the discourse of magic.

The speech is a rhetorical tour de force, brilliantly redefining not just Apuleius's own identity but the nature of each of the charges brought against him.[27] Apuleius is accused not only of performing erotic magic but also of obtaining *venena*, of causing a local boy to go into a trance, and of engaging in unspecified secret and nocturnal rituals. In response to these condemnations of him as an outsider to the community of Oea engaged in non-normative practices, Apuleius provides a depiction of himself as an insider, a respectable member of the community—not of marginal Oea, out in the wilds of the African provinces of the Roman Empire, but rather of the elite educated community established in the cosmopolitan centers of the Empire: Athens and Rome, Carthage and Alexandria. The only community that really matters, Apuleius maintains, is this elite community, of which he is a member, not the communities of the insignificant fringes. Not only does he redefine the center and peripheries of the community at issue, but he likewise shifts the nature of each of the actions of which he is accused, redefining them not as the non-normative magical practices characteristic of an outsider, but rather as the erudite philosophical practices of an intellectual elite.

The key to Apuleius's strategy is convincing his judge, Claudius Maximus, himself a member of the educated elite, whose work as proconsul and other offices of the imperial system took him across the broader world of the Empire and who was himself a Stoic philosopher and the teacher of the emperor Marcus Aurelius. In his speech, with countless flattering references to their shared philosophical and cultural knowledge, Apuleius places himself firmly in the center with his judge, relegating his accusers to the margins and characterizing them as objectively profane with their provincial ignorance and behavior. With his social location established, he can redefine the activities of which he is accused as the kind of practices befitting such a philosopher as himself and Maximus.

Apuleius turns a number of the most significant charges on their head, treating first the accusation that he procured *venena*. His opponents appear to have claimed that he sought and obtained certain poisonous sea creatures, including the *lepos marinus* or sea hare, a poisonous sea slug famous for its deadly power.[28] They also accused him of procuring fish whose

---

[27] For analyses of Apuleius's legal and rhetorical strategies, see Bradley 1997 and Rives 2008, as well as the introduction in Hunink 1997.

[28] Pliny, *HN* 9.77 (155) cites it as an example of a deadly sea creature whose mere touch

names resemble the words for sexual organs for the purposes of using them in erotic magic. Apuleius mocks his opponents for being so ignorant as to suppose that a similarity of names could indicate a similarity of powers (blithely ignoring the vast number of parallels for just such symbolic reasoning in lore about plants, stones, and animals of all kinds), as well as so ignorant as to suppose that magical substances ever come from sea creatures (citing a plethora of literary works that fail to mention fish), and he further mocks them for their provincial squeamishness at mentioning the words for genitalia in public (in contrast to his own sophisticated urbanity). While he denies that he ever got a sea hare, he further argues that he was acquiring a large variety of fish because he was engaged in writing a treatise, in the scientific and philosophical tradition of Aristotle, on the reproductive systems of fish. He offers to read portions of his treatise, so that Maximus, who is already so well acquainted with the Aristotelian tradition of works on the generation of animals, may appreciate it and so that his opponents, though already sunk in senile decay, may yet learn something new—although he worries lest they in their ignorance just think all the strange fish names are magical words instead of technical terms. In this section, Apuleius defines himself as a natural philosopher of the Aristotelian tradition and his opponents as ignorant and superstitious provincials, who blush at the mention of genitalia and think that fish with strange names must be magic. He aligns himself with Maximus against his accusers, and, instead of denying the actions attributed to him, he provides a plausible explanation of the behavior of which he is accused by redefining it as scientific inquiry.

His strategy with the next charge is even more risky. Faced with the accusation that he caused a youth to fall on the ground in a trance, he mocks his accusers for being too ignorant of the discourse of magic even to fabricate a plausible description of the nocturnal ritual. He fills in the missing elements of the trope himself—the boy should have been pure and virgin, and he should have made prophetic utterances in his trance to complete the divinatory ritual of which Apuleius was being accused. Apuleius claims that he knows such details as an educated person, having read the accounts of Varro and other philosophers; his opponents are once again characterized as ignorant boors in contrast to his own elite and educated status. He taunts them because their ignorance of these details led them to make up this story about a boy who is anything but pure, since he has suffered his whole life from epilepsy and is constantly falling into fits and soiling himself. He then provides an explanation of the disease, with many

---

can cause harm. Philostratus, *VA* 6.32 claims that Domitian poisoned his brother Titus with the sea hare, "the most deadly thing on land or sea," and that mixing it into their food was a favorite device of Nero's for getting rid of a number of his enemies.

citations of Plato and other philosophical authorities, and claims that he examined the boy, Thallus, with his medical knowledge in hopes of helping the wretched child, just as he was asked to do by the doctor of another woman with epilepsy who was brought to him for examination. As Graf points out, while he mocks his opponents for their failure to fabricate a divination rite properly, he entirely omits to mention anything about the possibility that the epileptics might have been brought to him for exorcism rather than divination.[29] Demonic attack was a common explanation for the violent fits characteristic of epilepsy, as the furious counterarguments in the Hippocratic treatise *On the Sacred Disease* attest, and a ritual expert might well have been asked to drive out the afflicting demon. Apuleius, however, once again presents himself as an educated philosopher, whose scientific activities have been misunderstood by the ignorant outsiders and imagined as magic instead of medicine.

Apuleius then challenges the other charges of non-normative ritual behavior, of keeping certain secret objects in his house, of having a special statue of a god made for him, and of performing nocturnal rituals in a rented house. Having already argued for his identity as a philosopher and member of the cosmopolitan educated elite of the empire, Apuleius can claim that the first two of these are evidence of his normative piety; the statue is proof of his special devotion to a particular deity, while the objects are the tokens of his performance of a number of mystery rituals, the kind of rites that demonstrate a special relationship with the divinity. Again, rather than pursuing a strategy of denial, Apuleius proudly proclaims the truth of what he is charged with, arguing that it is only his opponents' ignorance and lack of piety that causes them to fail to understand. Apuleius is exemplary in his pious performance of honors to the gods, even to the extent of performing extra special rites, whereas his opponents are so profane that they are unacquainted even with ordinary pious actions.

As a result, Apuleius can dismiss their accusations that he performed mysterious nocturnal rituals in a rented house with complete scorn and contempt, throwing in a vicious character assassination of the man on whose testimony they are relying. For a charge whose proof can depend only on the reliability of the witnesses (he mocks his opponents adducing feathers and burned spots as if they could provide credible physical evidence), he relies on the normative status he has established for himself and hurls invective to further demolish the status of his opponents. Apuleius can then treat the accusation that he used erotic magic on Pudentilla as the fabrication of the envious Aemilianus, who had hoped to wed Pudentilla himself, and of the horrible Rufinus, who wished to add the in-

---

[29] Graf 1997: 77–78.

heritance of his son-in-law Pontianus to his other ill-gotten gains. Rather than an outsider who illegitimately managed to seduce the prize widow of the community away from her respectable and appropriate suitors, Apuleius presents himself as a wealthy cosmopolitan who condescended to stop in the backwater of Oea out of affection for the personal qualities of Pontianus and Pudentilla and has been pestered by the envious slanders of the rustics who lack his status and resources.

While previous scholars have often remarked that Apuleius reveals that he knows an awful lot about magic for someone who claims to be innocent of its practice, his deployment of his knowledge in his strategy of redefining his social location has not always been fully appreciated.[30] Apuleius's defense speech shows, more clearly than any other piece of evidence, the crucial importance of the cue of social location in the discourse of magic and the ways that it could be manipulated in the ancient Greco-Roman world. In section 26, Apuleius does make a brief use of one of the common tropes about magic that appears in the rhetorical manuals, the paradox that if his accusers believed he was truly a magician, they would be too afraid of his power to accuse him, but if they believe he is a charlatan, they have no basis on which to make their charge.

This trope plays with the paradox of extra-ordinary efficacy, albeit in a different way than the love poets do when they describe the omnipotent sorceresses who are unable to retain the affections of the men they love. In one of his orations, Libanius invents the scenario of a plague afflicting the city, which an oracle proclaims can only be stopped by the sacrifice of a child. The lot falls on the son of a sorcerer, but the magician promises to stop the plague himself if the community will spare his son. Libanius argues that, if the magician actually has the power to stop the plague, then he should be executed for not having done so earlier, when so many others were dying. If, however, he is merely lying to save his son and has no power to stop the plague, then he should be executed all the same for his treachery. Whether the extra-ordinary efficacy is above normal or a subnormal scam turns out not to matter; the magician who claims it deserves to die.[31] While the focus in the imaginary rhetorical exercises is on the extra-ordinary efficacy, since there is no actual social situation involved,

---

[30] As Hunink 1997: 13 notes, "On reading the speech as a whole, one becomes aware that he knows quite a lot about magic," while Collins 2008a: 151 adds, "So much, in fact, that to a modern reader the conclusion is virtually inescapable that he is capable of practicing it." See, in addition to Hunink and Collins, the analysis in Graf 1997: 65–88.

[31] Libanius, *Declamation* 41. Cp. the scenario in the speech of Hadrian of Tyre, preserved in the *Declamationes* of Polemon (44–45). When a witch magically prevents herself from being burned by the community, another witch volunteers to ensure by magic that she does burn. Hadrian argues that the second witch should also be burned because of her extra-ordinary power.

the actual trials hinge instead upon the negotiation of the social situation. If, like Theoris of Lemnos, the defendant cannot avoid the classification of herself as someone with a social location outside the normal (foreign and female), then she will suffer the consequences of being labeled with the discourse of magic. If, by contrast, the defendant manages to redefine himself as more normative than his accusers, as Cresimus and Apuleius did, then he can redefine the acts with which he is charged as not outside the bounds of normative practice.

In the other-labeling in the legal contexts, then, in contrast to the kind of labeling of another with the discourse of magic in literary or other imaginative evidence, the cue of social location is more valid for determining whether the label is successfully applied. While in the literary texts, extra-ordinary efficacy or weird performance may dominate the depiction, such elements remain secondary and dependent on the social location in the agonistic contexts of the legal arena—and, no doubt, in the other kinds of agonistic social contexts that fail to leave evidence for later scholars to analyze, the endless, petty, jealous struggles within small communities carried out through gossip, slander, and social manipulation.[32]

SELF-LABELING OF MAGIC

Oh, my name is John Wellington Wells,
I'm a dealer in magic and spells,
In blessings and curses
And ever-filled purses,
In prophecies, witches, and knells.
If you want a proud foe to 'make tracks,'
If you'd melt a rich uncle in wax,
You've but to look in
on our resident Djinn,
Number seventy, Simmery Axe.
We've a first-class assortment of magic,
And for raising a posthumous shade
With effects that are comic or tragic
There's no cheaper house in the trade.
Love-philtre, we've quantities of it,
And for knowledge if any one burns,
We keep an extremely small prophet, a prophet
Who brings us unbounded returns. . . .

[32] Eidinow 2016 provides an illuminating investigation into such undercurrents of envy, but more exploration remains to be done, particularly with the evidence from comedy and other comic genres.

In contrast to the attempts to avoid the label of 'magic' in the ancient Greco-Roman legal contexts, Gilbert and Sullivan's Sorcerer cheerily proclaims himself a magician, singing his own praises as a commercial purveyor of all sorts of magical services. This sort of self-labeling is comparatively rare in the evidence from the ancient Greco-Roman world, and indeed from cultures all over across time, in comparisons with all the accusations by others. However, among the multiple and complex strategies Apuleius deploys in his own defense against being labeled by his opponents as a 'magician' is the surprising strategy of self-labeling. At the end of his introductory sections, where he spends time and effort undermining his opponents' characterizations of him as an impoverished and deviant outsider, he then draws a distinction between this common portrait of a magician as a subnormal individual and another category of magicians, among whom, he proclaims, he would be proud to be numbered.

> If a magician in the Persian language is what a priest is in ours, as I have read in many authors, what kind of crime is it to be a priest and to have the right information, knowledge and mastery of the ceremonial rules, ritual requirements, and sacred laws? Provided of course that Plato understands what magic is when he recalls the lessons that the Persians use to initiate a youth in kingship. I remember the very words of that inspired man, and you, Maximus, may recall them together with me.[33]

The true definition of a magician, a *magos*, is a pious Persian priest, not an itinerant charlatan, and Plato himself provides the authority for such a definition, as educated men of the world such as Apuleius and his judge Maximus well know. Those with extra-ordinary knowledge of natural science, such as Anaxagoras or Demokritos, or extra-ordinary knowledge of the workings of the gods, such as Orpheus, Pythagoras, or Ostanes, are called 'magicians,' and Apuleius says, "I congratulate myself therefore on being admitted to such distinguished company."[34]

Apuleius proudly takes on the label of 'magician' in this sense of a distinguished philosopher or pious religious expert, accepting the cachet of this extra-ordinary status as a way of deflecting the stigma of the characterization of extra-ordinarily low status that his opponents are attempting to fasten upon him. Apuleius here engages in a form of what may be known

---

[33] Apuleius, *Apologia* 25. *Nam si, quod ego apud plurimos lego, Persarum lingua magus est qui nostra sacerdos, quod tandem est crimen, sacerdotem esse et rite nosse atque scire atque callere leges cerimoniarum, fas sacrorum, ius religionum, si quidem magia id est quod Plato interpretatur, cum commemorat, quibusnam disciplinis puerum regno adulescentem Persae imbuant—uerba ipsa diuini uiri memini, quae tu mecum, Maxime, recognosce.*

[34] Apuleius, *Apologia* 27. *gratulor igitur mihi, cum et ego tot ac tantis uiris adnumeror.*

as 'stereotype appropriation,' taking on the stereotypical characterization imposed by another but converting it to one's own advantage.[35]

What advantage might there be to appropriating the label of 'magician' for oneself, of deliberately labeling oneself as a practitioner of non-normative ritualized acts? Why should one risk legal prosecution or even social ostracism by labeling oneself as deviant in such a way? John Wellington Wells provides one answer, the profit motive of prophets seeking to advertise their extra-ordinary expertise, but other reasons for such self-labeling appear in the evidence. Although still less common than other-labeling, the sources from Greco-Roman antiquity actually provide more evidence of self-labeling than most of the cultures studied in the ethnographies of anthropologists, where accusations of witchcraft and magic predominate and self-labeling is almost nonexistent. Examples of self-labeling thus provide some of the most interesting insights into the discourse of magic in Greco-Roman antiquity.

The most basic reason to claim the label of extra-ordinary ritual practice for oneself is simply for the claim to be extra-ordinary in a positive sense. Even if the theurgists avoided the label of *goētia*, they nonetheless insisted that their ritual practice made them exceptional, exceptionally pure, and exceptionally blessed by the gods. Iamblichus explains that "the gods in their benevolence and graciousness unstintingly shed their light upon theurgists, summoning up their souls to themselves and orchestrating their union with them," while the Emperor Julian boasts that the divine favor provided by theurgy is something unknown to ordinary folk.

> And if I should touch on the secret teaching of the Mysteries in which the Chaldaean, divinely frenzied, celebrated the God of the Seven Rays, that god through whom he lifts up the souls of men, I should be saying what is unintelligible, yea wholly unintelligible to the common herd, but familiar to the happy theurgists.[36]

One reason to label oneself as a non-normative practitioner is precisely to differentiate oneself from the 'common herd.' The common herd suffers through an ordinary life, while the theurgist attains extra-ordinary felicity through his rituals that give him closer contact with the gods. Demokritos is credited with a description of alchemists that likewise puts them among

---

[35] Frankfurter 1998: 224–233 applies this concept to the Egyptian priest as magician in the Greco-Roman world.

[36] Julian, *Hymn to the Mother of the Gods* 172e. εἰ δὲ καὶ τῆς ἀρρήτου μυσταγωγίας ἁψαίμην, ἣν ὁ Χαλδαῖος περὶ τὸν ἑπτάκτινα θεὸν ἐβάκχευσεν, ἀνάγων δι' αὐτοῦ τὰς ψυχάς, ἄγνωστα ἐρῶ, καὶ μάλα γε ἄγνωστα τῷ συρφετῷ, θεουργοῖς δὲ τοῖς μακαρίοις γνώριμα· Cp. Iamblichus, *de myst* 1.12. Διὰ τῆς τοιαύτης οὖν βουλήσεως ἀφθόνως οἱ θεοὶ τὸ φῶς ἐπιλάμπουσιν εὐμενεῖς ὄντες καὶ ἵλεῳ τοῖς θεουργοῖς, τάς τε ψυχὰς αὐτῶν εἰς ἑαυτοὺς ἀνακαλούμενοι καὶ τὴν ἕνωσιν αὐταῖς τὴν πρὸς ἑαυτοὺς χορηγοῦντες.

the demiurgic divinities: "O natures, artificers [*demiourgoi*] of natures! O greatest natures that conquer natures with your transformations! O natures above nature, which delight in natures!.," and a poem attributed to the astronomer Ptolemy celebrates the blessedness that derives from practicing astrology: "I know that I am mortal, the creature of one day. But when I explore the winding courses of the stars I no longer touch with my feet the earth: I am standing near Zeus himself, drinking my fill of Ambrosia, the food of the gods."[37]

While such blessedness may be an end in itself, this extra-ordinary status may also have instrumental uses, which make claiming it a worthwhile strategy for anyone who wishes to sell his services as a ritual expert. Such self-labeling by ritual experts is a common feature in the evidence about such figures, even if much of that evidence comes from a critical perspective that condemns those who make such claims. Plato provides one of the earliest of such critiques of the self-advertising experts:

> Wandering priests and prophets approach the doors of the wealthy and persuade them that they have a power from the gods conveyed through sacrifices and incantations, and any wrong committed against someone either by an individual or his ancestors can be expiated with pleasure and feasting. Or if he wishes to injure any enemy of his, for a small outlay he will be able to harm just and unjust alike with certain spells and incantations through which they can persuade the gods, they say, to serve their ends.[38]

Plato is scornful of such charlatans and condemns their lack of a moral compass in providing services that can do harm unjustly and free the unjust from the consequences of their injustice, but his condemnations make clear that people really did claim that they had extra-ordinary power through incantations and rituals, that is, that they labeled themselves as magicians even if they did not use the term *magos*.

Ripat acutely points out the ways in which astrologers must have made use of similar strategies to enhance their reputation for power; to be considered one of the astrologers expelled by the edicts against astrology was a powerful badge of authority, a sign that one possessed expertise too potent to be permitted in ordinary society.[39] Self-labeling oneself as an

---

[37] Demokritos, *Physika kai mystika* 15 Martelli; Ptolemy, *Anthologia Palatina* 9.577.

[38] Plato, *Republic* 364b–c. ἀγύρται δὲ καὶ μάντεις ἐπὶ πλουσίων θύρας ἰόντες πείθουσιν ὡς ἔστι παρὰ σφίσι δύναμις ἐκ θεῶν ποριζομένη θυσίαις τε καὶ ἐπῳδαῖς, εἴτε τι ἀδίκημά του γέγονεν αὐτοῦ ἢ προγόνων, ἀκεῖσθαι μεθ' ἡδονῶν τε καὶ ἑορτῶν, ἐάν τέ τινα ἐχθρὸν πημῆναι ἐθέλῃ, μετὰ σμικρῶν δαπανῶν ὁμοίως δίκαιον ἀδίκῳ βλάψει ἐπαγωγαῖς τισιν καὶ καταδέσμοις, τοὺς θεούς, ὥς φασιν, πείθοντές σφισιν ὑπηρετεῖν.

[39] See Ripat 2011: 140: "Perhaps this is one explanation why astrologers were never cast once and for all from Rome or Italy: in theory, the city could be rid of astrologers without a

expellable astrologer might in theory open oneself to prosecution, but in practice it could be an excellent advertisement of one's extra-ordinary power, bringing in the government's evaluation of one's prowess as a kind of testimonial to win clientele. In the competitive context where ritual experts vied for authority, self-labeling could be a strategy to mark oneself as outside the common herd, risky perhaps, but potentially profitable.

How might an expert convincingly self-label, when a timely edict did not provide an opportunity to act out one's identity as an expellable astrologer? One route would be to cater to the expectations of the potential clients, performing the identity that fits the preconceived notions of the magician. Ethnic identity might provide one means: the *magoi* are Persians, witches are Thessalian, while the astrologers are Chaldaeans. The Jews specialize in prophecy, Etruscans make the best haruspices, while the Egyptians know ancient secrets.[40] Costumes and other external trappings could complement names that suggested ethnic identity as ways of claiming non-normative social status as a foreigner outsider—and therefore possessor of alien wisdom.[41] Such stereotype appropriation provides a way to define oneself as a magician to a public audience of fellow mortals who might be in the market for a ritual expert.

But the most important audience for a ritual performance might not be the potential clientele on the horizontal axis; a ritual performer might mark himself or herself as a magician in private, alone on the horizontal axis, with only the divine entities on the vertical axis as witnesses. In such a case, the crucial cues would not be the external trappings that mark one's alien status within the community, but rather the performance of the ritual itself as a symbolic communication that involves a level of self-definition. Just as the performance of the normative ritual of the wedding redefines the bride as a married woman instead of an unmarried girl, so too the

---

single person leaving, provided everyone who had embraced the identity gave it up. But the identity could be just as easily readopted when it seemed safe to do so. There is, however, every reason to suppose that some self-proclaimed astrologers did physically, and perhaps even ostentatiously, leave the city in response to various bans of the early empire. Given the public nature of their pursuits, when faced with renewed legislation, self-proclaimed astrologers would have the choice either of relinquishing the activity and staying in the city, or of embracing the persona of an Expellable Astrologer and leaving. Leaving the city would have the pragmatic advantage of being able to continue business elsewhere, and also the desirable effect of proving definitively to the population at large that one was not some inconsequential diviner, but an Expellable Astrologer of great and dangerous skill."

[40] Ripat 2011: 129 notes, "Those who did make a point of advertising 'foreignness' thus generally had an ulterior motive for doing so; for example, as Marie-Laurence Haack has demonstrated, some *haruspices* chose to adopt location-specific Etruscan names in a bid to prove their qualifications." Wendt 2016 provides a fascinating study of such freelance experts, noting the ways that Paul makes use of his identification as a Judean to bolster his religious authority.

[41] See now the study of such strategies in Wendt 2016.

performance of a non-normative ritual such as a clandestine curse marks the performer as involved within the discourse of magic, as a magician—at least for the moment.[42] Seen in this light, the epigraphic evidence of curse tablets, erotic enchantments, protective amulets, and the like attest to acts of self-definition of magic throughout the Greco-Roman world. By inscribing the *defixio*, sticking nails in the doll, or binding on the amulet, the performer labels himself or herself as involved with magic.

Unfortunately, most such acts provide little information for the analysis of the modern scholar seeking to understand the discourse of magic in the ancient Greco-Roman world from an etic perspective. Whatever the impact on the performer's understanding of herself, the performance provides no access for the modern scholar into such pyschological levels and indeed usually fails to provide even superficial details like name, family, date, or social context. In the aggregate, however, curse tablets and similar evidence can provide insights into the cultural patterns of self-definition, how a performer would define himself as practicing magic. Only a few sources provide more richly complex information, if not about the performers themselves then at least about the process of the ritual. Among all the sources from Greco-Roman antiquity, none are so rich as the corpus of so-called Greek Magical Papyri, the recipes for magical rituals preserved on papyrus in the sands of Egypt and dating mostly from the first to fourth centuries CE.

Greek Magical Papyri

While some of the papyri are little more than scraps containing executed examples of curses or amulets that provide little more than the executed examples on lead or gemstone, it is the lengthy recipe books that not only provide the most insight into the process of creating such examples of magic but also the most insight into the practitioners who compiled them. These are texts created by self-defining magicians for the use of self-defining magicians, not simply because of the presence of certain words of high cue validity in the texts, such as *mageia* or *katadesmos* or the like, but because of the ways the rituals are depicted as performances with high coefficients of weirdness, teeming with collections of incomprehensible *voces magicae*, bizarre ingredients, and unusual ritual actions. Although we have examined individual texts from these papyri throughout this study

---

[42] Of course, such an act may not actually permanently shift the identity of the performer in the way that the marriage ceremony does. Someone who creates one curse tablet may not continue to think of himself as a magician after the rite is over, just as someone who once engages in shoplifting may not continue to think of himself as a thief. While the persistence of identity categories across time is a complex issue, the process of self-definition through a ritualized act at least serves to define the performer's identity while performing the act.

as evidence for particular kinds of practices, it is worth examining the texts as self-definitions of their creators as practitioners of non-normative ritual acts, of magic.

The story of the modern discovery of these texts is sensational in itself, and their importance for understanding ancient religion is perhaps even greater than the discovery of the Dead Sea Scrolls or the Nag Hammadi cache of texts. The story has been told by other scholars at greater length, but a brief summary will suffice here to explain their place in the scholarship of ancient magic.[43] In the middle of the nineteenth century, a collection of papyrus texts were sold to various museums and collections in Europe by the current Swedish-Norwegian Consul-General to the Pasha of Egypt, a certain Jean d'Anastasi.[44] The fascination with the age and majesty of Egyptian civilization, which was prevalent even among the ancient Greeks and Romans, had revived with particular fervor in Europe after Napoleon's expedition (1799–1801).[45] When Champollion (with the aid of the famous Rosetta stone) managed to decipher Egpytian hieroglyphics in 1822, a wide range of evidence was now decipherable that had remained incomprehensible to everyone (Egyptians included) for over a millenium and a half. Anastasi capitalized on this Egyptomania by purveying a variety of Egyptian antiquities to the European market, including a set of papyri, which he reported had been discovered sometime before 1828 by native Egyptian workers 'in a tomb' somewhere in the vicinity of Egyptian Thebes. Anastasi sold these texts to a variety of buyers around Europe, but interest in them remained somewhat limited until the beginning of the twentieth century. The texts from Anastasi's collection, along with others of a similar ilk, were brought together into a corpus of Greek Magical Papyri (Papyri Magicae Graecae or PGM) by Karl Preisendanz, a German scholar interested in the survival of earlier Greek folk religion in

---

[43] Cp. Brashear 1995: 3398–3412; Fowden 1986: 168–172; Gordon 2012: 147–151.

[44] This Giovanni Anastasi (as he later called himself) was an Armenian born in Damascus (Syria) around 1780. Around 1797, he went to Egypt with his father who became a merchant for French troops serving with Napoleon in his attacks on Egypt. After the French defeat, Anastasi's father died in bankruptcy, but Anastasi re-established himself and became an exceptionally wealthy merchant. He managed to have himself appointed Swedish-Norwegian Consul-General to the Pasha of Egypt from 1828 to his death in 1857, and in this eminent position, he ran a number of commercial ventures, including a lucrative trade in Egpytian antiquities for which there was a thriving market in Europe.

[45] The Arab conquest of Egypt in 641 CE had cut Egypt off from European tourists for nearly 700 years, and even after the Middle East became more open to European visitors in the Renaissance, Egypt remained a land of mystery. Mozart's *Magic Flute* (1791) shows the kind of late eighteenth-century 'Egyptomania,' the fascination with ancient wisdom and culture. These grand hopes of secret lore were dampened when the first ancient Greek papyrus from Egypt was published in 1788 and turned out to be a bureaucratic list of workers on a canal project in 193 CE in an unknown place called Tebtynis.

these texts, dating mostly from the third- to fifth-century CE Egypt. Because of his interests, Preisendanz excluded from the collection texts he deemed to be too Christian and texts that were in Demotic Egyptian, as well as texts that did not fall under his definitions of magic.

As a result, two of the papyri that seem to have come from Anastasi's 'Theban cache,' two codices of alchemical recipes in the same scribal hand, were not edited and included with the Greek Magical Papyri (P. Holmiensis, the Stockholm Papyrus, so called after the museum to which it was sold, and P. Leid. J 397, which went to the Leiden collection). The same scribe, however, also produced a 1,078-line collection of Coptic and Greek spells in codex form, which Preisendanz did include in his collection as PGM XIII. The loose page of papyrus known as PGM Va was found among the pages of the Stockholm alchemical papyrus. While the three papyrus rolls from the Berlin collection that Preisendanz numbered as PGM I, II, and III probably did not come from the same Theban cache, they bear many resemblances to PGM IV (a 36-page codex of spells in Coptic and Greek, 3,274 lines long) and PGM V (a 7-page codex of spells in Greek, 489 lines long), which did come from that collection. Another scribe seems to have been responsible for producing several other texts in this collection. PGM XII is a long papyrus roll with 19 columns of spells on one side in Demotic and Greek, dating to fourth century CE, while on other side is a Demotic literary text from the second century BCE. The same scribe composed PGM XIV, a papyrus roll of 29 columns on one side and 33 on the other with spells in Old Coptic, Greek and Demotic, as well the papyri exclusively in Demotic known as the great Demotic Magical Papyrus and the PDM supplement. Neither of these last two texts were included in Preisendanz's collection of Greek Magical Papyri because they were in Demotic Egyptian, rather than Greek, despite the fact that the same scribe had composed other texts in Greek. Preisendanz did include many other similar papyri containing recipes for magical rituals, and scholars have added more to the collection in the intervening years.[46]

The range of rituals included in these recipe books, as well as the ways in which they were compiled, provide vital insights into the discourse of magic in the ancient Greco-Roman world. The long spell books, in particular, provide an unparalleled collocation of different kinds of rites: curses, erotic spells, protections and exorcisms, petitions to various divine forces for a multitude of things, divinatory rites of all sorts, astrological calculations, alchemical recipes, and even theurgic rites that bring together

---

[46] Preisendanz and Henrichs 1973 represents the latest revision of the Greek texts from Preisendanz's collection. More texts have been published in the *Supplementum Magicum* (Daniel and Maltomini 1990 and 1992), and the collection in Betz 1992 provides a translation of the Greek texts collected in these volumes along with many others, both in Greek and Demotic.

material and spiritual forces to connect the performer with the divine. To the compilers of these texts, at least, all these things belong together as part of the discourse of magic, even if some of the modern editors wanted to excise parts that failed to correspond to their own definitions of ancient Greco-Roman magic, such as astrology, alchemy, invocations to Christian religious figures, or texts that were not in Greek.

It is precisely the multiplicity of languages in these texts, however, that provides some of the best insights into the identity of their compilers. Although most of the texts of this collection are written in Greek, the presence of sections in Demotic Egyptian, glosses in Coptic and Hieratic, and texts in the same scribal hand that are entirely in Demotic, indicates that the writers of these texts were experts proficient in all these languages—not a common skill set in any era. Moreover, formal features of the texts' composition, such as the style of the scribal hand, the formal divisions of the sections, and the marking off of the magical words by word separation or overlining, all indicate the professional expertise of the scribes (in contrast to the often haphazard production of curse tablets and other epigraphic materials). Some of the longest and most complicated papyri, notably PGM IV, show evidence of having been collated from multiple manuscripts, as the scribe notes that in another source the recipe reads slightly differently.[47] Such features of the texts provide a picture of their authors as highly educated professional scribes with access to collections of texts in a variety of languages and an interest in the kinds of rituals included in the spell books.[48]

As scholars such as Frankfurter and Dieleman have pointed out, the historical type that best fits these qualifications are the lector-priests (ḥry ḥbt) of the Egyptian temples. They seem to be among the very few who

---

[47] Sometimes the notation is explicit, as in PGM II.1–64, where at line 50, the scribe notes, "In another text, I have found the following." ἐν ἄλλῳ δὲ οὕτως εὗρον. The Mithras Liturgy in PGM IV.475–829 shows several signs of redaction from multiple sources, e.g., line 500: "in another [text]," ἐν ἄλλῳ, or 591 "but some [have]," οἱ δέ, as well as the revision of the ritual procedure at the end of the instructions, 793–799, "But the god said to me: 'Use the ointment no longer, but, after casting it into the river, [you must] consult while wearing the great mystery of the scarab revitalized through the 25 living birds, and consult once a month, at full moon, instead of 3 times a year.'" εἶπεν δέ μοι ὁ θεός· 'μηκέτι χρῶ τῷ συγχρίσματι, ἀλλὰ ῥίψαντα εἰς ποταμὸν <χρὴ> χρᾶσθαι φοροῦντα τὸ μέγα μυστήριον τοῦ κανθάρου τοῦ ἀναζωπυρηθέντος διὰ τῶν κε ζῴων ὀρνέων, χρᾶσθαι ἅπαξ τοῦ μηνός, ἀντὶ τοῦ κατὰ ἔτος γ′, κατὰ πανσέληνον.' Alternate forms of divine epithets or voces magicae are often noted, e.g., PGM IV.464 and 466, 1277, 2731, etc. Cp. the alternate procedures in PGM IV.1106, VII.204, and XII.204, or the alternate titles listed in XIII.731.

[48] Cp. Gordon 2013b: 179: "Variety of authorial voices, supplementation, practical theory, and implicit ethical hierarchization in the Group 1a formularies [the Anastasi cache] suggest the possibility that the composition of such books, performed by unusually skilled and dedicated scribe-editors, contributed to the construction of an implied reader with a variety of capacities and expectations."

would have the fluency in Greek and Demotic (as well as Coptic, Hieratic script, etc.) to have composed such texts, and their interests in such rituals may well be understood as an adaptation by these ritual experts to the shifts in the institutional power of the temples under centuries of Roman rule. It remains unclear what kind of clientele they may have served, but the texts themselves provide insights into the way they defined their own authority for their ritual performances. Even if the authors were lector-priests working within the temples, the ritual authority for the performers of the spells is not grounded in the temple or its traditions, but within the performance of the spell itself.[49]

It is worth briefly examining a particular spell to demonstrate how such a ritual text serves to label the performer as a magician. One of the recipes in the spellbook now in the National Museum in Paris (PGM IV.154–286) has a number of notable features, both explicit and implicit, that define the magician who uses the recipe. Although the implicit ways that the text defines the magician must be sifted from the setup of the text, the explicit self-definitions come in the main ritual itself.

The spell provides a procedure for making contact with the sun god, Helios, to imbue the magician with the power to perform all sorts of miracles whenever and wherever he likes. "You will observe through bowl divination on whatever day or night you want, in whatever place you want, beholding the god in the water and hearing a voice from the god which speaks in verses in answer to whatever you want."[50] The procedure itself follows the common tripartite pattern of a rite of passage that transforms an individual from one status to another: acts of separation from the old status, acts betwixt and between the old and new, and then acts that reinforce the incorporation into the new status.[51] To remove himself from his status as an ordinary person, the magician goes to a rooftop and removes all his clothing, lies down on a pure linen sheet and is wrapped up like a corpse (perhaps a mummy). For the crucial middle phase, the liminal moment, the magician invokes the god to bring about a divine encounter

---

[49] Once again, the distinction in J. Smith 2003 of religion of there vs. religion of anywhere is illuminating for understanding these strategies of authorization. Gordon 2013b: 170 suggests, "The majority, however, deliberately evoke Egypt and aspects of Egyptian temple-practice." Such evocations, however, do not suggest an actively functioning temple context but rather claim that the spell came originally from the inner shrine of a temple or other sacred point of origin. The rites have been relocated to suit the new conditions. On 'stereotype appropriation' in such contexts, see Frankfurter 1998: 198–237; Dieleman 2005: 185–284; Moyer 2011: 248–273.

[50] PGM IV.162–165. σκέψη διὰ λεκάνης αὐτόπτου ἐν ᾗ βούλει ἡμέρᾳ ἢ νυκτί, ἐν ᾧ βούλει τόπῳ, θεωρῶν τὸν θεὸν ἐν τῷ ὕδατι καὶ φωνὴν λαμβάνων ἐν στίχοις παρὰ τοῦ θεοῦ, οἷς βούλει·

[51] Such a pattern, as set out by van Gennep 1960, can be found in a wide variety of rites in cultures throughout time and space. Marriages, funerals, and maturation ceremonies for adolescents are perhaps the most common, but the pattern is broadly applicable.

(*systasis*). After the prayer has been repeated, the encounter occurs by a falcon swooping down and striking the (bound and blindfolded) magician with its wings; this direct contact with divinity is bearable because the magician is possessed of a "magic soul" (*magikēn psuchēn*). After this divine epiphany, the magician arises, dresses in white, and burns incense while performing a set of self-identifying utterances.

> "I have been attached to your holy form. I have been given power by your holy name. I have acquired your emanation of the good things, Lord, god of gods, master, daimon. ATHTHOUIN THOUTHOUI TAUANTI LAŌ APTATŌ." Having done this, return as lord of a god-like nature which is accomplished through this divine encounter.[52]

The tripartite structure of the rite of passage is a familiar pattern within the ritual tradition, one that signifies the transformation that it enacts. Both verbally and performatively, the ritual thus explicitly defines the performer as one who has acquired a godlike nature through the encounter with the divine, thus enabling the performer to succeed in various forms of divination (specifically bowl divination and necromancy) for which further instructions follow.

Such overt forms of self-definition, however, are only part of the way the text constructs its reader and defines his identity; other, more subtle and implicit markers may be seen by considering the text more closely. First is the mere location of this recipe within such a large collection; only someone interested in the performance of magic would own or consult such a peculiar work.[53] The text itself marks itself as containing an extraordinary ritual practice, since it styles itself as a letter from an Egyptian magician to an Egyptian king.

> Nephotes to Psammeticos, immortal king of Egypt. Greetings. Since the great god has appointed you immortal king and nature has made you the best wise man, I too, with a desire to show you the industry in me, have sent you this magical procedure which, with complete ease, produces a holy power. And after you have tested it, you too will be amazed at the miraculous nature of this magical operation.[54]

---

[52] PGM IV.215–220. "συνεστάθην σου τῇ ἱερᾷ μορφῇ, ἐδυναμώθην τῷ ἱερῷ σου ὀνόματι, ἐπέτυχόν σου τῆς ἀπορροίας τῶν ἀγαθῶν, κύριε, θεὲ θεῶν, ἄναξ, δαῖμον αθθουϊν θουθουϊ ταυαντι· λαω απτατω." ταῦτα ποιήσας κάτελθε ἰσοθέου φύσεως κυριεύσας τῆς διὰ ταύτης τῆς συστάσεως ἐπιτελουμένης.

[53] Cp. the Roman legal rulings that make the mere possession of such books a crime, e.g., *Pauli Sententiae* 15.23.14–19.

[54] PGM IV.154–162. Νεφώτης Ψαμμητίχῳ, βασιλεῖ Αἰγύπτου αἰωνοβίῳ, χαίρειν· ἐπεί σε ὁ μέγας θεὸς ἀπεκατέστησεν βασιλέα αἰωνόβιον, ἡ δὲ φύσις κατέστησεν ἄριστον σοφιστήν, καὶ ἐγώ σοι βουλόμενος ἐπιδείξασθαι τὴν ἐν ἐμοὶ φιλοπονίαν ἀπέστειλά σοι τήνδε τὴν πρᾶξιν ἐν πάσῃ εὐκοπίᾳ

The king is wise and powerful because of divine favor, and the text explicitly describes him as the leader of magicians (*magōn kathēgemōn*); in terms of valid cues, it is worth noting that this text uses both the noun *magos* and the adjective *magikē*, marking itself with the terminology of magic. Moreover, Nephotes claims to be a magician with power that will amaze anyone who makes use of it—that is, the one who reads the text and performs the ritual. The reader of the papyrus is the target of this advertisement, a celebrity endorsement that validates the authority and power of the rite. Of course, not only the performer himself will be amazed, but anyone else who is in the audience for the performance will be astounded at the extraordinary nature of the rite and its performer.

More subtle markers also appear. The text provides an alternate reading at one point in the invocation to Helios Typhon, which indicates that the scribe who wrote the recipe in the codex had at least two versions of this ritual procedure to consult. The performer, moreover, is presumed to be qualified to decide between the rival readings in his performance. The performer is also characterized by a certain level of previous ritual expertise, since the text includes several instructions in 'shorthand,' abbreviated forms that presume prior knowledge. The prayer invokes "ABERAMENTHŌOU (formula)," that is to say, a particular *vox magica* formula that appears spelled out in other texts as a long palindrome:

ABERAMENTHŌOUTHLERTHEXANAXETHRELTHUOŌTHENEMAREBA.[55]

The magician is expected to know the whole formula and to be able to insert it into the prayer at the appropriate point. Likewise, when another hymn to the god concludes with "add the usual," the magician is expected to know the customary formulae for making specific requests at the end of a petitionary hymn.[56] Thus, like an advanced cookbook that presumes a chef of a certain level of experience (one who knows, for example, how to caramelize onions or to make a roux), this text defines its performer

---

ἱερὰν ἐπιτελουμένην ἐνέργειαν, ἣν καὶ <σὺ> δοκιμάσας θαυμάσεις τὸ παράδοξον τῆς οἰκονομίας ταύτης· Cp. 243: μάγων καθηγεμών.

[55] The indication of alternate reading appears in PGM IV.189. Cp. PGM I.294; II.125–126; III.116–117; V.180; XIV.25 (= pdm xiv.689); CXXVIa.13–15, etc. In PGM III.67–68, the palindrome is to be spelled out in a diminishing triangle, "in heart form, like a bunch of grapes," καρδιακῶς, ὡς βότρυς.

[56] This is another feature common in the Greek Magical Papyri, cp. PGM III.14, 40, 53, 81–82*, 76, 84, 93, 112, 115, 119, 123, 161, 437; IV.87, 273, 2668; V.330, 488; VII.203, 309, 316, 380, 384, 389, 393, 404, 410, 416, 422, 461, 465, 589c, 627, 657, 660, 685, 702, 715, 996, 1025; IX.6; XIV.27; XIXb.2; XXXVI.255, 347, 359, 370; LXI.58; LXII.18, 23. It is worth noting that the term κοινά often appears with some form of 'whatever you wish,' indicating that the magician is to fill in the blank with the specifics of the target or aim of the spell. This usage is disproportionately the case in the two papyri, III and VII, that make most use of the formula.

as someone well versed in the ritual procedures of such magical spells, with knowledge of the common formulae and familiarity with a range of variations.

An analysis of other features of this recipe, such as the myth evoked in the prayer to Typhon or the hymn in Greek dactylic hexameter, would provide further insights, but the analysis of even just these formal features points to the kind of user these texts construct. Such a reader must be, in terms of social location, among the educated elite, the scribes who are proficient not just in the Greek that is the common written language of Egypt at this point, but in the Demotic, Coptic, and others that are the purview of scholars. The user seeks extra-ordinary power, divinatory success that will amaze and astound with its efficacy, and to this end he performs a ritual filled with non-normative elements, like being wrapped up like a mummy and chanting incomprehensible palindromic magical words. All these cues clearly indicate the magician, and the performer is voluntarily and deliberately applying them to himself through the performance of the ritual in the text. In this way, the Greek Magical Papyri offer unusually rich evidence for self-labeling of 'magic' in the ancient Greco-Roman world, and this evidence deserves further examination and analysis in the scholarship.[57]

Alien Wisdom: The Cross-Cultural Experience of Magic

Although most of the texts are written in the Greek language, the Greek Magical Papyri are not purely Greek (whatever that might be imagined to mean); they are produced in Egypt in the first several centuries CE while Egypt is under the domination of the Roman Empire. They incorporate references to divinities not merely of the Greek tradition but also the Egyptian, as well as the Jewish, Christian, and even ancient Babylonian, traditions, and they make use of ritual patterns and procedures that can be found in all those traditions. In other words, the Greek Magical Papyri are products of the particular historical context in which they were composed—like any text. While scholars interested in origins have argued about how Greek, how Egyptian, how Jewish, and so forth, various pieces of the Greek Magical Papyri may be, these texts provide evidence for the discourse of magic in the ancient Greco-Roman world at the time and place of their composition and compilation, precisely because that discourse includes the cross-cultural, multilingual interactions that appear in the texts.

---

[57] Graf engages in such analysis of PGM I.1–42, the so-called Spell of Pnouthis, in Graf 1991 and Graf 1997: 96–117, which also include some analysis of the Nephotes spell from PGM IV analyzed here. Graf, however, focuses more on the parallels with mystery cult initiations than on self-definition.

It has often been objected, however, that the category of magic cannot apply to certain of the elements, such as Egyptian procedures or invocations, since those elements have their place in the normative religious discourse of Egyptian religion.[58] Procedures such as execrations (curses) or bowl divination are not marked in the Egyptian tradition as non-normative in the same way they are in the Greco-Roman tradition, and the Egyptian word most often translated as 'magic,' *heka* (*ḥk3*), does not indicate non-normative ritual practice, but simply ritual power of any kind. That Heka is personified in Egyptian tradition as a deity whose power provides the efficacious force of ritual practices seems to reinforce the normative status of *heka* in the Egyptian tradition.[59] However, *heka* can be used *both* for normative *and* non-normative ritual practices. It is not that the Egyptian tradition did not have a discourse of non-normative ritual practice that might be, from an etic perspective, labeled as 'magic' in the sense used in this study; it is rather that *heka* is not the emic term that marks such a distinction.[60] The tendency to translate *heka* as 'magic' stems from the failure of earlier scholars to separate the emic categorizations within the Egyptian religious tradition from their own etic judgments

[58] Ritner 1993: 13 asserts in his still fundamental study of Egyptian ritual practice, "However magic may be defined, in Egypt the practice was in itself quite legal. . . . Kings, priests, and commoners used the same methods on a daily, normative, and legal basis." Ritner, however, defines magic as any kind of use of ritual power, rather than specifically the non-normative uses.

[59] As Ritner 1995: 3353 notes, "Heka's hieroglyphic symbol means simply 'power,' and late hieroglyphic 'ciphers' use his image to spell the 'divine force' embodied as 'gods' and in 'temples.' Orthodox temple ritual regularly invoked the use of such force, and the god himself received a standard cult."

[60] Ritner, however, considers the substantive question of *what* was done as the primary criterion to classify magic, regardless of the criteria considered throughout this study. For him, the private practices of execration, for example, "are nonetheless equivalent in meaning and method to the more elaborate state production, differing only in scope" (Ritner 1993: 184). Since the terminology for and the practices of execration and divination remain essentially the same whether performed by a priest in a temple or a private individual, Ritner concludes that *who*, *where*, and *when*—that is, the cues that mark the social location of the practitioner—have no impact in how the act is regarded. "Neither terminology nor technique separates public from private ritual sorcery" (Ritner 1993: 189). Ritner points out that, when the 'Harim conspiracy' sought to assassinate Ramses III (c. 1182–1151 BCE), a *pḥ-ntr* was used by the conspirators. "The resulting prosecution of the conspirators was not a trial against sorcery, but rather a trial for treason, in which magic had served as one weapon. The hostile ritual had been taken from the royal library, and the practitioner, as usual, was a priest" (Ritner 1995: 3354). This example, however, shows the similarities with the prosecutions involving *pharmaka* or *venena* in the Greek and Roman contexts, and it is only in the later Roman Empire, when the Roman laws are expanded to make *magia* prosecutable in itself, that *heka* (or, rather, its later Coptic equivalent) becomes regarded as inherently problematic. "Only now could the practice be termed 'magic' in the Western sense (i.e., 'illegal' and 'private') and then only from a Roman perspective" (Ritner 1993: 218–219). Cp. Ritner 1993: 236 and Ritner 1995: 3372.

about what looked like magic to them.[61] Curses, even if performed in communal execration ceremonies by official priests, looked like magic, especially if they involve manipulation of figurines through performative persuasive analogies. Thus, a whole range of normative ritual procedures in the Egyptian tradition were regarded as magical, with the result that Egyptian religion as a whole could be regarded as magic (or, alternately, that the Egyptians had no magic at all, only religion). Such problems are inevitable with an approach to magic that focuses only on the formal or substantive features of the practices—the *what* question, instead of the more complex factors of the performance: *who, where, when*, and so forth. Similar confusions have arisen with various religious traditions in the ancient Near East, from Babylonia to Phoenicia, the Levant, and Asia Minor, with terminology for ritual power used in rites that seemed, to nineteenth- and twentieth-century scholars, to smell like magic.[62] In each cultural context, different cues have validity for distinguishing normative from non-normative ritual activity, and the lexical categories are often more misleading than helpful.

These confusions, however, are not merely the result of modern philologists operating with modern categories of religion; the blurring of lines from an outsider perspective occurs in antiquity as well, as members from various cultural traditions in the ancient Mediterranean world attempt to make sense for themselves of other traditions that they encounter. Egyptian or Babylonian or Jewish religion, seen through the eyes of an ancient Greek, presents a different spectrum of normativity than it would from the perspective of someone within the Egyptian or Babylonian or Jewish tradition, since what is normative practice for the insider appears exotic and

[61] Ritner 1993: 1 explicitly chooses to remain within the emic category of *heka* in his study, designating as magic in the etic modern Western sense "any activity that seeks to obtain its goal outside the natural laws of cause and effect," thus including pretty much all of ritual practice. He critiques previous scholars who have mixed the etic and emic classifications. Cp. pp. 67–72 and the concluding discussion, pp. 236–246.

[62] See, for example, the discussion of Babylonian magic in Thomsen 2001: 13, where the scope of magic is defined by the substance of the rituals that seem like magical rituals in the Western tradition: curses and cures, divinations and prayers. "The methods and purposes of the rituals are very similar, at least in principle, to those known from magic practices in other cultures." She insists, however, that in the Babylonian tradition magic is the same as normative religion. "An important difference, however is that magical practices in Mesopotamia were not in opposition to an 'official' religion. They were not regarded as superstitious or forbidden, or laughed at. The rituals called 'magical' were the ordinary way of dealing with illness and misfortune" (Thomsen 2001: 14). She nevertheless admits that all the evidence concerns the practices of professionals at court and that "we have no information about the performance of rituals in the lower levels of society" (Thomsen 2001: 14). Her analysis still represents an advance over the older studies of Near Eastern magic that stick with the idea of magic as part of a 'primitive' worldview that works *ex opere operato*. Cp., e.g., Bottéro 2000: 66, 68.

non-normative to the outsider. The social location of the exotic is, as Bourdieu would classify it, always objectively profane.[63]

The complexities of such cultural interactions may be seen in the story that a certain Thessalos attaches to the introduction of his treatise on the impact of astrological configurations upon the medicinal properties of plants. This Thessalos has often been identified with Thessalos of Tralles, a medical expert in the time of Nero famous for his introduction of new medical theories—and for his flamboyant trashing of his rivals.[64] However, whether this treatise is by the historical Thessalos of Tralles, or (more likely) a work forged under the name of Thessalos of Tralles, or even a work by another Thessalos who was later confused with the more famous one from Tralles, the work itself can be dated fairly securely to the second century CE through the astrological calculations mentioned in the work.[65] In the prologue, Thessalos tells the tale of how he obtained the special knowledge of the workings of plants that he records in the treatise from a magical ritual performed by an Egyptian priest. Egyptologists have shown clearly that the rite Thessalos describes is a fairly standard divination ritual that was performed by temple priests, a normative part of Egyptian religion. For Thessalos, however, and for his audience in the Greco-Roman world, the ritual is marked as magic by a number of cues.

The story has been analyzed in different ways by a number of scholars, but the main points are worth rehearsing here. Thessalos, who has already proved himself a brilliant medical expert, comes across a treatise by the legendary Egyptian magician-king, Nechepso, which contains a set of recipes for healing every part of the body by means of stones and plants with special astrological correspondences. Thrilled at obtaining this ancient Egyptian wisdom, he writes back to family and friends, boasting of his newfound powers, only to discover, when he tries the remedies, that their

---

[63] As Redfield 1991: 104 insightfully comments of the ritual practitioner, "Such a person has a social role which changes with social conditions—even if practices and doctrines remain unchanged. A guru, even though he changes his teaching not at all, becomes someone different when transported from Bhutan to Los Angeles."

[64] Pliny, *HN* 29.9. "The same generation in the principate of Nero rushed over to Thessalus, who swept away all received doctrines, and preached against the physicians of every age with a sort of rabid frenzy. The wisdom and talent he showed can be fully judged even by one piece of evidence: on his monument on the Appian Way he described himself as *iatronices*, 'the conqueror of physicians.' " *eadem aetas Neronis principatu ad Thessalum transilivit delentem cuncta placita et rabie quadam in omnis aevi medicos perorantem, quali prudentia ingenioque aestimari vel uno argumento abunde potest, cum monumento suo, quod est Appia via, iatronicen se inscripserit.*

[65] See Moyer 2011: 293–297 and Moyer 2015. A second-century date need not rule out authorship of the treatise by the first-century Thessalos of Tralles, since the calculations might have been updated by a later copyist, but it does rather strongly suggest that the connection was made later, most likely by a pseudepigrapher taking the name.

efficacy is not extra-ordinarily high, but extra-ordinarily low. Having made himself a laughingstock in Alexandria, he goes off to Diospolis (Egyptian Thebes) in search of authentic Egyptian wisdom and inquires among the Egyptian priests there about obtaining efficacious ritual power—magic (*ti tēs magikēs energeias*). Unimpressed (or perhaps rejected) by most of these priests, Thessalos discovers one old priest who seems to be capable of some real magic, and, having befriended this worthy fellow, he begs him to perform a bowl divination rite (lekanomancy), dramatically threatening suicide if he can't obtain what he wants.

The priest puts him through three days of purification before leading him to a specially prepared pure dwelling. When he asks Thessalos whether he wants to converse in the bowl divination with a god or a dead spirit, Thessalos surprises him with a request to speak face to face with the god Asclepius, rather than through the mediation of the bowl. The priest reluctantly agrees, so Thessalos (prepared in advance with paper and pen) has his encounter with the divine presence.

> He would, though not happily—for the features of his face revealed this, but he had promised. So he enclosed me in the chamber, and ordered me to sit opposite the throne on which the god would sit. After summoning the god through his ineffable names and exiting, he closed the door.[66]

The god appears in indescribable glory and tells Thessalos that Nechepso's treatise is not completely useless, but only missing a crucial bit of information.

> King Nechepso, a man of most sound mind and adorned with every virtue, did not obtain from a divine voice anything which you seek to learn; having made use of a noble nature, he observed the sympathies of stones and plants, but the times and places in which it is necessary to pick the plants, he did not know. For according to the seasons, everything waxes and wanes with the emanation of the stars; and that divine, most refined spirit which exists throughout all substance especially pervades those places where the emanations of the stars were in the time of the cosmic nativity.[67]

[66] Thessalos, *de virt. herb.* prol. 23. ὅμως οὐχ ἡδέως μέν (τοῦτο γὰρ ἐνέφαινον οἱ τῆς ὄψεως χαρακτῆρες), πλὴν ἐπηγγείλατο. καὶ ἐγκλείσας με εἰς τὸν οἶκον καὶ καθῖσαι κελεύσας ἄντικρυς τοῦ θρόνου, εἰς ὃν ἔμελλεν ὁ θεὸς καθέζεσθαι, προαγαγὼν διὰ τῶν ἀπορρήτων ὀνομάτων τὸν θεὸν καὶ ἐξελθὼν ἔκλεισε τὴν θύραν (trans. Moyer).

[67] Thessalos, *de virt. herb.* prol. 27–28. ὁ βασιλεὺς Νεχεψώ, ἀνὴρ φρενηρέστατος καὶ πάσαις κεκοσμημένος ἀρεταῖς παρὰ μὲν θείας φωνῆς οὐδὲν ὧν σὺ μαθεῖν ἐπιζητεῖς εὐτύχησε· φύσει δὲ χρησάμενος ἀγαθῇ συμπαθείας λίθων καὶ βοτανῶν ἐπενόησε, τοὺς δὲ καιροὺς καὶ τοὺς τόπους ἐν οἷς δεῖ τὰς βοτάνας λαμβάνειν οὐκ ἔγνω. ὥρια γὰρ πάντα τῇ τῶν ἄστρων ἀπορροίᾳ αὔξεται καὶ μειοῦται· τό τε θεῖον ἐκεῖνο πνεῦμα λεπτομερέστατον ὑπάρχον διὰ πάσης οὐσίας διήκει καὶ μάλιστα κατ' ἐκείνους

With the aid of this divine revelation, Thessalos gains access to the magical power of the plants and stones, allowing him to make good his previous boasts to his acquaintances and even leading him to address the prologue of his book to the emperor, informing him of his magical power and how he acquired it.[68]

On one level, this story is a straightforward example of the discourse of magic in the ancient Greco-Roman world. Thessalos acquires magical power to heal from a divination rite, which he obtains when he seeks something he explicitly labels as 'magical' (*magikē*) from the Egyptian priest. Thessalos's quest fits with a common trope in the literature of the period, the brilliant youth who journeys to exotic places in his search for alien wisdom. The hero of Apuleius's novel, Lucius, goes off to Thessaly to find the magic of Thessalian witches, for example, while, in the *Recognitions* attributed to the early Christian Clement, the narrator (identified as the companion of the apostle Peter who became Pope Clement I) resolves to seek out an Egyptian magician to perform a necromantic ritual in order to prove that the soul is immortal.[69] Both Nechepso's original treatise and the Egyptian priest's rite are marked as magic by the cue of social location; from Thessalos's perspective, they are not the normative practices but rather those of the exotic Egyptians, who are marked not only by cultural (and thus spatial) distance from the Rome of the Emperor to whom the treatise is addressed, but also by temporal distance—the priest is aged, while Nechepso belongs to the legendary past. The performance is filled with ineffable words, giving it a high coefficient of weirdness. Most importantly for Thessalos, the efficacy of both is extra-ordinary; the treatise provides remedies superior to all the medical arts of the doctors with

τοὺς τόπους, καθ᾽ οὓς αἱ τῶν ἄστρων ἀπόρροιαι γίνονται {τῆς} ἐπὶ τῆς κοσμικῆς καταβολῆς (trans. Moyer).

[68] The Greek manuscript (cod. Matrit. Bibl. Nat. 4631) that preserves this prologue contains only a portion of the treatise, more of which survives in other Greek manuscripts and in later Latin versions (some of which also have the framing material of prologue and epilogue).

[69] Ps. Clementine, *Recognitions* 1.5. *quid igitur agam? hoc faciam: Aegyptum petam atque ibi hierofantis vel prophetis qui adytis praesunt, amicus efficiar et pecunia ab eis invitatum magum precabor, ut educat mihi animam de infernis, per eam quam necromantiam vocant, tamquam de aliquo negotio consulere cupienti. mihi vero haec erit consultatio: si inmortalis est anima.* "What, then, shall I do? This shall I do. I shall proceed to Egypt, and there I shall cultivate the friendship of the hierophants or prophets, who preside at the shrines. Then I shall win over a magician by money, and entreat him, by what they call the necromantic art, to bring me a soul from the infernal regions, as if I were desirous of consulting it about some business. But this shall be my consultation, whether the soul be immortal." The text survives in a Latin version by the fifth-century CE Rufinus, but scholars agree that the original story probably goes back several centuries earlier. Cp. Apuleius, *Metamorphoses.* In the prologue to the Cyranides treatise, Harpokration seeks wisdom in Syria, while Lucian's Menippus goes to a Chaldaean magician.

whom Thessalos has studied, while the priest's rite is not just an efficacious divination through the medium of a bowl, but the even more unusual and efficacious encounter with the god himself. Thessalos explicitly and triumphantly trumpets his acquisition of magical power as a way of providing his treatise with extra-ordinary authority. "I alone," he claims, "among the men of all time have accomplished something marvellous. For having set my hand to matters which transcend the limits of mortal nature, I have, through many trials and dangers, brought to these matters the proper completion."[70]

But there is another side to this story, one that helps illuminate the complexities of defining magic within the context of cross-cultural contact. Not only the lekanomancy but even the direct vision of the god were normative rituals within Egyptian temple religion, something that an Egyptian priest would consider validated through centuries of religious tradition.[71] The performance of such a *ph-ntr* would consist of the traditional ritual formulas and actions, without a particularly high level of weirdness or deviation from the normative. The priest is the appropriate person to perform such rituals. So, is Thessalos's 'magic' ritual not magic after all?

Of course, from Thessalos's perspective, outsider that he is to traditional Egyptian religion, the rite is still most definitely and deliberately magical, but I would argue that, even from the perspective of the Egyptian priest, his performance of the divinatory ritual for Thessalos would appear as magic. *What* he is doing remains the same, but *where* and *when* he is doing it, for *whom*, and *why*, all differ from the normative performance. The ritual is not performed in a normal temple religion setting with a normal interaction between the priest and his usual audience, but rather in a different place as the result of a different kind of negotiation with a foreigner.[72] As Moyer has argued, the Egyptian priest is engaged in stereotype appropriation in this interaction, playing off the stereotypical expectations of a Greek like Thessalos about what an Egyptian priest would do and making use of the label of 'magic' that Thessalos seeks to apply to him. Rather than offering his services for an ordinary, normative ritual, the priest offers to perform the magical rite Thessalos seeks, even if the performance, for him, is just another performance of a standard *ph-ntr* rite. In the process of

[70] Thessalos, *de virt. herb.* prol. 1–2. μόνος δοκῶ τῶν ἀπ' αἰῶνος ἀνθρώπων πεποιηκέναι τι παράδοξον. ἐπιχειρήσας γὰρ πράγμασιν, ἅπερ θνητῆς μέτρα φύσεως ὑπερβαίνει, τούτοις γε μετὰ πολλῶν βασάνων καὶ κινδύνων τὸ καθῆκον τέλος ἐπέθηκα (trans. Moyer).

[71] For lekanomancy and *ph-ntr* as parts of traditional Egyptian practice, see Ritner 1995: 3346–3348. For a more detailed discussion of *ph-ntr*, see Ritner 1993: 214–220.

[72] There has been some dispute in the scholarship as to whether the 'dwelling' (*oikos*) in which the rite takes place could refer to the priest's temple or must indicate a separate space, but, given Thessalos's interest in appropriating the wisdom of the Egyptian temple tradition, some mention of the temple would be expected if that is where the rite was taking place.

translation, the normative *pḥ-ntr* becomes a magical *autoptos systasis*, a one-on-one meeting with the god that is deliberately non-normative.[73]

If Thessalos's story relates how he managed to win the secret ancient magical wisdom of the Egyptians for himself from one of their venerable priests, the priest's version of the story might relate how he convinced an ignorant foreigner that an ordinary rite was something magical and extra-ordinary—thus obtaining an extra-ordinary reputation and possibly getting paid a lot more for it. Thessalos's story mentions nothing about payment, but dramatic threats of suicide aside, the priest was presumably induced to perform the ritual with the promise of some of the large sums of money with which Thessalos set off for Egypt.[74] The reputation for extra-ordinary ritual power, however, may well have been the more important consideration in this kind of stereotype appropriation, providing for the Egyptian priest a kind of social prestige within the milieu of Greco-Egyptian interactions in the Roman Empire worth far more than any payment, and, indeed, the later Latin versions mention that the priest accompanied Thessalos when he went back to Alexandria to show off his new powers.[75] While, of course, the whole story is a creation of the author writing under the name of Thessalos, its embeddedness within the cultural context of Greco-Roman Egypt enables us, from a modern scholarly perspective, to locate the agency of the character of the priest and analyze the ways in which such cultural interactions, in historical reality, were not a one-way obtaining of secret magic from the Egyptians, but rather a complex set of negotiations.[76]

CONCLUSIONS

From the earliest uses of the words, *magos* and *mageia* have indicated the Greco-Roman perspective on non-normative ritual practice as something

[73] See Moyer 2003. Cp. the title of the recipe in PGM IV.930–1114, as well as a number of other rites in the PGM that are labeled as a direct encounter with a god (e.g., VII.505 *systasis* with one's own daimon; VI.39 with Selene; VI.1 or III.197 with Helios).

[74] Thessalos, *de virt. herb.* prol. 4 μετὰ συχνοῦ ἀργυρίου. See Moyer 2003: 54–55.

[75] Moyer's treatments of the scene as a commodity exchange in Moyer 2003 and Moyer 2011: 248–273 remain the most illuminating analyses, building upon the approach set out by Frankfurter 1998:198–237. For the process of stereotype appropriation, he adduces the parallel of Carlos Castaneda and his shaman Don Juan, while Frankfurter refers to Native American rituals performed as tourist attractions. Further study of this process of cultural interactions from the perspective of the Egyptian priests appears in Dieleman 2005: 185–284.

[76] Moyer and Frankfurter rightly emphasize the active agency of the Egyptian in this process of cultural appropriation by a dominant from a subaltern culture. Cp. Frankfurter 1998: 198–237; and Moyer 2011: 248–273.

that comes from outside the normal order, rather than being a straightforward description of the historical realities of the other cultural traditions in the ancient Mediterranean world. Tiresias was never a Persian priest, despite Oedipus's characterization of him as a *magos* in Sophocles, and the *magoi* to whom the Derveni author refers probably had as little to do with actual Persian religion as the figure of Ostanes who becomes such a figure of magical authority in the Hellenistic and Roman periods.[77] While the cultures of Mesopotamia had complex religious traditions of their own, the Chaldaeans as they appear in the Greco-Roman sources are at best heavily refracted images of such practices. For the most part, 'Chaldaean' becomes a label for astrological specialization, although the *Chaldaean Oracles* of the Neoplatonic theurgists reflect another usage of the extra-ordinary prestige of the Chaldaean tradition.[78] As the cultural orbit of the Greco-Roman world expands, the Judaeans are imagined as extra-ordinary for their prophets, while the Brahmans of India become the ultimate idealized figures of far-off alien wisdom.[79] Even before the *magoi* provide the word for magic, Helen in Homer's *Odyssey* obtains her magic *pharmakon, nepenthe,* from Egypt, and the Thessalian *pharmakides* are notorious for drawing down the moon.[80]

Some kind of alien social location thus appears to be one of the most valid cues for the label of 'magic' throughout the evidence, as the Greeks (or Romans) view the ritual activities of those outside their own cultural tradition as non-normative and therefore characterize non-normative ritual activities in their own communities as alien. As the Greco-Roman cultural tradition develops, certain cues accumulate particular meanings, so that the specific cue of Thessalian or Chaldaean or whatever is linked to the particular activity or other circumstantial factors, but any of them can contribute to the plausibility of the label.

Social location tends to correlate with markers of performance, since one manifestation of alien location is ritual performance with high coefficients of weirdness. Foreign words or completely incomprehensible *voces*

[77] The study of Bidez and Cumont 1938 collects the evidence for such Greek receptions of Persian figures, and, even if their methodological assumptions about cultural interchanges reflects the limitations of the period, it was nonetheless a groundbreaking study.

[78] This cachet of alien origin remains the most significant element even if the *Chaldaean Oracles* did actually originate from a temple of the Chaldaean god Bel. See Athanassiadi 2005.

[79] The Brahmans appear in Philostratus, *Life of Apollonius of Tyana* 3.15 as exceptionally holy religious figures (like Apollonius), while in Nonnos, *Dionysiaca* 36.344–349 they are even characterized as being able to draw down the moon. Wendt 2016 makes an intriguing point about the ways Paul may have exploited the reputation of the Judaeans as expert in prophecy to bolster his own religious authority.

[80] Homer, *Odyssey* 4.219–239. For Thessalian witches, cp. Aristophanes, *Nub.* 746–757; Pliny, *HN* 30.7, etc.

magicae, unfamiliar or contrary ritual patterns, and ritual performances outside their normal time and place are actions taken as characteristic of the objectively profane, with the result that someone deliberately performing in a non-normative manner is likewise marked as non-normative, intentionally profane. Non-normative performance appears far more often in the evidence (and with more validity) as a cue for magic than non-normative ends. The most significant cue throughout the evidence, however, tends to be non-normative efficacy, whether that efficacy is miraculously above normal or ineffectively below. Curses that provide an unfair advantage in competitive situations—mercantile, athletic, or erotic—are not non-normative because the end they seek (victory over competitors) is non-normative, but rather because they disrupt the normal system of competition with their extra-ordinary power. Modes of divination likewise are labeled as 'magic' not because the aim of receiving communications from the gods is socially unacceptable, but because their extra-ordinary efficacy makes them appear either as uncanny miracles or useless superstitions. Likewise, the debates over the legitimacy of such arcane arts as astrology, alchemy, and theurgy hinge on the question of their efficacy. Either these practices involve needless complications designed only to baffle the uninitiated and conceal their uselessness, or they provide extra-ordinary power to the one who is schooled in their erudite systems. At times, their extra-ordinary efficacy is condemned because such abnormal results could only be obtained through bargains with evil demonic powers, whereas their defenders claim that their superior understanding enables them to tap into the divine power of the cosmic system. Both sides in such debates, however, agree that these procedures are extra-ordinarily powerful and non-normative, whether they consider it a good or a bad thing.

The range of things that can receive the label of 'magic' in the ancient Greco-Roman world is wide, for the discourse of magic is rich and complex. Theurgy, alchemy, astrology, divination, healing, protection, love spells, and curses all fall at times within its purview. Looking at the collocations of activities within evidence such as the Greek Magical Papyri shows the astonishing range. As Otto comments in exasperation,

> The PGM subsume an irritatingly wide range of ritual practices under μαγεία: among the most common ritual goals are divination, evoking love between two persons, defence and protection, controlling or damaging other people, healing or the achievement of wealth, luck, and fame; if wealth has been stolen, a ritual may be conducted to identify the thief; if a healing rite has been unsuccessful, a ritual for reawakening the corpse may be useful; other miraculous abilities like interrogating a dead body, becoming invisible, controlling one's own

shadow, breaking up bonds, opening closed doors or extinguishing a fire (unsurprisingly, without water) are also described.[81]

The discourse is too broad to be encompassed by the things indicated by the cues of particular words, and even things given the label of 'magic' in one context or by one source may appear elsewhere unmarked, accepted as unproblematically normative. Nevertheless, attention to the contexts of labeling reveals the significance of the cues of non-normative social location, ends, performance, and efficacy for the application of those labels.

Ultimately, of course, the complexities and uncertainties ensure that the category of magic in the ancient Greco-Roman world remains as mysterious to us as modern scholars approaching it from an etic point of view as it no doubt was to the people of the ancient Greco-Roman world themselves. By refining our etic definitions, however, with our analyses of the emic classifications, we can nevertheless bring our categories closer to theirs, providing richer insights into the ways the people of the ancient Greco-Roman world thought and acted. We can better comprehend their interest in astrology or alchemy, the way they deployed curses and charms within the networks of envy, gossip, and slander that made up the agonistic social contexts of the Greco-Roman world, or the way they marked off certain modes of interacting with the gods as normative and non-normative in their prayers and sacrifices. Through such definitions and analyses, in the end, we can even gain insight into that most mysterious and marvelous of rites, drawing down the moon.

[81] Otto 2013: 332–333.

Bibliography

Abbink, J. 1993. "Reading the Entrails: Analysis of an African Divination Discourse." *Man* 28 (4): 705–726.

Abt, Theodor, and Salwa Fuad. 2007. *The Book of Pictures by Zosimos of Panopolis.* Zurich: Living Human Heritage Publication.

Addey, Crystal. 2014. *Divination and Theurgy in Neoplatonism: Oracles of the Gods.* Farnham and Burlington: Ashgate.

Adkins, A. W. H. 1969. "Εὔχομαι, Εὐχωλή, and Εὖχος in Homer." *Classical Quarterly* 19: 20–33.

Adler, Margot. 1981. *Drawing down the Moon: Witches, Druids, Goddess-Worshippers, and Other Pagans in America Today.* Boston: Beacon Press.

Ahearne-Kroll, Stephen P. 2014. "The Afterlife of a Dream and the Ritual System of the Epidaurian Asklepieion." *Archiv für Religionsgeschichte* 15: 35–52.

Armstrong, Arthur Hillary. 1955. "Was Plotinus a Magician?" *Phronesis* 1 (1): 73–79.

Athanassiadi, Polymnia. 2005. "Apamea and the Chaldaean Oracles: A Holy City and a Holy Book." In *The Philosopher and Society in Late Antiquity: Essays in Honour of Peter Brown,* edited by Andrew Smith, 117–143. Swansea: The Classical Press of Wales.

Aubriot-Sévin, Danièle. 1992. *Prière et conceptions religieuses en Grèce ancienne jusqu'à la fin du Ve siècle av. J.-C.* Lyon-Paris: Maison de l'Orient Méditerranéen-de Boccard.

Audollent, Auguste, ed. 1904. *Defixionum Tabellae Quotquot Innotuerunt Tam in Graecis Orientis Quam in Totius in Corpore Inscriptionum Atticarum Editas.* Luteciae Parisiorum: Albert Fontemoing.

Auffarth, Christoph. 2005. "How to Sacrifice Correctly—Without a Manual?" In *Greek Sacrificial Ritual: Olympian and Chthonian. Proceedings of the Sixth International Seminar on Ancient Greek Cult, Organized by the Department of Classical Archaeology and Ancient History, Göteborg University, 25–27 April 1997,* edited by Robin Hägg and Brita Alroth, 11–21. Stockholm: Skrifter utgivna av svenska Institutet i Athen.

Ausfeld, Carolus. 1903. *De Graecorum Precationibus Quaestiones.* Lipsiae: Teubner.

Bachvarova, Mary. 2012. "The Transmission of Liver Divination from East to West." *Studi micenei ed egeo-anatolici* 54: 143–164.

Barton, Tamsyn. 1994. *Ancient Astrology.* Sciences of Antiquity. London and New York: Routledge.

———. 1995. *Power and Knowledge: Astrology, Physiognomics, and Medicine under the Roman Empire.* Ann Arbor: University of Michigan Press.

Beck, Roger. 1976. "Interpreting the Ponza Zodiac I." *Journal of Mithraic Studies* 1 (1): 1–19.

Beck, Roger. 1977a. "Cautes and Cautopates: Some Astronomical Considerations." *Journal of Mithraic Studies* 2 (1): 1–17.

———. 1977b. "Interpreting the Ponza Zodiac: II." *Journal of Mithraic Studies* 2 (2): 87–147.

———. 2006. *The Religion of the Mithras Cult in the Roman Empire: Mysteries of the Unconquered Sun.* Oxford: Oxford University Press.

———. 2007. *A Brief History of Ancient Astrology.* Malden, MA: Blackwell Publishers.

Bélis, Mireille. 1999. "The Use of Purple in Cooking, Medicine, and Magic: An Example of Inference by the Imaginary in Rational Discourse." In *From Myth to Reason? Studies in the Development of Greek Thought,* edited by Richard Buxton, 295–316. Oxford and New York: Oxford University Press.

Bettarini, Luca. 2005. *Corpus Delle Defixiones Di Selinunte.* Alessandria: Edizioni dell'Orso.

Betz, Hans Dieter, ed. 1986. *The Greek Magical Papyri in Translation: Including the Demotic Spells.* Chicago and London: University of Chicago Press.

———. 1990. "The Delphic Maxim ΓΝΩΘΙ ΣΑΥΤΟΝ in Hermetic Interpretation." In *Hellenismus und Urchristentum: Gesammelte Aufsätze I,* 92–111. Tübingen: J. C. B. Mohr.

———, ed. 1992. *The Greek Magical Papyri in Translation: Including the Demotic Spells.* 2nd ed. Chicago and London: University of Chicago Press.

———. 2003. *The "Mithras Liturgy": Text, Translation, and Commentary.* Tübingen: Mohr Siebeck.

Bhamla, M. S., et al. 2017. "Hand-Powered Ultralow-Cost Paper Centrifuge." *Nature Biomedical Engineering* 1 (0009): 1–7.

Bidez, Joseph, and Franz Cumont. 1938. *Les mages hellénisés : Zoroastre, Ostanès et Hystaspe, d'après la tradition grecque.* 2 vols. Paris: Les Belles Lettres.

Blänsdorf, Juergen. 2010. "The Texts from the Fons Annae Perennae." In *Magical Practice in the Latin West. Papers from the International Conference Held at the University of Zaragoza, 30 Sept.–1 Oct. 2005,* edited by Richard Gordon and Francisco Marco Simón, 215–244. Leiden and Boston: Brill.

Böck, Barbara. 2000. *Die babylonisch-assyrische Morphoskopie.* Archiv für Orientforschung 27. Vienna: Institut für Orientalistik der Universität Wien.

Bonnechere, Pierre. 2003. *Trophonios de Lébadée. Cultes et mythes d'une cité béotienne au miroir de la mentalité antique.* Religions in the Graeco-Roman World 150. Leiden: Brill.

———. 2007. "Divination." In *A Companion to Greek Religion,* edited by Daniel Ogden, 145–159. Malden, MA: Blackwell Publishing.

Bonner, Campbell. 1950. *Studies in Magical Amulets, Chiefly Graeco-Egyptian.* Ann Arbor: University of Michigan Press.

Bottéro, Jean. 2000. "Magie, exorcisme et religion en Mésopotamie." In *La magie: Actes du colloque international de Montpellier, 25–27 Mars 1999.* Vol. 1, *Du monde babylonien au monde hellénistique,* 63–76. Montpellier: Université Paul Valéry, Montpellier III.

Bouché-Leclercq, Auguste. 1879. *Histoire de la divination dans l'antiquité.* 4 vols. Paris: Ernest Leroux.

———. 1899. *L'astrologie grecque*. Paris: Ernest Leroux.

Bourdieu, Pierre. 1971. "Genèse et structure du champ religieux." *Revue française de sociologie* 12 (3): 295–334.

Bowden, Hugh. 2005. *Classical Athens and the Delphic Oracle Divination and Democracy*. Cambridge: Cambridge University Press.

Braarvig, Jens. 1999. "Magic: Reconsidering the Grand Dichotomy." In *The World of Ancient Magic: Papers from the First International Samson Eitrem Seminar at the Norwegian Institute at Athens, 4–8 May 1997*, edited by David R. Jordan, Hugo Montgomery, and Einar Thomassen, 21–54. Bergen: Norwegian Institute at Athens.

Bradley, Keith. 1997. "Law, Magic, and Culture in the Apologia of Apuleius." *Phoenix* 51 (2): 203–223.

Brashear, William M. 1995. "The Greek Magical Papyri." *Aufstieg und Niedergang der römischen Welt II* 18.5: 3380–3684.

Bremmer, Jan N. 1999. "The Birth of the Term 'Magic.' " *Zeitschrift für Papyrologie und Epigraphik* 126: 1–12.

Brenk, Frederick E. 1986. "In the Light of the Moon: Demonology in the Early Imperial Period." *Aufstieg und Niedergang der römischen Welt II* 16.3: 2068–2145.

Briquel, Dominique. 1999. "La religion étrusque." In *Les religions de l'antiquité*, edited by Yves Lehmann, 7–75. Paris: Presses universitaires de France.

———. 2014. "Etrusca Disciplina and Roman Religion. From Initial Hesitation to a Privileged Place." *Latomus* 343: 112–132.

Brisson, Luc. 1992. "Le corps 'dionysiaque': L'anthropogonie décrite dans le *Commentaire sur le Phédon de Platon* (1, Par. 3–6) attribué à Olympiodore—est-elle orphique?" In Σοφίης Μαιήτορες *«Chercheurs de Sagesse»: Hommage à Jean Pépin*, edited by Marie-Odile Goulet-Cazé, Goulven Madec, and Denis O'Brien, 481–499. Paris: Institut d'études augustiniennes.

Burkert, Walter. 1983. "Itinerant Diviners and Magicians: A Neglected Element in Cultural Contacts." In *The Greek Renaissance of the Eighth Century B.C.: Tradition and Innovation. Proceedings of the Second International Symposium at the Swedish Institute in Athens, 1–5 June, 1981*, edited by Robin Hägg, 115–119. Stockholm: Svenska institutet i Athen.

———. 1992. *The Orientalizing Revolution: Near Eastern Influence on Greek Culture in the Early Archaic Age*. Cambridge, MA: Harvard University Press.

———. 2005. "Signs, Commands, and Knowledge: Ancient Divination between Enigma and Epiphany." In *Mantikê: Studies in Ancient Divination*, edited by Sarah Iles Johnston and Peter T. Struck, 29–49. Leiden: Brill.

Caley, Earle Radcliffe. 1926. "The Leyden Papyrus X: An English Translation with Brief Notes." *Journal of Chemical Education* 3 (10): 1149–1166.

———. 1927. "The Stockholm Papyrus: An English Translation with Brief Notes." *Journal of Chemical Education* 4 (8): 979–1002.

Carastro, Marcello. 2007. "Quand Tirésias devint un *mágos*: Divination et magie en Grèce ancienne (Ve–IVe siècle av. n. È.)." *Revue de l'histoire des religions* 224.2 (February): 212–230.

Chaniotis, Angelos. 1995. "Sich Selbst Feiern? Städtische Feste des Hellenismus im

Spannungsfeld von Religion und Politik." In *Stadtbild und Bürgerbild im Helle-nismus*, edited by Paul Zanker and Michael Wörrle, 47:147–172. Munich: C.H.Beck'sche.

Chaniotis, Angelos. 1997. "Theatricality beyond the Theater. Staging Public Life in the Hellenistic World." In *De la scène aux gradins. Théâtre et représentations dramatiques après Alexandre le Grand dans les cités hellénstiques. Actes du collo-que, Toulouse 1997 (Pallas, 41)*, edited by B. Le Guen, 219–259. Toulouse: Presses universitaires du Mirail.

——. 2008. "Priests as Ritual Experts in the Greek World." In *Practitioners of the Divine: Greek Priests and Religious Officials from Homer to Heliodorus*, edited by Beate Dignas and Kai Trampedach, 17–34. Cambridge, MA: Harvard University Press.

——. 2009. "Ritual Performances of Divine Justice. The Epigraphy of Confession, Atonement and Exaltation in Roman Asia Minor." In *From Hellenism to Islam. Cultural and Linguistic Change in the Roman Near East*, edited by Hannah M. Cotton, Robert G. Hoyland, Jonathan J. Price, and David J.Wasserstein, 115–153. Cambridge: Cambridge University Press.

Clarke, Arthur C. 1973. *Profiles of the Future: An Inquiry into the Limits of the Possible*. New York: Harper & Row.

Clarke, Emma C., John Dillon, and Jackson P. Hershbell, trans. 2003. *Iamblichus: On the Mysteries*. Writings from the Greco-Roman World 4. Atlanta: Society of Biblical Literature.

Collins, Derek. 2002. "Reading the Birds: Oiônomanteia in Early Epic." *Colby Quar-terly* 38 (1): 17–41.

——. 2003. "Nature, Cause, and Agency in Greek Magic." *Transactions of the American Philological Association* 133: 17–49.

——. 2008a. *Magic in the Ancient Greek World*. Blackwell.

——. 2008b. "Mapping the Entrails: The Practice of Greek Hepatoscopy." *The American Journal of Philology* 129: 319–345.

Connor, W. R. 1988a. " 'Sacred' and 'Secular': Ἱερὰ καὶ Ὅσια and the Classical Athe-nian Concept of the State." *Ancient Society* 19: 161–188.

——. 1988b. "Seized by the Nymphs: Nympholepsy and Symbolic Expression in Classical Greece." *Classical Antiquity* 7: 155–189.

Copenhaver, Brian P. 1992. *Hermetica: The Greek Corpus Hermeticum and the Latin Asclepius in a New English Translation, with Notes and Introduction*. Cambridge and New York: Cambridge University Press.

——. 2015. *Magic in Western Culture: From Antiquity to the Enlightenment*. Cam-bridge: Cambridge University Press.

Costanza, Salvatore. 2009. *Corpus Palmomanticum Graecum*. Papyrologica Floren-tina 39. Florence: Edizioni Gonnelli.

Cramer, Frederick H. 1954. *Astrology in Roman Law and Politics*. Philadelphia: Amer-ican Philosophical Society.

Cumont, Franz. 1911. *The Oriental Religions in Roman Paganism*. Chicago: The Open Court Publishing Company.

Cunliffe, Barry, and R. S. O. Tomlin, eds. 1988. *The Temple of Sulis Minerva at Bath, II: The Finds from the Sacred Spring*. Vol. 2., *The Finds from the Sacred Spring*.

Oxford University Committee for Archaeology Monograph 16. Oxford: University Committee for Archaeology.

Daniel, Robert. 1975. "Two Love-Charms." *Zeitschrift für Papyrologie und Epigraphik* 19: 249–264.

———. 1991. *Two Greek Magical Papyri in the National Museum of Antiquities in Leiden: A Photographic Edition of J384 and J395 (= PGM XII and XIII).* Abhandlungen der Rheinisch-Westfälischen Akademie der Wissenschaften, Sonderreihe Papyrologica Coloniensia 19. Opladen: Westdeutscher Verlag.

Daniel, Robert, and Franco Maltomini, eds. 1990. *Supplementum Magicum.* Vol. 1. Papyrologica Coloniensis 16. Cologne: Westdeutscher Verlag.

———, eds. 1992. *Supplementum Magicum.* Vol. 2. Papyrologica Coloniensis 16. Cologne: Westdeutscher Verlag.

Dasen, Véronique. 2008. "Le secret d'Omphale." *Revue Archéologique* 46 (2): 265–281.

———. 2014a. "Healing Images. Gems and Medicine." *Oxford Journal of Archaeology* 33 (2): 177–191.

———. 2014b. "Sexe et sexualité des pierres." In *Les savoirs magiques et leur transmission de l'antiquité à la renaissance*, edited by Véronique Dasen and J. M. Spieser, 195–220. Florence: Sismel.

———. 2015. "Probaskania: Amulets and Magic in Antiquity." In *The Materiality of Magic*, edited by Jan Bremmer and Dietrich Boschung, 177–203. Paderborn: Wilhelm Fink Verlag.

Dasen, Véronique, and Jérôme Wilgaux. 2013. "De la palmomantique à l'éternuement, lectures divinatoires des mouvements du corps." *Kernos. Revue internationale et pluridisciplinaire de religion grecque antique* 26 (October): 111–122.

Daxelmüller, Christoph. 1993. *Zauberpraktiken: Eine Ideengeschichte der Magie.* Zurich: Artemis & Winkler.

Delatte, Armand. 1932. *La catoptromancie grecque et ses dérivés.* Bibliothèque de la faculté de philosophie et lettres de l'Université de Liège 48. Liège and Paris: Imp. H. Vaillant-Carmanne; Librairie E. Droz.

Depew, Mary. 1997. "Reading Greek Prayers." *Classical Antiquity* 16: 229–258.

Dickie, Matthew W. 1999. "The Learned Magician and the Collection and Transmission of Magical Lore." In *The World of Ancient Magic: Papers from the First International Samson Eitrem Seminar at the Norwegian Institute at Athens, 4–8 May 1997*, edited by David R. Jordan, Hugo Montgomery, and Einar Thomassen, 163–193. Bergen: Paul Aströms.

———. 2000. "Who Practised Love-Magic in Classical Antiquity and in the Late Roman World?" *The Classical Quarterly* 50: 563–583.

———. 2001. *Magic and Magicians in the Greco-Roman World.* London and New York: Routledge.

Dieleman, Jacco. 2005. *Priests, Tongues, and Rites: The London-Leiden Magical Manuscripts and Translation in Egyptian Ritual (100–300 CE).* Religions in the Graeco-Roman World 153. Leiden: Brill.

Dieterich, Albrecht. 1903. *Eine Mithrasliturgie.* Leipzig: Teubner.

Dillery, John. 2005. "Chresmologues and Manteis: Independent Diviners and the Problem of Authority." In *Mantikê: Studies in Ancient Divination*, edited by Sarah Iles Johnston and Peter T. Struck, 167–231. Leiden and Boston: E. J. Brill.

Dillon, John. 2007. "Iamblichus' Defence of Theurgy: Some Reflections." *The International Journal for the Platonic Tradition* 1: 30–41.

Dillon, Matthew. 1996. "The Importance of Oionomanteia in Greek Divination." In *Religion in the Ancient World: New Themes and Approaches*, edited by Matthew Dillon, 99–121. Amsterdam: Adolf M. Hakkert.

Dodds, E. R. 1951. *The Greeks and the Irrational.* Berkeley: University of California Press.

Dufault, Olivier. 2006. "Magic and Religion in Augustine and Iamblichus." In *Religious Identity in Late Antiquity*, edited by E. DePalma Digeser and Robert Frakes, 59–83. Toronto: Edgar Kent.

———. 2008. "Augustine and the Invention of Magical Dissent." In *Augustine and World Religions*, edited by K. Paffenroth, J. Doody, and B. Brown, 3–20. Lanham: Lexington Books.

Durling, D. C. 1983. "Testament of Solomon (First to Third Century A.D.): A New Translation and Introduction." In *The Old Testament Pseudepigraphia*, edited by James H. Charlesworth, 1: 935–987. Garden City, NY: Doubleday.

Dzwiza, Kirsten. 2012. "The Catalogue and Statistical Analysis of the Charakteres Project: A First Introduction." In *Contesti magici*, edited by Marina Piranomonte and Francisco Marco Simon, 307–308. Rome: De Luca Editore D'Arte.

Edelstein, Emma J., and Ludwig Edelstein. 1945. *Asclepius: A Collection and Interpretation of the Testimonies.* 2 vols. Publications of the Institute of the History of Medicine, Johns Hopkins University. Baltimore: Johns Hopkins University Press.

Edmonds, Radcliffe G. 2003. "At the Seizure of the Moon: The Absence of the Moon in the Mithras Liturgy." In *Prayer, Magic, and the Stars in the Ancient and Late Antique World*, edited by Scott B. Noegel, Joel Thomas Walker, and Brannon M. Wheeler, 223–239. University Park: Penn State University Press.

———. 2004. "The Faces of the Moon: Cosmology, Genesis, and the Mithras Liturgy." In *Heavenly Realms and Earthly Realities in Late Antique Religions*, edited by Ra'anan S. Boustan and Annette Yoshiko Reed, 275–295. Cambridge and New York: Cambridge University Press.

———. 2006. "To Sit in Solemn Silence? 'Thronosis' in Ritual, Myth, and Iconography." *The American Journal of Philology* 127 (3): 347–366.

———. 2010. "Necromancy." In *The Homer Encyclopedia*, edited by Margalit Finkelberg, 563. Chichester, West Sussex; Malden, MA: Wiley-Blackwell.

———. 2013. "The Ephesia Grammata: Logos Orphaïkos or Apolline Alexima Pharmaka?" In *The Getty Hexameters: Poetry, Magic, and Mystery in Ancient Selinous*, edited by Christopher A. Faraone and Dirk Obbink, 97–106. Oxford and New York: Oxford University Press.

———. 2014. "There and Back Again: Temporary Immortality in the Mithras Liturgy." In *Conversion and Initiation in Antiquity: Shifting Identities, Creating Change*, edited by Birgitte Bøgh, 185–201. Early Christianity in the Context of Antiquity 16. Frankfort: Peter Lang.

———. 2015. "Imagining the Afterlife." In *The Oxford Handbook of Ancient Greek Religion*, edited by Esther Eidinow and Julia Kindt, 551–563. Oxford: Oxford University Press.

Eidinow, Esther. 2007. *Oracles, Curses, and Risk among the Ancient Greeks*. Oxford: Oxford University Press.

———. 2011. "Networks and Narratives: A Model for Ancient Greek Religion." *Kernos. Revue internationale et pluridisciplinaire de religion grecque antique* 24 (January): 9–38.

———. 2012. "Risk and the Greeks: A New Approach to Understanding Binding Curses." In *Contesti magici*, edited by Marina Piranomonte and Francisco Marco Simón, 13–19. Rome: De Luca Editore d'Arte.

———. 2016. *Envy, Poison, and Death: Women on Trial in Classical Athens*. Oxford: Oxford University Press.

Eidinow, Esther, Julia Kindt, and Robin Osborne, eds. 2016. *Theologies of Ancient Greek Religion*. Cambridge: Cambridge University Press.

Ekroth, Gunnel. 2009. "Thighs or Tails? The Osteological Evidence as a Source for Greek Ritual Norms." In *La norme en matière religieuse en Grèce ancienne: Actes du XIIe colloque international du CIERGA (Rennes, Septembre 2007)*, edited by Pierre Brulé, 125–151. Liège: Presses universitaires de Liège.

———. 2011. "Meat for the Gods." In *«Nourrir les dieux?» Sacrifice et représentation du divin. Actes de la VIe rencontre du groupe de recherche européen «Figure. Représentation du divin dans sociétés grecque et romaine» (Université de Liège, 23–24 Octobre 2009)*, edited by Vinciane Pirenne-Delforge and Francesca Prescendi, 15–41. Liège: Centre international d'étude de la religion grecque antique.

Evans-Pritchard, E. E. 1937. *Witchcraft, Oracles, and Magic among the Azande*. New York: Oxford University Press.

Fabiano, Doralice. 2013. "La nympholepsie entre possession et paysage." In *Perception et construction du divin dans l'antiquité*, edited by Philippe Borgeaud and Doralice Fabiano, 165–195. Geneva: Librairie Droz.

Faraone, Christopher. 1985. "Aeschylus' Ὕμνος Δέσμιος (Eum. 306) and Attic Judicial Curse Tablets." *The Journal of Hellenic Studies* 105: 150–154.

———. 1991a. "The Agonistic Context of Early Greek Binding Spells." In *Magika Hiera: Ancient Greek Magic and Religion*, edited by Christopher A. Faraone and Dirk Obbink, 3–32. New York : Oxford: Oxford University Press.

———. 1991b. "Binding and Burying the Forces of Evil: The Defensive Use of 'Voodoo Dolls' in Ancient Greece." *Classical Antiquity* 10: 115–153.

———. 1992a. "Aristophanes, Amphiaraus, Fr. 29 (Kassel-Austin): Oracular Response or Erotic Incantation?" *Classical Quarterly* 42: 320–327.

———. 1992b. *Talismans and Trojan Horses: Guardian Statues in Ancient Greek Myth and Ritual*. Oxford: Oxford University Press.

———. 1993. "The Wheel, the Whip and Other Implements of Torture: Erotic Magic in Pindar Pythian 4.213–19." *The Classical Journal* 89: 1–19.

———. 1999. *Ancient Greek Love Magic*. Cambridge, MA: Harvard University Press.

———. 2001. "The Undercutter, the Woodcutter, and Greek Demon Names Ending in -Tomos (Hom. Hymn to Dem 228–29)." *The American Journal of Philology* 122: 1–10.

———. 2005. "Necromancy Goes Underground: The Disguise of Skull- and Corpse-Divination in the Paris Magical Papyri (PGM IV 1928–2144)." In *Mantikê:*

Studies in Ancient Divination, edited by Sarah Iles Johnston and Peter T. Struck, 255–282. Leiden: Brill.

Faraone, Christopher. 2009. "Does Tantalus Drink the Blood or Not? An Enigmatic Series of Inscribed Hematite Gemstones." In *Antike Mythen: Medien, Transformationen und Konstruktionen*, edited by Ueli Dill and Christine Walde, 248–273. Berlin and New York: Walter de Gruyter.

———. 2010. "A Greek Magical Gemstone from the Black Sea." *Kernos. Revue internationale et pluridisciplinaire de religion grecque antique* 23: 91–114.

———. 2011a. "Magic and Medicine in the Roman Imperial Period: Two Case Studies." In *Continuity and Innovation in the Magical Tradition*, edited by Gideon Bohak, Yuval Harari, and Shaul Shaked, 135–156. Leiden: Brill.

———. 2011b. "Magical and Medical Approaches to the Wandering Womb in the Ancient Greek World." *Classical Antiquity* 30: 1–32.

———. 2011c. "Text, Image and Medium: The Evolution of Graeco-Roman Magical Gemstones." In *"Gems of Heaven": Recent Research on Engraved Gemstones in Late Antiquity, c. AD 200–600*, edited by Chris Entwistle and Noel Adams, 50–61. London: British Museum.

———. 2012a. "At the Limits of Efficacious Speech: The Performance and Audience of Self-Curses in Ancient Near Eastern and Greek Oaths." *Mètis* 10 ("Serments, vœux et construction rituelle des actes de parole efficaces," edited by Clifford Ando and Christopher A. Faraone): 120–133.

———. 2012b. *Vanishing Acts on Ancient Greek Amulets: From Oral Performance to Visual Design*. BICS Supplement 15. London: Institute of Classical Studies, School of Advanced Study, University of London.

Faraone, Christopher A., and Amina Kropp. 2010. "Inversion, Adversion, and Perversion as Strategies in Latin Curse-Tablets." In *Magical Practice in the Latin West: Papers from the International Conference Held at the University of Zaragoza, 30 Sept.–1st Oct. 2005*, edited by Richard Gordon and Francisco Marco Simón, 381–398. Leiden: Brill.

Faraone, Christopher A., and Dirk Obbink, eds. 1991. *Magika Hiera: Ancient Greek Magic and Religion*. New York: Oxford University Press.

Faraone, Christopher A., and Dirk Obbink, eds. 2013. *The Getty Hexameters: Poetry, Magic, and Mystery in Ancient Selinous*. Oxford and New York: Oxford University Press.

Festugière, A. J. 1944. *La révélation d'Hermès Trismégiste: L'astrologie et les sciences occultes*. Vol. 1. Paris: J. Gabalda.

Flower, Michael. 2008a. "The Iamidae: A Mantic Family and Its Public Image." In *Practitioners of the Divine: Greek Priests and Religious Officials from Homer to Heliodorus*, edited by Beate Dignas and Kai Trampedach, 187–206. Cambridge, MA: Harvard University Press.

———. 2008b. *The Seer in Ancient Greece*. Berkeley: University of California Press.

Fontenrose, Joseph. 1978. *The Delphic Oracle: Its Response and Operations with a Catalogue of Responses*. Berkeley, Los Angeles, and London: University of California Press.

Forbes, R. J. 1964. "The Origins of Alchemy." In *Studies in Ancient Technology*, 2nd ed., 1:125–148. Leiden: E. J. Brill.

Fowden, Garth. 1986. *The Egyptian Hermes: A Historical Approach to the Late Pagan Mind*. Cambridge: Cambridge University Press.

Frankfurter, David. 1997. "Ritual Expertise in Roman Egypt and the Problem of the Category 'Magician.' " In *Envisioning Magic: A Princeton Seminar and Symposium*, edited by P. Schäfer and H. Kippenberg, 115–135. Leiden and New York: E. J. Brill.

———. 1998. *Religion in Roman Egypt: Assimilation and Resistance*. Princeton, NJ: Princeton University Press.

———. 2005. "Voices, Books, and Dreams: The Diversification of Divination Media in Late Antique Egypt." In *Mantikê: Studies in Ancient Divination*, edited by Sarah Iles Johnston and Peter T. Struck, 233–254. Leiden: E. J. Brill.

Fraser, Kyle A. 2004. "Zosimos of Panopolis and the Book of Enoch: Alchemy as Forbidden Knowledge." *Aries* 4 (2): 125–147.

———. 2007. "Baptised in Gnôsis: The Spiritual Alchemy of Zosimos of Panopolis." *Dionysius* 25 (December): 33–54.

Frazer, James G. 1952. *The Golden Bough: A Study in Magic and Religion*. New York: MacMillan.

———. 1979. "Sympathetic Magic." In *Reader in Comparative Religion*, edited by William A. Lessa and Evon Z. Vogt, 337–352. New York: Harper & Row.

Furley, William D., and Jan Maarten Bremer. 2001. *Greek Hymns: Selected Cult Songs from the Archaic to the Hellenistic Period*. Studien und Texte zu Antike und Christentum 9–10. Tübingen: Mohr Siebeck.

Furley, William D., and Victor Gysembergh. 2015. *Reading the Liver: Papyrological Texts on Ancient Greek Extispicy*. Studien und Texte zu Antike und Christentum 94. Tübingen: Mohr Siebeck.

Gager, John G., ed. 1992. *Curse Tablets and Binding Spells from the Ancient World*. New York and Oxford: Oxford University Press.

Gautier, Paul. 1988. "Pseudo-Psellos: Graecorum Opiniones de Daemonibus." *Revue des études byzantines* 46: 85–107.

Gellar-Goad, T. H. M., Zinon Papakonstantinou, and Werner Riess. 2018. "Magic in Ancient Athens: A Complete Translation of Attic Curse Tablets." In *Colloquium Atticum I–III: Neuere Forschungen zur Archaik, zum athenischen Recht und zur Magie*. Stuttgart: Steiner Verlag.

Gennep, Arnold van. 1960. *The Rites of Passage*. Translated by Monika Vizedom and Gabrielle Leboeuf Caffee. Chicago: University of Chicago Press.

Georgoudi, Stella, Renée Koch Piettre, and Francis Schmidt, eds. 2012. *La raison des signes: Présages, rites, destin dans les sociétés de la méditerranée ancienne*. Leiden and Boston: E. J. Brill.

Gertz, Sebastian, John Dillon, and Donald Russell. 2014. *Aeneas of Gaza: Theophrastus with Zacharias of Mytilene: Ammonius*. London: Bloomsbury Publishing PLC.

Gordon, Richard. 1987a. "Aelian's Peony: The Location of Magic in the Greco-Roman Tradition." *Comparative Criticism* 9: 59–95.

———. 1987b. "Lucan's Erictho." In *Homo Viator: Classical Essays for John Bramble*, edited by Michael Whitby, Philip Hardie, and Mary Whitby, 231–241. Bristol: Bristol Classical Press.

———. 1995. "The Healing Event in Graeco-Roman Folk-Medicine." In *Ancient Medicine in Its Socio-Cultural Context: Papers Read at the Congress Held at Leiden University, 13–15 April 1992*, edited by Ph. J. van der Eijk, H. F. J. Horstmanshoff, and P. H. Schrijvers, 2:363–376. Amsterdam and Atlanta: Rodopi.

———. 1997. "Quaedam Veritatis Umbrae: Hellenistic Magic and Astrology." In

Conventional Values of the Hellenistic Greeks, edited by Per Bilde, Troels Engberg-Pederson, Lise Hannestad, and Jan Zahle, 128–158. Aarhus: Aarhus University Press.

Gordon, Richard. 1999a. "Imagining Greek and Roman Magic." In *Witchcraft and Magic in Europe: Ancient Greece and Rome*, edited by Bengt Ankarloo and Stuart Clark, 159–275. Philadelphia: University of Pennsylvania Press.

———. 1999b. " 'What's in a List?': Listing in Greek and Graeco-Roman Malign Magical Texts." In *The World of Ancient Magic: Papers from the First International Samson Eitrem Seminar at the Norwegian Institute at Athens, 4–8 May 1997*, edited by David R. Jordan, Hugo Montgomery, and Einar Thomassen, 239–277. Bergen: Paul Aströms.

———. 2002a. "Another View of the Pergamon Divination Kit." *Journal of Roman Archaeology* 15: 188–198.

———. 2002b. "Shaping the Text: Innovation and Authority in the Graeco-Egyptian Malign Magic." In *Kykeon*, edited by H. F. J Horstmanshoff, 69–111. Leiden: E. J. Brill.

———. 2004. "Raising a Sceptre: Confession-Narratives from Lydia and Phrygia." *Journal of Roman Archaeology* 17: 177–196.

———. 2011a. "Archaeologies of Magical Gems." In *"Gems of Heaven": Recent Research on Engraved Gemstones in Late Antiquity, c. AD 200–600*, edited by Chris Entwistle and Noel Adams, 39–48. London: British Museum.

———. 2011b. "Signa Nova et Inaudita: The Theory and Practice of Invented Signs (Charaktêres) in Graeco-Egyptian Magical Texts." *MHNH: Revista Internacional de Investigación sobre Magia y Astrología Antiguas* 11: 15–44.

———. 2012. "Memory and Authority in the Magical Papyri." In *Historical and Religious Memory in the Ancient World*, edited by Beate Dignas and R. R. R. Simon, 145–180. Oxford and New York: Oxford University Press.

———. 2013a. "Cosmology, Astrology, and Magic: Discourse, Schemes, Power, and Literacy." In *Panthée: Religious Transformations in the Graeco-Roman Empire*, edited by Laurent Bricault and Corinne Bonnet, 85–111. Leipzig and Boston: E. J. Brill.

———. 2013b. "The Religious Anthropology of Late-Antique 'High' Magical Practice." In *The Individual in the Religions of the Ancient Mediterranean*, edited by Jörg Rüpke, 163–186. Oxford: Oxford University Press.

———. 2013c. " 'Will My Child Have a Big Nose?': Uncertainty, Authority and Narrative in Katarchic Astrology." In *Divination in the Ancient World: Religious Options and the Individual*, edited by Veit Rosenberger, 93–137. Stuttgart: Franz Steiner Verlag.

Gordon, Richard, and Francisco Marco Simón. 2010. "Introduction." In *Magical Practice in the Latin West: Papers from the International Conference Held at the University of Zaragoza, 30 Sept.–1st Oct. 2005*, edited by Richard Gordon and Francisco Marco Simón, 1–49. Leiden: E. J. Brill.

Gould, John. 1973. "Hiketeia." *The Journal of Hellenic Studies* 93: 74–103.

Graf, Fritz. 1991. "Prayer in Magic and Religious Ritual." In *Magika Hiera: Ancient Greek Magic and Religion*, edited by Christopher Faraone and Dirk Obbink, 188–213. New York and Oxford: Oxford University Press.

———. 1994. "The Magician's Initiation." *Helios* 21 (2): 161–177.

———. 1997. *Magic in the Ancient World*. Cambridge, MA: Harvard University Press.

———. 1999. "Magic and Divination." In *The World of Ancient Magic: Papers from the First International Samson Eitrem Seminar at the Norwegian Institute at Athens, 4–8 May 1997*, edited by David R. Jordan, Hugo Montgomery, and Einar Thomassen, 283–298. Bergen: Norwegian Institute at Athens.

———. 2002a. "Augustine and Magic." In *The Metamorphosis of Magic from Late Antiquity to the Early Modern Period*, edited by Jan N. and Jan R. Veenstra Bremmer, 87–103. Leuven: Peeters.

———. 2002b. "Theories of Magic in Antiquity." In *Magic and Ritual in the Ancient World*, edited by Paul Mirecki and Marvin Meyer, 93–104. Leiden: E. J. Brill.

———. 2005. "Rolling the Dice for an Answer." In *Mantikê: Studies in Ancient Divination*, edited by Sarah Iles Johnston and Peter T. Struck, 51–97. Leiden: E. J. Brill.

———. 2009. "Serious Singing: The Orphic Hymns as Religious Texts." *Kernos. Revue internationale et pluridisciplinaire de religion grecque antique* 22: 169–182.

———. 2015. "Magie et écriture: Quelques réflexions." In *Ecrire la magie dans l'antiquité: Actes du colloque international (Liège, 13–15 Octobre 2011)*, edited by Magali De Haro Sanchez, 227–237. Liège: Presses universitaires de Liège.

Greenbaum, Dorian Gieseler. 2010. "Arrows, Aiming and Divination: Astrology as a Stochastic Art." In *Divination: Perspectives for a New Milennium*, edited by Patrick Curry, 179–209. Burlington: Ashgate.

———. 2016. *The Daimon in Hellenistic Astrology: Origins and Influence*. Leiden and Boston: E. J. Brill.

Grimes, Shannon L. 2006. "Zosimus of Panopolis: Alchemy, Nature, and Religion in Late Antiquity." Dissertation, Syracuse: Syracuse University.

Grottanelli, Cristiano. 2003. "Evenius Becomes a Seer (Herodotus 9.93–5): A Paradoxical Initiation?" In *Initiation in Ancient Greek Rituals and Narratives: New Critical Perspectives*, edited by David Dodd and Christopher A. Faraone, 203–218. London and New York: Routledge.

———. 2005. "Sorte Unica pro Casibus Pluribus Enotata: Literary Texts and Lot Inscriptions as Sources for Ancient Kleromancy." In *Mantikê: Studies in Ancient Divination*, edited by Sarah Iles Johnston and Peter T. Struck, 129–146. Leiden and Boston: E. J. Brill.

Gundel, Wilhelm. 1936. *Dekane und Dekansternbilder: Ein Beitrag zur Geschichte der Sternbilder der Kulturvölker*. Glückstadt and Hamburg: J. J. Augustin.

Hadot, Pierre. 1995. *Philosophy as a Way of Life: Spiritual Exercises from Socrates to Foucault*. Translated by Arnold Davidson. Oxford and New York: Blackwell.

Hale, John, Jelle De Boer, Jeffery Chanton, and Henry Spiller. 2003. "Questioning the Delphic Oracle: Overview / An Intoxicating Tale." *Scientific American*, August, 67–73.

Halleux, Robert, and Jacques Schamp. 1985. *Les lapidaires grecs*. Collection des universités de France. Paris: Les Belles Lettres.

Hallum, B. C. 2008. "Zosimus Arabus: The Reception of Zosimos of Panopolis in the Arabic/Islamic World." Dissertation, London: Warburg Institute, University of London.

Haluszka, Adria. 2008. "Sacred Signified: The Semiotics of Statues in the Greek Magical Papyri." *Arethusa* 41: 479–494.

Hamilton, William, and Johann Tischbein. 1791. *Collection of Engravings from Ancient Vases Mostly of Pure Greek Workmanship: Discovered in Sepulchres in the Kingdom of the Two Sicilies but Chiefly in the Neighbourhood of Naples during the Course of the Years MDCCLXXXIX and MDCCLXXXX Now in the Possession of Sir Wm. Hamilton . . . with Remarks on Each Vase by the Collector.* Naples: W. Tischbein.

Hansen, William, ed. 1998. "The Oracles of Astrampsychus." In *Anthology of Ancient Greek Popular Literature*, translated by Randall Stewart and Kenneth Morrell, 285–324. Bloomington: Indiana University Press.

Harris-McCoy, Daniel. 2012. *Artemidorus'* Oneirocritica*: Text, Translation, and Commentary.* Oxford: Oxford University Press.

Heim, Ricardus. 1893. "Incantamenta Magica Graeca et Latina." *Jahrbücher für classische Philologie* Supplement 19: 462–575.

Henrichs, Albert. 2010. "What Is a Greek God?" In *The Gods of Ancient Greece: Identities and Transformations*, edited by Jan Bremmer and Andrew Erskine, 19–39. Edinurgh Leventis Studies 5. Edinburgh: Edinburgh University Press.

Hephaestion of Thebes. 1998. *Apotelesmatics: Book II.* Translated by Robert H. Schmidt. Cumberland: The Golden Hind Press.

Hershbell, Jackson P. 1987. "Democritus and the Beginnings of Greek Alchemy." *Ambix* 34: 5–20.

Hopfner, Theodor. 1932. "Mittel- und neugriechische Lekano, Lychno-, Katoptro- und Onychomantien." In *Studies Presented to F. LL. Griffith*, edited by Stephen Ranulph Kingdon Glanville, 218–232. London: Oxford University Press.

———. 1983. *Griechisch-ägyptischer Offenbarungzauber. 2 Vols. Studien zu Paläographie und Papyruskunde 21 und 23.* Amsterdam: Verlag Adolf M. Hakkert.

Howie, Gordon. 1991. "Pindar's Account of Pelops' Contest with Oenomaus." *Nikephoros* 4: 55–120.

Hunink, Vincent. 1997. *Pro Se de Magia Apologia: Apuleius.* Amsterdam: J. C. Gieben.

Jackson, Howard M. 1978. *Zosimos of Panopolis: On the Letter Omega.* Society of Biblical Literature Texts and Translations 14. Missoula: Scholars Press.

Jakobson, Roman. [1956] 2002. "The Metaphoric and Metonymic Poles." In *Metaphor and Metonymy in Comparison and Contrast*, edited by René Dirven and Ralf Pörings, 41–47. Berlin and Boston: De Gruyter Mouton.

Jameson, Michael H. 1991. "Sacrifice before Battle." In *Hoplites: The Classical Greek Battle Experience*, edited by Victor Davis Hanson, 197–227. London and New York: Routledge.

Janowitz, Naomi. 2002. *Icons of Power: Ritual Practices in Late Antiquity.* Magic in History. University Park: The Pennsylvania State University Press.

Jim, Theodora Suk Fong. 2012. "Naming a Gift: The Vocabulary and Purposes of Greek Religious Offerings." *Greek, Roman, and Byzantine Studies* 52: 310–337.

Johnston, Sarah Iles. 1990. *Hekate Soteira: A Study of Hekate's Roles in the Chaldean Oracles and Related Literature.* Atlanta: Scholar's Press.

———. 1992. "Riders in the Sky: Cavalier Gods and Theurgic Salvation in the Second Century A.D." *Classical Philology* 87: 303–321.

———. 1995. "Defining the Dreadful: Remarks on the Greek Child-Killing Demon."

In *Ancient Magic and Ritual Power*, edited by Marvin W. Meyer and Paul Allan Mirecki, 361–390. Leiden and New York: E. J. Brill.

———. 1997. "Rising to the Occasion: Theurgic Ascent in Its Cultural Milieu." In *Envisioning Magic: A Princeton Seminar and Symposium*, edited by Peter Schäfer and Hans G. Kippenberg, 165–194. Leiden and New York: E. J. Brill.

———. 1999. *Restless Dead: Encounters between the Living and the Dead in Ancient Greece*. Berkeley and Los Angeles: University of California Press.

———. 2001. "Charming Children: The Use of the Child in Ancient Divination." *Arethusa* 34 (1): 97–117.

———. 2002. "Sacrifice in the Magical Papyri." In *Ancient Magic and Ritual Power*, edited by Marvin Meyer and Paul Mirecki, 344–358. Leiden: E. J. Brill.

———. 2003. "Describing the Undefinable: New Books on Magic and Old Problems of Definition." *History of Religions* 43 (1): 50–54.

———. 2004. "Working Overtime in the Afterlife; or, No Rest for the Virtuous." In *Heavenly Realms and Earthly Realities in Late Antique Religions*, edited by Ra'anan S. Boustan and Annette Yoshiko Reed, 85–100. Cambridge: Cambridge University Press.

———. 2005. "Delphi and the Dead." In *Mantikê: Studies in Ancient Divination*, edited by Sarah Iles Johnston and Peter T. Struck, 283–306. Leiden: E. J. Brill.

———. 2008a. *Ancient Greek Divination*. Malden, MA: Blackwell Publishing.

———. 2008b. "Animating Statues: A Case Study in Ritual." *Arethusa* 41: 445–477.

———. 2010a. "Homo Fictor Deorum Est: Envisioning the Divine in Late Antique Divinatory Spells." In *The Gods of Ancient Greece*, edited by Jan Bremmer and Andrew Erskine, 406–421. Edinburgh: Edinburgh University Press.

———. 2010b. "Porphyry, Sacrifice, and the Orderly Cosmos: On the Philosophy to Be Derived from Oracles Fr. 314 and 315." *Kernos. Revue internationale et pluridisciplinaire de religion grecque antique* 23: 115–132.

———. 2010c. "Sending Dreams, Restraining Dreams: Oneiropompeia in Theory and Practice." In *Sub Imagine Somni: Nighttime Phenomena in Greco-Roman Culture*, edited by Emma Scioli and Christine Walde, 63–80. Testi e Studi Di Cultura Classica 46. Pisa: Edizioni ETS.

———. 2012. "Sosipatra and the Theurgic Life: Eunapius Vitae Sophistorum 6.6.5–6.9.24." In *Reflections on Religious Individuality: Greco-Roman and Judaeo-Christian Texts and Practices*, edited by Jörg Rüpke and Wolfgang Spickermann, 99–117. Berlin: De Gruyter.

Johnston, Sarah Iles, and Peter T. Struck, eds. 2005. *Mantikê: Studies in Ancient Divination*. Leiden and Boston: E. J. Brill.

Jordan, David. 1985. "A Survey of Greek Defixiones Not Included in the Special Corpora." *Greek, Roman, and Byzantine Studies* 26 (2): 151–197.

———. 1994. "Late Feasts for Ghosts." In *Ancient Greek Cult Practice from the Epigraphical Evidence: Proceedings of the Second International Seminar on Ancient Greek Cult, Organized by the Swedish Institute at Athens, 22–24 November 1991*, edited by Robin Hagg, 131–143. Stockholm.

Jung, C. G. 1967. "The Visions of Zosimos." In *Alchemical Studies*, translated by R. F. C. Hull, 59–108. Princeton, NJ: Princeton University Press.

Kahlos, Maijastina. 2016. "Artis Heu Magicis: The Label of Magic in the Fourth-Century Conflicts and Disputes." In *Pagans and Christians in Late Antique Rome:*

Conflict, Competition, and Coexistence in the Fourth Century, edited by Michele Renee Salzman, 162–177. New York: Cambridge University Press.

Karanika, Andromache. 2011. "Homer the Prophet: Homeric Verses and Divination in the Homeromanteion." In *Sacred Words: Orality, Literacy and Religion*, edited by André Lardinois, Josine Blok, and M. G. M. van der Poel, 255–277. Leiden: E. J. Brill.

Kelhoffer, James A. 2008. " 'Hippolytus' and Magic. An Examination of Elenchos IV 28–42 and Related Passages in Light of the Papyri Graecae Magicae." *Zeitschrift für antikes Christentum* 11: 517–548.

Keyser, Paul. 1990. "Alchemy in the Ancient World: From Science to Magic." *Illinois Classical Studies* 15 (2): 353–378.

Kingsley, Peter. 1995. *Ancient Philosophy, Mystery, and Magic: Empedocles and Pythagorean Tradition*. Oxford: Oxford University Press.

Kippenberg, Hans G. 1997. "Magic in Roman Civil Discourse: Why Rituals Could Be Illegal." In *Envisioning Magic: A Princeton Seminar and Symposium*, edited by Peter Schäfer and Hans G. Kippenberg, 137–164. Leiden and New York: E. J. Brill.

Kissling, Robert Christian. 1922. "The Ὄχημα-Πνεῦμα of the Neo-Platonists and the *De Insomniis* of Synesius of Cyrene." *The American Journal of Philology* 43 (4): 318–330.

Komorowska, Joanna. 2009. "Astrology, Ptolemy and Technai Stochastikai." *MHNH: Revista Internacional de Investigación sobre Magia y Astrología Antiguas* 9: 191–204.

Kotansky, Roy. 1994. *Greek Magical Amulets: The Inscribed Gold, Silver, Copper, and Bronze Lamellae: Text and Commentary*. Abhandlungen der Rheinisch-Westfälischen Akademie der Wissenschaften. Sonderreihe Papyrologica Coloniensia 22. Opladen: Westdeutscher Verlag.

Kropp, Amina. 2008. *Defixiones: Ein aktuelles Corpus lateinischer Fluchtafeln: Dfx.* Speyer: Kartoffeldruck-Verlag.

———. 2010. "How Does Magical Language Work? The Spells and Formulae on the Latin Defixionum Tabellae." In *Magical Practice in the Latin West: Papers from the International Conference Held at the University of Zaragoza, 30 Sept.–1st Oct. 2005*, edited by Richard Gordon and Francisco Marco Simón, 357–380. Leiden: E. J. Brill.

Laín Entralgo, Pedro. 1970. *The Therapy of the Word in Classical Antiquity*. Translated by L. J. Rather and John M. Sharp. New Haven, CT: Yale University Press.

Langholf, Volker. 1990. "Prognosis and Divination." In *Medical Theories in Hippocrates: Early Texts and the "Epidemics,"* 232–254. Berlin and New York: Walter De Gruyter.

Larson, Jennifer. 2001. *Greek Nymphs: Myth, Cult, Lore*. New York: Oxford University Press.

Lehoux, Daryn. 2007. "Drugs and the Delphic Oracle." *Classical World* 101 (1): 41–57.

Letrouit, Jean. 1995. "Chronologie des alchimistes grecs." In *Alchimie: Art, histoire et mythes: Actes du 1er colloque international de la société d'étude de l'histoire de l'alchimie (Paris, Collège de France, 14–15–16 Mars 1991)*, edited by Didier Kahn and Sylvain Matton, 11–93. Paris: S.É.H.A.

———. 2002. "Hermétise et alchimie: Contribution à l'étude du Marcianus Graecus 299 (=M)." In *Magia, alchimia, scienza dal '400 al '700. L'influsso di Ermete Trismegisto*, edited by Carlos Gilly and Cis Van Heertum, 85–105. Venice and Amsterdam: Bibliotheca Philosophica Hermetica.

Lévi-Strauss, Claude. 1963. "The Structural Study of Myth." In *Structural Anthropology*, 206–231. New York: Basic Books, Inc.

Lewis, Nicola Denzey. 2014. "Living Images of the Divine: Female Theurgists in Late Antiquity." In *Daughters of Hecate: Women and Magic in the Ancient World*, edited by Kimberly B. Stratton and Dayna S. Kalleres, 274–297. Oxford: Oxford University Press.

Lewy, Hans. 1956. *Chaldaean Oracles and Theurgy: Mysticism, Magic and Platonism in the Later Roman Empire*. Le Caire: Imprimerie de l'Institut français d'archéologie orientale.

LiDonnici, Lynn. 1995. *The Epidaurian Miracle Inscriptions: Text, Translation, and Commentary*. Atlanta: Scholars Press.

———. 1998. "Burning for It: Erotic Spells for Fever and Compulsion in the Ancient Mediterranean World." *Greek, Roman, and Byzantine Studies* 39 (1): 63–98.

———. 2001. "Single-Stemmed Wormwood, Pinecones and Myrrh: Expense and Availability of Recipe Ingredients in the Greek Magic Papyri." *Kernos. Revue internationale et pluridisciplinaire de religion grecque antique* 14: 61–91.

———. 2002. "Beans, Fleawort, and the Blood of a Hamadryas Baboon: Recipe Ingredients in Greco-Roman Magical Materials." In *Magic and Ritual in the Ancient World*, edited by Paul Mirecki and Marvin Meyer, 359–377. Leiden, Boston, and Cologne: E. J. Brill.

Lindsay, Jack. 1970. *The Origins of Alchemy in Graeco-Roman Egypt*. London: Frederick Muller.

Long, A. A. 1982. "Astrology: Arguments Pro and Contra." In *Science and Speculation: Studies in Hellenistic Theory and Practice*, edited by Jonathan Barnes, Jacques Brunschwig, Myles Burnyeat, and Malcolm Schofield, 165–192. Cambridge: Cambridge University Press.

Love, Edward O. D. 2016. *Code-Switching with the Gods: The Bilingual (Old Coptic-Greek) Spells of PGM IV (P. Bibliothèque Nationale Supplément Grec. 574) and Their Linguistic, Religious, and Socio-Cultural Context in Late Roman Egypt*. Berlin and Boston: De Gruyter.

Luck, Georg. 1999. "Witches and Sorcerers in Classical Literature." In *Magic and Witchcraft in Europe: Greece and Rome*, edited by Bengt Ankarloo and Stuart Clark, 91–158. Philadelphia: University of Pennsylvania Press.

———. 2000. "Theurgy and Forms of Worship in Neoplatonism." In *Ancient Pathways and Hidden Pursuits: Religion, Morals, and Magic in the Ancient World*, 110–152. Ann Arbor: University of Michigan Press.

———. 2006. *Arcana Mundi: Magic and the Occult in the Greek and Roman Worlds: A Collection of Ancient Texts*. 2nd ed. Baltimore and Ann Arbor: Johns Hopkins University Press and University of Michigan Press.

Lupu, Eran. 2005. *Greek Sacred Law: A Collection of New Documents*. Religions in the Graeco-Roman World 152. Leiden and Boston: E. J. Brill.

Majercik, Ruth. 1989. *The Chaldean Oracles: Text, Translation, and Commentary*. Leiden: E. J. Brill.

Malinowski, Bronislaw. 1935. *Coral Gardens and Their Magic*. New York: American Book Co.

Manetti, Giovanni. 1993. *Theories of the Sign in Classical Antiquity*. Translated by Christine Richardson. Bloomington: Indiana University Press.

Martelli, Matteo. 2013. *The Four Books of Pseudo-Democritus*. Leeds: Maney Publishing.

———. 2014a. "L'alchimie en Syriaque et l'ouvre de Zosime." In *Les sciences en Syriaque*, edited by Émilie Villey, 191–214. Paris: Geuthner.

———. 2014b. "Properties and Classification of Mercury between Natural Philosophy, Medicine, and Alchemy." *AION Annali dell'Università degli Studi di Napoli «L'orientale»* 36: 17–47.

Martín Hernández, Raquel. 2014. "Using Homer for Divination: Homeromanteia in Context." *Center for Hellenic Studies Research Bulletin* 2 (1). http://nrs.harvard.edu/urn-3:hlnc.essay:MartinHernandezR.Using_Homer_for_Divination_Homeromanteia_in_Context.2013.

Martín Hernández, Raquel, and Sophia Torallas Tovar. 2014. "The Use of the Ostracon in Magical Practice in Late Antique Egypt: Magical Handbooks vs. Material Evidence." *Studi e Materiali Della Storia Delle Religioni* 80 (2): 780–800.

Martinez, David. 1991. *A Greek Love Charm from Egypt (P. Mich. 757)*. American Studies in Papyrology 30. Atlanta: Scholars Press.

Mastrocinque, Attilio. 2002. "The Divinatory Kit from Pergamon and Greek Magic in Late Antiquity." *Journal of Roman Archaeology* 15: 173–187.

———. 2004. *Sylloge Gemmarum Gnosticarum*. Vol. 1. Bollettino di Numismatica, Monografia 8, 2. Rome: Instituto Poligrafico e Zecca della Stato.

———. 2008. *Sylloge Gemmarum Gnosticarum*. Vol. 2. Bollettino di Numismatica, Monografia 8, 2. Rome: Instituto Poligrafico e Zecca della Stato.

———. 2014. *Les intailles magiques du département des monnaies medailles et antiques*. Paris: Bibliothèque nationale de France.

Maurizio, Lisa. 1995. "Anthropology and Spirit Possession: A Reconsideration of the Pythia's Role at Delphi." *The Journal of Hellenic Studies* 115: 69–86.

———. 1997. "Delphic Oracles as Oral Performances: Authenticity and Historical Evidence." *Classical Antiquity* 16: 308–334.

———. 2001. "The Voice at the Center of the World: The Pythias' Ambiguity and Authority." In *Making Silence Speak: Women's Voices in Greek Literature and Society*, edited by André Lardinois and Laura McClure, 38–54. Princeton, NJ and Oxford: Princeton University Press.

Mauss, Marcel. 1967. *The Gift: Forms and Functions of Exchange in Archaic Societies*. Translated by Ian Cunnison. New York : London: W. W. Norton.

———. 1972. *A General Theory of Magic*. Translated by Robert Brain. London: Routledge & Kegan Paul.

Mazur, Zeke. 2003. "Unio Magica: Part I: On the Magical Origins of Plotinus' Mysticism." *Dionysius* 21: 23–52.

———. 2004. "Unio Magica: Part II: Plotinus, Theurgy, and the Question of Ritual." *Dionysius* 22: 29–56.

Mehl, Véronique. 2008. "Parfums de fête. Usages de parfums et sacrifices sanglants." In *Le sacrifice, vestiges, performances, stratégies: Actes du colloque de Lam-*

peter, 29 Août–3 Septembre 2006, edited by Pierre Brulé and Véronique Mehl, 167–186. Rennes: Presses universitaires de Rennes.

Meiggs, Russell, and David Lewis. 1969. *Selection of Greek Historical Inscriptions to the End of the Fifth Century B.C.* Oxford and New York: Clarendon Press.

Merkelbach, Reinhold, and Maria Totti-Gemünd. 1990. *Abrasax: Ausgewählte Papyri religiösen und magischen Inhalts.* 5 vols. Opladen: Westdeutscher Verlag.

Merlan, Philip. 1953. "Plotinus and Magic." *Isis* 44: 341–348.

Mertens, Michèle. 1995. *Les alchimistes grecs. Tome IV, 1ère partie. Zosime de Panopolis. Mémoires authentiques.* Paris: Les Belles Lettres.

Michel, Simone. 2001. *Die magischen Gemmen im Britischen Museum.* Edited by Peter Zazoff and Hilde Zazoff. 2 vols. London: British Museum.

———. 2004. *Die magische Gemmen: Zu Bildern und Zauberformeln auf geschnittenen Steinen der Antike und Neuzeit.* Studien aus dem Warburg-Haus 7. Berlin: De Gruyter.

Michels, Agnes Kirsopp. 1967. *The Calendar of the Roman Republic.* Princeton, NJ: Princeton University Press.

Mouterde, P. René S. J. 1930. *La Glaive de Dardanos: Objets et inscriptions magiques de Syrie.* Beyrouth: Imprimerie Catholique.

Moyer, Ian. 2003. "Thessalos of Tralles and Cultural Exchange." In *Prayer, Magic, and the Stars in the Ancient and Late Antique World,* edited by Scott Noegel, Joel Walker, and Brannon Wheeler, 39–56. University Park: The Pennsylvania State University Press.

———. 2011. *Egypt and the Limits of Hellenism.* Cambridge and New York: Cambridge University Press.

———. 2015. "A Revised Astronomical Dating of Thessalus' De Virtutibus Herbarum." In *The Frontiers of Ancient Science: Essays in Honor of Heinrich von Staden,* edited by Brooke Holmes and Klaus-Dietrich Fischer, 437–450. Berlin: De Gruyter.

Moyer, Ian, and Jacco Dieleman. 2003. "Miniaturization and the Opening of the Mouth In a Magical Greek Text (PGM XII.270–350)." *Journal of Ancient Near Eastern Religions* 3: 47–72.

Muellner, Leonard. 1976. *The Meaning of Homeric Eukhomai through Its Formulas.* Innsbruck: Innsbrucker Beiträge zur Sprachwissenschaft.

Murdock, George. 1980. *Theories of Illness: A World Survey.* Pittsburgh: University of Pittsburgh Press.

Murray, Gilbert. 1925. *Five Stages of Greek Religion.* New York: Columbia University Press.

Naiden, Fred S. 2013. *Smoke Signals for the Gods.* Oxford: Oxford University Press.

Neugebauer, O., and H. B. Van Hoesen. 1959. *Greek Horoscopes.* Memoirs of the American Philosophical Society 48. Philadelphia: American Philosophical Society.

Nissinen, Martti. 2010. "Prophecy and Omen Divination: Two Sides of the Same Coin." In *Divination and Interpretation of Signs in the Ancient World,* edited by Amar Annus, 341–351. Oriental Institute Seminars 6. Chicago: The Oriental Institute.

Noegel, Scott. 2007. *Nocturnal Ciphers: The Allusive Language of Dreams in the Ancient*

Near East. American Oriental Series 89. New Haven, CT: American Oriental Society.

Ogden, Daniel. 1999. "Binding Spells: Curse Tablets and Voodoo Dolls in the Greek and Roman Worlds." In *Magic and Witchcraft in Europe: Greece and Rome*, edited by Ankarloo and Clark, 1–90. Philadelphia: University of Pennsylvania Press.

———. 2001. *Greek and Roman Necromancy.* Princeton, NJ: Princeton University Press.

———. 2009. *Magic, Witchcraft and Ghosts in the Greek and Roman Worlds.* 2nd ed. Oxford: Oxford University Press.

O'Neill, William. 1965. *Proclus: Alcibiades I.* The Hague: M. Nijhoff.

Otto, Bernd-Christian. 2011. *Magie: Rezeptions- und diskursgeschichtliche Analysen von der Antike bis zur Neuzeit.* Religionsgeschichtliche Versuche und Vorarbeiten 57. Berlin and New York: De Gruyter.

———. 2013. "Towards Historicizing 'Magic' in Antiquity." *Numen* 60: 308–347.

Otto, Bernd-Christian, and Michael Stausberg. 2013. "General Introduction." In *Defining Magic: A Reader*, edited by Bernd-Christian Otto and Michael Stausberg, 1–15. London: Equinox Publishing, Ltd.

Pachoumi, Eleni. 2013. "The Religious-Philosophical Concept of Personal Daimon and the Magico-Theurgic Ritual of Systasis in the Greek Magical Papri." *Philologus* 157 (1): 46–69.

Park, George K. 1963. "Divination and Its Social Contexts." *The Journal of the Royal Anthropological Institute of Great Britain and Ireland* 93 (2): 195–209.

Parke, H. W. 1988. *Sibyls and Sibylline Prophecy in Classical Antiquity.* London: Routledge.

Parke, H. W., and D. E. W. Wormell. 1956. *The Delphic Oracle: The Oracular Responses.* 2 vols. Oxford: Blackwell.

Parker, Robert. 1983. *Miasma: Pollution and Purity in Early Greek Religion.* Oxford: Clarendon Press.

———. 1997. "Gods Cruel and Kind: Tragic and Civic Theology." In *Greek Tragedy and the Historian*, edited by Christopher Pelling, 143–160. Oxford: Clarendon Press.

———. 2000. "Greek States and Greek Oracles." In *Oxford Readings in Greek Religion*, edited by Richard Buxton, 76–108. Oxford: Oxford University Press.

Parsons, P. 1989. "3831. Homer Oracle." *The Oxrhynchus Papyri* 56: 44–48.

Pease, Arthur Stanley. 1979. *M. Tulli Ciceronis de Divinatione.* Reprint of 1920 edition. 2 vols. New York: Arno Press.

Peek, Philip M., ed. 1991. *African Divination Systems: Ways of Knowing.* Bloomington: Indiana University Press.

Peek, Werner. 1941. *Kerameikos, Ergebnisse der Ausgrabungen.* Vol. 3, *Inschriften, Ostraka, Fluchtafeln.* Berlin: De Gruyter.

Peirce, Charles Sanders. 1991. *Peirce on Signs.* Edited by James Hoopes. Chapel Hill: University of North Carolina Press.

Peirce, Sarah. 1993. "Death, Revelry, and 'Thysia.' " *Classical Antiquity* 12 (2): 219–266.

Petrovic, Andrej. 2012. "Tieropferrituale in den griechischen Zauberpapyri aus ästhetischer Sicht." In *Ästhetik des Opfers: Zeichen/Handlungen in Ritual und*

Spiel, edited by Alexander Honold, Anton Bierl, and Valentina Luppi, 35–62. Munich: Wilhelm Fink Verlag.

Pfister, R. 1925. "Teinture et alchimie dans l'orient hellenistique." *Seminarium Kondakovianum* 7: 1–59.

Phillipp, Hanna. 1986. *Mira et magica: Gemmen im Ägyptischen Museum der Staatlichen Museen Preussischer Kulturbesitz, Berlin-Charlottenburg.* Mainz: von Zabern.

Phillips, C. Robert. 1991. "Nullum Crimen Sine Lege: Socioreligious Sanctions on Magic." In *Magika Hiera: Ancient Greek Magic and Religion*, edited by Christopher Faraone and Dirk Obbink, 260–276. New York: Oxford University Press.

Pike, Kenneth. 1967. *Language in Relation to a Unified Theory of the Structure of Human Behavior.* 2nd ed. The Hague and Paris: Mouton & Co.

Pingree, David. 2014. "Hellenophilia versus the History of Science." *Transactions of the American Philological Association* 104 (3): 3–15.

Piranomonte, Marina. 2002. *Il santuario della musica e il bosco sacro di Anna Perenna.* Rome: Electa.

———. 2010. "Religion and Magic at Rome: The Fountain of Anna Perenna." In *Magical Practice in the Latin West. Papers from the International Conference Held at the University of Zaragoza, 30 Sept.–1 Oct. 2005*, edited by Richard Gordon and Francisco Marco Simon, 191–214. Leiden and Boston: E. J. Brill.

———. 2012. "Anna Perenna: Un contesto magico straordinario." In *Contesti Magici*, edited by Marina Piranomonte and Francisco Marco Simon, 161–174. Rome: De Luca Editori D' Arte.

Plass, Paul. 1982. "A Greek Alchemical Formula." *Ambix* 29 (2): 69–73.

Preisendanz, Karl, and Albert Henrichs. 1973. *Papyri Graecae Magicae: Die Griechischen Zauberpapyri.* 2nd ed. Stuttgart: Teubner.

Prince, Meredith. 2003. "Medea and the Inefficacy of Love Magic: Propertius 1.1 and Tibullus 1.2." *Classical Bulletin* 79 (2): 205–218.

Principe, Lawrence M. 2013. *The Secrets of Alchemy.* Chicago: University of Chicago Press.

Pulleyn, Simon. 1997. *Prayer in Greek Religion.* Oxford Classical Monographs. Oxford and New York: Oxford University Press.

Raphals, Lisa. 2013. *Divination and Prediction in Early China and Ancient Greece.* New York: Cambridge University Press.

Rapinesi, Ida Anna, and Jarmila Polakova. 2012. "La conservazione dei materiali magici del Santuario di Anna Perenna. Il Restauro." In *Contesti magici*, edited by Marina Piranomonte and Francisco Marco Simón, 175–182. Rome: De Luca Editore D'Arte.

Redfield, James. 1991. "The Politics of Immortality." In *Orphisme et Orphée: En l'honneur de Jean Rudhardt*, edited by Philippe Borgeaud, 3:103–117. Geneva: Librairie Droz S. A.

Reiner, Erica. 1995. *Astral Magic in Babylonia.* Transactions of the American Philosophical Society 85. Philadelphia: American Philosophical Society.

Renberg, Gil. 2010. "Dream-Narratives and Unnarrated Dreams in Greek and Latin Dedicatory Inscriptions." In *Sub Imagine Somni: Nighttime Phenomena in Greco-Roman Culture*, edited by Emma Scioli and Christine Walde, 33–62. Testi e Studi Di Cultura Classica 46. Pisa: Edizioni ETS.

Renberg, Gil. 2017. *Where Dreams May Come: Incubation Sanctuaries in the Greco-Roman World.* 2 vols. Leiden and Boston: E. J. Brill.

Renehan, Robert. 1992. "The Staunching of Odysseus' Blood: The Healing Power of Magic." *American Journal of Philology* 113 (1): 1–4.

Rice, David, and John Stambaugh. 2009. *Sources for the Study of Greek Religion: Corrected Edition.* Atlanta: Society of Biblical Literature.

Riess, Werner. 2012. *Performing Interpersonal Violence: Court, Curse, and Comedy in Fourth-Century BCE Athens.* De Gruyter.

Riley, Mark. 1987. "Theoretical and Practical Astrology: Ptolemy and His Colleagues." *Transactions of the American Philological Association* 117: 235–256.

Ripat, Pauline. 2011. "Expelling Misconceptions: Astrologers at Rome." *Classical Philology* 106: 115–154.

Ritner, Robert K. 1993. *The Mechanics of Ancient Egyptian Magical Practice.* Chicago: The Oriental Institute.

———. 1995. "Egyptian Magical Practice under the Roman Empire: The Demotic Spells and Their Religious Context." *Aufstieg und Niedergang der römischen Welt* II 18.5: 3333–3379.

Rives, James. 2002. "Magic in the XII Tables Revisited." *The Classical Quarterly* 52 (1): 270–290.

———. 2003. "Magic in Roman Law: The Reconstruction of a Crime." *Classical Antiquity* 22 (2): 313–339.

———. 2008. "Legal Strategy and Learned Display in Apuleius' Apology." In *Paideia at Play: Learning and Wit in Apuleius,* edited by Werner Riess, 17–49. Groningen: Barkhuis Publishing.

———. 2011. "Magic in Roman Law: The Reconstruction of a Crime." In *Oxford Readings in the Religious History of the Roman Empire: Pagans, Jews, and Christians,* edited by J. A. North and Simon Price, 71–108. Oxford and New York: Oxford University Press.

Rochberg, Francesca. 2004. *The Heavenly Writing: Divination, Horoscopy and Astronomy in Mesopotamian Culture.* Cambridge: Cambridge University Press.

Rochberg-Halton, F. 1988. "Elements of the Babylonian Contribution to Hellenistic Astrology." *Journal of the American Oriental Society* 108 (1): 51–62.

Rohde, Erwin. 1925. *Psyche: The Cult of Souls and Belief in Immortality among the Greeks.* Translated by W. B. Hillis. London: Kegan Paul, Trench, Trubner & Co., Ltd.

Rosch, Eleanor, and Carolyn B. Mervis. 1975. "Family Resemblances: Studies in the Internal Structure of Categories." *Cognitive Psychology* 7: 573–605.

Roth, Paul. 1982. "Mantis: The Nature, Function, and Status of a Greek Prophetic Type." Dissertation, Bryn Mawr: Bryn Mawr College.

Ruelle, C. E. 1908. "Hermès Trismégiste: Le livre sacré sur les décans. Texte, variantes et traduction française." *Revue de Philologie* 32: 247–277.

Rüpke, Jörg. 2007. *Religion of the Romans.* Translated by Richard Gordon. Cambridge: Polity.

Saffrey, Henri-Dominique. 1995. "Historique et description du manuscrit alchimique de Venise Marcianus Graecus 229." In *Alchimie: Art, histoire et mythes: Actes du 1er colloque international de la société d'étude de l'histoire de l'alchimie*

(Paris, Collège de France, 14–15–16 Mars 1991), edited by Didier Kahn and Sylvain Matton, 1–10. Paris: S.É.H.A.

Santangelo, Federico. 2013. "The Haruspices and the Rise of Prophecy." In *Divination, Prediction and the End of the Roman Republic*, 84–114. New York: Cambridge University Press.

Saunders, Trevor. 1991. *Plato's Penal Code: Tradition, Controversy, and Reform in Greek Penology*. Oxford: Clarendon Press.

Saussure, Ferdinand de. 1986. *Course in General Linguistics*. 3rd ed. Translated by Roy Harris. Chicago: Open Court Publishing Company.

Scarborough, John. 1979. "Theophrastus on Herbals and Herbal Remedies." *Journal of the History of Biology* 11: 353–385.

———. 1991. "The Pharmacology of Sacred Plants, Herbs, and Roots." In *Magika Hiera: Ancient Greek Magic and Religion*, edited by Christopher A. Faraone and Dirk Obbink, 138–147. New York and Oxford: Oxford University Press.

———. 2010. *Pharmacy and Drug Lore in Antiquity: Greece, Rome, Byzantium*. Farnham: Ashgate.

Schibli, Hermann Sadun. 2002. *Hierocles of Alexandria*. Oxford and New York: Oxford University Press.

Scott, Walter. 1924. *Hermetica, the Ancient Greek and Latin Writings Which Contain Religious or Philosophical Teachings Ascribed to Hermes Trismegistus*. Oxford: Clarendon Press.

Serafini, Nicola. 2016. "Sacerdoti mendicanti e itinerant: gli *agyrtai* nell' Antica Grecia." *Museum Helveticum* 73: 24–41.

Shaw, Gregory. 1995. *Theurgy and the Soul: The Neoplatonism of Iamblichus*. University Park: The Pennsylvania State University Press.

———. 1999. "Eros and Arithmos: Pythagorean Theurgy in Iamblichus and Plotinus." *Ancient Philosophy* 19: 121–143.

Sheppard, Anne. 1982. "Proclus' Attitude to Theurgy." *The Classical Quarterly* 32 (1): 212–224.

Sider, David, and Carl Wolfram Brunschön. 2007. *Theophrastus of Eresus. On Weather Signs*. Leiden: E. J. Brill.

Smith, Andrew. 1974. *Porphyry's Place in the Neoplatonic Tradition: A Study in Post-Plotinian Neoplatonism*. The Hague: Martinus Nijhoff.

Smith, Jonathan Z. 1978a. *Map Is Not Territory: Studies in the History of Religions*. Leiden: E. J. Brill.

———. 1978b. "Towards Interpreting Demonic Powers in Hellenistic and Roman Antiquity." In *Aufstieg und Niedergang der römischen Welt*, II 16.1: 425–439.

———. 1982. *Imagining Religion: From Babylon to Jonestown*. Chicago Studies in the History of Judaism. Chicago: University of Chicago Press.

———. 1995. "Trading Places." In *Ancient Magic and Ritual Power*, edited by Marvin W. Meyer and Paul Allan Mirecki, 13–27. Leiden and New York: E. J. Brill.

———. 2003. "Here, There and Anywhere." In *Magic in History: Prayer, Magic, and the Stars in the Ancient and Late Antique World*, edited by Scott Noegel, Joel Walker, and Brannon Wheeler, 21–36. University Park: The Pennsylvania State University Press.

Smith, Morton. 1996a. "The Eighth Book of Moses and How It Grew (PLEID. J 395)." In *Studies in the Cult of Yahweh: New Testament, Early Christianity, and*

Magic, edited by Shaye J. D. Cohen, 2:217–26. Leiden, New York, and Cologne: E. J. Brill.

Smith, Morton. 1996b. "P Leid J 395 (PGM XIII) and Its Creation Legend." In *Studies in the Cult of Yahweh: New Testament, Early Christianity, and Magic*, edited by Shaye J. D. Cohen, 2:227–234. Leiden, New York, and Cologne: E. J. Brill.

Smith, Nicholas D. 1989. "Diviners and Divination in Aristophanic Comedy." *Classical Antiquity* 8: 140–158.

Spiller, Henry, John Hale, and Jelle De Boer. 2002. "The Delphic Oracle: A Multidisciplinary Defense of the Gaseous Vent Theory." *Clinical Toxicology* 40 (2): 189–196.

Stahl, William. 1952. *Commentary on the Dream of Scipio (Macrobius, Ambrosius Aurelius Theodosius)*. New York: Columbia University Press.

Stolzenberg, Daniel. 1999. "Unpropitious Tinctures. Alchemy, Astrology & Gnosis According to Zosimos of Panopolis." *Archives internationales d'histoire des sciences* 49 (142): 3–31.

Stratton, Kimberly B. 2007. *Naming the Witch: Magic, Ideology, and Stereotype in the Ancient World*. New York: Columbia University Press.

———. 2013. "Magic Discourse in the Ancient World." In *Defining Magic: A Reader*, edited by Bernd-Christian Otto and Michael Stausberg, 243–254. London: Equinox Publishing, Ltd.

Stroud, R. S. 2013. *The Sanctuary of Demeter and Kore. The Inscriptions (Corinth XVIII.6)*. Princeton, NJ: Princeton University Press.

Struck, Peter T. 2001. "Pagan and Christian Theurgies: Iamblichus, Pseudo-Dionysius, Religion and Magic in Late Antiquity." *Ancient World* 32 (2): 25–38.

———. 2003. "The Ordeal of the Divine Sign: Divination and Manliness in Archaic and Classical Greece." In *Andreia: Studies in Manliness and Courage in Classical Antiquity*, edited by Ralph M. Rosen and Ineke Sluiter, 167–186. Leiden: E. J. Brill.

———. 2004. *Birth of the Symbol: Ancient Readers at the Limits of Their Texts*. Princeton, NJ: Princeton University Press.

———. 2016. *Divination and Human Nature: A Cognitive History of Intuition in Classical Antiquity*. Princeton, NJ: Princeton University Press.

Styers, Randall. 2004. *Making Magic: Religion, Magic, and Science in the Modern World*. New York: Oxford University Press.

Tambiah, S. J. 1973. "The Form and Meaning of Magical Acts: A Point of View." In *Modes of Thought: Essays on Thinking in Western and Non-Western Societies*, edited by Robin Horton and Ruth Finnegan, 199–229. London: Faber & Faber.

———. 1979a. "The Form and Meaning of Magical Acts: A Point of View." In *Reader in Comparative Religion*, 4th ed., edited by William A. Lessa and Evon Z. Vogt, 352–362. New York: Harper & Row.

———. 1979b. "A Performative Approach to Ritual." *Proceedings of the British Academy* 65: 113–169.

Tanaseanu-Döbler, Ilinca. 2013. *Theurgy in Late Antiquity: The Invention of a Ritual Tradition*. Göttingen: Vandenhoeck & Ruprecht.

Tardieu, Michel. 2010. "L'oracle de la Piere Mnouziris." In *Die Chaldaeischen Orakel: Kontext-Interpretation-Rezeption*, edited by Helmut Seng and Michel Tardieu, 93–108. Heidelberg: Universitätsverlag Winter.

Taylor, F. Sherwood. 1930. "A Survey of Greek Alchemy." *The Journal of Hellenic Studies* 50: 109–139.

Thomas, Keith. 1997. *Religion and the Decline of Magic: Studies in Popular Beliefs in Sixteenth and Seventeenth Century England.* New York: Oxford University Press.

Thomassen, Einar. 1997. "Is Magic a Subclass of Ritual?" In *The World of Ancient Magic: Papers from the First International Samson Eitrem Seminar at the Norwegian Institute at Athens, 4–8 May 1997,* edited by David R. Jordan, Hugo Montgomery, and Einar Thomassen, 55–66. Bergen: Norwegian Institute at Athens.

Thomsen, Marie-Louise. 2001. "Witchcraft and Magic in Ancient Mesopotamia." In *Witchcraft and Magic in Europe: Biblical and Pagan Societies,* edited by Bengt Ankarloo and Stuart Clark, 1–95. Philadelphia: University of Pennsylvania Press.

Timotin, Andrei. 2012. *La démonologie platonicienne: Histoire de la notion de Daimōn de Platon aux derniers néoplatoniciens.* Philosophia Antiqua 128. Leiden and Boston: E. J. Brill.

Todorov, Tzvetan. 1978. "Le discours de la magie." In *Les genres du discours,* 246–282. Paris: Éditions du Seuil.

Tomlin, R. S. O. 1988a. "Tabellae Sulis: Roman Inscribed Tablets of Tin and Lead from the Sacred Spring at Bath." In *The Temple of Sulis Minerva at Bath, II: Finds from the Sacred Spring,* edited by Barry Cunliffe, 59–105. Oxford: Oxford University Committee for Archaeology.

———. 1988b. *Tabellae Sulis: Roman Inscribed Tablets of Tin and Lead from the Sacred Spring at Bath.* Oxford: Oxford University Press.

———. 2010. "Cursing a Thief in Iberia and Britain." In *Magical Practice in the Latin West. Papers from the International Conference Held at the University of Zaragoza, 30 Sept.–1 Oct. 2005,* edited by Richard Gordon and Francisco Marco Simón, 245–273. Leiden: E. J. Brill.

Turfa, Jean Macintosh. 2012. "Diarium Tonitruale: Johannes Lydus, de Ostentis 27–38." In *Divining the Etruscan World,* 73–101. Cambridge: Cambridge University Press.

Turner, Victor W. 1975. *Revelation and Divination in Ndembu Ritual.* Ithaca, NY: Cornell University Press.

Ustinova, Yulia. 2013. "Modes of Prophecy, or Modern Arguments in Support of the Ancient Approach." *Kernos. Revue internationale et pluridisciplinaire de religion grecque antique* 26: 25–44.

Van den Berg, R. M. 2001. *Proclus' Hymns: Essays, Translations, Commentary.* Leiden: Brill.

Van Straten, Folkert. 1981. "Gifts for the Gods." In *Faith, Hope, and Worship,* edited by H. S. Versnel, 65–151. Leiden: Brill.

———. 1988. "The God's Portion in Greek Sacrificial Representations: Is the Tail Doing Nicely?" In *Early Greek Cult Practice: Proceedings of the Fifth International Symposium at the Swedish Institute at Athens, 26–29 June, 1986,* edited by Robin Hägg, Nanno Marinatos, and Gullög Nordquist, 51–68. Stockholm: Paul Aströms Förlag.

Várhelyi, Zsuzanna. 2001. "Magic, Religion, and Syncretism at the Oracle of Claros." In *Between Magic and Religion: Interdisciplinary Studies in Ancient Mediterranean Religion and Society,* edited by Sulochana Ruth Asirvatham, Corinne

Ondine Pache, and John Watrous, 13–31. Lanham, MD: Rowman & Littlefield Publishers, Inc.

Vernant, Jean-Pierre. 1989. "At Man's Table: Hesiod's Foundation of the Myth of Sacrifice." In *The Cuisine of Sacrifice among the Greeks*, edited by Marcel Detienne and Jean-Pierre Vernant, translated by Paula Wissing. Chicago and London: University of Chicago Press.

Versnel, Hendrik. 1981. "Religious Mentality in Ancient Prayer." In *Faith, Hope, and Worship*, edited by H. S. Versnel, 1–64. Leiden: E. J. Brill.

———. 1985. " 'May He Not Be Able to Sacrifice . . .' Concerning a Curious Formula in Greek and Latin Curses." *Zeitschrift für Papyrologie und Epigraphik* 58: 247–269.

———. 1991a. "Beyond Cursing: The Appeal to Justice in Judicial Prayers." In *Magika Hiera: Ancient Greek Magic and Religion*, edited by Christopher A. Faraone and Dirk Obbink, 60–106. New York : Oxford: Oxford University Press.

———. 1991b. "Some Reflections on the Relationship Magic-Religion." *Numen* 38: 177–197.

———. 1998. "And Any Other Part of the Entire Body There May Be . . . : An Essay on Anatomical Curses." In *Ansichten griechischer Rituale: Geburtstags-Symposium für Walter Burkert*, edited by Fritz Graf, 217–267. Stuttgart and Leipzig: B. G. Teubner.

———. 1999. "Κολάσαι Τοὺς Ἡμᾶς Τοιούτους Ἡδέως Βλέποντες· (Punish Those Who Rejoice in Our Misery): On Curse Texts and Schadenfreude.' " In *The World of Ancient Magic: Papers from the First International Samson Eitrem Seminar at the Norwegian Institute at Athens, 4–8 May 1997*, edited by David R. Jordan, Hugo Montgomery, and Einar Thomassen, 125–162. Bergen: Norwegian Institute at Athens.

———. 2002. "The Poetics of the Magical Charm: An Essay in the Power of Words." In *Magic and Ritual in the Ancient World*, edited by Paul Mirecki and Marvin Meyer, 105–158. Leiden: E. J. Brill.

———. 2010. "Prayers for Justice, East and West: New Finds and Publications since 1990." In *Magical Practice in the Latin West: Papers from the International Conference Held at the University of Zaragoza, 30 Sept.–1st Oct. 2005*, edited by Richard Gordon and Francisco Marco Simón, 275–354. Leiden: E. J. Brill.

Viano, Cristina. 1995. "Olympiodore l'alchimiste et les présocratiques: Une doxographie de l'unité (De arte sacra, §18–27)." In *Alchimie: Art, histoire et mythes: Actes du 1er colloque international de la société d'étude de l'histoire de l'alchimie (Paris, Collège de France, 14–15–16 Mars 1991)*, edited by Didier Kahn and Sylvain Matton, 95–150. Paris: S.É.H.A.

———. 2005. "Les alchimistes gréco-alexandrins et le Timée de Platon." In *L'alchimie et ses racines philosophiques: La tradition grecque et la tradition arabe*, edited by Cristina Viano, 91–107. Paris: Librairie philosophique J. Vrin.

Vlachou, C., J. G. McDonnell, and R. C. Janaway. 2002. "Experimental Investigation of Silvering in Late Roman Coinage." In *Material Issues in Art and Archaology VI*, edited by Pamela B. Vandiver, Martha Goodway, and Jennifer L. Mass, 464–469. Warrendale, PA: Materials Research Society.

Voutiras, Emmanuel. 1998. *Dionysophōntos Gamoi: Marital Life and Magic in Fourth Century Pella*. Amsterdam: J. C. Gieben.

Wellmann, Max. 1928. *Die Physika des Bolos Demokritos und der Magier Anaxilao aus Larissa.* Abhandlungen der Preussischen Akademie der Wissenschaften. Berlin: Walter de Gruyter.

Wendt, Heidi. 2016. *At the Temple Gates: The Religion of Freelance Experts in the Roman Empire.* New York: Oxford University Press.

Westerink, L. G. 1976. *The Greek Commentaries on Platos' Phaedo.* Vol. 1, *Damascius.* Amsterdam, Oxford, and New York: North-Holland Publishing Co.

White, R. J. 1975. *Artemidorus Daldianus: The Interpretation of Dreams: Translation and Commentary.* Park Ridge: Noyes Press.

Wilburn, Andrew. 2012. *Materia Magica: The Archaeology of Magic in Roman Egypt, Cyprus, and Spain.* Ann Arbor: The University of Michigan Press.

Williams, Michael A. 1996. *Rethinking "Gnosticism": An Argument for Dismantling a Dubious Category.* Princeton, NJ: Princeton University Press.

Winkler, John J. 1991. "The Constraints of Eros." In *Magika Hiera: Ancient Greek Magic and Religion,* edited by Christopher Faraone and Dirk Obbink, 214–243. New York and Oxford: Oxford University Press.

Wünsch, Richard, ed. 1897. *Inscriptiones Atticae Aetatis Romanae, Defixionum Tabellae.* Appendix. Inscriptiones Graecae, iii. 3. Berlin: Reimer.

———. 1898. *Sethianische Verfluchungstafeln aus Rom.* Leipzig: B. G. Teubner.

Zago, Michela. 2008. "L'emploi des noms divins dans la kosmopoiia (PGM XIII)." In *Religioni in contatto nel mediterraneo antico. Modalità di diffusione e processi di interferenza, atti del 3 colloquio su «Le religioni orientali nel mondo greco e romano», Loveno di Menaggio (Como), 26–28 Maggio 2006,* edited by Corinne Bonnet, Sergio Ribichini, and Dirk Steuernagel, 205–217. Pisa and Rome: Fabrizio Serra editore.

Zografou, Athanassia. 2010. "Magic Lamps, Luminous Dreams: Lamps in PGM Recipes." In *Light and Darkness in Ancient Greek Myth and Religion,* edited by Menelaos Christopoulos, Efimia D. Karakantza, and Olga Levaniouk, 276–294. Plymouth, UK: Lexington Books.

———. 2011. "Des sacrifices qui donnent des ailes : PGM XII, 15–95." In *«Nourrir les dieux?» Sacrifice et représentation du divin. Actes de la VIe rencontre du groupe de recherche européen «Figure. Représentation du divin dans sociétés grecque et romaine» (Université de Liège, 23–24 Octobre 2009),* edited by Vinciane Pirenne-Delforge and Francesca Prescendi, 149–163. Liège: Centre international d'étude de la religion grecque antique.

———. 2013a. *Papyrus magiques grecs: Le mot et le rite. Autour des rites sacrificiels.* Παράρτημα 85. Ioannina: Επιστημονική Επετηρίδα Πανεπιστημίου Ιωαννίνων.

———. 2013b. "Rencontrer les dieux en rêve dans l'antiquité tardive: La 'programmation' des rêves dans les Papyri Graecae Magicae." In *Perception et construction du divin dans l'antiquité,* edited by Philippe Borgeaud and Doralice Fabiano, 211–233. Geneva: Librairie Droz S.A.

———. 2013c. "Un oracle homérique de l'Antiquité tardive." *Kernos. Revue internationale et pluridisciplinaire de religion grecque antique* 26 (October): 173–190.

Index Locorum

#52.12, 117, 128
#60, 74

Harpocration
  s.v. Theoris, 382
Heliodorus
  6.14, 24
Hephaestion
  Apotelesmatica 11.15 Pingree, 131
  Apotelesmatica 12.20–23 Pingree, 131
  Apotelesmatica 160.18–20 Pingree, 247
Heraclitus
  fr. 92, 196
  fr. 93, 214
  fr. 121, 327
Hermetica
  Asclepius 3, 332
  Corpus Hermeticum I, 311
  Corpus Hermeticum I.18, 332
  Corpus Hermeticum I.24–26, 250
  Corpus Hermeticum IV, 311
  Corpus Hermeticum XI.20.4–6, 297
  Corpus Hermeticum XI.20.12–18, 297
  Corpus Hermeticum XIII, 369
  Stob. Herm. 6 1.21.9, 257
  Stob. Herm. 26.13, 299, 362
  Stob. Herm. 26.28–29, 299, 362
Hermias
  in Plat. Phaedrum 87.4, 137
  in Plat. Phaedrum 87.4–9, 347
Herodotus
  1.46–54, 214
  1.51, 162
  1.53, 200
  4.151.1, 192
  5.63, 230
  5.90.2, 216
  5.92, 222
  6.57.4, 216
  6.66, 230
  6.84, 230
  7.141.3–4, 232
  8.134, 211
  8.20, 216
  8.77, 216
  8.96, 216
  9.33–35, 227
  9.43, 216
  9.92–94, 227
  9.95, 228

[Herodotus]
  Life of Homer 30, 105
Hesiod
  Theogony 38, 193
  Theogony 535–557, 165
  Works and Days 109–93, 327
  Works and Days 11–24, 68
  Works and Days 335–341, 168
  Works and Days 383–387, 244
  Works and Days 564–573, 244
  Works and Days 609–623, 244
  Works and Days 618–695, 126
  Works and Days 825–828, 205
Hierocles
  in aurum pyth. 26.3–4, 330
  in aurum pyth. 26.22, 330
Hippocrates
  de morbo sacro I, 139
  de morbo sacro IV, 13
  de morbo sacro IV.1–8, 25
  de morbo sacro IV.8–10, 26
  de morbo sacro IV.17–19, 26
  de natura hominis 7, 138
  de prisca medicina 1.1, 138
  Epidemics 1.2.5, 209
  On Regimen IV.86–93, 218
  Prognosis 1.1, 193
Hippolytus
  Haer. 1.21.2, 262
  Haer. 4.28–42, 198
  Haer. 4.35–36, 355
  Haer. 4.37, 27
Homer
  Iliad
    1.34–40, 156, 186
    1.57–120, 230
    1.62–67, 192
    1.69–70, 193
    2.1–36, 219
    3.40, 95
    6.235–6, 154, 157
    9.497, 185
    14.197–210, 100
    15.106, 340
    16.514–516, 204
    19.139, 203
    23.65–93, 222
    24.221–224, 213
    24.527–528, 233
  Odyssey
    1.174, 204

Subject Index

libations, 80, 159, 164–65, 168, 172, 185, 222, 345, 348–49n99, 357, 369
Libra, 243, *248*, 255
Libya, 23, 67, 192n14, 391
linguistics, 6nn5–6, 11
lion, 131n36, 218, 325n24, 334, 355, 356, 364n145
liver, 104, 189, 196, 196n23, 197n28, 207–8, 208n62, 208n64, 209n65, 233
lots, 202, 203, 212, 258, 258n36
Lucan, 20, 20n28, 21, 23, 23n47, 24n49, 25n53, 84n71, 149, 196n24, 215n88, 225, 225n125, 226n129, 229
Lucian, 21, 101, 109–10, 111, 111–12n43, 113, 198, 350, 350n101, 413n69
Lucius, 43, 211, 263, 266n61, 344n82, 369n158, 413
Lydia, 30, 67n23, 200, 219n106, 222, 380
lyric, 14, 42

Macedonia, 98
Macrobius, 250, 250n23
Magi, 118n6, 272n6, 309, 312, 356
mageia, 13, 14, 31, 38, 380, 384, 397n33, 401, 409n60, 415
magica, 13, 407, 413
magos, 13, 38, 231, 268n65, 272n7, 304n91, 311, 397, 397n33, 399, 407, 415
Maia, 166
mania, 189, 195, 214
Manilius, 241, 245, 245n16, 254n28
mantike, 189, 214. See also divination
mantis, 189, 189n5–6, 191n12, 195, 209, 218n100, 382. See also divination
Marcellus of Bordeaux, 120–21, 131
Marcus Aurelius, 263n52, 264, 317, 392
Maria the Jewess, 275, 284, 290, 290n53, 292, 308n99
Marinus, 29
marriage, 18, 77, 90, 98, 101–2, 109n37, 190, 209, 247n21, 254, 391, 401n42, 405
Mars, 247, 250–52, 255, 283, 366n148, 367
marvelous, 1, 24, 70, 184, 352–53n106, 418
Maximus of Ephesus, 242, 319–20, 347, 347n93, 392–93, 397
Medea, 1, 23n47, 25, 29, 103, 112–13, 115, 135
Medes, 14n24
medicine, 14, 43, 89n83, 110, 117–18, 118n6, 121, 130–31, 134, 138–39, 158,

209, 209–10n68, 218n99, 227, 236–37, 261, 261n26, 295, 389, 394, 411, 413–14
Melampous, 209
Melissa, 222
Menander, 20, 20n37, 175n63
Mene, 179
Menelaus, 157, 227
Mercury, 247, 250–52, 255, 283, 366n148, 367
mercury (Hg), 274, 283, 287, 291, 291n55, 293, 294n60, 299, 312–13n116
Meroe, 21n41, 28, 111–12, 112n45
Mesopotamia, 3, 20n36, 60n12, 89, 89n83, 208, 208n62, 208n64, 209n65, 210n70, 221, 224n121, 226n127, 240n7, 270, 277, 307–8, 410n62, 416
metal, 12, 24, 53, 55, 57, 63, 67, 83, 88, 119, 123, 220, 226, 273–74, 280–82, 285–87, 285n39, 290, 294, 312
metallurgy, 11, 39, 284
metaphor, 46–48, 84, 84n70, 137n47, 244n14, 287n40, 334
meter, 47, 85, 144, 162n28, 205, 215, 242, 355
metonymy, 46–48, 84, 84n70, 137n47
Middle Ages, 269
Middle Platonism, 318
Mithraism, 243n12, 266, 322, 333, 359n128, 361, 361n134, 364–65, 368–69, 388
Moirai, 31, 177n70
moon, 1, 3–4, 5, 14, 1, 20n36–37, 20n39, 21–28, 23n47, 24n49, 25n52, 26n56, 29, 31, 32, 43, 49, 74, 109, 112, 149, 173, 173n58, 176, 198n32, 244–46, 245n15, 247, 254, 258, 269, 310, 311, 322, 345, 348, 350, 353, 353n108, 355, 356, 358n121, 359, 364, 365, 366, 404n47, 416, 416n79, 418
moon divinity, 2, 19, 24n49, 25, 25n52, 28–29, 29n58, 31, 74, 105, 128, 179, 242, *244*, 247n21, 250–52, 255, 283, 334, 355–56, 358, 358n121, 367
moonfoam, 23–24. See also *aphroselenon*
Musaeus, 216
Mysteries, 159, 236, 317, 398. See also Eleusinian Mysteries
myth of Er, 327

Nechepso, 131n35, 239, 255n29, 264, 411–13

CPSIA information can be obtained
at www.ICGtesting.com
Printed in the USA
LVHW020738201021
700899LV00001B/1

9 780691 230214